PETER O'TOOLE

HELLRAISER
SEXUAL OUTLAW
IRISH REBEL

AWARD-WINNING ENTERTAINMENT
ABOUT HOW AMERICA INTERPRETS ITS CELEBRITIES

WWW.BLOODMOONPRODUCTIONS.COM

"Dishing with abandon, the authors spare no one—especially not the dead."
—The New York Post

"If you love smutty celebrity dirt as much as I do (and if you don't, what's wrong with you?) then have I got a book for you!"
—The Hollywood Offender

"These monumentally exhaustive collections of sins, foibles, failings, and sexual adventures are the ultimate guilty pleasure."
—Books to Watch Out For

"The grittiest, most unvarnished, and most comprehensive biography of the dashing, charismatic movie star and roué ever written."
—Celebrity Dish

"There are guilty pleasures. Then there is the master of guilty pleasures, Darwin Porter. There is nothing like reading him for passing the hours. He is the Nietzsche of Naughtiness, the Goethe of Gossip, the Proust of Pop Culture. Porter knows all the nasty buzz anyone has ever heard whispered in dark bars, dim alleys, and confessional booths. And lovingly, precisely, and in as straightforward a manner as an oncoming train, his prose whacks you between the eyes with the greatest gossip since Kenneth Anger. Some would say better than Anger."
—Alan W. Petrucelli
The Entertainment Report
Stage and Screen Examiner
Examiner.com

"Insouciant, offensive, brilliant, promiscuous, and brash, Peter O'Toole was said to have matched Don Juan's legendary total of 1,033 seductions. It's all here in this latest blockbuster biography from those blokes at Blood Moon, no doubt hellraisers themselves when it comes to stirring up scandal."
—Fab

A Word About Phraseologies

Since we at Blood Moon weren't privy to long-ago conversations as they were unfolding, we have relied on the memories of our sources for the conversational tone and phraseologies of what we've recorded within the pages of this book.

This writing technique, as it applies to modern biography, has been defined as "conversational storytelling" by *The New York Times,* which labeled it as an acceptable literary device for "engaging reading."

Blood Moon is not alone in replicating, "as remembered" dialogues from dead sources. Truman Capote and Norman Mailer were pioneers of direct quotes, and today, they appear in countless other memoirs, ranging from those of Eddie Fisher to those of the long-time mistress (Verita Thompson) of Humphrey Bogart.

Some people have expressed displeasure in the fact that direct quotes and "as remembered" dialogue have become a standard—some would say "mandatory"—fixture in pop culture biographies today.

If that is the case with anyone who's reading this now, they should perhaps turn to other, more traditional and self-consciously "scholastic" works instead.

Best wishes to all of you, with thanks for your interest in our work.

Danforth Prince
President and Founder
Blood Moon Productions

PETER O'TOOLE
Hellraiser, Sexual Outlaw, Irish Rebel

Darwin Porter and Danforth Prince

www.BloodMoonProductions.com

Manufactured in the United States of America

ISBN 978-1-936003-45-7

Special thanks to the Stanley Mills Haggart Collection,
the Woodrow Parrish-Martin Collection, the H. Lee Phillips Collection, the Fredric
and Grace Smithey Collection, and Elsa Maxwell Café Society.

Cover designs by Richard Leeds (Bigwigdesign.com)
Videography and Publicity Trailers by Piotr Kajstura

Distributed worldwide through National Book Network
(www.NBNbooks.com)

1 2 3 4 5 6 7 8 9 10

PETER O'TOOLE

Hellraiser, Sexual Outlaw, Irish Rebel

DARWIN PORTER & DANFORTH PRINCE

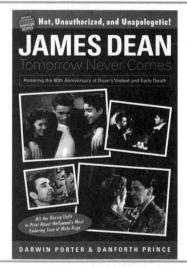

OTHER PUBLICATIONS BY DARWIN PORTER
NOT DIRECTLY ASSOCIATED WITH BLOOD MOON

NOVELS
The Delinquent Heart
The Taste of Steak Tartare
Butterflies in Heat
Marika
(a roman à clef based on the life of Marlene Dietrich
Venus
(a roman à clef based on the life of Anaïs Nin)
Bitter Orange
Sister Rose

TRAVEL GUIDES
Many Editions and Many Variations of
The Frommer Guides, The American Express Guides, and/or
TWA Guides, et alia to:

Andalusia, Andorra, Anguilla, Aruba, Atlanta, Austria, the Azores, The Bahamas, Barbados, the Bavarian Alps, Berlin, Bermuda, Bonaire and Curaçao, Boston, the British Virgin Islands, Budapest, Bulgaria, California, the Canary Islands, the Caribbean and its "Ports of Call, " the Cayman Islands, Ceuta, the Channel Islands (UK), Charleston (SC), Corsica, Costa del Sol (Spain), Denmark, Dominica, the Dominican Republic, Edinburgh, England, Estonia, Europe, "Europe by Rail," the Faroe Islands, Finland, Florence, France, Frankfurt, the French Riviera, Geneva, Georgia (USA), Germany, Gibraltar, Glasgow, Granada (Spain), Great Britain, Greenland, Grenada (West Indies), Haiti, Hungary, Iceland, Ireland, Isle of Man, Italy, Jamaica, Key West & the Florida Keys, Las Vegas, Liechtenstein, Lisbon, London, Los Angeles, Madrid, Maine, Malta, Martinique & Guadeloupe, Massachusctts, Morocco, Munich, New England, New Orleans, North Carolina, Norway, Paris, Poland, Portugal, Provence, Puerto Rico, Romania, Rome, Salzburg, San Diego, San Francisco, San Marino, Sardinia, Savannah, Scandinavia, Scotland, Seville, the Shetland Islands, Sicily, St. Martin & Sint Maartin, St. Vincent & the Grenadines, South Carolina, Spain, St. Kitts & Nevis, Sweden, Switzerland, the Turks & Caicos, the U.S.A., the U.S. Virgin Islands, Venice, Vienna and the Danube, Wales, and Zurich.

BIOGRAPHIES
From Diaghilev to Balanchine
The Saga of Ballerina Tamara Geva

Lucille Lortel
The Queen of Off-Broadway

Greta Keller
Germany's Other Lili Marlene

Sophie Tucker
The Last of the Red Hot Mamas

Anne Bancroft
Where Have You Gone, Mrs. Robinson?
(co-authored with Stanley Mills Haggart)

Veronica Lake
The Peek-a-Boo Girl

Running Wild in Babylon
Confessions of a Hollywood Press Agent

HISTORIES
Thurlow Weed
Whig Kingpin

Chester A. Arthur
Gilded Age Coxcomb in the White House

Discover Old America
What's Left of It

CUISINE
Food For Love
Hussar Recipes from the Austro-Hungarian Empire

AND COMING SOON, FROM BLOOD MOON

Bill & Hillary
So This Is That Thing Called Love

James Dean
Tomorrow Never Comes

Thanks for the Memories

THIS BOOK IS DEDICATED TO

KENNETH GRIFFITH
AND
JAMES VILLIERS

Ω

PLUS A CAST OF HUNDREDS OF OTHER PLAYERS

OUTRAGEOUS COMMENTS FROM THE MAD IRISHMAN, PETER O'TOOLE

"I grew up in Leeds, but I was born an Irishman, which accounts for my gift of gab, my unruly behavior, my passionate devotion to women, and the bottle, and my loathing of any authority figure."

"I believe in reincarnation. I can solve for you one of the great murder mysteries in English history. I was Jack the Ripper. There was nothing more exciting to me than taking a butcher knife and slitting open a whore's belly, watching her entrails spew forth."

"I hid my true personality from my fans—my hair-trigger temper and my violent tendencies. I inheritied those from my drunken Irish bookmaker dad. I once hit a cop, a restaurateur, a film critic—and I was notorious for smashing television sets like Elvis Presley."

"I'm not from the working class. I'm from the criminal class."

"The greatest problem facing any young actor on the English stage, especially one as gorgeous as I was, is avoiding the clutches of some of England's most stately homos, Laurence Olivier, John Gielgud, Noël Coward, *et al.*"

"I'm not an actor. I'm a movie star."

"Why did millions of gay men assume I was one of them after seeing *Lawrence of Arabia?*"

"I've never looked for women. When I was a teenager, perhaps. Then I met this stripper from Barcelona, name of Bubbles LaRue, who taught me everything I needed to know about sex—and a lot I didn't need to know. I'd still be with her had she not tried to hire me out as a boy whore."

"I will not be a common man. I will stir the smooth sands of monotony."

"I woke up one morning to find I was famous. I bought a white Rolls-Royce and drove down Sunset Boulevard, wearing dark specs and a white suit, waving like the Queen Mum."

"My favorite food from my homeland is Guinness. My second choice is Guinness. My third choice would have to be Guinness."

"Always a bridesmaid, never a bride my foot! Did you hear that, you bloody Oscar pickers?"

"Pope Paul III (1534-1549) was the greatest thief in the history of the Church."

"Public crucifixion is no fun."

"There are only three indispensible things: the audience, the actor, and the author. The rest is dross."

"There's always a hunger, when you're young, to go from peak to peak and avoid the valleys."

"As a star, I had a reputation to live up to every night of my life. At a Hollywood party, I spotted little Peter Lorre, that heavy-lidded, campy, thrilling eccentric and world-weary sardonic. I walked over to him, grabbed him, and kissed him madly, ramming my serpent-like tongue down his throat from which emerged the famously sinister voice on screen. After withdrawing my tongue, I bit his tongue like a vampire, tasting his blood. What else was there for me to do?"

"At one point I was far too gone to worry that April Ashley had been born a boy. She was a world-class beauty."

"I have a darling idea, Dickie (Burton). In the opening scene of *Becket,* we're screwing the same wench. Let me go with you to your suite at the Dorchester and join you and Elizabeth in bed for the night. It can be a rehearsal for our upcoming scene Monday morning."

"Ursula Andress is a bloody sex symbol and all that, but a really nice woman. She told me that all she had to do was run through a film with nothing on."

"The night after Princess Margaret seduced me, I was seen driving around London in her Rolls-Royce Phantom, which she had discarded for a new one."

"When we made *Lion in Winter,* I called Katharine Hepburn a female impersonator. But I just adored the dykey bitch. Even when she hauled off and slapped my face. We had a violent relationship, which was fine with me. I've always had this masochistic streak in me."

"How can I compete with the bosom of Sophia Loren in *Man of La Mancha?* To do so, the director will have to photograph me in a jockstrap."

"You know my favorite review for *The Ruling Class?* Vincent Canby of *The New York Times* claimed that with my blonde wig, I looked like Barbara Stanwyck in *Double Indemnity.* High praise indeed, to be compared to this stately dyke, (who's) second only to Katharine Hepburn in the lez department."

"The director of *Caligula*, Tinto Brass—I called him Tinto Zinc—gave me this Sumerian girl to follow me around. I nicknamed her Betty, the Collapsible Crutch. I was also followed by thirteen naked men as my guards. They were selected for their very large penises and given only Robin Hood hats to wear, nothing else. "I was willing to appear nude and with an erection in *Caligula* if called for. But Tinto Zinc told me that at this stage of his life, Tiberius could only be sexually aroused by being penetrated. When I saw those four-foot phalluses being brought onto the set, I opted out."

"I want my *Macbeth* to be the bloodiest in history, darlings. Do you know that if you stab a living man with a sword, blood spurts out seventeen feet. After opening night, critics claimed that my *Macbeth* was the worst in history. I was compared to Bette Davis in *What Ever Happened to Baby Jane?* I was as popular as a pork sausage in a synagogue."

"Elizabeth Ashley told me she smoked a lot of dope. She also made it with a lot of guys. She was almost as pretty as Audrey Hepburn. Neither of them had any tits."

"It's a razor's edge, a romance with an old man and a young woman."

"The only exercise I take is walking behind the coffins of friends who took exercise."

"As for my final curtain, I chased my own rainbow to the end. No, I didn't find a pot of gold... Only an empty crock. It didn't smell like Chanel No. 5."

"Over time, I went on to become the greatest stage and screen actor of the 20th Century, as immodest as that sounds. So, I'm a braggart. Well, I've got bloody something to brag about!"

"I've done everything that's possible to be done."

Contents

Rumanian Aristocrat, He Flees from World War II. Later, as Robinson Crusoe, He Escapes from Cannibalistic Caribbean Natives.

Chapter 1

Young Peter O'Toole

Offensive, Brilliant, Promiscuous, Brash,
& Born to Raise Hell,
The Golden Boy of Ireland Invades England

Beaten by Nuns & Molested by Priests, Peter Becomes a Lager Lout at
Thirteen, "A Member, Like Dad, of the Criminal Class"

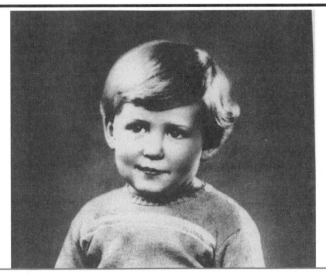

"At five years old, I was an Irish laddie. I looked like a cherubic saint, and I was named after a saint. But, trust me, I was no bloody saint."

When he was sixteen, the future actor, Peter O'Toole, proclaimed, "God put me on this Earth to raise hell, and I intend to do just that."

By then, he was accustomed to making proclamations. "God, if there is such a woman, bestows on a man her greatest gift if she makes him an Irishman. And if born in Ireland, as I was, there is no more beautiful place to wander dale and stream than to see the light of day in Connemara. *[Gaelic: Conamara].*

"The night before my birth on August 2, 1932, Mum and Pop told me that the evening sky turned a color known as royal purple. That was perhaps because I was born a direct descendant of the ancient Kings of Ireland. But when darkness came, it rained all night, not just mere rain, but a violent thunderstorm, as if to punish man and beast who inhabited the land."

"With such a grand entrance into the world for a bloody little infant boy, with everyone checking my wee-wee to see which sex I belonged to, it was only appropriate that I be named after an Irish saint."

Peter's mother took his full name, Peter Seamus Lorcan O'Toole, from Lorcán Ua Tuathail, also known as Saint Laurence O'Toole (1128-1180), who was archbishop of Dublin at the time of the Norman invasion of Ireland.

Peter was born a decade or so after the establishment of the Irish Free State. A sister, Patricia, had preceded him, her name inspired by the patron saint of Ireland.

Even though he was to leave his beloved Connemara early in life, as an adult, he would frequently return to his native land for retreats to his cottage, which he designed and had constructed just as he wanted it.

"I can't really say I was a soil-reared Irish boy, and that is much to my regret. But I'm an Irishman in my heart, and that's all that matters. There was a time when no Irishman was allowed to wear green, on orders of the

"In 1939, war clouds were looming, but dear old mum tended her flowers and took care of us," said young Peter.

Captain Pat O'Toole was a part-time shipwright and full-time racetrack bookmaker. This picture was taken in 1938, when Pop was "rapdily going skint. Boracid lint. Broke, potless," as phrased in the colorful language of his son, Peter.

The Teenage Prodigy Morphs into "the Chief Wanker of Leeds"
& Falls into the Honeypit of the Catalan Stripper, "Bubbles LaRue"

King of England. Today, I never go out the door without wearing green, at least green socks, and, on occasion, chartreuse underpanties."

"Oh Connemara, dear Connemara," he said. "I always take you with me wherever I go, from the sands of the Sahara to the mansions of Beverly Hills."

[Connemara lies in the territory of West Connacht, part of County Galway, in western Ireland. Originally, the land consisted of several ancient kingdoms. Galway is home to Lough Corrib, the largest lake in the Republic of Ireland, and Ne Beanna Beola (Twelve Bens), a mountain range.]

"As a professional actor, I always retreat to Connemara when the world grows too cold and cruel. Sometimes, when I felt no one is listening, I'd stand on a hill, the wind blowing through my hair, and sing, 'The Hills of Connemara,' that old Irish drinking song.

"I love the way Connemara ponies roam freely, grazing the world's greenest grass. After a day spent in the fields, I retire to one of my favorite pubs and order Connemar, the name of my favorite brand of Irish whiskey produced at the Cooley Distillery. God bless their wicked hearts for turning all the stalwart men of Connemara into drunkards."

The green, green grass of Connemara always lured native son Peter back to the home of Connemar whiskey, Connemar ponies, and Connemar women.

"Many of the legends of Ireland are true if you've had enough Guinness," Peter said. "The wee people might pay you a visit on certain nights. Perhaps some bow-legged fiddler, dressed in Robin Hood green, will play for you to dance an Irish jig for him."

One afternoon, while walking under gray clouds, I came across a fellow stalker in the countryside, Mr. John Ford, the American film director. His real name is actually Sean O'Feeney."

[John Ford, arguably one of the handful of truly great American film directors, was born John Martin Feeney in Cape Elizabeth, Maine, to John Augustine Feeney and Barbara "Abbey" Curran, on February 1, 1894. His father, John Augustine, was born in County Galway, Ireland in 1854. Barbara Curran had been born in the Aran Islands.

3

Ford's parents had arrived in Portland and Boston, respectively, within a few days of each other in May and June 1872. They were married in 1875, and became American citizens five years later on September 11, 1880, eventually producing eleven children.]

"I'll let you in on a bloody secret. Ford is known in this area as an old sod who likes to fly here from America to feast on Irish boy cock, which Truman Capote once told me was the tastiest in the world, and he should know."

"But in Connemara, we don't make too many moral judgments. Every household has dark secrets, especially the male species of the family. Most of us would like to keep those secrets buried in those megalithic tombs around the little town of Clifden."

John Ford... "A bloody old sod, but who am I to judge?"

"All good things must come to an end, or so my Mum says. When I was six, Pop decided that his wife, his son, and his daughter were to begin a vagabond existence that would, in time, lead us away from our beloved Ireland to face the real world. It would take us into one of the worst ghettos of industrial England, into the land of the enemy of the Irish people, our bloody oppressors. But I always knew I'd come home again, heeding the siren call of my native land."

"I was born an Irishman, and I will die an Irishman. I have all the characteristics of an Irishman. I loathe authority, especially British authority... and I believe rules are made to be broken. It is said that even as a child, I had a golden tongue, the famous Irish gift of gab. If that is so, I will reveal my technique of conversational seduction. In talking even with the most distant stranger, I have this ability to draw them in like some sort of conspiracy we're sharing."

Separated From His Beloved Ireland, Young O'Toole Sets Out "To Eat of the Fruit of all the Trees in the Garden of the World"

The future International film star, Peter O'Toole, was born into a poor family. His father, Patrick Joseph O'Toole, was known as "Paddy," "Patty," "Captain O'Toole," or even "Spats" because of the leather gaiters he wore over his shoes.

"Even though he was called captain, I don't know if he ever set foot on a boat, much less a ship," Peter said. "After a few drinks in his pub, he told amazing stories of how he commanded a crew, which had all sorts of adventures at sea. At one point battling a ferocious prehistoric monster attempting to devour them."

"Rough and rugged, he'd been a star athlete until his footballing legs grew weak in the knees. He never held any job for long, but had been trained as a metal plater and shipwright. His real profession was that of a larcenous, itinerant racetrack bookmaker. He carried a blackboard around with him, on which he wrote down the bets of the day's punters."

Is it a sea monster?
Is it a Lamprey Eel?
Did Paddy O'Toole really kill one?

"He was a bookie, not a 'turf account-ant,' as he often claimed," his son said. Actually, he was listed in the phone directory as a financial consultant.

He had been taught bookmaking by his crusty old mother, who concealed her illegal gambling operations under the guise of running a secondhand furniture store. Most of her merchandise had been retrieved from the street, discarded objects set out for the garbage collectors.

As a bookmaker at the racetrack, the captain always counted on a horse to lose if one of his clients had bet on it. If it paid off, the captain would grab his son's hand and stir up a dust bowl while fleeing from the premises.

"I'm not technically a criminal," the captain told his son, "although I do run away to keep from paying off a bet at the racetrack. But that is just good business practice. As for those goods I sometimes bring home, they fall off a lorry, and I retrieve them. I'd hardly call that stealing."

"My pop was a criminal, an idiot, a charmer, a bastard, and a very nice gentleman," Peter said.

As he later wrote, "Pop taught me poker, chemmy shoes, spinning wheels, balls of all sorts, dicing, and especially the art of horse racing. Gambling was his Lady Truelove."

In 1928, Captain O'Toole had wed "a bonnie lass," Constance Jane Eliot (*née Ferguson),* a Scottish orphan who eventually evolved into a nurse. As a child in Scotland, she had been transferred from one household to another, with no one seemingly wanting her. She was lucky to get a cold scone in the morning along with tepid tea.

"Connie," as she was called, was liked by the locals, and Saturday night would find her at the local pubs, "kicking up her legs" at a country dance.

"No one could dance an Irish jig better than dear ol' Mum," Peter said. "And she wasn't even Irish."

He both loved and admired his mother, "A dainty, wee lady. Mummy's beauty seemed wraithed by her ineffable sadness, *[which were]* quite at variance with her manner and quality, which were both joyous and generous and fused by acuity and authority. The bad times left her little time for repose, less for reflection. Connie-Jane set to keeping the crippled SS O'Toole buoyantly afloat. Never one for walking when she could run, sitting when she could stand, sleeping when she could wake, my little Mum fair tore into troublesome tasks and made them seem glad duties. Work of all sorts, washing, windows, scrubbing floors, dusting, ironing, sweeping, lifting, shoving, baking, mending."

By the time he turned six, his Pop [in Peter's words] "was a busted flush. A very Humpty Dumpty one. His good fortune had taken a fierce tumble."

After leaving Connemara, the O'Tooles moved to the little town of Tralee in County Kerry, in the verdant and folkloric southwestern region of Ireland. There, they rented a broken-down farmhouse on the outskirts, whose owner had long ago fled to a prosperous life in Boston. The roof leaked, there was no plumbing, and "we had to chase out the bloody rats—one the size of a cat with red eyes. The chimney was falling in, filling the house with more smoke than a busy pub in Dublin on a Saturday night."

In just a few weeks, O'Toole, senior, informed them that he had never paid the first installment on the rent, and the sheriff would likely arrive to evict them that very day. "We're off to Dublin, bag and baggage, though there's not much of either. Someday I'm going to buy your mother a fancy wardrobe that would make Lady Astor jealous."

Peter's earliest memories were of the capital on Ireland's east coast at the mouth of the River Iffey. Founded as a Viking settlement, Dublin would continue to attract the adult O'Toole at frequent intervals throughout the rest of his life. In the 1960s, he would star at both its Gaiety Theatre and its Abbey Theatre.

The O'Tooles lived in a tenement "along with some bloody rats," as Peter remembered it. "We had potato stew night after night."

"Pop was delighted that the Guinness Brewery had been founded here, and all the local pubs were amply stocked," Peter said. "In fact, the brewery may have been the city's biggest employer."

Peter was often sick, and didn't attend school regularly. His mother shouldered the task of teaching him how to read and write. He became adept at both. His choice of novels was more geared to adults than to children. He became very interested in the literary works of men associated with Ireland, beginning with Dublin's native-born son, Oscar Wilde.

The first novel he ever read was Wilde's *The Picture of Dorian Gray* (1890), although he didn't really understand it until he re-read it when he was older.

"Wilde was an old sod, but a brilliant writer," Peter said. "I heard he had a sharp wit and dressed flamboyantly. Except for the sodomy aspects, I found him fascinating, a possible role model when I grew up. I didn't really understand sodomy. Perhaps Pop could demonstrate it for me. Also, the first play I ever saw, *The Importance of Being Earnest* (1895), was also by Wilde. I think it influenced me to become an actor."

"A dreamer is one who can only find his way by moonlight, and his punishment is that he sees the dawn before the rest of the world."

Oscar Wilde

In later life, Peter ordered a wooden plaque with words from Wilde's De Profundis.

[De Profundis (Latin: "from the depths") is a grim and (justifiably) embittered letter written by Wilde in 1897 during his imprisonment in Reading Gaol, to his disloyal lover and to some degree, the cause of his imprisonment, Lord Alfred Douglas. In it, Wilde relays an overview of their ostentatious partnership, public exposure of which led to Wilde's conviction and imprisonment for gross indecency.

Whereas autobiographical elements within printed versions of the letter were systematically removed by literary censors, its full text didn't appear until 1962. The words from it cited by Peter O'Toole were:
"To regret one's own experiences is to arrest one's own development.
To deny one's experiences is to put a lie into the lips of one's own life.
It is no less than a denial of the soul."]

Peter claimed, "[Although] my sexual habits differed from those of Mr. Wilde, the words he wrote in prison at Wandsworth in London, jailed for his homosexuality, helped form my philosophy of life."

["I wanted to eat of the fruit of all the trees in the garden of the world. And so, indeed, I went out, and so I lived. My only mistake was that I confined myself so exclusively to the trees of what seemed to me the sun-lit side of the garden, and shunned the other side for its shadow and gloom."]

Before he set sail with his family from Ireland, the Captain told his eight-year-old son, "God I love Ireland better than any man alive, but I just can't make a living here."

[After his departure from Ireland, the Captain said that from that point on, he preferred to be called "Paddy." He would never return to his native land, living in England for forty years until his death at the age of eighty-six in 1975.]

"And so I moved on from the shores of Ireland to the shores of England, although English people terrified me," Peter said. "After all, Ireland's greatest export is its handsome, studly, virile men, each a maiden's dream, a great lover unless we're too besotten. We're great writers, too, and born leaders. For the most part, we've done well in foreign lands. Take Joseph Kennedy, for example. He became a multi-millionaire selling bootleg Irish whiskey, and his womanizing son ended up running America for those Yanks."

When a Priest Insists that There Is No Sex in Heaven, Peter Abandons the Church

After a stormy crossing of the Irish Sea, the O'Tooles journeyed to the town Gainsborough in the West Lindsey district of Lincolnshire, in the English Midlands on the River Trent, 55 miles from the North Sea.

[Gainsborough had been one of the biggest settlements of the early medieval kingdom of Mercia, which, from around 600 to 900 C.E. had dominated most of what's now known as central England, before being partially overrun by the Vikings. In 868, King Alfred "The Great," (ruling much of medieval England from 871 to 899), married his queen, Ealswitha, daughter of a local nobleman, here. Gainsborough became the inspiration for the fictional town of St. Ogg's in George Eliot's The Mill on the Floss *(1860).]*

For a while, Paddy worked as a traveling salesman for Smiffy's, an enterprise founded in 1894 as a wigmaker, selling its products throughout England. Since he was often drunk, he had a poor sales record, and was eventually fired. One month, he sold only eight wigs, and that was because his wife, Connie, dyed them pink. They sold as a novelty item for women or drag queens to wear at flamboyant parties. Pink hair, as it still is today, was a daring and edgy innovation in those days.

Drunk, Paddy returned home one night to announce to Connie, Peter, and Patricia his loss of a job. "We're going to try our luck in Leeds. I hear that West Yorkshire is riddled with racecourses. There's big money to be made there."

In Leeds, Paddy found that the cheapest rents were in Hunslet, the "Mick ghetto," a run-down inner-city district of South Leeds that George Bernard Shaw had called "a black stain on the face of the British Empire."

The rundown town had expanded rapidly during the Industrial Revolution as hordes of workers migrated there from farms throughout the Midlands. Most households were headed by a men who toiled as day laborers in any of dozens of factories churning out products that included rubber, cotton, wool, iron, and tin, within a landscape riddled with gas works and freight yards.

As Peter remembered their home, it was "one of those brick-built rabbit hutches that had been studded up, squad and meager, back to back, row upon row of crisscrossing cobblestone miles of nasty, sunless narrow streets."

Paddy took his son once a week to a public bathhouse to wash off the soot and grim. Along the way, they passed a lunatic asylum, countless pubs, churches, a dance hall, pawnbrokers, and the headquarters of a rugby club known for its fistfights on the playing field.

At the busy police station, thieves were often whipped, bareback, with cats-o'-nine tails.

At night, Paddy would drop Peter off for a supper of bangers and mash before retreating into one of the gaming houses along "Murder Mile," the most dangerous strip in Leeds, where many a man met his death getting stabbed.

"It was a rough neighborhood," Peter recalled. "The boys I grew up with turned out to be Jack the Ripper types, with an occasional murderer. We had our share of rapists, child molesters, crooks, drug addicts, prostitutes, wife beaters, degenerates, drunkards, bums, and Peeping Toms. We had at least one old wretch of a man who wore an overcoat, nothing else, and liked to flash at little girls on the playground, although I heard he didn't have all that much to flash."

As he was growing up, Peter got rid of myths, sometimes painfully, As the holidays approached, he was eager to find something under the Christmas tree, except there was no tree. As Pop explained it, Father Christmas had committed suicide, "so he won't be leaving any whiskey in my tumbler."

As Pop read the racing form every evening, Connie read to her son from the works of Charles Dickens, Robert Burns (her personal favorite,) John Galsworthy, and Shakespeare (Peter's favorite).

Oddly enough, when O'Toole sat down to write the first volume of his autobiography, which almost no one understood, he entitled it *Loitering With Intent—The Child.*"He devoted more space to Hitler than to anyone else in his pages, referring to the Nazi dictator as Schickelgrüber, his birth name. He also called the former paperhanger an untalented artist, a failed beer hall *putschist,* and "the Mad Muftie of the Long Knives."

By the end of the year, Peter was defining the *Führer* as "the cowardly rat cowering in a bunker in Berlin, committing suicide rather than facing the Russian invaders." Stalin had wanted Hitler alive so that he could subject him to almost unspeakable humiliations.

Peter's father would take him to the News Cinema, with its hour-long "programme," followed by a creamy treat at the Moo Cow Bar, where Peter would slurp his milkshake flavored with chocolate.

"As a very young kid, I thought old Schickelgrüber was a bloody movie star. The people booed his screen appearances."

As a little boy, he was carried along the street on his father's broad shoulders, his bony legs wrapped around the man's powerful neck, his ankles resting in Pop's cupped fists as they might have in the stirrups of a saddle. Sometimes, he'd place his chin on the Captain's billcock bowler.

"Of all the newsreel actors, FDR, with that long cigarette holder, was a better actor than *Der Führer* and Goebbels, who were too hammy."

The imp in the boy would shove the bowler down over his father's face, impairing vision that was already blurred from too much lager.

Not knowing the difference between a newsreel and a feature-length movie, Peter remembered the first "film star" to whom he attached a name. It was Adolf Hitler, filmed in Berlin by news cameras as he was addressing crowds of cheering Nazis. He remembered how the audiences hissed and booed every time *Der Führer's* image came onto the screen. As Peter later wrote, "The booing was for comical villainy to be encouraged by a raspberry jeer."

As movie stars went, Peter preferred the "louche, noble courage" of Franklin D. Roosevelt, with his long cigarette holder.

After their refreshment at the Moo Cow Bar, the Captain liked to retreat to his favorite local, where he'd order a "whiskey from the wood and a pint of plain," repeating the order countless times throughout the remainder of the evening.

Peter did not attend school on a regular basis until he was eleven years old, as he was stricken with various illnesses which began when he was six. They included tuberculosis, peritonitis, and eye trouble requiring at least a dozen painful operations. "If it was a disease, I had it!" he later wrote.

During the first decade of his life, O'Toole was raised as a girl, as Connie had not wanted to be the mother of a boy. "It's amazing I didn't turn into a homosexual," he later said. "For a long time, I had this stammer and a lisp. When I did go to school, the boys beat me up because they thought I was a poof."

"I never got over that eye trouble, by the way," he said. "Even when I was forced to stop drinking, my eyes always seemed to be bloodshot. Ever seen me in a close-up?"

Thanks to home schooling by his very bright and well-read mother, Peter was not that far behind when he was enrolled in the Holy Rosary and Saint Anne's Catholic Primary School on Leopold Street in Leeds. It was run by nuns. Later, he was educated by Jesuit priests, one of whom, as Peter alleged, molested him. He provided no further details, asserting, "There are some aspects of one's life not meant for conversation."

At school, Peter excelled in composition, although the nuns took a ruler and brought it down hard on his knuckles if he were caught writing with his left hand. One sister told him. "Write with your right hand. God considers it a sin to write with your left hand. Left-handed boys grow up to become evil-doers and most often end up in prison."

"The nuns called me 'Bubbles,' a name I detested. I asked one of the daffy ones, 'Why Bubbles?'" She said it was because of my unruly mop of blonde hair. How do you get Bubbles from that? Nuns aren't that smart anyway. Imagine denying yourself cock all your

"These black-robed nuns swept down on me like fluttering bats. My crime? I'd drawn a horse pissing."

life. If I were a heterosexual woman, I would take on at least six men a night from early morning to midnight."

In art class, Peter was asked to draw a horse. He'd seen enough of them on the tracks with his father. His teacher, a nun, found his depiction rather thin, and asked him to add something. As Peter recalled in his memoirs, he attached a penis to the horse—"a huge thick black truncheon of a penis"— and configured it so it seemed to be "pissing a waterfall."

When the nun saw it, she summoned her sisters. He remembered a severe beating as he faced "rattling beads, white celluloid breasts, winged sleeves, and white bony hands striking him as blows from the Brides of Christ."

"'Tis only a gee-gee having a wee-wee, you cruel, mad old ruins," he shouted at them.

In 1972, during a rare interview with a writer from *The New York Times,* he discussed his school days being taught by nuns. "Their whole denial of womanhood was so horrible—the black dresses, the shaving of the hair, so terrifying. Of course, that's all been stopped. They're sipping gin and tonics in the Dublin pubs now. A couple of them recently flashed their pretty ankles at me."

For a while, young Peter functioned as an altar boy for John Cardinal Heenan, Primate of the Roman Catholics in England. Perhaps Peter libeled the good cardinal in later years, when he mocked him as "being to the Right of Attila the Hun. If not that, he was at least Torquemada sending heretics to be burned at the stake during the Inquisition. He could not quite control an unruly lad like me. When I displeased him, which was every day, his heavy jaw cracked as if he had masticated an early Christian."

"He was also concerned with blasphemy. He had a fit punishment for those accused of that horrific crime. He preferred the medieval method of cutting a hole in each cheek followed by removal of one's tongue. However, in democratic England, the King, or rather, Parliament, frowned on that method, so Heenan had to restrain himself."

During the relatively brief period he operated as a church-going Catholic, Peter preferred the noon mass because it was brief. "That's when out-of-work actors, failed writers, untalented painters, and other debris showed up because the service was short," Peter said. "The priest could race through it, because he, like the rest of us, needed to get back to the bottle."

"What really turned me against the Catholic Church was a talk I had with a Jesuit priest. I asked him how many girlfriends would God allow me when I got to Heaven. He told me there was no sex in Heaven. 'Bloody hell!' I said. 'No sex? Then why go there?' I asked the befuddled fellow."

"Another reason I left the Church was that I got handmaiden's knees from all that kneeling to pray," O'Toole said. "I never believed in all that crap they were preaching or teaching. Imagine living forevermore. Who in the fuck would want to do that? One life is far more than enough. We'll be bloody lucky if we get through just one life alive."

"I decided to become a retired Christian," he said. "But I stayed on for a while as an altar boy because I liked all the pomp and circumstance that went with Catholic ritual. It made me think I was acting in some grand medieval theater. In the back of my brain I thought I might become a real actor one day. I was already memorizing the roles of *Hamlet* and *Macbeth*."

Peter and His Pop Become Racetrack Sharpies, Disappearing Whenever Winning Bettors Tried to Collect

Before Peter was ten years old, he considered himself as an expert on horse racing, a pastime that had been showcased since the Roman occupation of Britain, with a history in Yorkshire stretching back to around 200 C.E.

Horseracing was, at the time, the second-largest spectator sport in Great Britain. Queen Anne, during the 18th Century, had kept a large string of horses, and was instrumental in the founding and promotion of Royal Ascot.

Wagering of bets on horse races is as old as the sport itself. To entice customers who were carrying cash, Paddy often waited outside Post Offices where "The Dole" (State pension money) was dispensed.

The son of a bookmaker spent many a day at the racecourses of Yorkshire. "Lager, horseracing, and nooky, the three favorite pastimes of an Englishman. In that order."

Both Paddy and his son became familiar faces at the York Racecourse in North Yorkshire, at the time, the third-biggest racecourse in the U.K. in terms of total prize money, and second in the U.K., behind Ascot in the amount of prize money per meeting.

Another favorite was the Doncaster Racecourse in South Yorkshire, one of the nation's oldest tracks, dating from the 16th Century. Historically, Doncaster was said to attract the largest number of "ruffians" in Britain. It's home to two of the world's oldest horse races: The Doncaster Cup, first run in 1766, and the St. Leger Stakes.

Paddy and son also patronized the Beverly Racecourse in East Riding, Yorkshire, dating from 1767. "It was not Pop's favorite. He called it 'unpretentious but agreeable if you've had a lager or two.'"

Catterick Bridge Racecourse in North Yorkshire, a racing tradition since 1783, is a racetract that's normally reserved for thoroughbreds. Sometimes, father and son would stay over for the Catterick Sunday Market, held on the racecourse grounds. "My Pop was the best bargain hunter in all of England, usually making deals when the vendors were closing for the day, with many perishable items left unsold."

The Wetherby Racecourse near the market town of Wetherby in West Yorkshire was closer to home, only 12 miles from Leeds, standing immediately opposite Wetherby prison. "Pop warned me that it was highly likely we might spend part of our days there, behind barbed wire."

At the Cinema, Peter Grows Disenchanted with Adolf as "A Movie Star." Then, He's Exposed to the "Wacko Facts of Life" by his Pop

As the World War II dragged on, Peter decided that Hitler was no movie star, but an "atrocity inflicted upon the world." As movie stars, he preferred Stan Laurel and Oliver Hardy, especially as they appeared in *Air Raid Wardens* (1943). Harpo Marx was also a favorite of mine."

13

"Hitler at the cinema, during his rants, was looking insane. We were told to wear our gas masks during the day because a surprise *Blitzkrieg* could hit us at any minute, like it did when we lived for a time outside the city of Coventry."

"I remember tin hats, big balloons overhead, soldiers, sailors, air-raid wardens, ration books, clothing coupons, my Mummy and Pop surviving during our time there."

Paddy found work as a wartime Bodger for the Royal Navy, "pounding bits of ships into proportionate slabs, which were then floated down the river out into the open sea, scooped up and assembled elsewhere. That had banjaxed everybody, family and all, no one had known where the old bugger had been going to or coming from."

"In the last years of the war, when the Yanks arrived, many girls I'd known in Leeds became whores," Peter claimed. "The oversexed Yanks arrived, and most of them had dollar bills and chocolate bars. After the Yanks went home in 1945, many of these same girls found some poor Englishman to marry them and settled down and raised three brats."

"I hope these kids didn't ask their mummies, 'What did you do during the war?'"

When his son turned twelve, Paddy waited for an evening when Connie was away working. He had decided that it was time his boy learned the facts of life, because he could hear him masturbating through the thin walls, just as Peter could hear his father making drunken love to his mother.

For the occasion, he brought home beer for them to drink, consuming most of it himself.

Beginning on that rainy night, Peter developed a taste for beer and became, at the age of twelve, a steady drinker, like so many of his contemporaries in Hunstret.

"Beer blurred reality for me at the time," he said. "The war-torn world, with its blacked-out windows at night, was such a dreary place. When we could get some money together, we could always get an older friend to buy the booze for us, so we could get pissed."

"The world views us Irishmen as more sexually inept and guilt-ridden than our debauched English enemies," Paddy said. "A little advice: If you want oral sex, don't ask your future wife. No self-respecting Irish woman will do that nasty thing to any man. For that, you must hire one of the whores who walk the street, especially if she is foreign-born."

"You might hear some Yankee men talk about a husband's duty to pleasure his wife," he continued. "That is pure bullshit. No woman finds pleasure in having sex with a man—any fool knows that. Sex is something women endure for the man's sake—or else to have babies, and God knows there are enough of those brats running around in their shitty diapers."

The Captain told him, "The English have always tried to judge the sexuality of us Irishmen. Edmund Spencer, who fancied himself an Elizabethan poet, swore that all of us were a bunch of lascivious bisexuals, who offered ourselves freely to both men and women. He called for the extermination of the Irish race. For that, we burned down his bloody castle in County Cork."

"Women should be warned about Irishmen," Paddy continued. "We are a dangerous breed. A girl is likely to get drunk, and then we take advantage of the poor thing before throwing her back on the street like some half-naked tub of lard. Maybe pregnant. We Irishmen are a fertile bunch."

"Women have told me that nearly everything an Irishmen does is sexy, even putting on our shoes in the morning. Naturally, the sexiest thing we Irishmen do is take off our underwear. A bitch gets to see us in all our uncircumcised glory. What a treat that must be for the poor dears."

As a Teenager, Peter Presides Over The Mutual Masturbation Society, as His Companions ("The Dirty Dozen") Loot, Swill Beer, & Circle Jerk

Peter admitted that he discovered the joys of sex at an early age, beginning as a schoolboy in Leeds, when he was twelve—"almost thirteen."

He rounded up eleven other horny schoolboys. With himself configured as its leader, he formed the "MMS" (Mutual Masturbation Society), otherwise known as "The Dirty Dozen." They met at five o'clock every afternoon for what they called a "circle jerk."

"I was the chief wanker, sometimes with a record of three eruptions before six o'clock, as night fell over Leeds."

"Lost somewhere back in Victoria's day, our ignorant school masters taught us that masturbation was a form of 'self-abuse' and 'self-pollution.' What did the idiots know? Our gang knew better than any of them."

"Although I was head of the group, the real ringleader, or at least its star attraction, was Lars Hansson. He was built like a Danish Viking and had come down from the Outer Hebrides. His ancestors must have raped and pillaged half the women in North England."

"He didn't have a cock, something more akin to a log. He also had chest hair and thick, hairy arms and thighs, and we didn't. All the girls were crazy about him. He had a brother who was twenty-two years old, and he got him

15

to buy beer for us so that after our eruptions, we could get pissed."

"As for money, I learned how to get some from observing Pop. The boys and I earned money by stealing goods from lorries and selling the merchandise real cheap. On occasion, we ventured into the most prosperous sections of Leeds and broke into homes, many of which were inhabited by owners of factories. They hired laborers from Hunslet, paying them slave wages. We distributed some of their ill-gotten gains to the poor—namely, ourselves. We thought this was fair, calling it a 'redistribution of wealth.'"

Beginning as an early teen, Peter became a chronic masturbator. He even studied masturbation and some of its quirky associations. During Victorian times, the makers of boys' trousers designed them so that the genitals could not be touched through the pockets.

"The chief wanker of Leeds takes time out for a drink in a local pub...and another lager, and another. When the money ran out, I went out and stole something."

To lessen the possibility that a boy might actually "do the dirty deed," A bland, meatless diet was recommended, mainly by the manufacturers of Kellogg's corn flakes and the creator of Graham crackers.

Peter later learned that he and fellow members of MMS were violating an 1847 government law that interpreted masturbation with another person as "an offence against public decency," carrying a prison sentence if convicted.

He much preferred the tribal customs of the Gambia tribe of New Guinea. They believed that frequent sex among teenagers was to be encouraged, but only through fellatio. Tribal leaders felt it was wrong to waste semen, viewing it as a form of male strength more precious than mother's milk.

In later life, Peter decided his favorite artwork in the world was a self-portrait of the Viennese artist Egon Schiele depicting himself "wanking off" in 1911.

Peter lived long enough to witness the collapse of those early teachings and warnings about masturbation. In fact, in 2009, the Health Ministries of the United Kingdom and other European nations encouraged teenagers to masturbate at least daily as a means of reducing sexual tensions. One of the benefits of this involved a measurable reduction in teen pregnancies. Britain's National Health Service suggested that "an orgasm aways keeps the doctor away."

In his dotage, Peter proclaimed, "Although we of the MMS knew what was right all along, it took decades for the bloody government to wise up."

A Barcelona Stripper Teaches Teenaged Peter O'Toole
"Every Trick She Ever Learned" in a Catalán Bordello

Fortified with Paddy's instruction in the facts of life, Peter set out to seduce his first prostitute. In those years, a colony of whores flourished in Hunslet.

His first encounter with a prostitute occurred at the age of thirteen. The experience traumatized him. He had saved up two pounds, and was ready to buy himself a woman. He approached a prostitute in a tight-fitting purple dress with black hosiery. Not known what to say to her, he reached for her hand and placed it on his penis.

"Lovely, ducky," she said. "I'm busy tonight. It's pay day at the factories, and there will be money to spend. But save that little thing of yours, and I'll get around to smoking it in the morning, after a hard night's work."

His manhood insulted, he returned to his familiar circle jerk in the late afternoon.

However, his luck changed one afternoon when he was coming home from school. He was accosted by a big-bosomed, Spanish-speaking woman with dyed blonde hair. She looked to be a well-preserved woman in her early 50s.

Apparently, she liked his looks and invited him back to her flat.

Offering him tea, she explained to him that her English husband, a factory worker, had recently died.

Her late husband, if indeed, she'd been married at all, had met her during a holiday in Barcelona. She had been working as a stripper in a seedy bar in the medieval *Barri Gòtic*, billing herself as "Bubbles LaRue."

Peter found a certain irony in that, as the nuns at school had also nicknamed him "Bubbles."

Over the next five months, he visited Bubbles at her flat almost every afternoon, later asserting, "She taught me every sexual trick I've ever known in life. She had worked in a whorehouse on the back streets of Barcelona, a place

"Bubbles LaRue was a walking sex manual, but I fled from her embrace when she tried to make me into a boy whore."

17

where her father, a refugee from Spanish Morocco, had deposited her at the age of nine. He had sold her to a madam who welcomed child molesters as clients.

His sex life became so intense with the former hooker that at one point, she suggested that when Peter became of age, she would be interested in taking him as her husband. "I've got some money stashed away, and I could help you get started in life. I could make you very comfortable. You wouldn't have to struggle."

He began to mistrust her motives, suspecting that she had never really married that English factory worker. She often worried about her immigration status with the British government, understanding that if she were married to a Brit, she might be entitled to certain financial and medical benefits as she grew older.

One afternoon, Peter told her, bluntly, that he did not plan to marry her or any woman. "I'm a loner, and I want to be free to make impulsive choices in life, not to be tied down."

During the course of the following week, she began to postpone or avoid altogether his usual rendezvous at her flat. He felt that she'd resumed her former profession, and he suspected that because of her "advanced" age, she could no longer attract young men, most of whom sought prostitutes their own age or younger.

When he found a set of whips and sex toys in her bathroom closet, he suspected she was catering to the "kink market," and was actually whipping or mildly torturing men who wanted to be punished for harboring sexual desires with children.

One afternoon, Peter spotted a girl who looked no more than twelve, leaving Bubble's flat with a man who looked old enough to be her grandfather.

Peter's sexual liaison with Bubbles came to an abrupt end when she tried to enlist him as a sex object for some of her new clients. Obviously, one or more of them preferred boys instead of young girls.

He was introduced to an older factory laborer.

"I drank two beers with them that day," he told his friends. "After I got drunk, I learned that Bubbles wanted me as a player in her act. It turns out that while I was screwing her, she wanted this bloke to sodomize my young, tight ass."

"I got out of there and quick, never to return. I decided that before nightfall, I had to get a new act together, and it didn't involve Bubbles."

***

Although he detested most of the nuns at St. Anne's, he fell under the spell of one beautiful novice who had come to Leeds from York. "Years later, when I saw Audrey Hepburn in *The Nun's Story,* I felt this young woman could have been her sister. I had such a passion for her that one afternoon, I did something reckless and stupid."

"I asked her if I could talk with her privately, in a corner of the library. There were only two or three students reading at the far end of the room. When I came face to face with this lovely girl, I felt I had to press my case, weak though it be."

"I looked into her eyes and told her that living the life of a nun was going against the will of God."

"What on earth do you mean?" she asked him. "I devote my life to God and to helping others."

"You are defying one of God's greatest creations, the source of all life on this planet. He created a man's package of jewels to provide both pleasure and procreation to women. I want to make you a woman according to God's divine wishes."

As he later reported, the nun looked astonished before bursting into tears and fleeing from the library.

The next day, Peter confronted the stern Mother Superior, who was a dead ringer for Dame Edith Evans during her later years.

"You have committed an unspeakable act against God and this school," the nun lectured him. "You are expelled. You are to leave the grounds at once before I am forced to call the police."

As he later relayed to his friends, both Paddy and Connie never heard the full story. All that they were told is that their son had been caught in "an unspeakable act."

"Both of my parents seemed to think I'd been caught in the cloak room having sex with another boy. Mum didn't want to talk about it, but Paddy seemed understanding. He took me for a walk along the streets of town, telling me that as a schoolboy in Ireland, he had 'fooled around' with other lads."

"It's part of the experience of a young boy on the dawn of his manhood," Paddy told Peter. "It's a spell you're going through, as all of us boys do. A few months from now, you'll discover the warmth, the splendor of a woman's bosom and some of her lower attractions, too, and you'll never want to leave home and hearth after that. There is nothing on Earth as good as a man and a woman."

After the St. Anne's scandals, Peter was still al-

"Hovering like winged bats over me, scary nuns evoked Dame Edith Evans, but didn't dress in her finery."

19

lowed, during a period that lasted a few months, to be taught by Jesuit priests in another school. But when that didn't work out, he abandoned school altogether, never to return to his studies, except independently, when he became a voracious reader. "I was self-educated," he later said.

He also had to make a living, and thus launched himself into the adult workplace, refusing to become a factory worker. "I did every sort of odd job to make a shilling or two," he said.

For a time, he wrapped packages being mailed out of a dreary warehouse, a holdover from the Industrial Revolution. "When business was slow, I always pulled out that paperback edition of Shakespeare's works that I had tucked into my back pocket."

"I didn't stay on that job very long. After all, I was my father's son. I wasn't paid much, so I decided to sneak off with a package every now and then, especially if it looked like it contained something valuable."

"My boss caught me and fired me."

***

"Since I had been praised for my composition in school, I decided to storm the citadel of journalism. A newspaper reporter, that's what I would be. After all, I fancied myself as talented as The Bard. I'd already written a mean verse or two, which I think measured favorably when stacked up against Shakespeare's sonnets. Let me toss you a line or two."

"I don't crave security.
I want to hazard my soul to opportunity."

Chapter 2

"Pop's Irish Laddie" Takes to the Stage

& Overworks His "Didgeridoo" With Floozie Show-Biz Wannabees

Dressed Like Bogie, & Smoking "Fags" Like Bette Davis, Peter Becomes a Heavy Consumer of "The Brew"

Peter O'Toole as a reporter for *The Evening Post* in Leeds. "I was a young and callow fellow, reporting on rape and murder, dating a commie wench, posing in the nude, getting hit upon by England's most stately perverts, and winning rave reviews on the stage as the next Olivier."

Before he fled from the restrictions of the Catholic church, the then-fourteen-year-old Peter O'Toole was befriended by a kindly priest, Leo Welch. "This one had my actual welfare at heart. He wasn't one of those casting couch Jesuits."

21

The priest discussed his future, asking him what he really wanted to do in life.

"Sell Jaguars," young Peter responded. "But only the expensive custom-made ones in a rainbow of colors," Peter responded. "If not that, then a journalist, specializing in crime reporting, but only the most violent ones, like rape and murder, not petty theft or stealing cars—and no domestic violence stuff."

As a friend of the general manager of the *Yorkshire Evening Post,* Welch volunteered to get Peter a job there. He warned Peter, "You'll have to start at the bottom rung of the ladder and slowly work your way up."

Founded in 1890, its name abbreviated as "*Y.E.P.,*" the *Evening Post* was published nightly from its headquarters on Albion Street in Leeds. On the political spectrum, it was viewed as Liberal/Central Left. It rounded up local news, political fights, and crime, with lots of coverage of both local and national sports events, with special emphasis on such regional teams as the Leeds Rhinos, or the Yorkshire County Cricket Club.

Is it raining?

Although he did not excel at Y.E.P., many of its readers became aware of O'Toole's brief and turbulent association with that newspaper.

To his editor, Peter stated his own political views. "I am a total, wedded, bedded, bedrock, ocean-going, copper-bottomed, triple-distilled Socialist."

At the newspaper, he started out as a "teaboy," moving from desk to desk taking orders from editors and reporters who wanted a "cuppa," a sandwich, and some biscuits, or whatever. Invariably, he got all the orders mixed up.

"I became the office's chief "gopher"—go for this, go for that. Eventually,

As a "Teaboy" and Crime Reporter at the Morgue, Young O'Toole, as a Journalist in Yorkshire, Uncovers an Illegal Stash of Pornographic "Quim" Pix

I was made a copyboy before graduating to an assistant to the photographer in the lab."

Peter's boss was Nils Swenson, a striking figure of a man, standing 6'4" with a physique that evoked the movies of the body-building actor then identified with Hercules, Steve Reeves. At a charity raffle, Swenson had been voted "the handsomest man in Leeds."

"Instead of tea and watercress sandwiches, this flesh-eating carnivore sent me out to this dreary little caff every day at noon to bring him back his bloody platter that had once been part of the body of a fine stallion of grace and dignity galloping through fields of grass."

"On my second day on the job, I discovered his stash of quim photographs," Peter said, referring to large box of pictures Swenson had taken just of the vaginas of many of the women and girls of Leeds. "No woman was too old or too young to have a picture of her privates taken by this guy, from eight to eighty, or so it seemed."

"Maybe it was all that horsemeat he ate every day," Peter said. "Or perhaps he had something in common with the horse. The question that remained unanswered was, 'How did he get all these floozies to pose for him?' Our work in the lab was constantly interrupted by phone calls from women wanting to date him."

On three different occasions, Peter was assigned to cover sporting events. One day, after showing up at a soccer match, he got the scores mixed up. "Not only was I dismissed as a sports reporter, soccer fans in Leeds nearly lynched me."

Most late afternoons, after work, Peter retired, along with many of the other hard-drinking reporters, to the Adelphi Pub, where he always ordered Tetley's Bitter, brewed nearby.

[The Adelphi became his favorite. A journalist in the late 1980s remembered him entering the pub wearing a cream-colored linen suit, a chartreuse tie, and green socks, potentially provocative garb for a man of Leeds.]

Since he had not attained the legal drinking age of eighteen, he disguised his look, appearing in what he called "my Humphrey Bogart trenchcoat with dark glasses. I screwed on my head a flat cloth cap that I used to conceal my person for the specific purpose of upping my age a couple of years. When ordering, I would always lower my voice to more manful register." Then

The influential journalist Keith Waterhouse, shown here as a young "Advice to the Lovelorn" columnist.

he added, "I smoked fags like I'd seen Bette Davis do in the movies."

Very briefly, he worked with the chief reporter who covered crime not just in Leeds and Hunstret, but in the surrounding county as well. His journalistic turf included "Murder Mile," the very street on which Paddy O'Toole strolled *en route* to the gaming houses.

One of the publication's best staff writers, Keith Waterhouse, claimed that this strip was "stuffed with criminals, idiots, charmers, bastards, and some exceptionally nice people."

Waterhouse moved on to greater glory, writing the "Cassandra Column" for 26 years for London's *Daily Mirror*. Eventually, he migrated to *The Daily Mail*. Ironically, Peter, in 1999, would star in a televised version of a stage play written by Waterhouse, *Jeffrey Bernard is Unwell*.

"A Woman of Substance," Barbara Taylor Bradford: "I write for fame, glory, and millions."

Waterhouse would eventually forge a writing partnership with another soon-to-be famous member of the Leeds *literati*, Willis Hall. Their best-known play was *Billy Liar* (1960); an adaptation of Waterhouse's 1959 novel with the same name. *[Its premise would later be adapted into a film, a musical, and a TV series. Eventually, the two authors would jointly produce a staggering 250 scripts for theater, cinema, and TV. Peter would star in* The Long And The Short And The Tall *in 1959 at London's Royal Court Theatre, a play written by Hall.]*

At the *Evening Post,* Peter also came into contact with the third most famous writer of Leeds, Barbara Taylor Bradford. Her debut novel, *A Woman of Substance* (1979), sold more than 30 million copies worldwide, making it one of the top best-selling novels of all time.

During his time on the newspaper, Peter's most sensational encounter occurred as part of a visit the county morgue. Accompanied by the paper's assistant news editor, he viewed the body of a seventeen-year-old girl who had been raped and murdered. "The morgue attendant looked like Dracula—after all, who would take a job like that, with all those dead bodies? He wheeled out this cadaver and

The morgue, O'Toole's favorite "news beat."

removed the sheet from her body. He told us that her killer had bitten off the nipples from both of her tits, as we could plainly see for ourselves"

"Later, my editor commented on what a good condition her body was in, except for those missing nipples. He told me a necrophile would delight in her body. I asked him to explain."

"When he claimed that necrophiles preferred sex with dead bodies, I thought he was bullshitting me. Years later, I was taken to this bar in Soho, which I was told was the London hangout for dead body devotees. The drinks-and-sandwich menu was printed on a facsimile of a tombstone. I learned that necrophiles do indeed exist."

"Not for me!" Peter quipped. "I like my women hot and breathing. I even prefer them to work up a sweat like a pig on the morning of his castration."

Surprisingly, Peter's editor allowed him to attend two university classes a week in English literature. "The subject fascinated me," he recalled. "The staff called me 'The Bard of the Bog.' At one point, I was allowed to review plays at the Theatre Royal in Leeds."

"All of this was leading up to my own debut on the wicked stage."

Dating a Commie, & Touting Infant Sexuality, Peter Ventures Upon the Wicked Stage

During that period of his life, Peter kept a diary, in which he detailed "only my printable acts, not the unprintable ones. I still suffered Catholic guilt, but I didn't let that slow me down."

He wrote, "I will not be a common man, because it is my right to be an un-common man. I will stir the smooth sands of monotony."

He joined a repertoire company at the Leeds Arts Centre, which ran a Civic Theatre presenting plays to the community.

In the basement was the headquarters of both the Leeds' Marxist Association and the Young Communist League. Each of the groups tried to lure Peter into party membership, but he considered these Left-wingers "glum sods," and rejected their overtures.

Barbara Grace, an aspiring young actress of that time, remembered Peter: "No one singled him out for having any particular talent. I remember he showed up drunk on some nights. Mostly, he was known among the girls as a horny bastard who would not take 'no' for an answer. He propositioned me eight times. I always turned him down. He just wasn't my type. I liked burly men, and he was a pack of bones. He had better luck with some of the other girls."

"He often argued with one of our directors. He was always questioning the motivation of his character. One director called him 'a pain in the arse.'"

Roger Tracey, an actor, remembered a young actress from the Communist League who dated Peter. "She told me that he was not interested in any political cause, and that he had a 'don't-give-a-fuck' attitude. She also told me that instead of kissing his mouth, he wanted her to make love to his nose. In those days, he had what we in the theater called 'a Shylock Nose.'" Years later, when I went to see *Lawrence of Arabia,* that Jewish nose of his had been whacked off by some beauty butcher."

O'Toole: A rebellious cold-war bohemian looking for love in some of the wrong places.

According to Tracey, "Peter told outrageous stories, asking me if I knew that babies could get erections. He said that by the time he reached the age of five, he was having at least two orgasms a day, but without all that creamy stuff."

Another actor, Charlie Storey, momentarily befriended Peter. "When we had money, we quaffed quite a few and then we quaffed some more. He was always telling me what he did to the floozies with his *'didgeridoo.'* I think he exaggerated a wee bit."

"He told me that one night, he was pumping it to this girl, even though he had the world's biggest boil on his left buttock. In the middle of the dirty deed, she grabbed both cheeks of his arse to push him to a lower depth. Suddenly, the boil burst, and he said he let out a blood-curdling scream. The girl fled in terror, running out into the hall dripping pus from her hand and with her dress flying behind her."

"I remember once Peter and I went on a trip to York to see a rugby game. He coolly smoked one fag after another. When he had to go, he pulled down the carriage *[i.e., bus]* window and watered the vegetation *en route*. He said he was too drunk to walk to the loo."

"He bragged on how far he could let a golden stream flow. He said if we ever got to London, he would piddle on Lord Nelson from atop one of the stately lions of Trafalgar Square."

"Peter and I hung out with three other wannabee actors. None of us had any money. Peter devised a way to get us into the cinema. We pooled our shillings and raised enough to buy one ticket for Peter. Once inside the theatre, he would slip us in by lowering the window in the loo at the rear of the building, or else he'd open the door marked EXIT that led to the street. Of course, we could slip in only after the lights dimmed."

"He told us that when he was only twelve, he was the head of a Mutual

Masturbation Society in Leeds. He described what a pledge had to do during initiation."

According to Peter, "We stripped him naked, blindfolded him, and then forced his nose into the ass of a 300-pound boy who could fart on cue. Fattie's farts were as deadly as the mustard gas used in World War I."

Another actor's illness just before showtime brought Peter his first big break in the theatre. The local actors were set to perform a play based on the 1862 novel by Ivan Turgenev, *Fathers and Sons.*

The conflict in the play focuses on the growing divide between two generations of Russians. The character of Yevgeny Bazarov, a nihilist and medical student, rejects the concepts of the old order. Turgenev's novel was the first Russian work to gain prominence in the West. Later, it was praised by everyone from Henry James to Gustave Flaubert.

At the last minute, Peter was asked to play the lead, since he was the only one in the theater who could memorized lines after only a few readings.

The play was a success, and the local press praised his debut as a stage actor. He delivered to his editors at the *Evening Post* his own critique. "I was a daisy," he exclaimed.

Ivan Turgenev
Fathers and Sons
A new translation by Richard Freeborn

OXFORD WORLD'S CLASSICS

"I played the lead in the dramatization of Ivan Turgenev's novel. My character was a lovely bloke, one to share a blather, crack a bottle, or steal a woman from."

Peter's "Best Bloke" Persuades Him to Pose as Goya's The Naked Maja "In All My Uncut Glory,"

Then He Befriends a Celebrated Child Molester

A flair for late 19th century dramatics.

Peter would enjoy many best friends through-out the various stages of his life. Depending on the circumstances and the period of his life, they would include Kenneth Griffith, Richard Burton, Oliver Reed, Richard Harris, and James Villiers, all of them actors.

But the first man who became his "best friend" was a year younger than he was. A painter named Patrick O'Liver, he became Peter's confidant and "comrade in various randy adventures." Peter described some of these in the first volume of his memoirs.

"My painter friend, Patrick O'Liver, asked me to pose nude for his portrait of me. I obliged."

The relationship began with a surprise referral from Peter's editor at the *Evening Post.* Over coffee, the editor said that one of his closest friends, a distinguished journalist, had a son that Peter might enjoy forming a bond with.

Patrick O'Liver was described as "precociously gifted, intelligent, charming, and a touch unruly, wayward, and rebellious—just like you, Peter."

It was agreed that a rendezvous between the two youths would be set up that Saturday night at a dinner. As Peter later claimed, "That began my hurly-burly friendship with Patrick. We pinned our ears back and snarled; I knew a bank were the wild thyme blows, and he knew all that was foul and fit to screech in." *[O'Toole sometimes spoke with such colorful syntax that at times, most people didn't know what he meant.]*

Patrick's father was a bit too stern and distinguished for Peter's taste, but "I found his Mum a randy imp of a girl. Patrick had inherited his artistic bent from her. She took us into her study, and she showed me a catalogue of her early sketches of the men she'd known before her marriage. She had drawn the balls and the tools of the fools who had bestrode her. There were quite a lot of them, too."

Perhaps taking after his mother, Patrick, in the coming weeks, asked Peter to pose nude for him. "He wanted to paint the male version of the famous portrait by Goya of *The Naked Maja,* allegedly modeled by the Duchess of Alba. During the course of a long weekend, I posed for him in all my uncut manly glory. I don't know what happened to the painting. It's probably hanging in some stately home today."

Goya's *The Naked Maja*, the role model for Peter's first nude painting.

In the months and years ahead, Patrick become "one of the most solid blocks in my life. No one— the good, the bad, or the loathsome mediocrities—had a greater and more timely influence *[on me]* than O'Liver."

Once, Peter invited O'Liver to accompany him for an interview with Jimmy Savile, at the time, one of the most famous personalities in England, and on the dawn of a Knighthood.

Jimmy Savile, Britain's most widely publicized child-molesting pervert, confidant of Margaret Thatcher, and marriage counsellor to Prince Charles and Diana.

[Savile was soon to become nationally famous as a DJ, TV presenter, media personality, and charity fund-raiser. He was also a semi-professional sportsman who sometimes wrestled in the ring.

Thanks to Savile's involvement in charities, which were to raise millions of pounds, he became a close friend of then Prime Minister Margaret Thatcher, and often spent the Christmas holidays with her and her family. He also became a close friend of Prince Charles, and at one point, although a bachelor himself, Savile offered Charles and his then-wife Diana marriage counseling in a (failed) attempt to prevent their divorce.]

When Savile returned to Leeds, Peter was sent to interview him. He found him a colorful character whose words could be morphed into enticing newspaper copy. When Peter and O'Liver met him for the first time, Savile was smoking a cigar. "Pop gave me my first cigar when I was seven years old, thinking that it would make me sick. It had the opposite effect. I've been addicted to cigars ever since."

Back in his office at the *Evening Post,* Peter, to his editor, made what appeared to be a highly exaggerated claim about Savile. "The bloke tried to get Patrick and me drunk. He went so far as to proposition us, promising he would take care of our wee-wees. We got the hell out of there, with our virginity intact."

At the time, the editor dismissed Peter's accusation, telling his assistant, "Imagine that O'Toole kid saying that about Jimmy Savile, who is one of the most masculine men I've ever met. There's no way in hell that he's a poof."

[With the passage of time, Peter was exonerated in his claim that Savile had tried to seduce O'Liver and himself. At the time of Savile's death in October of 2011, he had come to be viewed as one of the most aggressively predatory sex offenders in Britain, scoring a series of seductions of both young girls and boys, perhaps 450 known cases. Some of his victims who cited rape were under ten years old at the time.

As early as the 1990s, when Peter heard stories of Savile's child molesta-

tion and other abuses, he claimed, "I could have told the authorities about that a half-century ago. It's amazing how Savile got away with his criminal activities for so long. But he had friends in high places, if you get my drift."]

***

When Peter woke up on the morning of his 18th birthday, he called O'Liver. "I've decided that I don't want to be a journalist. I don't want to write about the affairs of other people. I want journalists writing about *my* affairs. I think I want to be a famous actor."

Later that day, when he told his editor about his career change, his boss agreed with him. "I heartily endorse your plan. You were never a journalist. Nor do I think you could ever have become one. Good riddance, kid."

That night over beer—he was now of legal drinking age—he told O'Liver, "I've decided to storm the formidable walls of London Town. I'm going on the stage where no doubt within months, I'll be hailed as the greatest actor since David Garrick. This is not overly exaggerated desire on my part. It is my destiny. I'm heading south to conquer. Get out of my way *[Sir Laurence]* Olivier, or else I'll knock you down and walk over your tired old body to claim my right in the spotlight."

As Peter described his youthful self later in life: "Young, dumb, full of cum, and a magnet for tarts."

"I think you just might pull this off," O'Liver said. "You're a bloody original."

"In the meantime, let's get pissed. Booze is the most outrageous of drugs. That's why it's my preferred choice."

Chapter 3

Seaman O'Toole:

"The Worst Sailor" in the History of His Majesty's Royal Navy

"I Fought Off the Homos at Night & Spent Most of My Time in the Brig"

"To fulfill my duty to Queen and country, I was forced into National Service. I was no bloody sailor, vomiting my way across the stormy seas and fighting off the amorous attention of my superior officer."

"The highlight of my tour of duty was shacking up with Mai Zetterling, the Swedish beauty. I got to her before Tyrone Power made her a live-in."

While he was still in the Navy, the beautiful Swedish bombshell, Mai Zetterling, became Seaman O'Toole's first movie star seduction, the first of many.

From the slums of Stockholm, she'd traveled the road to the glitter of London and Hollywood, having affairs with actors Herbert Lom, Tyrone Power, Peter Finch, and O'Toole long before he became a star himself.

"I came to London to become an actor—actually I already was one—but His Majesty's Government had other plans for me," O'Toole said.

"In 1950, I turned eighteen, and there was this thing called National Service that ate away at two years of your life, especially the year when boys turned nineteen and were at their sexual peak. During that crucial time, they're surrounded with other young men in the service and not a bird in sight until they go ashore. I don't know what bloody fool figured that out."

"At first, I considered objecting to service on religious grounds, even though I was a lapsed Catholic. Then I thought about registering as a conscientious objector. Some blokes who did that ended up in prison or else were forced to work in a coal mine."

"Paddy, my father, still calling himself 'Captain O'Toole,' urged me to follow in his footsteps. That from a man who never sailed anywhere except on a ferryboat across the Irish Sea to England. He just pretended to be a sea captain, although he had stopped telling tales of how he once fought off a sea monster in the middle of the Atlantic Ocean."

O'Toole definitely didn't want to be a British foot solider, so he chose the Royal Navy. But it was hard to get in. There were several problems. A prospective sailor had to be British born. Although he had

Royal Navy seamen circa 1936. A hard-knock life. Regimentation of this sort was NOT for Peter O'Toole.

HMS Victory
Royal Naval Barracks
Portsmouth
Prior to modernisation and renamed HMS Nelson

Old, Imperial England and its Maritime ways.

His Affair with Britain's "Swede-Heart," Actress Mai Zetterling

been born in Ireland, he maintained that his father, Patrick Joseph O'Toole, had been born in Ireland when it was under British rule.

"Inspired by Paddy, I fibbed to my recruiting officer, a young and rather naïve man. I told him that I had descended from a long line of courageous seafarers, who had extended the boundaries of the British Empire. I also claimed that I was a dedicated man, who wanted to make my life's career in the Royal Navy. What a crock!"

He was accepted in the Navy and told to report to duty at Portsmouth. He read a book extolling the exploits of the Royal Navy, whose origins went back to the 16th Century. From the end of the 17th Century until well into the 20th Century, it was the most powerful navy in the world, playing a key role in establishing and expanding the British Empire, which at its peak stretched from the Falkland Islands to Hong Kong.

When he was inducted into the Royal Navy, because of economic hardships in post-War Britain, it was in a state of decline. The increasingly powerful U.S. Navy was assuming Britain's former role as a global naval power and police for the Atlantic and Pacific.

Portsmouth, the seat of the Royal Navy for 500 years, had been almost leveled by the *Luftwaffe* during World War II. Most of its docks, wharves, and naval facilities had been rebuilt in June of 1944, when Allied troops used it as their port of departure for the storming of the Nazi-controlled beaches of Normandy. The epic battles resulting from that invasion eventually turned the tides of World War II.

At Portsmouth, O'Toole was subjected to an aptitude test comprised of twenty questions. Its outcome would determine if he might be a candidate for officer training. He answered only one of the questions, and his wording was flippant.

In the aftermath of his (failed) aptitude test, instead of entering an officer training program, he was assigned to submarine duty as a signaler, decoding naval messages and enabling communications among land, sea, and air forces, including Royal Marine Commandos in the field. Most of his communications were about weather patterns and ship movements.

During his period of enlistment, O'Toole found that one of the major preoccupations of the Royal Navy involved its role as an anti-submarine force, hunting Soviet intruders. "The Cold War was freezing half the Globe," he said.

"As a signalman, I was supposed to know the semaphore code and how to receive it and transmit it. Not once at sea was I ever able to demonstrate this skill. Instead, I blundered into wanking a teleprinter, dashing around with messages, and generally making myself helpful to all those stationed at the signals office on the bridge."

"Being confined to the cramped living quarters of a submarine was bloody hell for me," O'Toole said. "Ever since I was a kid in Leeds, I suffered from history's worst case of claustrophobia. I'd walk up twelve flights of stairs to avoid having to get inside a lift *[i.e., elevator]*."

"In the military, you always have to march. I was not fit for parades. I was always out of step. I'd get confused. I was never able to tell my left foot from my right. Each of my feet has always operated independently of each other."

"I never got Navy lingo down pat. My officers called it a deck. Aboard ship—I always called it a boat—a deck was a floor. Instead of a porthole, I called it a window, and instead of the ship's funnel, I referred to it as a chimney."

"On most nights, the men off duty engaged in heavy bull sessions. Their favorite topic was all the dazzling beauties they left behind. No one had an ugly girlfriend. All of them, to hear these guys tell it, had a woman far more beautiful than Elizabeth Taylor."

Invariably, the biggest braggart would be a little shrimp of a man. To hear him tell it, he ripped apart vaginas with his mammoth lethal weapon. I once spotted one of these braggarts in the shower. It was a tiny piece of okra."

"There was nightly talk of a Sylvia, a Deborah, or a Vivien, the girl left behind before the men took to sea. A large majority of them had plans to marry once their tour of duty was over, providing their girlfriends hadn't wed some other bloke in the meantime."

Despite his status as a signalman, O'Toole simply did not understand decoding messages. To him, it seemed a dreadful waste of time. Most of the messages were weather reports or about movement of His Majesty's battleships.

"There was no Soviet spy shit—nothing like that," he said.

His problem was solved one night when he wandered into Portsmouth's longtime sailor favorite, The Ship & Castle Pub on The Hard.

Here, he met Barbara Leicester, a member of The Women's Royal Naval Service (its members are officially designated as "Wrens") working at Portsmouth's naval base decoding communications among ships. Before the night was over, he'd not only made love to her, but obtained her agreement that she'd henceforth give him readable transcriptions of each ship's messages so he

The Women's Royal Naval Service: recruitment posters hinted at more than just career advancements.

wouldn't have to spend hours trying to decode them himself.

As a sailor, he'd been provisioned with a "Brown Card," identification that allowed him easy passage to and from his ship. He met frequently wlth Leicester, who gave him the decoded messages, which he would then forward to his commanding officers and to other ships.

This went on for about three weeks, as did his love-making with this beautiful young woman. However, someone in her office learned about what she was doing, and O'Toole was reported to Naval authorities. And whereas Leicester lost her job, O'Toole ended up in the brig, the first of about a dozen other "lockups," he suffered before he "retired" forever from the Navy.

He devoted scant attention to his service in the Navy within the first volume of his memoirs, in which he wrote, "My sea had been black; black and gray, with great lumps of white water crashing over our bows to rush swilling along the lurching deck. Often I stood, gloved hands gripping a rail or a stanchion, just gazing, awed by this immense world of black and brutal water. Northern waters had been our lot."

From the Western Islands of Scotland, his ship proceeded through bodies of water that included the Atlantic, the Irish Sea, the North Sea, the Pentland Firth, the Skagerrak, the Kattegat, the Baltic, and the Gulf of Bothnia.

In lieu of simply ignoring this period of young O'Toole's life, his time in the Navy has been reconstructed by comments he made to friends over the years, particularly Kenneth Griffith, his acting collaborator and would-be memoirist.

After the release of *Lawrence of Arabia,* after O'Toole became famous, many men who had known him during his naval service came forward with recollections about their soon-to-be movie star associate.

The Loneliness of a Mariner Named "Nellie," Vomiting from "Mal de Mer" during Graveyard Shifts in the North Atlantic

"I was often accused of insubordination, ending up in the brig," O'Toole said. "On our boat, I was the most frequently jailed of all the sailors. I got used to hearing some commanding officer tell me, 'It's off to the brig for the likes of you.'"

"Some of the offenses that sent me to the brig I recall," he said. "Others, I have long forgotten. One night, I made off with a bottle of rum. It was a very cold night, and I needed to warm my insides. On another occasion, I was caught masturbating on duty. One time, I was spotted wearing a pair of women's bloomers. Some jealous bloke reported me."

"I had a reason for that. One night, I was shacked up with this bird, and I overslept, as was my tendency. Rushing to get dressed in the dark, I slipped into her panties, grabbed my jeans and shirt, and made a run for it. This guy later saw me undressing, and spread the word. For weeks, I was called 'Nellie,' and reported to be a secret cross-dresser."

"The first time I was locked away in this cell, I became panicky, since I suffered from claustrophobia. The shits never told you how long they were going to keep you confined. It was part of their mental torture of you."

"I lay on this steel cot, trying to think about my future and not the pain of the past. A solitary guard would march back and forth every hour or so."

There were some benefits to his confinement. He got to read and memorize lines from the works of William Shakespeare.

"After six weeks at sea, I decided that the Royal Navy was not for me. I was doing the Navy no good, and, bloody hell, it was doing me no good either. I wanted to go to London to become an actor."

"A fellow seaman told me that if I drank a lot of alcohol and then swallowed a bottle of aspirin, that I would become so ill, so pale, and in such desperate need of hospitalization, that I would be discharged. On the first night ashore, I went to this pub and invested all my bob in eighteen bottles of wine, which I consumed, followed by those lethal aspirin pills. My recovery took three days in the hospital, the longest and most severe hangover of my illustrious career as a drunk. Even when I so-called recovered, I stumbled about groggy for a week or more."

"The only good thing for me in the Navy was when I was allowed to join the boat's band. I was assigned the bass drum. Fortunately, I'd had some experience in Leeds when Leadbelly was my favorite singer."

"I was never cut out to be a sailor. I spent most of my time in the service vomiting. The rocking of the boat always made me violently ill. In fact, I polluted the Seven Seas with my green slime. It seemed I spent more time vomiting in the toilet bowl than I did crapping in it."

After being fired as a decoder, his next assignment was the least desired among the ship's duties. He was assigned the "graveyard shift," which put him on patrol between midnight and four in the morning.

His evening began when he made the rounds of the vessel, with the assignment of ensuring that the sailors assigned to duty had not fallen asleep. Some of them had.

After three tours of the ship, he was allowed to go to the mess hall for cups of coffee. It was a lonely place at that hour, with barren tables and only one light bulb burning.

"On some nights, all alone on my shift, I was mesmerized by the incredible stillness of the ocean when the waters were calm. It was a stillness like none possible on land. I'd often stand at my lookout station, staring out at the dark, distant horizon, wondering if the men who sailed with Columbus to the New World felt the same as I did. Perhaps they were fearful of going over the edge, since they believed that the world was flat. I had no such fear, of course, but I did feel we were out in this incredible body of water that had swallowed up countless thousands of men."

"I always welcomed the first streaks of dawn, a rosy glow in the sky. You could hear the screech of seagulls. Nothing is as fresh as a morning breeze in the North Atlantic. I was sucking air into lungs grown stale from breathing all that smog from the Industrial Revolution in Leeds."

"I could stand for hours mesmerized by the phosphorescent whitecaps created by the boat's movement through the dark waters. I even came to like the sound of the engines, knowing that one day, they would bring me back to shore and my freedom. My favorite nights were when there was a full moon, illuminating the waters. Only once did I see a blood moon. It was one of the most dramatic sights I'd ever seen in my life."

The worst nights were when the ship rolled through the heavy seas, churning, heaving and rolling, much like O'Toole's delicate stomach. He always got sick on those nights.

He recalled how one night, after duty in the North Atlantic, he climbed down a narrow ladder into a hallway lit by a single lightbulb. "Before taking off my dungarees and tying my shoes, I sat down on a toilet in this cramped compartment before heading back to my bunk. I shed tears, but muffled my sobbing. No sailor wants to be caught crying like a baby. But the tears came and I couldn't turn them off. I felt desperately homesick, and all alone."

After each of his all-night duties, just as he tried to sleep, the sounds of morning filled his ship. He heard men banging lockers, talking in loud voices. A lot of sailors wanted more sleep and could be heard cursing. The sounds of short and long blasts could be heard. Announcements were blasted over the loudspeakers, "Now hear this! Now hear this!"

O'Toole's Chief Officer Gets Amorous With the Lonely Sailor on Night Watch

Throughout the illustrious and complicated history of Britain's Royal Navy, attitudes about homosexual activity have ranged from benign neglect to fervent attempts at suppression. As if to illustrate the prevalence of male-to-male bonding at sea, during an argument with a Member of Parliament, Sir Winston Churchill once said, "The only Navy traditions are rum, sodomy, and the lash."

Even when O'Toole served during the early 50s, he saw and experienced evidence of rampant homosexuality aboard his ship. He did not choose to participate, although he was frequently solicited by horny shipmates, sometimes aggressively so.

In the coming years, especially during the mid- to late 1960s, there would be investigations of scandals associated with homosexual liaisons aboard British ships, even of activities pursued by British sailors on leave in various ports. These included patronage of transvestite prostitutes.

One of O'Toole's shipmates told him about the night he picked up a beautiful prostitute. "When I undressed her, I found she was he. 'Blimey, you're all there!' I said. But by then, I was too far heated up to back out. Transvestites will do all things to a man that no decent woman ever would."

Admiral Sir John Fitzroy Duyland Bush, head of the British Western Fleet, said, "There is, regrettably, ample evidence that homosexual practices are rife in the fleet. I have a strong belief that many of the men are not perverts, but basically normal men whose standards of behavior are thoroughly lax."

BOYS AT SEA

Sodomy, Indecency, and Courts Martial in Nelson's Navy

B. R. Burg

O'Toole later told friends, "It was not my cuppa, but more than half the men aboard my ship were into it. They were desperate, poor guys."

The book, *Boys at Sea*, is the story of homoerotic life aboard ships of the Royal Navy in the age of fighting sail. It traces sexual activity from the reign of Queen Anne almost to the dawn of the Victorian Age.

"The guys who suffered the worse were the young, unwilling sailors, upon whom some of the older officers forced themselves."

One investigative report concluded: "Fifty percent of the fleet have sinned homosexually at some time in their naval career. Because of rapidly changing views on sexual morality in the Western world, it was suggested in some quarters that a few youthful indiscretions might be overlooked, since expulsion of so many men would threaten the national security of Britain. 'We would lose half of the young men we'd trained so expensively,' one commander noted."

O'Toole later related the details of his own encounter with a homosexual aggression from a superior officer: "Every night, my chief would come on deck, as he called it, and fraternize with me while I stood guard duty. I'd been told that officers were not to hang out with enlisted men, but he didn't bother following that rule."

"He was a family man with a wife and three kids left behind in Shropshire."

"My chief was in his late thirties, but a life at sea had hardened his features. The first signs of wrinkles had already appeared under his eyes."

"I was embarrassed at all the attention he paid me. He seemed to be taking a fatherly interest in me, or at least I hope that was what it was. Sometimes, he put his arm around me as we'd stand just looking out at the sea, without saying a word."

One night when he joined me on watch, he seemed to be drunk on rum. His speech was slurred as he spoke of the beauty of the sea. "The sea is like a gorgeous doll," he said. "No matter what angle you turn her, she's still gorgeous."

Suddenly, he made a move toward O'Toole. "You're gorgeous, too, kid. I've been wanting to do this for a long time." He groped O'Toole and began kissing his neck.

Terrified and not knowing what to do, O'Toole withdrew as gently as he could. After all, this was his superior officer.

When he realized that O'Toole had pulled away, the officer did not force the issue. He looked up at the sky and at the ocean on the horizon. "Well, I guess I'd better hit the sack," he said. "Good night."

That was the last time the officer visited him during his night watch. For the rest of the trip, he barked orders at O'Toole without any further personal talk. It was an embarrassment between them best left unmentioned.

In a Tongue-Kissing Contest, O'Toole Becomes "The Homo Bitch" of a Brutish Russian Sailor Intent on Winning One for the Kremlin

O'Toole's battleship—aka "my boat," as he insisted on calling it—sailed into the Port of Stockholm, marking the first time a vessel in the British fleet had visited Sweden since the outbreak of World War II in 1939. It would be for an extended stay, and would be the most important time for him of the months he spent in the British Navy.

Although the sailors, depending on their assignments, could party on shore at night, they had duties during the day. O'Toole would botch his first on-shore assignment, landing him two nights in the by-now-familiar brig.

Along with a junior officer, O'Toole was given a walkie-talkie, which he carelessly slung over his shoulder, not securing it as navy regulations required.

The British admiral was scheduled to greet King Gustav VI Adolf aboard a Swedish battleship. A heavy fog had descended, so O'Toole and a junior officer, John Shepherd, were to coordinate the coming together of the two vessels.

To that effect, O'Toole and Shepherd boarded a small boat and set out to locate the Swedish ship. Visibility was so poor that O'Toole could not make out anything. Peering out, he bent too far over in the boat and his radio, suspended from its strap, fell from his arm into the sea.

He never found out if Sweden's King ever met with the British Admiral, because he was summoned ashore and hauled off once again to the brig, this time for two nights.

COLD WAR POLITICS
HRH Queen Elizabeth II with Sweden's
King Gustav VI Adolf in 1954

After his release, during his first night on leave, he and eight other sailors headed for a rough sailors' dive in *Gamla Stan*, Stockholm's Old Town. His shipmates still called him "Nellie," but had come to admire him for his insubordination and his many times in the brig.

After a pub crawl, the sailors ended up at a place called Pub Engelen in a dingy cellar dating from the 15th Century. Some members of the Soviet fleet, based

What Western Europe and the U.S.
feared. Why there was NATO.

Soviet Naval Militia during the Cold War

aboard a ship docked in Stockholm's harbor, were also drinking heavily in the same cellar.

"It was either going to be an all-out brawl, or an endurance contest," the chief bartender predicted. Through a translator, the "limey" sailors learned the details of a most unusual Soviet challenge.

To determine which men were stronger, the Russians wanted to see which sailor could endure the longest in a bout of tongue kissing. The first one who backed away would be the loser, with the understanding that the vanquished would have to pay for the drinks of the winning team.

The British selected "Nellie" as their choice to engage the Russian. O'Toole objected strenuously, but since he had been designated as his shipmates' unanimous choice, he felt he had to "stand up for Western democracy."

His opponent was "a huge monster of a Russian sailor, grossly overweight, with reddish blonde hair and a matching beard and mustache. "When I faced him, I felt I was a goner," O'Toole recalled.

"My challenger was a fierce fire-breathing dragon with a tongue at least a foot long that clogged my wind tunnel," O'Toole claimed. "He had breath so foul that it would make the sewers of Paris smell like Chanel no. 5. I thought I was going to smother to death during his assault."

On leave in Stockholm, Soviet sailors like those depicted above often encountered their British counterparts in pubs.

There, they engaged in some unusual endurance contests, testing their manpower and might against what they called "the Limeys," about the only English word they knew.

O'Toole became the victim of one of them.

"It went on and on, and he showed no sign of giving up. I finally had to cry 'uncle' myself and pulled away. I wanted to slug him, but I knew he would make mincemeat of me. Our tongue battle was timed. I endured seven minutes of an oral attack from this commie brute."

"My shipmates were horribly disappointed in me, and the Russians drank up and cheered the winner, knowing they wouldn't have to pay the bill."

"The brute shouted something at me and I asked the translator what he was calling out. It turned out to be something like this: 'I made the homo my bitch!' he was boasting."

"Every Man, at Least Once in His Life, Should Have an Affair with a Swedish Actress"

— Peter O'Toole

He went ashore again, this time making his way to the *Kungliga Dramatiska Theatern* (Royal Dramatic Theater), where Greta Garbo got her start as an actress, and where Sweden's foremost director, Ingmar Bergman, staged productions.

A lecture about stage techniques was being delivered that afternoon by the beautiful, Swedish-born actress, Mai Zetterling, who had found success and popularity in Britain. O'Toole, who continued to dream of becoming an actor if he ever got out of the Navy, was allowed to sit in on her lecture. Zetterling delivered it in English, since a number of foreigners, including Americans and Brits, were in attendance, and because all the Swedish students spoke English, which was mandatory in schools.

In her first movie role, Alf Sjöberg directed Mai Zetterling in *Frenzy (aka Torment; 1944)*. Its screenplay was by Ingmar Bergman, who liked her performance so much, he agreed to audition her in his bedroom.

Seven years older than O'Toole, Zetterling was returning to her roots. Her breakthrough role had been in in Bergman's 1944 film, *Torment,* in which she played a controversial role as a shop girl. But her greatest success had been with British moviegoers for films she had made in London. Peter had seen only one of them, *Quartet* (1948), based on the short stories of W. Somerset Maugham. He admired her talent greatly, although knowing she would never match the record of her Swedish competitors, Ingrid Bergman or Greta Garbo.

In her segment of *Quartet,* a separate feature entitled *The Facts of Life,* Zetterling appeared with a young actor, Jack Watling. She played a gorgeous woman who befriends Watling but turns out to be a thief.

After the lecture, O'Toole went backstage to introduce himself. She was charmed by his youth, male beauty, and his genuine appreciation of her talent as an actress. She invited him to dinner in her suite at Stockholm's nearby Grand Hotel.

He was honored to accept the invitation.

Unknown to him, Zetterling was coming to the end of her wartime marriage to Tuttle Lemkow, a Norwegian actor and dancer known mostly for playing villainous roles in British films.

Ironically, Lemkow would appear with O'Toole and Richard Burton in the 1964 *Becket.*

As O'Toole would later relate to James Villiers back in London (he knew Zetterling), "The sexual chemistry between us was just right. We clicked. Every bloke should make love to a Swedish actress at least once in his life."

The following morning over breakfast, she invited him to stay with her whenever he wasn't needed aboard his ship.

As he later claimed, "The most remarkable thing about Mai was that at the peak of the Cold War, she was a dedicated communist. I couldn't believe it. Even more than her dedication to her acting career, she had the commie line down pat and most convincing. But she didn't convince me to desert and join that Russian ship in the harbor, not with that big brute of a tongue kisser aboard."

[Unlike their U.S. equivalent during the Cold War, neither the British or Swedish governments maintained a "blacklist" populated with the names of Left-leaning members of their stage and film communities. Zetterling's politics did not appear to harm her career as an actress.]

There's speculation that rugby—probably the most brutal of the "recognized" sports on earth—was first played by the military as a diversion from other, less healthy pastimes...

Before he left Sweden, O'Toole the sailor would confront another disaster, this one quite violent.

It an error in judgment, his superior officers ordered him to take part in a rugby game featuring British seamen against Stockholm policemen. The venue lay on a rugby field about six miles from Stockholm's city center. He was supplied with the address.

Granted three days leave in conjunction with the timing of the sporting event, he planned to spend those nights with Zetterling. On the afternoon of the game, he lost the paper on which he had written the address. When he contacted his ship to retrieve it, he wrote down the wrong address, then handed the scribbled paper to Zetterling. Consequently, she drove him to the wrong rugby field, where he was told that the game he was scheduled to play in was about three miles away.

O'Toole finally found the stadium, arriving in the changing room only a few minutes before the game was scheduled to begin. His coach was furious, demoting him from the star position he'd understood he'd be playing, and assigning him instead to a (arguably more injury-prone) position on the tightly huddled starting lineup known as the scrum.

The opposing team was composed of well-trained quasi-military bruisers who looked as if they had murder on their minds.

After the first round, O'Toole had been mauled, but instead of taking him out of the game, he was assigned a defensive role as a fullback.

Always a rebellious iconoclast, O'Toole didn't necessarily play rugby by the rules—in fact, he probably didn't even know what the rules were. This seriously pissed off one of the bruisers on the Stockholm team.

In a fast maneuver, O'Toole caught the ball, but then fell to the ground. His mouth was open as one of the beefiest of the police team members kicked him in the chin with his booted foot. O'Toole's teeth clamped down on his tongue, partially severing about an inch of it. Screaming in pain, he began bleeding profusely.

Rushed into the emergency division of the nearest hospital, he was wheeled directly into surgery, where doctors skillfully sewed his tongue back together.

To his amazement, when it healed, he derived an unexpected benefit: Before his injury, he had had a slight stammer and lisp. But speaking with his restored tongue, he said, "My Bogart lisp has vanished. I now sound like Olivier."

During his recovery, Zetterling came to visit him in the hospital every day, bringing some small gift. On her final visit, she kissed him goodbye and promised to see him again when both of them were back in London.

His officer had notified him that he was to leave the hospital early the next morning, based on his ship's imminent departure for the North Sea.

He got up in enough time to board a train into central Stockholm, but by mistake, he boarded the wrong train, one heading for the city of Gothenburg in the west. When he realized his mistake, he got off at the first stop and changed trains, this time boarding one heading east toward Stockholm.

When he finally arrived at the harbor, he saw his ship sailing away.

In desperation, he hired the owner of a speedboat festooned with balloons at Tivoli Gröna Lund. *[In Stockholm, it's a carefully landscaped amusement park and concert venue, established in the 1860s, that's evocative of a larger, better-known equivalent in Copenhagen.]* Its captain chugged its way toward the British ship, from which a sailor uncoiled a rope ladder and passed it down to O'Toole, who climbed aboard, only to be sent for a final lockup in the ship's brig.

***

After eighteen months of service in His Majesty's Navy, O'Toole was judged unfit for military service. He was discharged and told that he would never again be called up for military service "even if Soviet battleships are coming up the Thames."

He left the ship wearing blue jeans, having stuffed his Navy uniform, including his sailor's cap, into a duffel bag.

When his train arrived at Waterloo Station, he headed for the nearest bridge. Into the Thames he threw his bell bottoms.

Then he traveled north to Leeds, where he worked for a brief stint at the *Yorkshire Evening News* until he accumulated enough money to head for London again, where he planned to enroll in the Royal Academy of Dramatic Art (RADA). He wanted to make his mark in a city that had witnessed a parade of famous people—Samuel Johnson, Elizabeth I, Sir Walter Raleigh, Henry VIII, Nell Gwyn, Oliver Cromwell, Charles Dickens, and, yes, Shakespeare himself.

"I was ready to embark on my career as an actor," O'Toole said. "In my youthful vanity, I was convinced of one thing: The name of Peter O'Toole would soon be added to those august personages of yesterday."

***

Back in London, he met again with Zetterling on several occasions, but there is no evidence that they ever resumed their affair. It appeared that she was a serial seducer of actors, often her co-stars. She went on to become romantically linked with Richard Widmark; Laurence Harvey ("What a mess," she said); Peter Sellers; the Prague-born actor, Herbert Lom; Richard Attenborough; and Stanley Baker.

She fell in love with Dirk Bogarde, but learned that he was gay. Her most notorious affair was with Tyrone Power, beginning in 1956 and continuing off and on until his death in 1958.

That same year, she wed David Hughes, the Welsh novelist with whom she collaborated on a number of films and books.

In the press, she was dubbed as "Britain's *Swede*-Heart," a designation she loathed.

She even engaged in a brief affair with O'Toole's friend, Peter Finch. At the Salisbury Pub in London, she talked about Finch: "I liked him very much, but he's a roamer, never wanting to settle down with just one woman, even if he's married to her. He is a true outlaw, a haunted, depressed man. He and his lover, Vivien Leigh, have much in common, the master and mistress of the sudden dark mood. I think he seduced so many women as a means of proving something to himself. He fears his homosexual nature. He had an affair with Olivier."

"And with Vivien, too," O'Toole said. "At least that's keeping it in the same family."

"Finch boozed too much, and I found that unacceptable," she said. "In the end, I came to view him as pathetic. He left me tired, bored, and sad."

O'Toole's final encounter with Zetterling transpired at the 1965 Cannes Film Festival. She was in a depressed mood, as the festival

Through Mai Zetterling, Seaman O'Toole got an early view of the rarefied world of *avant-garde* filmmaking of the 1950s.

Though relatively tame by today's standards, *Loving Couples*, the film she directed, broke most of the taboos of that era. Peter, as an ambitious but unknown actor, soaked it up ravenously.

45

judges had refused to show her latest film, *Ålskane par (Loving Couples),* a celluloid portrait of three women from different backgrounds in the hospital giving birth. The judges rejected the film because of its sexual explicitness and full-frontal nudity.

The well-known critic, Kenneth Tynan, in *The Observer,* appraised the film as "one of the most ambitious directorial debuts since *Citizen Kane."*

Zetterling also seemed very bitter about Hollywood, telling O'Toole, "You can take that town and shove it. I felt like a creature from another planet there. I refused to conform in that sex-crazed, pinup hungry town. I'm now setting out to make it as a director, but only on my own terms."

She told him that she'd like to direct him one day as the star of one of her future films.

"I'd be most willing," he said.

It was a promise dangled before him that was never kept.

Mai Zetterling once screened her controversial film, *Loving Couples,* for O'Toole and even gave him a review of her own movie, a scene from which is depicted above:

"It is severe, funny, often a moving critique of family life and hypocrisy in human relationships. It is very Swedish, much like Ingmar Bergman, but it has a universal theme. It is about women and their deeper attitudes to the fundamentals of life: birth and marriage, sexual relations, human feelings, freedom."

Chapter 4

O'Toole in Training

at the Royal Academy of Dramatic Art
(How It All Began)

Mixed Advice from Veteran Stars of the British Stage:
"Give Up the Theatre Altogether" &
"Put More Cock Into Your Voice!"

"Not all the drama students at RADA became great actors."

So spoke Peter O'Toole as he walked through the doors of 62-64 Gower Street in London's West End.

"A lot of us were from the north country, a sort of 'Yorkshire Mafia.' I knew I was heading for greatness. There were some hopefuls: Albert Finney, Alan Bates (he came on to me), and Richard Harris. None quite had my talent, though."

As a seaman in His Majesty's Navy, Peter O'Toole, as he admitted himself, had been "a bloody failure. It was a nightmarish experience, most of my time spent locked in the brig."

"All my reading of Willie Shakespeare, while confined, had imbued me with an overriding desire to become an actor on the stage. At that time, I never dreamed or even wanted to be a star of the cinema."

With his new best friend, Patrick O'Liver, an aspiring painter, O'Toole hitched a ride with a lorry *[i.e., truck]* driver from Leeds into London. His mother, Connie, had packed a large picnic basket for them, which O'Toole shared with Patrick and the driver.

In London, the driver dropped them off at Euston Station. In parting, he told them, "You two young blokes look like queer bait. Better keep it zipped up."

The two young and aspiring artists had exactly five pounds between them. O'Toole had envisioned dropping in on his sister, Patricia, and "hitting her up for a few bob and maybe using her apartment as a crash pad." But she was not in London at the time.

Bewildered, he turned to O'Liver for advice. His friend suggested that since O'Toole was an attractive male, he might consider hanging out at the loo in the Underground Station at Piccadilly Circus. O'Liver had learned that if a young man stood, unzipped, at one of the long line of urinals in the men's loo, "He might attract the interest of some old sod."

O'Toole didn't have the inclination for that. "I'm more of a grower than a shower," he told O'Liver. "I don't think I would be all that alluring if I flashed it."

Getting food in their stomachs was a real problem, but O'Liver knew how to solve that, since he'd been broke in London before.

O'Liver took him to the Lyons Corner House halfway between Piccadilly Circus and Leicester Square, which consisted of several restaurants on different floors. Somewhere along the way, they'd picked up two plastic bags. Following O'Liver's example, the two young men passed through the rooms, their eyes closely focused on any diners leaving a table. The "pickings" were good

> History will record O'Toole's name within the register of artists who were virtually starving.
>
> In O'Toole's case, that meant scavenging table scraps off restaurant tables before he was "discovered" by one of the most prestigious schools of drama (RADA) in the world.

O'Toole Falls In Love With a Virginal but Suicidal Country Girl

O'Toole Vs. James Villiers:
Intimate Friends? An Indiscreet Fling? A Love Affair?

on the just-vacated tables, and they scooped up the contents of the roll baskets, often rescuing half-eaten pieces of roast chicken and, in one case, an unfinished slab of roast beef with plenty of meat still left on the bone. O'Toole made off with a slice of gooseberry pie which a previous consumer had only nibbled at.

After devouring their feast on a park bench, they decided to head to the *As You Like It* Coffee House on Monmouth Street. *[Ironically, that was the name of the first play in which O'Toole would appear on the London Stage.]*

It had been decorated by an aspiring playwright who had a fetish for American movie stars. Its walls were lined with photos of Greta Garbo, Betty Grable, Carmen Miranda, and Carole Lombard. For two bob, O'Toole and O'Liver ordered afternoon tea, demanding refills.

O'Toole learned that this café was a hangout for aspiring actors, which meant that most of the other clients were looking for a job. They shared a table with Michael Hartley, who had come to London from Bournemouth to become an actor.

He led them to a cheap hostel on Tottenham Court Road, where they each rented a dormitory bed for the week. Since Hartley, a regular clientele, vouched for them, they didn't have to pay in advance.

The next day, whereas O'Liver, in his capacity as a painter, wanted to visit the National Gallery, O'Toole headed for the Royal Academy of Dramatic Art (RADA) on Gower Street. Founded in 1904, this was one of the oldest drama schools in Britain, and certainly the best. It was located in Bloomsbury, the academic heart of London.

Every aspiring actor wanted to be admitted to RADA, which often benefitted from generous legacies and donations. Before his death in 1950, George Bernard Shaw had bequeathed whatever royalties were generated from his play, *Pygmalion,* to RADA. When his play was adapted into *My Fair Lady* 1964), it generated a cash windfall for the school.

Former and future students of RADA included John Gielgud, Kenneth Branaugh, Ralph Fiennes, Edward Fox, Anthony Hopkins, Derek Jacobi, Helen Mirren, Diana Rigg, Lord Snowdon, Timothy Dalton, Maggie Gyllenhaal, John Hurt, Glenda Jackson, Vivien Leigh, Joe Orton, Roger Moore, Harold Pinter, Susannah York, and Joan Collins.

At the entrance, he met a formidable male secretary sitting at a desk by the door. Anyone hoping to enroll in the school had to fill out a questionnaire, list

NO LOWER CLASS HOOLIGANS NEED APPLY:

The guardian of RADA's gate resembled "Sir Cedric Hardwicke (depicted above in 1956) on a bad hair day."

49

ing their schooling and previous experience.

O'Toole knew how unimpressive his credentials were, as he'd had only two years of formal schooling. He decided to take an aggressive approach, protesting having to fill out a questionnaire.

"A Decent Bloke"
RADA's Director,
Sir Kenneth Barnes

"I was twenty years old at the time, and full of piss and vinegar," he claimed. "I practically got into a fight with this stern guard, who no doubt was descended from the executioner who chopped the heads off the wives of Henry VIII."

In the middle of O'Toole's "battle," a distinguished, gray-haired gentleman approached to see what the ruckus was about.

It turned out to be Sir Kenneth Barnes, the principal (i.e., director) of RADA since 1909, who was just two years from retirement. When Barnes identified himself, O'Toole told him, "If RADA rejects me, they'll be turning down the Olivier of tomorrow."

Amazingly, there was something so audacious, but so compelling, about O'Toole that Barnes invited him into his office for an extensive interview. Perhaps Barnes was having a slow day, but he kept O'Toole in his office for two full hours, during which O'Toole impressed the principal with his dedication to learning how to act.

Years later, O'Toole recalled Barnes: "His face seemed to me to have gripped and gnarled itself into an expression that one might easily have found in the features of a displeased medieval bishop."

At one point, Barnes shared his views about the difference between British and American actors. "There is a sort of mutual envy and a shared inferiority complex between the Yank and the Brit on stage. Without a doubt, we Brits are the great stage actors, but the Americans seemed to have mastered screen acting, especially the close-up, which they invented. I think American actors excel in raw emotional power, a sort of shoot-from-the-hip style. British actors are more technically proficient and have greater voice control. They are also more text-based."

At the end of their interview, Barnes dismissed O'Toole, after establishing a time for him to return to RADA for an audition the following afternoon.

At his temporary lodgings in the hostel, O'Toole borrowed a suit from a young salesman who had been fired from his job, promising he'd give him a pound note, which he didn't have. But he'd worry about that later.

The next day, looking more polished than before, O'Toole arrived at RADA for his audition. In front of Barnes, three members of the staff and a number of students, he delivered lines from *Hamlet,* recited two sonnets by Shakespeare, and even performed a scene from George Bernard Shaw's *Pygmalion.*

O'Toole would later refer to his success that day as "the luck of the Irish." Barnes must have been impressed, because he asked O'Toole to return within a few days.

Then, inside his office, the principal told him the good news: RADA was going to award O'Toole with a scholarship, which would pay for his tuition, his books, and his kit. The two-year scholarship would begin in the autumn of 1953.

Young Albert Finney... Our heart was young and straight.

That very day, O'Toole met his fellow students, many of whom would become his friends. He was introduced to Shirley Dixon, Brian Bedford, Bryan Pringle, Roy Kinnear, Rosemary Leach, Alan Bates, Albert Finney, Ronald Fraser, and Frank Finlay.

With O'Toole's keen eye, he quickly sized up his classmates, ultimately deciding that Finney and perhaps Bates would represent the strongest competition.

O'Toole was correct in that assessment.

Years later, he was asked what his first impression of Finney was. "Did you suspect that he might be a better actor than you?" a journalist asked.

"Not at first. I was more concerned about whether he had a bigger dick than mine."

Young Alan Bates... Our heart was young and gay.

[In time, Finney would be the original first choice to star in Lawrence of Arabia, *but he turned it down. Like O'Toole, he would be nominated for a Best Actor Academy Award based on his performance in* Tom Jones *(1963);* Murder on the Orient Express *(1974);* The Dresser *(1983); and* Under the Volcano *(1984). He would also be nominated for an Oscar as Best Supporting Actor for his performance in* Erin Brockovich *(2000), opposite Julia Roberts.]*

Since many of the aspirant actors at *RADA* were from the north of England, they were collectively nicknamed "The Yorkshire Terrorists."

Unable to pay the bill at their hostel, O'Liver and O'Toole slipped out and found nighttime refuge for a while sleeping under a bandstand in Green Park.

With no money, O'Toole met some of his fellow Irishmen, laborers and/or supervisors of construction projects. One of them gave him a job "humping" bags of cement at an electric power station in South Kensington.

O'Toole eventually struck up a friendship with a fellow student at RADA, James Villiers, who was a year younger than he was. Along with actor Kenneth

Griffith, he would become one of O'Toole's closest friends. It was said by some that "Villiers came to know Peter O'Toole better than his future wife, Siân Phillips."

The two handsome young men came from radically different backgrounds. Many of their fellow classmates at RADA came to believe that they were having an affair, but there is no proof of that.

Whatever the force was that drew them together, it was so strong that Villiers became like O'Toole's loving brother, in spite of their different backgrounds.

James Villiers, a descendant of England's *haute* aristocracy, shown here as he appeared in *Blood From the Mummy's Tomb* (1971), a British horror flick that, ironically, became one of his best-known roles.

Villiers had an aristocratic lineage, boasting a family tree dating from the 2nd Marquess of Rockingham (Prime Minister of England from 1765-1766), with direct ancestors that included the Earls of Clarendon. Educated at Wellington College, he became stage struck as a boy. He made his stage debut in 1953, the year he and O'Toole became friends. He'd starred in summer Theatre in Frinton, *[Located in Essex, on the seacoast east of London, Frinton is home to the longest running weekly professional repertory theatre company in the UK.]* with a part in the Agatha Christie thriller, *Ten Little Niggers* (1953).

[The politically incorrect title of that play, and the title of later film and TV adaptations, was later revised to And Then There Were None, *or* Ten Little Indians.*]*

That was followed in 1954 by Villiers' first West End of London appearance with the Shakespeare Memorial Company.

O'Toole's stage voice, with his ripe and plummy articulation, may have been heavily influenced by Villiers.

O'Toole and Villiers, to their friends, at least, seemed so interconnected that they often completed each others' sentences. Since O'Toole never found any form of sustained work during most of the months he studied at RADA, Villiers frequently took him to dinner, and probably gave him money.

Every time the two men came together, they embraced and kissed each other on the cheeks, although that did not necessarily prove a homosexual attachment, as hugging and kissing were common among their theatrical crowd.

O'Toole occasionally said something to suggest their intimacy. As remembered by Alan Bates, "I never wear any of my dull gray underwear. I always encase my plumbing in James' undies. He has the best, most elegant, and most expensive underwear in London, specially purchased on Savile Row, the same type of drawers Prince Philip wears, and from the same tailor."

The Secret Question O'Toole Faced at RADA:
"Was Albert Finney's Endowment Larger Than His?"

The first winds of the autumn of 1953 were blowing through London when O'Toole returned there to begin his apprenticeship at RADA. He joined 46 would-be actors and 31 actresses. In future years, their membership enrollment would be considerably reduced.

"For the first time in my life, I proclaimed, 'God, it's good to be an Englishman,'" O'Toole said.

He began with a rigorous array of seemingly endless classes, including voice coaching from Clifford Turner, who later wrote a definitive book on "stage speech," *Voice and Speech Training in the Theatre.*

Lessons in stage diction were administered to both O'Toole and Finney by a well-known actor, Denys Blakelock.

"A hint of the vicar hovered around Blakelock," O'Toole said. "Attach a straw hat, bicycle clips, and a dog collar to him, let him judge a marrow, solemnize a marriage, raise funds for a steeple, and there you'd have him, your perfect platitude of vicarhood."

Classes in movement were conducted by Amy Boalth, stagecraft by Howard Williams, and stage technique by John Gabriel.

In fencing class, O'Toole's partner was Frank Finlay. "Peter pictured himself a dashing Errol Flynn in *Captain Blood* (1934), and *The Adventures of Robin Hood* (1938). I was more like Douglas Fairbanks, Sr., in *The Thief of Baghdad* (1924)," Finlay said.

Six years older than Flynn, Finlay was the son of a Lancashire butcher who refused to follow in his father's profession, preferring instead to pursue a career on the stage. In time, he would play Iago opposite Laurence Olivier in a 1965 stage presentation of *Othello.* That same year, he starred in the film version of that production, for which he received a Best Supporting Actor Academy Award nomination.

"Frank could play anyone from Adolf Hitler to Don Quixote's Sancho Panza," O'Toole said. "He was even made a Com-

Frank Finlay...Swordfighting
with O'Toole.

mander of the Order of the British Empire. But we were never that close. I was too much of a hellraiser, and the gentleman was a devout Catholic."

Of all his many lessons, the one that O'Toole would remember the most were the ballet classes he and Finney took with Madame Fletcher. As he once jokingly told Villiers, "At last I got to answer the burning question about how Albie (Finney) was hung, "O'Toole said. "Those leotards we wore left little to the imagination."

As he wrote: "I remember the 'fruity' dialogue and the orders from the Madame: 'Grab the *barre,* plonk down one foot in disjointed fashion, pointing sideways from the body, add the heel of one's other foot to the heel of the plonked foot, stick it out in a similarly unnatural way, and they you have it, the First Position."

Beside him was Finney, "all relaxed and poker straight, with feet akimbo."

"After my first six weeks in London, I decided that the world did not fully appreciate my talent as much as I did," O'Toole said. "I was surrounded with actors far more educated than I was, and I was racing to catch up with them."

"Soho, that age-old hunting cry, became the stamping ground for my footfalls," he said. "A dish of grub at Burglar's Restaurant, a wander along Charlotte Street, wriggle a little, straight on, plod over to Oxford Street and there one was right in the Crooked Mile itself. Rackety, rickety, glamorous, and seedy, old as sin and streaming with novelties, uniquely itself sprawled the lanes, yards, alleys, courts, passages, streets, the mazy old voluptuous body of these parts that West Central London lets squeeze right up to Shaftesbury Avenue, fair buggering the backsides of those posh theaters standing there."

"London was awash with actors and actresses lining up at the casting offices in and around Soho," he said.

He remembered hoping to get work as an extra, even as a stunt man, "but there were forty other young men and women waiting there for hours and hours."

"I drifted off to a pub, where I met a bloke who told me about this bordello four doors down, with real cheap prices. It was run by Chinese women from the British colony of Hong Kong. I went there and was told that I had to pay a pound to use one of the girls, but that for two shillings, I could 'get a wank.' Yes, these women had learned British slang. I took the wank option. But what I got was an old crone with a clammy hand. I still had to pay up, even though I couldn't get an erection. The bitch mocked me, 'Limey's had too much lager.'"

***

For an upcoming stage presentation in RADA's Little Theatre, O'Toole was cast in Shakespeare's *As You Like It.*

Barnes had told him that because of the density and difficulty of the language, this play was often chosen "as a dish for beginners to gobble on." O'Toole's intention involved understanding "the compound of its humor, its lewdness, its melancholy, and its robustness."

In it, O'Toole was cast as Oliver, the eldest son and heir of a recently deceased nobleman. He was well aware that in spite of critical disputes, including attacks from George Bernard Shaw, *As You Like It,* probably written in 1600, remains one of the Bard's most frequently performed comedies. The longest-running production on Broadway (1950) had starred Katharine Hepburn. She, of course, had interpreted the star role of Rosalind.

Finney was cast as George the Wrestler. "Albie spoke his lines with an unashamed Salford *[i.e., a metropolitan borough of Manchester]* accent. As the bloke told me himself, he was 'unsophisticated, ungainly, clumsy, and a bit uncouth.'"

"George the Wrestler was not the finest role to have dropped off Shakespeare's pen," O'Toole wrote. "But Albie had given it vigor, menace, and a rollicking display of athleticism."

On the opening night of *As You Like It,* O'Toole was told that Dame Sybil Thorndike was in the audience. He felt intimated. "Right before my entrance, I rushed to the loo, hung my head over the toilet bowl, and vomited."

O'Toole knew that Bernard Shaw had written *Saint Joan* (1920) especially for her, and he was awed by her reputation. She'd made her first stage appearance in 1904, in Shakespeare's *The Merry Wives of Windsor,* and in 1931, she'd been made Dame Commander of the Order of the British Empire.

[After World War II, it was discovered that Thorndike's name had been entered into Hitler's "Black Book" (Sonderfahndungliste G. B.)*, his roster of Britons who were to be arrested and executed in the event of a successful Nazi invasion of the U.K.]*

When the performance ended, Dame Sybil came backstage to greet the players. When she failed to compliment O'Toole on his performance, he blatantly asked her what she thought.

When Dame Sybil Thorndike, one of the three or four grandest of the *grande dames* of the British Theatre, and an Edwardian terror in her own right, met the neophyte actors, Peter O'Toole and Albert Finney, she made it clear that she was not impressed and that she was not amused.

55

She looked him up and down with a skeptical eye. "Since you ask my opinion, I will give it. My suggestion is that you and Mr. Finney pursue some other work than the theater. As you know, there are a lot of construction jobs in the East End in the wake of the Blitz. Whole blocks need to be rebuilt. I'm sure you gentlemen will find gainful employment there."

In the spring of 1954, Edward Burnham helmed O'Toole in RADA's production of *Trelawny of the Wells,* a comic play from 1898 by Arthur Wing Pinero.

O'Toole appeared as Tom Wrench, an aspiring playwright who dreams of staging plays in a more realistic style than the routine Victorian dramas that dominated the stage. In 1928, Norma Shearer, Hollywood's Queen of MGM, had starred in a silent screen adaptation of the drama.

The English actor, producer, and director, Sir Robert Atkins, watched O'Toole perform, and he went backstage with some advice: "Take the crucifixion out of your voice and put some cock into it."

O'Toole was at RADA when the legendary Ernest Milton joined the teaching staff. In O'Toole's usually enigmatic style, he proclaimed Milton as a teacher in the "actor-laddie tradition."

Born in San Francisco in 1890, Milton was a Shakespearean stage actor and playwright, who had been with the Old Vic since 1918, during which time he seemed to relish his involvement in eccentric or villainous parts.

Milton directed both Finney and O'Toole in George Bernard Shaw's 1897 *You Never Can Tell,* with O'Toole cast as a penniless dentist, Valentine, who falls for Gloria, an ardent feminist. In essence, it was a subversive comedy of errors about the negotiations of men with women about independence and marriage. One critic said, "On stage, O'Toole is exactly what he is in real life: a student actor."

Milton returned to direct O'Toole in Shakespeare's *Twelfth Night,* in the role of Malvolio, a steward in the household of Olivia, a wealthy countess, whom he courts. O'Toole followed countless actors who had performed the role since its premiere in 1602. O'Toole had seen *Twelfth Night* at the Old Vic in a production that had starred Richard Burton. Consequently, he modeled his performance of Malvolio on the way

(I am) More Divine than Thou:

Ernest Milton
as Henry IV in 1938.

56

the actor, Michael Hordem, had played it.

"Coming from a very low-class background, O'Toole was an imposing figure on the stage because of his height and his swaggering charm," Milton said. "No doubt about it: He was a masterful blagger." *[i.e., a reference to someone who can sell ice to an Eskimo.]*

He next joined Hugh Miller's production of *The Trail of Mary Dugan.* Written in 1927, it was a melodrama about a sensational courtroom trial of a showgirl accused of killing her millionaire lover. The play was performed in summer at Regent's Park. Norma Shearer had made a 1929 film of the drama.

He then returned to RADA for an *Alice in Wonderland* panto where he had three roles, the March Hare, the Carpenter, and the White Knight.

[British pantomime, which, unlike its French and Italian counterpart, does not usually involve silent performers in white-face, takes familiar children's stories and fairy tales—Dick Whittington and His Cat, Snow White, Aladdin and his lamp – and injects vaudevillian, musical hall razzmatazz and audience participation to create boisterous entertainment for children and adults. Some scholars attribute the 15th and 16th century traditions of La Commedia del Arte *for its conventions and archtypes.]*

As RADA's Director and Principal, Barnes did not try to inhibit the individualism of his actors. One wannabee actress even walked around the theater with a boa constrictor around her neck.

"Albie reminded me of James Dean, always going around with his head down," O'Toole said. "I once asked him why he did that. He told me, 'I go downstage with my head down, then I look up and give the audience my eyes.' Okay. But what I didn't tell him was that my eyes were bluer and more beautiful than his. I didn't want to make him jealous of me."

Long before O'Toole played Shakespeare's Troilus, he attended a performance of Finney starring in *Troilus and Cressida* in London. The production called for its actors to wear modern dress.

Kenneth Tynan, the controversial young critic for London's *The Observer,* reviewed Finney's performance with such lavish praise that O'Toole became "furiously jealous."

Although O'Toole had compared Finney to James Dean, Tynan published other, loftier comparisons. "Here is Albert Finney, a young actor playing Troilus. He is a smouldering young Spencer Tracy, an actor who will soon disturb the dreams of Mssrs. Burton and Scofield."

"I finally decided that the only thing Finney and I have in common is that we're both the sons of bookmakers."

Finney told O'Toole, "Having a father for a bookie is the perfect training for an actor's vagabond life—no security."

Piercing Hymens, Discovering "Glorious" Richard Burton, And Surviving Catastrophic Car Crashes

O'Toole's nights were spent going to wild parties and inventing schemes for making money, such as selling balloons in the parks. His pub crawling continued at a hectic pace, and day and night, as he confessed, "I chased the dolly birds. I thrived on a tin of meatless spaghetti with tomato sauce, spending what money I had on the brew."

Almost as much as "bedding the birds," his favorite pastime involved slipping into West End Theatres to see plays. He expressed delight in a performance by Sam Levene as Nathan Detroit in *Guys and Dolls.* But usually, he preferred more high-brow stuff. He learned much about acting by attending some of the great moments in English theatre during a golden period.

Richard Burton became his favorite actor, even since he witnessed his performance as *Hamlet* at the Old Vic in 1953. O'Toole grew addicted to Burton, slipping into some of his other performances at the Old Vic during the '53-'54 season. He watched Burton's portray Philip the Bastard in *King John;* Sir Toby Belch in *Twelfth Night;* the title role in *Coriolanus*; and Caliban in *The Tempest,* with his off-screen lover, Claire Bloom.

Of all the roles Burton played, his interpretation of Philip the Bastard remained O'Toole's favorite. He later wrote: "When Burton strutted his Bastard onto the stage, he fetched with him a virility and poetry which neither before nor since have I seen matched in any playhouse. Power he brought, and insouciance; laughter, energy, danger; a rapidity of action and mental agility which throbbed; a relaxation and stillness which magnetized; an eye and presence which commanded, and a glorious voice which rang and hushed and boomed and stung with every sounding inch of the auditorium."

Across the street was a pub where he'd see Burton, surrounded by admirers, "make merry, impressing me with his joy and vitality. I longed to be part of his company, and, in time, I got my wish."

O)'Toole also managed to slip into theaters

Young Richard Burton: "I was never this beautiful, before or since."

58

where Dorothy Tuttin and Eric Porter were appearing in Graham Greene's *The Living Room;* Trevor Howard in *The Devil's General;* Herbert Lom and Valerie Hobson in *The King and I;* Peggy Ashcroft and Michael Redgrave in *Anthony and Cleopatra;* Laurence Olivier and Vivien Leigh in *The Sleeping Prince;* and John Gielgud and Ralph Richardson in *A Day By the Sea.*

O'Toole later recalled, "Little did I know at the time that I would get personally involved with most of these stars, befriending the men while making a cuckold of their wives, notably the old girls married to Burton and Olivier."

"I somehow managed to seduce a dollybird a night, usually a pickup in a pub," O'Toole confessed to his friends. "If the hour grew later, and I'd had the luck, I could always get one of the whores trolling the 'Dilly' *[i.e., Piccadilly Circus].* The later the hour, the cheaper they sold their wares."

In the midst of all this rampant promiscuity, along came love in the form of a beautiful young actress named Jeannie Graves.

As O'Toole later described her, "She was graceful, slender, shy, with long black hair and wide light eyes, possessing a disturbingly dark shade." He'd met her during rehearsals for *As You Like IT.*

At the time, he told Villiers that she was the only known virgin at RADA. Convent-educated, she was living in a Catholic hostel for girls.

"She's like a girl from the country, with country manners. She even calls me 'sir,' and I've got to relinquish that title very soon."

He later claimed that it was Jeannie herself, who after a spaghetti dinner, during their walk back to RADA, asked him about "this hymen business."

He set out to explain to her what the deflowering of a virgin involved: "I was forced to tell my sweetheart what happens to a woman when her membrane pops."

"I confirmed that after the grief, the lovers can rub bacons together to their genitals' content and poke happily ever after or until one or the other or both hollers 'nuff."

"I told her that it was the tradition in places like Sicily for the bridegroom on his wedding night to open the window and display a bloody sheet to show his family and friends waiting below that he'd pierced the hymen of his virgin bride. "In time, Jeannie would want a physical demonstration of the piercing of the hymen, and O'Toole was happy to oblige," Villiers said. Once penetrated, she wanted it repeated, and so it became a ritual between them."

Like most young lovers at RADA, they soon drifted off, and whereas he found countless other companions, she focused on just one.

Discussing her later love interest, O'Toole said, "I met them in a coffee house in one of the warrens off Tottenham Court Road," he said. "He was a painter, with a good jaw, so we gave our tongues a fling. I later heard that she'd married the bloke and had a kid."

"They lived somewhere in the country, Hampshire, I think. I heard the terrible news at RADA. She'd walked into a wooded glade one day with a plastic bottle of mineral water and a bottle of sleeping pills. She then proceeded to commit suicide. I wept and wept some more. I guess I never understood her, but maybe I did. I remember that dark shadow I sensed that long ago day when I first gazed upon her beauty. Was she still thinking of me when she popped that last pill?"

***

It was roughly estimated that during his time at RADA, an itinerant O'Toole may have occupied as many as two dozen "crash pads." They included a short time at Chalk Farm, just up the hill toward Belsize Park. He often spent his nights in Soho, within various flats of "dubious repute."

When he was briefly hired to solder wires onto model cars, he lived in a dreary flat in Greater London's East Croydon, about ten miles south of London Bridge. For some reason, he left suddenly in the middle of the night, taking his meager belongings to another flat owned by a recently divorced housewife in a district of North London named Muswell Hill.

One of most unconventional temporary homes was aboard an old and rickety rented houseboat whose 40-foot length was permanently moored on the Thames. It was named *Venus,* which coincidentally would be the title of his Oscar-nominated film in 2006.

One night, he invited his fellow students on board for a house party. So many people came aboard that during the raucous party, the houseboat sank. O'Toole managed to escape with his few bits of clothing. In the aftermath of the disaster, one of his classmates let him move into a flat in Archway, in Inner North London.

As a child, O'Toole had frequently been ill, and during this stressful period of his early twenties, he often became so incapacitated that he sometimes ended up in the hospital. His intestines were frequently inflamed, a condition perhaps accelerated by his heavy drinking.

During the course of his early career in the 1960s, he wanted to conceal his many illnesses, fearing that directors would not hire him if it appeared that his health was precarious in any way. In 1975, when he hovered between life and death, he'd undergo several life-threatening operations.

By chance, O'Toole encountered Wilfred Lawson, who was thirty-two years his senior. At the time, Lawson was famous English character actor known for his heavy boozing and his many starring roles. He, too, came from the West Riding District of Yorkshire.

O'Toole had gone to see him in Strindberg's *The Father,* and had come backstage to congratulate him on his perform-ance.

He had been the star of one of O'Toole's fa-vorite movies, George Bernard Shaw's *Pygmalion* (1938), a film starring Leslie Howard and Wendy Hiller. In this hit film, Lawson had played the role of Eliza's dissipated but extroverted father, Alfred P. Doolittle. As a boy, O'Toole had seen Lawson perform in John Ford's *The Long Voyage Home* (1940), starring John Wayne.

When O'Toole met him, Lawson's star power, because of his frequent bouts of alcoholism, had faded, and his roles had become smaller.

"We struck up a great friendship and started pubbing together," O'Toole said.

Later in life, he cited Lawson as "one of the greatest influences in my life. He lent me money when I was down to my last bob. He picked up

Wilfred Lawson as Eliza's father, Alfred P. Doolittle, in *Pygmalion*, the 1938 film that co-starred Leslie Howard and Wendy Hiller.

my lager bill in the pubs. He nursed me in and out of my many ill-fated ro-mances. He helped me as an actor, and often criticized my lazy tongue, trying to wake it up by giving me the most difficult passages to read in English liter-ature. He even taught me how to drink and still remain standing. Better yet, he gave me some pointers about how to screw a dolly bird. The fucking lessons he taught me held me in good stead until the day when my wager wagged no more."

In 1966, O'Toole descended into a morbid depression when he learned that Lawson had died in London at the too-early age of sixty-nine.

After a brief visit to Leeds, O'Toole—as a passenger in a friend's car—was rushing back to London to attend a production at RADA. On the A1 motorway, the vehicle crashed into a lorry. Whereas O'Toole sustained some serious in-juries, his friend was disabled for life.

O'Toole was due that night in London for an appearance in Dylan Thomas's *Under Milk Wood,* one of his favorite plays. But the hospital staff detained him. After a delay of five hours, he still had not received a report based on the X-rays taken of his injured legs.

Trembling with anxiety, he slipped out of the hospital and entered a local pharmacy, where he stocked up on painkillers. Then he boarded a fast train to London, and made it to the theater just in time for the opening curtain.

He later claimed that he was in acute pain during his performance and then collapsed after the curtain went down. He was rushed to the nearest hospital, where more X-rays reveal that his leg had been broken.

Before midnight, his leg had swollen to almost twice its size. "I was out of commission for a while. Even when released, I had to hop around London like a cripple. I was up for any roles in a wheelchair."

"Somehow, I was never good behind the wheel of a car," he said. "In fact, in my future I would learn to ride a camel quicker than I could master the intricacies of being a driver."

"No sooner had my leg healed than I was driving a Riley, again on the A1," he said. "I'd had a few nips at the pub before heading out from Leeds. Somewhere along the way, I fell asleep at the wheel. When I woke up, I found myself going down this embankment. There was nothing to do at this point but put my feet up on the dash and wait for the inevitable."

Leaving the scene of his accident bruised but not seriously injured, he called the AA (British Automobile Association) to tow the wreck away. "I never saw that junk heap again."

He had a good reason for leaving the scene of the accident. Although he drove frequently, he never, until 1959, bothered to get a license. "There was another problem," he confessed. "When I fell asleep (at the wheel), I was pissed, not just pissed, but really, really pissed."

***

In 1955, as O'Toole describe it, "an English summer—and you know what that is, my darlings—descended on the countryside." His days as a student at RADA had ended. In the aftermath of his sojourn at RADA, he headed west to the old city of Bristol, where he planned to become a star in the repertory company at Bristol's well-respected Old Vic Theatre. He would spend his next three years there, starring in some of the most demanding roles, including *Hamlet,* in the English Theatre.

Chapter 5

O'Toole in Training at Bristol's Old Vic

Talented but Inexperienced, Former Seaman Peter O'Toole Joins a Repertory Theatre, Playing Diverse Roles Ranging from Jupiter to Hamlet

A Ball-Clanking "Angry Young Man" Excites England's Theatrical Elite. "Move Over Gielgud. Move Over Olivier!"

Peter O'Toole, before his nose job, at the Bristol Old Vic opposite Wendy Williams in *Man and Superman.* He referred to his snout as, "my magnificent hooter."

"I came, I saw, I conquered," Peter O'Toole scribbled on a postcard to his painter friend, Patrick O'Liver, in Leeds. He was referring to his arrival in the ancient city of Bristol on the River Severn in the West Country of England. He was a bit off. Although he never actually conquered Bristol, he would at least make a stab at doing so.

He had been accepted into the ranks of the repertory company of the prestigious Bristol Old Vic. During the three years he spent there (1955-1958), he would achieve nationwide fame, attracting theater-goers and critics from London, especially during his notable and remarkable performance as Hamlet.

The Bristol Old Vic, viewed from the gracefully symmetrical side known as Cooper's Hall.

Positioned across the Bristol Channel from Wales, this historic inland port is linked to the sea by seven miles of the navigable Avon River. It is steeped in maritime tradition. In 1497, John Cabot sailed from here, a voyage that led to the discovery of the northern half of the New World.

An extension of London's Old Vic, the Bristol company functioned more or less independently from its more famous sibling. Established in 1946, in the immediate aftermath of World War II, it was headquartered within the landmarked and gracefully symmetrical Theatre Royal. Built in 1764, it was the oldest continually operated theater in England.

"At the callow age of twenty-three, I began my ball-clanking walk up the steps to the Bristol Old Vic," O'Toole said. "Great actors had preceded me. With each step, I was sending a signal that a new generation of actors had arrived."

Before leaving London, O'Toole had revealed his steely determination to his close friend, fellow actor James Villiers. "In just a few months, I expect to become a leading stage star. Some old sods dismiss the Bristol Old Vic as a

Sexual Overtures from Cary Grant

Storing Rhubarb Wine With Industrial Waste in a Carboy,

Deflowering the Virgins of Bristol
("Or whatever's left of them after the departure of those oversexed Yanks")

mere 'nursery' for actors heading toward the West End. But I intend to make it more than that. London critics will be beating a pathway to my door just to see me on stage."

As part of the application process for a scholarship, O'Toole had to be auditioned at the Old Vic in London, on Waterloo Road in front of spectators from the theater's branch in Bristol.

The director of the Old Vic in Bristol was the aptly named John Moody, who in previous chapters of his life had worked as both an actor and singer in productions with Charles Laughton and Laurence Olivier. On the day of O'Toole's audition, Moody came down with the flu and designated his assistant, Nat Brenner, to appear in his place. In time, Brenner would spend the next thirty years at the Bristol Old Vic, rising through its ranks to become its general manager and director of its theatre school.

On the day of its auditions in London, about a hundred hopeful actors and actresses showed up. O'Toole arrived on the scene at 3AM that morning and slept under a blanket on the sidewalk, designating himself as the first in line.

When he walked out onto the stage later that morning, he wore a moth-eaten red sweater and a pair of corduroy trousers long past their expiration date. Standing before Brenner, he was "tall and thin and looked like a half-starved street urchin," Brenner recalled. "He had piercing blue eyes which I noted as he performed a scene from *Cyrano de Bergerac.* He certainly had the nose for it."

In Edmond Rostand's play, Cyrano, a 17th century wit who longed for the love of a beautiful lady, was disfigured by his long, misshaped nose.

"O'Toole was riveting. I was mesmerized by this quirky fellow," Brenner said.

O'Toole followed his *Cyrano* skit with a scene from *Berkeley Square* by John L. Balderston. It was the story of a young American who is transported backward through time to a location in London during the revolution of Britain's North American colonies.

In the scene, which O'Toole executed beautifully, he had to maintain a dialogue with two imaginary women.

Brenner chatted only briefly with O'Toole, but arranged to interview him more extensively the following day. He later said, "I thought he had amazing potential, but I sensed something self-destructive about him. It was just a hunch. I asked him if he were a drinking man."

"I've been known to have a lager or two on Saturday night at my local," he lied.

"Don't go beyond that," Brenner advised.

When Moody recovered from the flu, Brenner arranged for O'Toole to audition with the same two scenes—excerpts from *Cyrano de Bergerac* and

Berkeley Square—he'd performed before.

Moody was not as impressed with O'Toole as Brenner was. Privately, Moody told Brenner, "We might cast O'Toole one day as a spear-carrier in the third act."

Eventually, however, Moody acquiesced to Brenner's "hysterical enthusiasm," telling him, "You must have the hots for this young man."

O'Toole was elated when he was accepted as a member of the Bristol Old Vic's repertory company. He was disappointed, however, when he realized that the first play of the season, Angus Wilson's *The Mulberry Bush,* had already been cast.

Playwright Angus Wilson, going around the mulberry bush.

He became friendly with Wilson three years later, in 1958, when the playwright was awarded the James Tait Black Memorial Prize for his play, *The Middle Age of Mrs. Eliot.* O'Toole interpreted Wilson as "an author to delight, a man of keen insight and judgment, writing in a strong satirical vein."

He became intrigued with Wilson's service record during World War II. He was one of the so-called "famous homosexuals," who worked in the British Naval Section of the code-breaking establishment at Bletchley Park, decoding secret messages from Fascist dispatches.

Alan Turing, hero of the *Enigma* program, winning World War II

There, he had met and befriended Alan Turing, who was the main inventor of "The Enigma," the computer machine that broke the Nazi code and kept abreast of Germany secret communications throughout the war.

Sir Winston Churchill later said that Turing cut two years off the war and may have saved fourteen million lives. Harassed by the police because of his homosexuality, this brilliant scientist was driven to suicide in 1954.

O'Toole immediately seized upon the idea that Turing's story would make a terrific movie unless it vi-

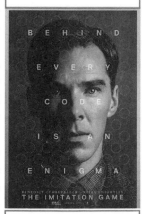

Benedict Cumberbatch, portraying Alan Turing in *The Imitation Game (2014)*

olated British secrecy rules. He often came up with film stories, some of which would not be made until the 21st Century. Such was the case with Turing's tragic but heroic saga. In 2014, Benedict Cumberbatch and Keira Knightley starred in *The Imitation Game,* which was nominated for an Oscar as Best Picture of the Year.

Wilson told O'Toole that his work at Bletchley had led to a nervous break-down. When he recovered, he returned to work at the British Museum, where he met a much younger man, Tony Garrett, who became his lifetime companion.

"Reeking of Horsehit,"
O'Toole Makes His Debut at the Bristol Old Vic

In 1955, at the time of O'Toole's arrival in Bristol, the three leading actors at the Old Vic were Eric Porter, Alan Dobie, and Derek Godfrey.

Ironically, Godfrey would eventually play Jack Gurney in the theatrical version of Peter Barnes' play, *The Ruling Class*. A few years later, in 1972, O'Toole would star in the film version of that play, which would bring him a Best Actor Oscar nomination.

Coming from West Riding in Yorkshire, Dobie would rack up an impressive list of stage roles. In 1955, he married actress Rachel Roberts. Whether Dobie knew it or not, his new wife began cheating on him with O'Toole even during the first year of their marriage. Later, Roberts would become far more famous, both as an actress and because of her marriage to Rex Harrison.

[For more on the O'Toole/Roberts affair, refer to Chapter 32.]

Arriving in Bristol, O'Toole was eager to work, but ran into a roadblock. The company had decided to launch a new production of *The Matchmaker*, and already had cast all the roles. A decision was made to let O'Toole act in a minor role. To do that, he and the director had to persuade Anthony Tuckey to give up his part.

"I was very disappointed, but I gave in," Tuckey later said. "When I saw O'Toole perform, I was so impressed that I became very jealous of him."

O'Toole had great praise and learned much from Eric Porter, one of the company's most veteran actors, who had been cast in the lead role in *The Matchmaker*. The son of a London bus conductor had failed to win a scholarship at RADA, but he had been granted one at the age of seventeen at the Shakespeare Memorial Theatre in Stratford-upon-Avon. In time, his ongoing performance as the brutal Soames Forsyte in the John Galsworthy TV saga would bring him fame.

"Eric was compelling in any role he took," O'Toole

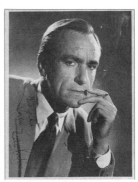

Eric Porter.
He found O'Toole "brash and cheeky."

said. "I never met a more versatile actor."

Porter took notice "of this new young upstart. He was very brash and so cheeky I knew he had talent. Only great stars are arrogant, and he had more than his share of that quality. I felt if he could do something about that Shylock nose of his, perhaps making a date with a plastic surgeon, he might even become a film star."

O'Toole was cast as a cabman behind a horse-drawn carriage in *The Matchmaker,* that Thornton Wilde comedy about a middle-aged widower who decides to get married. *[The play was later musicalized as* Hello Dolly.*]*

In heavy makeup that made him appear more aged, O'Toole came onto the stage "reeking of horseshit!" To render his character more authentic, he'd paid a farmer on the outskirts of Bristol to let him sleep in his barn before the night of the play's premiere.

O'Toole followed with a cameo in *Ondine,* the story of a knight-errant who falls in love with a water sprite. It had been written in 1938 by the French dramatist, Jean Giraudoux., "Watching him come out in *Ondine* convinced me that my first judgment at that audition back in London was right," Brenner said. "The moment he walked onto the stage, even in a cameo, he dominated the action. Even John Moody changed his mind about Peter."

O'Toole was also granted a small role in Ben Jonson's *Volpone* in which Eric Porter played the lead. *Volpone* (Italian for "sly fox") was a 1605 comedy by the English playwright, a merciless satire on greed and lust, one of the finest of Jacobean comedies. O'Toole was cast as Corvino ("the Carrion Crow"), a merchant.

[Ironically, in 1967, O'Toole would vie for but lose the lead role in The Honey Pot *(1967), a movie based on the play, Volpone. Rex Harrison starred in this role opposite Susan Hayward.]*

O'Toole next role was that of a Georgian peasant in *Uncle Vanya,* a play by the Russian playwright, Anton Chekhov. Once again, he played a stableman whose character called for him to wear an old man's makeup.

As before, O'Toole devoted much attention to perfecting his cameo, emerging "smelling of horseshit" from yet another night in an actual stable.

He knew that Josef Stalin had begun life as a Georgian peasant, and he made himself up to look like the Soviet dictator. He had only one line, "Dr. Astrov, the horses have arrived."

"I spoke my line like a dedicated commie showing his distaste for the Russian aristocracy," O'Toole said. "I even walked with a limp like Stalin had."

Upon seeing him for the second time as an old man, a well-intentioned Bristol theater critic wrote: "Peter O'Toole is an actor in his sixties, or maybe his seventies, and at this point in an actor's life, he knows he'll never make it as a star. Nonetheless, he is clearly a delight, showing no bitterness or resentment for forever being assigned to the most minor of roles at his age."

Even though he had only one line, O'Toole studied *Uncle Vanya* in great detail, finding it thematically preoccupied with frustration and filled with laments over "wasted lives." A mood of melancholy pervaded each of the characters. O'Toole vowed that one day, he would star in the play as Uncle Vanya himself.

[That would culminate during the 1973-74 season at the Bristol Old Vic. He would also take Uncle Vanya *on tour in 1978, visiting Washington DC, Chicago, and Toronto.]*

After a year and still no breakthrough role, O'Toole called the Bristol Old Vic "the best repertory company in the world."

His next assignment involved playing a "pantomime dame" *[a man in drag playing an exaggerated and campy archetype of a woman]* in *Ali Baba and the Forty Thieves.* In it, he was cast as Ali Baba's wife.

A Pantomime Dame, depicted above, is a stock character from British vaudeville.

During intermission, the performers mingled with the audience, selling refreshments to the patrons. O'Toole was given cups of ice cream to peddle to the audience in the stalls.

The second person he encountered during his hawking of refreshments was a distinguished-looking man with a face familiar to movie audiences the world over.

"Would you like a cup of ice cream, sir?" O'Toole asked.

"I would indeed, Mrs. Baba," the spectator answered. "Whatever you're selling." With that, he raised a provocative eyebrow at O'Toole.

"I'm honored," O'Toole said. "For Cary Grant, there is no charge."

Cary Grant Makes A Forward Pass at O'Toole During a Visit to His Hometown of Bristol

Ever since co-stars Marlene Dietrich and Tallulah Bankhead had "outed" Grant in the Hollywood of the 1930s, his reputation as a homosexual had crossed the pond, at least as far as the theatrical circles of London. O'Toole had heard about Grant's longtime relationship with actor Randolph Scott.

O'Toole wasn't interested in going the casting couch route with Grant, but he did want to meet him. For the first time in his life, he was considering the possibility of breaking into films. He had read that Grant had formed his own film company, Granart Productions, which planned to make independent films distributed by Warner Brothers. O'Toole hoped that Grant might consider him for a possible role.

When Grant came backstage, O'Toole invited him into his dressing room, where he sat in his underwear removing his makeup. It was only too obvious that Grant was checking him out. The actor invited him to a late night dinner at his hotel.

"I'd be thrilled to share a meal with Cary Grant," O'Toole said. "I'm sure at least half the people in the world would envy me."

Young O'Toole turned down Cary Grant's invitation for "a sleepover...or whatever."

At the hotel, O'Toole and Grant dined on roast beef and chatted, Grant telling him he had been born in Bristol in 1904 as Archibald Leach.

He had returned to Bristol to visit his mother, Elsie Maria Leach, who was in a mental hospital. He had married the actress, Betsy Drake, in 1949, but she had not come with him.

After dinner, Grant invited O'Toole upstairs to his suite for a nightcap. After room service had delivered their drinks, and after consuming yet another Scotch, O'Toole knew that a pass was inevitable.

Grant was subtle about it, inviting him to spend the night, since it was getting late. O'Toole turned him down, but in a most graceful manner, asking for a raincheck.

He didn't want Grant to feel rejected. At the door, he kissed him on the lips and thanked him for dinner.

As O'Toole would later tell James Villiers, "Grant was a perfect gentleman. He wasn't angered by my rejection, but invited me for lunch the following day."

Over a late lunch, there was no more talk of sex. Grant discussed his visit to his mother. "To her, I am just her Little Archie come home again. She doesn't seem to realize that I've gone to Hollywood and become a movie star. She urged me to get married and have children. I'm on my third marriage. I've brought her up to date about me, but she doesn't accept me as an adult."

After lunch, they parted with an embrace. Although they would never appear together in any movie, they would see each other from time to time in the future.

"I've always envied Grant," O'Toole told Nat Brenner. "He can so easily slip into farce, and it's such a struggle for me."

Years later, an intoxicated O'Toole encountered Grant at a party in Mayfair. "Why didn't you ever cast me in a movie?" Is it because I didn't drop trou for you that night back in Bristol?"

"No, not at all, you cheeky devil," Grant said. "You're too good an actor. I was afraid you'd show me up."

Later, Grant turned down the chance of working with O'Toole when he was asked to interpret the role of General Allenby in *Lawrence of Arabia.*

In 1965, when O'Toole was appearing in a play, *Ride a Cock Horse*, at London's Piccadilly Theatre, he told a reporter, "I don't want to get typecast like Cary Grant. He's a fine actor, but all Hollywood does is cast him in light comedies."

Based on that comment, O'Toole seems to have ignored Grant's many dramatic roles, including those in such Alfred Hitchcock classics as *Suspicion* (1941), *Notorious* (1946), and *To Catch a Thief* (1955), as well as such wartime dramas as *Destination Tokyo* (1943).

O'Toole's business partner, Jules Buck, was always urging O'Toole to develop "that Cary Grant image—well dressed, clean cut, with all his secrets kept hidden in the closet."

It was only once that O'Toole deliberately tried to replicate Grant's screen appearance, and that was in 1965, when he made *How to Steal a Million* opposite Audrey Hepburn.

Before appearing in that film before the camera, he had at least a dozen Grant comedies screened for him as a means of studying and learning from the actor's technique. "The role was tough for me to pull off, but it would have been so easy for Grant. He could have called it in."

Onstage, O'Toole, as "The Angel," Threatens Sodom & Gomorrah With Brimstone

In repertory at the Bristol Old Vic, O'Toole would eventually appear in 79 plays, some of which he remembered, if at all, only very distantly. He recalled playing an angel in *Sodom and Gomorrah* by the French dramatist, Jean Giraudoux. It was the only play that Giraudoux produced during the Nazi occupation of Paris.

The play begins with O'Toole as "The Angel," proclaiming that the people of these two notorious cities would be destroyed unless they could show among themselves examples of true love.

[His role was very similar to the film in which director John Huston cast him as three angels in his splashy epic, The Bible: In the Beginning *(1966), a*

personal interpretation of the Old Testament's Book of Genesis. During the course of its filming, O'Toole briefly resumed his affair with Ava Gardner.

Gardner had been cast as Sarah. On greeting O'Toole, she told him that after reading the script, "I almost have come to believe in circumcision."

The picture failed at the box office. One critic wrote, "Hated the picture, loved the book."]

* * *

Next, in a marked departure from mimicking the behavior of an angel, O'Toole was cast as a general in *Romanoff and Juliet,* a play written by the talented actor, Peter Ustinov. Set in the mythical Kingdom of Concordia, its king is being wooed by both the United States and the Soviet Union as a spoof of the Cold War. In 1957, without including O'Toole in its reprise, Ustinov brought the play to Broadway.

One of O'Toole's most memorable acting experiences during his time in repertory at Bristol's Old Vic involved appearing in *King Lear* (1956) with Eric Porter in the title role. O'Toole was cast as the Duke of Cornwall, the husband of Reagan, Lear's second daughter.

At the close of the play, O'Toole told the press that Porter was the best of all King Lears. "I haven't seen all the actors who ever played Lear, but I know that what I said is true and honest."

Originally drafted in 1603, the Shakespeare drama's title role is still coveted by some of the world's greatest actors.

In 1956, O'Toole was also cast as Bullock, a country clown, in *The Recruiting Officer.* Written in 1706, by the Irish author George Farquhar as a Restoration era comedy, it follows the social and sexual exploits of two military officers in pursuit of good times and good fortune.

Laurence Olivier attended the premiere in Bristol and liked the play very much. Backstage, he congratulated all the cast, but didn't single out any particular actor, much to O'Toole's disappointment.

[In 1963, Olivier brought The Recruiting Officer *to the National Theatre in London, where he assigned the lead role to himself. "I noticed that Larry didn't cast me, and I know why," O'Toole said. "By then, I was too big a star, taking only leads myself."]*

As 1956 marched on, O'Toole was cast as Peter Shirley in *Major Barbara,* a play about income inequality and the class struggle by George Bernard Shaw first published in 1907. In various performances, the play had already fared well in both England and America. Generating reams of social commentary, it had lured such stars as Glynis Johns, Eli Wallach, Burgess Meredith, and Charles Laughton.

Based on its success in Bristol, Moody and Brenner made arrangements for their repertory company, with O'Toole, to perform *Major Barbara* at the Old Vic in London.

"I feel I had really arrived at that point," O'Toole said. "Here I was appearing in the West End in a major play which would be attended by Fleet Street critics."

Before they'd begun rehearsals, O'Toole and the cast were shown the 1941 film adaptation of the play, starring Rex Harrison and Wendy Hiller.

At the Bristol Old Vic, O'Toole starred as "The General" in a production of *Romanoff and Juliet.*

During his stay in Bristol, he also played a eunuch, a hermaphrodite, a dwarf, and a vulture.

"Had I been of the right age, I'm sure I could have played the role better than Harrison."

One reviewer did notice me," O'Toole said. "I think he was a homo. His critique consisting mostly of praise for how good looking I was, my trim physique, and my grace of movement. As for my acting, he called me undisciplined."

In reference to the other reviews, O'Toole claimed, "I guess the old sods didn't wear their glasses or else they would have noticed me."

He was amused at a review that appeared in some minor publication. "The twit wrote that George Bernard Shaw attended opening night, but walked out after the first act. I doubt if that were true since Shaw died in 1950. So much for the critics."

Before 1956 ended, O'Toole was cast as Lodovico in *Othello* at the Bristol Old Vic. [*O'Toole had long been fascinated by this tragedy about love, betrayal, jealousy, and repentance written by Shakespeare in 1603. In 1955, O'Toole had seen Richard Burton perform Othello at the Old Vic in London. Later, in 1964, he'd see Olivier in an acclaimed performance as Othello at the Royal National Theatre. The play's most noteworthy production had been staged in 1943 with a cast that included the African American actor, Paul Robeson, as Othello. It was the first production ever in America to feature a black actor within an otherwise all-white cast.*]

Looking Back in Anger While Waiting for Godot To National Acclaim, O'Toole Interprets the Plays of "Misogynistic" John Osborne & "Absurdist" Samuel Beckett

The year that came, 1957, was a peak moment in his life, that saw him cast in four major works, along with some minor parts as well.

One of O'Toole's favorite roles came when he was cast as Alfred P. Doolittle in George Bernard Shaw's *Pygmalion* whose plot involves Professor Henry Higgins claim that he can radically transform the manners and speech patterns of a bedraggled cockney flower girl, Eliza Doolittle, in Covent Garden. Critics hailed the play as a lampoon on the rigid and judgmental English upper class and as a commentary on women's independence.

The Eliza role originated in 1912, when it starred the famed actress who demurely billed herself as "Mrs. Patrick Campbell."

O'Toole as Doolittle, Eliza's father, is motivated with the sole purpose of extracting money out of Higgins, seemingly having little interest in his daughter. "I played him as a member of the undeserving poor who plans to continue that way for the rest of his life," O'Toole recalled. "Doolittle was an odd character who was intelligent but lacked education."

O'Toole would be bitterly disappointed when he lost the role of Henry Higgins to Rex Harrison in *Pygmalion's* film adaptation, *My Fair Lady* (1964). But twenty years later, he did get to play the professor in 1984, appearing in London's West End at the Shaftesbury Theatre opposite Jackie Smith-Wood as Eliza. He later made his Broadway debut in *Pygmalion.*

In Shakespeare's *A Midsummer Night's Dream,* written somewhere between 1590 and 1596, O'Toole played Lysander, who is in love with Hermia at first, but later loves Helena before switching the direction of his love back to Hermia again.

"At least they didn't cast me as one of the dancing fairies," he said.

This much performed comedy, with its ambiguous sexuality, was never one of his favorites. "At least I fared better than Titania. That love potion she swallowed forced her to fall in love with an ass."

"At last a role with some meat on it," O'Toole told Nat Brenner after reading *Look Back in Anger,* which had been written the year before (1956). It concerns a love triangle, featuring Jimmy Porter (O'Toole) as an intelligent and educated but disaffected young man of the working class.

The play by John Osborne was such a success in London that it spawned the theatrical term "angry young men" as a description of writers who brought a harsh, glaring reality to stage dramas that stood in stark contrast to the escapist themes of plays that had preceded them.

O'Toole won praise for his deliveries of Jimmy's tirades, some of them focused on middle-class snugness, although some of his oral assaults are aimed at female characters.

Many theater-goers expecting a glamorous, witty evening were shocked by the setting, a one-room flat in the Midlands that was "unspeakably dirty and squalid." Among the lines that O'Toole uttered was one that referred to an effeminate male friend as "a female Emily Brontë."

One critic claimed that Osborne didn't actually contribute to the British theater, but instead "set off a landmine and blew most of it up."

[O'Toole got good reviews for his performance, and later sent them to director Tony Richardson, hoping to get cast in the play's film adaptation. But Richardson rejected him, preferring to cast Richard Burton instead. Years later, O'Toole would lament, "Some of my most desired film roles went either to Rex Harrison or Burton, Alas, woe is me."]

During its run in Bristol, Osborne had attended some of O'Toole's performances as Jimmy Porter. In turn, O'Toole seemed fascinated by the playwright's "post Atomic Age" political activism, one aspect of which questioned the point of the monarchy, a revolutionary and much-condemned platform at the time. O'Toole interpreted Osborne as iconoclastic, especially as regards "the ornate violence of his language."

Osborne revealed to him that he wrote *Look Back in Anger* in only seventeen days while occupying a deck chair on Morcambe Pier in Lancashire. When it was finished, he had sent the play to many producers, receiving bitter rejections until the English Stage Company premiered it at London's Royal Court Theatre in 1956, heralding the advent of the sometimes brutally realistic movement known as "kitchen sink drama."

Laurence Olivier attended one of O'Toole's performances in London. At the time, Olivier was feuding with Marilyn Monroe, who was working with him, unhappily, in the filming of Terence Rattigan's screenplay, *The Prince and the Showgirl* (1957). When O'Toole spoke to Olivier in the lobby of the London theater, Olivier said to him, provocatively, "Dear Boy, I hear you're doing that dreadful Osborne play. I found it bad theater, unpatriotic, and a travesty to England."

[Before very much time had passed, Olivier very obviously changed his mind about Osborne, appearing as a key player in his The Entertainer *(1957).]*

Osborne gave O'Toole some advice about how to deal with women, telling him to have many wives and far more mistresses. "And don't be afraid to mistreat wives and lovers alike," the playwright—who would marry five times and take countless lovers—advised.

O'Toole continued to see Osborne over the years, especially during his marriage to Jill Bennett, his fourth wife.

In the press, during their much-publicized

Playwright John Osborne...
"Down with the Queen."

breakup, Bennett referred to Osborne as "impotent," and denounced him as a homosexual. In the wake of that, Osborne presented O'Toole with a strange request. "From all reports, you are straight, and God knows I am. However, let's make it with each other tonight and find out what all this homosexual attraction is all about. Perhaps we'll go for it. Who knows until we try it?"

"A charming offer, darling," O'Toole responded, "but I'm wearing the wrong underwear tonight."

Years later, Osborne shared with O'Toole his counterattack on Bennett. "She never bought a bar of soap in all the time she lived with me. She had no love in her heart for people and only a little more for dogs. Her frigidity was almost total. She loathed men and pretended to love women, whom she hated even more. She was at ease only in the company of homosexuals, whom she also despised, since their narcissism matched her own. My only regret is that I did not flob (spit) into her open coffin."

[Bennett had committed suicide in 1990.]

After Osborne's death in 1994 based on complications from diabetes, O'Toole told a reporter, "I will always be grateful to John for teaching me how to handle women."

In July of 1957, O'Toole appeared in London at the Garrick Theatre, starring as the ailing Uncle Gustave in *O Mein Papa*. The theater stood on Charing Cross Road, and had presented its first play in 1889. It was named after the famous stage actor, David Garrick.

At first, Brenner had been reluctant to release O'Toole from his commitment to the Bristol Old Vic, fearing that *O Mein Papa* might be a hit and would run for a year. He needed the increasingly popular O'Toole for performances in Bristol.

He need not have feared, as reviews were mediocre, and *O Mein Papa* closed after three months.

In it, O'Toole sang a duet with Rachel Roberts, the Welsh actress five years his senior. Notoriously unstable, she'd been another RADA graduate. She was married to Alan Dobie but that didn't seem to diminish her interest in O'Toole.

The O'Toole/Roberts onstage duet later evolved into an even more intimate duet off stage. O'Toole was sexually attracted to her, but admitted to James Villiers that she was mentally disturbed.

Their on-again, off-again relationship would last until her suicide in 1989. *For more details on that, and on her affair with O'Toole, refer to chapter 32.]*

On opening night, the audience of *O Mein Papa* booed the actors, but O'Toole bravely carried on, as did the rest of the cast. Many patrons left, but several stayed to continue their catcalling as the final curtain descended.

So upset was O'Toole that he got disastrously drunk that night.

A policeman in Holborn caught him "harrassing" an insurance building, and arrested him. O'Toole was jailed for the rest of the night.

When he faced the judge the next morning, he said, "I felt like singing and so I began to woo this building." The judge fined him five pounds, with a warning not to show up in court again.

In need of a meaty role after the theatrical debacle of *Oh Mein Papa*, O'Toole returned to Bristol, where Brenner handed him the script for Samuel Beckett's *Waiting for Godot*. In this play for two actors, the role of Vladimir was offered to him for its 1957 premiere.

[Twelve years later, in 1969, O'Toole would again appear as Vladimir at the Abbey Theatre in Dublin.]

In the play, Vladimir encounters Estragon, and both of them seem to be waiting endlessly for the mysterious Godot who never appears. The script calls for Vladimir to look up at the sky and muse about religious and philosophical matters.

Both actors wore bowlers and other broadly comic accessories, wardrobe choices that reminded some members of the audience of Laurel and Hardy, who in their films often played tramps wearing bowler hats.

O'Toole would later be angered at critics who found homoerotic qualities in the play, whose text contains very few references to female characters.

As a couple, Vladimir and Estragon were defined as "quasi-marital" by one newspaper reporter. "They bicker, they embrace each other, they depend on each other. They might be thought of as a married couple." Some reviewers cited Estragon's stage business of "sucking on the end of his carrot" as an example of his homoeroticism.

"In my dressing room, before I was to go on at the night of the premiere, I vomited three times," O'Toole later admitted. "Surely, no woman giving birth went through my agony. I performed my role as child labor. It's difficult to explain, but my role seemed to be a marriage of Peter O'Toole the man and Peter O'Toole the actor. Before going on, I lay down for an hour on the floor of my dressing room, 'Waiting for Godot' you might say—and I imagined I was a fetus, my eyes were covered with black eyepads, as I imagined myself in my mother's womb, minutes before she went into labor."

Rachel Roberts...
performing "duets" with O'Toole both on and off the stage.

Critic Vivien Mercier wrote that the play "achieved a theoretical impossibility—a play in which nothing happens, that keeps the audience glued to their seats. What's more, since the second act is a subtly different reprise of the first, he has written a play in which nothing happens twice."

One critic for a Bristol newspaper hailed O'Toole's performance "as one of the most exciting nights of my life in the theater."

Over the course of years, he would meet several times with the play's author, Samuel Beckett, the Irish avant-garde playwright and theater director, who had been born in Dublin. O'Toole gravitated toward Beckett's outlook on life, a bleak, tragicomic portrait of human nature in a heady mixture of black comedy and gallows humor. Beck-ett had become a key player in the "Theatre of the Absurd," which in 1969 brought him the Nobel Prize for Literature.

As "Vladimir," O'Toole (right) starred in Samuel Beckett's *Waiting for Godot*, along-side his counterpart, "Estragon."

At one point, Beckett came to see one of O'Toole's performances at the Gaiety Theatre in Dublin, starring as Jack Boyle in *Juno and the Paycock,* a play by Sean O'Casey, which dealt with the Irish Civil War. Later, Laurence Olivier revived this tragi-comedy for his National Theatre in London.

Beckett complimented O'Toole for playing down the more comic elements of the play, and for allowing the tragedy to assert itself.

Even when O'Toole went out drinking with Beckett later that night, he still wore his character's red mustache and shaggy wig. As Jack Boyle, he was with Beckett when the first review came in. It was by Sean Day-Lewis *[son of Cecil Day-Lewis, poet-laureate of the U.K. from 1968-1972, and half-brother of the brilliant actor, Daniel Day-Lewis]*, who wrote in *The Daily Telegraph:* "Peter O'Toole gives his best stage performance in years, more than simply power-ful. He has a nervous struggle with the accent, at times his vowels get no fur-ther west than Liverpool, but he is truly involved with the captain, and the aggressive bluster of his delivery is most effective."

O'Toole told Beckett, "Back on the stage has convinced me that this is where the heart lies. Movies are just lucrative drudge."

Meeting Beckett years later, O'Toole found the playwright objecting to a then-newfangled concept of assigning the two male roles in Godot to women. "They're ruining my play. It has to be performed by men because women don't have prostates."

[He was referring to the fact that Vladimir frequently has to exit from the stage to urinate.]

At one point, O'Toole asked Beckett, "Exactly who was Godot?"

"My play was performed by prisoners in Lüttringhausen Prison near Wuppertal in Germany. They understand. I received word that inmates enjoyed my play—'thieves, forgers, toughs, homos, crazy men, and killers spend this bitch of a life waiting...and waiting...and waiting. For what? Godot? Perhaps."

When he was an international star, O'Toole desperately tried to adapt *Waiting for Godot* into a low-budget teleplay, for which he raised £20,000 pounds. He approached Beckett himself to request film rights, which were reluctantly granted by the playwright with a warning, "*Waiting for Godot* cannot be made into a movie. It just won't work."

Samuel Beckett called O'Toole "a true son of Ireland."

As events unraveled, it became apparent that in this, at least, the playwright's words were prophetic.

Beaten up by Teddy Boy Hooligans, Extolled for Hamlet, & for Fathering Baby Hercules

In 1958, in another meaty role at the Bristol Old Vic, O'Toole would star as Jack Tanner in *Man and Superman,* a play written by George Bernard Shaw in 1903. It was based on the legend of the amorous Don Juan, who was said to have seduced 1,003 women. "Why the extra three?" O'Toole asked. I thought he'd be exhausted after the first thousand."

O'Toole played Tanner as a "political firebrand and confirmed bachelor," a spiritual descendant of Don Juan, or at least a modern representation of him. O'Toole's leading lady in the play was the lovely actress, Wendy Williams.

In Act III, Shaw compares Don Juan's resemblance to Tanner's.

"Besides, in the brief lifting of his face, now hidden by his hat brim, there was a curious suggestion of Tanner, a more critical, fastidious, handsome face, paler and colder, without Tanner's impetuous credulity and enthusiasm, and without a touch of modern plutocratic vulgarity, but still a resemblance, even an identity."

[Reviews for O'Toole's performance were favorable, and O'Toole liked the role so much that more than twenty years later, in 1980, he shouldered the role of Tanner again at London's Theatre Royal on the Haymarket. Two years after that, in 1982, he arranged to have it filmed as a teleplay.]]

"If George Bernard Shaw were alive today, he would applaud O'Toole in his role of Jack Tanner," wrote one critic. "In the play by Ireland's leading modern dramatist, O'Toole performs one of the best roles of his career." Another critic noted that "Shaw's words just glided smoothly off O'Toole's silvery tongue."

Only once did a stage role by O'Toole catalyze a physical attack upon him. In *The Pier* (1957) he played a "Teddy Boy" so convincingly that he offended some actual Bristol Teddy Boys in the audience. Furious at how they were portrayed on stage, five of them ganged up on O'Toole in an alleyway behind the theater. They attacked him and gave him a beating, but no serious injury.

He later said, "The chaps gave me a dusting off. Except for some bruises, I survived. Actually, I took the beating as a perverse compliment."

After his beating, O'Toole invited the Teddy Boys for "a lager on me," at a local pub.

[In the 1950s, Teddy Boys became famously associated throughout Britain with rock and roll, hooliganism, and for form-fitting, updated versions of Edwardian suits that later, in the early 1960s, influenced some of the designers on Carnaby Street. Critics referred to Teddy Boys as "zoot-suiters, and spivs."]

O'Toole had appeared on stage dressed in a tightly form-fitting, double-breasted suit with a Trilby hat *[a modernized version of a Fedora]* and lace-up shoes, known as "creepers," with thick, crepe rubber soles.

A late 1950s British Teddy Boy. Somehow, they always looked undernourished.

Somehow, before the night ended, he convinced these Teddy Boy thugs who attacked him in that Bristol alley, that in *The Pier*, he was actually paying them tribute, not satirizing them.

He was even invited to join their gang and informed that they were about to inaugurate a brawl with a rival gang from the neighboring town of Clifton. One of the Teddy Boys told O'Toole that their weapons of choice for this upcom-

In *The Pier*, O'Toole, in an uncharacteristic role, dances the night away, later donning Teddy Boy drag.

ing battle included "knuckle dusters, coshes, razors, and meat skewers."

O'Toole politely rejected their invitation for him to join them.

On the last night of his performance in *The Pier*, two young men in neo-Edwardian dress came to see O'Toole's performance, and afterwards, went backstage to congratulate him. They even gave him a present. Later, when he opened the package, he found two items of clothing representative of his status as an "adopted member of the Teddy Boy mystique." They included, as O'Toole later noted in his memoirs, without further description, a pair of "Winkle Picker Boots" and a "Kiss-Me-Quick" cowboy hat.

***

O'Toole's next big challenge at the Bristol Old Vic involved the most thrilling role of his career so far, the title role in their 1958 production of *Hamlet*.

He spoke with great candor to the press about his involvement with the role. Many of his words were later censored by editors. "I wanted to play the Prince of Denmark with the clear suggestion that he was definitely fucking Ophilia and that he had had incest written on his face when he bestowed lascivious kisses on dear old Mum."

"Even in rehearsals, I was hailed as a virile Hamlet, more so than Olivier's version, and without the Gielgudian pathos which can be a bit much and queeny at times."

"If I may review myself, I packjammed the graveyard scene with wit and utter fascination—at least that's what Nat Breener told me. I was heavenly. But I do carry on a bit too long, and perhaps the audience will grow rebellious and storm the stage and damage my family jewels."

In Hamlet, O'Toole played the Prince of Denmark with a beard. As he asked Brenner, "Why should Hamlet be the only bloke at Elsinore Castle with a razor?"

During a lecture in London, Gielgud told wannabee young actors that each of them should play Hamlet before they turned thirty.

O'Toole said, "I heeded Gielgud's advice."

Even before *Hamlet's* opening night, theater critics were writing about a new breed of British actors, as exemplified most visibly by Richard Burton, Albert Finney, Alan Bates, and a theatrical stewpot of other contenders. "Is it goodbye to Gielgud and Olivier except for grandfather roles?" asked one reviewer.

"In England today, it is the era of angry young men in the theater," another reporter wrote. "Except for Shakespeare, modern plays are signaling goodbye to Noël Coward, goodbye to Terence Rattigan."

Before opening night, O'Toole hyped his upcoming performance. "I want to bring fresh blood to *Hamlet,* a real character who farts and pisses against the wall, minus all that Gielgudian deity, all that mellifluous diction. A Prince who knows how to get it hard when the time comes."

None of those remarks were replicated in the Bristol press.

What the papers did print after *Hamlet's* premiere were rave reviews

The Daily Telegraph claimed that O'Toole's Hamlet lacked nobility, but for the most part, other critics wrote raves. O'Toole even got an endorsement from the notoriously acerbic Kenneth Tynan, who came to Bristol from London to see his performance. Tynan predicted major stardom in the theater for O'Toole, including him in a roster of working class actors—such as Finney, Burton, and Tom Courtenay—taking over the art form.

O'Toole's most important and influential visitor was Sir Peter Hall, the director of the world-famous Shakespeare Memorial Theatre at Stratford-upon-Avon. Hall spoke to the press after *Hamlet's* premiere. "I see sparks of genius in this actor. Genius is not too strong a word. There are minor problems, of course, in one so young. Sometimes, he didn't deliver a line as I would have preferred, and the meter wasn't always perfect, but on the whole, it was a splendid night in the theater."

Hall was so impressed that he signed a contract in 1960 for O'Toole to appear in three works at Stratford, each a play by Shakespeare.

Ironically, in 1963, Olivier, the master Hamlet himself, would direct O'Toole in the title role of *Hamlet* at the National Theatre.

Following his success as Hamlet, O'Toole fulfilled his contract with the Bristol Old Vic by appearing as Jupiter in a modern, English-language translation of the ancient Roman play, *Amphitryon* by Titus Maccius Plautus. Categorized as a tragi-comedy, it depicted Amphitryon's jealous reaction to his wife's seduction by Jupiter (O'Toole).

The play *[which many theatregoers interpret as heavy lifting, an ancient work that's confusing and for the most part of scholastic rather than popular interest]* generated lackluster reviews. O'Toole brushed off the criticisms, claiming, "I prefer plays in modern dress, although it was flattering to be cast as the father of Hercules, skinny, bony me."

"Mothers of Bristol, Lock Up Your Daughters!"
(Peter O'Toole Has Hit Town, and He's on a Rampage!)

During his sojourn in Bristol, performing in repertory at the Old Vic there, O'Toole began to receive his first press clippings, hailing him not just as a brilliant actor, but as a hellraiser.

"I remember going to see Rosalind Russell in the film version of *Auntie Mame* (1958). I may be misquoting her, but she said something like, 'Life is a banquet and most people are starving to death.' I didn't want that to happen to me. In spite of the long hours at the Old Vic, I still had the energy in those days to chase after dollybirds after midnight, and I encountered many of them raring and ready to go with a bloke like me. Some of them wanted repeats, and that kept me exhausted. I will say this about Bristol: The young women there (or at least they used to be) were the horniest in England. The Yanks had awakened their sexual appetites during World War II, and they got turned on and were insatiable."

Continuing his pattern of portraying senior citizens, O'Toole was cast in the role of the Pope in a play about Galileo's discoveries in physics and the church's rigorous opposition. Joseph O'Conor, one of the repertory company's leading actors, had high praise for him.

"O'Toole is able to immerse himself in any role, and I'm sure he could even play the Shirley Temple part in *Rebecca of Sunnybrook Farm* if called for."

In spite of the differences in their ages, O'Conor would often go pub crawling with O'Toole, a fiery young man whose Irish blood was raging and whose hormones were out of control.

"What amazed me even back then was his determination to become a star," O'Conor said. "He constantly said 'when I make it,' not 'if I make it.' There was no question in my mind that he would make it, perhaps sooner than later."

A fellow graduate of RADA, O'Conor was sixteen years older than O'Toole. He was known mainly as a Shakespearean actor, having appeared in the title role of plays that had included both *Othello* and *Hamlet*.

He and O'Toole became a regular at "Mead Parties," which were fashionable at the time. [*Mead, whose origins go back at least to the Middle Ages, is a beverage fermented from a mixture of water, honey, malt, and yeast. Its alcohol content can reach 20%, depending on how it's made.*]

Night after night, O'Toole, O'Conor, and various companions, downed cupfuls of it. "It turns me into a roving caveman with a club, hitting a female over the head and dragging her back to my cave," O'Toole claimed.

When O'Toole's sister, Patricia, showed up for a reunion with her brother in Bristol, she joined O'Conor and O'Toole on their nightly rounds. Caught on the street by a bobby with a club at 2AM, the police officer asked them, "What are you drunken pieces of trash doing out on the streets this late at night? Looking for trouble, no doubt."

Still holding a bottle of mead, Patricia struck the policeman over the head with it, knocking him out. Then all three of them fled into the night.

For two months, O'Toole became so attached to mead that he went to the library to research whatever he could learn about it. Known during some eras as "honey wine," it had been drunk by the ancient Egyptians.

Sometimes it's mixed with fruit juices, spices, grains, or hops, and some devotees professed to prefer it with "aged" rainwater. "In my view, mead should be drunk more often," O'Toole said. "It is a healthy elixir, and it was even consumed by Tolstoy and Dostoevsky."

The more O'Conor drank, the more he and O'Toole argued. The older actor had a strong spiritual side, and O'Toole had long ago abandoned the church, asserting that he found it filled with "pedophiles."

The two actors also didn't agree politically, as O'Toole was against the government and opposed the British invasion of Suez. O'Conor, on the other hand, was more conservative.

"In spite of their differences, the two men would bear hug at night during their goodbyes after evenings on the town. "Peter would kiss me passionately on the lips, a theatrical affectation I could do without. After all, he didn't look like Marilyn Monroe."

Often, O'Toole didn't have money to go out drinking unless he was invited. "I devised this plan of making my own brew, something Americans call moonshine, except mine was rhubarb wine. To get the rhubarb, I raided a neighboring farm, harvesting the plant after midnight. I made my own rhubarb wine in the bathtub. A taste of it would send you to the next dimension."

"I needed storage space for it, and I found this abandoned carboy in a junkyard."

[In Britain, the word "carboy" has been in documented use since the 1970s as the nickname for any large container designed for the storage of liquids. In this case, the carboy salvaged by O'Toole had apparently once held a corrosive acid.] "I don't think it had been thoroughly washed before I filled it with rhubarb wine. Maybe it was that residual acid that caused all the damage to my intestines that I would experience in later years."

One night in Bristol, O'Conor accepted an invitation to migrate with O'Toole to a party in the neighboring district of Clifton. "At one point during the drive, we got lost, and he ended up driving his Riley down a series of concrete stars, something I had seen done only in the movies up to then."

When not delivering brilliant performances at the Theatre Royal, O'Toole often showed up at a local pub with an odd name, *The Naval Volunteer,* in Bristol on King Street. It boasted that it provided the best Guinness and Bass Ale in Bristol.

"He seemed to seek out the most unsavory characters in the pub,"

O'Conor claimed. "Perhaps an ax murderer who had been released from prison after serving twenty-five years. Perhaps a Peeping Tom who hung out at playgrounds getting turned on by eight-year-old boys, trailing them to the loo when they took out their little wee-wees to wee-wee."

"Peter gravitated to broken down old trollops, who had served the boys during the war, and who were a bit long in the tooth back then. He didn't want to leave the pub with these old battle axes, but he loved talking to them, hearing their stories, especially if kinky enough. One whore said that she once went to bed with a soldier who had two penises."

O'Toole's carousing buddy and mead connoisseur, Joseph O'Conor

"One old soldier had been a member of the Royal Guard," O'Conor said.

"He told Peter that he used to plow it nightly to Edward, Prince of Wales before he became Edward VIII, King of England."

One night at a local pub, Peter got really pissed and went over to a table and insulted one of the regulars, a very burly man who worked for the railroad," O'Conor said. "Peter said something about his wife's tits, suggesting that they were sagging down to her navel."

The bloke seized O'Toole and dragged him out a rear door and beat him up in the alley.

Nat Brenner encountered O'Toole the next day and found him badly bruised. He warned him that if he continued, he might get knifed one night, but he never listened. "He continued on this self-destructive forays into the night. Always up to no good and looking for trouble and then finding it."

On several nights, O'Toole ended up in the hospital, always summoning Brenner to extricate him from his latest trouble.

Brenner admitted that one night, "I did a bad thing. I went to the hospital were Peter was being cared for after a bad fall. X-rays had been taken, but the results had not come in. He'd been there five hours. With his permission, I slipped him out of the hospital, helped him get dressed in his stage costume, and let him go on in his condition. He was in great pain but performed well. Only later did we discover that he had broken his arm. Fortunately, the play did not call for sword-fighting."

Actor Frank Finlay, O'Toole's RADA chum, arrived in Bristol one night. Not associated in any way with Bristol's Old Vic, he was performing with a troupe of traveling players going from town to town on one-night stands.

Learning that Finlay was staying in Room 401 on the fourth floor of the local YMCA, O'Toole arrived far too late. The gates were already locked as part of the organization's nightly curfew. Ignoring the signs, O'Toole scaled the fire escape and entered the YMCA's dimly lit hallway, knocking on Finlay's door at 2AM.

They spent the pre-dawn hours drinking mead which O'Toole had brought, and reliving their raucous days at RADA.

For a while in Bristol, O'Toole became part of "The Three Musketeers, pubbing and wenching" alongside Patrick Dromgoole and the playwright, Tom Stoppard.

Born in Chile, and two years older than O'Toole, Dromgoole later became a well-known producer and director.

Playwright Tom Stoppard... deadly wit.

At the time O'Toole met Stoppard, the Czech-born playwright and future Oscar and Tony winner was a reporter for *The Western Daily Free Press* a regional newspaper covering parts of southwestern England, mainly Gloucestershire, Wiltshire and Somerset.

Years later, partly in tribute to their good times in repertory theatre in Bristol, O'Toole would attend the premiere of Stoppard's play, *Rosencrantz and Guildenstern Are Dead* (1966). It was a play about Hamlet as told from the point of view of two of his courtiers. In theatrical circles, "Stoppardian" became a term for descriptive works that employed both wit and comedy while addressing philosophical concepts.

"Back when I knew Tom in Bristol," O'Toole recalled, "He was known for his failed attempts at humor and for his unstylish garb. But he showed the bloody bastards and became a big fucking deal, one of the most internationally performed dramatists of his generation who grew up during the war."

Ill health continued to plague O'Toole in Bristol. When he was appearing in London, he checked with a doctor, who told him that he was developing cysts over his corneas. He checked into a hospital for eye surgery.

In recovery for two days, he slipped out to see his close friend, James Villiers, perform in a play called *Tomorrow With Feeling* at the Duke of York Theatre in London's West End.

At curtain, he rushed backstage to hug and kiss Villiers, feeding him his tongue, as was his custom. "Darling," O'Toole told Villiers. "You were the most magnificent thing since the invention of soda pop."

After three years association with the repertory theatre, just before he abandoned Bristol for the stages of London, O'Toole hugged and kissed Brenner farewell.

"You are always welcome to come back to our theater one day," Brenner told him. "Thank you for not burning it down."

[On two different occasions, O'Toole had accidentally set his dressing room on fire.]

O'Toole Returns to the Bristol Old Vic to "Save Its Bacon" From Financial Doldrums
—In a Mishap, He Accidentally Shoots another Actor

Beginning in 1973, O'Toole decided to take a sabbatical, wandering through the green glens of Ireland or digging ditches for sewerage at his new house in Clifden. *[Clifden, in County Galway, is sometimes called "the capital of Connemara."]*

Scripts arrived daily, but none of them intrigued him. His wife, Siân, however, continued her acting work, frequently from a base in London.

That allowed O'Toole the freedom to pick up an Irish lassie or two as he wandered down various country lanes.

"If Siân is having a fling in London, I don't want to know," he told his friend, Kenneth Griffith. "I put a ring on her finger, not on her nose."

He was in recovery from the failure of his most recent film, *Man of La Mancha* (1972), in which he had co-starred with Sophia Loren.

He'd lost so much weight making the film that Siân had nicknamed him "The Bone."

Then an offer came in from his old friend, the director Nat Brenner at the Bristol Old Vic, where O'Toole had launched his theatrical career during the 1955-58 seasons. Recently, thanks partly to the advent of television, attendance there had dropped considerably at the Theatre Royal, where he'd performed his notable rendition of *Hamlet.*

Although at the time he was rejecting offers from the West End, from Broadway, from the British film industry, and inevitably from Hollywood, he eventually decided—perhaps for sentimental reasons—to return to Bristol's Old Vic. It certainly wasn't for the money, since the salary the theater could pay was negligible.

Brenner had lined up three plays as vehicles for O'Toole's formidable talents—Anton Chekhov's *Uncle Vanya;* George Bernard Shaw's *The Apple Cart;* and Ben Travers' farce, *Plunder.* As a trio, the roles were widely varied, and O'Toole welcomed the challenge of performing before live audiences again.

Each of the three plays would feature a different director: Val May, David Phethean, and Brenner himself.

Brenner even found him a home in Bristol's leafy suburb of Clifton, his former stamping ground when he'd been the city's most visible and celebrated hellraiser. "The house was built long ago from profits made by shipowners in the tobacco and slave trades," O'Toole said.

"Lean and mean, Peter was better than ever," Brenner later said. "He'd learned a lot since the 1950s. He was, indeed in marvelous nick. He did what I hoped he would. He brought locals back to the Theatre Royal, and lured Londoners to take the fast train to the West Country."

O'Toole worked with familiar faces from the past, especially Nigel Stock, who appeared in all three plays, as did Edward Hardwicke and Judy Parfitt. "Each was a veteran pro," O'Toole said. "They were a back-up choir in case I warbled off key."

His first appearance was in the title role of *Uncle Vanya.* He announced that, "I want to do the definitive Uncle Vanya." He was allowed to select his own translation from the Russian, as there seemed to be more than a dozen different English-language versions available to him.

Rehearsals went smoothly except for one incident. In the play, the professor tells his fellow housemates that he's going to sell Vanya's land.

As Vanya, O'Toole views that as treachery.

"I couldn't believe it," May recalled. "He became a wild man. He even tossed furniture around and broke vases. I thought he was going to attack all of us, especially the professor. But he calmed down. I have never in all my life seen any actor rehearse that intensely."

In October of 1973, opening night produced a standing ovation, which was repeated night after night. "Our old audience came back to see Peter, and he performed *Uncle Vanya* brilliantly, truly captivating in the role. At the cast party that followed the premiere, I think he danced with every girl, some of them swooning to be in the arms of *Lawrence of Arabia."*

There was one horrible night, however. In one scene near the end of the play, Nigel Stock, playing the professor, was scheduled to be shot. Every night, O'Toole had gripped a pistol, holding it in his right hand and shooting upward. But on one Friday night, he gripped the pistol in his left hand and pointed it downward. He stood less than two feet from Stock, his (character's) intended victim.

"I felt this horrible sensation in my right calf," Stock later asserted. "I felt my leg had been bashed by an iron bar. I fell back into my chair and could not rise to my feet at curtain call. The blank cartridge had hit me. For the rest of the run of *Uncle Vanya,* I had to sit down or else hobble about the stage."

O'Toole preferred one review among the many raves. It was by the theater critic for *The Guardian,* David Foot, who wrote: "Peter O'Toole shuffled down the steps into the garden. His mouth sags in geriatric despair. His red-rimmed eyes are filled with Chekhovian pain. He is old before his time. It is an entrance worth waiting fifteen years for."

The second play, *Plunder,* was by the English playwright Ben Travers, first presented in London in 1928 and later adapted into a film in 1933. O'Toole claimed that Travers was "Pre-Orton, one of the most talented of British *farceurs."*

At Bristol, O'Toole was to star in the first revival of the play since its original staging in 1928.

During rehearsals, when O'Toole learned that Travers was still alive, he took the train to London to meet with him. The writer had been born in 1886 during the colonial and Empire-building heyday of Queen Victoria.

Meeting with the playwright, O'Toole talked about the recent abolition of theater censorship in Britain during the early 1970s.

"The removal of censorship has made me want to return to writing," Travers told him. "I have found it hard to write without focusing on sexual activities."

True to his word, after O'Toole left him, Travers set to work on *The Bed Before Yesterday* (1975), which was eventually staged in London when he turned eighty-nine years old. It became the longest-running of his stage plays. O'Toole went to see it, watching Joan Plowright, who was married at the time to Laurence Olivier, discover the pleasures of sex.

O'Toole's standing ovations continued, although not all of the critics were won over. Eric Shorter in the *Daily Telegraph* wrote: "Mr. O'Toole gangles and dithers nicely as the silly ass who gets caught up in the crookery but asininity is not really in his line."

The Times interpreted *Plunder* as "a very entertaining piece of nonsense," and praised O'Toole's performance. Another reviewer found O'Toole "in top-top form," even though his health at the time was rapidly deteriorating.

Shorter was kinder to O'Toole in his evaluation of his performance as King Magnus in George Bernard Shaw's *The Apple Cart.* "O'Toole's presence at the Theatre Royal had not only put the company on its feet by enduring full houses throughout the season, it has drawn first-rate players in support."

Shaw, O'Toole's favorite dramatist after Shakespeare, had written this "Political Extravaganza," as he called it, in 1928. As King Magnus, O'Toole spars with, and ultimately outwits, Prime Minister Proteus and his cabinet, who, it's learned as the plot unfolds, are trying to strip the monarchy of its rapidly waning political power.

"My goal every night was to reduce the Prime Minister to a cipher," O'Toole said. "As King, he abdicates the throne and puts himself up for election as Prime Minister."

Shaw claimed that he had based the character of King Magnus on himself. For the pivotal character of the enigmatic Orinthia, he based it on the actress who billed herself as "Mrs. Patrick Campbell." She shot to fame in the role of Eliza Doolittle in Shaw's *Pygmalion.*

On the final night, when O'Toole bid farewell to the Bristol Old Vic, the director and Old Vic spokesperson Val May declared to the press, "He saved our bacon. We never looked back after that. Even though I had never considered him as such before, when I saw him perform in these three plays at our theater, I knew I was seeing a genius at work on that stage."

O'Toole later summed up why his experience in Bristol had meant so much to him. "It all happened for me in Bristol. I arrived a boy and left as a famous actor. It was in Bristol that I discovered myself. Before that, I had been a series of pieces to a jigsaw puzzle. In Bristol, I put those pieces together and became a whole man again. When I returned to Bristol in 1973, it was to gain reassurance because I'd lost my way. Bristol was like a second home to me because it was here that I came to be *me.*"

Chapter 6

O'Toole's Affair with Vivien Leigh

"I Wanted Scarlett O'Hara. Instead, I Got Blanche DuBois."

Breaking Into Show-Biz while Pursuing England's Most Beautiful Actress.
Her Links to "Finchy" and Her Subsequent Breakdowns

As Scarlett O'Hara in *Gone With the Wind*, Vivien Leigh became a household word.

Vivien Leigh, boarding an airplane with her lover, Peter Finch, O'Toole's friend and rival. Inset photo: O'Toole waiting for a shot at Miss Scarlet, the "Antebellum Belle of Georgia."

As a teenager still living in Leeds, young Peter O'Toole had a dream: He wanted to become a jazz musician. To that end, he bonded with some locals to form a band provocatively named "Coming Down Hard."

During a period of three or four months, the group performed every Saturday night at some out-of-the-way pubs. As payment, they were given free lager and allowed to pass a collections plate.

O'Toole tried to imitate the highly energetic and flamboyant style of Chicago-born Gene Krupa, the jazz and big band drummer. His favorite recording was "Drum Boogie" from the 1941 film, *Ball of Fire,* in which a dubbed version of Stanwyck's singing voice had been inserted. O'Toole played "Drum Boogie" repeatedly.

Peter's other musical inspiration was the Louisiana born "Lead Belly," the American folk and Blues musician noteworthy for his strong vocals and virtuosity on the twelve-string guitar. O'Toole's favorite songs, which he played endlessly, included "Looky Looky Yonder," "Take This Hammer," and "Julie Ann Johnson."

O'Toole, before his nose job, in a swashbuckling minor role in *Kidnapped.*

He also decided he wanted to play the bagpipes. As a means of achieving that goal, he took lessons from an elderly, former blacksmith who had moved to Leeds from Perth in Eastern Scotland. He taught O'Toole how to play, and with money he'd saved from his job earnings, he bought himself a Scottish kilt.

He became so adept at playing the instrument that he was allowed to join Lord Kolmarry's Own Hibernians, an Irish piping and dancing group which had settled in Leeds.

O'Toole later said, "Leeds was the only place left for these hellraising hard drinkers. They got kicked out of every other place."

At the age of 18, after having abandoned newspaper reporting as a career goal, he journeyed to London to study acting at RADA. Needing to eke out a living, he decided to do what many young actors at RADA were doing: That involved finding work, any kind of work, in the movies, especially at Pinewood Studios outside London.

The jobs available to him included stints as a stunt man, and they involved a high risk of injury.

[Ironically, one of his most famous movie roles was The Stunt Man *(1980), for which he'd be nominated for an Oscar.]*

For obscure reasons of his own, as a stuntman, he adopted pseudonyms that included Arnold Heartthurg, Walter Plings, and Charlie Staircase. He later

> *"I have a husband, and I have lovers like Sarah Bernhardt"*
>
> *— Vivien Leigh*

said, "Instead of O'Toole, I should have billed myself in the future as Peter Heartthurg, or would Heartthrob be better?"

"When I worked as a stunt man, my lilywhite body was constantly black and blue. I ended up with only a few broken bones. At least I didn't get my neck broken, although I came close, and I didn't end up in a wheelchair for the rest of my life, as many poor blokes do."

In His Film Debut, O'Toole is "Kidnapped"
As His Costume, He's Assigned the "Garb of the Gods"

During his studies at RADA, O'Toole encountered Peter Finch, one of the best actors around. Although born in London, Finch had grown up in France, India, and, ultimately, Australia. He was sixteen years older than O'Toole, and had a certain world weariness about him.

O'Toole liked him, and one night, invited him to The Queen's Elm, a pub in Chelsea, to hear him join with three Scotsmen in a bagpipe concert evocative of the Scottish Highlands.

Having a drink after the show with him, O'Toole mentioned casually that he'd like to break into the movies. Finch had learned that Albert ("Cubby") Broccoli was in London at the time, casting a James Bond 007 movie, *Dr. No*, and that there might be a role in it for O'Toole. "I know Cubby, and if you're interested, I can arrange for you to see him tomorrow."

"I'm more than interested," O'Toole said. "I'm hot to trot."

Two days before, Broccoli had fired one of his supporting actors because of his heavy drinking. That was unknown to O'Toole when he showed up at Broccoli's office at Pinewood Studios. As O'Toole later recalled, "I'd had a nip or two because I was nervous as hell."

Regrettably, as he entered the office, he stumbled, and a pint of Irish whiskey fell out of his overcoat's pocket.

When he saw that, and ascertained that the new job candidate was already moderately drunk, Broccoli yelled at O'Toole, "Get the fuck out of my office."

In 1962, when *Dr. No* was released by United Artists, O'Toole went to see it with his friend, Kenneth

"The object of his affection": Ursula Andress in *Dr. No*

Griffith. After the screening, with Griffith in a pub, he told him, "I regret not getting cast in that movie. It's not missing out on the role so much as it is losing the chance to plug Ursula Andress."

Director Robert Stevenson cast Finch as Alan Breck Stewart, the lead in the 1959 film, *Kidnapped,* based on the Robert Louis Stevenson story.

The director told Finch that he was looking for an actor who could play the bagpipes. "I know one who does," Finch said. "I'll call him to come and see you."

This time for his audition, O'Toole deliberately arrived sober, and wearing a kilt. In addition to an interview, his audition included playing the bagpipes.

He got the role, and was instructed to report to work the following Wednesday morning.

***

During his first day on the film set of *Kidnapped,* he almost got fired. The night before, he and Kenneth Griffith had gone on a pub crawl through Soho. Instead of getting up at 5AM the next morning, he slept through his alarm. Griffith had stayed over that night and was asleep in the living room downstairs, where he was awakened by the persistent ringing of a telephone.

Peter Finch in *Kidnapped:*
"I was no Errol Flynn."

"Where in hell is O'Toole?" came an angry voice over the phone. That voice belonged to a production assistant on the set of *Kidnapped.* "The fucker is late!"

Despite his splitting hangover, Griffith "vamped until ready," as he later said. He honestly didn't know where O'Toole was, but he assured the assistant that he was already on his way to Pinewood.

After a thorough search of the house, Griffith found O'Toole asleep on the floor of his bedroom closet.

"I stripped off his clothes, dragged him into the shower, held him up under the Arctic cold water, and woke the bastard up," Griffith said. "Downstairs, I poured three cups of scalding black coffee down his gullet and drove him to

Roosters with Swords:
Peter Finch with Peter O'Toole in
Kidnapped

Pinewood. Fortunately, Stevenson had not had time to cast another actor. How many actors played the bagpipes?"

As it happened, Finch had not showed up on time that morning either. He arrived on the set an hour later, after O'Toole had already donned his kilt and was rehearsing with his bagpipe.

Finch whispered to O'Toole, "I had a reunion with Vivien Leigh last night. We both got pissed. I took me some time to pull myself together this morning."

"You're a man after my true soul," O'Toole told him. "Tonight, let's become two 'piss-ups' together."

"It's a deal, my good man," O'Toole said. "Incidentally, your breath is lethal!"

"Yours could ignite a fire that would burn down the Tower of London."

O'Toole told Stevenson, "I want to be authentic in the scene, which means I'll not be wearing any bloomers. As you know, a true Scot wears no panties beneath his kilt, preferring 'the Garb of the Gods.' If I have to do any high steps, the camera might get to photograph me in all my glory."

Cast in a minor role as Robin MacGregory, O'Toole had begun his movie career. His only scene was with Finch, when both of them competed to see which was the better bagpipe player. Finch conceded that O'Toole clearly won.

The director, Stevenson, was pleased with O'Toole's brief performance. He later said. "I sensed a rising star here. I think we'll be hearing a lot more from this actor—that is, if Finch and O'Toole don't drink themselves into an early grave. Those two guys have discovered each other. Two fellow boozers."

The famous plot of *Kidnapped* unfolds in 18th-Century Scotland when the young David Balfour (James MacArthur) is lured aboard a ship, where the captain shanghais *[i.e., kidnaps]* him. At sea, he realizes that he's been sold into indentured servitude.

During a thick fog, the ship collides with another vessel, and Alan Breck Stewart (Finch) comes aboard. The greedy captain plots to kill him for his money. Stewart and Balfour become allies, plotting to save themselves. After many dangerous escapades, the pair eludes their enemies on land and at sea. By the finale, back on the Scottish mainland, young Balfour is free to claim the inheritance and the castle that had been stolen from him.

O'Toole rather liked MacArthur, who had dropped out of Harvard during his sophomore year to make two Disney movies, *Kidnapped* and *Swiss Family Robinson*. He was the adopted son of playwright Charles MacArthur and his wife, actress Helen Hayes. Lillian Gish was his godmother, and he was friends with everybody from John Steinbeck to Harpo Marx.

Reviewing the film's screen credits, O'Toole later said, "The picture belonged to Finch and MacArthur. I was sandwiched between two other minor actors, Alex Mackenzie and Andrew Cruickshank."

The movie—aimed as it was by Disney, Inc., at the kiddie's market—made money in spite of the generally negative reviews it generated. Eugene Archer, film critic for *The New York Times,* wrote, "Either Mr. Disney, who made a vigorous *Treasure Island* ten years ago, has lost his touch in the intervening decade, or the kids have been spoiled by *Gunsmoke* and *Peter Gunn.* Yesterday's audience was definitely not amused."

Finch wasn't pleased with the reviews. One critic claimed that as a swashbuckler, he needed "more swash in his buckling. A young Errol Flynn might have pulled off the role."

Although another reviewer published high praise for O'Toole's mastery of the bagpipe, in an apparent contradiction, he wondered, "Was his music playing dubbed?"

As O'Toole later recalled, "Finch not only got me that small role in that Disney movie, he introduced me to Vivien Leigh, an actress on whom I had had a crush ever since my father took me to see *Gone With the Wind* (1939).

A Pair of "Gigglebums" Prowl London, Devouring Hearts ...Literally

On their first night of pub crawling together, Finch soon became "Finchy" to O'Toole. "He was the only bloke I ever met who could down more lager and whiskey than I could—and still remain standing," O'Toole told his friend, Kenneth Griffith.

O'Toole often spoke frequently about Finch as a talented actor with whom he enjoyed a life-long relationship. "I know what people say about Finchy," he told Albert Finney at RADA. "They called him a wild man, a maverick, a loner, and a nomad. I find him a curious mixture of intellect and alarming frankness, with the sensitivity of a moth. Even when he breaks up with one of his girlfriends, he most often remains a loving, loyal friend that can be counted on in a crisis."

"I know there's a lot of talk that when he was much younger, like Richard Burton, he was bisexual. Burton admits that he was, but I think Finchy is very heterosexual. He was involved with Larry Olivier, but that was for career advancement, not sexual desire or passion. All I know is that he's a world-class guzzler like myself and my great drinking buddy. And to clear up these sexual rumors, he never sucked my cock."

Yolande Turnbull, Finch's second wife, was a scriptwriter and TV actress long associated with South Africa. She described Finch in a memoir she entitled *Finchy, a drunkard, a womanizer, a genius.*

"Finchy was a pisspot and a hellraiser, but he was also a happy drunk, a *gigglebum and very, very good company. He was handsome, with a great dig-nified head; wide, deep blue eyes whose corneas were ringed with black; a bone structure that defied a bad angle, with cheekbones as high as an Amer-ican Red Indian's, with deep hollows beneath, and a pursed, sensual mouth I have heard ladies describe as 'bee-stung.' His hair was curly and the color Vivien Leigh gave it, baby elephant. For a beach bum from Australia, Finchy had a lot of class."*

On his second night boozing with O'Toole, Finch announced, "I'm so hun-gry I could eat a baby's asshole through a wicker chair. Right now, I'd devour anything except a goldfish sandwich."

"What have you got against goldfish?" O'Toole asked.

"One late afternoon in Australia, this bloke and I were starving," he said. "We didn't have one pence between us. Someone had left this bowl of gold-fish in an open window. We stole it, and cooked the fish over a campfire and then made a sandwich out of it, with some bread we'd lifted. Fried goldfish is the most disgusting meal in the world."

Then, Finch demanded that O'Toole get into a taxi with him for a jaunt to a restaurant he liked. They were they were driven to a grimy joint in London's East End that smelled of offal.

Inside the dive, an alleycat cockney waitress reminded O'Toole of Mildred in *Of Human Bondage,* as portrayed by Bette Davis in 1934. She took their order. According to O'Toole, the specialty of the house was a "Viscera Platter, consisting of a pig's heart, tripe, sweetbreads, kidneys, and even the asshole of a cow."

"I hope that cow didn't have diarrhea and that it's been washed out since the last bull mounted her," O'Toole said.

During the days, weeks, and years ahead, O'Toole claimed, "I came to love Finchy, learning about his flaws and virtues. I also identified with him in so many ways. We were so different, but so very much alike."

He was eager to lean how Finch had moved into the rarefied world of Vivien Leigh and Laurence Olivier, even as the union of that famously roman-tic pair was grinding to an end. "Larry was not really her Heathcliff, and Vivien was not really his Scarlett O'Hara," Finch told him. "That was an invention of the press."

"I've got to admit, I'm a bit jealous of you for getting so close to that pair," O'Toole said. "I mean, they're the greatest thing since butter on bread was invented."

"Beware of what you want, for you might get it," Finch warned. "If you get too close to either Larry or Vivien, you might have to drop trou."

"I'll take my chances," O'Toole said.

***

During their 1948 stage tour of Australia—a much-publicized event arranged in collaboration with the Old Vic in London—the Oliviers had attended an unconventional stage presentation of an English-language translation of Molière's *Le Malade Imaginaire* (*The Imaginary Invalid*), staged for the workers at O'Brien's glass factory in Sydney. It starred a young Peter Finch in the title role.

Olivier later commented that he found the actor "compelling, especially his penetrating blue eyes, intelligent and alert responses, and his ruggedly masculine features."

For a time, Laurence Olivier and Vivien Leigh were the most talked about, gossiped about, and some say, "beloved" actors in Britain.

Here, in a scene from the 1937 film, *Fire Over England*, they play Cynthia and Michael. Their real-life romance off-screen sometimes seemed to eerily echo their on-screen performances.

As Finch told O'Toole, "With the two greatest actors sitting out there watching me, I was afraid I'd forget my lines."

How Sir Laurence and Lady Olivier Lured Peter Finch into a Murky Love Nest Envied by O'Toole.

[Born in London in 1916, the remarkable Peter Finch had an intensity for life and a brilliant talent as an actor. He was the illegitimate son of a Scotsman, Major Wentworth Edward Dallas Campbell, an army officer in the Poona Horse Regiment. Enduring a tumbleweed childhood, young Finch traveled from England to France and on to India before settling in Australia.

During World War II, he'd been a gunner in the Australian Army, serving with the North African Troops. He broke into show business as a straight man to a stand-up comedian, and he eventually formed Peter Finch's Mercury Theatre Company, touring Queensland and New South Wales.

It was easy for Finch's young disciple, Trader Faulkner, to understand his mentor's attraction to Laurence Olivier. "I'm heterosexual," Faulkner claimed, "but I could see Sir Laurence's enormous attraction for both men and women, a charismatic personality. In his elaborate makeup as Richard III, he impressed me as a bluebottle fly in color, but like a scorpion underneath. When he walked about, there was something lethal in his movements. Even off stage he gave the feeling that he wasn't a person to go too near. He created an illusion of physical danger."

It has been suggested that Larry was sexually attracted to Finch. It was also suggested that somehow in the handsome young actor named Peter Finch, Larry saw a mirror of himself at the end of the 1930s when he had cut a more dashing and romantic figure.

"I think Larry felt that if he could possess Finch, some of his brashness and virility would wear off on him," said actor Harcourt Williams. "Broken and bent by his health and by his increasing problems with Vivien, Larry seemed to turn to Finch as a source to renew his own vitality, in the same way a middle-aged man turns to a younger woman for what's called a renewal."

"Like Larry, Vivien was sexually attracted to Finch from the first day they met," said Williams. "No doubt she envisioned him as the strikingly handsome young courtier in her future."

Vivien told Williams, "Peter has that kind of passion that drew me to Larry back in 1936. There is a lust for life in him that I find most appealing in an actor. He must be a demon in bed."

Many accounts assert that Larry told Finch during their time together in Sydney, "If you ever come to London, look me up."

But the reality was far more intimate than that. Larry and Vivien invited Finch and his first wife, Tamara Tchinarova, a Russian ballerina, to dinner after one of their performances. Over a late night supper, they solidified their intentions, Larry promising to find work for Finch as an actor in London, either at the Old Vic or in one of his own productions.

Tamara was more or less left out of the excitement. She remembered her husband coming together with Larry and Vivien as a "lovefest" in which she was not included.

Finch told Larry and Vivien that he had long planned to come to London, along with Tamara, of course, and he eagerly awaited his next reunion with the Oliviers.

Outside the restaurant, a taxi was hailed for Larry and Vivien. Both actors shook Tamara's hand and told her how delighted they'd been to meet her.

But she couldn't help but notice that during their farewells, both Vivien and Larry gave her husband rather passionate kisses on his lips.

As Finch would later recall, "both kisses held out much promise to me. I couldn't wait to get to London and be with them again. But had I not met them, had I not come into their lives, so much heartbreak could have been avoided."]

***

O'Toole learned that Finch's affair with Vivien began in 1949, when she was performing the title role in Jean Anouilh's *Antigone* at the New Theatre in London. At the same time, he was star-ring next door in *Daphne Laureola* at the Wyndham. "It began in her dressing room, and became something more, so much more."

After their third night together, O'Toole decided that he knew Finch well enough to ask him some questions about his love life.

"A raging libido and a sense of life's absurdities can breed queer bedfellows," Finch replied. "Richard Burton and I shared a similar past, when we were trying to launch ourselves on the stage in London. I landed in some pretty queer situations, and I know Richard did, too. Perhaps you'll escape with your virginity intact. We didn't."

Two "bathing beauties," Peter Finch and Vivien Leigh, take a break under the intense sun of Ceylon during their filming of *Elephant Walk* (1954). Finch and Vivien by then had launched a romance.

"But my love, my passion, is for the dollybirds and an occasional wife. I'm versatile. Kay Kendall, Mai Zetterling, a Sabena Airlines stewardess, a German princess, the daughter of an African chieftain, a professor of Greek, many prostitutes, lots of starlets. Of them all, Vivien had the style and wit to match her beauty. I really fell in love with her when we tried to make *Elephant Walk* (1954) together in Ceylon. As the world knows, on location there, she suffered a complete nervous breakdown, and she couldn't finish the picture."

"I hope she's fully recovered," O'Toole said.

"As you know, Elizabeth Taylor had to step in and take over her role," Finch said. "Larry temporarily rescued the tormented and tortured Vivien, and I came under the magical spell of another enchantress, the much younger and more beautiful Elizabeth Taylor. If I ever write my memoirs, I'll call them *The Errant Heart*."

"I fell hard for Elizabeth," Finch continued.

Before her mental breakdown on the set of *Elephant Walk*, in Ceylon (now Sri Lanka), Vivien Leigh agreed to pose with a "cobra necklace." The snake, it was made clear at the time, was de-fanged.

"It began when she invited me over night after night to eat popcorn and watch horror movies. We have a passion for them. She was married at the time to Michael Wilding, but had grown disenchanted with him. Imagine me getting to fuck both Scarlett O'Hara and Maggie the Cat. How lucky can a guy get?"

"I understand that you and Vivien aren't as hot and heavy as you once were, but still get together on occasion for old time's sake," O'Toole said.

"You've got that right, mate," Finch replied.

"Perhaps I could have drinks or dinner with you guys, then disappear into the woodwork and let you top off the evening with a heavy duty commando invasion."

"I'll introduce you," Finch said. "In fact, I'm seeing her five nights hence for dinner at The Ivy. It would be good if you came along. You can be our beard, throwing off the scent of the hound dogs from the press."

During his chat about Vivien, Finch painted a portrait of his sometimes on-, sometimes off- lover, with insights that hadn't been revealed in the press.

"Her moods change as fast as a kaleidoscope. Although I'm not a licensed psychiatrist, it's fairly clear that she's a manic depressive. At times, she'll be the most exhilarating person in the room, bathed in the red light of euphoria. Then a cold, chilly darkness will descend. To an increasing degree, she's show-ing signs of psychosis. One night, she was apprehended by the police in Soho, walking the streets like the prostitute she played in *Waterloo Bridge* back in 1940."

"Vivien's life story could be played by Joanne Woodward," Finch contin-ued. "I'm sure you saw her in *The Three Faces of Eve*. Vivien has at least two distinctly different faces: the good Vivien and the bad Vivien. She's on a lonely island that exists separate from her true self on the mainland. She flirts with suicide and has attempted it before. At times, her judgment is a horrid pot of porridge, bubbling over on the stove of her emotions. At those times, she be-come rash and reckless, losing her ability to reason and to think clearly. Dur-ing those moments, her libido goes wild, like some crazed nympho. You never know when her shift into another personality will descend, sometimes with-out warning."

"You must—just *MUST*—introduce me to this goddess of darkness and light," O'Toole said. "I feel capable of wandering into the shadows of night and then venturing out in the morning for a breakfast of kippers."

"All right, but you do so at your own peril," Finch said. "I will accept no blame for what happens."

"The woman sounds intriguingly dangerous," O'Toole said. "Margaret Leighton came into RADA one afternoon. She told me that Vivien likes to play this bizarre parlor game. It's called 'Ways to Kill a Baby.' Her fellow players have to come up with very inventive, often original methods to commit infanticide."

"That is absolutely true, and you'd better be good at it if you want to continue playing games with Vivien," Finch said. "What can I say? Vivien Leigh—or Lady Olivier, a term she hates—is a flawed masterpiece, with an emphasis on 'masterpiece.'"

O'Toole Is Lured Into the Psychotic Orbit of Vivien Leigh

During dinner at The Ivy with Peter Finch and Vivien Leigh, O'Toole encountered a woman in great turmoil. Her overriding concern seemed to be the status of her crumbling marriage to Laurence Olivier. Despite their many previous public appearances together, when they embarked on separate vacations in 1957, the press became aware that Britain's most romantic couple perhaps weren't that romantic after all.

Vivien was at the airport to kiss Olivier goodbye when he flew to New York to star on Broadway in *The Entertainer* (1958). Friends later made her aware that her husband was falling in love with a younger actress, his co-star, Joan Plowright.

At dinner, Vivien spoke of broken dreams, telling O'Toole and Finch that producer Mike Todd, Elizabeth Taylor's former husband, wanted to finance a movie adaptation of *Macbeth* starring Olivier and herself. That dream collapsed in 1958 when Todd had died in an airplane crash.

Playwright John Osborne, who saw a lot of Vivien at the time, later claimed, "She was in a condition of shock after learning that Larry was in love."

At dinner, O'Toole found Vivien solicitous and charming, asking about his career, his marriage, and his background. But despite her best efforts, it was obvious that she was coming unglued.

There was something mesmerizing about her, drawing O'Toole to her side, as if he wanted to protect her from the storms raging around and within her. He admired her courage, and how she carried on in the face of her almost blinding inner turmoil. She constantly reached for his hand for reassurance.

Even though her fabled beauty was decaying, O'Toole later told Kenneth Griffith, "She is still a lovely creature, very fragile, very delicate, almost begging for love and reassurance."

During the spring of 1958, he'd gone to see her perform opposite Claire Bloom in *Duel of Angels* at the Apollo Theatre on Shaftesbury Avenue.

"I knew that Claire had been intimate with Larry when they'd co-starred together in *Richard III,* but I didn't want to come on like some horrid fishwife, so I was kind to her," Vivien claimed.

O'Toole complimented Vivien for her recent debut on "that dreaded medium of television." On March 17, 1959, Vivien had reprised her stage role of Sabina in Thornton Wilder's *The Skin of Our Teeth,* her first and only star role on live TV. As she candidly admitted, "I was so terrified that I almost forgot my lines. Oscar was Wilde, but Thornton is wilder."

James Agate had written about her performance: "Vivien Leigh flittered and fluttered in an enchanting piece of nonsense-cum-allure, half dabchick and half dragonfly."

At the time of O'Toole's dinner with her, she was appearing on stage in Noël Coward's *Look After Lulu!* at the New Theatre.

Based on a French farce by George Feydeaux, *Look After Lulu!* generated mostly negative reviews, the *Sunday Times* claiming, "Coward was too witty, Vivien Leigh too beautiful."

She invited O'Toole to be her guest, promising to leave two seats for him at the box office.

"I prefer to come alone," he said. "Perhaps we could meet after curtain."

"I'd be delighted," she said.

At this point, according to O'Toole, "Suddenly, she assumed the coquettish demeanor of Scarlett O'Hara in the opening scenes of *Gone With the Wind*, where she is surrounded by beaux."

Backstage, on his way to his rendezvous with Vivien, O'Toole encountered *Lulu's* playwright, Noël Coward.

The playwright looked depressed. "I'm terrified of being eaten alive by the critics," Coward said. "I know the play's bad, but I don't know how to fix it. Vivien told me that she's appearing in it only because she needs the money."

"Even so," O'Toole lied, "it was a delightful night in the theater."

"You are too kind," Coward said. "I've seen your work. You're very talented, and I'm glad you're kind to Vivien in her dreaded hour of need. She feels so terribly alone in the world."

"I'm fond of her, but I hardly know her."

"To know her is to love her," he said. "But I must admit our friendship is like a roller coaster ride, zooming high in the sky only to fall dangerously toward the ground. We've had our good times and some absolutely horrid times. I believe in her ultimate goodness. But little devils inhabit her soul, and at time, these little creatures come out of hiding to terrorize the world."

Coward told O'Toole that he had invited

A *bon vivant*, and professionally witty, Noël Coward

Vivien to spend Christmas with him at his chalet in Les Avants, a mountain resort in the Vaud region of Switzerland. "You are most welcome to join us."

"I'm deeply flattered and would adore going, but I'm in this marriage thing. I think I'll be expected at home."

"Too bad, dear boy," Coward said. "I was hoping to get to know you better, maybe cast you in one of my plays."

"Perhaps we can meet when you return from Switzerland," O'Toole said. "I'd certainly like to get to know you better."

"I'll look forward to the night we meet again," he said, walking away to join a crowd of well-wishers.

From his position backstage, O'Toole went over and knocked on the door of Vivien's dressing room, where she called out for him to enter. He immediately complimented her "for a most amusing night in the theater." It was agreed that he'd take her to The Ivy for another dinner. Once there, she drew applause as she walked through the restaurant to her table. Many of the diners had seen her performance as Lulu.

Both of them ordered platters of Dover sole, but she only picked at her food, looking very despondent. "It's happened," she finally said. "Larry wrote me today. He told me that he's fallen in love with this little strumpet, Joan Plowright, and that he wants to divorce me and marry her."

"Are you going to contest it?" he asked.

"Not at all," she said. "You can't hold onto a person who wants his freedom. I'm telling him I understand his need for a chance at a new life. He told me he's going to go to Hollywood for Stanley Kubrick to film *Spartacus* (1960) with Kirk Douglas. He said he would not be returning to Notley."

[Notley Abbey was an Augustinian abbey founded in the 12th Century in Buckinghamshire. A team from Oxford excavated it in 1937 before it was renovated and acquired, along with 70 acres of field, pasture, and forest, as a country home by the Oliviers. Vivien painstakingly restored and furnished it as a showplace for their weekend guests.]

"I assume, then, that you'll sell Notley?" he said. "I always wanted to see it. I've heard so much about it. You must have had so many good times there."

"We did more or less during the first ten years of our marriage," she said. "But the last decade has been hell. We mostly went our separate ways. We continued to be seen in public on certain occasions, but that was merely to keep up appearances, pretending a love and a passion that had died. I still love Larry, and I think he still loves me, but it is the love a devoted sister might have for her older brother."

"I wonder if a career-oriented actor and actress should ever marry," he said. "As you know, I'm married to Siân Phillips, a really talented actress. We're relatively new to our marriage, but already there have been conflicts. Sometimes, I just have to get away. I don't necessarily tell where I'm going."

[Like Vivien and Olivier, O'Toole had entered into a marriage with the Welsh actress that would last twenty turbulent years.]

"Frankly, I think the bonds of matrimony are too binding," he said. "I never wanted to surrender my freedom to love."

After a long emotional talk, where she frequently held his hand, she looked imploringly into his eyes. "Please understand what I am about to say. My bedroom is very lonely tonight. I need some man to take me in his arms to reassure me that I am still beautiful, still desirable. I hope you will be my savior. By morning's light, you will be free to disappear, later returning only if it is your wish. It's entirely up to you."

"Never in my wasted life have I received such a divine offer," he said. "Your wish, my command. But it is a command that I desire to follow with all my heart."

That night marked the beginning of a friendship that would endure, going through various stages and degrees of intensity, until the day of her death in 1967.

Glimmering in the Twilight of Her Years, Vivien Leigh Replaces an Old Love with New Loves

When Notley Abbey was advertised for sale in real estate listings, there was a flurry of interest in buying it, including from prospective customers in North America. O'Toole eagerly accepted Vivien's invitation to drive there with her for a farewell. Most of her possessions had already been hauled away.

Leaving London early, they arrived on a Sunday. Fortunately, the sun had already broken through a cloudy English morning, so she could wander through her beloved gardens.

"I spent some of the best and some of the worst moments in my life in these gardens," she told him.

She pointed out her roses, many of which she had planted herself. She was particularly proud of the lime trees she had nurtured, and she showed him where hornbeams and beech had thrived, and continued to thrive, on the abbey grounds.

Cows were grazing in the pasture. She had named some of them after famous characters she had portrayed: Blanche, Cleopatra, Emma, Juliet, and Sabina.

"Which one is Scarlett?" he asked.

"Only I am named Scarlett," she answered.

She told him that she'd first come to Notley in 1943, one of the darkest of the wartime years in Britain. She said that the owners of the Abbey had fishing rights from the land that fronted the edge of the River Thames. She noted the vines she'd planted and trained to climb up the austere and in some cases, medieval stone walls.

As she ushered him through the manor's formal and stately salons and the bedrooms upstairs, she cited many of the famous people who had slumbered there—Marlene Dietrich, "Princess" Merle Oberon, Orson Welles, Rex Harrison, Noël Coward, John Gielgud, Tennessee Williams, and, among many others, Dame Sybil Thorndike.

"Dietrich made us her famous omelette for breakfast. And Merle made a play for Larry when I went into town to shop."

"It is one of the loveliest places I've seen in England," he said.

In her living room, he mused, "I wish I could have been in Olivier's shoes, sitting here by the fireplace on a winter's night, reading plays by George Bernard Shaw or Shakespeare to decide which roles we wanted to play. Any female part in Shakespeare would be ripe for you," he continued, "from Juliet to Lady Macbeth."

"More likely Lady Macbeth these days," she said.

In the fading light of an afternoon, he drove her down the lane leading to the main carriageway to London. She turned and looked back at her beloved abbey for a final time. "Goodbye, Notley," she said. "Goodbye, marriage. Goodbye, forever."

***

When the Olivier's divorce was finalized, O'Toole read about it in newspaper headlines. In an interview with a reporter, Vivien said, "After living half my life with Larry, he suddenly left me for a younger woman, an actress, no less."

O'Toole waited until after a respectable delay before contacting her again. Instead of finding her morbid and depressed, she seemed in a cheerful mood, inviting him to drive with her for an overview of her new country residence, Tickerage Mill.

As they headed north from London, she told him she learned about the property through a tip from actor Dirk Bogarde. It was in the hamlet of Black Boys, Sussex, near the town of Uckfield. Built in the Queen Anne style, it had functioned, for a while as the family home of Anthony Armstrong Jones.

[Armstrong-Jones later became Lord Snowdon, based on his marriage to Princess Margaret.]

Tickerage Mill sat on 90 acres of rolling countryside, and, like Notley, it was one of the beauty spots of England. Inside, she showed him around, pointing out that the Oscar she'd won for her portrayal of Blanche DuBois in *A Streetcar Named Desire* was being used as a doorstop.

"And the Oscar for Scarlett O'Hara?" he asked.

"I've assigned it to the bathroom," she answered.

"I don't dare ask what its duties there are," he said.

Over drinks, she fretted about "all the fearful stories being printed about me. I'm considered such a nympho that I've gone through all the guards at Buckingham Palace. There is so much written about my mental disorders that I've almost become afraid of appearing in public, although I'm going to a psychiatrist. I'm recovering from my fear, and may even go on tour again. But I can't help feeling that when people see me, they're just watching to see if I'm going to crack up right before their eyes."

"I don't know about your alleged past disorders, but tonight, you seem like the most sane person I know. Of course, I know mostly people in the theater world, very few of whom are sane."

"Oh, dear heart, I was feeling especially old until I saw you again. You make me feel young. As I'm getting older, reporters are younger. The other night, this moron from some London paper wanted to interview me. He asked me what role I played in *Gone With the Wind.* I told him, 'End of interview.'"

***

O'Toole did not attend her gala fiftieth birthday party, but called her two weeks later to arrange a private rendezvous with her. "I want to give you your present."

A few nights later, she informed him that everyone had been cleared out of her London house at 54 Eaton Square, and that she wanted him to visit her there at 8PM that evening.

He found her looking lovely in a champagne-colored dress. He had arrived with a bouquet of roses, which she at first assumed was her birthday gift.

She showed him around her London townhouse, which she'd decorated herself. She was especially proud of a painting by Degas depicting a woman washing, and of a Cellini drawing. She also showed him an unfinished sketch of herself by the well-known Welsh portraitist, Augustus John.

In her living room, while drinking champagne, he told her that he wanted to give her "the greatest gift I have to offer."

"And what, dear heart, might that be?" she asked.

"A gift from the gods. I present myself."

"How utterly delightful," she said. "I've always wanted something delivered directly from Heaven."

"When I later undress, you'll see that I have tied a red ribbon around it."

"Ever since I was a young girl, I have taken special pleasure in untying red ribbons."

That night, he made love to her in her upstairs bedroom within a four-poster that was a duplicate of one of the furnishings at Tara in *Gone With the Wind.* The bed was canopied with a rose motif.

He later told Kenneth Griffith, "It was a bit off-putting to make love to Vivien in a room with nine photographs of Larry Olivier. Off-putting to say the least. But nevertheless, I rose to the occasion."

The Twilight of a Goddess

Before departing from Vivien the following morning, O'Toole heard a confession from her about an incident that until then, he had interpreted as an unfounded rumor.

She had fallen in love with actor Jack Merivale.

The handsome actor had known Vivien for years, but their romance had bloomed when he'd been cast as her husband in *Duel of Angels,* a stage play.

John Herman Merivale, widely known in acting circles as "Jack," was born in Toronto in 1917, son of Philip Merivale, the famous English actor. Jack's stepmother, through her marriage to Philip, was one of the most formidable *grande dames* of the British stage, Dame Gladys Cooper, DBE.

Jack, for the most part, had been educated at Oxford before launching a career on the stage. He had made his theatrical debut at the age of 21 when he was an understudy in *A Midsummer Night's Dream.* "That's when I first met Vivien," he later said, "but she didn't know I existed at the time."

Vivien Leigh with Jack Merivale

She told O'Toole: "That Larry, bless his cheating heart. He auditioned Jack in every sense of the word before I got my chance."

"Jack worshipped the boards that Vivien trod on at the theatre," claimed Dame Mae Whitty. "She eventually adopted him like a surrogate brother or son. He was gorgeous, but timid. Some women, of course, are won over by that. He fell madly in love with Vivien, but had to cool his passion for her until she was free of Larry. Larry got to sample Jack's charms before Viv did."

Early in his life, Merivale was sharp enough to realize that he had much to gain by attaching himself to Olivier and Vivien.

His future mistress, the actress, Nina Foch, with a certain bitterness, asserted, "Jack would hustle men or women to get a meal ticket in life. He didn't expect to become rich in the theater, so he attached himself to those who had already arrived—Jan Sterling, myself, Larry Olivier, and ultimately, Vivien Leigh. She became his longest-running engagement."

One afternoon, Vivien called and invited O'Toole to her London townhouse to have dinner with Merivale upon his return from touring through the provinces of England.

She had told him that Merivale had entered her life at the right time to help restore her self-esteem. "It meant a lot to know that a handsome younger man found me alluring in my twilight years. I think he's a bit dazzled by me, and why not?"

"I am dazzled by you, too," O'Toole said. "So is half the world."

Over drinks and dinner, O'Toole understood why Vivien wanted and needed Merivale in her life.

He would later share his impressions of the evening with Griffith, who always wanted to hear all the details of any encounter with Vivien, on whom he had long harbored a crush.

When Vivien went into the kitchen to check on dinner, Merivale confessed to O'Toole his initial anxiety at becoming her lover. "They were such a legendary couple that I felt they were Siamese twins that I had to separate. But what to divide? I didn't know which organs they might share in common. To cut away at the wrong ones would have killed Vivien."

He told O'Toole that he was more aware of Vivien's unstable condition than anyone. "I plan to stand by her through all her ordeals. I told her not to be ashamed if she has various lapses here and there. I'm prepared to love her through all the good days and all the bad times that are inevitable."

Back in the living room, Vivien sat with Merivale on the sofa and declared her love for him in front of O'Toole. "It is his patience with me I find so endearing, so dependable. His tenderness with me touches my heart. Larry could be brutal at times. I've become extremely dependent on Jack and my love for him grows daily."

Since he had an early call, Merivale retired early, providing O'Toole and Vivien with an opportunity to discuss things in private.

"I think you've found something quite wonderful in Jack," he said. "He truly loves you, and he'll see you through. He lacks Larry's enormous ego, and that is all for the good."

"I view my life with Jack not as an end, but as a beginning," she said. "But what about us?"

"Let's define our time together, memorable though it was, as 'a brief interlude.'"

"That sounds like the title of a play," she said.

"David Lean directed *Brief Encounter* in 1945," he said. "Perhaps you saw it. Two strangers meet, both of them are married, but they find themselves drawn to each other for a short, poignant romance that is both intense and unforgettable. I'm stepping out of the picture to allow this wonderful love affair between the two of you to proceed at its own pace, without any interference from me."

"Are you telling me goodbye?" she asked.

"Not at all," he said. "It's goodbye until we say hello again. Meeting you, sharing intimate moments with you, has been one of the highlights of my life. I will cherish our times together as long as I live. If you ever need or want me, all you have to do is call and I'll come running."

"I believe you would, my dear."

He kissed her goodbye as she set out, with Merivale at her side, on the last professional ventures of her life.

He watched as once again she played a Tennessee Williams heroine in *The Roman Spring of Mrs. Stone* (1961). Wearing a blonde wig, she was cast as an aging actress who falls for the charms of a handsome Italian gigolo (Warren Beatty).

From afar, O'Toole continued to follow the saga of her final world tour, whose intinerary included live performances in South America, Australia, and New Zealand. He later read of her involvement in the Tony Award-winning musical, *Tovarich,* in 1963, on Broadway, opposite Jean Pierre Aumont.

After she and Merivale returned to England, O'Toole dined with them at Tickerage Mill. "We sat outside for drinks," he recalled. "I heard the sound of a meadow lark. It was a tender moment for all of us."

She told him that from Australia and New Zealand, she'd brought back seeds of plants that included coral trees and viburnums "which Jack and I plan to plant in our gardens."

O'Toole later remembered the night he "found Jack and Viv more in love than ever, totally dependent on each other."

She coughed frequently, and he feared for her health. She told him that she had agreed to star in *Ship of Fools* (1965), a movie based on the bestselling novel by Katherine Anne Porter. She said that Katharine Hepburn had wanted the role of the 46-year-old divorced Mary Treadwell, but it had gone to her, instead. "Katharine is my friend, but I don't know if she'll forgive me for taking a second role from her, the first being Scarlett O'Hara."

When he went to see *Ship of Fools* at a cinema in London, he was struck by Vivien's brilliant performance, fearing it would be her last film. Merivale had told him she was increasingly ill.

He asked Griffith to see the film with him. "The scene that stuck in my heart," O'Toole told his friend, "was when she sat at her vanity mirror aboard the ship. I can recite her exact lines:"

"You are not young, Mrs. Treadwell. You have not been young for years. You just didn't want to grow up. Behind those old eyes, you hold a sixteen-year-old heart, you poor fool."

Over lager in a pub, O'Toole told Griffith, "Those lines could have been written by Vivien to describe herself."

One night, a very distressed Merivale called O'Toole and asked him to come over to see Vivien, who was asking for him. "I fear she has not long to live. She seems to grow weaker every day, and she's coughing a lot."

Two hours later, he was at her bedside, enjoying time alone with her without Marivale, who had gone down to the study as a means of leaving them alone. Her face was tired and drawn. Without makeup, this once-fabled beauty looked like an old lady who had aged way beyond her actual years. He noticed a white handkerchief stained with fresh blood on her vanity table.

Cynical, *über*-jaded, and tragic, Vivien Leigh nonetheless managed to satirize the "aging of a diva" process in these shots from *Ship of Fools*.

Lee Marvin, sharing a ship's railing with her, is about to attempt to rape her.

Later, he did not tell Griffith what they had talked about, as was his usual custom. He only recited her final lines to him:

I have finally decided who you were in my life. You are my Ashley Wilkes, the unobtainable, the man I loved from afar. Our time together was all too fleeting, but it left me with a loving memory. Perhaps we'll meet again on some far and distant shore."

***

Along with the rest of the world, O'Toole learned that Vivien had died of tuberculosis on July 8, 1967, just as *Gone With the Wind* was about to be launched on its most successful reissue.

Vivien's ashes were scattered over the lake at Tickerage Mill. A few days later, O'Toole held Merivale's hand as they sat silently for nearly an hour watching the sun set over the lake.

When he left that evening, he hugged and kissed Merivale. "Thank you for letting me come and see you."

In London, Peter Finch called, reading the printed account of what he'd said to the press: "I remember Vivien as if it were yesterday, walking like an eager boy through the temples of Ceylon—walking in the wind at Notley. I will always see her hurrying through life. I'll always remember those bright eyes, always in laughter."

O'Toole shared his loss with Lady Diana Cooper one evening in the West End. In her words:

"Vivien was delicate but also so dynamic. She was brilliant, unique, a goddess who had to coddle a demon who lurked inside her, trying to burst out at any moment. She had such grace of movement, such shining kindness in her as she faded like Camille. A great light has been extinguished. It will not come on again. *Adieu*, Vivien."

Rest in Peace
Vivien Leigh
1913-1967

[Additional references to the fascinating life of Vivien Leigh are available within Blood Moon's 2011 publication, Damn You, Scarlett O'Hara, *a hot, startling, and unauthorized probe of the two most famous and gossiped about English actors of the 20th Century, Miss Leigh and her very complicated husband, (Lord) Laurence Olivier.]*

Chapter 7

Robbing the Bank of England

Peter O'Toole, as His Majesty's Guardsman, Is Hailed as "The Next Laurence Olivier"

Valiantly defending the financial security of England,
O'Toole confronts the handsome American would-be bank robber, Aldo Ray.

Peter O'Toole's second film, *The Day They Robbed the Bank of England* (1960), would have a major effect on both his life and career. When director David Lean saw him in it, he decided to lobby the film producer, Sam Spiegel, to cast O'Toole as *Lawrence of Arabia* (1962).

The Day They Robbed the Bank of England was a period piece, taking place in 1901 London when England was locked in a battle with Ireland during that nation's struggle for independence.

The lead role was the character of Charles Norgate, an Irish-American known as the most skilled bank robber in America. Irish revolutionaries, as a means of funding their guerilla activities, recruit him to undertake the robbery of one of the world's most heavily guarded banks.

At first, O'Toole, as Lt. Monte Fitch, one of the security supervisors, befriends Norgate, but then grows suspicious of him. The die is cast.

Initially, Jules Buck [the film's producer and later, O'Toole's partner in Keep Films] and the film's director, John Guillermin, wanted O'Toole to interpret the role of Norgate. But after reading the script and meeting with Buck and Guillermin, O'Toole rejected their offer. Later, however, he agreed to play the minor role of Fitch, who foils the Irish activists' clever attempt to rob the bank.

Projecting the image of the spirit that made Britain Great; the cinematic newcomer fresh from the classrooms of RADA and Bristol's Old Vic—Peter O'Toole.

"The part of the tearaway Irishman was intriguing, but I preferred to play the hero instead of the bandit," O'Toole said.

Buck agreed, because at the time of casting, O'Toole was being hailed as Britain's "hottest, newest—and best—stage discovery," based on his performances at Stratford-upon-Avon.

Ironically, O'Toole's wife, Siân Phillips, was for a while, considered for the film's female lead, Iris Muldoon, the widow of a martyr in the movement for Irish independence.

Siân, wearing [in her words] "a boring good dress," scheduled a meeting with Buck in his MCA office near London's Hyde Park Corner. She found him very American, chugging out smoke from a large cigar evocative of Darryl F. Zanuck at Fox in Hollywood.

She was rejected for the role, the part eventually going to Elizabeth Sellars. A Glaswegian actress trained at RADA, who was nine years older than O'Toole, Sellars had performed for the Royal Shakespeare Company and had broken into British films in 1949, when she appeared in *Floodtide*. [*Defying his family, a young Scotsman becomes a ship designer, works his way up the firm, marries the boss's daughter, and revolutionizes shipbuilding.*] Sellars went on to perform minor roles in major films such as *The Barefoot Contessa* (1954), co-starring Humphrey Bogart and Ava Gardner. That same year, she had also appeared in *Désirée*, with Marlon Brando miscast as Napoléon.

Born in London of French parents, Guillermin was a director, producer, and screenwriter. After serving in the Royal Air Force during World War II, he drifted to Hollywood to learn how to make films.

In time, he became known for his action movies. When O'Toole met him, he'd just completed *Tarzan's Greatest Adventure* (1959), starring Gordon Scott as Tarzan. In that movie, Guillermin had cast Anthony Quayle as the co-star, playing a ruthless, murdering profiteer.

Before working with Guillermin, as a means of gathering information about his upcoming director-to-be, O'Toole set up a meeting with Quayle. Over drinks, in reference to Guillermin, Quayle said, "Always smoking that pipe of his, always demanding perfection, always in search of the right camera angle. But he's a prick to work with, very demanding."

A Frenchman at heart, John Guillermin helmed everyone from Tarzan to Peter O'Toole.

"He was hated by cast and crew, demanding perfection when so few could deliver it," O'Toole claimed.

Quayle was not alone in his harsh appraisal. Over the years, those who worked on films with the director echoed similar sentiments.

Elmo Williams, producer of *The Blue Max* (1966), claimed that Guillermin was "the most demanding director, indifferent to people getting hurt as long as he got realistic action. The crew disliked him."

Producer David L. Wolper, on the set during the filming of *The Bridge at Remagen* (1969), claimed Guillermin was "the most difficult director with whom I've ever worked."

After a week of working with Guillermin, O'Toole had developed his own appraisal. He told Kenneth Griffith, "He's a skinny guy, rather dark, with the sharp features of a bird of prey. He's a royal pain in the ass, horribly demanding, an irascible personality. He's the last person you meet before you enter the Gates of Hell."

When Guillermin invited O'Toole to see a screening of *Bank of England's* first rushes, he was horrified. "Seeing myself on the screen made me self-conscious, which is disastrous for an actor. For days, I felt immobilized. I was unable to act for a time. I just strutted about, trying to strike a pose. I farted like an idiot instead of my usual blast of wind. I was determined never to watch rushes again. I certainly never had any intention of ever sitting through complete versions of one of any of my future films. I felt that if I did, I'd never act again."

During filming on *Bank of England,* O'Toole lunched several times with actor Kieron Moore, cast as Walsh, one of the Irish revolutionaries who dislikes Norgate, and who is convinced that there is no "Achilles' Heel" to be found in the security systems associated with vaults at the Bank of England.

Like O'Toole, Moore had been born in Ireland. He discussed his own promising launch of a film career, when the British producer Alexander Korda had signed him to a seven-year moviemaking contract.

"For years, I carried around his appraisal of me in my wallet."

Korda had told the press, "Moore has a brilliant acting talent. Then he has six-feet-two of brawn, a mobile photogenic face, rich expressive eyes, and the ability to adapt himself to any kind of role—ultra romantic or the last word in villainy. Very soon, he will be one of the big names on world screens."

Moore went on to say, "And then along came the time I was horribly miscast in the role of the suave Count Vronsky in *Anna Karenina* (1948), with Vivien Leigh and Ralph Richardson. I received the worst notices of my career. I've never recovered from the critical attacks. Right now, I seem to be specializing in robbery films."

A few months before his work on *Bank of England,* Moore had been in a somewhat equivalent heist film *The League of Gentleman* (1960). In it, he played a disgraced former Fascist who's being blackmailed for homosexual indiscretions, and recruited to take part in a big upcoming robbery.

The Welsh actor, Hugh Griffith, was cast in *Bank of England* as one of the Irish revolutionaries. "Actually, I set out to be a banker, starting out as a clerk," he told O'Toole. "Imagine me, a banker. No one's money would be safe. Then I decided to hell with it and became an actor"

Griffith had starred on Broadway with a fellow Welshman, Richard Burton, in *Legend of Lovers* (1951). O'Toole congratulated him for winning an Oscar as Best Supporting Actor in *Ben-Hur* (1959).

"I went pubbing with Griffith one night," O'Toole said. "Would you believe me, I had collapsed under the table, completely drunk, and he was just getting started."

[Griffith later descended into chronic alcoholism.]

After O'Toole rejected the lead role of Norgate, the part went to the American actor and heart-throb, Aldo Ray. When O'Toole got to know him, he later proclaimed, "Aldo is a bigger hellraiser than I am."

Destroyed by his own greed, Aldo Ray tries to haul off more gold bars than he can reasonably carry.

A former football player and, during World War II, a Navy frogman, Ray drifted into films and became known for his tough but sexy persona, a husky frame, a thick neck, and a raspy voice. "With my gargle voice and my jarhead look, I was a natural to play a sergeant leading an Army platoon," he told O'Toole.

Over drinks in pubs, Ray revealed colorful stories about his former life and how he broke into the movie business. "When I was a young fucker, along the road to my horizon, I got into a lot of trouble. When I played football, I got this cheerleader pregnant, and we needed money for an abortion."

"Fortunately, I knew this gay photographer who wanted me to pose for nudes. I did, and raised the money to get rid of the kid."

"My film career got launched by another gay man, the director, George Cukor," he said. "He fell in love with my big dick. He wanted it real bad. All of a sudden, I was a film star."

"He didn't like everything about me, though," Ray said. "He felt I walked like a football player, so he sent me to ballet classes."

Cukor cast Ray in *The Marrying Kind* (1952) opposite Judy Holliday. That same year, Cukor also cast him as the dim-witted boxer in *Pat and Mike* opposite Katharine Hepburn and Spencer Tracy.

As a Marine private, Ray had appeared in the box office hit, *Battle Cry* (1955), and was also cast as the psychotic officer in *The Naked and the Dead* (1958), based on Norman Mailer's bestselling novel set amid the battlefields and anguish of World War II.

O'Toole had also seen him in *Miss Sadie Thompson* (1953), based on W. Somerset Maugham's *Rain*. "I ended up in the tropics with Rita Hayworth," Ray said. "By then, I had dropped Cukor and was plugging Rita—that is, during those rare moments that drunken Argentine singer, Dick Haymes, wasn't monopolizing her.

"Rita was really fucked up," Ray said. "I felt sorry for her."

When Ray saw the first cut of *Bank of England*, he said, "My voice sounds like sandpaper, and O'Toole comes off as an elegant soprano in some Victorian drawing room."

At the end of filming, before his departure from London for New York, Ray told O'Toole, "I know all my tough soldier roles have an expiration date. If I'm going to stay in films, I'll need to find another gig."

"It was great working with you, my friend," O'Toole said. "Until we meet again." Then he hugged and kissed him.

"I'll have a memory of your standing with me at the urinal pissing away all that good-tasting English beer."

As regards his own work on *Bank of England,* for the most part, O'Toole received excellent reviews in a mediocre film. Dilys Powell, a leading film critic, wrote: "Peter O'Toole is the new gift to British cinema and to the theater."

In the *Evening News,* Felix Barker claimed, "A magnetic spark seems to come out of the screen at the birth of a great star. O'Toole is going to blaze a fiery trail over our screens that will make some other reigning satellites look stale."

MGM distributed the film mostly in Britain, with more limited outlets in Canada and the United States, where it generated only $180,000 at the box office. When the tally was counted, its producers were dismayed to realize that *The Day They Robbed the Bank of England* suffered a net loss of $57,000.

But for O'Toole, at least, there was a silver lining. In *The Daily Express,* Peter Evans asked, "Is Peter O'Toole the next Olivier?"

Perhaps his Victorian-era character evoked a more confident, more imperialistic, less "challenged" Britain than the one into which this postwar film was released.

Regardless, O'Toole's breezy elegance brought his talents to the attention of movie directors whose need for a romantic lead (T. E. Lawrence) would launch him to world stardom.

Chapter 8

Hollywood Producer
Jules Buck
Discovers His Golden Boy (Peter O'Toole) And Morphs Him Into Hollywood Royalty

O'Toole Parties with John Huston, Ava Gardner, & Burt Lancaster. Despite His Seduction of Ava, O'Toole Defines Frank Sinatra as "A Tough Act to Follow."

Marilyn Monroe with Jack Paar in *Love Nest* (1951), as produced by Jules Buck

In later life, Peter O'Toole would equate his coming together with the American producer, Jules Buck, as an occasion more important than Stanley meeting Livingstone in the wilds of darkest Africa.

Buck would become co-founder and O'Toole's partner in Keep Films, Ltd. That entity either produced or co-produced almost every movie O'Toole made between 1960 and 1975. In the clear-eyed evaluation of cinematic history, almost everyone agrees that except for *Lawrence of Arabia* (for which David Lean and Sam Spiegel claim credit) Jules Buck was the major force responsible for launching O'Toole's film career.

In 1959, Buck and his wife, Joyce Gates (née Joyce Ruth Getz) attended a performance of *The Long And the Short And The Tall* at the Royal Court Theatre in London. Buck later asserted, "I was bowled over by the performance of this 26-year-old Irish actor, Peter O'Toole, with the melancholy blue eyes and the blonde locks."

The business links of O'Toole to his "Svengali," Jules Buck, extended deep into their family lives too.

Depicted above are Joan Buck and Siân Phillips, tending baby Katy (center) at a pub in Stratford, presumably while their respective husbands were off signing deals, or whatever.

After their first day together, wandering around London, Buck cast him as the young security guard in *The Day They Robbed the Bank of England* (1960). That was the film that eventually persuaded David Lean to cast O'Toole as the male lead in *Lawrence of Arabia*.

Working with Buck on *Bank of England*, his second-ever film, O'Toole developed a close friendship with him and began to formulate the idea of establishing an ongoing working relationship in their future.

In front of Buck, O'Toole quickly sketched his background, which before London, had consisted of appearing in about a dozen plays at the Bristol Old Vic.

O'Toole was unfamiliar with Buck's former life in Hollywood, and the producer quickly established his credentials. Before the release of *Lawrence of Arabia*, Buck had already told his wife and others that he thought O'Toole would become one of "the biggest stars on the planet, and I wanted to get in on the ground level before half of the hound dogs of Hollywood dangled contracts in front of this promising new film star."

During their early moments together, Buck explained why he had left Hollywood and moved to Paris and later to London. "The anti-communist witch hunts organized in Hollywood by J. Edgar Hoover and Joseph McCarthy drove

O'Toole Rejects the Role of a Native American Plagued With Syphilis

me out. I, myself, was never blacklisted, although many of my friends there were. I'm a liberal idealist, and I didn't want to work in such an oppressive environment."

Buck went on to inform O'Toole that he was one of the founders of the Committee for the First Amendment, whose membership had included Humphrey Bogart, Lauren Bacall, Lucille Ball, Bette Davis, John Garfield, Judy Garland, Katharine Hepburn, Edward G. Robinson, and Frank Sinatra. They were united to defend Free Speech in America and to protest against the "witch hunts" which at the time were destroying the careers of members of the film colony accused of supporting communists.

In 1947, some members of this group, with director John Huston, had flown to Washington to protest the actions of the House Un-American Activities committee. "Faced with enormous pressure and threats from all sides, we sort of blew it," Buck confessed, "and Bogie more or less recanted to save his career."

Born in St. Louis in 1917, Buck had come to Hollywood in the 1930s, working as a photographer, taking candid pictures of such superstars as Joan Crawford, Errol Flynn, Clark Gable, and W.C. Fields.

When World War II began, Buck was promoted to the rank of captain, and—designated as a cameraman for the U.S. Army Signal Corps—made wartime documentaries and "U.S. propaganda films" with John Huston, a lieutenant in the Corps.

After the war, as Buck's association with Huston continued, he worked as assistant producer on Robert Siodmak's fatalistic *The Killers* (1945). Although Huston had been a co-writer of its script, he was not credited because at the time, he was bound by an exclusive contract to Warner's.

Buck eventually joined Huston and Sam Spiegel to found Horizon Pictures, an independent production company. Later, when the company failed to thrive, Huston began referring to their enterprise as "shit creek productions."

Their first movie project was *We Were Strangers* (1949), a thriller starring John Garfield playing a Cuban rebel plotting to overthrow a right-wing dictator. The film was later denounced as "Leftist propaganda," and Garfield was blacklisted In Hollywood. Eventually Huston himself would become fed up with all this "commie witchhunting" and would move both his family and his film operations to more tolerant Ireland.

[We Were Strangers *had almost prophetically depicted a shocking presidential assassination. It was later revealed that in October of 1963, Lee Harvey Oswald was watching the film on television weeks before he fatally shot President John F. Kennedy as he rode in an open-topped car as part of a motorcade in Dallas.]*

Director Jules Dassin hired Buck to work as associate producer on *Brute*

Force (1947) and *Naked City* (1949), two noteworthy *films noir* of the late 1940s. Later, Dassin found himself blacklisted.

Despite his residency overseas, Buck continued as a creative force in the film industry throughout the 50s. He joined forces with John Steinbeck to work on early drafts of a screenplay for Elia Kazan's *Viva Zapata* (1952), a film that had co-starred Marlon Brando with Anthony Quinn. It brought Quinn an Oscar as Best Supporting Actor. Brando was also nominated for an Academy Award for Best Actor, but lost to Gary Cooper for *High Noon*.

In 1951, Buck had produced *Love Nest*, a comedy-drama starring June Haver, William Lundigan, Frank Fay, Jack Paar, and a relatively unknown Marilyn Monroe, who stole every scene she was in.

Buck confided in O'Toole that Marilyn did the casting couch routine but in reverse. "I didn't have sex with her until after she'd finished the picture. She asked to meet with me one night. I couldn't believe it. She wanted to thank me for casting her in the film the only way she knew how. She stripped off all her clothes in front of me. What else was a red-blooded male like me to do?"

At the time Buck met O'Toole, the producer had just completed a TV series, *O.S.S.*, twenty-six episodes detailing the exploits of the Office of Strategic Services during World War II. The O.S.S., of course, was the predecessor of the Central Intelligence Agency (CIA).

[Running for 26 half-hour episodes during the 1957-1958 season, it was broadcast in the United States by ABC. It showcased the adventures of Frank Hawthorne, a fictional O.S.S.agent operating behind Nazi lines in occupied France.]

Since Buck felt that O'Toole was on the dawn of a great film career, and he believed that Buck was going to rise even higher as a producer, both of them formed a partnership in Keep Films, Ltd. O'Toole was asked the reason for the name. "It means I keep what I earn and don't give it away to somebody else, notably a greedy studio."

Peter and Siân and Jules and Joan: A Conjoined Quartet Sharing the Ups and Downs of their Turbulent Lives

The soon-to-be married Peter O'Toole, with his future wife, actress Siân Phillips, formed a tight emotional bond with Jules Buck and his wife, Joyce Getz, a gifted interior designer.

[She had been a beautiful child actress and later, as a late teenager, a cover girl model in Hollywood. It was there, in 1945, that she'd met and married Buck, who had just returned from Army service overseas.

When Joyce died in 1996, Siân wrote her obituary, claiming "Peter, Joyce, Jules, and I were together for some two decades, seeing each other on almost a daily basis. We shared many highs and lows. Self-absorption and whining were not the style of this American. From her, I learned to keep a stiff upper lip and apply more lipstick in times of trouble."

Joyce became Siân's confidant during the troubled years of her turbulent marriage to Peter.

"My new wife, Jules and Joyce, and I became very tribal," O'Toole said. "For many years, we had this ritual of spending every Christmas together in Venice."

Their first Christmas together, however, in 1959, was spent not in Venice, but in Ireland. "The Four Musketeers" decided to pay a visit to the 100-acre estate, St. Clerans, of Buck's longtime friend, John Huston.

John Huston's and Peter O'Toole's Shared Talent for The Blarney

In Ireland, O'Toole Listens to Huston Discuss Sex & Deception in Hollywood

Newlyweds Peter O'Toole and Siân Phillips "tagged along" with their friends, Jules and Joan Buck, during their Christmas, 1959, visit to John Huston and his family at their carefully restored Georgian-style manor house, St. Clerans, in Ireland. Set on the rolling "green, green grass" at the edge of Galway Bay, it lay near Craigwell in County Galway, a 90-minute drive from Shannon Airport. It had been built on the site of an 11th Century monastery that had fallen into neglect.

Huston had told gossip columnist Louella Parsons, "As a kid, I never had a home. I was always on the prod, living out of dressing rooms and hotels. Now I've found a place to settle down."

When they arrived, Huston wasn't there to greet them, but a staff member (one of eight servants) showed them inside, directing them to the colonnaded courtyard with fountains in the middle and stone lions flanking the main entrance. They crossed a hall floored in black marble and found a fireplace blazing in every room.

The first of the Hustons O'Toole met was the director's daughter, Anjelica. Born in 1951, she was only eight years old, the daughter of Huston's third wife, Ricki Soma, a model. She told them that her father would be right down after he'd taken some libation for his enduring hangover.

"He's back from a tiger hunt in India," she said. "He's such a romantic traveler, always bringing me home exotic gifts. Sometimes, he arrives with other women he picked up in his travels."

O'Toole would later recall meeting Anjelica with "her little weasel face, very pointing, playing with her braids."

Anjelica remembered O'Toole as "looking like a god with his blonde hair and crystal blue eyes. He spoke in a theatrical way, with an Irish reflection," she said.

While waiting for her parents to come down, Anjelica offered to entertain them with her impressions. She asked O'Toole, "Would you prefer me to imitate Sandra Dee or Greta Garbo?"

"By all means, Madame Dee," O'Toole replied.

An hour later, Huston made his way downstairs to greet his houseguests. He introduced himself to O'Toole, who saw up close that the director had a certain simian handsomeness. He stood tall and wiry, his loose-fitting pants held up with purple suspenders. He had a courtly charm, and, like O'Toole himself, spoke with a certain theatricality.

In spite of his hangover, he invited his guests, especially O'Toole, to join him in some rare Irish whiskey that he'd acquired

St. Clerans, the Huston's "away from home home" in County Galway

John Huston directing a tricky scene in *The Asphalt Jungle*

at great expense. "I see my reputation as a drinker has preceded me," O'Toole said.

The actor later recalled, "I didn't seek his approval. We were about the same height, and we both had talent and charisma, except I was just starting out and he had this enormous track record—oh, my god. *The African Queen* (1951) and all that."

"Over drinks before the fireplace, I think I impressed him by telling him that *Beat the Devil* (1953) was my favorite of all his movies," O'Toole said. "It had starred Humphrey Bogart, Robert Morley, and Jennifer Jones, with Truman Capote hired as the scriptwriter."

Huston seemed appreciative that O'Toole had cited one of his lesser known and less appreciated films. "I remember it well, shooting along the Amalfi Coast. There was this burly lesbian chasing after Jennifer. I let Capote suck my cock. He even got to Bogie's cock as well. He had foolishly bet Capote that he'd let him give him a blow-job if he lost a wrestling match with him. Bogie thought he'd win over this mincing little creature. Lo and behold, Capote beat Bogie and he had to let him go down on him. But he warned our little friend that he was not to swallow. Of course, Capote didn't follow Bogie's command. Of course not."

Throughout O'Toole's visit, he found Huston a marvelous raconteur, filled with fascinating stories about Old Hollywood and bragging of his many affairs with actresses, including Olivia de Havilland, whom he called "Livvy."

"I seduced them all—yes, Ava Gardner. I think I seduced Elizabeth Taylor one night, but we were too drunk to remember. Like everyone else, I got Marilyn Monroe when I cast her in *The Asphalt Jungle*."

"I married Evelyn Keyes, Scarlett O'Hara's younger sister. As I said, I'd already had Melanie (De Havilland) from *Gone With the Wind*."

One night, Huston screened two documentaries he'd made with Buck during their time in the Army.

The first, *Report from the Aleutians*, was a 47-minute documentary propaganda film that Huston had directed and narrated, with Buck doing the camera work. *[Filmed in color, it was nominated in 1943 for an Oscar as Best Documentary.]* Though it contained very little combat footage, it depicted the dreary live of the U.S. service stationed on Adak Island. Their mission involved the orchestration of flying missions over nearby Kiska, bombing Japanese military installations there.

[In June of 1942, a small Japanese force occupied the remote Aleutian islands of Kiska and Attu. The islands' strategic value was their ability to control the Northern Pacific's shipping routes. In 1935, U.S. General Billy Mitchell had stated to the U.S. Congress, "I believe that in the future, whoever holds Alaska will hold the world. I think it is the most important strategic place in the world."]

The second film on which Huston and Buck worked impressed O'Toole even more. Thirty minutes long, *The Battle of San Pietro* (1944) was the only wartime propaganda film that showed the complete record of an infantry battle. One critic asserted that it was "unmatched in evoking the physicality and human price of war."

It became the first film to show American war dead, and, as such, much of the Army brass had wanted to suppress it. However, by 1945, Army Chief of Staff, General George C. Marshall, reversed the ban, claiming that every American solider in training should see it. "It will not discourage them, but rather will prepare them for the initial shock of combat."

Without telling Huston, O'Toole later said, "It was just too grimy, too realistic, especially those scenes of dead soldiers being loaded into body bags. It was almost more than my peace-loving Irish soul could abide."

While the men watched battle scenes, Siân and Joyce, the interior designer, went on a tour of the building's public rooms. Joyce commented on Huston's taste in décor. "There are primitive blood stuff everywhere," she said. "See that mounted water buffalo he shot? Not my taste at all. I don't like to be surrounded by dead things. I prefer life."

O'Toole preferred to explore field and stream on his own, including a trout stream on the estate. From the Huston stable, he borrowed a horse and rode to the little town of Loughrea, seven miles away. He later told Buck what happened that afternoon.

"I stopped into a pub for a few lagers and some Irish whiskey," he said. "There, I encountered two busty barmaids who agreed to meet me upstairs in one of the rooms over the bar for a little love in the afternoon when the pub closed. One was a blonde, bleached, the other with hair as red as that of Maureen O'Hara's."

"Would you believe it, the two dames in bed with me became jealous, each one claiming that I was paying more attention to one than the other. I had to remind these ladies that I had only one cock."

At some point, Siân and O'Toole departed from the Huston manse to travel to their own home in Connemara, a 70-mile, 90-minute drive to the west.

As he was leaving, Huston told him, "One day, sooner than later, I'm going to cast you in a picture."

Years later, the very grown up Anjelica would remember encountering O'Toole as "he was putting his hands and feet in concrete in front of Grauman's Chinese Theater in Hollywood." After the ceremony, he invited her for a meal at Musso and Frank's. "We talked of my dad."

Later, O'Toole spoke of his dinner with Anjelica to Buck. "I find it hard to believe that this lovely, sensitive, talented creature was Jack Nicholson's chief cocksucker for such a long time."

The Sultriest of the Cinematic "Femmes Fatales" —
O'Toole's Close Encounters with Ava Gardner

Back in London, Jules Buck called O'Toole to join him for drinks and dinner with "two dear friends."

Each of those two amigos, as it turned out, were superstars: Ava Gardner and Burt Lancaster.

Buck had become their friend when he'd worked as assistant producer to

Mark Hellinger on Director Robert Siodmak's classic film noir, *The Killers* (1946), based on a short story by Ernest Hemingway.

When Buck heard that Gardner and Lancaster were in London at the same time, he decided it was time for a reunion. He also wanted to introduce them to his rising new star.

Meeting for drinks in Gardner's suite at the Savoy Hotel in London, O'Toole found that the sultry Tarheel beauty lived up to her billing as the most beautiful woman in the world. He'd later share his memory of her to his friend, Kenneth Griffith. "She was the temptress of the ages, who made strong men weak, including Howard Hughes and John F. Kennedy. She was an international playgirl who'd married Mickey Rooney, Artie Shaw, and Frank Sinatra. From reports, she lived for kicks, was a world class drinker, the patron saint of any bullfighter who looked like he was bulging out of his suit of lights, and the last patron to close a nightclub in Paris, Rome, London, Madrid, and Hollywood."

Both Buck and O'Toole spoke to her about their recent holiday visit to the Irish mansion of her friend, John Huston.

It had been Buck himself who had originally introduced Gardner to Huston, after inviting both of them to his home in Tarzana, in California's San Fernando Valley.

"I miss John," she said. "He always seems to be somewhere, directing Bogie and Hepburn in deepest Africa, killing some tiger in India, off boozing in Ireland. I hope we make a picture together some day before I'm playing grandmothers."

Buck told O'Toole, "John fell for Ava bigtime when I brought them together. He'd written most of the script, but couldn't be credited because his contract with Warners forbade it."

"I remember the night so very well," she answered. "John chased me around the bushes in his moonlit garden."

Lancaster arrived an hour late. O'Toole later confessed "a certain jealousy" in meeting this former circus acrobat in the flesh, a rough-and-tumble kid who had grown up in the Depression-era neighborhood of New York City's East Harlem. He was strikingly handsome, the quintessential *bête du cinéma*, one of the biggest stars on the planet. Buck had told O'Toole, "Burt is bi. Maybe he'll make a pass at you."

"I'd rather have Ava," O'Toole said.

He felt left out of the conversation in the beginning, since it focused almost exclusively on the making of *The Killers* (1946), that not only had introduced Lancaster to movie fans, but had been Gardner's breakthrough role after all those lackluster roles she'd play during her early days in Hollywood.

Lancaster told O'Toole that he had not been the first choice to play "The

Swede," a hapless victim in the picture, an ex-boxer unwittingly roped into the criminal underworld and into the dangerous embrace of the sultry and duplicitous femme fatale, Kitty Collins (played by Ava).

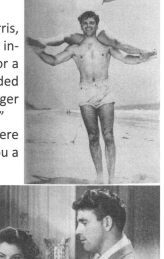

"Mark Hellinger originally wanted Wayne Morris, that big blonde bruiser. Not getting him, he went instead for Van Heflin, Jon Hall, and Sonny Tufts. For a while Edmond O'Brien was considered, but he ended up in the role of the insurance investigator. Hellinger got me because I was the cheapest actor in town."

"I wanted you from the beginning, although there were objections," Buck said. "Some guys called you a block of muscles—and little else."

"Fuck them!" Lancaster said. "I showed the pansies."

"As you know, Ernest Hemingway was my friend," Gardner said. "He told me that *The Killers* was the only movie adaptation of his work that he liked."

"What did he think of me?" Lancaster asked.

"He called you bait for homosexuals, darling," Gardner said. "You're so God damn sexy and attractive, just the type gay men swoon over."

"And let's not leave out millions of women," Lancaster shot back.

Two views of Ava Gardner with Burt Lancaster. *Top photo*: An early publicity shot, and *(lower photo)* in *The Killers* (1946).

"I showed my appreciation for you when we played our first love scene together," he said. "I'd never kissed a woman in front of so many people. Nor one as beautiful. I got a raging hard-on."

"I took that as a compliment," Gardner said, "and invited him to my dressing room that afternoon for a private audition."

[Ironically, Ronald Reagan's last motion picture, The Killers (1964), was conceived and filmed as a TV movie in which he co-starred with JFK's former mistress, Angie Dickinson. Unusual for him, Reagan played a villain, who in the film notoriously slaps Dickinson across the face. The movie was deemed too violent for TV and subsequently released as a feature movie in cinemas. It's known today as the film that effectively ended Ronald Reagan's film career. After critics responded with lackluster evaluations of his performance, he had to search for other gigs.]

"I remember for a while you were known as a brawny Apollo, a brute of a man with the eyes of an angel," Buck said to Lancaster.

"I no longer have to be modest about my rise In Hollywood," Lancaster said. "*Cosmopolitan* claimed that my skyrocketing to fame was faster than that of Garbo, Gable, or Lana Turner. As for my appearance, my hair looked like a bird-nest, going all over the place."

"I'm predicting the same meteoric rise for Peter here that you experienced after the war," Buck said to Lancaster.

"Good luck, kid," Lancaster said. "But I have to be frank with you. I'm always a bit leery meeting tomorrow's competition."

"When we met, I had hoped Burt might become my steady piece," Gardner said, "But the next thing I knew, he was shacked up in Malibu with Marlene Dietrich. She was forty-five years old, if a day, and had just returned from her wartime romance with Jean Gabin."

"Sometimes antique pussy is the best," Lancaster said. "Marlene would get out of bed at five o'clock in the morning to see me off to the studio. She'd cook my breakfast. As you know, she's celebrated for her omelette. She'd pack me a paper bag lunch—bagels, lox, cream cheese, and fresh doughnuts."

"I'd rush back to Malibu at quitting time, ready for her embrace. She always welcomed me with lip service. She has a preference for oral sex."

"A lot of people do," Gardner said. "Especially Peter Lawford."

The repartee between Lancaster and Gardner puzzled O'Toole. Was this how superstars spoke to each other? Both of them seemed to know that most intimate details about each other.

"I went over to see Burt when he was making *Brute Force* (1947)," Gardner said. "But I found out he'd forgotten all about me and was banging Yvonne de Carlo. She told me that you'd first seduced her in her backyard when you spread out her mink coat and fucked her under her oleander bush."

"Yvonne told me that you also made a pass at her," Lancaster said.

"*Touchée*," Gardner responded.

O'Toole later told Buck, "For the first time, I got a preview of how big stars banter with each other. No subject is off limits, no vulgar detail left out. If I ever go to Hollywood, I will have to learn a new lingo, not the Queen's English."

When Buck raised the subject of Sinatra, Gardner looked angry. "I don't want to talk about him. Frankie and I were fighting all the time. Fighting and boozing. But he was good in the feathers. Our real trouble began when I rose from bed and headed for the bidet."

Over dinner, both Lancaster and Gardner told fascinating stories about life in Hollywood. No one topped Gardner when she spoke of her life in Madrid, telling them she lived in a duplex directly above the apartment of

Juan Péron, the deposed military dictator of Argentina. He was living there, in exile, with his second wife, Isabel.

His former wife, Eva ("Evita") Duarte de Perón, whom he'd married in 1945, had died of cervical cancer in 1952.

"I was shocked when I was first invited down to have drinks with them," Gardner said. "Both Juan and Isabel are big movie fans. To my amazement, Evita's coffin, with her embalmed body inside it, was in their dining room. When he opened it for me, and I gazed about her amazingly well-preserved remains."

"We sat there facing this open coffin, downing empanadas. Isabel makes the best in the world. After a second bottle of wine, Juan told me that during the coup, Evita's body had been stolen. He claimed that she had been violated

The official state portrait of Juan Perón, military dictator of Argentina, and his controversial wife, Eva.

by at least twenty Argentine soldiers who had always wanted to fuck her. Here was their chance."

"How ghoulish," O'Toole exclaimed. "I can't imagine how anyone could get it on with a cold, dead body, but I've heard of such things."

"The second time I was invited down for drinks, the coffin was still there. This time, I was introduced to this giant of a man. He'd been a doorman at the Hilton, where the Peróns had met him. It turned out he was a Warlock, and he performed a *macumba* ceremony for us right there in the living room. Isabel dabbles in the occult."

At around 1AM, after a night of heavy drinking, Lancaster and Buck, along with O'Toole, prepared to leave, but Gardner invited O'Toole to stay for a nightcap.

O'Toole agreed to meet Buck the following day for lunch. Lancaster held out the promise of a future movie with O'Toole.

[That was no idle promise. They would co-star together in *Zulu Dawn* (1969), a colonial saga with thousands of cast members, filmed in South Africa.]

"I went to shake Burt's hand," O'Toole later told O'Liver. "He ignored that and gave me a real deep-throated kiss. Now I know what Deborah Kerr experienced on the beach with Burt in *From Here to Eternity* (1953).

O'Toole confessed to O'Liver that he spent three "blissful, passionate nights in the arms of Ava. She's rather demanding, insisting on controlling the fuck, but she takes a man on a journey to a kind of sexual Nirvana that he's not likely to experience again. I have nothing but praise for the woman. She told me I was ten times the lover that Gable was, but not quite the equal of Robert Mitchum."

"How do you feel about her having made these comparisons?" O'Liver asked.

"I count myself lucky she didn't size me up to Sinatra."

O'Toole's Early Success With David Lean & Jules Buck, Vs. His Later Box Office Failures Without Them

In partnership with Jules Buck, O'Toole would make some of his most distinguished films as well as some of his artistic and commercial failures.

They set out on a high note with the screen adaptation of Jean Anhouilh's dramatic play, *Becket,* a film that paired O'Toole with Richard Burton. Hal B. Wallis produced it for a Paramount release in 1964.

That was followed by Richard Brook's worthy but flawed adaptation of Joseph Conrad's *Lord Jim* (1965). From that, the two men went on to make *Great Catherine* (1968), with the French actress, Jeanne Moreau cast as the flamboyant queen in a film adaptation of a one-act play by George Bernard Shaw.

And so it went, year after year. Buck understood O'Toole as no previous producer ever had. "Everything depends on Peter's mood for the day. If it's his Yorkshire mood, then it will be okay. He's sensible and makes the right choices. But if he's in an Irish mood, run for the hills."

In 1971, O'Toole, Richard Burton, and Elizabeth Taylor released a "vanity project," Dylan Thomas' *Under Milk Wood*. Buck noted, "Those three actors seemed to be living in each other's crotches. I'm sure they were having a three-way...at least that!"

That same year, Buck and O'Toole released their most controversial film, *The Ruling Class*, a scathing satire of the depravity of the English aristocracy and a send-up of organized religion. Critics were sharply divided.

That was followed by such disasters at the box office as that dreadful flop, Man Friday (1975) an unconvincing reworking of Daniel Defoe's novel, *Robinson Crusoe.*

As the 1970s began to wind down, so did O'Toole's business partnership with Buck in Keep Films. "Our relationship with Peter had become very strained. I had wanted to produce films that had a better chance at the box office, whereas he preferred more artistic choices. Some of these were not only losers at the box office, but films that interested no one but Peter himself."

"We had a relationship where I was the forever giving father, and he was the errant son. It was time for us to break up. We behaved like gentlemen— no recriminations, no accusations. Both of us were responsible for our many failures."

"Another big reason for moving on was that the infusion of American cash into British films had virtually come to an end. We had depended on the flow of the Yankee dollar, and then it was gone. Studio space was at a minimum, and box office takes were reduced to an all-time low. The film world had changed drastically from 1960 when we started."

Buck would produce one final film without O'Toole called *Great Scout and Cathouse Thursday* (1976), a quirky Western that, among others, starred Oliver Reed as a Native American.

"When I saw the final cut, I realized I should remove myself from making films," Buck said.

The movie, distributed by American International, also starred Lee Marvin and Sylvia Miles. The advertising was accurate: "THEY WERE NOT FORGOTTEN BY HISTORY, THEY WERE LEFT OUT ON PURPOSE."

O'Toole had rejected the role that eventually went to Reed. The review in *The New York Times* asserted that Reed's "ridiculously stereotypical portrayal of an Indian with the clap goes down in film history as the most absurd casting of a Native American role since the birth of the movies."

After 28 years in exile, the Bucks returned to Hollywood, where Jules assisted his wife in her decorating business, as she set out to upgrade the homes of Vincent Price, Jane Wyatt, Ralph ("This Is Your Life") Edwards, and Sam Jaffee.

Siân missed her friendship with Joyce more than O'Toole missed his relationship with Jules.

Siân recalled that Ralph Waldo Emerson was right when he said, "The best effect of a fine person is felt long after we have left their presence."

Without Buck, O'Toole wondered what lay in his film future, perhaps fearing dusty oblivion like so many stars of the 1960s and 70s. To make matters worse, he picked up the morning newspaper to read, "Has Peter O'Toole reached the end of his tether charm?"

Chapter 9

Portrait of a Turbulent Marriage

O'Toole Weds and Stays Married to a Welsh Actress for 20 Years, Telling Friends, "I Will Never Be Faithful"

Through "Mad & Impulsive Times," Siân Phillips & O'Toole Become One of the Theater World's Most Fabulous Couples

O'Toole in *The Long And The Short And The Tall*.	Siân Phillips, around the time of her inaugural romance with O'Toole.
"No wonder I got the part. I looked the role of an angry young soldier with a fag in my mouth, trapped in a malarial swamp."	"The first hour I met him, I decided to marry him."

In the mid-1950s, in London, a troupe of actors, each a RADA student, took a lunch break from their rehearsals of their upcoming play. *En route* to a spaghetti house for a cheap meal, the group encountered several other actors.

To Siân Phillips, one of them stood out more than all the rest. She was introduced to a young Peter O'Toole, a name already familiar to her. He was known as a bad boy, a shining star at the Bristol Old Vic, where, in 1958, he had delivered a performance of Hamlet that was hailed as brilliant and compared favorably with other, better-known interpretations of the play by Laurence Olivier and John Gielgud.

Years later, she would recall his "curly hair and blue, blue eyes set into a quizzical face. Looking like 'The Actor' in Disney's *Pinnochio*. But that actor was a wolf. O'Toole the wolf wore a green velvet jacket and a neckerchief."

Siân

At the spaghetti house, she ordered risotto with an egg on top and wondered when it would be that she would become the bride of this O'Toole wolfman.

Siân had been born in 1933, a year after O'Toole, in Gwaun-Cae-Gurwen in West Glamorgan, an industrialized part of South Wales, the daughter of a teacher and a steelworker-turned-policeman. Throughout most of her childhood, she spoke only Welsh, finally teaching herself English by listening to the BBC.

Both Siân and O'Toole had risen to prominence on the stage during the late 1950s. In 1958, a year before she married O'Toole, Siân had performed as St. Joan in George Bernard Shaw's *Saint Joan* at the Belgrade Theatre in Coventry, where O'Toole, as a boy, had briefly lived during World War II. In reference to

...more Siân

her performance, one critic claimed, "This girl doesn't act Joan, she *is* Joan—in short, perfection."

In 1957, while still a scholarship student at RADA (where she'd studied alongside both Diana Rigg and Glenda Jackson), she made her first appearance in London's West End. There, she'd starred in Hermann Sudermann's *Magda*. This drama about an opera diva, a role that had not been performed since Sarah Bernhardt had last played her, was a great success, earning her rave notices. Soon after, she won the Bancroft Gold Medal for her performance in Ibsen's *Hedda Gabler,* for which the press hailed her as "a natural successor to Bernhardt." Her skill, presentation, and tenacity led to the offer of a three-film contract in Hollywood. She rejected that proposal, preferring stage work in the U.K. instead.

After Desertions and Chronic Infidelities,
Siân Abandons O'Toole For a Younger Lover

Around the time Siân first met O'Toole, he had been "outed" in the London press as a "hellraiser," along with Trevor Howard (an actor whose talent he admired), Peter Finch, and Brendan Behan, the Irish playwright, who was never known to turn down a drink. O'Toole became drinking buddies with all three of them.

Lacking conventional good looks, gruff-voiced, crag-faced Howard, an alumnus of RADA, had been one of O'Toole's role models ever since he'd appeared in *Brief Encounter* (1946). A reporter in London once asked Howard to comment on that season's emerging crop of new actors, especially O'Toole.

Trevor Howard
...scathing and trenchant

Howard did not answer the question directly. "I've heard that the poor laddie worships me. But I could never see myself as a guru."

Years later, Howard also said, "There was some talk that both of us were to star in *Mutiny on the Bounty* (1962), but I ended up with Marlon Brando—God deliver us, and O'Toole instead went off to make some desert picture with the bloody Arabs."

The next time O'Toole encountered Siân, he asked her out on a date, and they attended a play together. Their relationship intensified when they were cast in a play, *The Holiday,* by John Hall.

Siân later admitted, "Both Peter and I knew it was a terrible play, but we stuck it out, touring in Birmingham, Leeds, Nottingham, even in Peter's native city of Leeds, before the play died its death in Scotland."

Siân and O'Toole played brother and sister. But as he told his painter friend, Patrick O'Liver, "At the end of each performance, after the curtain went down, those siblings were guilty of incest."

"As brother and sister, we did look alike," Siân said. "It was verse drama, and verse drama was virtually dead on the stage at the time. 'Kitchen sink' plays were all the rage."

[In the British theater of the 1950s, "kitchen sink" was used to identify a new breed of brutally realistic dramas that focused on the working class. John Osborne's Look Back in Anger *was the best example of this emerging stage motif.]*

Also in the cast was Jack Merivale, who was on the dawn of his (real-life) role as Vivien Leigh's last lover, following her very public separation and widely publicized divorce from Laurence Olivier.

At one point, O'Toole told his friend, director Tony Richardson, "John is moving in on Miss Leigh, a woman I've slated on my calendar to deflower.

May the best man win, and, darling, you know who that is."

Back in London, Peter continued to court Siân, who had moved on to appearances with Richard Burton and Emlyn Williams in a recording of *Treason,* a play by Saunders Lewis which the BBC was recording in both English and in Welsh, with the understanding that all three of its performers were proficient in both languages. At the time, O'Toole suspected that Siân might be having an affair with Burton. "Why not?" he asked O'Liver. "Burton's fucking anything that moves."

After that, O'Toole and Siân began to date seriously, but in secret, which was the most discreet thing to do, since Siân was already married—though separated—from Donald Roy, whom she'd wed in 1956.

At the time Siân married him, Roy was a post-graduate student at the University of Wales. Almost from its debut, that marriage wasn't successful. Siân later claimed, "I never lived with Don, so I like to think that the marriage never happened."

Siân's dating of O'Toole intensified in 1959, when he starred alongside Robert Shaw in Wallis Hall's anti-war play, *The Long And The Short And The Tall* at London's Royal Court Theatre.

In it, O'Toole was cast as Private Bamforth, an angry young soldier, part of a lost patrol of British soldiers surrounded by the Japanese army in the steaming "malaria jungles" of Malaya.

Co-stars Robert Shaw and Ronald Fraser received praise for their performances, but Alan Dent, of the *News Chronicle,* defined O'Toole's interpretation as "an outstanding moment in the theatre."

[A film adaptation of the play was released in 1961, starring Laurence Harvey, Richard Harris, and Richard Todd.]

O'Toole's understudy was an aspiring young actor, Michael Caine. One night, O'Toole seriously injured his knee, requiring surgery. But he postponed it, claiming, "What? And let Mick on stage in my part? No chance, thank you very much."

Years later, in recalling his status as O'Toole's much-abused understudy, Caine said that in addition to learning the lines, his duties included fetching drinks for O'Toole and researching where the hot parties would be on any given evening. "I love a party," Caine said, "but I couldn't keep up with Peter. At some point in the evening, I usually ducked out."

An exception occurred one Saturday night, when O'Toole extended an invitation to the Golden Egg, a fast-food joint in London on Leicester Square.

The next thing Caine remembered was waking up

Young Michael Caine, almost before everything else began...

in an unfamiliar flat, lying next to O'Toole. "I nudged Peter and asked him what time it was."

"Never mind what time it is," O'Toole said. "What day is it?"

Neither actor knew. Their hostesses, however, whom Caine later referred to as "two dubious-looking girls," told him that it was 5PM on Monday afternoon. The curtain for the play's next performance was scheduled to rise at 8PM that evening.

When they arrived—rumpled, disheveled, and eager to appear in control of the situation—at the Royal Court, the stage manager there informed them that the manager of the Golden Egg had come in to tell him that "from this day and forevermore, both Peter O'Toole and Michael Caine are banned from the Golden Egg."

Caine wanted to know what they had done in his fast food joint.

O'Toole cautioned him: "Never ask. It's better not to know."

***

Fellow actor Frank Finlay remembered standing in O'Toole's Royal Court dressing room when Caine, having ascertained that no one really knew where O'Toole was, was preparing to go on.

Suddenly, two minutes before curtain, O'Toole rushed in with a "pub plate special" of bangers, eggs, and beans. As he frantically applied his makeup, he was shoveling those beans into his gullet.

"I hope the bloody beans don't make me fart on cue on stage," he quipped.

Stripping down and getting into his soldier's uniform, he grabbed a sausage, downing it as he headed toward the stage.

On his way there, he told Finlay, "I'm in love for the first time in my life. It's Siân. She's the girl of my dreams. I'm already a familiar visitor to her quim."

On another occasion, as Caine prepared to go on for O'Toole, [once again, he'd been visibly absent with no communication of any kind], the actor came hurtling through the stage door three minutes before the curtain was to go up. Casting off his street clothes, he shouted at Caine, "I'm here! I'm here! No need to go on!"

Caine finally got to perform in O'Toole's role when he went abroad for the filming of Lawrence of Arabia. The Hall play, this time starring Caine, toured through the British provinces for four months.

[Years later at an Academy Awards ceremony in Hollywood, O'Toole encountered Caine. "You and I stand tall," O'Toole said. "So does Sean Connery. But the midgets are taking over the business—Tom Cruise, Jude Law, Robert De Niro, Al Pacino, Dustin Hoffman."]

Siân and O'Toole began to be seen together in public, affectionately holding each other's hands. He referred to her as "darling," but that was not unusual, as he called both men and women darling, sometimes after he'd known them for only a few minutes.

Caught up in the passion of his first serious romance, O'Toole wanted to spend all of his nights with Siân, his new discovery. He tried to teach her to drink, preferably Scotch or Irish whiskey. Before making love, they often configured "musical evenings," which involved him playing the guitar and her singing. He taught her Irish songs; she taught him Welsh tunes.

Their romance almost came to an angry ending before it ever really begun. He had told her a secret in confidence. A few days later, she inadvertently revealed it to a friend of his, thinking that he was already in on the secret. He was not. When that friend confronted O'Toole with Siân's revelation, O'Toole approached Siân and, from a position outside the Royal Court Theatre, provoked a monumental row with her, castigating her loudly, in public.

Sobbing from his denunciations, she ran from the conflict, convinced that their romance had come to a crashing finale.

But a few nights later, she heard a tapping on her ground-floor window. Aroused from a deep sleep, and still deeply troubled over their broken relationship, she discovered O'Toole outside her window, which she unlocked and raised. He emerged through the opening, landing on her floor.

"All six feet of him straightened itself cheerily and seemed to sketch a little bow," she later wrote.

He told her that he had access to a car. "Coming for a cup of tea?" he asked her.

"It's three in the morning," she protested.

"So?" he responded.

They were back together again. That "cuppa" he'd promised had to wait until long past the morning light that filtered into their room, but which failed to awaken the exhausted lovers.

At the time, Siân was starring frequently in teleplays. As she moved in with him, she remembered O'Toole drinking incredible quantities of alcohol. "Drink apart, it was easy living together and with wonderful sex thrown into the mix, it was ecstatic."

The "anemic" scrambled eggs they ate every afternoon in his dressing room were less to her satisfaction.

When Siân's divorce from Roy came through, O'Toole proposed marriage, scheduling their wedding for December of 1959. As he told Caine, "My seed is quite fertile. I've already knocked her up."

For Peter, "Carnal Pleasures Within Wedlock— Wonderful, Ecstatic Sex"

O'Toole's marriage to Siân transpired without any particular flamboyance at the Registrar's Office in Dublin. "*[There will be]* no church wedding for a wayward whore like me," O'Toole said.

As his best man, he asked Kenneth Griffith to fly to Dublin, but regretfully, the actor refused, citing his commitment to a film he was shooting. "The bloody bloke said no to me," O'Toole protested. "He felt that working on some stupid movie was more important than my getting hitched. Perhaps he was right, so I must forgive him."

Siân recalled that at her wedding ceremony, Joyce Getz Buck was "either my best man or she gave me away." *[Joyce was the wife of Jules Buck, O'Toole's business partner in their recently formed movie production venture, Keep Films, Ltd.]*

Also according to Siân, "The wedding party was attended by Irish poets, singers, actors, a politician or two, and considerable riff-raff as it 'wound' its way through the Dublin night."

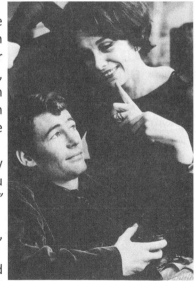

As she remembered it, at 5AM on the morning of her wedding, she found herself in a room with differently patterned wallpaper on each of its four walls, stars on the ceiling, and an alarming cabbage rose linoleum on the floor. "An unknown child was asleep in an armchair, and I was seated at a table groaning with Guinness bottles."

Henry Brogan, an actor at Dublin's Abbey Theatre, began flirting with her. "Did you ever read James Joyce's *Finnegan's Wake?*" he called out to her.

Taking a dainty sip of Guinness, she said, "No, but I rather feel I'm in it right now."

After the ceremony, and after Siân and O'Toole flew back to London, they moved temporarily into the tiny flat of Griffith, who at the time was living with Dora Noar, who would later become his second wife.

In defiance of his policy about avoiding appearances in the same production together, O'Toole and Phillips opted to so-star in *Ride a Cock Horse*, a scene from which is depicted above.

Sian's marriage to Peter was kept as more or less a secret until both of them made an appearance at Llangollen, a charming town in North Wales on the banks of the River Dee, which flowed between two parallel mountain ranges. The stone bridge, which had gracefully spanned the Dee since the 14th century, is often defined as one of the Seven Wonders of Wales.

O'Toole had accompanied Siân to Llangollen's *Eisteddfod,* a midsummer festival devoted to the choral music and culture, an international event that attracted dancers, folk singers, and choirs from around the world.

The O'Tooles lodged at the Royal Hotel (a historic coaching inn formerly known as the King's Head) on Bridge Street, in a room once occupied, before her coronation, by the future Queen Victoria.

Peter and Siân did not attempt to conceal the nature of their relationship, and soon the press figured out what was going on. They were so pestered with requests for information that after the festival, they fled back on London in a taxi that charged the then-astronomical sum of 25 pounds.

Next, sheltered within the relative anonymity of London after their secret marriage in Dublin, O'Toole and his bride co-starred together in *The King's Daughter,* a BBC-TV play.

In March of 1960, their first child, a daughter, was born, although Peter had been hoping for a son. They named her Katherine, a name inspired by Katharine Hepburn, with the understanding that the child would be called Kate.

Like her parents, and like her namesake, Kate O'Toole would also become an actress.

O'Toole's parents, Connie and Paddy, arrived in London to celebrate the birth of their granddaughter. Long after Siân and Connie had retired to their respective bedrooms, Paddy and his son stayed up drinking. When she went downstairs the next morning to make breakfast, Connie discovered her son and her husband passed out and lying side by side on the living room floor.

After giving birth to Kate, Siân was too busy with her career to operate as a full-time mother. Consequently, the O'Tooles hired a "cook-cum-nanny," Lonnie Trimble, a black woman who O'Toole nicknamed "Le Mumbo."

In Stratford-upon-Avon, Sir Peter Hall allowed infant Kate to make her stage debut during the christening scene of Shakespeare's 1623 romantic comedy, *The Winter's Tale.*

Almost simultaneous with his marriage came sudden stardom. After years of a relatively secret existence, except for stage appearances at Bristol's Old Vic, O'Toole found he was suddenly in the news. "My every indiscretion seemed to get into the bloody press. I couldn't even take a fart without getting a mention. Stardom is not really so bad, however. Look, when it hits some people, they bounce around like corks because they have no middle of themselves to measure from. But I have a very definite middle. My centerpiece is Siân. I measure everything from there. Without Siân, I could never have made it at all. Not this far, not this fast. She's got a grip on a pretty wild, roaring Irishman and pointed him in the right direction."

Since the working couple earned good money, they decided to purchase Guyon House, at 98 Heath Street in Hampstead, a stylish neighborhood on the northern edge of London. Direly in need of massive repairs, the five-story house dated from 1740. The O'Tooles paid £13,500 for it.

Before its acquisition by the O'Tooles, the building had functioned as a crash pad for underemployed actors, many of whom maintained a hot plate in their bedrooms. After they bought it, a restoration, which eventually stretched out over a period of five years, was launched.

Starving Bohemians Get Bourgeois, Gentrified, and Grand

The stately looking 18th-century facade of Guyon House in Hampstead, renovated and inhabited by Siân Phillips and Peter O'Toole.

Siân learned early in her marriage that her husband was no financial wizard—far from it. One day, Peter Evans, the popular columnist for London's *Daily Express* and author of several books, came to interview O'Toole at his home.

"I'm skint," Peter told Evans, "having spent all the money I earned from *Lawrence of Arabia.* The only difference between me today and me yesterday is that I am luxuriously broke."

As if to illustrate that point, Evans noticed Kate's bonnet perched atop a statue. "It looked like something that a baby of a poverty-stricken couple in a Charles Dickens novel might wear, but it was draped over a *[very costly]* statue by Jacob Epstein," Evans said.

"If I up and became cautious with a shilling, Siân would bundle Kate up under one arm and hop it to God knows where."

He went on to tell Evans that he wasn't as politically radical as he had been when he was younger. "I still have this self-destructive streak, though. But there is nothing like a few bob to cure a man of socialism. I have a house here in Hampstead, and children. I'm not the big bad wolf ready to huff and puff and blow the house down. I've worked too bloody hard for it."

Then he challenged the visiting columnist. "All experience, in my experience, corrupts. You learn too many tricks. Tell me any experience that you've had that enables you. Go on!"

As his marriage matured, O'Toole continued to have affairs. "Surely, Siân doesn't expect me to be faithful," he told O'Liver. "I don't know if she's getting something on the side. If so, she certainly has that right."

As his fame as a movie star grew, he found some of the most beautiful women in the world, including a member of the British Royal Family, pursuing him.

"Dickie Burton and I have the same problem," he told fellow actor, James Villiers. "He may have the most beautiful woman in the world at home in his bed (Elizabeth Taylor), but that doesn't mean he ceases to pursue that extra piece. In his case, that included, on one occasion a toothless, broken down hotel maid in Jamaica."

"Otherwise, Burton is seducing Zsa Zsa Gabor, Jackie Kennedy, Ava Gardner, Susan Strasberg, Sophia Loren, Barbra Streisand, and Lana Turner, not to mention Rachel Roberts and Jean Simmons."

Despite his sexual success, one drunken night at the Salisbury pub in London, Burton confessed to O'Toole, "Most actors are latent homosexuals, if not overtly practicing ones. We cover it with drink. When I started out as an actor, I was a homosexual, but it didn't take."

"I love Siân dearly," O'Toole repeated, frequently, year after year. In apparent contradiction, however, he once told a reporter for *The New York Times,* "Marriage is an impossible institution. I can't be expected to remain faithful forever. This notion of two people being bound to each other can't be legislated. When a marriage works, it's a complete accident, a delightful shock. I truly believe that a couple are not held together by some marriage contract. They are held together by mutual esteem. I'm dreadfully fond of Siân."

"Actually, I liked Siân as my mistress more than as my wife," he continued.

Possibly, he was referring to the time they lived together prior to their marriage in 1959. He might also have been referring to their 1965 performance at London's Piccadilly Theatre, when she played his character's mistress in *Ride a Cock Horse.*

Because both Siân and O'Toole were often absent from their house in Hampstead at the same time, pursuing various acting jobs, they suffered through occasional burglaries. Once, thieves broke into their home and made off with two paintings by Jack Yeats, a gift from producer Hal. B. Wallis after O'Toole had completed his filming of *Becket* (1964).

Although Siân and O'Toole always maintained that working together was a quick detour to the divorce courts, each of them followed the other's career with avid devotion. Whenever possible, he was on hand to applaud Siân at her opening nights. He recalled one occasion in 1964, when he attended one of Siân's performances with the very distinguished Dame Edith Evans in *Gentle Jack.*

Peter O'Toole to Michael Bryant, depicted above: "YOU CUNT!"

On that particular night, he encountered another member of the cast, Michael Bryant, *en route* to Siân's dressing room.

"Siân acts better than you ever could," Bryant provocatively informed O'Toole.

"You cunt," O'Toole said. "I've got more hairs on my cock than you've got on your head."

Bryant and O'Toole would later appear together in *Goodbye, Mr. Chips* (1959).

Siân always claimed that Bryant was one of the best actors in England, and so he was. A lynchpin of National Theatrical Productions for nearly forty years, Bryant was not a showy actor, but more of a fastidious perfectionist in the style of Alec Guinness. He played T.E. Lawrence in the touring version of Terence Rattigan's play, *Ross,* which had starred Guinness during its run in London.

Early Discord in Their Marriage

From the beginning, Siân admitted to O'Toole that before she met him, she had led "a life of carnal pleasure without wedlock."

When drunk, he often threw her past up in front of her, and he sometimes attacked her to his friends. He would often order her out of the house. Riding with her in a car, often with friends, he would tell her to get out, leaving her abandoned on the street, often late at night, trying to find a taxi.

Even when he wasn't working, such as when he was in Ireland digging ditches for the sewerage of his new house there, he urged Siân to take work in films, on the stage, or in teleplays. "She's a free woman. Just because she's married doesn't mean she has to be a servant to her man. There's a wedding ring on her finger, not on her nose."

Sally Phillips, Siân's mother, moved into Guyon House to look after the family. She always seemed to be preparing cauldrons of beef broth—"With tons of cow blood," the way O'Toole preferred it for maximum potency. "After drinking a quart of Mother's hearty broth, I'm a bull," he boasted.

Surviving the vagaries of their marriage, with its ups and downs, in June of 1963, O'Toole announced that Siân was pregnant again. "We're returning to Ireland. I want my son to be born an Irishman like his father."

The baby, who was, indeed Irish based on having been born on Irish soil, turned out to be a daughter. She was named Patricia in honor of Peter's older sister, and would grow up to become a theater's stage manager.

In Dublin, in anticipation of Patricia's birth, Siân checked into an Irish maternity ward. There, it was understood that she would endure an old-fashioned Irish birth *[i.e., very little pampering and a lot of actual pain for the mother.]*

During Patricia's birth, Peter retired to his favorite pub in Dublin with his friend, producer Kevin McClory, "who was still mourning getting dumped by Elizabeth Taylor, who had, long ago, promised to marry him."

Over Guinness, O'Toole said he could just imagine what was going on back in that maternity ward. "Some sweaty rugby-player-turned-doctor is shouting at her, '*Go, girl, go*! Then the bloke yanks the baby out, slaps its red butt, and listens to it scream at being uprooted from such a warm place. No doubt, before Siân goes under, she'll sing the Welsh National anthem."

When he heard that he was the father of a newborn baby girl, he ordered another pint of Guinness before making his way back to the ward. Wearing a green corduroy jacket, a green polka dot tie, loafers dyed green, chartreuse socks, and showing up drunk, there could be no doubt that he was a new Irish father.

The next day, he rose early and "downed a Guinness or two—maybe more," before heading with McClory to the horseracing track, the former stamping ground of his father, Paddy.

O'Toole's Hard Drinking Takes Its Toll

News Reporters Write His Obituary

"I Avoided the Grim Reaper but Lost My Guts"

In looking back, O'Toole said, "The Queen of England, addressing the nation, once spoke of her *annus horribilis.*"

[In her public address, Queen Elizabeth II was referring to 1992, the year that included naughty behavior from her children and the destruction, by fire, of parts of Windsor Castle],

"For me," O'Toole continued, "my 'horrible year' was 1975, the most crucial of my life. I not only had to deal with a premature visit from the Grim

Reaper, but my professional and personal life was coming unglued. What a time! I faced disasters of Biblical proportions. Even my dear dog Scobie died."

For more than five years, he had been denying his abdominal pains, refusing to see a doctor and stridently resisting checking into a hospital.

Then, one night, his pain became so intense that he could no longer deny the dangers it implied.

An ambulance was summoned to haul him to London's nearby Royal Free Hospital. As he was rushed into one of its emergency rooms, he began moaning with almost unbearable pain.

With beard he grew for the role of Judas, a part he never played, O'Toole, with Siân, as he's about to enter a hospital.

After a series of examinations—"most invasive," he'd later complain—the chief surgeon ordered some exploratory surgery. The results were enigmatic. Stomach cancer had been feared, but no evidence of such a disease was immediately diagnosed.

Nonetheless, O'Toole was very, very ill, enough so that he had to be fed by a tube that channeled nutrients through his nose into his stomach—no more solid food.

He said, enigmatically, "The surgeons spotted something that should not have been there."

[He was eventually diagnosed with chronic and acute pancreatitis, an inflammation of the pancreas, a long, flat gland in the upper ab-

Ill and vulnerable in 1977. "Death came knocking, but I didn't answer the door."

domen that produces enzymes that assist digestion and hormones that help regulate the way a body produces glucose.]

This was followed with at least three more surgical procedures. "Doctors had to remove my guts yards at a time, not all at once. I would no longer halfway recover than I was wheeled in for surgeons to cut out more of my intestines. I feared there would be nothing left, just an empty vessel of a man."

"Friends arrived with fruit and flowers," he said. "My steadies, such as James Villiers and Griffith, even a surprise visit from Noël Coward, who was always enchanted with me."

"I trust they didn't remove your pride and joy," Coward said to him.

"No, they didn't. But don't get your hopes up. It's not in working order right now."

There was a rumor that, among other removals, he would have to have his pancreas removed. However, he issued strict orders that no member of the hospital's medical staff would reveal exactly what his operations had entailed.

Snoopers who tried to delve into his medical records discovered that they had mysteriously disappeared from the hospital altogether.

"I had so much surgery done that I told my doctor that he should install a zipper so he wouldn't have to cut me open so bloody much. There was so little left of my digestive system that even the smallest amount of booze could prove fatal to me."

"The worst period of my illness was between the ages of thirty-nine and forty-one. At forty, I was so desperately ill, I couldn't act for a whole year."

As he recovered, he said, "I found out that half of my entrails had been removed. Probably fed to some ravenous cats in the alley."

The press picked up on his confinement, at first defining his problem, in print, as alcohol poisoning. Reporters began calling Siân for help in writing O'Toole's obit.

During his recuperation, he developed a full growth of beard. When a male nurse began preparations to shave him, in a very weak voice, he protested, "Bloody hell! Don't do that. I need my beard!"

Before his diagnoses, he had been scheduled to play Judas Iscariot in Lord (aka Sir Lew) Grade's TV epic, *The Life of Jesus Christ,* starring Robert Powell.

Sir Lew was disappointed that O'Toole's health problems prevented him from playing Judas. Nevertheless, he decided to cast both Siân and O'Toole in his next production, leaking to the press that he was going to offer O'Toole the role of the World War II German ace, "The Red Baron," Manfred von Richthofen, with Siân cast as his wife, Frieda.

When it came time for the actual filming, however, O'Toole was far too ill to play either the Red Baron or anyone else, for that matter, so Sir Lew had to look elsewhere for a suitable actor.

"My doctors told me that I would have to abandon the liquid of life," O'Toole said. "I was told to be a boozer no more, or else I would end up six feet under." As he would later proclaim, ruefully, "Publicans have lost their best visitor from Ireland."

He followed his doctors' advice and gave up liquor, though he continued to attend pubs regularly. "I like the smell of urine and beer, and all that healthy smoke," he said. He'd order a tonic and lime, or else lemonade.

Based on the belief that he was dying, O'Toole summoned Griffith to his hospital bed, where he admitted that Griffith knew a lot about him already—"Too much, if you ask me."

He went on to say that he wanted a biography written "of my wasted life. I'll tell you things I've never told anybody, especially about my early life and my time in the Navy."

But when O'Toole recovered, he announced to Griffith that he wanted him to abandon any work he might have started on the biography. "I'm going to write my own autobiography in three volumes, to be entitled: *Loitering with Intent, The Child; Loitering with Intent, the Apprentice;* and *Loitering with Intent, the Adult.*"

Although the first two of the proposed three volumes were completed in a format which most readers interpreted as confusing, opaque, mysterious, and unclear, he never lived to finish the third, a book which, had it been brought to conclusion, would undoubtedly have been the most intriguing, and titillating, of the three projected volumes.

Sometimes, during his later years, he would become enraged with Griffith, accusing him of "dining out on Peter O'Toole stories. Apparently, you never learned during the war that loose lips sink ships. At times, I think you know more of my biography than I do. I've forgotten so much, or else I don't care to remember."

He remained "at death's door" *[his words]* in the hospital for two full months. At checkout, he was cadaver white and extremely frail, having lost forty-five pounds. In states of undress, whenever he confronted a mirror, he was horrified at the fifteen-inch scar he saw. He was still in pain, often enduring prolonged coughing spasms.

[In 1987, when O'Toole was appearing in Manhattan in Pygmalion, *he was asked about his surgery. "I was troubled with my stomach since I was a child. From age 19 and on, I would have great flare-ups of pain. Then, when I was in my 40s, I was hemorrhaging very badly and nearly died. So a surgeon opened me up like a purse and had a fiddle around my innards. Something was removed."*

"Malignant?" asked a reporter.

"It wasn't benign," O'Toole responded, tersely.]

Additional devastating news was on the way. To add to O'Toole's woes, he received a call from his mother, Connie, telling him that Paddy had been hit by a car. "He was just leaving a betting shop. The car picked up his body and deposited him next door at the entrance to a pub. He was badly injured. The doctors don't expect him to pull through."

His father died two days later, but not before pleading with the nurses to give him a shot of Irish whiskey.

As if all this weren't enough, Jules Buck notified Peter in 1978 that their partnership, Keep Films, was insolvent. In reporting its demise, London headlines referred to O'Toole as "The Faded Boy of the British Theatre."

Accusing Her of Robbing a Cradle, O'Toole Confronts His Wife's New Beau, Defining Him as "A Young Geezer, a Toy Boy, Mr. Siân Phillips"

In Divorce Court, Siân Charges O'Toole as "A Dangerous, Disruptive Human Being"

In the year that O'Toole was enduring his surgeries, Siân was cast in a farce, Arthur Wing Pinero's *The Gay Lord Quex*. Dame Judi Dench was designated as the star of the play. Also cast in a part was a young actor, Robin Sachs, who was 17 years younger than Siân. During the run of the play, they fell in love.

From the sidelines, O'Toole watched with great satisfaction as his wife successfully starred in teleplays adapted for or by the BBC. The most memorable of these involved her interpretation of Livia in the teleplay based on the Robert Graves' novel, *I, Claudius* (1976).

At the time she filmed it, she was immersed in her clandestine relationship with Sachs. Their romance had not yet been discovered by O'Toole.

Even as their marriage crumbled, O'Toole remained her champion. When she starred as Beth Morgan in *How Green Was My Valley* (1975), a critic attacked her, asserting that she had been miscast—"Far too aristocratic."

When O'Toole read that, he burst into anger. "Too aristocratic? Bloody hell! She's a bloody peasant. Born on a farm in Gwaun-Cae-Gurwen. You can't get more peasant than that. You should see her when I'm getting the scorching tongue. Ah, every man should have his Siân."

Siân, as Livia in 1976, proved that her husband was not the only O'Toole capable of portraying ruthlessly decadent ancient Romans.

When asked about the status of her marriage, she answered, "Like a fine wine, my marriage gets better as it matures. We remain a beloved couple and devoted parents to our two daughters."

Eventually, the truth came out. Someone informed O'Toole of his wife's clandestine affair with Sachs.

He urged her to break off with Sachs, referring to her relationship with him as "ridiculous." Do you realize that when you're fifty-seven, old and gray, he'll be only forty years old. If you want to be foolish, maybe the gods will forgive you. I won't."

From then on, he referred to Sachs as his wife's "toy boy," sometimes calling him "a young geezer," and continuing, spitefully, with "And in public, he'll be known as 'Mr. Phillips.'"

Siân Phillips with Robin Sachs, the younger lover for whom she abandoned Peter O'Toole.

O'Toole told his friends that he was still in love with Siân and held out the possibility that she'd "forgive me my many sins and transgressions and return to home and hearth on the Heath."

He told Griffith, "I think I have lost Siân forever. She's found a far younger and more reliable penis than my withered wand of lust that will only stand up and salute the flag on occasion."

Finally, when he knew that clinging to the shreds of his marriage was hopeless, he asked Siân to move out of Guyon House. In the aftermath of that request, she purchased a house in Islington and set up housekeeping there with Sachs.

The end of her marriage did not imply an end to her career. Here is Siân as Lady Bracknell in Oscar Wilde's *The Importance of Being Earnest.*

At some point, O'Toole and Siân finally stopped "living a lie" and admitted the truth to the press.

"Siân has given me the Greasy E," he said. "It happens to a lot of men my age. I harbor no rancor, only deep regrets. Today, divorce is commonplace. We've become just another statistic. How many marriages go the full trip, from youthful passion to a blithering old age, drooling at the mouth?"

In the wake of their divorce, Siân issued a statement: "I regret that my marriage to Peter O'Toole came to an end. But these things happen, and I'd already had one disastrous student marriage by the time we met. My marriage to Peter just drifted away from us."

In August of 1979, the long-delayed divorce of O'Toole from his Welsh bride of yesteryear was legally concluded. In court, Siân had asserted, "My husband and I have not lived together as man and wife for more than two years."

Four months later, on Christmas Eve of 1979, Siân married Sachs, a union that would end in divorce in 1991.

Ironically, despite her daughter's divorce from O'Toole, Sally Phillips, Siân's mother and O'Toole's ex-mother-in-law, would continue to live in O'Toole's house in Hampstead, taking care of the home and its occupants, which (obviously) no longer included her daughter.

After their divorce was finalized, Siân and Peter's daughters, Kate, 17, and Pat, 14, were given the choice of which parent they wanted to live with.

Both of them chose their father.

***

[As a performer, Robin Sachs eventually achieved his greatest success in the United States, where he took an American wife, marrying Actress Casey Defranco in 1995.

Ultimately, his most famous role involved the interpretation of Ethan Rayne in Joss Whedon's cult TV series, Buffy the Vampire Slayer. *Through it, he established a large fan base as the benevolent owner of a costume shop who, in reality, was a master of the black arts, a sorcerer, and an arch enemy of Giles (played by Anthony Head) and the Scooby Gang.*

Sachs, who died in 2013, divorced his second wife in 2006.

He once confessed to one of his former directors, John Gielgud, "I went alone to a matinee in London—I forgot the name of the play—and after the first act, I went to the loo. I think all men check out each other's cocks when they're taking a leak. I observed the cock pissing next to me. Suddenly, when I looked up, I was staring into the face of Peter O'Toole."

"How delightful," Gielgud responded with a characteristic touch of bitchery. "Checking out what turned Siân on before she dumped him for you?"

Chapter 10

The Savage Innocents

O'Toole Co-Stars with Anthony Quinn
"At the Top of the World"

Plastic Igloos, Peroxided Polar Bears, A Casting Couch Director, and a "Pidgin-English-Mexicano" Cast as an Eskimo

Victorian Scruples: O'Toole, of the Canadian Royal Police, "defending Imperialism and the white man's culture."	The Mighty Anthony Quinn as an Eskimo, a Noble Savage, and in the words of its Italian producers, an *"Innocenti."*

"At last, I have come face to face with the poet of American disenchantment," Peter O'Toole said upon his first meeting, in London, with director Nicholas Ray.

"He was not at his peak when I met him," O'Toole recalled. "His glory days, brief though they were, had come and gone."

[By the late 1950s, in an era that produced a succession of noteworthy films, Ray's most famous movies seemed like statements from the distant past. Knock on Any Door, with Humphrey Bogart, had been released in 1950; the campy Johnny Guitar with Joan Crawford, had been released in 1955; and

Rebel Without a Cause, *with the doomed James Dean, had been released in 1956.]*

Ray seemed broke and disillusioned when he met O'Toole. His recent years had been devoted to drinking, drugs, aimless wandering, gambling, and lack of work as a director.

He had stumbled upon a novel by Hans Ruesch, a Swiss racecar driver, novelist, and animal rights activist who campaigned against vivisection. Although Ruesch had never met an Eskimo, he'd written a novel, *Top of the World,* which *The New York Times* had critiqued as "a brilliant feat of poetic imagination." It was a saga about the cultural clash between an Eskimo living by his wits in the cold Arctic, who comes into a violent confrontation with "the white man's culture."

Director Nicholas Ray with James Dean. "I'm mad about the boy."

Basing his work on Ruesch's novel, Ray was writing the screenplay himself, with the intention of directing it, and changing its title to *The Savage Innocents* (1960).

In 1958, Ray had married Betty Utey, and it was she who had seen O'Toole in London's West End play, *The Long And The Short And The Tall.*

Author and animal rights activist Hans Ruesch, attacking vivisection.

She recommended to her husband that he cast O'Toole as the Canadian police trooper who arrests the Eskimo, Inuk, and attempts to take him to a remote trading post to stand trial for his (unintentional) murder of a misguided Christian missionary.

"Even though my role was small, I jumped at the chance to work with Ray," O'Toole later claimed. "I thought, at least at the time, that he was my kind of guy."

As a young man in Leeds, O'Toole had gone to see *Rebel Without a Cause* several times, becoming entranced by both its director, Ray, and its star, James Dean.

After His Voice is Silenced and His Lines are Dubbed in the Final Cut, O'Toole Threatens a Lawsuit if His Name Is Not Removed from the Credits

---

Meeting for the first time over drinks and dinner one evening in London, Ray appeared intoxicated as he began the evening, and became increasingly incoherent and indiscreet as the night progressed.

He told O'Toole that originally, in *Rebel,* he'd wanted to cast Marlon Brando in the James Dean role, but that it had taken years before he was given a green light to shoot the movie.

"I have to admit I took director's privilege. Jimmy wasn't the only one who landed repeatedly on my casting couch. I also seduced Natalie Wood and Sal Mineo, even though they both were (underaged) jailbait at the time."

Gloria Grahame developed a taste for the lovemaking skills of a 13-year-old boy.

Another aspect of Ray's life that fascinated O'Toole was his marriage (from 1948 to 1952) to the *film noir* blonde, Gloria Grahame. O'Toole had taped a poster of Grahame to his bedroom wall years ago. "I must confess," O'Toole said. "She was my masturbatory fantasy on many a night. I dreamed of having her in my bed."

"I actually occupied her bed until one afternoon," Ray said. "I came home early from the studio one day and caught my son, Tony, in bed with my wife/his stepmother. Tony was my son from my first marriage to the journalist, Jean Evans. The kid was only thirteen. But judging from what I saw that day, he was fully developed, at least in one department."

"What did you do?" O'Toole asked.

"I kicked him out of my house and, not much later, I divorced Gloria."

[In 1960, to the shock of Hollywood, Gloria married her former stepson, making him the stepfather of Timothy, a child she had given birth to during her marriage to Ray.]

Two nights later, O'Toole met Maleno Malenotti, the producer, screenwriter, and director. Before tackling *The Savage Innocents,* he had turned out a number of biographical pictures, including *The Young Caruso* (1952); *The Life and Music of Guiseppe Verdi* (1953); and *Beautiful but Dangerous* (1958), starring Gina Lollobrigida as the operatic soprano, Lina Cavalieri.

Before Malenotti left London, he had signed O'Toole to a part in *The Savage Innocents.*

In 1976, O'Toole was saddened to learn that Malenotti had been kidnapped at his estate in the province of Pisa in Italy. His kidnappers had demanded a ransom which was paid by his family. Malenotti was never returned, and later, was officially listed as dead.]

Before O'Toole reported for work at Pinewood, he learned that a catastrophe had already descended on the picture. All of the outdoor scenes shot in the Canadian Arctic had been lost when a private plane carrying them had gone down in the wilderness. As replacement for the lost footage, igloos and icy landscapes, all of them fabricated from plastic, were being replicated on the lot at Pinewood Studios, even though it was July during the hottest summer recorded in England in thirteen years.

Polar bears were shipped in from the Dublin Zoo, but they didn't look white enough, so the makeup department coated their bodies with peroxide. Irritating their skin, it drove the beasts mad.

O'Toole became reacquainted with Anthony Quinn, who had been cast as a good-humored Eskimo named Inuk. He was clearly the star of the picture. O'Toole had recently seen him on the stage on Broadway, playing Henry II opposite Laurence Olivier in the stage version of *Becket.* Soon after that performance, both Quinn and O'Toole migrated to Jordan for their joint appearances in *Lawrence of Arabia.*

O'Toole met some of Quinn's friends, including mob boss Frank Costello, depicted above. Like Frank Sinatra, Tony Quinn had a taste for gangsters.

Ray told O'Toole, "I cast Tony because he looks like an Eskimo, even though he was born in Mexico. But I made it clear to this over-the-top actor that I did not want our film to be 'Tony in the Arctic.' I want the real stars to be the cold, the ice, the snow, and the sun that never sets."

"I'm always cast as an exotic," Quinn complained. "Hollywood producers are racists."

From the beginning, Ray encountered problems with both Quinn and O'Toole. The bright lights made O'Toole's eyes squint, and he had to wear darkened contact lenses to shut out the light. As for Quinn, he seemed to want to direct the picture himself and rewrite his own dialogue.

When O'Toole lunched with Quinn, the actor told him he was reaching a turning point in his career, having been in the movies since 1936. He claimed that it was Hollywood racism that had hindered his chances as a leading man. "Directors didn't want a mug like mine," he said. "They wanted Tyrone Power or Gregory Peck."

He revealed that Cecil B. DeMille conflicted with him when he'd cast him as an Indian in *The Plainsman* (1936). He gave me a rough time. But I got even. I married his daughter (Katherine DeMille) and give the old geezer five grandchildren."

"Since the years are racing by too fast for me, I'm going to have to re-invent myself. I've got to come up with a new character. That means letting my gut get bigger, my hair turn gray, and my swarthy face become even more rugged and weathered by the years."

O'Toole later recalled, "Tony was clearly a genius and the most versatile actor I've known. Once in New York, he invited me to dinner with him at 21. Let's call it, 'Guess Who's Coming to Dinner?' It turned out to be mob boss Frank Costello."

Eskimos Anthony Quinn and Yoko Tani with a new generation of *Savage Innocents*.

When he met with O'Toole, Quinn told him that to prepare for his role, he'd read all he could about Eskimo culture. "When a man dies, his friends and family gather for five days to honor his life. They tell amusing stories about him, really personal things. They even discuss the size of his 'thing.' They make small talk about the smell of his sweat, how he chewed his food. After that and by the fifth day, they never mention his name again."

As the film progresses, at a trading post, Inuk accidentally kills a well-intentioned but self-righteously priggish missionary. The

The corrupted face of misguided "civilization" as personified by Royal Canadian Police Officer, Peter O'Toole.

priest had insulted Inuk by refusing to take advantage of what Inuk had (generously) offered as a gesture of hospitality: a sexual interlude with Inuk's wife. When Inuk slams the missionary against a wall, inadvertently killing him, he's pursued by a vengefully obsessive officer of the Canadian police (as played by O'Toole) and his fellow officer (Carlo Giustini).

As Inuk, Quinn says, "No matter how many times you lend your wife, she always comes back like new."

The Japanese actress, Yoko Tani, was cast as Asiak, Inuk's wife. She had been born in Paris where, as she matured, she became a nightclub entertainer. In that capacity, she'd been billed as "an exotic Oriental beauty who performs sexy geisha dances, removing her kimono at the end of her act."

At the debut of her film career, Tani had been discovered by a film director who spotted her performance at Le Crazy Horse in Paris, the most famous strip club in France.

Eventually, she appeared in international films, including MGM's 1958 film adaptation of Graham Greene's *The Quiet American*. That same year, she got an even bigger role in *The Wind Cannot Read* opposite Dirk Bogarde.

[Years later, in 1977, director David Lean met with O'Toole for drinks in London. He told O'Toole that he had seen Yoko Tani in São Paulo, Brazil, where she was starring in a drag show. Lean had originally been assigned the task of directing her in The Wind Cannot Read.

O'Toole told Lean, "Let's face it. Show business has its ups and downs. As for me, I would never be hired as a stripper, even as a young man. I never had the body for it."]

Yoko Tani

In a dramatic scene set in a frozen and desolate wilderness, Canadian police officers, as played by O'Toole and Giustini, arrest Inuk. They have to forcibly transport him back across an Arctic wasteland to stand trial at the trading post. Along the way, Trooper Giustini falls into icy water and dies instantly. When O'Toole's hands become frozen, Inuk, technically a prisoner of O'Toole, rescues him from amputation or death by killing one of his huskies, ripping open its belly with a knife, and then plunging O'Toole's hands into the warm bloody guts of the dying dog. As circulation is restored to his frozen hands, O'Toole cries out in pain, to which Inuk responds, "Good. That means life is coming back. Only death is painless."

In *Marco Polo* (1962), Rory Calhoun, playing an Italian explorer, rescues Yoko Tani, who's playing Princess Amurroy, daughter of the Mongol leader Kublai Khan.

With their sledge gone, vanished into the icy water, O'Toole and Quinn need to remake one in a frozen landscape that's devoid of any building materials. That was a weak spot whose details were never resolved within Ray's script. As a means of creating a graceful segue, O'Toole suggested that Inuk kill him, eat him, and then fashion a sledge from his skin and bones.

"We're not making that kind of picture," Ray shot back.

In the film's closing scenes, Trooper O'Toole is grateful to Inuk for saving his hands and his life. In a reversal, he opts to release Inuk and Asiak so that they can return to the wilderness from which they came.

***

O'Toole had gotten along fabulously with Ray until he saw the film's final cut. The director had dubbed his voice with the soundtrack from another actor. Whereas O'Toole had delivered his lines with an Irish accent, Ray had hired Robert Rietty to lip-read O'Toole as he delivered his lines, and then record them in a Canadian accent.

In reaction, O'Toole threatened to sue and demanded that his name be removed from the credits. He denounced Ray to the press. "I was vain and arrogant enough to want my own voice retained. And why not? I have an absolutely divine speaking voice. I'm outraged at what Ray has done. I don't want anything to do with the promotion of this film. The whole thing is a disaster."

Quinn called O'Toole, warning him "to cool it. Your attacks on Ray might harm you. Future directors might regard you as too much trouble to cast again. Combine that with tales of your heavy drinking and outrageous behavior and you may have a problem. I'm speaking as a friend. I love your spirit and I'm all for you. But you might scare off the Wall Street boys who invest in films."

"Great advice, Tony darling," O'Toole said, "although you know deep down in those big *cojones* of yours that I'll never take it."

Distributed by Paramount Pictures, *The Savage Innocents* was premiered at the Cannes Film Festival in 1960. It did not do good business and had a limited release in the United Kingdom and the United States. In Italy, it was released as *Ombre Bianche,* and in France, its title was *Les Dents du Diable.*

Bob Dylan wrote the song "Quinn the Eskimo (The Mighty Quinn)" in tribute to that actor's portrayal of Inuk in *The Savage Innocents.*

Variety wrote of Quinn talking "pidgin-English-cum-Eskimo. His memorable moments are hunting down foxes, bears, seals, walruses, and the majesty of bleak wastes, the ice, the storms, and primitive living conditions. The human elements don't come out of it quite so well, mainly because Ray's screenplay contains some pretty naïve lines rubbing shoulders with out-of-character talk."

Writing in *The New York Times,* Eugene Archer said, "Most of the qualities that have made Nicholas Ray one of America's most highly praised directors abroad while leaving him relatively unpopular and unknown at home are clearly apparent in *The Savage Innocents.* Even though the movie is badly cut and a bitter drama, Mr. Ray's highly individualist preoccupation with moral tensions expresses itself in a series of unusually provocative scenes. This strange, disturbing drama will leave most of its viewers dissatisfied and some outraged, but few will remain indifferent."

Some of the best reviews came from the public at large, "Kenneth B." giving it four and a half stars. "Unfairly dismissed at the time of its release, *The Savage Innocents* is one of Ray's greatest films. The ambitious parable about the culture clash between the civilized and the savage benefits greatly from its semi-documentary style and beautiful imagery."

Other reviews were more critical, including that posted by "Brother Deacon": "If Johnny Weissmuller traded his Tarzan loincloth for seal-skin pantaloons and a polar bear parka, he'd fit ever so snugly into this mindless Eskimo yarn. Instead, we have Anthony Quinn as the Rousseau-styled Noble Savage blathering in pidgin English.

By 1963, Nicholas Ray had forgiven O'Toole for his outbursts. While living in Madrid, he was at work on a script called Road to the Snail, *whose leading role he planned to offer to O'Toole. If that hadn't worked, he'd intended to present it either to Peter Ustinov or to James Stewart.*

The project died.]

His role was small, but even so, O'Toole's name, as he requested, is conspicuously absent from this movie poster.

158

Chapter 11

Great Catherine

French Avant-Garde Diva, Jeanne Moreau, opposite
O'Toole, Interprets the German-born Russian Empress

Peter O'Toole's Lifelong Allegiance to the Welsh Actor

Kenneth Griffith,

"A Vision of Chartreuse Appears Before Me, Feeds Me His
Tongue, & Calls Me 'Darling'"
—Thus Begins a To-The-Grave Friendship

| Diplomatic immunity? O'Toole plays a resourceful and cooperative 18th Century English envoy to the court of a "*what she wants she gets*" Russian autocrat, played by Jeanne Moreau. | Catherine the Great, Empress of all the Russias, ruled from 1762-1796. Were those rumors about sexual relations with her soldiers and their horses really true? |

Peter O'Toole and Kenneth Griffith met in London when Rediffusion Studios decided to make a low budget quickie entitled *The Pier* in 1957. At the

Bristol Old Vic that same year, O'Toole had been cast as a "Teddy Boy" in neo-Edwardian dress, and he was asked to repeat his role for broadcast on "the British telly."

For three days, the director, Peter Zadek, waited for O'Toole to show up in the basement of the Irish Club, in the Islington section of London, where the film was being shot.

On the fourth day, O'Toole, dressed all in chartreuse except for his lime-green "Irish socks," walked in. "Hello darlings," he called out to the director and crew. "I'm here. Sorry to be so late."

"The Griffith" Bromances
"The Toole"

Griffith, as the leader of a gang of Teddy Boys, was asked to perform a scene with O'Toole from the James Forsyte script.

At the end of their scene, O'Toole approached Griffith, looking him straight in the eye. "I think you were bloody marvelous, darling," he said. Then he grabbed Griffith and passionately kissed him on the lips, feeding him his serpentine tongue. "From the taste of his tongue, I knew this tall young tramp had had shepherd's pie for a pub lunch," Griffith said.

"I assumed Peter was gay, and that he found me immensely attractive," Griffith recalled. "How wrong I was. After the scene, I just stood there, thoroughly kissed, the best kiss of my entire life, but I came to realize that as an actor, I faced the most formidable competition that I had dreaded to meet. His performance was word perfect and flawless. I actually believed he was a Teddy Boy, [i.e., a member of a British hooligan movement during the 1950s and

"My Terrible Beloved Friend Peter O'Toole Will Drive Me to the Gates of Hell, But I Can't Resist the Ride." —Kenneth Griffith

"Kenneth Griffith Is a Dangerous Marxist." —Prime Minister Margaret Thatcher

"Kenneth Griffith is the Most Distinguished of British Troublemakers." —Peter O'Toole

160

early 1960s, identified by their dandified, neo-Edwardian dress code] hanging out with the other fops at the Brighton Pier.

O'Toole had never heard of Griffith, a man eleven years his senior. Reared by his grandparents in Wales, Griffith as a schoolboy became "a lively rugby union scrum-half." At the age of sixteen, he became a stage actor, appearing in a modernized production, wearing contemporary street clothes, of *Julius Caesar* at Cambridge. In 1938, he'd made his debut in London's West End, taking a minor role in Thomas Dekker's *Shoemaker's Holiday.* After that, he functioned as what the Brits call "a regular jobbing repertory actor," touring from town to town.

With the outbreak of World War II, Griffith joined the RAF in Canada, where he came down with scarlet fever. "I was invalided *(sic)* out of the war," he said.

After his return to England, he starred in his first film role in 1941. That launched him into a career that would span some one hundred movies between 1941 and 1980.

O'Toole and Griffith traveled together, sharing a dressing room during their performance in *The Pier* on a stage in Manchester. The first question O'Toole asked was, "What fucking half of the mirror do I get to gaze upon my divine puss, a gift from the Gods, darling?"

After Manchester, from his then base in London, Griffith made three trips west to Bristol for performances of O'Toole in repertory at the Bristol Old Vic.

In his second memoir, O'Toole recalled countless evenings spent with Griffith in pubs. "He swilled a mouthful of Black Porter down his Welsh throat while informing me he was one of the 'Untouchables' of India, having been made an honorary member of that caste while filming a documentary in their midst. He defined the Untouchables as 'Children of God.'"

On many of their pub crawls, Griffith's eccentricities became obvious, thanks to his wearing of the the uniform (red coat, black trousers, and white pith helmet) of the 24th Regiment of the South Wales Borderers when they were massacred by the Zulus in the Battle of Islandwana in 1879.

Despite their status as intimate friends, O'Toole and Griffith referred to each other by their last names, except when tipsy. During those moments, Griffith called his friend "Dainty Duck."

Griffith and O'Toole became the closest of confidants. They talked endlessly about their darkest secrets, their most awesome fears, their hopes, their dreams, their ambitions, even their feelings about women. They even discussed homosexuality, during which O'Toole assured Griffith that although a whiff of homosexuality was probably buried deep within everyone, he, at least, was thoroughly heterosexual.

"Dainty Duck didn't just tell me he was straight, he demonstrated it night

161

after night with the dollybirds who chased after him when he became a big-time movie star," Griffith said.

During the days, weeks, months, and years to come, O'Toole and Griffith would be 'bound-at-the-hip-blokes,' as O'Toole so colorfully put it. "We are, in fact, Siamese twins."

Some of their acquaintances assumed that they were lovers. As Griffith later told friends, "Dainty Duck and I drank together, pissed together in the loos, hung out nude together in hotel rooms, and even slept together, but sexual passion was not part of our repertoire in spite of what people said. I emphatically deny it."

A favorite subject of conversation involved the theatre. O'Toole told Griffith, "Most of show business is a monumental shithouse, and I'm going to be a big shithouse keeper."

"Peter O'Toole was one of the handful of people who radically changed my life—and for the good," wrote Griffith in his memoir, *The Fool's Pardon.* "Before I met him, he was unknown to me. I knew he had talent clearly from his first cough. I wondered what sort of human being lay inside this explosive theatrical pirate. His big contribution to my life was painting it large. He urged me to go all out for the roof of the Sistine Chapel."

"As an actor, O'Toole was no mumble-mumble Marlon Brando," Griffith said, "and he did not suffer the frigid intellectualizing of Laurence Olivier. He was also honest. Because he picked his nose in private, he insisted on doing so in public as well. Since he pissed in private, he sometimes pissed in public right on the sidewalk."

"No deception," O'Toole said.

Patricia Neal (a Married Woman) Gets Hit Upon by the Married Peter O'Toole, Who Declares Himself a Better Lover than Ronald Reagan

Around the time O'Toole became close friends with Griffith, he met actress Siân Phillips, who in 1959 would become his first and only wife.

In a memoir, Siân wrote, "Griffith adored and admired O'Toole, and the feeling was mutual. He welcomed me as a fellow Welsh countryman, but he opposed my marriage to O'Toole."

"You cannot marry this wonderful man," Griffith told her. "Understand me, he is a genius, but he is not normal."

"I was so deliriously in love that I couldn't understand why Griffith was worried," Siân said.

After O'Toole married Siân in Ireland in 1959, they went to live with Griffith in his "shoebox" of a mews house on a relatively unfashionable edge of the otherwise very fashionable district of Belgravia. It opened onto a view of the back side of the headquarters of the National Coal Board. They shared the house with Doria Noar, whom Griffith would later marry.

"The bed Siân and I shared was held up with postage stamps," O'Toole recalled, a reference to his friend's postal history catalogues.

With a new wife and needing a flat of their own, O'Toole sought extra work, even venturing into television. For a 1961 release of a TV series *Rendezvous,* he appeared in three episodes as a character called "John." In one airplane drama, he co-starred with Patricia Neal. He was captivated by her, comparing her to "a healthy belt of Kentucky bourbon," a reference to her native state.

Patricia Neal, as she appeared in *Hud* (1963) two years after working with O'Toole on a TV episode in 1961.

Prior to that, she had starred in several movies and sustained a brief romance with Ronald Reagan, pictured below with her in his oh-so-brief panties.

At a dinner party in 1951 hosted by Lillian Hellman, Neal had met the British writer Roald Dahl, marrying him in 1953.

O'Toole knew that at the age of twenty-one in 1947, Neal had met and fallen in love with Gary Cooper, who was a married forty-six at the time. In 1949, when she went to London to film *The Hasty Heart* with Ronald Reagan, they had had a brief affair. *[At the time, Reagan was recovering from his divorce from Jane Wyman, and she was agonizing over her tumultuous relationship with Cooper.]*

Even though Neal was married to Dahl at the time, O'Toole was attracted to her subtle charm and beauty and a voice that he found could be alternatively sexy yet comforting. One night, she politely rejected "your lovely offer" after he propositioned her.

As he later told Griffith, "She did it in a style so charming that I did not feel rejected as a man. I assured her that I would be a far better seducer than Ronald Reagan, but I did-

n't know about Gary Cooper. He had quite a reputation back then."

O'Toole and Neal parted on friendly terms, and he later expressed delight when she won an Oscar as Best Actress for her performance opposite Paul Newman in *Hud* (1963).

Although the best of friends, O'Toole and Griffith often aired their differences. One point of dispute was over Siân. According to Griffith, "Dainty Duck could not forgive his wife for having known other lovers. She'd even been married before. He found her previous life beyond pardon.'"

In the presence of Griffith, she once heatedly said to her husband, "Forgive me for having lived a life before I met you."

"Sometimes, Peter would go raging through the house," Griffith said. "To my knowledge, he never struck her, but he was known to break the crockery in his fury."

"Although he chastised Siân for her past, he somehow overlooked his own philandering during marriage," Griffith said. "Once, he looked me straight in the face and told me that he was never unfaithful to her. He'd seemingly forgotten that only the previous night, he'd told me about going to bed with two sisters at the same time."

One night when O'Toole stumbled into the house and didn't find Siân at home, he tossed what he called her "bourgeois wardrobe" into the street, where it was immediately hauled away by scavengers. For the next few days, until she could replace her clothing, she was seen wearing castaways from her husband's wardrobe.

A few months after their marriage, O'Toole and Siân performed together in a Saunders Lewis play, *Siwan,* for Welsh TV. She had previously performed that role at the reopening of the Hampstead Theatre Club, while pregnant with her daughter, Kate, concealing her condition in a 13th century costume.

She called Lewis a great Welsh writer who "helped me change my life by leaving Wales for London and RADA."

She later claimed that "My big concern was, would O'Toole help me with the baby?"

"Dainty Duck" Conquers Stratford-Upon-Avon
Swilling Beer with Young Men on the Make at the Dirty Duck

For the 1960 Season in Stratford-upon-Avon, O'Toole had signed with Sir Peter Hall, founder of the Royal Shakespeare Theatre there, to appear in three of his Shakespearean productions.

Since he and his wife, Siân, would be in Stratford for several months,

O'Toole rented themselves a large Edwardian house. Previously, it had been lived in by playwright John Osborne during his tumultuous relationship with Mary Ure.

Griffith arrived for their housewarming and found O'Toole in a foul mood. "He was drinking a lot at the time, even though it was seriously damaging his body. At times, he became Dracula-like and very abusive. I put up with him because I loved him dearly. But he had this serpentine tongue which was used for more than kissing. He would turn into a vicious-like cobra. Siân was his victim. I feared their months-old marriage was doomed. I don't know how she stuck it out."

During that period, although O'Toole seemed in constant pain with stomach cramps, he refused to see a doctor. According to Griffith, "He consumed this bloody awful milky ulcer medicine, while downing vast amounts of Scotch. And if his excessive drinking weren't enough, he also chain-smoked those strong Gauloise cigarettes. Sometimes, he'd recover for a few days, then the stomach pain would reoccur. I feared that one day, he'd end up on an operating table or else on a slab of marble in the morgue."

The Royal Shakespeare Company had launched its 1960 season with a production of *Two Gentlemen of Verona,* starring Paul Scoffield. Reviews were lackluster and attendance was poor. Hall was hoping that O'Toole's upcoming appearance as Petruchio in *The Taming of the Shrew* would rescue the company from its doldrums.

Rehearsals had gone well, but on the night the curtain rose for the production's premier, O'Toole had disappeared. Hall pleaded with Griffith to find him.

Griffith searched his house, but no O'Toole. Finally, Griffith went out into the building's rear garden and found him asleep in a swing.

"I slapped him into reality," Griffith said. "When he finally came to, he told me he'd taken 'a long, very long, and longer still snooze.' I rushed him to the theater and virtually dressed him to go on. He just made it as the curtain went up."

In spite of O'Toole's condition, he performed the role brilliantly and even received a standing ovation. With this Shakespeare play, he became officially recognized, even by London's Fleet Street critics, as an exciting new talent to be reckoned with.

The Taming of the Shrew—always a crowd-pleaser—as performed here by Peter O'Toole as Petruchio opposite (Dame) Peggy Ashcroft as Katherine, the Shrew.

He followed his initial success with major

roles in two more Shakespeare plays. They included a stint as the controversial Shylock in *The Merchant of Venice,* and later that season, as Thersites in *Troilus and Cressida,* with Denham Elliott and Dorothy Tutin in the title roles.

Many admirers of O'Toole rode the northbound trains from London to Stratford to see the plays. Unfortunately, the last train from Stratford back to London left before the curtain went down, and consequently, many of these Londoners couldn't return home until the following morning.

In a gesture of goodwill, O'Toole repeatedly invited many of these guests to spend the night in his rented home, invitations which transformed the place into a sort of communal crash pad. To the exasperation of Siân, she would often find ten to twelve guests sleeping in her living room. O'Toole would arrive after a performance with his fans, demanding that Siân serve food to them. On one summer evening, some twenty overflow guests had to sleep on blankets in the front yard.

O'Toole as Shylock in *The Merchant of Venice* (1960).

Siân told Griffith that she needed a nanny, and he showed up the next day with a young American man, Lonnie Trimble. "He was black, an ex-marine from Atlanta," she later wrote. "He'd tasted unsegregated life in the *[U.S.]* Navy and found it impossible to resume a segregated existence by returning to Georgia. He was in England with no job, no work permit, and he needed some humble employment to keep him

O'Toole as Thersites in *Troilus and Cressida* at the RSC (1960)

afloat for three years so he could become a legal resident and pursue his career goal of becoming a chef."

Consequently, after the O'Tooles hired him as their nanny, he looked after Baby Kate and tended to chores around the house. He also proved himself adept as a barbecue chef, feeding O'Toole's constant flow of overnight guests.

On and off throughout the day, and during otherwise unoccupied parts of the evening, O'Toole frequented The Dirty Duck, a pub in Stratford that was popular with actors in the Shakespeare Company. One night, O'Toole set a record by downing a "yard of ale" (two and a half pints) in forty seconds.

When Griffith wasn't in Stratford hobnobbing with O'Toole, Dinsdale Landen and Jackie McGowan became his drinking companion. Every night, O'Toole was surrounded by admirers, mostly wannabe actors who found him a dashing hero, and they seemed to dote on his every pronouncement.

As Griffith noted, "A lot of these handsome young men assumed that O'Toole was gay, and many of them made themselves sexually available to him. He spurned offers of sex. However, he did tongue kiss these young men and call them *darling*. Could that have been what caused them to think Dainty Duck at the Dirty Duck was gay? I wonder."

Diva This, Diva That!
Sultry-Eyed Jeanne Moreau, Darling of the French New Wave, Plays an Autocratic Russian Empress

"Dainty Duck (O'Toole) and I had many plans to work together," Griffith said, "but we never became the Katharine Hepburn and Spencer Tracy of films. When we did work in the same movie, *Great Catherine* (1967), it was a spectacular flop."

O'Toole's concept of what would be an ideal vehicle for them as actors was a film version of Samuel Beckett's *Waiting for Godot,* in which O'Toole had performed so successfully at the Bristol Old Vic. Despite the playwright's warning that he did not think that his play would translate well into, or be successful, as a film, O'Toole, as producer, forged ahead with it anyway.

As financing for his production, O'Toole managed to raise £20,000, after which he set about working on a script. It was clearly understood that in his film version of *Waiting for Godot,* he would be cast in the star role of Vladimir and Griffith would be cast as Estragon.

Difficulties arose, and the cherished project was never made.

However, when O'Toole and his partner, Jules Buck, acquired the film rights to George Bernard Shaw's one-act 1903 play, *Whom Glory Still Adores,* O'Toole, again as its producer, found a role in it for Griffith. Shaw's play was devoted to Catherine the Great, the powerful and charismatic Empress (ruling from 1762 until her death in 1796) of Russia.

O'Toole, naturally, played the male lead, a British officer sent by the British government as envoy to the Russian court of Catherine the Great. For the key role of Catherine, he considered many possibilities. At one point, he even met with Elizabeth Taylor, but after her experience of playing another great queen,

Cleopatra (1963), she turned him down. She did, however, invite him to spend a "layover" with her, as she had the following two nights free.

Many actresses had played Catherine before, even Mae West in her 1944 stage play, *Catherine Was Great*. A year later, In Ernest Lubitsch's *A Royal Scandal* (1945), Tallulah Bankhead "rattled the palace windowpanes," according to one critic.

O'Toole finally decided on the French actress, Jeanne Moreau, who had entered a peak period in her career during the 1960s.

O'Toole, as Britain's Military Envoy, dabbles in international diplomacy.

The daughter of a French restaurateur and an English chorus girl, Moreau was an actress, singer, writer, and director. Film critic Molly Haskell labeled her, "A glorious fantasy, appealing to both sexes, to men as eternal mistress, to woman as a Nietzschean Superwoman."

Although it had been a long time since the press had celebrated Moreau as "The New Bardot," during the course of her career, she had

Jeanne Moreau, darling and muse of the *avant-garde* French Left.

worked with such magnetic directors as Michelangelo Antonioni, Luís Buñuel, Elia Kazan, Rainer Werner Fassbinder, Carl Foreman, and Orson Welles, who had called her "the greatest actress in the world."

The turning point in her life occured in 1957, when she and French filmmaker, Louis Malle, made a modernist *film noir* masterpiece called *Ascenseur pour l'échafaud [released in the U.S. as* Frantic *and in the U.K. as* Lift to the Scaffold]*, and the notorious, sexually frank drama, *Les Amants.*

Many of the stellar lights of cinema also enjoyed affairs with her. A partial list includes Jean Gabin, Edouard Molinaro, and Jacques Becker.

Notable achievements included *Dangerous Liaisons*, with the semi-pornographic Roger Vadim; *Jules et Jim* with François Truffaut; eccentric choral master Jacques Demy *(La baie des anges),* Spanish surrealist Luís Buñuel, and exiled and the "blacklisted by the McCarthyites" American genius, Joseph Losy.

At the time of her casting in *Great Catherine,* Moreau had recently married Teodoro Rubanis, the Greek actor/playboy. Consequently, although she became known for her affairs—including interludes with fashion designer Pierre Cardin and jazz trumpeter Miles Davis—O'Toole didn't expect much action from her after dark.

He knew that she moved in literary circles, enjoying friendships with such writers as Jean Cocteau, Jean Genet, Henry Miller, and Marguerite Duras.,

[Moreau's marriage ultimately failed, and in its aftermath, she fell into the arms of film director Tony Richardson, who left his wife, Vanessa Redgrave, for her. Moreau and Richardson never married.] "With that impressive roster, what would Moreau need with a ghetto boy from Leeds?" O'Toole asked Griffith.

In the film, the autocratic Empress of all the Russians craftily lures the handsome O'Toole away from his perky English fiancée.

O'Toole and Buck hired Elliott Silverstein as their film's director, but he soon left the picture, telling the press, "I will not be a lackey to the star." O'Toole then hired George Flemyng to replace him.

The new director described O'Toole as producer and star as "darting about in full costume like a greyhound smelling an electric hare."

Insofar as props were concerned, O'Toole scored a coup by persuading the London-based owners of the Romanov's crown jewels to lend them to his production company. Ironically, when Moreau appeared in some of her scenes wearing the actual jewelry owned by that doomed family, O'Toole publicly asserted that they were paste, fearing, as he did, a major jewelry heist.

For the key role of Patiomkin, O'Toole hired Zero Mostel, a personal friend who, when he was in London, often visited his home in Hampstead for dinner.

Mostel's antics stole the picture. As the one-eyed, cross-eyed Potiomkin, Chancellor to the Empress, "He pulls down the place with his bare hands," wrote the critic for *The New York Times.* "He comes on so strong in the opening minutes and explodes thereafter with such wild, slapstick abandon that the rest of the picture pales and teeters uncertainly."

"Jamming on a disheveled wig and slashing at it with a hairbrush, amid clouds of powder, Mostel is overpowering" the critic claimed. "Whether he is raging, whining, denouncing Voltaire, or funneling wine, the picture is his—and Shaw's, in that order."

At the end of the movie, Mostel had to work two days over the time limit established in his contract. "He practically held me up for ransom, which ended our friendship," O'Toole said. "I've never seen such a greedy beast trying to squeeze the last bob out of me as producer."

The Russian character actor Akim Tamiroff also appeared in the movie, as he had three years before in O'Toole's

Zero Mostel, Chief Majordomo to the Empress, playing a barely gentrified pig in silk undergarments.

Lord Jim (1965). In *Great Catherine,* he was cast as a Russian sergeant.

In a sentimental gesture, O'Toole cast his friend, Jack Hawkins, as the suave British ambassador to Moscow. Calling him "The Hawk," O'Toole and Hawkins had bonded when they'd made *Lawrence of Arabia* together back in 1962.

This was the first role that Hawkins had played since an operation to remove his larynx. He had

Jack Hawkins...with his larynx removed

Akim Tamiroff... Bombastic, smarmy, and edgy

great difficulty in uttering any sound, and his lines proved a daunting task for the recording department, who worked overtime to make his (dubbed) words flow smoothly.

[In 1973, long after the completion of Great Catherine, *Hawkins endured an operation whose intention involved the installation of an artificial voicebox to allow him to speak in his almost normal voice. An infection developed from the incision in his throat. He kept hemorrhaging, resulting in his premature death on July 18 at the age of sixty-three.]*

A highlight of *Great Catherine* occurred when a horde of fiery Cossack dancers bursts onto the screen before a sedate ballroom crowd for some dazzling choreography.

Great Catherine was both an artistic and financial failure. *TV Guide* wrote: "They waited 55 years to make Shaw's play into a film, and would have been well-advised to wait another 55 years. What a mishmash!"

The picture did win a rave for its lavish décor, costumes, and color photography.

In spite of the blasts from critics, Griffith, an ever-faithful friend, commended O'Toole's performance, calling it "a role he pulled off with anarchic brilliance."

At the end of filming, O'Toole announced, "I will never star *and* produce a movie ever again. *Great Catherine* was my lesson in disillusionment."

A Radical Filmmaker (Griffith)
And a "Theatrical Pirate" (O'Toole)
Evoke the Ire of Britain's Prime Minister

In addition to being an actor, Griffith was known for making radical documentaries. Britain's Prime Minister, Margaret Thatcher, denounced him as a "dangerous Marxist." O'Toole called him "the most distinguished of British troublemakers."

Over the decades, O'Toole avidly followed his best friend's political activities and controversial filmmaking. Griffith became the most banned filmmaker in England, referring to his censors at the BBC as "those priggish cuckoos."

"His troubles with the bluenoses left poor Griffith a frustrated and bemused figure, but in time, at least by 1993, his documentaries were screened to more sophisticated world," O'Toole said. *Screenonline* defined Griffith as "a world class documentary filmmaker, who knows that refusing to compromise his views had damaged his career."

Griffith was also a fiery supporter of the Afrikaners of South Africa, and a renowned Boer War historian. His entire house, even its bathrooms, were filled with artifacts from the Boer War.

His controversial Boer War documentary film was released in 1967 as *Soldiers of the Widow.*

In 1973, the BBC banned Griffith's documentary about Michael Collins, the Irish military and political leader. Entitled *Hang Up Your Brightest Colours,* when it was shown in Ireland, it brought death threats from British loyalists in Northern Ireland.

Griffith and O'Toole became so close they often went on holiday together. Italy and Switzerland were their favorite destinations.

Griffith tended to handle O'Toole's quirky behavior with a certain delicacy. Driving with him in the Swiss Alps near the Brenner Pass, he said to him, "I say, old boy, you're doing very well, but you should not try to change gears with your hand brake." At one point, in a diplomatic way, he suggested that O'Toole should get a driver's license.

From Switzerland, as part of a short holiday, the two actors drove south to Lake Como in Italy. It was there, at a lakeside hotel, that O'Toole announced one drunken night that he was going to commit suicide in the dark but moonlit waters of the lake.

"I didn't swim, and I went in a panic, fearing I would be unable to rescue him without drowning myself.

The Terror of the British Left:
Prime Minister and Iron Lady
Margaret Thatcher

About twelve feet from me, he plunged into the sea. I feared that all was lost. Then he rose from the water. It seemed that the lake was only two feet deep at that point."

Dripping wet, he came back with me to his room, where I stripped him down and dried him off. He didn't drown, but caught a bloody cold."

Griffith later said, "Life with O'Toole might be unhealthy, it might even be hazardous to your life if you were on an alpine peak, but it was always filled with adventure."

As he became well known as an actor, O'Toole "did not jump up and dance at every offer that came in," Griffith said. "Sometimes I would answer his phone since we were together so much. He'd be lying on the sofa, instructing me, 'Griffith, be a darling and tell whoever it is I'm having a kip'—his word for a much-needed rest when he was usually recovering from an all-night drunk."

Griffith suffered through O'Toole's ongoing roster of Oscar losses at various Academy Awards presentations. "The Academy clearly had to nominate him—you can't ignore such a person who, as an actor, is in a class all his own. But so deeply do they resent his independence, and his cheeky refusal to show respect, where rarely any respect is due, that they would go to the very lengths that they have to deny him first prize. Posterity will give him an Oscar."

During his twilight years, Griffith suffered from Alzheimer's Disease. O'Toole visited his bedside whenever he could. "I was sad, so very sad. I was there, offering friendship long after he ceased to know who I was."

Griffith died at the age of eight-four in June of 2006.

O'Toole was one of his pallbearers.

Chapter 12

Lawrence of Arabia (Part One)
A Towering Moment in the History of Cinema

Cast as a Desert Warrior, Peter O'Toole
Skyrockets into International Stardom

The real (relatively short) T. E. Lawrence (left); and the (tall) actor who portrayed him (Peter O'Toole, on the right) both headed to the desert for greatness.

Lawrence stated in his novel, *The Seven Pillars of Wisdom,* "All men dream, but not equally. Those who dream by night in the dusty reesses of their minds wake up in the day to find that it was vanity, but the dreamers of the day are dangerous men, for they may act their dreams with open eyes, to make it possible. This I did."

T.E. Lawrence's portrait was taken in 1918 by Harry Chase, cameraman to Lowell Thomas. O'Toole's, on the right, was snapped as part of the pre-production costume fittings for the movie that made him famous, *Lawrence of Arabia.*

Released in December of 1962, the film epic, *Lawrence of Arabia,* was produced by Sam Spiegel and directed by David Lean. It transformed the Irish-born actor and hellraiser, Peter O'Toole, known for his carousing and drinking, into an international star.

Today, the film is widely considered as one of the greatest movies of all time. In 1997, it was deemed "culturally, historically, and aesthetically significant" for preservation in the United States' Library of Congress.

Spiegel recalled, "Getting the rights, casting it, setting up the desert locations in a hostile terrain, and the actual filming, along with countless personal disasters, involved a strategy that evoked General Eisenhower's planning of the D-Day landing on the beaches of Normandy in 1944. I do not exaggerate when I say that *Lawrence of Arabia* shaved ten years off my life...at least."

O'Toole's appearance on

Their collaboration went deep:

Director David Lean (left), though behind the scenes, deserves almost as much acclaim as that generated by his actors, having nursed and nurtured the production through obstacles ranging from the contemporary to the medieval.

One of his self-assigned tasks involved teaching O'Toole (right) how to handle a firearm and shoot.

the screen in flowing white robes brought a charismatic actor to the attention of the world. He was cast as the enigmatic T. E. Lawrence, the guerilla leader of Arab tribesman during World War I in the battle against the Turks of the Ottoman Empire, who were on the side of the Kaiser's German soldiers during this epic war.

O'Toole dazzled audiences as he never had before and would never again. "It was my shining hour," he recalled, "actually my shining hours. The damn thing ran for four hours under that blazing desert sun beating down on my lily-white body."

The film elevated Lawrence into a bigger legend than he had been during his lifetime. It transformed this controversial British soldier-adventurer into an almost mythical hero. His exploits were displayed against an eye-popping

"One of the Seven Wonders of the Cinematic World"

— The Los Angeles Times

Arabian spectacle which included dazzling displays of foreboding desert, racing camels, larger-than-life sheiks, raging battles, and lots of blood, gore, explosions and gunfire.

In 1963, at the 35th Academy Awards presentation in Santa Monica, California, an event hosted by Frank Sinatra, *Lawrence of Arabia* was nominated for ten Oscars, seven of which it won, including Best Picture and Best Director. O'Toole received the first of his eight Oscar nominations, all of which he subsequently lost.

International stardom was nonetheless his. He was deluged with fan letters, many from women proposing seductions and including naked pictures. He also developed a wide array of devoted admirers from homosexual communities around the globe.

Near the end of his life, and in the wake of a long career, O'Toole predicted, "When I die, newspapers will herald my passing with this headline— PETER O'TOOLE, STAR OF *LAWRENCE OF ARABIA*, DIES...You fill in the year."

His words were prophetic. The actual date of his death was December 14, 2013. He remained employed as an actor until the very end.

Who in the Hell was T. E. Lawrence?
The World Wanted to Know, but He Died
"A Mystery Wrapped in an Enigma"

Lawrence of Arabia opens with a depiction of the 1935 motorcycle crash that took the life of T.E. Lawrence, and an insight into his subsequent funeral. At his burial at St. Paul's Cathedral in London, a war correspondent portrayed by Arthur Kennedy extols Lawrence's heroic qualities. Then, in an undertone, he claims, "He was the most shameless exhibitionist since Barnum & Bailey." His muttered critique nearly erupts into a fistfight on the steps of St. Paul's. The character who said that was based on Lowell Thomas.

Like most legends, an air of mystery envelops an overview of T.E. Lawrence. There is no doubt that he performed unique heroic deeds, but much of his legend was invented by the media, notably by Lowell Thomas (the character played by Kennedy in the movie). Thomas' bestselling 1924 book, *With Lawrence in Arabia,* did much to introduce "this modern Arabian knight" to the American public.

Thomas—a world traveler, writer, photographer, and radio broadcaster— met Lawrence in Jerusalem and wrote of his adventures, returning to America early in 1919 to launch a series of lectures backed up by dramatic film footage. These highly dramatic portraits of Lawrence, flamboyantly attired in

Arab dress, fanned his exotic legend in the West in an era when Rudolf Valentino, hero of Silent Films, was reinforcing the romantic image of "The Sheik of Araby."

East is East and West is West, and never the twain shall meet—unless it applied to T. E. Lawrence, the "culturally schizophrenic" subject of both of the photos above.

Thomas' lectures and film clips depicted Arabs in flowing white robes, camels racing through the desert with dashing Bedouin cavalry riders on their backs, and mysterious veiled women, seemingly from the pages of *Arabian Nights*.

Although Thomas extolled the glamor of Lawrence, he could also be critical. "He pretended to be publicity shy, but he had a genius for backing into the limelight."

About four million people saw the film and heard Thomas lecture, netting him a profit of $1.5 million, a vast sum in the mid-1920s.

Born in Wales in 1888, Lawrence was the illegitimate son of a British Lord, Sir Thomas Chapman, and Sarah Junner, a governess who was herself illegitimate. His father bestowed a false name on his son, baptizing him as Thomas Edward Lawrence, later shortened to T. E.

Educated at Oxford (1907-10), Lawrence set out to be an archeologist in the Middle East.

At the outbreak of World War I in 1914, he joined British Army Intelligence and was assigned to make a military survey of the Negev Desert. At the time, the Ottoman Turks, who occupied all but the most barren parts of the region, were allied with the German Kaiser's army.

Lawrence became celebrated for his liaison role during Britain's Sinai and Palestine Campaigns and again during the Arab Revolt against the Ottoman Turkish Empire. He later referred to the Arab revolt against the brutal Turks as "a sideshow of a sideshow."

In 1917, he and his forces captured the strategic town of Aqaba (whose name translates from the Arabic as "The Obstacle"), a Jordanian coastal city that opens onto the northeastern tip of the Red Sea. It is Jordan's only seaport, with a history going back to 4,000 B.C. The capture of Aqaba alleviated the threat of a Turkish offensive against Britain's control of the strategic Suez Canal.

After taking the city, the British promoted Lawrence to the rank of Major, and defined him as the new commander-in-chief of their Egyptian Expeditionary Force. The Sherif of Mecca called Lawrence "a very inspiring gentleman adventurer." The Britisher was also involved in the capture of Damascus, the most important city in Syria, from the Ottomans during the final weeks of World War I.

After all this worldwide publicity, in August of 1922, Lawrence enlisted in the Royal Air Force, using the pseudonym "John Hume Ross." Unable to avoid his previous notoriety, his identity was exposed in February of 1923, and he was forced out of the RAF. Changing his name to "T.E. Shaw" he then opted to join the Royal Tank Corps.

Unhappy there, he was readmitted to the RAF in August of 1925. In 1926, he was assigned to a remote base in British-ruled India, where he remained, quietly, until the end of 1928. He then returned to Britain, where he continued to serve in the RAF until his enlistment ended in March of 1935.

In 1922, he'd written a memoir, *Seven Pillars of Wisdom,* its title deriving from some lines within the Old Testament's Book of Proverbs. It became an international bestseller. The reading public was enraptured by his exploits, although many historians took a dim view, critic Charles Hill evaluating his autobiography as "a novel traveling under the cover of autobiography."

Ironically, he lost its first draft while changing trains in Reading (England), and later, painstakingly, had to reconstruct it.

The book was dedicated to "S.A." There was speculation that the initials stood for Selim Ahmed, a handsome teenaged boy from Syria. Lawrence was rumored to have fallen in love with the boy, who died at the age of nineteen from typhus right before Lawrence's offensive to liberate Damascus.

Before his autobiography was printed, and prompted by fears of libel, certain sections were eliminated. Sir Winston Churchill called it "one of the greatest books ever written in the English language." George Bernard Shaw also read the original "warts-and-all" edition, later denouncing its heavily edited International Edition as "an abridgement of an abridgment. I hold it in disdain."

T. E. Lawrence, on a motorbike equivalent to the one he was riding when he was killed.

In 1935, at the age of 46, only two months after his exit from the RAF, Lawrence died. A keen motorcyclist, he was riding near his cottage, Clouds Hill, in Dorset. At a dip in the road, where his view was obstructed, he swerved to avoid hitting two boys on their bicycles. Losing control, he was thrown over his handlebars. He died six days later in a local hospital.

Churchill said, "Though Mr. Lawrence is dead, he will live as a man for the ages."

"Meeting Katharine Hepburn Was a Pisser"
She Defines O'Toole as "Crown Prince of the Theater"

O'Toole recalled a turning point in his life that occurred in 1959 in London, where he was appearing on stage in the West End in *The Long And the Short And The Tall.*

[Set in British Malaya during World War II, O'Toole, one of a group of British soldiers headquartered in an abandoned tin mine, confronts a malfunctioning radio and an intrusion by a Japanese soldier.]

"There came a break in the play when I wasn't needed on stage," he said. "So I ducked out for a pint or two...I think it was at the Cricket, whose sticky floor was last mopped when Henry VIII was on the throne. I got tanked up."

"I rushed back to my dressing room, as nature sent out an urgent alarm. The star of the play was Robert Shaw. He had the sole crapper in his dressing room. I had only a little lavatory. I whipped it out for the piss of a lifetime. My kidneys were floating. All of a sudden, my door opened. I heard this voice. It was distinctive, one of the most recognizable on the planet."

"Good evening, Mr. O'Toole. I am Katharine Hepburn."

"I couldn't turn around. I couldn't stop. The gusher was going and I could not turn it off."

"Miss Hepburn, as was her naturally curious and nosy self, insisted on coming over for a closer inspection."

"Sorry," she said, looking down at what he called "my pride and passion."

"I thought your faucet had broken and was gushing water," she said. "I'm a pretty damn good plumber if I say so myself."

"Miss Hepburn," he said, shaking off the final drops of urine. Then he put

Über-diva and "sacred monster" Katharine Hepburn

his penis back in his trousers and zipping up, he turned to face her. "It's an honor to meet you. I'd shake your hand, but since you know where it's been, perhaps that is not a good idea."

"Of course, I'll shake your hand," she said in her formidable, almost aristocratic way. "I'm not afraid I'll be tainted by a human touch."

She had only high praise for his performance on the stage. "I think you have the potential to be a great stage star. If Olivier is the King of the British Theatre, you are at least its Crown Prince, waiting in the wings to take the crown from him."

"I'll convey that to him. I know he'll be delighted to hear that."

"Don't be impertinent with me, young man," Hepburn said, "though I recognize that such impudence is the hallmark of genius."

She turned to go. At the door, she looked back at him. "You'll be hearing from me...and others. Talent such as your must be shared with the world."

As he recalled that moment, he said, "I'm sure that many actors got their first big break by whipping it out for some cocksucker producer or director. In a sense, I launched myself into major stardom also by unzipping, but with a very different twist."

"There was a downside, however. In zipping up so fast, I seriously damaged my foreskin. For the next three days and nights, I was out of commission and had to endure a sexual famine until that wound could heal."

***

At Skepperton Studios outside London, producer Sam Spiegel and director Joseph Mankiewicz were filming Tennessee Williams' controversial *Suddenly, Last Summer,* starring Katharine Hepburn, Elizabeth Taylor, and Montgomery Clift. As the monstrous Violet Venable, Hepburn had been cast in her most unattractive screen role, as a tarantula mother who wanted a doctor to perform a lobotomy on Taylor to erase from her brain information about how her son, Sebastian, had died. *[As part of a sexual solicitation of their services, he was eaten alive by boy sex objects-turned-can-*

Who Is The Craziest Person In The Photo Above? *(Left to right*: Katharine Hepburn, Montgomery Clift, and Elizabeth Taylor.)

It depicts the difficult context O'Toole would have entered had he been "shoehorned" into the role of a surgical psychiatrist if the notoriously unstable Clift been fired.

179

nibals.]

Clift was in terrible shape, having been mended together again with the help of plastic surgeons after he'd survived a disfiguring car accident. He was physically and emotionally tormented, drinking heavily and taking drugs. Both Spiegel and Mankiewicz didn't think he'd be able to complete his work on their film.

Spiegel had arranged for actor Laurence Harvey to step into the role should Clift collapse. But in her meeting with both Mankiewicz and Spiegel, Hepburn felt that O'Toole would be much more talented as Clift's replacement. Based entirely on Hepburn's judgment and savvy, Speigel ordered a screen test for O'Toole.

He remembered a silver Jaguar sent for him to his lodgings in London, piloted by a hostile chauffeur. "I found out later that he was Monty's driver and that he didn't want his boss to lose the role."

After a transformation by Skepperton's makeup and wardrobe department, O'Toole appeared on the set dressed as a doctor ready to perform a lobotomy. He didn't seem to be taking the test too seriously. In one pivotal scene, he was required to hold up an X-Ray and examine it. He was given no line of dialogue, but told instead to improvise. Cheekily, he held up the X-ray and said, as the camera rolled, "Mrs. Spiegel, I don't think your son will ever play the violin again."

Spiegel was furious. "What impertinence. Get this ass out of here."

O'Toole took his time in leaving, at one point slipping onto a sound stage to witness a desperately ill Clift act his way through a difficult scene. In the script, he was supposed to be performing a delicate lobotomy in front of a gallery of future doctors. He had half a page of dialogue. Again and again, Mankiewicz ordered retakes.

Finally, after seventeen attempts, the director held up his gloved hands (he was suffering from a skin disease at the time), and ordered, "print the last one. It'll have to do."

"To me, Clift appeared on the verge of a nervous breakdown," O'Toole said. "I'm an expert on nervous breakdowns, so I should know."

In spite of his failed screen test, Hepburn still had faith in O'Toole. She came to tell him goodbye, wearing pants. Her hair was severely knotted into a bun. She wore no makeup and looked far older than her years. She kissed him on the cheek. "You're a damn good actor," she assured him. "We'll meet on some distant shore, of that I'm certain."

When he went outside to be driven back to Central London, the chauffeur-driven limousine had disappeared. In his pocket, he had just enough bus fare to make it back.

At this point, he spotted a completely made-up Elizabeth Taylor, accompanied by a wardrobe assistant, heading for a sound stage. He approached her, "Miss Taylor, I need your help. I'm Peter O'Toole. Spiegel hauled me out here to make a screen test. I said something smart ass, and now he's told the driver not to take me back."

At first, she seemed reluctant to get involved, but a pleading look on his face attracted her attention.

He looked into her eyes. "They weren't really violet," he later said. "Something between indigo and the deep blue sea. She seemed to be a really warm person."

"It's wrong for Spiegel, that asshole, to dump you like this," she said. "I'll have my personal driver take you back to London."

He leaned down to kiss her cheek in gratitude, but she backed away. "I can't allow that, because I have to pick cotton."

He later said, "I spent years trying to figure out what in hell she meant by that."

Since the 1920s, Producers Had Failed to Bring the T.E. Lawrence Saga to the Screen. Even Marilyn Monroe Sabotages the Project

Long before Sam Spiegel and David Lean launched their epic *Lawrence of Arabia,* many other producers had tried to make a movie out of T.E. Lawrence's *Seven Pillars of Wisdom,* or other books by or about the desert warrior.

In September of 1926, Lawrence was heavily in debt. He approached a young producer, Herbert Wilcox, a film mogul who had founded Astra Films at Kew, outside London, in 1919. Lawrence wanted him to make a film about his desert exploits during the Arab revolt. Lawrence came to him because of the producer's own military background, having served in the Royal Flying Corps during World War I.

British film mogul Herbert Wilcox, founder of Astra Films. Though interested at first, he was distressed by some of the vaguely homoerotic aspects of T. E. Lawrence's memoirs.

Wilcox described meeting Lawrence in his memoirs, finding him "Not very prepossessing. His story line was extremely interesting but not good cinema and in spots rather sordid. He told me of the homosexual advances of a Turkish chief and how in desperation one night, he fought him off with what he called 'a knee kick,' which resulted in the chief becoming disinterested in homo or any other form of sexual activity for a week or so, and the author being scourged and tortured for his attack. I ventured the opinion that I could not see cinema audiences seeking entertainment being attracted to such a subject. Lawrence did not agree, telling me that one day, it would make an outstanding film. He failed to sway me—but how right he was."

By 1927, a much-chastened Lawrence had paid off his debts and rejected a proposal by British director M.A. Wetherall to film his saga. When Lawrence was allowed to join the RAF, it was with the promise that he would avoid future publicity.

In 1934, the British film mogul, Alexander Korda, expressed interest in filming the story of Lawrence's life among the Arabs. Actor Leslie Howard bore a slight facial resemblance to Lawrence, and he was asked if he'd portray

> Alexander Korda, a Hungarian cosmopolite, was one of the many promising European directors who emigrated to Hollywood during the 1920s.
>
> In 1930, he left Hollywood, having rejected the strictures of its studio system to become an empire-builder in Europe, specifically Britain, where he wanted to film the T. E. Lawrence saga.

him on the screen. He agreed, with Lewis Milestone (*All Quiet on the Western Front*) directing.

At the time, Korda was the biggest name in British cinema. In 1933, he had scored an international success with the release of *The Private Life of Henry VIII*, starring Charles Laughton.

Ironically, Lawrence seemed to sabotage the project from its inception, making many demands, including that no females be depicted. "From end to end of it, there was nothing female in the Arab movement, but the camels."

Finally, during a dinner with Korda, Lawrence withdrew his consent to have his life portrayed on film. In a letter to author Robert Graves, he wrote, "I loathe the notion of being celluloided. My rare visits to cinemas always deepens me in a sense of their superficial falsity and vulgarity."

Following the death of Lawrence in 1935 in a motorcycle crash, Korda, though he denied it to the press, called Graves, asking him to write a script for a Lawrence movie.

Graves' task was eventually shifted to John Monk Saunders, who had written *Wings*—winner of the first Best Picture Academy Award, in 1927. He had also won an Oscar for *Dawn Patrol* (1930) for Best Original Screenplay.

Saunders was the husband of actress Fay Wray of *King Kong* fame.

Actor Walter Hudd, who resembled Lawrence somewhat, was to star in the film's title role. Lawrence himself had once suggested Hudd as *"the actor to play me on the screen."*

Hudd, a Londoner born in 1897, had appeared as a stage actor under the direction of the Old Vic and Stratford-upon-Avon theatrical companies. He didn't actually make a movie until the year of Lawrence's death, when he had a film role in Anthony Asquith's *Moscow Nights.*

Korda ordered his wardrobe department to dress Hudd in the robes of Lawrence for photographers. The producer liked the results, claiming that "Hudd actually looks like Lawrence, at least there's a resemblance."

Walter Hudd (1897-1963) was the actor most preferred by T.E. Lawrence to portray him in any biopic of his life.

Ironically, Hudd died the year O'Toole's film about Lawrence was released.

Korda later stopped production on the film because of the political unrest and fighting raging at the time in Palestine. Throughout much of 1936, Arabs in revolt were trying to drive out the British.

In the autumn of 1937, Leslie Howard, months before he played Ashley Wilkes in *Gone With the Wind,* was asked once again to star in a film entitled *Lawrence of Arabia,* with William Howard directing. Korda planned to shoot the film not in Palestine, but in the desert of Egypt.

When Howard accepted other roles, Korda, in 1938, produced *The Four Feathers,* a picture that became an epic success. Like O'Toole's *Lawrence of Arabia*, *Four Feathers* also would take two years to complete.

In spite of his earlier failure, Korda still nursed his dream of producing a movie about Lawrence. With Howard involved in his defining role as Ashley Wilkes in Hollywood, Korda asked both Laurence Olivier and later, Robert Donat to play Lawrence. Both of them had other commitments.

As a film producer, Korda was facing some thorny political issues since, at the time, Britain was friendly with the Turks, and they would be brutally depicted in the Lawrence film. Based on political alliances of that era, and under instructions from the British government, the Board of Censors threatened to forbid the release of the film in the United Kingdom.

However, once again, in 1939, on the eve of World War II in Europe, Korda announced the resumption of production on the Lawrence film, only to abandon it. Churchill asked him not to make the movie because, "We need the Turks on our side in the upcoming war against Germany." Korda was later revealed to be a secret agent working for the British government.

Ironically, at one point in the mid-1930s, Chruchill, a "closeted" screenwriter who recognized the nationalistic passion in the Lawrence saga, had been asked by Korda to write a scenario for the film, since the statesman so greatly admired the desert warrior's exploits and had such high praise for the *Seven Pillars of Wisdom.*

In 1954, producer Anatole de Grunwald acquired the rights to Liddell Hart's biography of Lawrence, paying 3,000 British pounds. Grunwald hired playwright Terence Rattigan to write the screenplay for the epic he hoped to film in the deserts of the Middle East.

Rattigan met with Grunwald, and the writer became intrigued with the project. "Lawrence and I have something in common," he confessed to Grunwald. "Like me, he is a homosexual."

Grunwald looked horrified. "That is your private business! We can't in any way portray homosexuality on the screen. The most we can do, perhaps, is to slyly suggest it in the torture scene by the Turkish soldiers when Lawrence is captured."

Two very avant-garde entertainment specialitsts tentatively collaborated on a film version of T. E. Lawrence's life: The Russo-British Film Producer, Anatole de Grunwald and......

Rattigan had a military background, having served in World War II as a tail gunner for the RAF. After the war, he became one of the best known of British playwrights, adept at both comedy and drama. His greatest success had come with such films as *The Winslow Boy* (1946).

Playwright Terence Rattigan

When he met Grunwald, he'd just completed his script for *Separate Tables* (1954), which became a film starring Rita Hayworth, Burt Lancaster, and David Niven.

Rattigan agreed that either Alec Guinness or Richard Burton should be asked to portray Lawrence on the screen.

The playwright had also penned a play entitled *The Sleeping Prince.* It was slated to be made into a film, retitled *The Prince and the Showgirl* (1957), a vehicle for Marilyn Monroe, with Laurence Olivier later cast as her leading man. The pairing was described as "the Oddest Couple of the Year," although the American director Josh Logan claimed it was "the best color combination since the invention of black and white."

Monroe and Olivier in promotional material for *The Prince and the Showgirl*, the film that derived, painfully, from Rattigan's play.

Jumping at the chance to write the screenplay for *The Prince and the Showgirl*, Rattigan abandoned his work on the Lawrence film.

In New York, Rattigan met with Monroe herself, who pleaded with him "to get Sir Larry to play the prince." He agreed, saying, "I will leave no stone unturned."

Not knowing he was a homosexual, she made advances to him to help her cause, but he graciously rejected her offers.

When she became aware of his gender preference, she told him, "I'm dating a very hot young man right now," she said. "If you wish, I'll turn him over to you during your stay in New York. He'll do anything I say."

He turned down that offer, too.

During the troubled production of *The Prince and the Showgirl* in London, Rattigan became so involved in the power struggle between its British and American stars that he later complained, "I forgot who T. E. Lawrence was."

He later claimed that Monroe "is a shy exhibitionist—a Garbo who likes to be photographed."

"Caught between Miss Monroe and Sir Larry has taken ten years off my life," he wrote to Grunwald. "If you proceed with the Lawrence film, you will have to use some other writer. Otherwise, I will return to the script if I survive Monroe. Talk about divas! In one scene, she has to nibble on a bite of caviar. It took two days, thirty-five different takes, and two dozen tins of Beluga caviar before she got the damn thing right! We never knew from day to day when she would show up. Apparently, in the beginning of the film, she seduced Sir Larry. Later, she humiliated him by talking about his so-called 'sexual inadequacy.'"

After *The Prince and the Showgirl* was finally wrapped, Rattigan did return to the Lawrence script and completed it. By that time, Grunwald had named Anthony Asquith as director, and he and Grunwald were scouting locations in Baghdad until they feared violence from some hostile Arabs, who spread the rumor that they planned to assassinate their king.

Asquith was nicknamed "Puffin" because of his slightly crooked nose. He was the son of Herbert Henry Asquith, the prime minister of Great Britain who had led his country into war against Germany in 1914.

Dirk Bogarde was selected to play Lawrence in a film with a whopping original budget of £500,000.

Ultimately, as the cost of making the film mushroomed to £700,000, the movie was abruptly canceled, causing anger among the stars and production crew engaged. Rattigan converted his film script into a stage production, entitled *Ross,* in February of 1959.

After all other producers, directors, and actors failed in their efforts to bring *Lawrence* to the screen, there was one man who was de-

Until his production unit collapsed, Dirk Bogarde almost played Lawrence

185

termined to film it.

He liked to chomp down on cigars like Darryl F. Zanuck at 20th Century Fox, and was known as a wheeler-dealer, a tough-as-nails negotiator. He was often described as rotund, though he preferred the word "stout."

Ever since he'd read a special unexpurgated version of *Seven Pillars of Wisdom* in 1926, he'd wanted to film the T.E. Lawrence saga.

In his own words, "There is no mountain high enough that I can't climb, no sea bottom deep enough I can't swim to."

"I had a dream," he announced to the world. He told colleagues, "Sam Spiegel is *chutzpah* on an epic scale."

"The Velvet Octopus" (Sam Spiegel) & "The Self-Enchanted Womanizer" (David Lean) Conspire to Bring Lawrence of Arabia to the Screen

Producer Sam Spiegel and director David Lean had pooled their resources and talents to release to the world *The Bridge on the River Kwai* in 1957. It starred William Holden, Alec Guinness, and Jack Hawkins. The film today is considered one of the greatest movies of all time, revolving around the construction of the Burma Railway during the war years of 1942 and 1943.

At the time of the Academy Awards, the film walked away with seven Oscars, including Best Picture (Spiegel); Best Director (Lean); and Best Actor (Alec Guinness).

When the director and producer got around to filming *Lawrence of Arabia,* they would once again cast Hawkins and Guinness.

Even before *Kwai,* Lean had used Guinness in *Great Expectations (1946),* based on the Charles Dickens novel. The actor had also starred in his 1948 *Oliver Twist.* Lean had come to consider Guinness "my good luck charm."

That good luck seemed missing when *Oliver Twist* opened, in which Guinness appeared as Fagin. Its first screening in Berlin in 1949 offended the surviving Jewish community and caused a riot. Likewise, in New York, charges of anti-Semitism was leveled by the Anti-Defamation League and the American Board of Rabbis. "I was shocked to be called an anti-Semite," Lean wrote. "We made Fagin an outsize and, we hoped, an amusing Jewish villain." The film's release was delayed until the summer of 1951, and Lean had to cut eight minutes out of the scenes depicting Fagin.

After that, both Lean and Spiegel searched for a subject worthy of an epic to bring to the screen. For about three weeks, they focused on the life of Mohandas Gandhi (born 1869). He had been assassinated in 1948. The son of a

Hindu merchant caste family, he was the pre-eminent leader of the Indian independence movement in British-ruled India. In a breathtaking sweep of British Colonial vigor, Queen Victoria had been officially honored with the title "Empress of India."

Both the producer and director found Gandhi's story inspirational, since his nonviolent civil disobedience had captured the imagination of the world, an incentive to promote freedom and civil rights in far and distant lands. But for reasons not clear, they soon discarded Gandhi as a possible subject, looking for another heroic figure instead.

In 1957, Spiegel once again read *Seven Pillars of Wisdom*. When he finished it, at three o'clock one morning, he called Lean, finding him in bed with two call girls. "Get in one last fuck," Spiegel told him, "and then kick out all the whores and read *Seven Pillars of Wisdom*. Lawrence of Arabia, more than Gandhi, is the man to bring to the screen."

It took Lean three days to get through the book. When he'd finished it, he called Spiegel, "Let's go for it."

Ferociously complicated problems—many of them nightmares—were about to descend upon them.

***

As a production and directorial team, Spiegel and Lean came to be known in Hollywood as "The Odd Couple."

Born in Poland (then part of the Austro-Hungarian Empire) in 1901, Spiegel was Jewish, his father a tobacco wholesaler. In 1933, the son fled Nazi Germany, arriving in the United States in 1938. Up until 1954, he billed himself as S.P. Eagle.

His nickname was "The Velvet Octopus" because of his propensity to entwine himself with beautiful young girls in the back seats of taxicabs. A busy man, he often seduced these prostitutes for quick release as he was dashing from one appointment to another.

Spiegel's taste for underage girls was sometimes interpreted as "creepy." He often hired as many as six girls, ranging in age from twelve to sixteen, to satisfy his lusts aboard his luxurious yacht, *Malahne,* notorious for the orgies that took place there.

In a biography of Spiegel, Natasha Fraser-Cavassoni defined him as, "a decidedly flawed protagonist, his wit, sophistication, and Old World charm make him a titanic figure, the likes of which the movie industry will not see again."

He really caught Hollywood's attention when he won an Oscar for Best Picture of 1954 with Elia Kazan's *On the Waterfront,* starring Marlon Brando.

[It was under the name of S.P. Eagle that Spiegel had produced the 1951

The African Queen, with Humphrey Bogart (he won an Oscar) and Katharine Hepburn.]

An Englishman born in 1908, Lean—on the surface—had little in common with Spiegel, although both of them were womanizers. Reared a Quaker, Lean was not allowed to view movies until he left his parents' home to join the film industry in London. There, he worked as a "tea boy," later as a "clapper/loader," followed by a job as an assistant in the cutting room. He was later elevated to the position of Assistant Director, and finally, the editor of *Movietone News.*

Two high-ego, high-maintenance, deeply driven moguls in high-stakes collusion. David Lean (left) and Sam Spiegel (right)

He would marry six times and keep many mistresses. His most famous bride, to whom he was married from 1949-1957, was the "ice blonde goddess," actress Ann Todd. Their acrimonious divorce left him nearly broke until he hooked up with Spiegel.

He would later tell both Spiegel and O'Toole that he could not afford to have his rotting teeth fixed. "Once in London, I was famished and pawned my gold cigarette case, a gift from Ann Todd."

Film critic David Thomson labeled the mercurial Lean as a "charming egotist, endlessly handsome, and in pursuit of women. He was a spellbinder with a frequent discomfort for dialogue scenes. He was also a romantic about himself, and those rewards may have persuaded him that he was too grand for small things. It was the Selznick syndrome."

Lean's co-writer and producer, Norman Spencer, claimed that his friend "had a boundless taste for women. He once confessed to me that he'd seduced 1,000 females. I told him that that record matched that of the legendary Don Juan."

Before the late 1950s, Lean had become known as a different type of director, noted for such quintessentially British films as the 1946 *Brief Encounter,* starring Trevor Howard, and the 1955 *Summertime,* featuring Katharine Hepburn.

In preparation for *Lawrence of Arabia,* both Lean and Spiegel determined that the only way to compete with the growing menace of television was to make Technicolor epics "bigger and bolder than the old movies shown on the little black box."

Before moving ahead, Spiegel had to acquire the rights to *Seven Pillars of Wisdom,* which were owned at the time by producer Arthur Rank. His vision involved casting the English actor, Dirk Bogarde, as Lawrence. Grunwald had also wanted Bogarde.

Spiegel had long harbored a deep-seated jealousy of Rank, who had risen from lowly beginnings in Kingston-upon-Hull in England, east of Leeds, where his father had owned a flour mill and had expected his son to follow in his footsteps. Although pronounced a "dunce" in school, Rank ultimately, after years of struggle, became one of England's greatest film producers, especially known for such hit British films as *Henry V* (1944) and *The Red Shoes* (1948).

At the time he was planning to produce the saga of T.E. Lawrence, he had been raised to the peerage as Baron Rank. In time, he presided over the biggest film empire in Britain's cinematic history.

In spite of his wide experience, Rank failed to come up with a suitable screen adaptation of the Lawrence saga. There was also the problem of financing.

He'd produced and, in 1946, released a film version of George Bernard Shaw's play, *Caesar and Cleopatra*, starring Claude Rains, Vivien Leigh, and Stewart Granger. Originally budgeted at £500,000, it ended up costing £1,000,000 under the direction of the flamboyant Hungarian. Gabriel Pascal. Spiegel warned Rank that bringing *Lawrence of Arabia* to the screen might cost as much as £25 million.

Time magazine recognized the growing power of film producer Arthur Rank, who at one time presided over England's greatest film studio. "I was a star maker," he proclaimed.

The saga of T. E. Lawrence, however, proved too much for him.

Perhaps anticipating another financial disaster, Rank eventually surrendered the rights of *Seven Pillars of Wisdom.*

Bogarde, at the time the matinee idol of Britain, was thirty-seven years old, but looked much younger. "The day I heard that the Lawrence film would not be made was the greatest disappointment of my life," he recalled. "I had never in my life, and would never again, lust after a role so much."

"I had read everything I could that had been written about T.E. Lawrence, and I even talked to people who knew him. I lost my own identity in what Americans call 'a period of total immersion.' Along came Peter O'Toole to take my dream away from me. Not only that, but I lost out on my greatest sexual fantasy, that of playing a blonde in the movies."

Bogarde later cynically remarked, "There are so many knocking about who were slated to play Lawrence. I'll form a private club of them, with me as President and Alec Guinness as vice president. I have even designed a necktie for members—a dark background with a motif of camel and burnoose."

What Bogarde may never have known is that Rank had learned of his recent arrest with a teenage student at Cambridge, where Bogarde was visiting. The actor and an engineering student were caught in a public toilet where the student was performing fellatio on Bogarde. For reasons not explained, the matter was dropped and not brought to court. At that time, male homosexual acts were criminal in Britain, certainly sex in a public toilet. Rank Studio contracts included a morality clause, which called for termination in the event of "immoral conduct" on the part of an actor, and that certainly included same-sex relationships. Bogarde's arrest and its associated embarrassment were not the only reasons for which Rank canceled his association with *Lawrence,* but it might have been a factor that influenced him.

[Referring to the time he had tentatively been offered the role of Lawrence, Bogarde later said, "I made the mistake of my life. I turned down the Gaston role in MGM's Gigi (1958), the part going to the French actor, Louis Jourdan."

Ironically, Bogarde was Lean's first choice to star in his 1965 Doctor Zhivago, the part ultimately going to Omar Sharif, O'Toole's co-star in Lawrence of Arabia.]

After Rank abandoned the project, the rights reverted back to Professor A.W. Lawrence, the brother of the desert hero and the literary executor of his estate.

Consequently, Spiegel persuaded him to sell the rights for a modest £20,000, with the promise that his brother's homosexuality would not become a feature of the desert saga. Spiegel's orders were relayed to his colleagues and crew: "There will be no scenes of T.E. sodomizing comely Arab youths."

"Sam and I had to walk across a shaky bridge with our story," Lean said. "Here was our hero, a repressed homosexual with a lust for getting punished. What a strange place for a Brit—in the center of the super-macho Bedouin world."

Spiegel and Lean decided to ask Michael Wilson to write the first draft of the *Lawrence* script. He'd performed well for them before as the co-writer of the script for *The Bridge on the River Kwai.*

Although a superb screenwriter, the Oklahoma-born Wilson had been blacklisted during the Joseph McCarthy communist "witch hunt" in the United States.

Beginning in 1941, he'd co-written some of the finest films in American cinema, including *It's a Wonderful Life* (1945), starring James Stewart, and *A Place in the Sun* (1952), co-starring Elizabeth Taylor and Montgomery Clift. He'd won an Oscar nomination for *5 Fingers (1952),* a spy thriller starring James Mason.

But because of having been blacklisted, he used a pseudonym or went uncredited for his writing of scripts for *The Bridge of the River Kwai* (1957) and *Lawrence of Arabia* (1962). His screenplay for *Friendly Persuasion* (1956) starring Gary Cooper was nominated for an Oscar, but was disqualified because no name appeared in the credits. In 1996, Wilson received posthumous credit for his contributions to that film. He would also be awarded, posthumously, an Oscar in 1984 for *Bridge on the River Kwai.*

After several weeks, Wilson came up with a first draft. Neither the director nor the producer liked it. "It did not encompass the power and grandeur of the epic" in Lean's words.

That's Hollywood: Screenwriters at War

Left: Blacklisted American scriptwriter Michael Wilson. Right: British scriptwriter Robert Bolt. Their dispute over who wrote what continued for decades.

Then Spiegel turned to Robert Bolt, who was the hottest playwright in London at the time, having scored a triumph with *A Man for All Seasons,* a play that exposed the moral conflicts between Sir Thomas More's personal struggle with Henry VIII, when the king asked for More's support in a break with the Pope and the subsequent establishment of the Church of England in the aftermath of Henry's divorce from Catharine of Aragón.

Although he'd be nominated for an Oscar for his screenwriting contribution to *Lawrence of Arabia,* Bolt would actually receive one for *A Man for All Seasons* and another for *Doctor Zhivago.* As a recurring theme in his dramatic works, he placed a protagonist in conflict with the prevailing society, as he did in *Lawrence of Arabia.*

At the time he worked on the script, his marriage to his first wife, Celia Ann Roberts, was coming to an end. They would divorce in 1963.

[In 1967, he married the British actress, Sarah Miles, only to divorce her in 1976. He remarried her in 1988, a union that lasted until his death in 1995. She had made her film debut as the husky, wide-eyed nymphet in Term of Trial *(1962), with Laurence Olivier, with whom she conducted a torrid affair.*

For a 1970 release, Lean turned to Bolt once again during the development of Ryan's Daughter, *starring Miles with Robert Mitchum and Christopher Jones. The film was evaluated as a notorious failure in its day, but found latter-day devotees as time went by. Later, Bolt wrote and directed her in the film,* Lady Caroline Lamb *(1972), in which she played his heroine.*

When he suffered a stroke in 1987, Miles returned to his side. O'Toole paid him a visit. Bolt told him, "I would be dead without Sylvia. When she's away, my life takes a nosedive. When she returns, my life soars."

"Oh, to be in love," O'Toole replied. "I never yet was there."]

Based on the final version that eventually reached the screen, Bolt and Wilson engaged in bitter conflicts over who had written the screenplay.

Whereas Bolt provided most of the movie's dialogue, Wilson, uncredited, had penned the story and its outline. Bolt alone, however, was nominated for an Oscar. Neither Lean nor Bolt ever officially recognized Wilson's contribution to *Lawrence of Arabia.*

Feeling secure about their ownership of the rights to *Seven Pillars of Wisdom,* Spiegel and Lean got another jolt when they learned that Alex Guinness was opening at London's Theatre Royal on Haymarket in a play called *Ross* by Terence Rattigan. The play's title came from the assumed name Lawrence took when he passed himself quietly, after the limelight (and embarrassments) of his fame, as "Aircraftman Ross" in the RAF.

IRONIES: in 1960, Alec Guinness played T.E. Lawrence in a stage play by Terence Rattigan entitled *Ross.*

Less than two years later, in David Lean's movie version, he played the Arab leader, Prince Faisal.

A deeply troubled homosexual, Rattigan brought some of his own issues to the front in *Ross,* where Lawrence confronts his sexual frustration, failed relationships, and a world of repression and reticence.

Both Spiegel and Lean were impressed with Guinness' *tour de force* performances as Lawrence. However, they knew he was too old to appear on screen in their epic, as he had been born in 1914. He did, however, bear a remarkable resemblance to Lawrence.

Both the director and producer were aware that Guinness, like Lawrence, was a closeted homosexual. Each of them had been mesmerized by the scene in Act Two, which became the buzz of the London theater world. Captured by the fierce Turks, Lawrence is "beaten and buggered" by his captors. Although Lawrence's rape takes place offstage, its undertones were made explicitly clear.

Author Evelyn Waugh seemed shocked that a play whose "plot was all buggery" would be presented at the Theatre Royal on Haymarket. After watching the play, Lean and Spiegel spent endless hours debating how Lawrence should be depicted on screen. The question for them involved whether they should openly portray Lawrence as gay, or whether they should merely suggest it.

Spiegel wanted to purchase the rights to Rattigan's play. He was horrified when he learned that the film producer, Herbert Wilcox, had already paid £100,000 for them, with the hopes of starring another gay actor, Laurence Harvey, in the title role.

Spiegel told Lean that he was "sickened" to read that Wilcox planned to launch his less elaborate cinematic overview of T.E. Lawrence's life in March of 1961, two months before Spiegel was to begin shooting his own version.

There was a certain irony here, as Wilcox, who had been approached by Lawrence himself to film his story in the 1920s, had, at the time, rejected the proposal.

Spiegel believed that Wilcox presented serious competition. The British film producer and director had begun making films during the Silent era, having established a "British Hollywood" at Elstree Studios.

His 1929 film, *Black Waters,* was one of the first British movies with sound. In time, he would produce more than a hundred films, directing about half of them himself.

In the 1950s, he had a desire to produce two filmed biographies, the one about Lawrence, and another about Vincent Van Gogh starring Trevor Howard.

Later, for reasons not fully explained at the time, Wilcox pulled the plug on both biopics.

[By 1964, Spiegel learned why Wilcox, famously married to the British actress, Dame Anna Neagle, never made the Van Gogh or Lawrence films. His company failed, and was declared bankrupt. As Spiegel remarked, "His company was going down, but had he made Lawrence of Arabia, he would have ended up in a debtor's prison from the Middle Ages—and of that, I'm absolutely certain."

With threatened competition eliminated, Spiegel and Lean moved ahead with their pre-production of *Lawrence of Arabia.* There remained a major hurdle, and that involved how to cast the movie, especially the difficult role of Lawrence. Neither man favored either of the choices of previous producers, especially Dirk Bogarde or Laurence Harvey as the male lead.

A decision had to be made. In the elegant bar of London's Dorchester Hotel, Spiegel decided, "The time has come to shit or get off the pot. Tomorrow morning we're going to make an offer to some actor for the role of Lawrence. Now who in the fuck is it going to be? The whole picture will ride on the star we choose. Let's name our best bet before we get drunk and head off for this evening's poontang hunt."

Spiegel: "Should We Hire a Fag to Play a Fag On Screen?"
Lean: "Why Not Cast a Hetero? Albert Finney? Peter O'Toole!"

Both Lean and Spiegel continued to grapple with "the elephant in the china shop," the issue of how to depict homosexuality as it applied to the saga of T.E. Lawrence. During pre-production, homosexuality was "the love that dared not speak its name" on the screen. The same problem had arisen during the 1958 release of Tennessee Williams' *Cat on a Hot Tin Roof,* starring Elizabeth Taylor and Paul Newman.

As *Lawrence of Arabia* faced the cameras, homosexuality was just beginning to be depicted on the screen.

Dirk Bogarde, who had failed to win the role of Lawrence, was filming *Victim* (1960), the story of a married barrister facing the public exposure of his homosexuality.

Lean later said, "Sam and I decided to remain where angels feared to tread and make Lawrence, not hetero, but asexual. There would be no love interest in the film, except maybe implied in the character of Farrah, an Arab servant boy devoted to his desert lord."

Lean wanted to know, "Should we subtly recruit a homosexual or bisexual actor to play Lawrence, one who could give off the right signals without being an obvious homo?"

"In that case, there's only one actor for the role," Spiegel said. "Marlon Brando. I did pretty well with him in *On the Waterfront.* Brando admitted to me that he's a bisexual."

Although a womanizer, Brando, who had played "Stanley Kowalski" in *A Streetcar Named Desire,* was known to have had sexual affairs with men, including fellow actors James Dean and Montgomery Clift.

Spiegel announced: "In a way, Brando and Lawrence are very much alike. Both have that mystic, tortured quality of doubting their own destiny. In 1917, Lawrence was barely thirty, and today, Brando is the same age. There is practically nobody else of international magnitude who could play the part."

When a reporter asked Professor Lawrence, who had already sold the screen rights to *Seven Pillars,* what he thought of Brando playing his brother, he answered, "I do not go to movies. Who is this Marlon Brando person?"

Lean did not warm to the idea of casting Brando. He pointed out the star's "entrenched mannerisms, his awkward speech patterns, and his conflicts with past directors. "Instead of *Lawrence of*

Marlon Brando, a contender for the role of T. E. Lawrence, was dyed blonde for his role as a Nazi in *The Young Lions*

194

Arabia, we are likely to get 'Brando of Arabia.'"

The question became moot when Brando wired back:

"I'LL BE DAMNED IF I'LL SPEND TWO YEARS OF MY LIFE OUT IN THE DESERT ON SOME FUCKING CAMEL. I'M VERY TEMPTED BY THE WHIP-PING SCENE. AS YOU KNOW, I'M ALWAYS INTRIGUED BY ANY ROLE WHERE I GET THE SHIT BEATEN OUT OF ME. BUT I MUST TURN IT DOWN FOR MUTINY ON THE BOUNTY."

[In another of Hollywood's casting ironies, O'Toole had been a contender to play Christian Fletcher in Mutiny on the Bounty *before Brando expressed an interest in the role.*

Later, when Brando had gone to see Lawrence of Arabia, *he told friends, "I was knocked down by the acclaim given to this O'Toole faggot. Perhaps you might say I've made a misjudgment. But I decided to follow Clark Gable in a remake of* Mutiny on the Bounty."]

After Brando's insulting response, Albert Finney was the next best choice. Born in Lancashire in 1936, he was the right age, although he bore no resemblance to Lawrence. At the time, Finney was known mainly for his per-formance in *Saturday Night and Sunday Morning* (1936), in which he played an aimlessly

Still from Albert Finney's screen test for his possible role as Lawrence.

young factory worker torn between two women.

He was intrigued at the idea of playing such a dashing, enigmatic character as Lawrence. He would have accepted the role had not Spiegel insisted on inserting a "poison pen" clause in his contract, calling for him to sign up for a three-picture deal for a combined fee of £125,000.

Even before his screen test, Spiegel had more or less decided that Finney would star as Lawrence. Few actors in the history of motion pictures received such an expensive and elabo-rate screen test, with more than £100,000 spent on exterior and lavish interior shots.

Shortly after rejecting a gig as T. E. Lawrence, Finney nabbed the lead role in the film version of the swashbuckling Restoration com-edy, *Tom Jones.*

A limousine was sent for Finney to transport him to MGM's studios at Borehamwood. He was stunned to find such a massive preparation. "My God, they're already shooting the film!"

He met both Spiegel and Lean, who had secured the services of Geoffrey Unsworth. On hand was Sir Anthony Nutting, 3rd Baronet, a British diplomat and Conservative Party politician. As former Minister of State for Foreign Affairs, he had resigned in 1956 over the Suez crisis.

Some well-known British character actors were employed to appear with Finney, including Laurence Payne and Marne Maitland.

Sir Anthony Nutting, 3rd Baronet, British diplomat and "nursemaid to O'Toole."

Entitled *Seven Pillars of Wisdom,* the test took four days to shoot, a total of two large reels, each lasting ten minutes. Nutting gave Finney some flowing robes for the test, each of which had been presented to him by a prince in Saudi Arabia. Finney was also photographed in a British military uniform.

Both Lean and the film's editor, Anne Coates, found him "magnificent" in the role. At the age of twenty-four, Finney was offered a meager £10,000 if he'd perform as Lawrence.

Perhaps daunted by the fee being proposed, Finney eventually rejected the role of Lawrence, telling its producers that he preferred to work on the stage in both *Billy Liar* and *Luther.*

[Finney's worldwide exposure came shortly thereafter when he starred in the Tony Richardson movie, Tom Jones *(1963), in which he was cast as the devilishly sexy 18th century English rogue.]*

For one brief interlude, Lean suggested Anthony Perkins, who had stunned movie audiences around the world in Alfred Hitchcock's *Psycho* (1960). In it, he'd played a troubled young serial killer with dementia in his eyes and a mother fixation on his brain. Lean had been impressed with Perkins' androgynous quality on the screen. "Rail thin, shy, and handsome, he could bring our quivering wacko of Lawrence to the screen," Lean told Spiegel.

"I doubt that," Spiegel said. "To me, Perkins comes across as just too, too gay. Instead of Lawrence, he might evoke 'Norman Bates of Arabia.'"

"The thing with Perkins is that he has shown the world that a seemingly innocent face can harbor shocking demons of violence and perversity. We need to capture that quality on screen with our Lawrence," Lean said.

"Could you just see Perkins flouncing around in the desert in his flowing white robe?" Spiegel asked. "He'd be mocked and laughed at. Case Closed!"

At least fifteen published sources stated that Montgomery Clift was also in the race to play Lawrence. But that actor told author Darwin Porter that he never received the slightest overture from either Spiegel or Lean about starring in the role.

He also confessed that he did not have the stamina to play such a physically challenging role. "I would also find it emotionally draining," Clift claimed.

Anthony Perkins in his most famous role, the homicidal and psychotically repressed Norman Bates, in *Psycho*.

Spiegel corroborated Clift's account. "I don't know where those looney tune writers came up with the preposterous idea I would ever have offered Clift the role. Drunk and drugged, and in failing health, he practically expired on the set of *Suddenly, Last Summer.* Those months in the desert would have pushed him into an early grave."

In his search for the right British actor to play Lawrence, Lean was seeing three movies a day in London. Finally, he wandered in to see *The Day They Robbed the Bank of England* (1060), starring O'Toole and Aldo Ray.

Lean later said, "There was our Lawrence, right up there on the screen in an unlikely, very un-Lawrence type of role. In fact, he played this silly-assed chap, an Englishman in a raincoat casting for trout. As unlikely as it seemed at the time, I saw T.E.

Monty Clift in *The Big Lift* (1950). "Lean never asked me."

Lawrence emerging from this dubious prospect. I left the cinema determined to cast O'Toole."

When Lean suggested O'Toole as their star to Spiegel, the producer went into a rage. "Over my dead body! I tested that jackass as a replacement for Clift in *Suddenly, Last Summer.* He's a silly little jerk with a prissy voice that is best confined to some fag bar in Mayfair."

Ignoring his producer's protests, Lean secretly contacted O'Toole and asked him to make a screen test. O'Toole showed up, and Lean directed the test himself. He found O'Toole most cooperative, really wanting the role. He told Lean, "This could be my really big chance. How many times does an opportunity like this knock on one's door?"

Two days later, Lean invited Spiegel into a screening room. "I've found our Lawrence," he announced before showing O'Toole's test.

When his image came onto the screen, dressed in the robes of Lawrence, Spiegel shouted, "Oh shit! Not that jackass!"

But Spiegel was an astute showman. As the test progressed, he had to admit that O'Toole had captured, if not Lawrence, then at least a charismatic screen interpretation of him. "He's got the part! Let's cast him and make the fucker an international star."

It was Spiegel himself who telephoned O'Toole to inform him that he and Lean wanted him to play Lawrence in a big Technicolor epic. The producer later reported to Lean what had transpired with that phone call: "Guess what? Instead of showing some elation, some gratitude, perhaps promising to lick my rosebud for casting him, the fucker came up with another of his stupid jokes."

On hearing about his good fortune, O'Toole facetiously asked Spiegel, "Is Lawrence a speaking part?"

"Is It True that Arab Men Actually Have Black Dicks?"

—O'Toole to Omar Sharif

Other than the role of Lawrence, Lean and Spiegel had the most difficulty hiring a suitable player for the role of Sherif Ali ibn el Kharish. The character was built from a composite of several historical figures, most notably Sherif Nassir, a first cousin of Prince Faisal, who led the Harith forces into battle against the Jordanian port city of Aqaba. In Bolt's script, "Sherif Ali" was used to represent a number of Arab war chiefs, since Lawrence joined several of them in battle.

Hollywood had long been known for casting actors into characters whose ethnicity was often radically different from their own, a famous example being the selection of Katharine Hepburn as a Chinese peasant girl in *Dragon Seed* (1944).

For the all-important role of Sherif Ali, Spiegel and Lean offered the part first to a German, then to a Frenchman.

Both Lean and Spiegel had been impressed with the screen presence of a young Berliner, Horst Buchholz, the first international star to emerge from post-World War II Germany. A handsome, intense young actor, he had attracted the attention of the producer/director duo at the Cannes Film Festival when he'd starred in *Sky Without Stars* (1959).

Lean thought Buchholz could convey Lawrence's ambivalent sexuality, surmising that he was a homosexual himself.

[In 2000, the actor gave an interview to the German magazine Bunte, *in*

which he outed himself. *"Yes, I also love men. Ultimately, I'm bisexual. I have always lived my life the way I wanted."*

He was married to the French actress Myriam Bru, a union that lasted from 1958 until his death in 2003. Whereas she lived mostly in Paris, he preferred his hometown of Berlin.]

Horst Buchholz... "I love men."

Spiegel learned that Buchholz had already signed with Billy Wilder to appear in the film, *One, Two, Three* (1961) as a hotheaded commie clashing with James Cagney, cast as an American businessman.

Alain Delon, hailed in fan magazines as "a French pretty boy," was just emerging as an international star when he attracted the attention of Spiegel and Lean. After the international success of *Purple Noon* (1960) and *Rocco and His Brothers* (1961), Delon was also labeled "France's answer to James Dean." Because he exuded sex appeal, especially in that bathing suit scene in *Purple Noon,* he became known as "the male version of Brigitte Bardot."

Alain Delon..."Pretty, but too French."

Two unconfirmed rumors were floated at the time about his possible casting in *Lawrence of Arabia,* the first being that he was actually offered the role of Lawrence himself. That seems a remote possibility, since he still had a French accent at the time, which would make it difficult for him to sound like an Englishman.

He was more likely offered the role of Sherif Ali.

According to published reports at the time, Delon turned down the role because he would have to wear brown contact lenses.

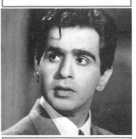

Dilip Kumar...Hindi-speaking matinee idol.

There is no doubt that he wanted to appear in American films, telling the press, "If you want to become an international star, you must establish yourself in American pictures, because only they will get adequate world-wide distribution."

"I am working to remove my distinctly French inflections so that I can play all Continental nationalities."

Another contender for the role was Dilip Kumar. Born in British India (now Pakistan), he was an actor known in films as "The Tragedy King" and described by the distinguished Bengali filmmaker, Satyajit Ray, as "the ultimate Method actor." He became the greatest actor in the history of Hindi Cinema. His most ardent fans called Kumar "The Greatest Actor Ever!"

Although Lean made a firm offer for Kumar to portray Sherif Ali, Kumar just as firmly rejected the role.

In preparation for casting actors into some of the Arab roles, Spiegel and Lean, accompanied by O'Toole, who was needed for screen tests, flew to Cairo. Egypt was the center of the Arabian film industry and was also known for having the best actors.

After looking at some 500 photographs of various actors, the face of Omar Sharif stood out. Spiegel and Lean's Egyptian assistant, a producer of local films, told them that in the Arab world, Sharif was already a matinee idol. Born in Alexandria in 1932 to Lebanese and Syrian parents, he was married to Faten Hamama, the reigning queen of Egyptian cinema. The couple had appeared in romantic films together.

The assistant arranged to screen two of Sharif's most recent movies for Lean and Spiegel.

Shown in a private screening room were two Egyptian movies, whose English titles were *Scandal in Zamalek* and *Struggle on the Nile,* both released in 1959. These savvy talent scouts liked Sharif's screen presence, along with his dark looks that hinted of Arab intrigue, exotica, and mystery.

A decision was made that day that would make the name of Omar Sharif known around the world, as he was about to become Egypt's only international star.

Though not well known outside the Arab world, Omar Sharif was a star in Egypt, thanks partly to his portrayal of the romantic lead in the Egyptian thriller and social drama, *Scandal in Zamalek,* released in 1959.

Spiegel's assistant located Sharif and called his home, asking him if he'd come over to meet the producer in his hotel suite. The interview was about a possible role in his upcoming *Lawrence of Arabia,* which Sharif, an avid reader of international movie news, had heard about.

As Sharif later related in his memoirs, *The Eternal Male,* he came into Spiegel's luxurious suite, finding him resting on a couch—"fat and with a big cigar in his mouth, a Hollywood *cliché.*"

Spiegel was delighted to learn that the actor spoke English with just a slight and undefinable accent. He was being interviewed for the role of Tafas,

Lawrence's Arab guide in the desert.

Spiegel asked Sharif to tell him something about himself, learning that originally, he had studied mathematics and physics at the University of Cairo and had worked for five years in the business of his father, Joseph Chalhoub, who specialized in the import and sale of exotic hardwoods to artisans throughout Egypt.

The producer was surprised that the deposed king of Egypt, "the fat and perverse Farouk," had been a family friend and met about once a week with Sharif's household to play card games. He always selected Sharif's mother, the former Claire Saada, as his partner.

Spiegel gave his stamp of approval to Sharif, and two days later, the actor was hustled onto a private plane that flew him to a remote location in the desert where screen tests were being conducted.

Once there, he was introduced to Lean within his large tent. He'd later remember him as having "the profile of a bird of prey, a terribly attractive man with a piercing gaze and an eagle's nose."

He recalled that "Lean undressed me with his eyes. I felt like a sex slave on the auction block. It was such an intense examination I feared he was going to ask me to unzip and show my cock."

Sharif hustled into wardrobe, where he was outfitted with a midnight black *djellaba.* For romantic effect, Lean added a stage mustache. Sharif liked his new look so much, he grew one for real.

As the camera rolled, he met a tall, blue-eyed fellow, Peter O'Toole, who was dressed as T.E. Lawrence of Arabia.

Right away, Sharif realized what an original and quirky personality the Irishman possessed. It was off-putting, yet fascinating to him.

"I hear that brown-skinned Arab men actually possess black dicks," O'Toole said. "Is it true?"

Fast with the quip, Sharif said, "You'll have to sample a few to find out for yourself. I hear the script calls for you to get raped, so I'm sure you'll learn the answer to that question then."

O'Toole burst into laughter. "We're going to blend together on camera, and perhaps off camera, as a perfect match. Maybe we'll become the screen's new romantic couple."

The test went smoothly, and Lean was stunned by the "on-screen chemistry" of Sharif and O'Toole. He'd later tell Spiegel "We can suggest that they are secret lovers in the desert, without any overt scene to actually show that—just a hint to tantalize the viewer."

Sharif would later record his impression of his newly found friend on that long-ago afternoon in the desert. "O'Toole was the very stereotype of the ham, representing an astonishing caricature of 'the Actor' with a capital A and, what's more, of the Irish actor. In his native land, an actor has to drink a lot, get into brawls, dress in a way different from others. Peter drank, brawled, and dressed with a great deal of originality, maintaining the traditions of the Abbey Theatre actors of his childhood."

"His inner self he doesn't let people see," Sharif continued. "He's like a prism that reflects the seven colors of the spectrum in a splendid rainbow. Peter the actor would identify readily with the scarf of Iris, the messenger of the gods. He's an actor on the set and also one in everyday life."

Sharif also tested with a French actor, Maurice Ronet, who was scheduled to play Sherif Ali.

Ronet was not only a film actor, but a director and writer, who, in time, would become one of the most popular and prolific actors in European cinema. After losing the role in *Lawrence of Arabia* because of his accent, he had a stroke of good fortune when Louis Malle cast him in his 1963 release, *Le feu follet (The Fire Within),* in which he played an alcoholic writer, a portrait of depression and suicide. Opposite Jeanne Moreau, he'd found his defining role, bringing him great acclaim.

When both Spiegel and Lean saw the screen test of the Egyptian and the Frenchman, a decision was made that night to offer the role of Sherif Ali to Omar Sharif.

O'Toole later kidded him, "Omar, you got the role because of your murky black eyes, the eyes of the Devil. The Frenchman had green eyes. Green wouldn't do, although as an Irishman, green is my favorite color."

At the end of the day, O'Toole told Sharif, "David wants a darkly romantic type to contrast with my sky blue eyes and blonde hair. It's a dye job. To make me an authentic blonde, do you think I should also dye my pubic hair, which right now is a bit ginger in color?"

"I think you should," Sharif said, "In case those winds from the desert blow your robe above your thighs. A movie magazine said Marilyn Monroe dyes her pussy hairs, so she can be blonde all over. Perhaps you can follow her example."

"I like your style, your wit, your charm," O'Toole said. "Let's fly back to Cairo, where I want you to take me on a tour of the fleshpots of the city, but only the most decadent ones."

He later claimed, "That hot afternoon in the god damn Egyptian sun that had once shone down on Cleopatra marked the beginning of a beautiful friendship."

With His Nerves Ablaze, O'Toole Heads a Cast of Marquee

Names in "This Galumping Camelodrama"

With Omar Sharif and Peter O'Toole under contract, Lean and Spiegel set about casting the rest of the picture. They decided to go for marquee names, actors who normally were featured as stars.

Spiegel hoped to convince these vain thespians that they should accept minor roles because *Lawrence of Arabia* would evolve into the most prestigious movie of that year.

"Let's start at the top," Spiegel told Lean. "Laurence Olivier as Prince Faisal."

Many of the characters in the film were fictionalized, but Faisal was real. He was the third of four sons of Emir Hussein, a tribal leader of the vast Hejaz territory, the western sector of the Arabian Peninsula. His father was the "Sherif" (religious leader) of the Muslim's holy cities of Mecca and Medina.

In his *Seven Pillars,* Lawrence had written, "Prince Faisal was the man I had come to Arabia to seek, the leader who would bring the Arab revolt to full glory. He was a man of moods, flickering between glory and despair. He looked older than thirty-one, and his dark, appealing eyes, set a little sloping in his face, were bloodshot, and his hollow cheeks deeply lined and puckered with reflection."

Olivier found the offer intriguing, but he also knew Lean, and believed that the director would not complete the film in six months. "David might drag this movie out for years chasing after the perfect sunset over the desert, perhaps waiting around for a rainbow to appear."

He wired his regrets and bowed out, pleading commitments to the Chichester Festival Theatre. He sent a wire to Spiegel: SANDALS AND SUN ARE GLORIOUS FOR A HOLIDAY, BUT NOT FOR ME."

The casting queries continued. Although he was considered too old to play Lawrence on the screen, Alec Guinness seemed ideal as a replacement for the role of Prince Faisal. Actually, he was too old for that part, too, but Lean and Spiegel never spent too much time worrying about historical accuracy.

Fresh from his success in Lean's *The Bridge on the River Kwai,* Guinness wired his acceptance.

After Guinness accepted the role, Spiegel wired Lean: "I'VE JUST SIGNED UP ONE OF BRITAIN'S MOST STATELY HOMOS AFTER ITS LEADING THEATRICAL HOMO TURNED US DOWN." The latter reference was to Olivier's bisexuality, widely known throughout Lon-

Laurence Olivier...
"No camel opera for me."

203

don's theatrical circles at the time.

During their previous work together, Guinness and Lean had had some big arguments, but the actor respected the director, later writing that he was "lithe and handsome, enchanting, affable, exciting."

The casting of Guinness turned out to be a wise choice. As critic Kenneth von Gunden wrote: "Faisal was the consummate politician and also a minimalist, just as Guinness is a minimalist actor. He parcels out emotion and expression sparingly."

In a private talk with Guinness, Lean assured him that he would find many an Arab boy receptive to the embrace of an older man. "They are somewhat shy with a sweet

As Prince Faisal, Alec Guinness drew this comment from a critic:

"His ethnicizing makeup and accent recalled all those white British thespians who at different times have fancied themselves as Othello."

reserve. You can feed them dates. I'm sure you'll find your Tadzio in the desert."

Lean was well aware of Guinness' closeted homosexuality. Lean had cast the actor in his 1946 screen adaptation of the Charles Dickens novel, *Great Expectations.* At that time, Guinness was arrested by the police, who had caught him performing fellatio on a young man in a public lavatory in Liverpool.

In court, Guinness gave his name as "Herbert Pocket," the name of the character he played in Lean's *Great Expectations.* He was fined £12. Lean helped him cover up a possible scandal.

Anthony Quinn was the first choice to play Auda ibu Tayi, based on a real character. The leader of the fierce Howeitat tribe in northwestern Arabia, the desert warrior was known for his daring exploits.

Spiegel offered Quinn 10,000 US$ for his involvement in the epic. The actor claimed that was "scandalously low. I demand $400,000."

Spiegel was flabbergasted at the price, warning Quinn that his financial backers would never agree to it. Amazingly, the producer called him back a week later.

"They went for it. You're our guy. But I've got to warn you. Playing this desert rat, you'll get sand in your foreskin, you Mexican wetback."

Really looking the role, Anthony Quinn played a larcenous, blood-thirsty Bedouin and demanded more money than any other actor.

Quinn also demanded third billing after O'Toole and Guinness. In what shaped up as an elongated cameo role, he was cast as the gluttonous, hawk-nosed chief of the marauding, murderous Howeitat tribesman.

Lean decided to base Quinn's character on T.E. Lawrence's description of him. "His black beard is tinged with white, but he is still tall and straight, loosely built, spare and powerful, and as active as a much younger man. His lined and haggard face is pure Bedouin broad: low forehead, high sharp hooked nose, brown green eyes, slanting outward, a large mouth."

"I told Lean I could play this desert lord of lords, the stud of studs," Quinn said. "Wasn't it type casting after all? As Auda, I was married twenty-eight times and deflowered 1,000 virgins. After I deflowered a virgin, I ordered my private surgeon to circumcise the girl."

The next casting decision confronted by Spiegel and Lean began with two odd choices. For the role of General Edmund Allenby, a historical character, both of them focused on Cary Grant. Grant wired back: *"IN CASE YOU HAVEN'T HEARD, I'M A STAR. I'M NOT REDUCED TO WALK-ONS."*

In a strange move, Lean once again invited Olivier to appear in the movie, this time as the British general. Once again, Olivier turned him down, pleading other commitments.

T.E. Lawrence and Allenby had a complicated relationship to convey on the screen. In *Seven Pillars,* Lawrence wrote, "He could not make out how much of me was genuine performer and how much charlatan. The problem was working behind his eyes, and I left him unhelped to solve."

When the English actor, Jack Hawkins, was offered the role of Allenby, he accepted immediately. From 1932 to 1940, he had been married to the distinguished actress, Jessica Tandy, who had created the original role of Blanche DuBois on Broadway in *A Streetcar Named Desire,* opposite Marlon Brando.

Lean thought Hawkins could draw on his World War II experience. (He had been a British colonel in India.) Lean had also cast him successfully in *The Bridge on the River Kwai.*

When Hawkins learned that the film was about T.E. Lawrence, he told Lean, "Politically, I'm a liberal, as you know, but I don't want to get involved in any homo scenes in the desert."

Earlier, Hawkins had turned down the role of a homosexual barrister in *Victim,* (1961) the role going to Dirk Bogarde. "It's important that I preserve my masculine image on the screen," Hawkins said. "No love scenes with O'Toole."

Jack Hawkins as General Allenby. "I won't sodomize Lawrence of Arabia if that's what you had in mind."

"It's a promise," Lean answered.

After casting Hawkins, Spiegel called Lean. "I hope this guy doesn't die on us. He smokes three packs a day, and he's got problems with his voice. I learned that a few months ago, he had to undergo cobalt treatments. Something about his larynx. I hope he makes it through the picture. I heard in private, he uses a mechanical larynx to aid his speech."

"As long as he's still standing, we can also dub his voice if his own speech fails him," Lean promises. "Let's take a chance. He'd be perfect as the stern British officer. Just perfect."

It was later revealed that Lean had originally wanted Hawkins to play the lesser role of Colonel Harry Brighton. But when both Grant and Olivier turned down the role of Allenby, Hawkins was shifted into that part instead.

In his book, *The Great Movie Stars* (1972), David Shipman called Jose Ferrer, the actor from Puerto Rico, "a jack of all trades, and master of most of them." Both Spiegel and Lean thought he'd be the most ideal choice to play the very jaded Turkish Bey, a brutal rapist, in *Lawrence of Arabia.*

It was a small role, but one of the most pivotal in the script. Ferrer would accept the part only if he were paid $25,000, more than the combined salaries of O'Toole and Sharif. The demand seemed outrageous, but Spiegel went for it, having already caved in to another gross demand from Quinn.

Although Ferrer initially held the role in contempt, he later recalled, "If I were to be judged by any one film performance, it would be my five minutes in *Lawrence of Arabia.*"

Jose Ferrer as the sadistic Turkish bey.

Jokingly, he later told friends, "I played a brute who got off piercing the hymens of beautiful, young, blonde-haired men."

His fans might disagree. When he was cast as the Dauphin of France with Ingrid Bergman in the 1948 *Joan of Arc,* he earned the first of his three Oscar nominations. He actually won the golden prize for his brilliant performance in *Cyrano de Bergerac* in 1950. Another Oscar nomination came in his amazing performance as Toulouse-Lautrec in the 1952 *Moulin Rouge,* with John Huston directing. In that film, Ferrer, a tall man, got down on his knees, with his legs strapped, to appear as the deformed artist. Ferrer was not just an actor, but a director and writer, too. On screen, he played cool, cerebral, and rather idiosyncratic characters.

"No one ever accused Ferrer of being a warm, cuddly type on the screen," Lean said. "He seemed perfect to play the sadistic, cruel Turkish rapist."

O'Toole said, "If any actor in that movie, a talented lot, were a challenge to my acting skills, it was Mr. Ferrer. I learned more about acting from him than I ever learned in an acting class."

In *Seven Pillars of Wisdom,* Lawrence called the Bey "Nahi," when in fact, he may have been General Hajim Bey of the Turkish Army, the District Governor of Daraa. Although leaving out many of the clinical details, Lawrence devotes five pages of his autobiography to his arrest by a Turkish Army sergeant, who escorted him to the headquarters of the Bey.

The alleged arrest and assault took place on November 20, 1917.

After being forced to wait for hours, he was ushered into the private chambers of the Bey, who wrestled him onto his bed. When Lawrence tried to escape, the governor called his guards, who pinioned him to the bed, ripping off his clothing. Once Lawrence was held captive, the Bey, "In a frenzy of both ardor and rage began kissing and also spitting on me, biting into my neck until he drew blood."

At this point, Lawrence was presumably sodomized. After the assault, the Bey ordered his guards to take the prisoner "out into the next room and teach him everything."

Lawrence claimed that at the mercy of the guards, he was stretched over a bench, where two brutal guards "knelt on my ankles, bearing down on the back of my knees, while two more twisted my wrists until they cracked, and then crushed them and my neck against the wood. Four guards then took turns lashing me with a whip on my back and buttocks hundreds of times. At last, when I was completely broken, they seemed satisfied."

"Before I was dragged back to the Bey's bedroom, I was hacked with the full length of a whip into my groin. I doubled over half screaming, or rather trying impotently to scream, only shuddering through my open mouth. Once in the general's bedroom again, he rejected me in haste, as I was a thing too torn and bloody for his bed."

The guards then dumped Lawrence into a courtyard, where, he alleged, he managed to escape, despite his beaten-down condition. Even so, he said he rode seventy miles on a horse stolen from the Turkish army, across the desert to find his allies.

Some Lawrence biographers have dismissed his account of torture in *Seven Pillars.* He had claimed that his body was pierced by a bayonet which "wavered down my side and dripped blood onto the front of my thigh." He also recalled that the general ran his fingertips over the blood, rubbing it across his stomach. He also recalled that he was kicked in the ribs as "a delicious warmth, probably sexual, swelled through my body."

After his release, he confided in the British colonel, Walter Stirling, "Hajim was an ardent pederast and took a fancy to me."

Over the years, Lawrence altered his version of the torture. In 1924, he confided a rather different tale to his friend, Charlotte Shaw, wife of the playwright George Bernard Shaw. To avoid additional torture, Lawrence may have surrendered to the sexual advances of the Bey, who later turned him over to his guards for a gang-rape.

All that is really known about that night was that *something happened* in Daraa.

With Bolt's script, Lean's direction, and the acting skills of Ferrer and O'Toole, that night of horror had to be re-created on the screen.

Two views of Claude Rains *(lower photo with O'Toole).*

And so it was.

Film critic Stanley Kauffmann later wrote, "Playing a diplomat, Claude Rains, always a fine and now vintage actor, is simply not on the screen long enough to suit us."

Lean had directed Claude Rains in the memorable picture, *The Passionate Friends* in 1949, co-starring Ann Todd and Trevor Howard. The director greatly respected the actor's talent and thought he'd be ideal for the role of the cynical British diplomat, Mr. Dryden. The character was based loosely on certain figures of the time, but mostly on Sir Ronald Storrs, the head of the Arab Bureau and later the governor of Palestine.

At first, Lean thought Rains might not go for such a cameo, but he wired his acceptance and was flown to Southern Spain, where a major segment of *Lawrence of Arabia* was filmed.

Rains was at the twilight of a distinguished career (*Casablanca; Now, Voyager; Mr. Skeffington*). Bolt claimed he created Dryden as a character "to represent the political and civilian wing of England's interest in Arabia to balance the military aims of General Allenby."

As predicted, Rains performed brilliantly. After all, during the course of his career, he had been nominated for four Best Supporting Actor Oscars. Like O'Toole, he never won one for his screen roles.

O'Toole had seen many of Rains' pictures and was eager to work with him. He praised the actor's "reliable drollery," as he put it.

When O'Toole lauded his voice, Rains said, "You should have heard me when I was thirteen. A thick cockney accent and a speech impediment."

"Here I am in a World War One story," Rains said. "I fought in that war along with my fellow thespians, Basil Rathbone, Herbert Marshall, and Ronald Colman. I suffered through an attack of mustard gas, which left me blind in one eye."

Like O'Toole, Rains was a heavy drinker. "The British can hold their liquor," Rains said, "unlike the Americans. Give them two drinks, and they're staggering around. I can manage four gins and tonic at lunch and still return to the set, knowing all my lines and how to perform them."

"Would that I could say the same for myself," O'Toole responded.

Anthony Quayle as the British colonel, Harry Brighton.

Quayle interpreted his source character, the historic figure of Lt. Col Steward Newcombe, as "a complete idiot."

When Hawkins was recast, Lean gave the role of the British colonel, Harry Brighton, to Anthony Quayle, the English actor and director. He was adept at playing military characters, having served during World War II as a British Army officer. He was also a noted Shakespearean actor and helped lay the foundations for the Royal Shakespeare Company in Stratford-upon-Avon.

He told Lean and O'Toole, "I can draw on my wartime experience to bring a certain authenticity to my part, which some of my fellow performers, who were non-combatants, cannot do."

Like some of the other characters in the film, Brighton was a composite of various British officers stationed in Arabia. More than any other individual officer, the character mostly resembled Lt. Col. Steward F. Newcombe, who had been Lawrence's predecessor as liaison officer to the Arab Revolt. Captured by the Turks in 1916, he later managed to escape. He was called Col. Newcombe in Wilson's original script, although changed to Brighton when Bolt rewrote the part.

Quayle set out to play the role of the colonel like the average English soldier might view Lawrence, claiming, "I conceived it like a bloke might admire Lawrence yet feel uncomfortable about all his foppish behavior in those flowing white robes and his pretense of grandeur."

He discussed acting with O'Toole, suggesting roles created by Shakespeare that might be ideal for him—"and not just *Hamlet* and *Macbeth.*"

"If you're an actor, you walk a tightrope between two extremes: justifiable pride and humility. You have to cultivate a complete carelessness of yourself or else become an egotistical, introspective monster."

"I prefer the latter," O'Toole shot back.

"Since it was an all-male cast, I didn't expect any romances to develop until I saw Guinness lusting after Quayle," Lean later claimed. "Every time this burly six-footer headed for the showers in our communal tent, Guinness also grabbed a towel and went after him, perhaps volunteering to scrub his back."

"Quayle admitted to me that he was not handsome enough for romantic roles," Lean recalled. "But he did tell me that when he takes off all his clothes, 'I can have anybody I want.'"

"I don't think Guinness got anywhere in his attempt to seduce Quayle—but who knows?" Lean said. "I noticed that Quayle, Hawkins, and Guinness became close friends during the shoot. They were always together at night, drinking, dining, or whatever."

The Man Who Made Lawrence of Arabia Famous

A former gold miner in Colorado, a cook on a ranch of cowboys, and later, a reporter on a newspaper, Lowell Thomas became one of the most famous American writers and broadcasters.

A "self-promoter without shame," he persuaded railroads and shipping lines to give him free passage in exchange for mention of their names and descriptions of their services in travel articles. In Alaska, he came up with the novel idea of making movies about faraway places.

With the coming of America's entry into World War I in 1917, Thomas wanted to configure himself as a war correspondent reporting on the action on the battlefields of Europe. But he didn't have the funds needed for the expedition. He had accumulated damaging information about the Chicago meatpackers. He threatened to expose these "cow and pig slaughterers" if they didn't finance his trip to the front. Fearing the damaging publicity, these meatpackers agreed to put up the money for his trip abroad.

As World War I droned on, Lowell began to find the conflict in Europe "boring" and instead became intrigued by General Allenby's campaign against the Ottoman Turkish Empire in Palestine. Aided by the British foreign office, he became an accredited War Correspondent.

It was in Jerusalem that Thomas came face to face with T. E. Lawrence, then a captain in the British Army. At the time, Lawrence was spending 200,000 British pounds every month as an incentive to provoke a Palestinian uprising against the Turks.

With his cameraman, Harry Chase, Thomas journeyed with Lawrence into the desert. He claimed he spent several weeks with the desert warrior, but Lawrence later claimed, "It was more likely several days."

Fired up by such a charismatic character as Lawrence—"A Brit in flowing white robes"—Thomas began to create a legend in the making.

Returning to America with copious notes and film footage, in 1919, Thomas launched a series of lectures illustrated with film footage of Lawrence in Palestine. The mysterious Middle East of *The Arabian Nights* came alive. Opening in Madison Square Garden in New York, the Lowell films and lectures became an immediate hit across the nation. He would eventually take his show to Covent Garden in London, always playing to packed houses.

His films, *With Allenby in Palestine* and *Lawrence in Arabia,* made T.E. Lawrence a household name. It did the same for Thomas in his role as a reporter.

At his shows, incense emanated from charcoal-fueled braziers as exotically dressed women (usually local showgirls) danced, wearing flimsy costumes inspired by the various hues of the rainbow.

Lawrence went to see the show in London and later told Thomas, "I hated it."

Nonetheless, as the reporter claimed, "T.E. had a genius for backing into the limelight. When I needed more pictures of him in Arab dress, he showed up at a studio in Chelsea and posed for all the portraits I wanted of him. I was also helping sell his own book, *Seven Pillars of Wisdom.*"

T. E. Lawrence was not the only Westerner who could dress in Arab drag. Reporter Lowell Thomas *(shown in both photos above)* brought Yankee razzmatazz and PR hype to a reticent denizen of Britain's Imperial military machine.

Lowell Thomas *(right)* with T.E. Lawrence, who wrote:

"I am painfully aware of what Mr. Lowell Thomas is doing. He came out to Egypt on behalf of the American Government, spent a fortnight in Arabia (I saw him twice in that time) and there he seems to have realised my 'star' value on the film. Anyway, he has been lecturing in America & London, & has written a series of six articles about me, for American & English publication. They are as rank as possible, and are making life very difficult for me, as I have neither the money nor the wish to maintain my constant character as the mountebank he makes me."

—T.E. Lawrence
in a letter to Sir Archibald Murray, 1920

Lawrence was introduced by Thomas as "The Uncrowned King of Arabia." He later wrote, "I first made the acquaintance of one of the most picturesque personalities of modern times, a man who will be blazoned on the romantic pages of history with Sir Walter Raleigh, Sir Francis Drake, Robert Clive, and Charles George Gordon."

Lawrence was shown moving through a world inhabited by fat sultans, caliphs with harems, and British statesmen.

Thomas proclaimed, "Lawrence freed Arabia, the Holy Land of millions of Mohammedans." Thomas exaggerated, but critics claimed he brought the romance and mystery of the Near East to America. "Cairo. Jerusalem, Damascus, Baghdad," Thomas said. "I took my listeners and viewers on a magic carpet to tales of 'The Thousand and One Nights.'"

In his 1924 bestseller, Thomas described Lawrence as a "five-foot-three Englishman who wore a *kuffieh* of white silk and gold embroidery, held in place over his hair by an *agal,* two black woolen cords wrapped with silver and gold thread. His heavy black camel's hair robe or *aba,* covered a snow-white undergarment fastened at the waist by a wide, gold-brocaded belt in which he carried the curved sword of a Prince of Mecca. This youth had virtually become the ruler of the Holy Land of the Mohammedans and commander-in-chief of many thousands of Bedouins mounted on racing camels and a fleet of Arabian horses. He was the terror of the Turks."

He always concluded his lectures by claiming, "Surely, destiny never played a stranger prank than when it selected, as a man to play a major role in the liberation of Arabia, this Oxford graduate whose life ambition was to dig into the ruins of antiquity, and to uncover and study long forgotten cities."

At one point, Lawrence claimed, "I had enough publicity to last five lifetimes." He wired Thomas to cancel upcoming shows devoted to him. Thomas ignored his requests.

Lawrence later recalled, "I never forgave Thomas for exploiting my image. He was a very vulgar American."

Some four million people flocked to see and hear Thomas' romanticized view of Lawrence, sowing the seeds of future fascination with a great film devoted to his exploits.

When Kirk Douglas Makes Too Many Demands, "John Kennedy" Grabs the Role

In Michael Wilson's original script for *Lawrence of Arabia,* the news reporter—a character named Jackson Bentley, who was based on Lowell

Thomas' role in Lawrence's life—functioned as the narrator in the original script. During pre-production, an offer was extended to a superstar, Kirk Douglas, to take on this key role.

Douglas already knew Lean—in fact, he had gone to him originally to produce his epic, *Spartacus* (1960). It was based on the novel by Howard Fast, who had once been jailed for being a member of the Communist Party.

Lean studied the project, but after he read the script, he turned it down. "I can't seem to fit myself into it style-wise," he told Douglas. "I couldn't bring it off."

After Lean's rejection, Douglas took the script of *Spartacus* to film director Stanley Kubrick, who agreed to take on the project with Edward Lewis designated as its producer.

Lean may have regretted not directing *Spartacus,* as it became the biggest moneymaker in the history of Universal. Its screenplay was written by Dalton Trumbo, one of the blacklisted "Hollywood Ten" accused of being loyal members of the Communist Party.

Although Lean had rejected any association with *Spartacus,* he called Kirk Douglas once again, asking him if he'd play the role of the reporter/narrator in *Lawrence of Arabia,* even though it was a minor part.

Kirk Douglas had been memorable in *Spartacus* (1960), but he wasn't offered the role of Lowell Thomas in *Lawrence of Arabia.*

Lean said, "He didn't want the part, he wanted a coronation."

Douglas said that the role intrigued him, but then proceeded to make demands that Lean interpreted as "outrageous." He not only wanted second billing after O'Toole, but demanded O'Toole's star salary. Lean had no choice but to turn him down. Not only was the salary demand absurd, but he had already promised Guinness second billing.

With Douglas gone from the role, Lean decided to reduce the character based on Lowell Thomas. He ordered Robert Bolt, who was reworking the original script by Wilson, to make the part less significant.

Instead of admiring Lawrence's achievements, as was the case with Thomas, Bolt's screen treatment depicted him as a cynical, middle-aged Chicago reporter, dubious of Lawrence's successes and mistrusting of his motives.

Edmond O'Brien was also tested for the role of the Lowell Thomas character, "but God had other plans for me."

Lean's first choice for the reporter's role was Edmond O'Brien, a New Yorker, who had won an Oscar as Best Supporting Actor for his performance as the harried publicity agent in *The Barefoot Contessa* (1952), starring Humphrey Bogart and Ava Gardner.

After taking a screen test, O'Brien suffered a heart attack and dropped out.

With the loss of both Douglas and O'Brien, Lean awarded the role to Arthur Kennedy, who accepted the part in spite of its reduced status in Bolt's revised script.

Arthur Kennedy plays Lowell Thomas

"My name is John Kennedy, and I'm from Massachusetts. David Lean didn't want me to use my real name—hence, Arthur Kennedy."

The Massachusetts-born Kennedy could play a wide assortment of roles, nice guys and villains alike, zigzagging between major and minor roles.

He facetiously asked lean, "Do you mind if I use my real first name in billing?"

"And what might that be?" Lean asked, "Archibald?"

"No, it's John A. Kennedy (my birth name) of Massachusetts."

"I think our president has staked that one out already," Lean said. "Better stick with 'Arthur.'"

Character actor Donald Wolfit, known for his touring productions of Shakespeare, was cast as the British General Murray.

O'Toole had seen Wolfit in *King Lear,* which had garnered the praise of Dame Edith Sitwell. She wrote that he "performed the role with cosmic grandeur...all imaginable fires of agony and all the light of redemption being in the production."

O'Toole later claimed that Wolfit was one of his most important mentors when it came to acting. One night he'd met Ronald Harwood, the actor's dresser. Harwood later based his play, *The Dresser,* on Wolfit. O'Toole's friend, Albert Finney, starred in *The Dresser's* 1983 movie version .

"In *Lawrence of Arabia,* Wolfit's part wasn't that big, but he pulled it off as he always did," O'Toole said. "Of course, Donald wasn't a pretty face."

Wolfit also had his detractors, none more so than fellow actor, Leslie French. "Wolfit is a joke, a terrible actor, with no sense of humor."

Peter O'Toole was sometimes compared to Donald Wolfitt.

Irving Wardle in the *London Times* wrote: "O'Toole gruesomely evokes the kind of thing one used to get from Sir Donald Wolfit on a bad night."

O'Toole tried to comfort Wolfit. "If my day ever comes, I'm sure that far worse will be said of me."

The script contained two other roles for young actors, the characters of Farraj and Daud, who attached themselves to Lawrence as his personal servants. In Lawrence's real life, two such Arab boys existed, and were rumored to have been more than servants, young lovers, in fact. Their characters were described as "desert imps."

Arriving in London from Rio de Janeiro, Michel Ray was hailed as the most promising teenaged actor in England. He was seventeen at the time he joined the cast of *Lawrence of Arabia.*

"Lean offered me my choice of roles," Ray said. "I asked him which was the larger part—the one who gets blown up by a detonator near the railway line, or the one who dies in quicksand. I played the quicksand victim and that was the role movie-goers remember, forgetting the part that went to John Dimech, who played Daud. *[Before getting involved in the desert saga, Dimech had been a waiter in Malta.]*

Even though at the time he was still a teenager, Ray claimed that he often went carousing in Beirut during visits there with O'Toole and Sharif. "That was real super. Countless women pursued those guys, and the parties were really cool...or hot, to be more specific."

"I was the Daniel Radcliffe of my day, starring in films such as *The Brave One* and *The Tin Star.* But I gave up acting."

Later, as an Olympic athlete, he met his future wife, Charlene de Carvalho-Heineken, the major shareholder in the Heineken Brewing Company. He had changed his name to Michel de Carvalho, and at this point he married her. By the late 21st Century, they were one of the wealthiest couples in Great Britain, with a net worth of some ten billion British pounds.

The role of Tafas, Lawrence's guide, was originally envisioned as appropriate for Omar Sharif, but instead, it went to Zia Mohyeddin, a household name in Pakistan at the time, and later, a fixture in British cinema, too.

The character was based on one of Faisal's guides. He was Sheikh Obeid el-Rashid, and he was specifically referred to several times in Lawrence's *Seven Pillars of Wisdom.* Lean would later cast Mohyeddin in his upcoming film, *A Passage to India.*

The British actor, Hugh Miller, originally from the Lake District of England, had worked in silent movies, appearing in such films as *The Love of Sunya* (1927), starring Gloria Swanson.

In *Lawrence,* he was cast as an RAMC colonel, and he also worked on several Lean pictures as a vocal coach. Lean found it cheaper to give small bit parts to members of his crew, so he wouldn't have to import them from England.

Gamil Ratib, cast as Majid, was an Egyptian actor, known to Sharif. He was fluent in French, and later appeared with the *Comédie Française* in Paris. At the time, his English had to be dubbed.

I. S. Johar, a well-known Bollywood actor in India, was cast as Gasim, the Arab whom Lawrence rescues from a horrible death in the desert. *[Lawrence is later forced to shoot him to prevent a blood feud among the tribes.]* Flying in from Bombay, Johar was a star in both Hindi and Punjabi movies, and he also wrote and directed films, some of which were inspired by the Bob Hope and Bing Crosby "road" movies.

Married five times, with countless affairs on the side, he was viewed as a libertine and a "dangerous" film maker. He was not afraid of controversy, releasing such films as *Nasbani (Vasectomy),* spoofing Prince Minister Indira Gandhi's failed policy of population control by coerced vasectomies. The movie was banned in India.

A prolific English character actor, Canterbury-born Jack Gwillim was a close friend of Anthony Quayle, who was instrumental in getting Lean to cast him as the obnoxious club secretary at the British Military Headquarters. Before that, he had been one of the youngest men ever to obtain the rank of Commander in the Royal Navy.

A Londoner, Jack Hedley had been born Jack Hawkins, but changed his name so as not to be mistaken for the more famous actor. Lean cast him as a reporter on the trail of Lawrence. Around the time he worked for Lean, Darryl F. Zanuck had cast him in *The Longest Day* (1962).

Another Londoner, Henry Oscar, played Silliam, a servant to Prince Faisal (Guinness). He'd been acting since 1911, appearing in such films as *Fire Over England* (1937), with Laurence Olivier and Vivien Leigh.

In *The Four Feathers* (1939), he'd played a Sudanese doctor and was often cast in ethnic roles.

As Elder Harith in *Lawrence of Arabia,* John Ruddock was a Peruvian-born British film and TV actor and a noted Shakespearean player, though he made a number of films too. They included *Lust for Life* (1956), the Van Gogh story, starring Kirk Douglas.

Yet another Londoner, Larry Fowler, was Corporal Potter. He had a career spanning sixty years and some 200 movie roles. O'Toole agreed with critic Terence Pettigrew's assessment of Fowler: "He was as English as suet pudding. His characters were neither honest nor irretrievably delinquent, merely wise in the ways of the streets, surviving through a combination of wit and stealth. He had a certain arrogance, but there was an appealing vulnerability, too."

In a casting oddity, the English film and television actor, Peter Burton, played a sheik from Damascus. He was fresh from having portrayed Major Boothoyd (better known as "Q" in the first James Bond film, *Dr. No* (1962).

Lean Tells O'Toole He's Got to "Have a Nose Job" Before Filming Begins

"Your contract is being drawn up," Lean told O'Toole. "It's not that I don't trust you, but I'm having my attorney write into that contract that you're going to have your nose reshaped. Our aim is to turn you into one of the pretty boys of England. A screen idol. Horny women and faggots will follow you wherever you go. By the time *Lawrence of Arabia* comes out, you'll learn the price of fame. If you get up in some club or restaurant to go to the loo to take a piss, you'll find that a stampede of other guys will follow you."

Regardless of his reservations about O'Toole, Spiegel knew how to put the proper spin on his meeting when he faced the press. "Mr. O'Toole is a heady blend of sensitivity and vitality, more so than any other actor I've known. Like T.E. Lawrence himself, Mr. O'Toole is a rare bird, even an exotic breed from distant shores. He is utterly mesmerizing on the screen."

O'Toole wanted to know how long it would take to shoot *Lawrence of Arabia*. Spiegel lied to him, telling him the schedule called for a wrap within six months. Privately, he told his associates at Columbia, "That fucking Lean will take at least two and a half years before a premiere."

O'Toole would later refer to his "captivity in Jordan" as the longest rehearsal period in the history of cinema.

On December 15, O'Toole kept another appointment with Spiegel in his Mayfair office of Horizon Films, which was working with Columbia to produce the movie.

His nose was covered with a bandage, and he also wore thick black sunglasses to protect his sensitive eyes from the light. He was dressed in the only suit he owned.

He explained to Spiegel, "I had the nose job done. But since you were paying for it, I threw in another job and had my eyelids operated on to correct my squint. I want movie audience to swoon over my baby blues."

That day over lunch, Spiegel introduced him to Sir Anthony Nutting, a world expert on Arab affairs, who had served in the British cabinet as Minister of State for Foreign Affairs. In spite of their widely different backgrounds, the two men bonded.

Nutting later told Lean and Spiegel, "I'll become O'Toole's mentor, turning this low-class bloke into a young Edwardian gentleman who has been educated at Eton before going on to Oxford."

O'Toole had agreed to fly with Nutting to Jordan three months before the debut of filming. "There, I want you to live with me like a Bedouin. You will have no more need for that cheap suit you're wearing. It obviously wasn't tailored on Savile Row. It'll be off with your trousers and on with a white robe and boots."

As a Jew, Spiegel had another reason for hiring Nutting. He wanted him to ease his transition into the Middle East, "Paving the way," as he put it, to King Hussein, whose cooperation was needed during filming.

David Lean Promises Belly Dancers from Cairo, but Then Warns O'Toole: "You May Not be Free to Play Lawrence"

With his new nose and dyed blonde hair, O'Toole checked his appearance in the mirror in a downstairs loo before wandering into the Salisbury Pub, where David Lean arrived to join him ten minutes later.

His first words to O'Toole were, "I was amused by your performance in *The Day They Robbed the Bank of England.* But you've transformed yourself into something gorgeous, absolutely stunning, a matinee idol in the making."

"Oh, my God," O'Toole said. "Are you gay? Does that mean I'll have to drop trou for you during my time impersonating T.E. Lawrence?"

"I wouldn't exactly call myself gay," Lean said. "Unless you call a man who seduced at least eighteen young birds a week gay. Then I'm gay. Right now, I'm working my way through all the beauties for sale in Soho."

"A man after my own heart," O'Toole answered.

"Don't get the idea I'll be soft on you," Lean said. "Because I won't. I am a monomaniac who can be ruthless when it comes to shooting a film."

"I was afraid you might object to a tall Irishman like me playing a runt like Lawrence." O'Toole said.

"Don't worry," Lean said. "I'll cut you down to size."

"That means I won't have to whip out Lawrence's sharp dagger from the leather belt around my white robe and chop off about a foot of my legs."

"Not at all," Lean said. "In fact, I wanted to cast Lawrence tall, the way a hero should stand. Mickey Rooney, although a fabulous actor, would not be right playing Lawrence."

"I'm looking forward to a great working relationship with you," O'Toole said. "It seems we're both womanizers. What will we do for ladies in the desert? Some Arab might cut off our balls if we go after all those veiled women."

"Have no fear," Lean said. "I plan to import a steady supply of available women from Cairo, but only the most beautiful and sexiest belly dancers. I have to do that. You see, I like to eat it before I fuck it, and nearly all the Arab women, except for the whores, are revolted by the idea of having their closely guarded Islamic pussies eaten, especially by a decadent man from the Western world."

"We'll have a blast," O'Toole predicted.

"Not so fast! It seems you may not be free to play Lawrence."

"What in bloody hell are you talking about?" O'Toole asked.

"I learned this morning the octopus-like tentacles from Peter Hall at the Shakespeare Memorial Theatre are about to reach out and ensnare you."

On Broadway to See Becket, O'Toole Tastes Olivier's Tongue and Sees Anthony Quinn "Naked As I Was Born"

At the age of twenty-nine, Director Peter Hall was a "bright young thing" on a search for other bright young things to appear at the newly formed Royal Shakespeare Theatre at its home base in Stratford-upon-Avon, the much-visited birthplace of William Shakespeare.

For his inaugural season, he wanted to make "a big splash." Consequently, he obtained the rights from playwright Jean Anouilh to produce *Becket,* his drama about the turbulent love/hate relationship of King Henry II and Thomas à Becket, whom he would disastrously appoint as the Archbishop of Canterbury, in whose "home cathedral" he would eventually be murdered.

In 1959, Hall had attended a performance at the Royal Court Theatre in London. O'Toole was performing as Bamforth in a play, *The Long And The Short And The Tall.* Dazzled by his acting, Hall invited O'Toole to appear in three Shakespeare plays at the RSC in Stratford during the 1960s.

O'Toole was to be cast in the role of Petruchio in *The Taming of the Shrew.* He also took the controversial role of Shylock in *The Merchant of Venice,* and was to finish the season as Thersites in Shakespeare's bleak tragedy, *Troilus and Cressida.*

His acting also attracted wide acclaim in the London press, as critics journeyed to Stratford to see this "new star of the British stage."

Since he'd proved himself as an actor of charm, wit, and versatility, Hall proposed that O'Toole sign a three-year contract, with an agreement that he would launch their season with *Becket.* O'Toole would be cast in the role of Henry II, with the very talented Eric Porter, one of the best of all English actors, playing Becket, the Archbishop of Canterbury.

The RSC was just getting launched in 1960, and *Becket* was "going to be our rocket to blast us into heavenly spheres," Hall was quoted as saying.

So convinced was he that O'Toole was taking the role, that RSC flew the actor to New York to see Laurence Olivier as Becket and Anthony Quinn as the King perform in *Becket* on Broadway.

Arriving on his first visit to New York, O'Toole set out to "raise some hell," ending up the night with two hookers—one Chinese, one black—who he'd picked up on the corner of 8th Avenue and 42nd Street. As he later told his friend, actor Kenneth Griffith, "Like London, New York is a city noted for its diversity, and I wanted to sample the various races. Each race smells differently, you know."

"I did not know that," Griffith said.

London newspapers carried headline stores that O'Toole was "invading" New York to see Olivier's performance in *Becket.* Many critics suggested that someone more appropriate than "a Mexican actor" (Anthony Quinn) might have been selected to star as Henry II.

"My fare cost the RSC £150," O'Toole later said. "I went wild. Didn't catch a wink. Walked the streets. Talked to people at random. I stayed at the Algonquin Hotel, where Tallulah Bankhead used to give those wild parties in her suite, receiving guests in the nude. Alas, Tallulah wasn't there. Neither was Dorothy Parker. I didn't meet one star."

Two tickets were waiting at the box office of the St. James's Theater on Broadway for O'Toole, but he chose to arrive alone so he could concentrate more fully on the drama unfolding on stage. Only that afternoon, he'd read a magazine story about "the end of England's greatest romance,"

Shakespearean Politics
(aka "Naughty Peter")

The photo above depicts Laurence Olivier and Anthony Quinn on Broadway together in a NYC production of *Becket*.

O'Toole's "research trip" from London to see it was paid for by the Royal Shakespeare Company, who desperately wanted O'Toole as the star of their upcoming production of the play at Stratford.

After whoring around NYC, O'Toole dropped out of the RSC production to make *Lawrence of Arabia* instead.

the dissolving of the marriage of Olivier to Vivien Leigh and news of her "replacement," the English actress, Joan Plowright.

In the lobby, O'Toole introduced himself to Peter Glenville, who was with his longtime companion, the American interior designer, Stanley Mills Haggart. The director and the actor instantly bonded, the beginning of a friendship that would lead to the casting of O'Toole as Henry II in the film version of *Becket,* opposite Richard Burton.

After the final curtain, O'Toole was most polite, not only congratulating the director, but going backstage to greet both Olivier—the introduction arranged by Peter Hall—and Anthony Quinn, who had already been cast by Lean as the desert warrior in *Lawrence of Ara-*

British Director Peter Glenville: "I was always a better actor than any actor I ever cast."

bia. O'Toole had already met Quinn, having appeared with him in a small role recently in *The Savage Innocents.*

It was only after returning to London that O'Toole shared his honest appraisal of the performance of the two stars. "Quinn was absolutely dreadful, hideous, in fact. He was hardly convincing as Henry II. Total miscasting. He dropped turds all over the stage, making an ass of himself. Olivier was hardly better, delivering one of his worst performances. Roddy McDowall could have done better. That's how bad it really was. Both actors stunk like a subway toilet on 42nd Street."

"In case I left it out, the play was simply fabulous, with two great roles," O'Toole said.

Backstage, O'Toole was ushered into Olivier's dressing room, finding him sitting at his mirror, taking off his makeup and wearing only a jockstrap.

O'Toole congratulated Olivier on his performance.

Olivier shared his experience of working with American actors: "They are like football players. They wait until they have the truth in their arms before they start running off with the ball. No English actor—and, I assume Irish actors such as yourself—do that. We start running when the curtain goes up and hope that the truth will catch up with us."

Olivier dressed quickly, claiming he had to rush to meet Joan Plowright for dinner. At the door, he turned to O'Toole, "Now give me a kiss and put some feeling into it. I'm sure we'll see each other soon on the daunting shores of England."

Before leaving, he told O'Toole that he had been invited to Washington by Frank Sinatra to attend the inauguration of John F. Kennedy.

"Are you going to kiss him, too?" O'Toole asked.

"Of course, dear boy," Olivier said. "It's time that Irishmen learned that in England, tongue is a delicacy."

Shown into Quinn's dressing room, O'Toole encountered the Mexican actor "jaybird naked, his body glistening with sweat from having performed a difficult role."

O'Toole noted that Quinn was extremely agitated.

"I've just got a sloppy wet one from Olivier," O'Toole said. "What can I expect from you?"

"As you can plainly see, I've got something *bigger* than a kiss to offer, but it's not available to you. Only a beautiful woman can get a rise out of me."

"I'm glad to hear that," O'Toole said. "We share something in common."

"I'm glad to hear that," Quinn said. "From the sound of your voice, I thought you were another fag like Olivier."

"It's been said that most English actors sound like fags," O'Toole said.

Quinn confessed, "Olivier is driving me crazy. I'm even going to see a psychiatrist. I just can't compete with him on stage. It is my agony and humiliation. He has this clarion tone in his voice. I sound like a *Mexicano* ordering tacos at a cantina."

"I thought your performance was magnificent," O'Toole said.

"You're an Irishman, I hear. I can see you're full of Blarney."

Before he stepped into the shower, Quinn told O'Toole to look at some of the reviews on his dressing table.

From *The New York Herald Tribune,* O'Toole read: "Against Quinn's clod-like vigor, Olivier's Becket has an easy swagger, a skipping verve."

Another critic wrote: "If only Olivier's Becket would also have played against Olivier's Henry II."

Emerging from the shower, Quinn asked, "What was your opinion of the play?"

"I thought Olivier as Becket had a secret homosexual crush on you—at least that's how he played it," O'Toole said.

"He should get so lucky," Quinn said. "You've got to excuse me. I've got a date with an old flame, Ruth Warrick. Perhaps you saw her as Hearst's wife in *Citizen Kane.* Perhaps you and I will work in a play together one day."

"I should be so lucky," O'Toole said, trying to flatter him in spite of his awful performance.

At that point, Warrick knocked

| Anthony Quinn... "So many women, so little time." | Ruth Warrick... "So many men, so little time." |

222

on the door, and Quinn introduced the 1940s movie star.

He excused himself to hear some new directorial instructions from Glenville, backstage.

O'Toole chatted with Warrick, as she watched Quinn rushing across the stage. "Tony once told me that his goal was to impregnate every woman in the world. I didn't realize till later how literally he meant that."

[At the age of eighty-seven, in 1993, Quinn fathered his latest child, reportedly with his secretary. According to Warrick, he sometimes preferred seductions of a mother and later, her daughter. An example of that was Ingrid Bergman, his co-star in A Walk in the Spring Rain *(1969), and a rumored involvement with her daughter, Pia Lindstrom.]*

The RSC Sues O'Toole to Prevent Him from Starring in Lawrence of Arabia

"*Becket,* with Peter O'Toole as its star, is going to skyrocket the RSC to acclaim," Peter Hall had boasted to the press. "He will be our guided missile."

Then one morning, after Hall read in one of the U.K.'s premier newspapers, *The Times,* that O'Toole had been cast in *Lawrence of Arabia,* he flew into a rage. "How could he do this to me?" he asked his associates at Stratford-upon-Avon.

"O'Toole was our shining star," Hall said. "We were counting on him. We've been betrayed by this quixotic rogue."

It was announced that *Lawrence of Arabia* would begin shooting in Jordan in February of 1961. That was in glaring contrast to Hall's arrangements for *Becket* to open on April 25 at London's West End theater of Aldwyck, where rehearsals had been scheduled to begin on March 20th.

In his rather foolish way, O'Toole thought he could wrap up his role in *Lawrence of Arabia* in enough time to make the London premiere of *Becket.* Hall, however, appraised it differently. He told his fellow RSC members that O'Toole might not be finished with *Lawrence* for perhaps two years. In that, his prediction would come true.

RSC Director (Sir) Peter Hall with his wife, the French *gamine*, Leslie Caron. They were married in 1956.

Hall took his case to the press, telling reporters, "Peter has let down his fellow actors, and me personally. I trusted him and believed in him. Now we at the RSC are in limbo."

He was greatly troubled, pouring out his woes to his wife, the French actress and dancer, Leslie Caron. She had become an international star based on films which had included *An American in Paris* (1951), with Gene Kelly, and later in *Gigi* (1958) with Louis Jourdan, who had been voted "the handsomest man in the world." Hall had directed Caron in the London stage production of *Gigi*.

Before helming her, he had directed such stellar lights as Dame Edith Evans, Dame Peggy Ashcroft, Laurence Olivier, and Charles Laughton.

Before being cast as T.E. Lawrence, O'Toole had already begun to rehearse in private with Eric Porter, a Londoner, star of film, stage, and TV. Porter was set to play Thomas à Becket, opposite O'Toole as Henry II.

He'd made his stage debut at the age of seventeen in Cambridge. In 1955, O'Toole had met him at the Bristol Old Vic where O'Toole would appear in stage roles during the 1955-58 season. He told Porter that he was enthralled with his performances in the title role of Ben Jonson's *Volpone.* O'Toole would later cite Porter as one of "my major mentors" in teaching me how to act."

Hall had planned for Porter and O'Toole to stage the premiere of *Becket* in London, not in Stratford. It would be a command performance attended by royalty. Other West End producers attacked Hall for scheduling his premiere at a locale and date that would compete with their own stage presentations, asserted that the RSC should present its plays only in Stratford or else in traveling road shows touring the provinces. Hall ignored their protests.

He also announced to the press that Anouilh would withdraw his permission for the RSC to stage his play unless O'Toole retained his role. O'Toole's non-appearance would, it appeared at the time, at least, sabotage the entire production.

[O'Toole and Lean both suspected that Hall was a liar in making this claim.]

O'Toole booked a shuttle bus from London to Paris. Once there, he went directly to where Jean Anouilh was living at the time. Fortunately, the playwright was at home. When he confronted Anouilh with Hall's assertion, he said, "I am so very sorry, monsieur, I've never heard of you. Laurence Olivier and John Gielgud, I know. You, I do not know."

O'Toole took the first shuttle back to London, armed with this new bit of information. Knowing that Anouilh had never made any threats to close down Hall's production of *Becket* made him feel less guilty for having to withdraw from the RSC's stage play.

Back in London, O'Toole met with Hall to press his case for dropping out of *Becket,* but O'Toole adamantly refused to perform in Hall's RSC production.

"I'm going to Jordan to appear in the desert as Lawrence—and that's my final word. It's the role of a lifetime. It could make me an international movie star. Some old play I can do at any time. Shakespeare never dies, and there are other grand plays. Maybe one day, I'll be Henry II in *Becket,* but not now, darling. I'll make money, too, not the fifty quid a week you pay. My only suit is becoming threadbare."

"It's too late at this point for me to cast another actor," Hall responded.

Reading of O'Toole's conflicts with Hall, the distinguished English actress, Dame Peggy Ashcroft, called O'Toole and invited him for lunch at The Ivy, a well-known dining establishment in London's West End.

Enraged, Dame Peggy Ashcroft accused O'Toole of "listening to the siren call of some Hollywood mogul."

He had appeared opposite her on stage in *The Merchant of Venice.*

Once seated she seemed bubbling with anger and did not waste time with polite niceties. "What are you doing? Selling your soul to the Devil? I can't believe you're double crossing Hall, who has done so much to help launch your career!"

Allowing him no time to respond, she pressed her case. "Your loyalty should be to the stage, not thrown away in some silly attempt to become a male Elizabeth Taylor. You need more stage roles to fine tune yourself as an actor. As an apprentice in the theater, I played male roles in Shakespeare plays. I've been a queen and a whore, even a Chinese silk merchant with a preference for red. At the Old Vic, I did Goldsmith, plays by Sheridan, and, of course, plays by George Bernard Show, that lusty old fart."

"I've had to kiss the lips of Olivier and of John Gielgud, not known where their mouths had been the night before."

She'd ordered only a glass of water, which she slammed down on the table. "Please give me your firm and honorable word that you will not desert Hall and the players of the RSC."

"That I cannot do, darling," he said.

"You're a vain, selfish young man," she said, rising from the table as her waiter arrived with her main course.

"May I see you to a taxi?" O'Toole asked, politely.

"I'm quite capable of managing on my own, thank you very much." She turned her back on him and walked toward the door.

[Ironically, in the years to come, O'Toole noted that when David Lean offered Dame Peggy the role of "Mrs. Moore:" in his 1984 A Passage to India, *based on the E.M. Forster drama, she eagerly accepted.*

225

For her appearance in that film, she was nominated for Best Supporting Actress of the Year. Perhaps as a jab at her for her stern lecture against accepting movie roles, he sent her a note, volunteering that he'd fly to Hollywood to accept the Oscar for her when he'd read that she could not attend the ceremony herself.

She did not respond, but asked Angela Lansbury to accept her Academy Award for her.]

Hall decided to pursue legal action against O'Toole in a London court, even though he did not have a signed contract, only an oral agreement. "Peter gave me his word," Hall protested.

Spiegel's aide, Anthony Nutting, met with Hall, urging him to drop charges. "No judge will accept a handshake as a contractual agreement," Nutting claimed. "To go after Peter is a wasted effort on your part. Recast the role of Henry II."

Then Spiegel called Hall, telling him, "You really can't force an actor to give a performance. Peter might appear in *Becket,* but, believe me, he would deliberately give the worst performance in the history of the English theater. Trust me, I know our star...or rather, our star to be."

O'Toole told Lean, "I think we have Hall by the balls, and we can squeeze really, really hard. I'm determined to play Lawrence. Only an arrow in the heart can stop me now."

Hall filed a writ in a London court, where he asked that O'Toole be prevented from appearing on the stage or on the screen until he'd honored his obligation to the RSC. In a surprise move, a judge in his chambers at the High Court ruled against Hall, claiming that O'Toole was not under any iron-bound agreement to appear in *Becket* or in any other play for the RSC.

Spiegel, grateful that he would not be forced to buy out O'Toole's commitment with the RSC, was among the first to hear the news.

As it turned out, Hall was able to replace O'Toole with Christopher Plummer. *Becket* opened at the Aldwyck, and the RSC continued to present plays at this West End theater for more than two decades.,

Ironically, O'Toole ended up playing Henry II two times, but on the screen—first in the movie version of *Becket* (1964), opposite Richard Burton; and later in another incarnation of Henry II in *The Lion in Winter* (1968) co-starring Katharine Hepburn.

Before filming on *Lawrence of Arabia* began, O'Toole was flown to New York to meet with executives at Columbia, the men who had arranged for the financing of the film. O'Toole's reputation as a hellraiser and a heavy drinker had reached them, and there was fear that he might sabotage this very expensive movie in the months to come.

Finally, one of the younger executives, who had been "practically undressing me" (O'Toole's words), delivered his verdict: "I see six million dollars in this actor, here."

O'Toole glared at him. "How would you like a punch in the throat?"

Back in London, he met with Lean. "I hated that shit. The creepy little suit made me feel like a prize bull."

He hurriedly packed his clothes, made any final arrangements, and kissed his wife, Siân Phillips, goodbye, promising to send for her at some point.

At the airport, he confronted a reporter before flying to the Middle East. "I'm going to spread my wings," he said. "Perhaps I'll become an angel."

***

[As time went by, after the success of Lawrence of Arabia, *O'Toole wrote to Hall, telling him that at some point he'd be available to play either* Hamlet *or* Macbeth *for the RSC. The director did not respond.*

At a party in Mayfair, in London, O'Toole spotted Hall across a crowded room. He weaved in and out of his fellow drinkers until he reached Hall.

According to actor Anthony Steel, who was talking to Hall at the time, "O'Toole pinned Hall to the wall, towering over him. He pressed his demand for Hall to cast him in a Shakespeare play."

Hall broke free of his "imprisonment" to confront O'Toole. "As God is my witness, you'll never appear in an RSC play again. The only way you'll work for us is over my cold dead body."

"Going Insane" in the Desert, Cinema's Camel Rider Tangles with Lean and Becomes Spiegel's "Tearaway"

In February of 1961, three months before the actual shooting of *Lawrence of Arabia* was to begin, O'Toole arrived in Jordan, even though a complete script was still being written. In fact, as he learned, to his dismay, only twelve pages of a shooting script had been completed.

Back in England, Robert Bolt, at his home in Richmond Green, was working twelve hours a day on the first draft. Progress was slow.

He closed his Venetian blinds to shut out the day, not wanting to be distracted by anything outdoors. "My entire soul has been taken over by Spiegel and Lean," he lamented.

In Jordan, Anthony Nutting was waiting to greet O'Toole, as he'd been assigned to teach the actor "the ways of the desert," including camel riding. In London, he'd been a charmer, but in Jordan, he was a stern taskmaster.

O'Toole did not like animals, and he had a special loathing for camels. "When I faced my first camel, my first impulse was to give up and go back to London. I was afraid of this unpredictable creature. Maybe I imagined it, but when I was introduced to the camel I would ride, he spat on me."

His first day was spent bumping around on the back of a very frisky camel. "My Irish arse was sore and bleeding after seven hours of riding. That night, an aide applied some germ-killing antiseptic to my tender buttocks. I'd arrived back in my tent with blood oozing out of my jeans."

When he was able to begin his second lesson, he went to the local souk, where he purchased a Dunlopillo rubber pad. "It was pink and I stuffed it under my saddle. I imagine the other camel riders were calling me a 'girlie man.'"

Subsequently, the Bedouins christened O'Toole Ab-al-Isfanjah, meaning "Father of the Sponge."

O'Toole began to feel kind toward his camel when the animal later saved his life during a scene. Some four hundred Arab horsemen were hired, along with fifty Bedouins, for a battle scene. During the height of the action, O'Toole was knocked off his camel. Although he feared he'd be trampled to death during the mock battle, the camel—as he'd been trained to do—stood guard over his body, protecting him from the galloping Arab horsemen.

[When the picture was finally wrapped, O'Toole estimated that he'd ridden 5,000 miles on the back of a camel.]

Unknown to O'Toole, Nutting sent a cable to Spiegel. "Peter is a delicate type, a hothouse flower. He actually detests sunlight, preferring the comforts of the damned in a smoke-filled pub, where the lager flows. He's suffered many injuries. He complains constantly. Tells people I want to keep him in a closed coffin like a vampire between takes. The whole production, as you know, hinges on my getting O'Toole through this picture. If he drops out, the project is doomed."

At night, Nutting's main job involved keeping O'Toole from emptying all the bottles of Irish whiskey he had brought with him into the desert. He told O'Toole, "Look, if you don't stay sober, you're going to get kicked out of Jordan on your skinny ass. I'm not going to tolerate your getting drunk all the time. You're the only actor we've got to play Lawrence. If you don't pull through for us, the film is over. The end."

There was the all-important question of wardrobe. O'Toole was given an ivory white *kuffia* and pristine white robes. Nutting told him to move about in them until they were as comfortable as his English dress. "He took to those damn robes," Nutting later said. "He literally flounced in front of the camera in his white flowing robe. When the film was later released, homosexuals around the world erroneously spotted O'Toole as one of their own."

At night, O'Toole slept alone in a sparsely furnished Nissen hut with no air conditioning. He told Nutting. "I've got to have a woman. I'm not used to such sexual deprivation."

He was assured that after Lean arrived, prostitutes would be imported from Cairo to satisfy his libido.

There were some heavily veiled Bedouin women about, but he was forbidden even to talk to them. Nutting told him that if a local woman were caught even speaking to a Western man, she might be stoned to death.

"I slept alone with my trusty, always reliable fist providing me some relief—that is, until one night, a sandstorm blew my hut away," O'Toole said. "By then, they'd found this dilapidated trailer for me."

Finally, Lean, flowed by Spiegel, arrived on the set, a forlorn desert outpost near Jordan's border with Saudi Arabia, where midday temperatures registered 130°F.

As filming began, O'Toole was on the verge of a nervous breakdown. He wired Siân, in London, to come to Jordan—"or else I will go insane."

She had to turn down a choice stage role, but she gave it up and flew to the Middle East.

As related in her memoirs, when she arrived on location, he rushed to greet her and to take her in his arms. She found him "gorgeous on the outside, but emotionally distraught. I'd expected to discover him gaunt and emaciated, but he'd never looked more glamorous, with his bleached blonde hair and even a suntan, more unusual for his milky white skin. He was a matinee idol in the making."

After one inaugural tift, wherein Siân threatened to immediately return to London, she fell into his arms for a long overdue reunion. "We started all over again," she later said.

To her horror, he confided that he was considering flying back to London and abandoning the film, although aware that that would probably end his movie career before it had even begun.

Lean was offering him no praise for any of his performances, even though he was valiantly trying to please his director.

"I get only criticism. He's pushing me to the brink. I can't turn to him for anything. I come back to this boiling hot trailer every night in total despair. In fact, I'll come right out with it. I think I'm incapable of portraying Lawrence."

Somehow, Siân managed to raise his spirits. Early the next morning, he was on the set, trying to follow Lean's directions precisely.

During the day, there wasn't much company, except for Lean's Indian wife, Leila Lean, who lived in a concrete bunker screened off from daylight. She spent her afternoons playing some stringed instrument, which the crew labeled "the joke banjo."

Siân was introduced to Anthony Quinn, "who borrowed my eyelash curlers." She spotted this buxom blonde who had been pursuing Quinn across the desert, one of dozens of female admirers he entertained during the course of the filming.

At night, O'Toole appeared on the verge of a nervous breakdown, as he poured out his woes to her. He claimed that "Spiegel doesn't trust me; he considers me a tearaway."

The producer himself was under enormous pressure, receiving urgent calls two or three times a week from New York. The backers wanted to know, "Is our hellraiser running wild? I hope you're keeping this wildcat on a leash."

At one point, O'Toole and Siân were invited to dine aboard Spiegel's luxurious yacht, *Malahne,* which was moored offshore the port of Aquba.

"As a Jew, I'm afraid to come ashore. Some hostile Arab might assassinate me."

His spies had told him that a rumor was being spread among the Arabs that he and Lean, during their direction of the film, had employed a crew of Jewish cameramen and editors intent on making an anti-Arab movie.

The big event was the arrival of King Hussein, who flew to the set to assure his fellow Arabs that those rumors weren't true. Hussein had agreed to extend to Lean and his crew major cooperation, including use of equipment and *materiel* owned or controlled by the Jordanian government. That included the use of many Jordanian soldiers, who served as extras in the movie.

A State occasion with Royal Protocol: O'Toole (right) meets Hussein

[Hussein, who claimed to be a descendant of the Islamic prophet Muhammad through his role as leader of the ancient Hashemite dynasty, functioned as King of Jordan from 1952 to 1999, throughout forty years of the Cold War and the Arab-Israeli conflict. Siân defined him as "the conquering hero of Jordan" and compared his supporters as "the followers of Henry V on the eve of Agincourt." She later recorded her impression of his arrival. "The Arabs adore him—they'll do whatever he asks them to do, and it's pretty plain that he loves them, as

King Hussein (above) shocked his subjects by marrying the daughter of a British Army officer.

well."]

Hussein spent time on the set, having lunch under a tent with Siân, O'Toole, and Lean, and watching some of the filming as it progressed. Later that same day, Hussein visited Lean's cluttered administrative headquarters in the desert to make a phone call. He was gone for two full hours.

When he returned, he appeared overjoyed. O'Toole told Lean, "He must have gotten some good news."

It was only later that they learned what had put a smile on the King's face.

He graciously invited O'Toole and Siân for dinner at his relatively modest palace in Amman.

Before dinner, he showed them into his carpet-strewn salon for mint tea. He told them that he'd recently had his appendix removed, without the use of anesthetic. "I was very brave. After the operation, I got up and walked out."

Siân found the King dashing, short of stature, and rather handsome, noting in her memoirs that he was fortunate that he had not become an actor, "since he was so much smaller than the most petite of actresses."

At the palace, O'Toole noted that Hussein was heavily guarded, no doubt fearing an assassin. He bragged not only about his bravery, but his fleet of Rolls Royces and private airplanes.

Under grilling from O'Toole, he admitted that the people of Jordan were very poor.

"I know how to make your country rich," O'Toole chimed in. "Round up a lot of empty Coke bottles and fill them with water from the River Jordan. Born Again Christians in America would buy these bottle like bargains in a fire sale."

For the most part, O'Toole steered clear of Middle Eastern politics. However, Lean—in advance of their arrival—asked him to remove the jeweled Star of David he had worn around his neck since the debut of his arrival in Jordan. It had been a gift from his mother, in recognition of her son's talent during his portrayal of Shylock, Shakespeare's most famous Jewish character, in *The Merchant of Venice.*

When taken to watch a day's shooting in the desert, Siân learned where the loo (toilet) was. She was given a shovel to cover up her waste in the sands.

She was also told not to be surprised if she saw Arab men walking around holding hands. It was pointed out that whereas this act might be interpreted differently in Britain, in Arabia, this hand-holding was a long-enduring form of male bonding.

That night in the desert, Arabs invited O'Toole and Siân to a sheep roast, a rather rare event. She learned that the locals consumed all parts of the slain beast, including the eyeballs and the testicles.

On his final night with Siân, O'Toole was said to have held her close, making love as a final farewell.

Back in London, she wrote, "I miss him terribly."

He later said, "That trip to Jordan was not the only time I'd send for Siân when I faced a crisis. The Old Girl always comes to my rescue."

Within a few days of Siân's departure, Hussein was back on the set again—in fact, he made several visits. He had two reasons for welcoming the cast and crew of *Lawrence of Arabia*. During the year the filmmakers were in his country, they would spend more than the total Jordanian tax revenue.

But Hussein's more compelling reason for flying to the film location aboard his Howker Hunter fighter jet was that he'd fallen in love with an English girl, Toni Gardiner, the on-site switchboard operator for Horizon Films. Like a desert flower, their romance was in full bloom.

In May, 1961, King Hussein married his English bride, Toni Gardiner, whom he'd met when she was working as a secretarial assistant and phone operator on the set of *Lawrence of Arabia*. Raised by English parents in British Colonial Malaysia, she produced four children with the king, one of whom became Jordan's King Abdullah II in 1999.

Even after her eventual divorce from the king in 1971, Toni, in her capacity as Princess Muna al-Hussein, continued to live as a figure of respect and dignity in Jordan, becoming deeply involved in the development and teaching of nursing and the medical professions.

When the announcement of their upcoming marriage was made at Aqaba, celebratory gunfire was heard throughout the port. Many locals thought that the gunfire derived from an Israeli attack upon their city. The celebratory mood was dimmed somewhat when the populace learned that the bride-to-be was British.

Nutting always regretted the marriage. He told the press "King Hussein just whisked her away, to the ever-lasting detriment of the phone exchanges at our headquarters. *[After her departure]* we never could get through another international call. Toni was the only one who knew how the system in the desert worked."

[Born Antoinette Avril Gardiner in England's East Suffolk, she was the daughter of a British Army officer. Hussein had divorced his first wife. When he took Toni as his bride, she became Her Royal Highness, Princess Muna al-Hussein. The royal couple would have four children before their divorce in 1972.]

In O'Toole's final summation of his experience in the Jordanian desert, he claimed, "You have to be insane to remain sane."

***

[When Spiegel sent Hussein the final print of Lawrence of Arabia, *the King loathed it, banning it from being shown in Jordan. He claimed, "The film does not respect Arab culture and its people."*

Other Arab countries followed his lead, all except Egypt. In Cairo, President Gamal Abdel Nasser praised the move for "its depiction of Arab nationalism."]

O'Toole in the Middle East—Beirut Bordellos, Gambling Casinos, & Belly Dancers from Egypt

When O'Toole was given two days off, he visited Bethlehem, but not for any particular religious reason, admitting, "I am a retired Christian."

At the time, the West Bank was under the control of King Hussein. Recalling his visit, O'Toole claimed, "I was horrified at the commercialization of Jesus in this shrine city. My God, they even called their leading movie house *The Manger Cinema.*"

"I looked to see what film was playing," he said. "My dearest friend, the actor Kenneth Griffin, was appearing in *Circus of Horrors* (1960). I bought a ticket and went inside, where I was treated to sadism, cruelty, and violence. In one scene, I spotted Ken wearing a sweater I had lent him and which he'd never returned. Perhaps the producers should pay me royalties for using my sweater as part of the movie's wardrobe."

The next day, he was back on the set.

O'Toole stood with Lean in the desert. Dozens of Arab extras had huddled like sheep under the overhand of a cliff to protect themselves from the blistering sun. Suddenly, a collective murmur arose from them *"AUDA TAY! AUDA TAY! AUDA TAY!"*

Lean took in the strange appearance of an imposing Arab chieftain. Then he turned to O'Toole and said, "Fuck Quinn! Let's fire him and hire this guy instead, whoever he is."

"It *is* Quinn," O'Toole said.

When Quinn came up to Lean, the director complimented him on his makeup. He told them that he had used a photograph of the real Auda as inspiration for his transformation into the desert warrior.

On location, Quinn and O'Toole began to spend some evenings together. One night over dinner, Quinn confessed to O'Toole, "I feel like a failure."

"Hell, you've been internationally acclaimed as an actor."

"It's not that. I'm talking about myself as a man. As a dark, lonely kid growing up with a twisted smile, I had a dream, and that was to be a Michelangelo, Napoléon, Shakespeare, Martin Luther, Pablo Picasso, and yes, Jack Dempsey—all rolled into one impressive package. I've got the impressive package, all right—just ask Evelyn Keyes—but that's not what I meant. I did try to be Dempsey, but dropped out because I lacked a killer instinct. Perhaps I'll end up a painter to give Picasso competition."

"When I was a kid, I once did a drawing of Douglas Fairbanks (Senior) when he was shooting *The Black Pirate* (1926). He gave me twenty-five dollars for it. That was a lot of money back then for a poor boy like me."

One Saturday afternoon, Quinn and O'Toole visited a local *souk*. In one booth, they met a tailor from Pakistan, who made suits for ten dollars each. Quinn ordered thirty of them, and later, gave them away.

O'Toole ordered even more. "I don't know what he did with his," Quinn said. "He told me that for years, he owned only one suit in his closet. I guess he was making up for his previous deprivation."

One afternoon of the following week, they went to a beach bordering the Red Sea. "We were told that the sea was filled with chicken fish, a horrible creature that looked like a small wet hen with feathers. Their sting could be deadly. I warned Peter not to go into the water, but he wasn't afraid. He told me, 'If one of those creatures tastes my blood, the bastard will die a ghastly death from alcohol poisoning.'"

When Omar Sharif arrived on location, O'Toole and Quinn saw less and less of each other, since Quinn had found a new companion. "Instead of hanging out with Peter, I took to my trailer, which I had demanded to be air conditioned. No longer with Peter, I spent my nights with this big tit blonde, a dead ringer for Dinah Dors. She had sex like there was no tomorrow."

When O'Toole had made a screen test with Sharif, he'd nicknamed him Cairo Fred, and that's what he continued to call him. "I found my soulmate," O'Toole said. "He's my kind of guy. He and I like the same things, notably women. He also liked to raise hell with me, and we're addicted to gambling."

The two actors often discussed the characters they were playing. Both of them stated that they felt that the screenwriter, Robert Bolt, had not clearly defined the nature of their relationship on screen. O'Toole claimed that because of Lawrence's closeted sexual preference, that he should have a homosexual fixation on Sherif Ali.

"Does that mean you're going to play Lawrence like a lovesick young girl lusting after my body?" Sharif facetiously remarked.

"Something like that," O'Toole answered. "I'll wing it."

When a break came in the shooting schedule, Sharif and O'Toole flew to Beirut, the capital of Lebanon, known at the time as "the Paris of the Middle East" and a city noted for its cosmopolitan sophistication, its decadence, and its debauchery.

O'Toole wasn't impressed with the Arab pilot, referring to him as "The Stepin Fetchit of the air." The reference was to a wide-eyed, slow-talking, shuffling, almost moronic black actor who perpetuated racial stereotypes on the screen.

Before the weekend in Lebanon ended, the two actors suffered gambling losses that ate up most of their earnings from the *Lawrence* film. O'Toole called the casinos of Beirut "crooked."

After their staggering losses, he suggested a visit to the city's most elegant bordello, "The House of Forbidden Pleasures," which was notorious at the time, advertising that "There is no desire we cannot satisfy."

In the reception area, they were greeted by "Queen Cleopatra" of Egypt, a 300-pound *Madame* in a beaded red dress and lots of purple eye shadow.

Looking them up and down, she evaluated both of them as homosexuals. "I've catered to your kind of gentlemen for years," she told them, "and I know what you want. I'm never wrong about these matters. I have in service tonight a lusty young blonde stallion from Germany, a French boy from Marseille who is celebrated for his tasty breasts, and an Arab boy from Syria noted for the sweetness of his breath, which has the aroma of a succulent date. That is only the beginning of my selection. Any age you want is available except the cradle."

"You've misjudged us, Cleo," O'Toole said. "We had women in mind."

"Oh, I see," she said. "What an unusual request for an Englishman. I can supply almost any woman: Sudanese, Lebanese, Spanish, French, or German. Perhaps you want a girl from Singapore? Most of them are sweet sixteen, also much younger. My special surprise tonight is an eight-year-old virgin from India. She is very, very expensive."

"I'll take the Lebanese," O'Toole said. "Sometimes it's best to enjoy the flavor of the land you're visiting."

After a night of debauchery, Sharif recorded that he woke up the next morning in a bed with a young woman. He stumbled into an adjoining room to find O'Toole asleep in bed and in the arms of a girl nearly identical to the one I just left in my bed."

To their dismay, they saw that they had overslept and missed their flight to Jordan. An enraged Lean would have to shoot without them that day.

Back in Jordan, around the campfire, Sharif learned what a marvelous storyteller O'Toole was. By the time he'd spun the tale of their adventure in

Beirut, the number of girls in each of their beds had climbed to six each, evoking the seductions of a sultan from a tale from *Arabian Nights.*

When news came in from New York, they learned that a new dance craze had taken hold in America. Called "The Twist," it had originated from a recording by Joe Dee, performed at the Peppermint Lounge in Manhattan. Since there were no women to dance with them, O'Toole played the record nightly and learned the dance movements with Sharif. He later said, "It was all in vain. By the time we finally reached London, the Twist was out of fashion."

Throughout the rest of the shoot, Sharif and O'Toole continued to go "slumming," patronizing only the most dangerous bars in Beirut and continuing to frequent bordellos and casinos, where they always seemed to lose.

O'Toole also found time to relate to his fellow co-stars. Cast as General Allenby, Jack Hawkins and O'Toole went over their lines together, frequently rewriting Bolt's script. This enraged Lean, who warned them to say their lines as written and already approved by him.

When he saw the growing friendship between O'Toole and Hawkins, Lean called O'Toole aside. "Onscreen, you must be aloof with Hawkins' character. Instead, you seem to be very friendly with him."

"We're both experienced actors, and what we do socially is not going to interfere with our acting," O'Toole answered.

He decided to ignore Lean's device, and went on to develop a strong bond with Hawkins, a bond made even stronger when, later, Hawkins co-produced *The Ruling Class,* in which O'Toole starred.

O'Toole also spent many evenings with Alec Guinness, who understood that he has lost the role of Lawrence because of his age, and not because of any lack of talent.

During his first evening with Guinness, O'Toole discovered that the veteran actor had misgivings about playing another foreigner. He'd balked at the idea of playing an Indian for Lean and Spiegel, when they'd come to him about starring as Ghandi in an epic movie. He also felt he'd been horribly miscast as the Japanese industrialist, Koichi Asano, in the 1961 movie, *A Majority of One.* He'd starred opposite Rosalind Russell, also miscast as a Jewish widow.

In the beginning, Guinness remembered O'Toole like this: "He has great wayward charm and is very striking in eye and carriage. Wife seems nice, too. There's a charming and most intelligent Egyptian actor here as well called Omar Sherif (*sic*), who is the matinee idol of the Middle East. A few others are a bit nondescript and uninteresting. O'Toole is marvelously good as Lawrence. He's dreamy good to act with, and has great personal charm and gaiety. He obviously goes off the trails every now and then, and I should think his wife—who has a sort of strength and wisdom about her—has got as much as anyone can handle. But he has a good heart and wit as well."

Guinness told O'Toole that he found inspiration for his character of Prince Feisal in Lawrence's *Seven Pillars of Wisdom.* He read a passage:

"I felt at first glance that this was a man I'd come to Arabia to meet, the leader who would bring the Arab Revolt to full glory. He was a man of moods, flickering between glory and despair. His dark, appealing eyes, set a little sloping in his face, were bloodshot, and his hollow cheeks deeply lined and puckered with reflection. In appearance, he was tall, graceful, and vigorous."

In spite of his initial fondness for O'Toole, Guinness' feelings had cooled considerably by the end of the shoot in Jordan. "I found a lot of O'Toole's drunken antics outrageous."

[As if to infuriate Guinness all the more, O'Toole in the years to come announced that he was taking over Guinness' Oscar-winning role as an English officer in a remake, then being discussed, of David Lean's The Bridge on the River Kwai *(1957). For O'Toole, that projected remake eventually died.]*

Fat Fátima, Dominatrix from Egypt, Teaches O'Toole "The Pleasure of Pain"

Through a connection he'd made with a bordello in Cairo, Lean secretly arranged a shipment of eager-to-please prostitutes to be sent to Jordan. A little heavy for typical American and English taste, these women provided "comfort" to O'Toole and some other lusty members of the cast, including Lean, who had a gargantuan sexual appetite.

Spiegel, aboard his yacht, *Malahne,* had his own underaged beauties imported from Lebanon. O'Toole told Quinn, "That fat Jewish pervert takes special delight in deflowering Arab virgins."

To prepare for his upcoming torture scene with Jose Ferrer, O'Toole made an odd request to Lean. He asked him to secure a dominatrix from Cairo who would teach him about "the pleasure of pain."

Lean thought that would be a very good idea. "I may shoot that scene when we transfer to Spain, but it's wise to rehearse in advance. It will be one of the most pivotal and controversial scenes in our film."

Two weeks later, Fátima arrived. "She would be called Fátima," O'Toole said. "How original."

She was a very big woman with too much makeup. "I have a belly on me, and you're a very skinny boy," she told O'Toole. "As you know by now, Arab men like women with bellies. That's why belly dancers are such popular attractions."

She had a good command of English, and also spoke French. In a stern voice, she insisted that he strip and lie on his back while she placed two leather straps on him, one across his chest, another restraining his thighs.

After he'd stripped, she removed all of her clothes as well.

She also had a large leather bag in which she stored her instruments of torture, including a six-inch hatpin used for the puncturing of a co-participant's skin.

"I sometimes work with Western men," she confessed to O'Toole. "Most of my clients are Arab men. They have dominated women for centuries. I take a special thrill in dominating them."

She began by taking sharp metal snaps, somewhat like a clothespin, and applying them to each of his breasts. When he winced in pain, and asked her to go easy, she slapped him really hard. "Take it like a man. From this moment on, you are in my power. You obey my orders. You must endure."

As O'Toole later confessed, Fátima told him that many of her clients have an orgasm during her rituals. "That didn't happen with me," he later said to Quinn. "If anything, I shrank."

She ran her long, jeweled fingers over his chest, complimenting him on how smooth and hairless it was. "In Cairo, at this point in my ritual, many of my clients prefer me to take a hot iron and burn the chest of my initiate. But Monsieur Lean has asked that I leave no marks on your body, no letting of blood."

She took a lithe strip of bamboo and began whipping his feet, the blows falling with clockwise precision, never relenting until she caused the most excruciating pain. She was careful not to break the skin, but she warned him that his pain would endure long after the end of the ordeal itself.

Her whipping was administered with such precision that she evoked a master cellist at his art. As she whipped, she chanted, "un autre coup," meaning "another lash."

Then she unstrapped him and had him turn over onto his stomach, where she proceeded to strap him down once again. Then she began to administer, with rhythmical precision, a beating to his buttocks. She continued with this for about twenty minutes as he moaned in agony. At this point, she blindfolded him.

As O'Toole remembered "Fat Fátima" from Egypt, "Her large nipples were pierced, and her mammoth breasts hung down to South Africa."

After that, she inserted her forefinger with its long, sharp nail, into his anus. He squirmed in discomfort, demanding that she stop that at once, but relentlessly she continued. Shortly after removing her finger, she jabbed what felt like a monstrous dildo deep into his rectum. He

238

screamed with pain, begging her to stop. That seemed to goad her into a fierce rape. As he later claimed, "It was pure agony, the worst pain I'd ever experienced in my life." This torture went on for ten excruciating minutes, but seemed much longer.

Later, when she'd freed him, he asked her, "Why in bloody hell did you do that? God damn you! I'm bleeding!"

"You must understand, *monsieur*," she said. "I was told that you'll be raped by four brutish Turkish soldiers. I'm certain that only your face will be depicted on camera. You can't fake it. After my own rape of you with a dildo, you can re-create the pain in your face so that it's realistic on camera."

"I know of such things. When a man is raped for the first time, it is important that the initial shock be painful. The realization must come that the victim has fallen under the control of another person who will use him to satisfy his own desires. Searing, burning pain must be felt by the victim, coupled with shock. That will lead to resignation, and, finally, ultimate acceptance. At one point, the victim will quit resisting and will submit to his captors. He will experience a loss of identity, but will come away with self-understanding. As someone once wrote, 'I am the helpless one who knows another's pleasure as pain.'"

At the end of her labors, which lasted for two hours, she dressed before unstrapping him. She wore a large black robe.

In her final words to him, she said, "My job was to provide ecstasy for you. To teach you that pain and suffering can be beautiful. Remember, I was far easier on you than those Turkish rapists will be."

He later shared the details of his brutal experience with Quinn, who demanded a detailed description. O'Toole defined Fátima as "a modern-day Marquise de Sade."

"I now have the sorest ass in the desert, not only from Fat Fátima, but from that damn camel riding," O'Toole claimed.

"I have learned a lesson in life," he said. "From now on, I want to be the penetrant, not the penetrantee."

Some critics defined the desert itself as the star of the picture. This shot shows "The Trek to Aqaba," as viewed from Jebal Tubeiq in Jordan.

Chapter 13

Lawrence of Arabia (Part Two)

Cast & Crew Invade Spain & Morocco

Royal Seductions & Slave Auctions in the Sahara

As Peter O'Toole later admitted, "I was never more glamorous than the night of the world premiere of *Lawrence of Arabia*. Even Her Majesty, with her diamond tiara, could not compete with
my male beauty. David Lean stood beside me looking like a schoolteacher from Harwich."

"I'm not really a Royalist, but had Her Highness summoned me to her boudoir that night, I, as
her obliging subject, would have answered the call to arms."

After 117 days of shooting in the desert, there came a temporary lull in the production of *Lawrence of Arabia*. With it came the opportunity
for cast and crew to embark on much-needed vacations.

In an effort to cut costs, Spiegel had closed his operations in Jordan, and
announced his intention of resuming his filming in Spain, a locale which of-

fered deserts, Moorish architecture, and crews of savvy technicians who were familiar with filming epics, earlier examples of which had included *El Cid* (1961).

As a Jew in Jordan, Spiegel had begun to fear assassination, convinced as he was that certain Arabs planned to poison him.

During an Entre'Acte in England, O'Toole Accidentally Pierces His Foreskin, and Is Jailed in Bristol for Drunk Driving

In Jordan, before O'Toole flew back to London and to his wife, Siân, he purchased a pair of earrings whose origins dated back to ancient Greece. It was illegal to export antiquities from Jordan, regardless of their original point of origin, so he decided to smuggle them through the stern and very thorough Jordanian custom inspectors.

As he later told Sharif, "I concealed them in my foreskin. I figured even the most thorough of custom inspectors wouldn't go there."

He was right. But aboard the plane, an accident occurred. The sharp point of one of the earrings pierced his foreskin, and he yelped in pain.

As he later confessed, "It took a week for my penis to heal. I was not able to fornicate. I could achieve orgasm only by having the tip of a delicate tongue gently darting in to lick the tip of my penis. It was most unsatisfactory."

"I had been a desert rat for six months, and I was in desperate shape," he recalled. "I wouldn't say that shooting *Lawrence* in the desert had been a dangerous experience, no I wouldn't say that, except for a blow to my groin that virtually destroyed my most valuable appendage. There was a skull fracture, too. My right anklebone was cracked, my thigh practically ripped off. Liga-

> **LOVE IS PAIN**
> A Token of O'Toole's Marital Esteem for Siân
>
> Depicted above are ancient Greek earrings more or less equivalent to the pair O'Toole described as having smuggled out of Jordan in his foreskin.

Hanging Out with the "Scruff & Slags"

ments in both of my hips were torn. The noonday desert sun gave me third degree burns, a camel attacked me, dreadful beasts. I almost lost two fingers and my thumb was broken. My spine was dislocated. I nearly broke my neck shooting one very difficult scene. Other than that, there were no problems."

Exhausted and in pain from his injuries, he checked into a hospital in Suffolk to "mend and repair my broken body."

He remained there for a week, receiving special attention from many of the nurses, including a "sweet little tart from Ashby-de-La-Zouch up in Leicestershire, land of King Lear and Ivanhoe. Her name was Priscilla, and she had more bosom than brains. She was a delightful little Florence Nightingale. Fortunately she had night duty. Hospitals at three in the morning are lonely places, and a red-blooded male needs the comforts that only a young woman can provide. Solace to the soul and other parts of the body, I call it."

[Editor's note: The name of the town that was referenced by O'Toole in the paragraph above is usually shortened to "Ashby," a name that linguists translate from the Vikings as "a settlement near a copse of ash trees." The town's longer name dates from the years after the Norman conquest of England, when it became a fiefdom under the control of a family named La Zouche during the reign (1216-1272) of Henry III.]

After his release from the hospital, Siân welcomed Peter to his new home in London, which she'd been creating for him. She found his luggage laden with Arabian robes, coffee pots in three sizes, and brass pestles and mortars for crushing cardamom seeds for blending into Arabic coffee, which she never made. The glass objects he brought home broke on touch. He renewed his relationship with his young daughter, Kate, who seemed to have forgotten him.

Siân later wrote, "He was bigger and handsomer than ever. In spite of his ordeal, he seemed fitter than ever. We all wanted to touch him. What it must be like for him to be back in England after all these months and still only half through this huge job."

During the work interim, Spiegel had ordered Omar Sharif to fly directly to London and to avoid a stopover in Cairo. He feared that if he were to touch down in Egypt, local authorities might not let him leave because he had been working for months for a Jewish producer.

In his memoir, in reference to their time in London, Sharif wrote "Peter and I spent our evenings and nights together, doing all the pubs and night clubs. One night, Peter broke with our tradition. He decided to take me to the theater."

In his book, *The Eternal Male,* out of discretion, Sharif drew the curtain on what he and O'Toole were doing during their carousing and instead, devoted the rest of the passage to praising the British theater.

Lean later summarized what his two co-stars were up to in London by saying, "Let me put it this way: Neither of them had trouble getting a date, maybe more than one."

Back in circulation again, O'Toole invited Sharif to one of his favorite pubs, The Queen's Elm along Fulham Road, down in Chelsea. There, they met the painter, Francis Bacon. O'Toole, enjoying a bottle of Irish whiskey, was reunited with his "mates" from RADA, actors Albert Finney and Alan Bates. Finney was particularly eager to learn of the shooting of *Lawrence of Arabia,* as he had previously rejected the title role.

"We were a rowdy bunch," O'Toole said, "In some of the snooty Mayfair bars, we were called lager louts, slags, and scruffs."

[Note: A scruff is someone who is unkempt and slovenly, and a slag is that scum formed on the surface of molten metal.]

Shortly before Christmas of 1961, O'Toole drove up to his new London home and presented Siân with a Yuletide gift: A new Morris Minor, tied and ornamented with a mammoth red ribbon.

The sight of the vehicle alarmed her, as she'd ridden with her husband before when he was behind the wheel. Whenever challenged for his reckless driving, he always said, "I am the captain of this vessel. We're going to have no *Mutiny on the Bounty* when I'm steering this carriage."

Then, in his characteristic way, he disappeared, with the car, for a week. He later explained his absence to Lean, who had warned him to stay out of trouble during this interlude in film production.

"After my release from the desert, and later from the hospital, I went bonkers. I drove to Bristol."

As he described it to Lean, "I left a lot of pretty little girls behind in Bristol when I became the terror of that city when I performed in all those plays at the Bristol Old Vic. I had pierced through a lot of maidenheads, and I was anxious to see how many little Peter O'Tooles were running about the city."

There, one night after a heavy drinking binge at the Hobgoblin on Bryon Place, he exited from the pub and got into his Morris. He was almost blind drunk.

Once inside the car, he floored the accelerator and had gone no more than a block before he crashed into the front of a warehouse. Miraculously, he escaped death, suffering only a few minor injuries.

Two policemen in a squad car arrived on the scene with sirens wailing and dome lights flashing.

Police later reported that O'Toole emerged from the wreckage relatively unscathed. He told the arresting officer, "Okay, Skip, let's go to the station. I'm drunk."

Hauled into court, O'Toole was fined 75 pounds and tossed into jail for the night. He also had his driver's license suspended for a year.

As for Siân's Morris Minor, it was hauled off to the junkyard.

The ever loyal Siân drove to Bristol to rescue her errant husband and haul him back to London, where he learned that another member of the *Lawrence of Arabia* team had also been jailed.

Its screenwriter, Robert Bolt, was behind bars.

***

During the break in filming *Lawrence of Arabia,* its screenwriter, Robert Bolt, arrived in London. He had already written the first half of the movie's screenplay, the part which had already been filmed in Jordan. His draft of the second part had been rejected by both Spiegel and Lean.

So far, Bolt likened his experience in writing the script as tantamount "to the erection of the pyramids. Working in Jordan was a continuous clash of egomaniacal monsters, wasting more energy than dinosaurs, and pouring rivers of money into the sand."

Taking time off from script writing, Bolt, on September 17, 1961, joined 10,000 other protesters, including Vanessa Redgrave, Bertrand Russell, and John Osborne, in blocking traffic in London's Trafalgar Square and on White-hall, the seat of the British government. These demonstrations were organized by the Campaign for Nuclear Disarmament.

The aim involved having Britain destroy its arsenal of nuclear weapons. The belief on the ground was that if the Soviet Union attacked the West, Britain would be spared destruction, since it would no longer present a threat. The group went on to conclude, loudly and as part of their civil unrest, that in the event of a nuclear war, whereas New York and Washington would be dev-astated, a disarmed London would survive more or less intact.

Bolt had been one of the organizers of the massive but massively disor-ganized protest. No permits had been granted, so the marches were illegal.

As one of the spokespersons for the movement, Bolt was arrested and

So *this* is how you spend your holiday? HMP (Her Majesty's Prison) Drake Hall and its screenwriting inmate, the very idealistic Robert Bolt (right).

hauled before the Magistrates' Court. There, he was given an option: Recant and swear not to participate in any additional protests or spend a month in the draconian "prison camp" known as Drake Hall in Staffordshire.

As the author of a play about Sir Thomas More (1478-1535), the Archbishop of Canterbury, standing up for his principles, Bolt could hardly recant. When he refused to recant, orders were issued for his incarceration in prison.

Once there, he believed that he would be given pen and pencil and allowed to continue working on the second half of the script for *Lawrence,* most of which, it was understood, would be filmed in Spain and Morocco.

But the warden, whom Bolt defined as sadistic, refused to allow him access to writing supplies, claiming that anything produced in Her Majesty's prison could and would be destroyed unless Bold signed a "recognizance of good behavior." The writer refused to sign it, and was subsequently informed that his script would be seized and burned. Actually, there could be no script because he was not allowed to have any writing materials.

Frantically, Spiegel sent Bolt long, detailed cables, warning him that the entire film would have to be shut down and perhaps never completed. "The financiers are ready to pull the plug," he wrote. "Hundreds will be unemployed. All of our work in Jordan might be tossed aside. We wouldn't be the first epic film to be ditched."

But none of Spiegel's arguments changed Bolt's mind.

In London, Spiegel sought legal recourse, but to no avail. Eventually, he opted to meet with Bolt face-to-face. As "extra ammunition" (his words), he demanded that O'Toole accompany him to Drake Hall. In Jordan, he had noted the easy working relationship between the writer and the actor, and he thought that O'Toole would be more effective in persuading Bolt to recant than he would.

Inside the gloomy confines of Drake Hall, Spiegel repeated all arguments, but Bolt remained unmoved. Using a different style, O'Toole used his wit and charm, an offensive that lasted for a full two hours, before Bolt very reluctantly agreed to recant.

From there, negotiations with the police and prison authorities took more than four hours before Bolt's imprisonment came to an end. Shortly before midnight, a Rolls Royce pulled up at the prison's main entrance. Climbing aboard for the trip back to London were Spiegel and O'Toole, along with the just-released inmate, Bolt himself.

Scriptwriting for the second part of *Lawrence of Arabia* could now resume.

[Long after the finished film was released, Bolt told a reporter, "I never forgave Spiegel for getting me out of prison. I betrayed my principles. It was the most shameful moment of my life."

In Seville, the Duchess of Alba Seduces
"A Poor Boy from the Ghetto of Leeds"

After a hiatus in England, cast and crew were flown to Seville, the capital of Andalusia in southern Spain, city of Don Juan, the *Reconquista,* and Carmen. After the bleakness of Jordan, it was like wandering into an oasis with orange trees, flower-filled patios, castanet-rattling gypsies, women wearing mantillas, and lovesick *torreos.*

From Jordan, the technical equipment for *Lawrence of Arabia* had been shipped by tramp steamer to the port of Cádiz, and then transported by truck north to landlocked Seville. Included were the "star camels," along with Arabian horses, even stuffed camels that gave off a sickening stench. The crew had purchased the skins from a slaughterhouse. There, the carcasses had been stuffed with straw in case David Lean needed them as distant props in certain scenes.

Lean said that he felt that the ancient city of Seville, once controlled by Moors from North Africa, could evoke a setting from the Middle East, thanks to its blasting heat and because it still had many examples of Moorish-Arab architecture remaining from before the Catholic conquest.

Sections of the city's sprawling Alcázar evoked ancient Damascus. Pedro the Cruel (ruling from 1350-1369) had constructed this magnificent 14th Century Mudéjar palace. Nearby, the Casa de Pilatos (theoretically, at least, a copy of Pontius Pilate's residence in Jerusalem) doubled as the 16th Century palace of the Dukes of Medinaceli. Recapturing the splendor of the past it combined Gothic, Mudéjar, and Plateresque styles in its courtyards, fountains, and salons. The building would be the defined by the filmmakers as the site of General Allenby's British military headquarters in Cairo. Other buildings, each evocative of sites associated with Lawrence's sagas in Cairo, Jerusalem, and Damascus, were located in and around Seville and rented as part of the filmmaking process.

Claude Rains arrived to film his scenes as the British diplomat, Mr. Dryden. He had dinner with O'Toole at the Corral del Agua, a historic restaurant in the medieval Barrio of Santa Cruz.

Rains told O'Toole that he had worked with Lean and his former wife, Ann Todd, before. "She was a man-eating machine who took every cent he had, except an old car she didn't want. Although he's gone on with his life, he's a broken man. Sometimes, a man never recovers from a former spouse. I, of all people, should know that."

Jack Hawkins arrived to shoot interior scenes associated with his role as General Allenby. He and O'Toole resumed the close bonds they had previously formed in Jordan. Hawkins said, "Here we are again, in a new twist on an old theme, transmuted to Iberia, continuing our ongoing dramas of tragedy and triumphs."

Hawkins told O'Toole that "Lean is enchanted by the sound effects of military boots clattering on marble. He insisted that steel tips be fitted to the heels and toes of my riding boots, and that I always wear my spurs rather loose for maximum clatter on the floors I walk upon. Every time I take a step, it sounds like knights in armor on a rampage."

[Hawkins constantly complained of throat trouble, ailments which would ultimately lead to the loss of his larynx and voice box from cancer. Despite these misfortunes, Hawkins would bravely continue to act as part of a career—with other men dubbing his voice—that continued fitfully even beyond the filming of Lawrence of Arabia. His life ended in 1973, when his body finally succumbed.]

The next day in the Palacio de Medinaceli/Casa de Pilatos, O'Toole and Hawkins were having a morning coffee, as technicians moved their filmmaking equipment to one of the upper floors for an interior shot wherein Lawrence confronts General Allenby.

In the center of the courtyard was a copy of ancient statue by Pheidias, the legendary sculptor of Periclean Athens, known throughout the ancient Hellenic world as "The Carver of the Gods."

As an electrical cable was being hauled up through a window, O'Toole suddenly screamed. The lower end of the cable had come into contact with the monumental statue. "Before we could shout a warning, someone gave it a terrific tug, and a reinforced junction hammered the arm off the statue— a kind of instant Venus de Milo in transformation," Hawkins said. "When the Duchess of Medinaceli arrived later and assessed the damage, she told O'Toole and Hawkins "Not to worry, my dears, it is *only* Roman."

Remembering Jack Hawkins: How he appeared in *Ben-Hur*.

***

Although not yet the international star he was to become, word of O'Toole's fame had spread across Seville. For the first time in his life, the poverty-stricken lad from a Leeds ghetto found himself being courted by the mega-wealthy aristocracy of Spain and by the many socialites, many of them expatriate and English, living along the Costa del Sol.

A hand-delivered invitation arrived for O'Toole from one of the richest and most flamboyant aristocrats of Europe, Cayetana Fitz-James Stuart, the 18th Duchess of Alba. This flamboyant *duenna* was known for her lavish lifestyle, her vast wealth, her art collection, and her fondness for handsome, much younger men. She had invited him to dinner two nights hence at one of her palaces in Seville.

Until that night at her palace, the only time O'Toole had even heard of the Duchess of Alba was from having watched Ava Gardner emote in her 1959 film, *The Naked Maja*.

[This was the story of the dramatic relationship between the 18th-century court painter, Francisco Goya, and the voluptuary María del Pilar Teresa Cayetana de Silva y Álvarez de Toledo, 13th Duchess of Alba (1762-1802). According to some authorities, and based on popular legend, she had posed as his nude model for the notorious painting, La Maja Desnuda (The Naked Maja).]

At the appointed time, and dressed in a rented tuxedo, O'Toole arrived at the entrance to her palace and was graciously invited inside, where he was directed to her antique-studded salon by a liveried doorman in 18th-century attire.

In a satin, emerald green gown, with a diamond-and-ruby necklace once owned by Marie Antoinette, the Duchess of Alba received him. He bowed and kissed her delicate hand.

"Welcome to my humble abode," she said in perfect English, acquired when her father was the Spanish ambassador to The Court of Saint James's in London during World War II.

Before meeting her, he'd been told that she was associated with at least forty honorific or aristocratic titles, making her the "most titled" person on the globe. "I don't know how you can keep track of all those titles."

She facetiously told him, "There are two advantages. I'm allowed by law to ride my horse into Seville Cathedral, and I don't have to kneel in front of the Pope when I visit him in Rome."

O'Toole learned that her husband was out of town. In 1947, she'd married Pedro Luís Martínez de Irujo Artàzcoz in the Cathedral of Seville, *The New York Times* hailing it at the time as the most expensive wedding in the world.

The next day over lunch, O'Toole recalled his first meeting with the Duchess. "She has a passion for flamenco," he said, "and even did a few steps for me when we had a glass of dry sherry before dinner."

He told Hawkins that in her salon were photos of her with famous people, including Spain's autocratic military dictator, General Francisco Franco (in power from 1939 to 1975) and the infamous Wallis Simpson, the American-born Duchess of Windsor, who had once been her guest.

He was also shown a photo of her at Seville's *Féria*—an intensely evocative equestrian and religious festival held every April—poised between Grace Kelly, the Princess of Monaco, and Jacqueline Kennedy. "They detested each other. I'm sure that Jackie had heard that Grace, when she worked as a model in New York, had had an affair with Jack Kennedy."

Positioned above the Duchess's fireplace was a reproduction of Goya's *The Naked Maja*. Noticing O'Toole as he gazed upon it, she said, "Of course, I wasn't around to pose for Goya, but I did pose for Richard Avedon and Cecil Beaton. Those devils had the bad taste to sell their pictures to *Time* and *Harper's Bazaar,* which ran them on

Three views of the very rich and very titled and very flamboyant Duchess of Alba

Top left: at her wedding, October, 1947, to Pedro Luís Martínez de Irujo Artàzcoz; *Top right*: in her studio at around the time of her involvement with O'Toole, and, *lower photo*, shortly before her death in November, 2014.

their covers. Lurid publicity, I would say. I hear that as soon as *Lawrence of Arabia* is released, you'll be on the covers of many magazines yourself."

"It's the price a working actor has to pay," he said. "I must say, I'm not quite prepared for it. You see, I'm a rather private man."

During one of their dialogues, Hawkins told O'Toole, "I hear the dame is worth between four and five billion dollars. That puts her up there in the same league as Queen Elizabeth."

"That makes her stinking rich," O'Toole said. "Actually, she has the smell of delicate orange blossoms. So far, the women I've sampled in Andalusia have lovely olive-colored skin, but they reek of garlic. It seems to ooze from their pores—garlic for breakfast, garlic for lunch, garlic for dinner, and a few cloves of garlic before midnight, too."

O'Toole told Hawkins that the Duchess had guided him through the rambling corridors of her palace, each of them lined end-to-end with paintings from her fabulous art collection. She revealed, "My greatest paintings are in my [neoclassical, built around 1770) Palacio de Liria in Madrid. I even display Columbus' first map of the Americas there. You must come and visit me as my guest there. I will let you sleep in the chamber personally decorated by Salvador Dalí."

O'Toole claimed that "I was served the most sumptuous meal of my life, far better than those bangers and mash my dear mum cooked for me in that tacky old kitchen in Leeds. I dined on a silver platters that had previously been used for serving supper to Queen Isabella."

He revealed that the meal was interrupted by a phone call from Aristotle Onassis. When the Duchess returned, she told him that she'd received an invitation for a cruise of the Mediterranean with the Greek shipping tycoon. "Perhaps you'll accompany me," she said. "My husband detests Ari, and I don't want to go alone."

"It would be the thrill of a lifetime," he said, "but you must not forget, there's this desert saga I'm making. "

"Oh, yes, forgive me," she said.

As O'Toole later told Hawkins, "That was the most prestigious invitation of my life, and I had to turn it down. What an invite for the son of a crooked bookmaker from Ireland."

"Let's skip all this flippancy and get down to the raw meat," Hawkins suggested. "Was there a sleepover?"

"Now you know I'm not a kiss-and-tell kind of guy," O'Toole said. "But indeed there was. Her Highness later told me that she could not discern much difference between an Irish dick and a Spanish dick. She stated she found both appendages rather similar, although she'd heard that Jewish men have a part of their penis removed when their owners are infants. I told her that I, too, had heard it was something like that, although I had never made a personal survey."

The following afternoon, the Duchess of Alba sent him a bouquet of red roses from her gardens with a note.

When Hawkins saw them, he told O'Toole, "I thought it was the male who was supposed to send the flowers."

The note thanked him "for a night of grand bliss" and also informed him that she'd be dressed and ready to see him after nine o'clock that evening.

This time, dressed in a black suit, he arrived at the palace on time. She was wearing a champagne-colored gown from Paris designed by Coco Chanel.

Over sherry, she told him that she had cleared her calendar and desired to see him on each of the following five evenings. The social highlight of those back-to-back *rendezvous* would be scheduled for the following Saturday, when she wanted O'Toole to escort Sarah Churchill to a reception that the Duchess would be hosting in her honor.

The Duchess revealed that she herself was a distant relative of Winston Churchill's, and that Sarah would be vacationing at a villa she owned along the Costa del Sol.

She also stated that her husband would be returning to Seville in time to attend her party, and that it would be more discreet if O'Toole arrived with a lady on his arm. "I don't know why I need to conceal anything from him, though," she said. "I've heard that he's been carrying on with some gypsy flamenco dancer in Madrid."

He told her that he'd be honored to escort her guest, and also that he'd seen Sarah in a film, *Royal Wedding* (1951), in which she had danced with Fred Astaire.

"Yes, the poor darling fancies herself an actress, but real stardom will never come for her," the Duchess said. "Perhaps you could convey that to her so that she doesn't have to pursue the impossible dream."

"Perhaps not," he answered.

Other "nights of bliss" followed before the elegant reception.

Both of them shared pillow talk. The Duchess told him that she believed a woman had to be married to give legitimacy to her children and to allow them to inherit wealth and titles. "But I feel lovers can be taken and discarded at random as a woman's mood shifts."

"My darling Cayetana," he said, taking the privilege of calling her by her first name, as she herself had suggested. "You and I share the same outlook on love and marriage."

During his final night with her before the reception, he wanted to ask her a question "that has been burning on my mind. Did your ancestor, the 13th Duchess of Alba, actually pose nude for Goya? It seems that there is an ongoing dispute about that."

"Of course she did, my dear," she answered. "Now turn over and get some sleep. I've got to wake you up at five in the morning to get you to the movie set. We'll have a lovely breakfast in my courtyard, listening to the sounds of chirping birds heralding another lovely day in Seville, the most romantic of cities."

[O'Toole did honor his commitment to escort the actress, Sarah Churchill, then in her late 40s, to the reception the Duchess of Alba hosted in her honor. When it concluded, the daughter of Britain's former Prime Minister and his wife, Clementine, asked O'Toole to drive her back to her villa in Marbella.

Descriptions of the adventures associated with O'Toole's time on the Costa del Sol are within Chapter 14.]

***

After filming ended in Seville, cast and crew were moved to the bleak, arid, and windswept town of Almería, on Spain's Mediterranean seacoast, 350 miles to the southeast, on March 19, 1962. A 50-truck convoy transported the equipment, props, and costumes. Set against jagged hills and sandy plains, Almería was "hot, barren, and rugged," as Lean remembered it. He said, "I can't believe I'm in Europe."

O'Toole appraised it with an oddly personalized reference, calling it "Pontefract with scorpions and sunshine."

The international crew didn't know what he was talking about, but Lean did. Pontefract was a historic market town in West Yorkshire, in northern England, east of the Pennine foothills. The town, which grew up around a Norman castle built in 1069, had absolutely nothing to do with the landscapes of Almería. O'Toole visited Pontefract on occasion during his illicit affair with a married woman in her thirties who lived there, wed to a traveling salesman who was often out of town.

Journalist Michael Anderegg was on the scene to file news reports of how the shooting was going. He wrote: "In a film where women are conspicuous by their absence, Lawrence—pale, effeminate, and a blonde and blue-eyed seraph—becomes a surrogate woman, a figurative white goddess."

At this point, O'Toole was almost enraptured with his flowing white robes. He said, "My robe is so comfortable that I have practically turned into a transvestite! I thought I'd literally end up running around in a nightie for the rest of my days."

Two major scenes were to be filmed in Almería: They included an Ottoman train wreck and its subsequent hijacking by the Arab Bedouins; and the Arab's attack, from the desert, on the (Ottoman-controlled) port of Aqaba, a scene originally planned to have been filmed in Jordan. Regrettably, in Jordan, flash floods had washed most of the filmmakers' set away, shortly after its construction.

Set designer John Box conceived the most disgusting scene shot IN ALMERIA. In *Seven Pillars,* Lawrence had described his visit to an Arab hospital with its "sickening stench."

Using that as his inspiration, Box ordered his staff to "shit it up in your usual way. We got cow's guts from a local *abbatoir* and rubbed all this crap all over the walls. A lot of it was rotting fish, so there were flies everywhere. When Peter came onto the set, he didn't have to act sick. He lost lunch."

At this point, having exhausted the possibilities of Spain as a site for the filming of his desert epic, Lean realized that Spain had run out of locations. In need of a bona-fide desert in which to shoot the final sequences, he turned his gaze southward, across the sea, to Morocco. In Rabat, its capital, Spiegel made a deal with King Hassan II and his brother, Crown Prince Moulay Abdallah. In the aftermath of those negotiations, Morocco's Royal Family agreed to let Lean's crew shoot their final desert scenes within the borders of their country.

Once again, the film's props, costumes, and technical equipment were hauled across the Mediterranean from Almería to North Africa. Spiegel sailed his yacht, *Malahne,* to Casablanca, the fabled Moroccan city on the country's Atlantic coast.

The film equipment arrived there, too, on the docks, where thirty "Queen Marys" were commissioned to transport it to the medieval Saharan outpost of Ouarzazate, on the distant side of the towering Atlas Mountains. *[A "Queen Mary" was a British nickname for a long-low-loader truck which could be driven directly into the fuselage of a transport plane.]*

For O'Toole, a new adventure was about to begin.

Filming A Manslaughter Orgy on a Grand Scale
A Slave Auction at a Saharan Outpost

From Spain, O'Toole took the ferryboat to Tangier, on the north coast of Africa. Ever since reading Robert Tuark's description of it in *As I Was Saying* (1950), he had long wanted to visit this exotic city, whose roots extend back to the 5th century B.C.E., and whose occupants had included the Carthaginians, the Phoenecians, the Romans, the Portuguese, the English, the French, and the Moroccan Sultans. According to Tuark: *"Sodom was a church picnic and Gomorrah a convention of Girl Scouts compared to Tangier, which contained more thieves, black marketeers, spies, thugs and phonies, beachcombers, expatriates, degenerates, characters, operators, bandits, bums, tramps, politicians, and charlatans than any place I've ever visited."*

Only the narrow Strait of Gibraltar separated the most southerly point in Spain from Tangier, a decadent and cosmopolitan semi-independent entity surrounded by the Kingdom of Morocco and known as the most wicked, corrupt, and debauched city in North Africa. From the beginning, O'Toole was mesmerized by its dazzling light, which had drawn painters who included Eugène Delacroix and Henri Matisse.

O'Toole had only three days and nights in Tangier. He later regretted not taking more time to explore its Medina and its ancient Kasbah. "I got 'waylaid' instead at the Sheherazade."

[He was referring to the most elegant and legendary bordello in Tangier,

whose nameless Madam was a Lebanese woman who dressed only in purple, magenta, and cerise. She was known for her collection of beautiful young girls gathered from all over the world—one a "milkmaiden" blonde from Norway; others including a lusty German girl from Berlin; a black-haired Andalusian temptress from Seville; a large-busted ebony beauty from the Sudan. The list went on and on. O'Toole wanted to sample them all, later asserting, "My desire was to introduce all these putas to an Irishman's finest possession."

He learned that about half of the bordello's patrons were expatriate pederasts. At one point, there were some 60,000 expatriates, many from England and the United States, living in Tangier. O'Toole was told that although many of them had been "evicted" from their home countries for debauchery or immorality, Tangier—provided that they had enough money— would open her arms to the departed, the despised, and/or exiled.

Although some clients requested extremely virile, masculine and well-endowed young men, a lot of them preferred pretty boys. Like their female counterparts, these boys came from all over the world, including Thailand, the Philippines, France, Spain, and one young blonde from California. He had been abandoned by his American father when he returned to San Francisco without him.

As O'Toole learned, these boys were mostly effeminate and "heavenly scented," each with a lipstick-coated mouth. The youths were frequently used as part of a heterosexual seduction. A French-language sign posted in the bordello's reception area asserted, "Nothing is so delightful during intercourse as the feel of a boy's delicate pink tongue probing the anus. Fifty dirham extra!"

O'Toole rented one of the elegantly furnished rooms upstairs, all part of a former sultan's harem. He later proclaimed, "I had never been worked over like this before—what joy, what pleasure—and I feared I'd never be pleasured like this ever again."

Outside, the July heat was scalding. "You could literally fry an egg on the sidewalk," he recalled.

After Tangier, the cast and crew were flown to Marrakech, where they boarded rented vans to carry them 127 miles south to the outpost of Ouarzazate, a desert-fronting garrison erected by the French Foreign Legion in 1927 on the site of an older Berber outpost.

The heat of the Sahara was so fierce that O'Toole labeled it "The Devil's Furnace. The temperature, I'm sure, evoked that part of hell reserved for the truly evil, guys like Hitler and Stalin, perhaps Attila the Hun."

As part of an arrangement whose fees were paid directly to members of Morocco's Royal Family, the Kingdom of Morocco agreed to supply 600 cavalry soldiers, along with 500 members of the Camel Crops, 800 footsoldiers, 180 mules, 1,000 World War I rifles, field kitchens, and some cannons staffed by

200 cannoneers.

Joining the Arab forces were 100 of the famous "Blue Men," nomads from the sub-Sahara.

Lean sent out word: "I want to depict an orgy of killing. Manslaughter on a Grand Scale."

Ouarzazate was the site Lean had chosen for the re-enactment of the bloodbath and subsequent annihilation of the ragged remnants of the Turkish Army. Historically, the United Saudi Arabs had been unified and spearheaded by Lawrence and his British overlords in 1918.]

Lean was slated to film his re-enactment of the Tafas massacre here, using Moroccan soldiers instead of Turks. As the film's director, he complained to O'Toole, "I couldn't get the bastards to perform like I wanted them to. They were impatient during camera setups and were the most uncooperative extras I've ever seen. To show their utter contempt, three soldiers once walked close into camera range, pulled out their dicks, and took a horse piss."

André de Toth, a Second-Unit director, wanted Lean to depict stage blood sprayed against the camera lenses during the battle scenes. The director rejected the idea as "just too gruesome." Furious, De Toth walked off the film.

When he wasn't needed for filming, O'Toole went exploring with his young guide and bodyguard, a 20-year-old Arab man with a bright red beard. O'Toole dubbed him "Redbeard."

He took O'Toole to the Kasbah of Taourist, former abode of "the Lords of the Atlas," a mile east of Ouarzazate. The region's ruling Pasha lived there with his harem.

After the intensity of Tangier, O'Toole found the limited diversions of Ouarzazate dull. They consisted mostly of sitting in the hotel's bar every night getting drunk.

One night, Redbeard told O'Toole that he might like to visit a slave auction. O'Toole said he'd be delighted—"Perhaps I could buy a woman! But I thought slavery went out of style years ago!"

"It's still a thriving business in Africa," the guide told him. He advised O'Toole to wear dark makeup, perhaps sunglasses, and to keep his head covered with the hood that was attached to his robe.

After night fell across the desert, his guide drove him to a dimly lit building some forty-five miles east of Ouarzazate.

"A Great, Galumping Camelodrama"
Above, O'Toole communicates with one of "the smelly beasts."

256

There, they were herded into a room filled with about fifty men, perhaps sheiks or chieftains from neighboring tribes. These buyers didn't look rich like the shieks of Saudi Arabia. Many of them ruled over nomadic herders.

On the auction block was a large, heavily muscled black man, standing about 6'5" tall. Exhibited in the

O'Toole, as T. E. Lawrence, crazed, vengeful, and thirsty for blood

nude, he glared at the buyers, almost daring one of them to purchase him. Redbeard told O'Toole that he might be used for stud duty to impregnate other slave women, or else he might be purchased for castration, and then used to guard a sheik's various wives.

What followed included the sale of three black women, each of them long past her prime, perhaps in their early thirties. Bidding was low, the guide suggesting that they would probably be used as domestics. Amazingly, each of them sold for the equivalent of around five British pounds.

Up until then, the Bedouins had not shown much interest in the slaves on the auction block. But a murmur of excitement arose among the buyers when a young and slender Arab boy, no more than twelve, was paraded out and onto the platform. His small hands covered his undeveloped genitals. He was shivering with humiliation and embarrassment.

Redbeard told O'Toole that desert Bedouins had a saying, translating it as, "A goat for use, a girl for enjoyment, a boy for ecstasy."

The Dallal who was auctioning off the slave forced the rather effeminate boy to turn around as a means of displaying his soft, round bottom. Two of the Dallal's attendants emerged and forcibly spread apart the boy's buttocks to display his anus. At this point, bidding increased. It was obvious to O'Toole why the buyers wanted the boy.

In the corner stood five members of the French Foreign Legion. O'Toole was too far away to hear how the bidding went. But the soldiers, perhaps pooling their assets, became the highest bidder for the boy. As he was turned over to these lusty men, he seemed to be trembling with fear.

"That kid has a rough life ahead of him," Redbeard said.

"Let's get the hell out of here before someone discovers my lily-white body and puts me on the auction block, too," O'Toole said.

***

When Lean's filming of the desert "bloodbath" ended, cast and crew headed home. O'Toole was ordered back to England for the re-enactment of the motorcycle crash that ended his character's life.

He later told Quinn: "David was really rough on me, at times acting like a bloody sadist. But up to now, he's been the most important influence on my life. I graduated in Lean, took my B.A. in Lean, working with him virtually day and night. I learned about the camera and the lens and the lights, and I now know more than some directors do. Do I like Lean, the man? Darling, that is an entirely different matter."

Before telling Sharif goodbye, Lean, in the presence of O'Toole, had some final advice for him:

"The day *Lawrence* comes out, you'll be a star and you're going to face great danger. Producers are going to offer you the usual crap—*Son of Sheik*, remakes of the Rudolph Valentino classics of the 20s. Perhaps things called *Eagle of the Desert.* You've got to turn them down, all of them. I know the appeal of money is strong, but you've got to sacrifice some of it to build up your career. If you need money in the meantime, I can lend you some, because I predict bigtime stardom for you."

"What about me?" a dejected O'Toole asked Lean.

"I have only one regret," Lean answered. "In that scene with the Turkish Bey, I should have had you actually penetrated. Of course, we wouldn't graphically depict the rape itself—only the pained look on your face. It would have made the shot more realistic."

At the end of the shoot, it was rumored that both Sharif and O'Toole flew to Casablanca, where they lost most of their final earnings in the casinos there. Their earlier earnings had been squandered in Beirut.

The Depiction of a Fatal Motorcycle Crash Almost Turns Fatal for O'Toole

Back in England, after a reunion with his wife, Siân, O'Toole was ordered to Chobham, Surrey, to shoot Lean's rendering of the motorcycle crash which, in 1936, had ended the turbulent life of T.E. Lawrence. Lean also had to depict a re-enactment of Lawrence's contentious memorial service at St. Paul's Cathedral in London.

Although Lean's depiction of Lawrence's motorcycle crash was inserted into the opening of the epic's final version, it was among the last scenes to be filmed. After the dizzying hazards faced on location in Jordan, Spain, and Morocco, it seemed especially ironic that O'Toole almost lost his life during the execution of his character's death scene in verdant, leafy England.

On the day of filming, Lean arrived on the set in acute pain. He would soon enter the hospital for surgery. In the desert, he had refused to wear sungoggles. "They interrupt my train of thought," he had protested when supplied with a pair. Unfortunately, during his filming of one of many battle scenes, sand had become embedded under his right eyelid, and later had to be surgically removed.

Of course, O'Toole wouldn't be filmed riding an actual run-of-the-mill motorcycle. His film version of a motorcycle was hooked to the back of a truck, on which was mounted the camera and the necessary crew. The actor merely had to pretend to be riding along, with the understanding that moving images of rolling English countryside would be inserted as a backdrop later.

The towing bar connecting the moving truck to O'Toole's motorcycle was tested and defined as adequate. But for extra protection, a length of rope was attached between the two vehicles as well.

When Lean called for action, the first two minutes of filming went smoothly. Then, suddenly, the driver of the trailer swerved abruptly on the pavement. As an after-effect, the metal tow-bar linking the trailer to the motorcycle snapped, perhaps a result of metal fatigue. Only that flimsy length of rope prevented O'Toole from being thrown onto the pavement and possibly killed, or at least severely injured. He saved himself by jumping to safety in the nick of time.

O'Toole later told Lean, "I don't know where T.E. Lawrence is tonight, perhaps in hell, maybe above. But I think he planned this possible accident for me. That's the fucker's way of getting even with us for daring to shoot his life story, or at least our version of it."

A final close-up of O'Toole's face was filmed at a studio in Hammersmith. Both Lean and the actor himself were shocked when "the thirty-one year old wreck of my countenance didn't match my twenty-nine year overlook. I had aged. The fucking film had actually aged me. I'd lost two stone (twenty-eight pounds) in weight. That came from digging deep within my gut to find the soul of Lawrence and extract it from me. In digging up Lawrence, I had to explore my lower depths. I also lost part of my own guts in doing so."

Lawrence of Arabia's Onscreen Blood Lust Plunges O'Toole into
"Insidious Stardom" Will Success Spoil Him?
"No! No! No!" O'Toole Exclaims, "I'm Already a Rotten Apple"

The date was December 10, 1962. The location, the Odeon Theatre, Britain's largest cinema, seating 2,000 on London's Leicester Square. The event was the long-awaited Royal World Premiere of *Lawrence of Arabia.* The screening would be attended by Queen Elizabeth herself.

Heralded by trumpeters of the Royal Horse Guards, Her Majesty, resplendent in a diamond tiara, made a spectacular entrance.

At the actual screening, O'Toole became so agitated and nervous that he could sit through only twenty minutes of the film.

Looking his most glamorous self, and wearing a tailored tuxedo from Savile Row, O'Toole shook the gloved hand of Her Majesty from a position beside David Lean.

The Times would define it as "a splendid night to behold."

For the most part, the film met with rave reviews, although there were the usual attacks, one reviewer dismissing the film as "moronic history."

The Daily Mirror wrote, "History is put through the mangle and comes out tattered, torn, and largely unrecognizable. If Lawrence is corny, romantic, and absurd, then I congratulate Mr. O'Toole on a masterly portrait."

Alexander Walker, in *The Evening Standard,* wrote: "Peter O'Toole brings to life the film's version of a flawed warrior who is corrupted by pride, soured by the empty victories, and betrayed finally by the jubilant jump of the heart every time he kills—so that he ends his career elbow-deep in needlessly spilt blood."

For *The Sunday Observer,* the astute critic, Penelope Gilliatt, wrote: "In Peter O'Toole's performance, there seem to be at least ten incompatible men living under the same skin, and two or three women as well. When he puts on a Sherif's robes for the first time and does an entranced ballet with himself in the desert, it made me think more than ever that one of the reasons for Lawrence's passion for Arab life might well have been that it allowed him to wear a skirt."

The Examiner defined the film as "an epic spectacle of the psyche which is both resolutely exterior and subtly interior—the desert outside and inside all of us."

Raves were heaped on O'Toole and onto the film itself, but T.E. Lawrence expert Liddell Hart Snidley remarked that "Peter O'Toole is good as *Peter O'Toole.* Silly exhibitionist dance on donning Arab clothes."

Lawrence's brother, A.W. Lawrence, thought "O'Toole paraded like a peacock through the film."

The public devoured it.

In the immediate aftermath of the film's success, O'Toole's reaction to his overnight fame was probed.

One London reporter from *The Observer* asked him directly, "Will success spoil you as an actor?"

"No, darling," he answered. "One is more likely to be amputated by failure than butchered by success."

Siân Phillips claimed that she realized that her husband had become an overnight sensation when she felt the stiletto heel of Gina Lollobrigida "pierce the arch of my foot in a hurtling frenzy to get to my husband."

After the premiere in London, Siân confessed, "I didn't see my husband for weeks. He had become the hottest property on the Continent."

Enjoying world acclaim, O'Toole said, "Stardom is insidious. It creeps through your toes, working its way to your nuts. When it grabs your balls, you know it's become not only painful, but dangerous."

"I've got this great thirst," he told Siân and others. To his male friends, he said, "I have three things my greedy heart desires—fame, money, and pussy." He left out the final desire when discussing his ambitions with Siân.

"*Lawrence of Arabia* launched me into super stardom, but it had a downside," O'Toole told a reporter. "I became obsessed with the character of T.E. Lawrence. A true artist should be able to jump into a bucket of shit and come out smelling like roses. But I spent two years and three months making that picture, thinking about nothing but (T.E.) Lawrence. It became bad for me."

O'Toole was asked if he'd deliberately played Lawrence as a homosexual. "There are so many ways of looking at things, and every word, every gesture, can be misinterpreted."

Was Lawrence Homosexual? And Will Success Spoil Peter O'Toole?

O'Toole was frequently queried about T.E. Lawrence's gender preference, and in response to these questions, he said, "He seems to have been a homosexual, and that's what several people got from the film. Others never sensed it. Obviously, in a story of a great man's life—or anybody's life—you have to omit plenty, for time's sake. So Lawrence's intriguing personal life wasn't developed sufficiently. The question is, was his private sexuality relevant to the things he did and to his place in history? I think there is too much sexual judging of human beings."

Obliquely, O'Toole denied that he welcomed the trappings of riches and celebrity. "What do I want? Three different Rolls-Royces in magenta, emerald green, and sunflower yellow. A hot blonde, brunette, and redhead, delivered fresh daily to my sultan's suite. An Olympic-size swimming pool filled with a bevy of young Esther Williams lookalikes, swimming below to service me. Perhaps a 90-room country estate on fifty manicured acres. A pad in New York. A palatial residence in Hollywood built by a vamp of the silent screen. No, I want none of that. I'm heading back to Connemara and the simple life."

[His reference, of course, was to a rural district of Ireland in West Galway.]

"I think that adorable boy didn't mean all that gibberish he was telling the press," said Noël Coward, his great admirer. "I think he was sending a signal that he didn't want to ignore his so-called criminal class roots. That he was still the ordinary chap he always was. Actually, he was enjoying the money, what he called 'the babes,' and his new found celebrity. Don't listen to his bullshit that he doesn't."

Coward appeared to have been accurate in his assessment. Perhaps O'Toole had forgotten that he'd once told a reporter, "I am just a bloody, greedy little grabber after money, success, and subsequent fame. When I was a young man, I made a promise to myself: I'll do anything, even dropping trou, for a producer or director, to get the rewards awaiting me at the end of the rainbow."

"The success I had after *Lawrence* did not spoil me," he said. "I was already the rotten apple in the barrel."

"For my next film, I need to appear with a bird (woman)," he said. "I've made movies with no birds. If I don't get romantic on screen soon, the public will think I'm queer."

In spite of the lack speaking roles for women in *Lawrence of Arabia,* critic D.K. Holm found that "the film comprises a series of love affairs—first between Lawrence and his two young and devoted servants, then between Ali (Omar Sharif) and Lawrence. Their relationship would almost be a traditional Hollywood story if one of them were a woman— they 'meet cute,' are antagonistic in the beginning, but end up admiring each other."

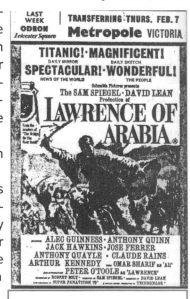

He could have written "even more than admiring," but didn't.

As *Lawrence of Arabia* opened in theatres throughout Britain, many of Lawrence's relatives complained about their kin's depiction by O'Toole. None was as vociferous as Professor A.W. Lawrence, who had, long before, sold the film rights of *Seven Pillars of Wisdom* to Sam Spiegel.

Publicity for the film's U.K. release

"I should not have recognized my brother

262

in this film, which is pretentious and false. My brother was one of the nicest, kindest, and most exhilarating people I've known. He often appeared cheerful even when unhappy. The film is a psychological recipe. Take an ounce of narcissism, a pound of exhibitionism, a pint of sadism, a gallon of blood lust, and a sprinkle of other aberrations, and stir well."

"Camel-Opera" Wows New York Audiences. Although Defined as a "Grand Slammer," Lawrence of Arabia is Also Attacked & Vilified

Regrettably, the American premiere of *Lawrence of Arabia* at the Criterion Theater in Manhattan opened on December 16, 1962, during the most contentious days of a citywide newspaper strike. Consequently, although reviews of the film were broadcast on radios and TVs, but, insofar as New York City was concerned, print reviews followed the broadcast reviews a short while later.

Kate Cameron of *The New York Daily News* gave it four stars. She said that was the paper's limit; otherwise, she would have given it even more. Fred Quinn of *The New York Mirror* rated *Lawrence of Arabia* "high on the list of all-time classics of the screen," as did Archie Winston of the *New York Post*.

The film's most immediately visible attack came from *The New York Times* through Bosley Crowther, who defined it as "a huge, thundering, camel-opera."

Writing in Manhattan's *The Village Voice*, Andrew Sarris claimed: "*Lawrence* is simply another expensive mirage, dull, overlong, and coldly impersonal. The objective is less to entertain or enlighten than to impress and intimidate. Some of its acting and technical effects are interesting, but on the whole, I find it hatefully calculating and condescending."

Critic Pauline Kael wrote, "If you went to see *Lawrence of Arabia* under the delusion that it was going to be about T.E. Lawrence, you probably stayed to enjoy the vastness of the desert and the pleasure of the senses that a huge movie epic can provide."

The premiere was such a success that the price of Columbia's shares on the stock market rose from $14 to $25 a share, and the box

Sharif and Spiegel at the film's NYC premiere. "I wanted the Arab to stay in Cairo, but O'Toole insisted."

office was confronted with endless lines of moviegoers that stretched around the block.

After Their Release from Jail, Two Stars are Born

The most memorable night in the life of Omar Sharif occurred when he and O'Toole flew to Hollywood for the West Coast premiere of *Lawrence of Arabia.* At first, Spiegel wanted all the publicity directed at O'Toole, preferring that Sharif remain in Cairo. But O'Toole threatened the producer, telling him, "I'll not attend the premiere at all unless you invite Cairo Fred, too."

For more than two years, Sharif and O'Toole had waited for this big night in America, having already endured the film's premiere in London. "We were certain that by dawn's early light, in the wake of the premiere, we would be big stars. But perhaps not. The fact that we'd gone over in London and also in New York didn't mean that we'd conquer the hearts of jaded Tinseltown."

Installed in luxury at the Beverly Hills Hotel, these women-chasing actors decided to inaugurate a "foxhunt." Behind the wheel of a rented car, O'Toole was not intoxicated, although other drivers would not have known that, judging by his reckless driving.

Along the way, O'Toole spotted the marquee of a theater where Lenny Bruce was performing at the time. "We've got to catch his act, and we're just in time for his eight o'clock show."

Because Bruce was not a household name in Egypt, a fast explanation from O'Toole to Sharif was in order.

Before going inside, O'Toole warned Sharif that Bruce was a Jew.

"As you should know by now, I have no problem with that."

[A stand-up comedian, social critic and satirist, the New Yorker, Lenny Bruce, was the most controversial performer in America at the time. His critics, often the police, viewed his act as "filthy and depraved." His defenders found that he told the truth in his sharp, hilarious way. Behind the scenes, he had an addiction to heroin.

His routines integrated sex, satire, religion, politics, and bracing jolts of vulgarity. Bruce's 1964 trial for obscenity unfolded two years after he

O'Toole, with Mr and Mrs. David Lean, at *Lawrence of Arabia's* premiere in Los Angeles

264

first met O'Toole. Today, that trial is interpreted as a historic landmark for freedom of speech in America.

For the first time on the stage, audiences heard words like "cocksucker," "come," and "schmuck" (i.e., Yiddish for "penis.")

O'Toole later praised Bruce like this: "Words were his power. He certainly asked the Americans: 'Can offensive speech really be free in the land of the free?'"

O'Toole became one of Bruce's early defenders, joining a loose but prestigious alliance that included Elizabeth Taylor, Gore Vidal, Woody Allen, Paul Newman, Susan Sontag, John Updike, and Playboy's *Hugh Hefner.]*

Bruce gave one of his most outrageous performances, which O'Toole found hilarious. Even Sharif was amused, but apparently less so. After the show, O'Toole took Sharif's arm, inviting him backstage to congratulate Bruce, who, fortunately, knew who they were based on advance publicity about the premiere of their film.

Two views of Lenny Bruce, "America's First Amendment martyr"

As he changed clothes in front of them, Bruce invited O'Toole and Sharif to join him for drinks and dinner at the West Coast version of P.J. Clarke's, a branch of the famous celebrity haunt in Manhattan.

Before one o'clock that morning, both O'Toole and Bruce were intoxicated. Sharif, however, was not a heavy drinker. Bruce invited the actors back to his apartment, where he whipped out a hypodermic syringe. After filling it with a liquid, he shot up.

Within less than thirty minutes, three policemen were pounding on his door. Apparently, they had been tipped off. Over O'Toole's shouts of rage, all three men were handcuffed and carted off to jail.

Sharif tried to explain his way out of the arrest, claiming that he and O'Toole had merely dropped in for a nightcap and had not indulged in any drugs.

In spite of that, all three men were strip searched, a process that included a thorough ransaking of their clothing. All that the police found were some pills in the pocket of O'Toole's suit. Sharif knew they were sleeping pills.

Then, abandoning whatever restraint he had left, O'Toole launched a verbal attack on the police, "accusing them of virtually everything but the Holocaust," Sharif later recalled. "To make matters worse, he told the police that those sleeping pills were morphine. It was off to the jail cells for us. I feared that if these drug charges were leveled against us, both Peter and I would be deported as undesirable aliens."

Sharif was allowed one phone call, and he made it to Spiegel, in his suite at the Beverly Hills Hotel, awakening him from a deep sleep. After denouncing Sharif for calling him at that ungodly hour, Spiegel was informed that he and O'Toole were in jail.

On the dawn of a glamorous world premiere, Spiegel reacted in horror to the possibility that his two stars were at the dangerous edge of a world-class scandal. "I'll take care of it," he said, slamming down the phone.

At 6AM that morning, a hastily dressed Spiegel arrived at precinct headquarters with six of the most expensive and high-powered lawyers in Beverly Hills. The negotiations that ensued between Siegel, his attorneys, and the police chief unfolded behind closed doors.

Finally, a guard, with keys, arrived at their cell to release the three performers.

Two Desert Warriors Are Propelled Into International Fame

Lawrence of Arabia's Hollywood premiere was a star-studded event, opening on December 21, 1962 at the Beverly Hills Cinema. *Tout* Hollywood showed up to see what all the excitement was about.

Out of jail, Sharif and O'Toole stood by as a parade of tuxedos, diamonds and designer gowns passed before them. Shirley MacLaine was one of the first stars to shake their hands with kisses on their cheeks. After she'd passed by, O'Toole whispered to Sharif, "Do you think she has red pussy hairs? As an Irishman, I find red quim most edible."

Bette Davis, Humphrey Bogart, Lauren Bacall, Peter Lawford, Kirk Douglas, David Niven, Joan Crawford, Jennifer Jones, Jane Wyman, and Rock Hudson filed by. Sharif remembered shaking the hand of Gregory Peck, who looked handsomer in person than on the screen, if such a thing were possible.

As the movie unreeled, Sharif at one point squeezed O'Toole's hand as he made his first appearance on the screen. Like a mirage, Sharif appeared as a black spot on horseback riding across the blazing sands of the desert toward the camera in one extended long shot. As Lawrence, O'Toole's

Who's the man a drugged and drunken actor in compromising circumstances should call after midnight to get him out of jail?

Sam Spiegel

eyes were riveted on the distant horizon. Finally, the exotically handsome features of Omar Sharif as Sherif Ali ibn el Kharish appears. The audience is mesmerized.

O'Toole became so nervous and edgy about his appearance on the screen that shortly after it began, he excused himself, promising to hook up with Sharif later.

Much of the rest of the evening was in blurred focus for both actors. Sharif remembered them being engulfed in "a sea of glossy mink and sable, with undulating bodies carrying both of us to a banquet room."

"I felt like Alice in Wonderland," Sharif said. "Hollywood was mine, at least for the night. We were the toast of the town."

At one point, O'Toole glided by Sharif before, as he described it, "being consumed by a coven of overly painted and overly bejeweled beautiful women." He had time for only a whisper in Sharif's ears. "Tonight, two international stars were born. But can either of us pay the price of fame?"

Most reviews of the film were favorable. In *The Hollywood Reporter,* James Powers wrote: "Peter O'Toole is a major star with this one role. A handsome, sensitive actor, he moves with grace and speaks with charm. His self-torture is great, and it is conveyed with compassion."

By the first week of January, the national magazines were publishing their own appraisals. *Time* magazine wrote, "In his performance, O'Toole catches the noble seriousness of Lawrence and his cheap theatricality, his godlike arrogance, and his gibbering self-doubt; his headlong courage,

Whoremongers, 27 years later, still the toast of the town, and still friends

Imitiation:
The Highest Form of Flattery

The fashion industry, promoting the then-novel concept of Dacron, borrowed themes from *Lawrence of Arabia* for its ad campaigns

girlish psychastenia [*def: a neurotic state characterized especially by phobias, obsessions, or compulsions that one knows are irrational*], Celtic wit, humorless egotism, compulsive chastity, and sensuous pleasure in pain."

Roger Sandall in *Film Quarterly*, wrote: "Acting, dialogue, and direction are so uniformly elephantine one feels that the film can't have been directed in the usual sense at all. It seems to have been 'panavisualised' instead, compounded by an unspeakably turgid score—O'Toole's tormented hermaphrodite (his cerebral tensions conveyed by such a fierce working of cheek musculature it's as if his nerves were on fire) would have had a hard time directing a revolt of disaffected palace eunuchs—let alone a military campaign."

After its opening, Spiegel called Lean, saying: "We've got a hit for years to come. Except I fear we've also created a Frankenstein in Peter O'Toole by making him such a big star."

As if to prove the accuracy of Spiegel's fears, O'Toole announced, "I'm now a *bona fide* movie star, top of the heap, bloody hell. I went out the next day and bought me a Rolls-Royce, the color of an elephant tusk. I also purchased a pair of sunglasses large enough to create envy in Jackie Kennedy. She'll probably be calling me any day to fuck her."

"In my new Rolls-Royce, I rode down Hollywood Boulevard, waving to passers-by like the Queen Mum. No one noticed me. The spectacle I was making was an ordinary event in Lotusland."

Lawrence of Arabia opened around the world from Moscow to London, from Sydney to Tokyo, from Miami to Nome, from Tijuana to Rio de Janeiro. With the exception of Egypt, Arab countries boycotted it. And although their government allowed it to be screened, the people of Turkey were not amused.

Although His Film Sweeps the Oscars, O'Toole, Nominated for Best Actor, Bites the Dust

April 8, 1963, the night Hollywood had been eagerly awaiting arrived: The 35th annual Academy Awards ceremony at the Santa Monica Civic Auditorium. The duties of the event's usual host, Bob Hope, had been commandeered by Frank Sinatra. Between segments of his running commentary, former Oscar winners would deliver the individual presentations.

Lawrence of Arabia had been nominated for eleven Oscars, including Best Picture, Best Director, and Best Actor. Sharif had been nominated as Best Supporting Actor.

O'Toole told a reporter, "Competing for the bloody Oscar is a terrifying competition. It's like a blood sport."

Shelley Winters launched the night's awards by announcing John Cox as the winner for Best Sound on *Lawrence of Arabia*. Since Cox could not attend,

Robert Wagner accepted for him.

For film editing, Anne V. Coates won for *Lawrence.* Not thinking she would win, Coates was on holiday with her family. Robert Stack accepted her Oscar for her.

Ginger Rogers came out to present the Oscar for Best Original Musical Score. Maurice Jarre was the winner for the symphonic work he'd composed for *Lawrence,* but since he wasn't present at the event, composer Morris Stoloff accepted the award in his place. *[Later, Jarre complained, "Wresting my award statuette from the iron grip of Spiegel was the most difficult task of all."]*

The first big award of the night involved the category of Best Supporting Actor. Sharif faced stiff competition from Ed Begley's performance as the sadistic political boss in Tennessee Williams' *Sweet Bird of Youth.* Other contenders included Victor Buono for his performance in *What Ever Happened to Baby Jane?;* Telly Savalas in *Birdman of Alcatraz;* and Terence Stamp in *Billy Budd* were also strong contenders.

Begley won, and in this case, the actor himself, and not a stand-in, was on hand to accept his Oscar.

Since there were no female roles in *Lawrence of Arabia,* the Best Supporting Actress Oscar, another major event, went to Patty Duke for her role in *The Miracle Worker.* Anne Bancroft also won that year as Best Actress for her role in *The Miracle Worker,* with Joan Crawford accepting for her.

The Best Art Director Award for a Color Film went to the team comprised of John Box, John Stoli, and Dario Simoni. Since none of them were present that year, actors Anne Jeffreys and Robert Sterling accepted the award in their names.

Joan Crawford's nemesis, Bette Davis, stepped forward to present the Oscar for Best Screenplay based on material from another medium. That award went to *To Kill a Mockingbird,* a blow to Robert Bolt and Michael Wilson.

One of the biggest awards of the evening involved the category of Best Director. Crawford read the list of nominees. They included Robert Penn Warren for *The Miracle Worker;* Robert Mulligan for *To Kill a Mockingbird;* Frank Perry for *David and Lisa;* Pietro Germi for *Divorce, Italian Style,* and David Lean for *Lawrence of Arabia.*

The Oscar went to Lean, who had previously won an equivalent award for *Bridge on the River Kwai (1957).*

He was brief, claiming, "This limey is deeply touched and greatly honored."

Freddie Young won for Best Cinematography in a Color Film for his work in the jungles of Malaya on *The Seventh Dawn.* Absent from the ceremony, his Oscar was accepted by Carol Lynley.

Performing in a play in London's West End, O'Toole was not present at the ceremony in California, even though Spiegel had promised to buy every ticket in the London theatre as a means of releasing him from his commitments and thereby allowing him to attend the Oscar event in Hollywood.

Joan Crawford, arguably the Hollywood actress most resistant to being directed by anyone, presenting the Best Director Award to David Lean for *Lawrence of Arabia*

Spiegel had told him that Gregory Peck was the sentimental favorite for Best Actor for his interpretation of the Southern lawyer, Atticus Finch, who defended a black man accused of rape in *To Kill a Mockingbird.*

The other nominees included Burt Lancaster for his work in *Birdman of Alcatraz;* Jack Lemmon for *Days of Wine and Roses,* and Marcello Mastroianni for *Divorce, Italian Style.* The award went to Peck, the first native Californian ever to win an Oscar. Shouts of "Bravo!" rang through the auditorium.

Olivia de Havilland, presenting Best Picture Award for *Lawrence of Arabia* to David Lean (left) and Sam Spiegel

That night marked the beginning of an Oscar "jinx" for O'Toole, who would begin a losing streak that extended through eight nominations but never a win.

The big moment came when Olivia de Havilland stepped forward to present the Oscar for Best Picture of the Year. Lean's competition included *The Longest Day; The Music Man, Mutiny on the Bounty,* and *To Kill a Mockingbird.* Once again, *Mockingbird* seemed a heavy favorite.

Lawrence of Arabia emerged as the winner, prompting Spiegel, with his paunch and massive head, to stroll grandly down to aisle to accept the award.

"After *Lawrence,* except for a few good roles, I was often offered the part of tormented bloody youths, romantic, blonde-haired, blue eyed twits,"

O'Toole later said.

Within a month of the Academy Awards ceremony, O'Toole won Best Actor at the British Film Academy Awards, with *Lawrence of Arabia* winning an award for the year's Best Film.

For the next twenty years, *Lawrence of Arabia* would be brutally cut and slashed, often so badly that in many cases, audiences didn't know what was really going on.

A Post-Mortem on Lawrence of Arabia
"One of the Greatest Movies in the History of Cinema"

Even though millions around the planet were flocking to see *Lawrence of Arabia*, O'Toole refused to watch it, not just at its premieres, but at any private screening in the years that followed.

Finally, on Christmas Eve in London (1975), he sat down to watch it as a re-run on TV. Even then, he could only sit through about half an hour of it.

"Too many bad memories came back," he said. "I remembered that when Omar (Sharif) came onto the set, he'd just emerged from his doctor's office, where tests had revealed that he had the clap. No, that's not right. It was I who had seen my doctor to learn I got the clap form a cheap whore in some long-forgotten bordello."

"When I did sit through some of *Lawrence* on that Christmas Eve, the moment I came on TV I hated my appearance. Fortunately, I was drunk before I came into the living room. When I saw myself on TV, I thought I looked like a faggot. I said out loud, 'Who is this bloody pudding?' I was pathetic, a coy twit with twinkling blue eyes. My God, I asked myself. 'Is that really Peter O'Toole?' Finally, I could take it no more. I staggered to my feet. It took three bottles of Burgundy before I passed out, trying to blot out my embarrassment and the awful memories. I passed out right on the living room floor, where I awoke the next morning in all my shame and humiliation."

When Spiegel showed his film's final cut to Professor A.W. Lawrence in 1962, he sat through it and then delivered his spectacularly negative verdict.

"To say that I am extremely disappointed is a gross understatement."

The final word on the family secret about T.E. Lawrence was not revealed until 1986. Professor A.W. Lawrence was being interviewed by Julia Cave for a BBC documentary entitled Lawrence of Arabia.

"T.E. hated the thought of sex," his brother revealed. "He had read a great amount of medieval literature about characters—some of them saints, some of them not—who had quelled sexual longings by beatings. And that's what he did. I knew about it immediately after his death, but of course said nothing. It's not a thing people can understand easily."

**

The American Film Institute ranked *Lawrence of Arabia* as one of the greatest achievements in the history of world cinema, and in general, the film almost always appears on the list of the ten greatest films of all time.

The American Film Institute went on to cite O'Toole's portrayal of Lawrence as among the ten greatest heroes in the history of the movies.

Chapter 14

O'Toole Devastates the Costa del Sol

Seducing Sir Winston Churchill's Daughter, &

His Affair with Europe's Most Famous Transsexual

A Multi-Million Dollar Film Offer from King Saud

| April Ashley... a question of gender | Sarah Churchill... daughter of a bulldog | King Saud... a walking sperm bank |

In the 1950s, the Costa del Sol, the seacoast along Andalusia's southernmost strip, had just come into vogue as a luxurious haven for vacationing Americans and British expatriates. It attracted the jet set of that era, royal families, heads of state, and Hollywood movie stars.

The Marbella Club in Marbella provided the most fashionable accommodations in Spain, a venue for the likes of the Duke and Duchess of Windsor, King Juan Carlos of Spain, Gina Lollobrigida, African princes, a Kennedy or two, Grace Kelly and Prince Rainier, Aristotle Onassis with Maria Callas, and three of Peter O'Toole's future co-stars and lovers: Ava Gardner, Audrey Hepburn, and Elizabeth Taylor.

In sharp contrast to the harsh desert landscapes of Jordan, O'Toole experienced a remarkably different life when cast and crew descended on Spain and Morocco for the final weeks of filming. O'Toole had become an international celebrity even before *Lawrence of Arabia* was wrapped and released.

Film offers were pouring in. In fact, there was a demand, in both Europe and the U.S., for more information about just who Peter O'Toole was.

His closest friend, Kenneth Griffith, arrived in Spain's port city of Almería to shoot a documentary about O'Toole for *Monitor,* the BBC Television Arts program. He shot footage of O'Toole at various locations, including a dramatic pose in his white robe on top of a hill in a stance that evoked some conquering hero.

"Darling," O'Toole told Griffith. "I have become the toast of international society. The decadent part, those who live just to fornicate on the Costa del Sol. It's the new gathering place for panty sniffers, child molesters, drunkards, prostitutes, pimps, gigolos, pillheads, and poon stalkers. I adore it. It seems that all the big names want to go to bed with me. A lucky few actually manage to accomplish that splendid feat."

A Night in Marbella with Sir Winston's Daughter, Sarah Churchill, "The Lamb Who Strayed"

At the Duchess of Alba's palace in Seville, the party for Sarah Churchill— her very, very distant relative—had been a huge success. As a young man working on a newspaper in Leeds, O'Toole had read some of the many pages of gossip about this actress/dancer, the "Black Sheep" of the Churchill clan, even though many critics believed that that dubious accolade should have been bestowed on Randolph, Churchill's frequently errant son, instead.

When O'Toole met Sarah, he found her vivacious, witty, and attractive. Her Titian red hair and her emerald green eyes were highlighted by her champagne-colored gown. She combined a certain innocence with worldliness.

Hellraising in Jerez de la Frontera & The Battle for Bond, 007

He was surprised at how flirtatious she was. He flirted right back, even though he was acutely aware that she was "pushing fifty" at the time he met her.

Before the Duchess' reception ended, both O'Toole and Sarah had more than their share of champagne. As her escort, he was obligated to take her back to her temporary residence in Seville.

When Sarah learned that he had two days off from filming, she came up with an idea: She invited him to come with her that following morning to a villa she occupied in chic Marbella, a 2 ½ hour drive southeast from Seville. At first, he was leary of the invitation, but finally decided, "What the hell?"

Outside her hotel in Seville, her chauffeur was waiting at 7AM in a Rolls-Royce the color of elephant skin. He wore an olive green uniform that looked very distinguished.

O'Toole had read that Sarah was about to be married to Lord Audley *[aka Thomas Percy Henry Touchet-Jesson, 23rd Baron Audley]*. As O'Toole would later relay to Jack Hawkins, "I wondered why an old girl about to be married to an English lord was running off with a handsome, dashing Irishman like myself."

"Perhaps a final fling before shouldering the bondage of marriage," as Jack Hawkins had suggested.

Publicity stills showed Sarah Churchill with a bulldog. There was no shame in reminding fans of her associations with Sir Winston.

Throughout their tortuous transit to Marbella, they talked "shop." She discussed having appeared as Rosalind in Shakespeare's *As You Like It* in England at Pembroke-in-the-Round, a theater in West Croyden.

She told him that she was completely surprised when her father, Sir Winston, showed up at the theater at the last minute

before curtain and took his reserved seat in the front row. "Within fifteen minutes, he was loudly snoring and snorting, much to my embarrassment. I guess that was his review of my performance."

What followed was a discussion of how challenging it was to perform Shakespeare. O'Toole shared his experience of performing "The Bard on the Boards."

At the Bristol Old Vic, in the mid-1950s, he'd starred in *King Lear, A Midsummer Night's Dream, Othello,* and the inevitable *Hamlet.*

As the ride seemed to go on and on, he was grateful for the bar in the passenger compartment of the Rolls-Royce. As his hostess, she mixed a batch or two of Bloody Marys.

Sarah Churchill in 1966, long after her dreams of making it big in the movies had faded.

"I was the lamb who strayed from the fold," she claimed. "My childhood was just too, too comfortable. At seventeen, I decided to make a break for it and test my luck in the cold, cruel world. I fear I made a mess of it—wild girl, and all that, you know."

In 1935, when she was twenty-one, she appeared on stage in London in a revue called *Follow the Sun.* "I wore a short skirt and frilly knickers and presented me befrilled bum to the world," she said in an exaggerated cockney accent.

She spoke sadly of her attempt to become a film star, having hoped that her appearance in *Royal Wedding* with Fred Astaire would help launch a big career for her on the screen. "As you know, that never happened. I got a couple of roles, but that was it."

"Probably the same thing will happen to me if we ever finish *Lawrence of Arabia,*" he said.

He found her an enchanting conversationalist, filled with amusing stories. She spoke of her work in photo intelligence when she'd served in the Women's Air Force. She also had inside stories about her traveling with Sir Winston to the 1943 Teheran conference with Franklin D. Roosevelt. She'd also accompanied her father the time he met again with Roosevelt at the 1945 conference at Yalta. "That lusty old Red fart, Stalin, crudely propositioned me."

"Oh, the war years," she said with a touch of nostalgia. "Since so many of our men were overseas, thank God the Yanks arrived on our shores to take care of our sex lives. I fell hard for John Gilbert Winant. You know, the U.S.

ambassador to Britain. Poor chap, and unluckily for me, he had a wife. John was adorable. I was so sorry to hear that he committed suicide in 1947."

"So sorry," he chimed in.

She returned to talk about her stage career, informing him that she'd played Eliza Doolittle in George Bernard Shaw's *Pygmalion.* He shared with her what he'd learned by being cast as Professor Henry Higgins in that play at Bristol's Old Vic.

"I'm afraid one night I'd had a nip too many, and I created this big, scandalous scene in a local pub," she said. "I was hauled off to prison like a common thief."

"The same thing happened to me in Bristol," he said. "The police claimed I was driving drunk when I crashed my new Morris Minor into the front of a warehouse."

Hawkins had also attended the Duchess of Alba's reception, and he had witnessed O'Toole leave the party with Sarah on his arm. The following Monday, over lunch, Hawkins was eager for news about O'Toole's weekend in Marbella.

"I don't want to be coy about what happened," O'Toole said. "But I don't really remember what happened, since we're both such heavy boozers. When I woke up Sunday, it was way past noon. I was jaybird naked in bed with her. But I swear on Shakespeare's grave that I don't know if we did it or not. I have no memory of stripping down and crawling into bed with her. She's an old girl, you know, and I mean that literally."

"Didn't she say something to indicate what happened?" Hawkins asked.

"She was in a desperate hurry to get to where Lord Audley was staying," O'Toole said, "and to allow that, she had to skip breakfast. She told me he was the love of her life. She did, however, take down my phone number, so she could call me when we both got back to London."

"Are you sure that there wasn't even a mention of the commando activities of the previous night?" Hawkins asked.

"Yes, I remember that there was indeed something," O'Toole said. "As she kissed me goodbye, she thanked me for one of the most memorable nights of her life. Her exact words were 'You're the answer to a maiden's prayer.'"

[Later that year, O'Toole read that Sarah had married Lord Audley, and that he had died within a year of their wedding. It was very unusual for him, but he mailed her a sympathy card.

Three days later, she called and invited him to this little inn down in Rye, along England's southern coast. He told her he'd get back to her, but decided not to respond. He figured that she was staking him out as her next lover. Perhaps she wanted him to divorce Siân and marry her.

She seemed to have recovered quickly from Lord Audley's death, and soon, he was reading that she was heavily involved with Lobo Nocho, the African-American émigré jazz singer and artist.]

Britain's First Trannie, April Ashley, Attracts O'Toole, Omar Sharif, Bing Crosby, Elvis, Salvador Dalí, Pablo Picasso, and Albert Einstein.

In Seville, invitations for O'Toole continued to pour in from international society, and not just from the Duchess of Alba. In this part of the world, he'd already "arrived," even though he was still involved with filming of *Lawrence of Arabia.* As far as local hosts and hostesses were concerned, he was already a big name to pursue, a challenge that many of them wanted to configure into their lives as an honored and prestigious guest.

One invitation intrigued him more than most, and that was from producer Kevin McClory, a tabloid name. The Dublin-born producer, also a writer and director, began life as a boom operator and location manager, eventually evolving into an assistant to director John Huston during the filming of *The African Queen* (1951), with Humphrey Bogart. He later fulfilled the same duties on the set of *Moulin Rouge* (1951) starring José Ferrer. McClory had also been assistant director on Huston's *Moby Dick* (1956), and later, an associate producer on Mike Todd's *Around the World in 80 Days* (also 1956).

During the making of that film, McClory's bride-to-be, Elizabeth Taylor, dumped him for Todd. That caused a serious rift in their friendship, but, according to the latest reports, McClory had made up with Todd and his new bride. If the gossip columns were to be believed, all had been was forgiven.

McClory was anxious to meet O'Toole because he'd heard that he was about to become the movie industry's next biggest star. At his party, he had little time to converse with O'Toole because of his duties as a host, but he promised he'd call him soon and get together for a long talk about his future before both of them flew back to London.

At the party, he introduced O'Toole to his lovely co-host, the air-

Kevin McClory at the Irish premiere of *Thunderball*

plane heiress, Frederica Ann ("Bobo") Sigrist. After Taylor had dumped him, Sigrist had helped McClory recover from his broken heart and then married him as part of the process. Together, they rented a luxurious residence, Villa Verde, from Carmen Franco, who was also at the party.

McClory asked O'Toole to come with him to meet the daughter of Spain's *El Caudillo,* the brutal dictator, Francisco Franco. King Juan Carlos would later honor her with the designation of an aristocratic title *[María del Carmen Franco y Polo, 1st Duchess of Franco, Grandee of Spain, Dowager Marquise of Villaverde (born in 1926 in Oviedo, Asturias, Spain) is the only child of Spain's Caudillo, dictator General Francisco Franco (who died in 1975) and his wife Carmen Polo y Martínez-Valdès.]*

O'Toole found her warm and gracious. "She can't help it if Franco was her father," he told Sharif. McClory had warned O'Toole not to bring up, for any reason, the incendiary subject of the politics, or even the name of her father.

Of all the gorgeous, beautifully gowned and bejeweled women at the party, there was one who stood out as more glamorous and chicly dressed than the rest.

Two Views of *El Caudillo's* Daugher

Top photo, as an anti-Royalist in 1921, and later, to the ironic cat-calls of many liberals in Fascist Spain, as the Duchess of Franco.

Arriving late in the foyer, she was greeted by him. "I'm Peter O'Toole," He studied her face carefully. "I know it's an old come-on line, but haven't we met before?"

"Indeed we have. I'm April Ashley."

He suddenly remembered being introduced to her in London at the fashionable Chelsea address of Duncan Melvin, the musical and ballet impresario. That night, O'Toole had arrived intoxicated at St. Leonard's Terrace to attend Melvin's celebrity-studded party. He'd chatted briefly with April, and was rather entranced, but he hadn't pursued her. She was still the stunning beauty he'd remembered, but only more so.

"I didn't recognize you at first," she said. "You're different. Dyed blonde hair and a nose job."

"You've nailed me!" he said.

Reportedly, he found April "delectably creamy," and she thought he was "ravishingly handsome."

For anyone who read gossip columnists at the time, April was a *Vogue* model with a jet-set lifestyle acted out in the salons of Paris and among the High Society in Spain; a fixture on the London scene; and a household name throughout Britain.

She'd been pursued by some of the most famous men on the planet—Elvis Presley, Bing Crosby, Salvador Dalí, Pablo Picasso, and even Albert Einstein.

By coincidence, she'd just moved out of the Villa Santa Cecilia which Sarah Churchill was renting at the time. "You must meet Sarah," April said. "She's absolutely divine."

"I've had the pleasure," he said.

At McClory's party, O'Toole introduced April to Sharif. "We call him Cairo Fred."

She remembered the Egyptian actor as being "at the height of his beauty, powerful and delicate, with stunning eyes."

All three of them bonded, drinking the night away until dawn arose over the Mediterranean coast. She invited them to come and stay with her at the Villa Antoinette, named after Marie Antoinette. The actual ownership of the villa appeared uncertain, although April said that it was a gift from her aristocratic English boyfriend. Rumors soon spread that the villa was sheltering a *ménage à trois.*

She later claimed, "We went bananas. Peter, this divine creature, could dive head first into a bottle. I shared a bed with him, while Cairo Fred slept in an adjoining bedroom with connecting doors, always open."

On some nights, she'd leave O'Toole's bed to join Sharif in the next room. After her return, O'Toole would whisper "traitor" in her delicate ear.

O'Toole learned that the villa had been given to her by the Hon-

Two views of April Ashley with her husband, Arthur Cameron Corbett. Both she and her husband liked to dress up in beautiful gowns.

orable Arthur Cameron Corbett, later the 3rd Baron Rowallan, the Eton- and Oxford-educated heir of Lord Rowallan. She told O'Toole that his lordship had proposed marriage, and that she'd accepted.

There was a problem. "Sometimes, Arthur liked to dress up and become 'She,'" April claimed. "He pays young men to come in and masturbate for him. 'She' becomes 'He' before morning."

"Quaint fun," O'Toole said. "Jolly good! All of us must have our amusements, and who is to say what is perverse?"

As his bedmate, he noticed that April did not let her upcoming marriage interfere with her love life. She had at least one ardent beau in hot pursuit of her.

The most prominent of these was Inigo del Infantado, son of the Duque del Infantado, who disapproved of his son's controversial English girl-friend. April told O'Toole that her lover was only twenty years old—"slender, solemn, and sensual. He can make love forever, day after day after day. It's all he wants to do. Me, too."

"What a noble occupation," O'Toole responded.

One day when O'Toole, with Sharif, arrived at the Villa Antoinette, April was in tears. "The Duke del Infantado is threatening to use his influence to have me deported from Spain if I don't release his son from some kind of sexual bondage. He's also threatening to disinherit Inigo, who wants me to flee with him to North Africa. What should I do?"

"Tell Inigo that he doesn't want to end up a pauper in Morocco," O'Toole said. "Follow the money trail to Papa in Madrid. Inigo can always slip around on the side to take care of business with you."

"Actually, I think that is very good advice," she said.

As "Florence of Arabia," O'Toole Rejects an Offer to Become Lady Corbett

One night, when April was away at a party, His Lordship, Arthur Cameron Corbett, the future 3rd Baron Rowallan, showed up. He was invited to join O'Toole for a night of drinking. Sharif had wandered off, presumably with an Andalusian beauty.

Although O'Toole knew that Corbett had been a closeted transvestite since childhood, he was amazed at the man's military background. He'd been awarded the *Croix de Guerre* for bravery in World War II. He had just come from Tasmania, where his father was the Governor (1959-63). At the time that O'Toole met His Lordship, Corbett's uncle, Jo Grimmond, was leader (1956-57) of the Liberal Party in Britain.

Apparently at the time, O'Toole never revealed what happened when he drove back to the villa where Corbett was staying. O'Toole did spend the night, but later told his actor friend, James Villiers, in London, "I don't think anything really happened. We both were too pissed by 3AM. All I remember was collapsing into bed with His Lordship. Perhaps a kiss or so. But then, I kiss everybody. Sometimes, often complete strangers."

"But maybe something did happen, because as I was leaving the next morning, His Lordship begged me to stay. He even promised to marry me and make me Lady Corbett. He'd seen pictures of me as Lawrence of Arabia, and was fascinated."

"And whereas I turned down the offer, April accepted. The following year, in April *[1962]*, she married darling Arthur in Gibraltar. But who wore the wedding gown?"

[In 1969, wanting a divorce but unwilling to pay alimony, Corbett applied for an annulment. The judge ruled that a person born male is legally male unto perpetuity. So in essence, Corbett vs. Corbett became the law of the land in the U.K until Britain's gender recognition act of 2004.

In 1993, after learning that Corbett, now 3rd Baron Rowallan, was dying, April flew to his side. She claimed that he told her that she was the only one that he had ever loved, and confessed that he had cheated her out of her rightful alimony.]

***

[On a drunken night many years later, O'Toole and his future bosom buddy, Richard Burton, began discussing April. The Welsh actor admitted that he'd screwed Sophia Loren, Ava Gardner, Barbra Streisand, and Lana Turner. But his fantasy woman had been April Ashley. "Of course, Elizabeth will always be number one.

"Of course," O'Toole said. "I'm sure April wouldn't turn you down."

"Few women can refuse me," Burton said. "Elizabeth tells me that she can achieve orgasm just listening to the sound of my voice."]

Remembered kindnesses from John Prescott (both photos above), later Deputy Prime Minister of England

282

Emerging from the Slums of Liverpool, an Abused Boy Becomes a Glamorous Model for Vogue, & a Celebrated International Beauty

Born George Jamieson in 1935 in the slums of Liverpool, the future April Ashley joined the British Merchant Navy at the age of 16 in 1951. But later, when he attempted suicide, the Navy abandoned him, releasing him with a dishonorable discharge. Later, as a civilian, he attempted suicide once again, this time ending up in a mental institution.

After his release, he went to work at the Hotel St. Asaph in Denbighshire, in Northeastern Wales, site of the smallest ancient cathedral in Britain.

In the hotel, he shared a bedroom with John Prescott, who worked at the hotel as one of the chefs. George's duties involved the removal of dirty dishes from the dining room.

George (aka Ashley) would later remember Prescott as "being incredibly nice and very handsome, like a young Marlon Brando. He was dapper and strapping, a lovely young man who wanted to be a boxer, though he was working at the hotel as a cook."

George Mathieson at 17. As a boy, a life of poverty and rejection.

As a woman, a life of international glamor and stardom.

It seemed inconceivable at the time that Prescott would eventually rise from such humble position to become Deputy Prime Minister (1997-2007) of Britain.

"I was probably a bit too exotic for Johnny," April recalled. "He found other digs quite quickly." Even so, Prescott and the newly glamorous April remained friends for years to come.

George, segueing into a self-identity as a woman, moved to London. There he became a drag queen, performing in Soho. Later, as "Toni April," he relocated to Paris, where he became one of the most popular entertainers at the well-known drag cabaret, *Le Carroussel,* which often attracted celebrities, even visiting movie stars.

One of Toni's most ardent admirers was Bing Crosby. "He pursued me," April admitted in her memoirs. She later referred to him as "lecherous."

April Ashley as an *haute* model a few years later

During summers, she migrated to *Le Carroussel's* "southern sister," its branch in Juan-les-Pins on the French Riviera. There, her show was attended by Bob Hope, who invited her to breakfast the following morning.

This led to her getting a small role as one of the six beautiful women in the picture he was filming at the time, *Road to Hong Kong* (1962), co-starring Joan Collins and Crosby, his partner.

Joan Collins, Bing Crosby, & Bob Hope in *Road to Hong Kong*. Nowhere to be seen is April Ashley, whose performance was excised from the movie's final cut when her secret became known.

During the shoot, Crosby continued to pursue her, singing "April in Paris" to her.

Regrettably, one of the jealous women in the cast "outed" Toni as a man to the film's director, who removed her name from the credits and cut out any scene that showed her face. "Only my back appears in the final cut," April said.

The famous and very eccentric surrealist painter, Salvador Dalí, was fascinated by drag queens and also frequented *Le Carroussel* in Paris. April recalled that in a single week, he showed up on six consecutive nights to watch her perform, and that "Dalí had this thing for chicks with dicks." The painter later claimed that it was he who had coined the term, "She-Males."

Salvador Dalí

Crazy, exhibitionistic, surreal, and—for a brief moment, at least—madly in love with April Ashley.

Dalí would arrive in her dressing room with chocolates and champagne, and he constantly urged her to pose in the nude for him. He wanted to depict her as Hermaphroditos, the son of Hermes and Aphrodite. Politely, she rejected his offer, later asserting, "I did not want to be immortalized on the wall of London's Tate Gallery with my little penis. Even then, before surgery, I knew I was a woman."

During the next summer season on the Riviera, from her base in Juan-les-Pins, she drove to the nearby Provençal village of Vallauris, where Pablo Picasso main-

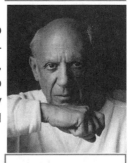

Pablo Picasso
Cynical and passionate

tained a studio devoted to the manufacturing, firing, and glazing of the ceramics he'd designed. He just happened to be at that studio the day April arrived. She remembered him as "looking like a Gila monster in shorts." Like Dalí, he, too, was fascinated by drag queens, and, like Dalí, he also wanted her to pose in the nude for him. As she later wrote: "I was afraid of him. He had a lecherous look, and I thought he would not be kind—either in bed or at the easel."

Elvis, through a pimp, invited intimacies with April.

Back in Paris at Le Carroussel for the winter season, April, still being billed as Toni April, picked up another world-famous admirer, Elvis Presley. For what he called "dirty weekends," he sometimes flew to Paris from West Germany, where he was stationed at a U.S. Army base.

As one of the members of his Memphis Mafia later revealed, "Elvis had the hots for this chick. I didn't know if she was male or female. She sure looked like a gal to me. Elvis even talked about wanting to marry her."

At the time, Elvis was on a mission, which involved his fantasy about seducing each of the forty long-limbed Blue Bell Girls, each a dancer at the (Paris) Lido. Elvis'

When he heard about it, Colonel Parker (above) "went ballistic."

aide said, "Boss man liked to deflower virgins, and he took the virginity of most of those showgirls." April knew about this, but she wondered how many actual virgins there had ever been within the ranks of the Blue Bell Girls.

April thought Elvis was one of the best-looking Americans she'd ever seen, writing later about his "blue-black hair, golden skin, lips so cherry red they looked artificial, and his brilliant green eyes."

On his second night at Le Carroussel, one of Elvis' aides went backstage and met with Toni. "Elvis wants to go to bed with you," he said. "How about it?"

She was stunned. "Elvis Presley wants to go to bed with *me?*"

She suggested in a memoir that Elvis' entry into her life was "just too premature," claiming that she never went off with him. Two of Elvis' aides dispute that, alleging that April and Elvis had a torrid affair. But prior to their allegations, these aides had been fired, and were trying to sell sensational stories about Elvis to the

Albert Einstein... "Just which gender are you?"

tabloids.

When Col. Tom Parker, Elvis' manager, heard that his breadwinner was involved in an affair with a drag queen, he went ballistic, ordering Elvis to dump her.

"The old colonel nearly choked on his cigar when he heard about Elvis and me," April later said.

Whether Elvis obeyed the colonel is a matter of conjecture. Elvis said, "You can throw ice water on a man who has the hots, but that doesn't mean you've put out the fire."

In May of 1960, when Toni had saved £3,000, she flew to Casablanca, where she submitted herself to sex reassignment surgery, a procedure that lasted for a full seven hours. Dr. Georges Burou performed this remarkable (for the time) surgery, which was successful, even though Toni had to endure horrible pain. In the aftermath, all her hair fell out.

Ashley as "Geronimo" at *Le Carroussel* (Paris) in 1959

When the newspapers finally learned of this operation, April became notorious as one of the earliest British men to transform into a woman through sex reassignment surgery.

In London, *The Daily Mail* called her "part Audrey Hepburn, part Princess Grace, with the earthiness of Honor Blackman *[The British actress who interpreted the role of Pussy Galore in* Goldfinger *(1964)]* thrown in."

Back in London, April met the renowned, then-elderly scientist, Albert Einstein, at a restaurant on Dean Street. It was she who approached his table. "Is it Mr. Einstein?" she asked.

"He had a question for her. "Are you a boy or a girl?"

"I think I'm a girl," she said.

"Whatever you are, you should be Madame Butterfly, with those long eyelashes."

Although she omitted it from her memoirs, Einstein then reportedly asked her to volunteer as a subject of a scientific examination of her body as a means of determining her gender. "It would be a very lovely scientific experience."

He went on to tell her that he found her "almost as beautiful as Marilyn Monroe."

After Einstein's death, it was revealed that for years after their meeting, he harbored a romantic fixation on her.

During her many seductions and romantic involvements that followed, one in particular stood out. It involved "a sensational one-night stand" with Michael Hutchence, the Australian musician who was the founder and lead singer of the rock band INXS. He later told friends, "This lovely creature can fill a man with an abiding passion." With a sense of regret and horror, April learned that the singer committed suicide in 1997.

Still alive at the time of this writing, April Ashley admits, "It hasn't been an easy life. You have to be resilient. You can't let people crush you."

Who a Visitor Might Have Met on the Costa del Sol in the Early 60s: "Auntie Mame," Gay American Playwrights, German War Widows, Spanish Gigolos, &

Peter O'Toole

Parading His "Gypsy Blood & El Greco Body" in a Bikini

When he wasn't needed for appearances before the cameras, Peter O'Toole and April Ashley made the rounds of the hot spots along the Costa del Sol, perhaps provoking the jealousy of her other beaux. Often, Omar Sharif, if available, joined them on their nightly rounds.

The evenings usually began in the medieval barrio of Marbella, where they went "tasca hopping," the English equivalent of a pub crawl. O'Toole enjoyed the local specialty, a *fritura malagueña,* a mixed fish fry whose individual components were based on the catch of the day, downing it with the local wines. Sometimes, they wandered along the waterfront, patronizing the local *chiringuitos* (tapas bars). Los Sardinales on Paseo de los Alicates became their favorite hangout.

Almost nightly, they dropped in at Tu Casa, a cozy Moroccan bar and tearoom off Plaza de los Naranjos. The owner was a friendly American woman, Roz McLester, who reminded O'Toole of Rosalind Russell in *Auntie Mame.* On cooler nights, they gathered around her fireplace, sometimes ordering her savory chili, followed by a large cup of Columbian coffee.

O'Toole became addicted to flamenco at La Pagoa Gitana because, as he told April, "It brings out the gypsy blood in my soul." The troupe which performed it there usually included some guitarists, about six singers, and an intensely dramatic *gran cantaora [principal folksinger]*.

He would later assert that these experiences helped him in re-creating the character of Don Quixote when he co-starred with Sophia Loren in his film version of *Man of La Mancha* (1972).

Often, their drinking binges took them over to the just-emerging and very hip and free-wheeling resort of Torremolinos, a former fishing village at the foot of the Sierra Mijas that seemed very far from the wealth, snobbery, and social pretense of Marbella.

He later wrote to Kenneth Griffith, asserting, "Torremolinos attracts a lot of Tab Hunter lookalikes, bikini-clad blondes, artists, writers, and past-the-30-mark English secretaries. To cater to all these single women, along with a lot of English pederasts, oily-haired Spanish youths from the hills descend on Torremolinos to fulfill the sexual desires of the expatriates. With their El Cordobés haircuts, they fancy themselves as *conquistadores.*"

"German war widows like to come here. I call them 'Brunhildes,' with their Andalusian Don Juans. So many Nazi men were killed in the war that these widows have to head to Spain to get laid. I spotted one Big Bertha strolling with a four-foot-nine-inch Spaniard in a pair of Don Quixote boots. As three lobster-red Swedish girls in reveal-everything bikinis strolled by, an aging Spanish *duenna,* her shoulders draped in a black shawl, crossed her heart."

James Leo Herlihy,
author of
Midnight Cowboy

O'Toole's favorite hangout became Pedro's at Torremolino's central Plaza Costa del Sol. There, he discovered young men in powder-pink dinner jackets escorting Vassar virgins, and an assortment of English and American writers and artists drawn to the incredibly cheap cost of living. A hamburger cost the equivalent of 30 American cents; a full meal comprising several courses cost $1.50, sometimes even less.

One night, he met two young American writers, James Leo Herlihy and James Kirkwood, who had rented a nearby villa. It turned out that the men were lovers, and would soon be receiving their close friend, Tennessee Williams, who was stopping off for a visit after his holiday in Tangier, across the Mediterranean.

Herlihy had written a novel, *All Fall Down,* which had been adapted into a movie starring Warren Beatty, Angela Lansbury, and Eva Marie Saint. Around the same

...in a love nest with
James Kirkwood,
famous for
A Chorus Line

288

time, one of his plays, *Blue Denim,* as directed by Joshua Logan, had been produced on Broadway. Herlihy would later write a novel, *Midnight Cowboy,* which, eventually, was adapted into a movie which won an Oscar in 1969 as Best Picture of the Year.

Kirkwood was also a novelist and playwright. He'd later write *A Chorus Line,* winning a Pulitzer Prize for his efforts.

Ashley later said," I always felt that Peter had a dislike of homosexuals, although he was always very kind to them."

As he once told her, "I felt both of these handsome, talented guys were going places big time, though maybe not as far as their friend, Tennessee. Why not be nice to them? They might write a prize role for me one day. Even though I plan to become a bigtime move star, I haven't given up my love for the stage. Make as many friends as you can on the way up, because in the theater, you'll meet them on the way down."

When O'Toole appeared on the beach wearing a bikini, he attracted a lot of attention. "It wasn't that he had the best body on the beach—he didn't, of course. It was that the Spaniards felt that a model for an El Greco painting had suddenly made an entrance from out of the past," April said.

One night, an invitation arrived for April, himself, and Sharif, to attend the premiere of an exclusive bodega in Jerez de la Frontera, the chic sherry capital of Spain, north of Seville. The invitation was from Pedro, the Marquis de Domecq d'Usquain, whose peerage had been created by Spain's King Alfonso XIII during the autumn of 1920. The honored guests would not only include visiting movie stars, but members of the Royal Family of Spain, which was still flourishing even though Franco had usurped their power.

One Rainy Night in Jerez, O'Toole Learns What a Surgeon Can Do to a Penis

The paparazzi had turned out for the event, and flashbulbs were going off at fifteen-second intervals as the *glitterati* arrived for the opening of the Marquis de Domecq d'Usquain's chic new bodega in Jerez de la Frontera. The Marquis, known as "Pedro" to his friends, stood near the entrance to greet his fashionable guests.

In many ways, the appearance of April Ashley stole everyone's thunder. She looked "drop-dead gorgeous," as she remembered it, in an emerald satin gown. Dressed in tuxedos, O'Toole was on one arm, Sharif on the other.

The *grandees* of Andalusia were there, along with others from Madrid. Pedro had gone all out to prepare a feast and the entertainment that followed.

Only the rarest of sherries were served with each course.

Everyone knew that *Lawrence of Arabia* was going to be the big new picture of the year, and that O'Toole was the male star of the evening, as everyone flocked around him.

But as the night wore on and as some of the guests (especially O'Toole) got more drunk, one of the liveried footmen, splendidly attired in 18th century costume, appeared before April, informing her that O'Toole could be found at the bar. "Señor O'Toole is weeping, wailing, howling. He wants you to come at once."

She rushed to his side to offer comfort. "Darling, darling, what is it? What has happened?"

He grabbed her in a tight embrace. "My dear, how can you hold up under the pain? What you must have suffered in life. Believe me, I didn't know. People can be so cruel to you."

"I don't have any pain," she said in astonishment. "I feel wonderful. It's such a gala night."

"You know...*the pain!*"

He wanted to leave the party at once, and both of them headed for the door.

On their way out, a man made a lewd remark about April, and O'Toole smashed his fist into his face, bloodying his nose. Another man then called out to him, mockingly, "You know, don't you, that you're fucking a dick that's been inverted?"

O'Toole took a swing at him, too, but he was so drunk that he missed.

Later, after April and O'Toole had returned to the room they were sharing at a local hotel, as she was getting ready for bed, she heard a door slam. She was nude, so she grabbed her coat, covering her body. Rushing outside into the hallway, and then down to the reception area, she was told that he had left the building.

It was raining outside. She ran to catch up with him, begging him to return to the hotel. He seemed "itching for a fight." It took a lot of persuading, but eventually, she was able to convince him that he was in no condition for combat.

Apparently, at some point, she began a discussion with him about her male-to-female conversion process. "I really wasn't much of a man," she reportedly said. She'd confessed to others that her male genitalia was "alien to me. To think of it still gives me goosepimples." She said her penis had always been very small, evoking a woman's clitoris. "(Having) a vagina wasn't my fancy, but a deeply rooted need."

As she stated clearly in her memoirs, "I was to be a woman or to be nothing. Otherwise, I was to evaporate from my torment."

She also admitted that, "No man who wanted me ever changed his mind when he found out that I had been a transvestite, later a transsexual. If anything, it made them more keen to be with me. Men are men. They are strange creatures, yet so predictable."

Back in London, O'Toole shared the details of his involvements with April with his friend, Kenneth Griffith. "If the vagina on a transsexual is delectably tight, and gives a man a spectacular orgasm, what does it matter what the ex organ used to be? The only thing that matters is that it's in working order at the moment. And, yes, it helps if the woman beneath you is more stunning than almost any other female on the planet."

"I see, old boy. That helps, of course," Griffith said, sardonically.

A Drunken O'Toole Goes on a Violent Rampage in the Sherry Capital, Tossing Champagne in Faces and Bloodying a Nose

Alec Guinness died in 2000. A year before his death, he authorized the novelist, Piers Paul Read, to write his biography, which was posthumously published in 2003. In it, Guinness revealed an incident that happened in Spain's sherry capital of Jerez de la Frontera when he and O'Toole were invited as guests of honor to an elegant dinner party. At this point near the end of the filming of *Lawrence of Arabia,* Guinness' initial affection for O'Toole had diminished because of his outrageous behavior when he was drunk.

Once again, their host was Pedro, the Marquis de Domecq d'Usquain, who had recently hosted the premiere of his elegant new bodega, an event which O'Toole, with April, had attended. Two other stars from the cast of *Lawrence,* Jack Hawkins and Anthony Quayle, had also been invited to the party by the marquis.

The Spanish *grandee* had prepared a Luculian banquet for the stars. As the night progressed, and as O'Toole's drinking increased, he began to attack Francisco Franco, the grip of the Catholic Church on the politics of Spain, and the then-Fascist Spanish government's collaboration with Nazi Germany during World War II. Anywhere in Spain at the time, any of these subjects was virtually incendiary in terms of the raw emotion and pain they each provoked.

During one particularly intense moment in his diatribe, O'Toole became so enraged that he tossed his glass of champagne into the face of his host, the Marquis.

Later, in a letter to his friend, Philip Barton, back in England, Guinness wrote: "O'Toole could have been killed, shot, strapped, or strangled, and I'm beginning to think it's a pity he wasn't."

"Fortunately, the host summoned his security, and two of his guards tossed O'Toole out on his ass onto the street of stones in front of the bodega."

During his departure that night, Guinness quipped to the Marquis, their host, "When I return to London, I'm advising Her Majesty not to invite Mr. O'Toole to her garden party."

In his memoirs, Guinness wrote about O'Toole's co-stars and director. "O'Toole's Arab servant, *Shufti,* looks about ready to use daggers on Mrs. O'Toole," a reference to Siân Phillips, who had flown in to visit her husband in Seville.

Guinness continued, "Jack Hawkins is here, and I think in a rather poor way, poor old thing. He's so very shaky—his hands tremble all the time, and having had the top of his head shaven to play Allenby (it looks like a blue egg—rather flat, though), he looks wounded in his pride. Claude Rains is here, too, and he is a dear."

O'Toole in *Night of the Generals* (1967). "I was a Nazi in uniform, but not in my heart."

"David Lean seems OK and less beady-eyed than usual—though not exactly cosy. I would have thought a drink might be offered, and an introduction to his sari-clad Indian wife. On the other hand, I got a vast bowl of dead carnations sent to my funeral parlour," a reference to his suite at one of Seville's most prestigious hotels, the Alfonso XIII.

As Guinness prepared to leave Spain, he wrote one final note to a friend. "Like all horrors, *Lawrence of Arabia* has come to an end, at least the shooting schedule for me. If there is a God, I know he is kind and merciful and will never force me to encounter Peter O'Toole ever again."

***

[*After the Spanish segments of the filming of* Lawrence of Arabia *were finished, O'Toole returned to England, bidding farewell to April Ashley and Omar Sharif. He and Sharif would remain friends for life, and would make future movies together. The most widely publicized was* Night of the Generals *(1967), in which they co-starred with Tom Courtenay in a picture directed by Anatole Litvak, former husband of the temperamental screen actress, Miriam Hopkins.*

"*I got to strut about in Nazi uniform and work for Sam Spiegel again," O'Toole said. "God, if there is such a person, is good. I was this Nazi general— mad, psychopathic, in charge of the Nazi war machine in Warsaw. The wonderful blood and carnage brought back fond memories of* Lawrence of Arabia.]

That Decadent Spendthrift, King Saud, Wants O'Toole to Portray Him as a Heroic Warrior in a Desert Epic —This One "Without the Jew"

King Saud of Saudi Arabia owned a luxurious vacation retreat along the Costa del Sol. During O'Toole's sojourn nearby, with the intention of visiting it, he flew to Málaga with some of his wives and some of his 115 sons and daughters. (He preferred sons, some of whom he called "little kings."

In addition to a holiday, he wanted to check to see if the public image of Saudi Arabia was being "misrepresented" in either the story line or the visuals of *Lawrence of Arabia*. When it became clear that neither Sam Spiegel nor David Lean seemed interested in returning his calls, King Saud turned to O'Toole as a source of information, especially when he was sufficiently drunk. Saud had hired spies, who had reported some of the gossip associated with O'Toole's fondness for the bottle.

O'Toole was occupied when Sharif and Ashley went to the Plaza de Toros in Málaga to watch a series of "deaths in the afternoon," as Ernest Hemingway had described the bullfights.

Both April and Sharif were impressed when King Saud *[Saud bin Abdulaziz Al Saud, King of Saudi Arabia from 1953 to 1964]* presented gold watches to the matadors.

That night at Pedro's in Torremolinos, they met one of the Saudi princes, who was accompanied by three blonde girlfriends, each of whom seemed to look, talk, and dress like Marilyn Monroe.

In a conversation with the Prince—they never specifically identified which of Saud's many sons he was—he commented on the ironies he faced as an oil-enriched desert lord. He told them that his father had to keep importing a string of Cadillacs in all colors from America. "I drive them to remote

King Saud on the cover of *Time's* edition of January, 1957.

Saud wanted O'Toole to portray him on screen—in a style akin to what he'd delivered as T. E. Lawrence—as a heroic desert warrior, "but without any Jews in the picture."

desert locales. They are badly made. When they run out of petrol, I abandon them—finders keepers—and ride a camel back to the palace."

April suggested that it might be less expensive to simply refill each of the Cadillac's gasoline tanks. On hearing that, the prince appeared as if he'd never heard of such economy.

Later that evening, he conveyed a personal invitation from King Saud to O'Toole, whom he wanted to entertain at his luxurious villa along the southern coast of Spain.

When O'Toole learned about the proffered invitation, he eagerly accepted. "It's about time Royalty started paying me some attention," he said to Sharif. "Queen Elizabeth has never even invited me into her boudoir at Buckingham Palace. I know she must be getting pretty god damn tired of Philip by now."

As an Egyptian, Sharif was far more informed about Saud than O'Toole, partly because Saudi Arabia was engaged in a bitter conflict with Soviet-backed Egypt. At the time, Saud was also involved in a power struggle with his brother, Prince Faisal.

Faced with declining oil revenues, Saud—a extravagant spendthrift by anyone's standards—had doubled his country's debt by spending millions upon millions on luxurious palaces and other luxuries—fleets of Rolls-Royces, trunk loads of diamonds and rubies; antiques; almost priceless paintings; extravagant living arrangements; and constant presents to his ever-growing corps of wives and royal children.

"He lives like some sultan despot from *The Arabian Nights.*" Sharif claimed.

"He sounds like a man after my own heart," O'Toole responded. "I must meet him."

The banquet at Saud's Andalusian villa featured belly dancers imported from Tripoli. Over a lavish banquet, Saud told him that he had long been fascinated with T.E. Lawrence, and asked many questions, not only about how he was being depicted on the screen, but how Arabs in general were being portrayed. "The fact that this film has a Jew producer has greatly alarmed me," Saud complained.

O'Toole quickly responded that Saud would be thrilled, since the film presented Arabs as heroic fighters for independence from foreign colonial powers.

Before the evening ended, Saud made an astonishing proposal. "I'm getting a lot of bad publicity. I want *my* true story depicted on the screen. Perhaps David Lean can direct another epic, with you portraying myself as a younger man. Of course, that blonde hair would have to go, and you'd have to cover your blue eyes with contact lenses."

Saud explained himself in great detail, having heard that *Lawrence of Arabia* had been budgeted at $15 million. "I can provide Lean with $25 million, more if needed, if he'll portray my own heroism on the screen. You see, I, too, was a desert warrior."

Saud told O'Toole that he had been just a teenager in 1921 when he battled and prevailed over his dynastic rivals, the Al Rashid clan, in their headquarters of Ha'il, a city that straddled the camel caravan routes to Mecca. Later, he had led Saudi troops fighting in Yemen, and he also battled in eight separate armed conflicts before his ascension to the throne. *[In addition to the above-mentioned destruction of Ha'il, they included the Grab War, the Yabet War, the Ikhwan Revolt, and armed hostilities at Truba, Alkuras, Alhijaz, and Almahmal.]*

"An impressive achievement, dwarfing Lawrence's victories," O'Toole said, in an attempt to flatter him.

Before the night ended, a drunken O'Toole promised that he would become Saud's chief advocate with Lean in his attempts to interest him in another desert epic.

Saud's final words to O'Toole were a warning that 'No Jew like Spiegel can produce such a glorious story of an Arab."

"Of course," O'Toole said, diplomatically.

It is not known if O'Toole ever even discussed Saud's proposal with Lean. Regardless, nothing ever came of it.

In 1964, before Saud could solidify his dream for a film about his military exploits with other directors and actors, he was replaced as King of Saudi Arabia and removed from power. In exile, he moved about, fitfully, finally settling in Greece, where he died in February of 1969.

On hearing the news, O'Toole told his friends, "Would anyone believe me on the screen as King Saud? Surely, it would be the miscasting of the century, although I'd look divinely delicious in my flowing white robes."

***

Actor Peter O'Toole was just as anxious to meet with the respected film producer, Kevin McClory, as McClory was to meet with him. Both men seemed to sense that each of them might be involved creatively with the other sometime in their immediate futures.

"We met for dinner one night, without anybody else hanging out with us," O'Toole said. "Two creative artists smelling each other out." Apparently, both the actor and producer interpreted the other as "charismatic."

Before their dinner, O'Toole had been brought up to date on the publicity during the 1950s that had enveloped McClory in the tangled web of Elizabeth Taylor.

Before she got involved with her eventual husband, producer Mike Todd, Elizabeth was going around telling such friends as Roddy McDowall that "in the future, I'm to be known as Elizabeth Taylor McClory."

McClory, a native of Dublin, had been descended from two of O'Toole's favorite authors, the literary sisters, Emily and Charlotte Brontë. Both of his parents had been actors on the Dublin stage.

McClory told O'Toole tragic, sometimes heroic, tales associated with his service in the British Merchant Navy during World War II. At one point, his ship was torpedoed in the North Atlantic, and many members of his crew drowned. But he drifted for the next 700 miles in a lifeboat in freezing waters before he was picked up off the coast of Ireland with four other survivors.

Elizabeth Taylor's Former Boyfriend Ponders Casting Peter O'Toole as James Bond, Agent 007

After the War, McClory had become friends with famous writers and directors who included John Huston, who defined him "as a man's man like Bogie." McClory was also a close friend of writer Ian Fleming, and he was one of the first to realize the cinematic potential of the exploits of Fleming's James Bond character. "Your secret agent would be the focal point of a dynamite series of movies," he told Fleming.

After a few drinks at dinner, McClory admitted to O'Toole that he did not break up Elizabeth's marriage to Michael Wilding. "She had already fallen out of love with him when I started dating her. It was all over, except for the divorce. I was crazy for her, and she was in love with me, too—and we planned to get married when her divorce came through. I warned her I was a man of limited means and couldn't afford to keep her in mink and laden with diamonds."

He reported that Elizabeth had said, "It doesn't matter. I'd live in a log cabin with no jewelry, scrub our floor, and cook Irish stew for you every night, serving it with cold beer, if you'll make me your wife."

The Battle for Bond

On seeing Sean Connery on the screen as James Bond, O'Toole said, "What a fool I was. It could have been me."

"Do you mean that, my darling girl?" McClory had asked her.

"I mean it as much as a man does when he tells a woman he'll put in only the first three inches," she said.

"That Elizabeth!" O'Toole said. "I've met her only briefly when she was filming *Suddenly, Last Summer* (1959), but she seems to have a wicked wit."

"That and other things," McClory said.

"If you'd like to meet her, I can arrange that when we get back to London."

"I can't wait," O'Toole responded. "She loaned me her car once when I was abandoned by the studio's driver after a failed screen test."

"Well, she's certainly heard of you," McClory said. "At this point, who hasn't?"

O'Toole was being discreet. He didn't want to confess to McClory that he'd already become very acquainted with Elizabeth Taylor. The reason for holding back was that he didn't want to arouse jealousy in a producer who might offer him some tantalizing acting jobs.

Before their evening ended, McClory and O'Toole discussed the possibility of several future projects together. Foremost among these was the cinematic treatment of the James Bond character. O'Toole had never read an Ian Fleming novel.

"Ian came to me in 1958, and I read his Bond books, but I rejected all of them," McClory said. "However, I thought he was on to something with 007. I worked on a script with Ian and two other men, Jack Whittingham and Ivar Bryce.

[Later, O'Toole made it a point to read one of Fleming's novels, but he was not that intrigued with the Bond character, interpreting 007 as a "comic book hero" preoccupied with action, including car chases and the like. He sought more substantial roles, and then spent the rest of his life regretting that he turned McClory down.

Eventually, McClory's collaborations and compromises would evolve into the movie Thunderball *(1965), with Sean Connery cast as Bond. McClory's material would also end up in another Bond film,* Never Say Never Again (1983), *a loose re-interpretation of* Thunderball *that once again starred Sean Connery.]*

Copyright disputes for these films would rage for some fifty years, until they were finally resolved in 2013, seven years after McClory's death.

At that dinner in Marbella, McClory also said that he had "another burning idea in the back of my head, and that is to make a bio-pic about Michael Collins."

[Collins (1890-1922) was an Irish revolutionary hero.]

O'Toole admitted that interpreting that role "would be dear to my Irish heart."

However, in 1968, when McClory decided to actually launch that film, he'd become intrigued with the idea of casting Richard Harris in the role of Collins.

"My big plans with Kevin never worked out," O'Toole recalled, regretfully. "He claimed to people that he was the man who *really* introduced me to Elizabeth Taylor. I didn't want to rain on Kevin's parade, but what he didn't know was that I already knew Elizabeth as David knew Bathsheba, but that's a story for another day."

007? With a License to Kill?

Chapter 15

Elizabeth Taylor Seduces O'Toole

Then, With Cleopatra in Chaos,
She Asks Him to Co-Star in it as Marc Antony

From left to right, Elizabeth Taylor with Eddie Fisher, who was married to Debbie Reynolds when this picture was shot and flashed around the world. Months later, Elizabeth protested to Peter O'Toole, "The press hound-dogs claim I stole Eddie from Debbie. It wasn't much of a god damn theft."

She wanted O'Toole as her new leading man, and perhaps a lot more. "I have assets," she told him.

Peter O'Toole's performances in plays at Stratford-upon-Avon were generating interest from filmmakers. They began sending signals, tempting him with possible roles.

The best example of this involved Elizabeth Taylor and her husband, Eddie Fisher. When they arrived in London, they were interested in testing him in a star vehicle for her.

"Of course, he'll have to settle for a second banana part opposite you, my darling," Fisher told Elizabeth and her in-house gay secretary, Dick Hanley.

"Do you want me to audition him first?" asked Hanley.

"Is your mind always on cock?" she asked.

"I guess that's why my mother named me Dick," he answered, jokingly.

"Of course, I want to appear in films where the woman always has the star role," she said. "But I can see O'Toole as a leading man. Instead of me appearing with a different actor in every picture, I want to try my luck with him as part of a screen team—you known, Myrna Loy and William Powell; Spencer Tracy and Katharine Hepburn; Gable and Harlow. I need to find out if O'Toole and I have the chemistry to burn up the screen. In other words, is he the man for me?"

"Don't put it that way," Fisher cautioned. "I'm the only man for you. O'Toole would be a mere actor."

"Right you are, my darling. For you, I've disgraced myself and now I'm denounced as an international Jezebel, if not a trollop.""

"If it hadn't been Eddie, then who?" Hanley asked.

"Probably Mike Todd, Jr., she said. "But if I'd married my late husband's son, that would have caused even more scandal than I got for stealing Eddie from Debbie Reynolds."

"We weren't really America's sweethearts," Fisher said. "I never loved her, and she sure as hell wasn't in love with me."

"We'll have to drive up to Stratford and catch O'Toole in a play," she said.

"Only if you make a promise to me," Fisher said, "and that is you'll not make a play for him."

"Darling, you ask the impossible," she said. "From what I've heard, no woman is safe with Mr. O'Toole."

Taylor Wants to Replicate Garbo's Success as Anna Karenina, With O'Toole Cast as Her Dashing Count Vronsky

In 1960, at Stratford-upon-Avon, O'Toole was appearing as Petruchio opposite Peggy Ashcroft in that Shakespearean romp, *The Taming of the Shrew*.

After the curtain went down, O'Toole received a surprise guest in his dressing room. It was Eddie Fisher. The singer complimented O'Toole profusely on his performance that night, although O'Toole wasn't really flattered since he considered Fisher no expert on Shakespeare.

"Mrs. Fisher wanted to drive up to Stratford with me tonight, but she's sick in bed with the flu at the Dorchester in London," Fisher said. "She's read wonderful reviews of your performance, and she also had *The Day They Robbed the Bank of England* screened for us. She just adored you in the role opposite that very flat Aldo Ray. He's such a jerk."

"I am deeply honored," O'Toole said.

"Elizabeth not only liked your performance, but she considers you one of the finest actors in the world, an emerging new talent with a distinctly different style from either Gielgud or Olivier."

"When she recovers, could I meet this divine wife of yours?" O'Toole asked.

"Even before she recovers," Fisher said. "She wants you to drop by our suite at the Dorchester tomorrow night at six. The stage manager said there is no performance here tomorrow."

Undressing in front of Fisher, and then putting on his street clothes, O'Toole invited the singer for a nightcap at his favorite watering hole, the Black Swan (aka "The Dirty Duck") on Waterside. Most of the patrons there recognized Fisher from his pictures in the newspapers, but the actors respected his privacy and didn't approach him for autographs.

"Actually, one day, Elizabeth wants to make a film version of *The Taming of the Shrew*," Fisher said. "But I doubt if she ever will."

[In 1967, Elizabeth and Richard Burton, under Franco Zeffirelli's direction, brought this comedy by Shakespeare to the screen.]

"For the moment, Elizabeth has her mind set on doing a remake of *Anna Karenina*," Fisher said. "As I'm sure you know, Garbo did her version in 1935 and Vivien Leigh did hers in 1948. Those are two tough acts to follow, but Elizabeth wants a challenge. You'd be following in the footsteps of Fredric March, in the Garbo version, and Kieron Moore in the Leigh version."

"I think I could bring Count Vronsky to the screen again,"

Anna Kareninas: Hard acts for Elizabeth Taylor (lower photo) to follow.

Other actresses who had stamped their identities on the role included Greta Garbo (upper photo) in 1935 and Vivien Leigh (center) in 1948.

O'Toole said. "I'm better looking than March, and I have more talent than Moore."

"I'm glad you said that," Fisher said. "I hate false modesty in an actor."

O'Toole drove down to London the following morning and wandered aimlessly around the West End Theatrical District, catching a movie matinee before heading to the Dorchester, where he was ushered upstairs to the Fisher suite promptly at six o'clock.

Fisher was there to show him in and to reacquaint him with Elizabeth after their ever-so-brief meeting several years before.

O'Toole thanked her for the use of her car when he was screen tested as a possible replacement for Monty Clift on the set of *Suddenly, Last Summer.*

She looked him up and down. He felt like a bull being auctioned off to the highest bidder at a cattle sale in Hereford. "I never had a chance to thank you for the wheels," he said.

"Actually, I felt a little guilty about that," she said. "I think I was the one who prevented you from getting the role of Sebastian. I told Joseph Mankiewicz that if he fired Monty, I was going to walk—and I meant it."

"It's just as well," he said. "perhaps I'll work with you in the future."

Elizabeth Taylor wanted O'Toole, as Count Vronsky, to co-star with her as Anna Karenina.

As such, they'd be following film precedents already trailblazed by Greta Garbo and Fredric March (top photo), and later by Vivien Leigh and—in a less successful mating—Kieron Moore (lower photo).

She launched into a discussion of her plans for *Anna Karenina,* outlining how she wanted to do a very different version from that of Garbo or Leigh. "As the Count, I think you and I would have a powerful chemistry on the screen.

Eddie will give you a copy of our screen treatment."

After the business was out of the way, she told him she was bored with her recuperation in bed and wanted him to play a game of blackjack with Fisher and her. They played until midnight. He later told his friends, "I won forty quid off her."

As he was preparing to leave, she said, "I'd kiss you, but I don't want to give you the flu."

"That's the second time you've come up with an excuse for not kissing me," he said.

"What on earth do you mean?" she asked.

"The day you loaned me your car, you said you'd kiss me were it not for the fact that you had to go pick cotton. I didn't know what in the hell you meant."

"A real movie buff would have figured it out," she said. "I was parroting a famous line from Bette Davis in *Cabin in the Cotton* (1932), one of her early films. She told her prospective beau, 'I'd kiss you but I just washed my hair.'"

As she sat up in bed, where she'd retired after their card game, he bowed and kissed her delicate hand. "We'll meet again to make future plans when I rise from my death bed. Before you go, could you try to locate that little jerk I married and send him in? And on your way out, get him to sing 'Oh! My Pa-Pa' for you. That's the only thing he does well."

"I'd love to work as your leading man in anything," he said. "I'd even play your sex slave if you get cast as the Empress of Rome or as the Queen of Egypt."

That was just a toss-off line he delivered, not knowing at the time that a film entitled *Cleopatra* was on the way.

"Okay, Big Guy," she said. "Call again and again and again. The next time, I'll be up and looking beautiful. As for those two kisses I've postponed with you, I assure you, I'll make up for them. When most men start kissing me, they can't stop."

"I'll take my chances."

In the corridor, he wondered if Miss Taylor Hilton Wilding Fisher was just a harmless flirt, or if she were really attracted to him. He knew one thing as he stepped into the elevator: He would soon find out.

Both O'Toole and his wife, Siân Phillips, read the screen treatment of Elizabeth's version of *Anna Karenina* written by some unknown. Both of them thought it was horrid.

With the money he'd won from Elizabeth at blackjack, O'Toole bought a new wardrobe and tossed out his old clothes. "He came home looking gorgeous," Siân later claimed.

The *Anna Karenina* project died. Elizabeth had a far more important role in mind for him.

O'Toole Gets Down and Dirty With "The Serpent of the Nile"

Far away in Hollywood, at the headquarters of 20th Century Fox, a film was being discussed that would spill over into the life of Peter O'Toole.

The studio was desperate for a hit, an epic, perhaps, that would bring much needed millions to their diminishing coffers.

Spyros Skouras came up with the idea of remaking *Cleopatra,* which in 1917 had been a huge success for the studio. It had starred the silent screen vamp, Theda Bara.

Over the years, other actresses had brought the "Serpent of the Nile" to the screen and stage. In 1934, Claudette Colbert had starred in Cecil B. De-Mille's kitschy screen epic, one of the seminal tearjerkers of the decade. In 1937, on Broadway, Tallulah Bankhead, in *Antony and Cleopatra,* "barged down the Nile—and it sank," in the words of one critic.

Near the end of World War II, Vivien Leigh had revived the doomed queen in Gabriel Pascal's *Caesar and Cleopatra.* The performance by the former Scarlett O'Hara left most critics cold.

Fox executives were undecided about what to do. In September of 1958, they brought in producer Walter Wanger to try to pull the project together and to decide whether they wanted to film a major epic, perhaps starring Sophia Loren or Elizabeth Taylor, or whether they preferred a $1.2 million "cheapie" starring Joanne Woodward. *[Woodward had just won an Oscar for Three Faces of Eve.]*

Other "budget choices" for the role of the Egyptian queen included Joan Collins, Millie Perkins, Barbara Steele, and Dolores Michaels. Whereas Skouras wanted to go with Woodward, Buddy Adler, production chief, preferred Collins.

Finally, it was decided that Woodward wasn't sexy enough. Suzy Parker was considered until Fox learned that she was pregnant.

As the central figure in a big budget film, Audrey Hepburn was briefly considered until Skouras complained, "She looks like an effeminate boy—she has no tits at all."

"If you want tits, how about Gina Lollobrigida," Wanger asked. "Better yet, how

ELIZABETH TAYLOR RICHARD BURTON REX HARRISON

CLEOPATRA

Despite some feverish politicking, O'Toole's name did not figure into the production of this film.

about Elizabeth Taylor."

Many different casting dramas, especially those associated with the role of Cleopatra herself, were percolating in the background when O'Toole arrived for a second time at the Dorchester suite of Elizabeth. This time, there was no Fisher. Elizabeth's secretary, Dick Hanley, ushered O'Toole in to greet Elizabeth, who stood in her living room dressed in a magenta gown with plunging décolletage. She'd obviously recovered from the flu and welcomed him warmly.

As he seated himself on the sofa with her, she wasted no time in getting to the point. "I've been asked by Fox if I'd play *Cleopatra* in this big Technicolor epic, although that bitch from Brooklyn, Susan Hayward, is also being considered."

"I didn't know you were in the sword-and-sandals picture business," he said.

"I know it's shit," she said. "But I need the money. I don't want to do it. I called my agent, Kurt Frings, and told him to tell Fox I'd do it for a million dollars. He protested that no actress had ever commanded such a figure. I told him, 'But that's not all, baby. I also want ten percent of the gross."

"Would you believe it?" she asked. "The suckers came back to me and agreed to all my terms. They're desperate for a star."

"So you've accepted?" he asked.

"Yes, I have, and here's where you come in, sugar," she said. "I want you to be my co-star as Marc Antony."

He seemed to almost jump in enthusiasm. "I could go for that big time. Wearing a toga comes natural to me. I always run around my house in a nightgown that's sort of like a toga. Nothing on underneath, of course."

After midnight, after much talk about the project, and a catered dinner from the kitchen below, he suggested that it was perhaps time that he left.

"Dear heart, don't rush off," she said. "Not to worry. Eddie's in Paris. I sent him on an errand. I want you to stay. It gets lonely here at night. The kids and my staff are safely locked up in another wing for the night, even my cats and dogs. We're alone."

He'd later relate the details of the evening to his friend, Kenneth Griffith.

"I knew what was about to happen," O'Toole said. "I was going to fuck Elizabeth Taylor, something at least half the men on the planet wanted to do. For the first time in my life with a woman, I was nervous, fearing she might critique my performance."

"Elizabeth, as you know, has been around the block," O'Toole said. "Perhaps she never took on forty-four soldiers in one night like Cleo did. But she's been bedded and frequently. Her first two husbands, Nicky Hilton and Michael Wilding, are supposed to be incredibly endowed. I don't know about what kind of Jewish dick Mike Todd had. He did tell the press one time, 'Any minute this little dame spends out of bed is totally wasted.'"

"Some critics award films between one and five stars. How many stars did you get from Elizabeth?" Griffith asked.

"How can I answer such a dumb question?" O'Toole asked. "You get dumber every day. I know this. She promised to call me frequently for a rendezvous when she gets rid of 'The Jerk'—her name for Fisher."

"Poor Eddie Fisher, the Jewish Sinatra," Griffith said. "He's out of his league."

[In later years, O'Toole confided to Griffith that, "Elizabeth must have liked my performance. I've been fucking her on and off over the years. Our farewell roll in the hay was when we made Under Milk Wood in '72."]

After his night with Elizabeth, a call came in two days hence from the producer, Kevin McClory, who had just flown in from Madrid. "I've talked to Elizabeth," he said. "She remembered meeting you on the set of Suddenly, Last Summer. She wants you to join us at the Dorchester this coming Sunday night. Eddie's back in town. Your buddy, Peter Finch, will be there. She wants him to co-star with her in her upcoming movie, Cleopatra."

"As Marc Antony?" he asked.

"No, as Julius Caesar," McClory answered.

"Did she mention who she would like to play Marc Antony?" O'Toole asked.

"Actually, she didn't," McClory said. "If she does, I'll suggest either Anthony Steele or Stephen Boyd."

Arriving at the Dorchester ahead of everyone else, O'Toole was shown to a table reserved for Elizabeth and her friends in the bar. He ordered a lager from an Italian waiter. In fifteen minutes, his long-established friend, Peter Finch, came in. "Welcome, Caesar," O'Toole said.

Finch and O'Toole had bonded during their filming together of Kidnapped (1960). Before that, Finch had been plunged into the turbulent world of Vivien Leigh, his ill-fated co-star in Elephant Walk (1954) until she had to drop out and be replaced by Elizabeth.

Elizabeth arrived an hour late, with McClory on one arm, Fisher on the other. "Cleopatra has arrived," she said, "ready to receive Caesar and Marc Antony."

As he later related to Griffith, "Elizabeth pretended she didn't know me. She didn't want to make Eddie Fisher jealous. As for Finch, I don't know if Fisher knew that he and Elizabeth had been hot for each other."

To O'Toole's surprise, over drinks, Elizabeth flirted outrageously with Finch, much to the annoyance of Fisher. After about an hour of that, the singer stormed out of the bar.

She was becoming intoxicated, and so were Finch and O'Toole. Since he was not involved in any way with Cleopatra, McClory seemed left out of the conversation and left the party early.

"As Cleopatra," she said, "I'm supposed to fuck both of you. Both of you are men named Peter. Such handsome Peters you are, though frankly, I prefer the name Dick. To me, Peter sounds like some piece of okra attached to a thirteen-year-old boy."

Belatedly, O'Toole realized that all the men seated at her table that night, not only Finch and himself, but McClory and most definitely Fisher, had already seduced Elizabeth.

Way past midnight, on their final bottle of champagne, the bill was presented. "I'll sign for it," she said.

"I'm glad the lady pays," O'Toole said. "The bill would empty out my bank account and then some."

She proposed the final toast of the evening. "Let's drink to making the greatest epic in the history of Hollywood and a fuck-you to Cecil B. DeMille."

***

Two weeks went by and O'Toole had heard nothing from Elizabeth. When he tried to get in touch with Finch, he was told that "Peter has had a nervous breakdown."

One morning over breakfast, he read that another Irish actor, Stephen Boyd, was under consideration for the role of Marc Antony.

Unknown to O'Toole, the director of *Cleopatra,* Rouben Mamoulian, had arrived in town. He'd rejected Elizabeth's idea of casting O'Toole as Marc Antony. Instead, he had offered the role to Marlon Brando, who had rejected the idea.

The director believed that "O'Toole's legs are too bony, toothpicks, really, and his voice too prissy and high pitched" to play a macho like the Roman warrior.

Mamoulian had learned that the director of *The Savage Innocents* had dubbed O'Toole's voice because it wasn't macho enough to belong to a Mountie in the northern forests of Canada. He told Elizabeth, "You're the Queen of the Nile. We don't need an actor who sounds like a queen."

Mamoulian went on to say, "I think

As Marc Antony:
Irishman Stephen Boyd?

Stephen Boyd would be ideal as Marc Antony. If you don't believe me, just watch him as Messala in *Ben-Hur*. He sure has the legs for it. Of course, he's gay as a goose, but comes across as really macho on the screen."

O'Toole had the week off between appearances in Shakespeare plays at Stratford-upon-Avon. Consequently, he agreed to meet Finch at their favorite London pub, the Salisbury. By coincidence, Dick Hanley was also there, waiting to have a drink with Shelley Winters, who was also staying at The Dorchester during her filming in London of *Lolita* (1962) with James Mason.

O'Toole told Hanley that he'd read in the papers that morning that Stephen Boyd "was trying to steal Fisher's wife."

"If Boyd is screwing either of them, it's Eddie, not Elizabeth," Hanley claimed. "As you know, Eddie is booked in a separate suite at The Dorchester. The other night, I saw Boyd leaving Eddie's room after midnight."

O'Toole wanted to be discreet, but he couldn't resist asking about how casting was going on Cleopatra, wondering if he were still in the running for the role of Marc Antony.

"Elizabeth has signed, but all the male roles, particularly Caesar and Antony, are up for grabs," Hanley said.

At that point, Shelley Winters arrived with kisses for all. She was her gossipy self. "I just came from having a drink with Elizabeth. We've been friends ever since we appeared together in *A Place in the Sun* with Monty *[Clift]*. She and Eddie have had this big blowout because he accused her of having an affair with Peter."

"Which Peter?" Finch asked.

"You, baby," Winters said.

When Hanley and Finch went off to the men's room, Winters cracked, "I think Dick went along to hold it for Finch." Then she leaned over and whispered, "Why don't you come up and see me some night at The Dorch?"

"I have a better idea, O'Toole said. "I'm going to be playing Shylock next week in *The Merchant of Venice*. Why don't you drive up to Stratford and see my performance? After the curtain goes down, we'll have a riotous good time."

"An invitation I can't refuse. I'll be there Saturday night."

Two days later, he heard over the BBC that Elizabeth had been rushed to a private clinic in London, suffering from meningitis.

He called Hanley to learn that she was recover-

Sexy and vulnerably vulgar: Shelley Winters

ing and would be out of the hospital in a week. Hanley told him that Lloyds of London, which had insured the filming of *Cleopatra,* had asked Fox to replace Elizabeth with a less illness-prone lead. "Kim Novak, Shirley MacLaine, and Marilyn Monroe have been suggested as alternatives."

"From what I've heard, hiring Monroe would make *Cleopatra* the most expensive epic ever filmed." O'Toole said.

"There's even a rumor that Dorothy Dandridge is being considered."

"A black Cleopatra!" O'Toole said. "How utterly delightful. Fox would never go for that."

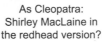

As Cleopatra:
Shirley MacLaine in the redhead version?

"Forty-four men a night would be a bit much for me."

As Serpent of the Nile:

Kim Novak in the lavender blonde version?

"Perhaps not," Hanley answered. "I also heard that Jennifer Jones is standing by."

"Give Elizabeth my love," O'Toole said.

When he called in a week, he learned that Elizabeth and Fisher had flown back to California for some R&R in Palm Springs.

Fox had shut down production at Pinewood. The remake of *Cleopatra* appeared to be in jeopardy.

In the meantime, Shelley Winters descended on Stratford-upon-Avon.

Shelley Winters Rates O'Toole as a Lover:
"He's as Good as Gable" (But Was That a Compliment?)

As she had promised, Shelley Winters made it to Stratford-upon-Avon in time to see O'Toole's performance as Shylock in *The Merchant of Venice.* At the time, she was still svelte, sexy, vampish, and known as a "Man Eater."

As she entered the theater, accompanied with a secretary/companion, there was a buzz within the audience. Known for her screen charisma and skill at portraying vulgar, brassy woman, Winters was a familiar face to these theater lovers.

Reporters tended to love her because she was so outspoken that she could be counted on to generate good copy. Earlier, she'd told a local newspaper reporter, "I was drowned by Monty Clift, who preferred Elizabeth Taylor to me. When I let that psychotic preacher, Robert Mitchum, into my bed, I ended up at the bottom of a lake with my throat cut. Now, I'm being run over by that pedophile, James Mason, so he can fuck my daughter, Sue Lyon. I've been strangled, raped, and murdered, but I'm still here."

After the performance, she went backstage to renew her acquaintance with O'Toole.

"Well, Shelley, what's your review of me as Shylock?" he asked her as he stripped down to his underwear during his change of clothing.

"I'll say one thing for you," she said. "You're not a Jew. I'm a Jew. I know Jews."

"So, you didn't like it?"

"I didn't say that," she answered. "All I said was 'you're not a Jew.'"

Ignoring her putdown, he said, "Perhaps you'll like my performance later this evening."

"I'm eagerly looking forward to it," she said. "No one, even my enemies, ever accused Shelley Winters of turning down a good fuck. I've had them all—Errol Flynn, Clark Gable, Marlon Brando, Ronald Colman, William Holden, Howard Hughes, Anthony Quinn, John Garfield, even Farley Granger."

"I thought Granger is gay?" he said.

"He's gay, but for me, he makes an exception," she said.

"John Ireland was the best-hung—a horse dick. Burt Lancaster had one of the smallest cocks but the fastest action."

Over dinner, Winters was such a font of information about insider Hollywood that he told her that if she became a gossip columnist, she would put Louella Parsons and Hedda Hopper out of business.

She'd spent the previous evening with Elizabeth Taylor, since they occupied adjoining suites at The Dorchester.

"Her entire entourage was running wild in the Oliver Messel suite," she said. "Her secretary, her chauffeur, a German couple who look after her, three kids, and that Eddie Fisher boy. Lots of dogs, even some cats. I'm amazed management allows that. The place smells. They'll have to redecorate when she checks out and pays for damages."

"I've had a few meals with her," Winters said. "Even though she's British, she prefers food from elsewhere—stone crabs flown in from Joe's on Miami Beach, steaks from Chicago, shrimp remoulade from New Orleans, linguini with clam sauce from Genoa, and white asparagus from the fields of France. Last night, we dined on chili flown in from Chasen's in Los Angeles."

"Her marriage to the boy singer is doomed," Winters continued. "He's not man enough for her. She bosses him around something terrible. Treats him

310

like an abused servant. She'll dump him soon, I'm sure. She spoke highly of you. I think she's got a crush on you. She also thinks you're a great actor, but the jury is still out on that. If you play your cards right, you could become the next Mr. Elizabeth Taylor."

"Come now," he said. "I'm happily married to a brilliant actress, Siân Phillips, and I'd rather be known as Mr. Peter O'Toole."

"Fisher was married to that little Debbie Reynolds before Elizabeth decided she wanted him. Lola gets what Lola wants."

"We'll see about that," he said. "How's *Lolita* going?"

"I'm from Venus, Mason and Peter Sellers are from Mars," she said. "Mason is very aloof, very technical. I find him sexy, but I hear he has this thing for Mediterranean boys. Sellers wanders off into outer space. I can't relate to him at all. I had to do this nude scene with Mason, pressing my naked bosom up against his back. I was so damn nervous, I broke his glasses and hit my head on the mike. Finally, Stanley Kubrick had to give me some gin, lots of gin, to calm my nerves before shooting could resume."

"Kubrick is a pain in the ass, but he understands the delicate mechanism of an actor's psyche," she said.

She discussed other actors, naming Frank Sinatra as her least favorite. "When we made *Meet Danny Wilson* (1952), he called me a 'bowlegged bitch of a Brooklyn blonde.' I told him he was 'a skinny, no-talent stupid Hoboken bastard.'"

"I don't hate all actors. The most charming I've met is Sean Connery. He's young, handsome, and one of the most masculine men I know. When I met him, he was very impoverished. Like a true Scot, he had deep pockets and short arms. When we shopped for food, he buys weird vegetables like parsnips and Brussels sprouts. Can you imagine eating such crap? He'll walk for miles to avoid paying for a cab."

Her bullet-like impressions of everyone even extended to the time she met Dylan Thomas in Hollywood at a lavish dinner. "I asked him why he was in Tinseltown. He told me he was here for two reasons—one, to touch the titties of every blonde starlet he could; and another to meet Charlie Chaplin so he could piss on the plants in his garden to make them grow larger. To get him started on his goal, I let him reach in and touch my tits."

James Mason

O'Toole never got the chance to prove that he could be a better pedophile than this "Yorkshire fag."

Apparently, Dylan didn't get around to Marilyn Monroe," she said. "You know she used to be my roommate. There are rumors going around that we used to bump pussies when we didn't have a man in bed with one of us. Right now, poor Marilyn is in bad shape. She's fucking up her life with these clandestine affairs with Jack Kennedy and his brother, Robert. Nothing good will come of that. She's also hanging out with Sam Giancana, Johnny Roselli, and Sinatra. At the rate she's going, she'll be dead before she's forty."

When he relayed the details of his evening with Winters to his voyeuristic friend and fellow actor, Kenneth Griffith, he wanted to know how Shelley rated his performance in bed, since she didn't seem to care that much for his performance as Shylock.

"Her review was enigmatic," O'Toole said. "She told me my penis was slightly bigger than that of Gable's, that I had the fast action of Burt Lancaster, that my foreskin matched that of Marlon Brando, and that I had the endurance of John Garfield's trusty Jewish dick."

"What's your final verdict on this Winters dame?" Griffith asked.

"I'd say she's the smartest dumb blonde I know."

When Elizabeth Taylor Nearly Dies, So Does O'Toole's Chance to Play Marc Antony

When Elizabeth returned to London late in 1960, she learned that the *Motion Picture Herald* had named her the number one box office attraction in America. Her ranking was followed by Rock Hudson, Doris Day, John Wayne, and Cary Grant.

O'Toole read that after settling once again into the Oliver Messel Suite at The Dorchester, Elizabeth was spending her evenings with Peter Finch and that Eddie Fisher was "drowning in martinis."

He also heard rumors that Elizabeth and Fisher had gotten into a screaming match in the lobby of The Dorch when she publicly accused him of trying to run over a drunken Finch in their Rolls-Royce.

Aware of her presence in London, O'Toole made an attempt to reach Elizabeth, but she did not return his urgent calls. He was on the stage almost every night at Stratford-upon-Avon.

Another item in the papers claimed that Fox had decided to cast Cary Grant as Julius Caesar and Burt Lancaster as Marc Antony.

Finally, Elizabeth returned his call, apologizing for not getting back to him. She told him that she had been stripped of the power to determine who would be cast in either of the film's male leads, but that he still had her strong support.

At this point, Rouben Mamoulian had been fired as *Cleopatra's* director and had been replaced by Joseph Mankiewicz, who had previously helmed

Elizabeth in *Suddenly, Last Summer* (1959).

Mankiewicz flew into London in January of 1961 to discover that only ten minutes of usable film footage had been shot, and that some two million dollars had already been spent. "The sets are a disaster," he announced, "and the fucking script is unshootable." He set to work to rectify that.

His first order of business involved rejecting Finch as Caesar. He also nixed having either Stephen Boyd or O'Toole play Marc Antony.

On hearing that, O'Toole was heartbroken, as he had set his heart on starring in *Cleopatra* opposite the biggest movie star in the world. "It was just what I needed to launch myself," he told his friends. He didn't know at the time that it would be *Lawrence of Arabia* (1962) that would fulfill that wish.

He later said, "Who knows how the history of Hollywood would have been rewritten if I'd gone to Rome to make love to Elizabeth. I might have broken up her marriage to Eddie Fisher, wed her, then divorced her, then remarried her, then divorced her a final time. Alas, it was not meant to be."

Mankiewicz announced a whole new concept for his film. "I want to make two motion pictures," he said. "One with Elizabeth co-starring with Rex Harrison called *Caesar and Cleopatra* and a second one with Elizabeth and Richard Burton named *Antony and Cleopatra.*"

Burton was on Broadway appearing in *Camelot* at the time with Julie Andrews and Roddy McDowall. Walter Wanger and Mankiewicz persuaded Burton to sign as Marc Antony for $250,000 and paid the producers of *Camelot* $50,000 to release him from his contract.

In February of 1961, while Mankiewicz was struggling to finalize a script for *Cleopatra,* Elizabeth and Fisher arrived in Munich to attend the annual pre-Lenten carnival *[Fasching]* and its roster of masked balls. She appeared as Marie Antoinette with Fisher impersonating Louis XVI. Upon her return to London, on March 4, illness struck again when she came down with a severe case of Asian flu. O'Toole followed what happened next in the London papers.

She was rushed by ambulance to the London Clinic, for a life-saving tracheostomy *[i.e., an opening surgically created through the front of the neck into the trachea (windpipe) to enable breathing through direct access to the wind pipe.]*

Her diagnoses involved acute *staphylococcus* pneumonia, an infection which in many cases then was fatal. As an after-effect of the tracheostomy, she would retain a scar on her throat for the rest of her life.

She had to be fed intravenously through her ankle. As such, when further complications and infections developed, she almost lost her left leg. Daily bulletins were issued about her condition.

When she had partially recovered, O'Toole visited her in the hospital, where he discovered that a metal object resembling a silver dollar had been placed into the opening in her throat. Outside, fans were maintaining an around-the-clock vigil.

Elizabeth told O'Toole, "The bastards are just waiting for me to die."

She apologized that the casting of *Cleopatra* had not worked out in his favor, and then promised to cast him in some of her future pictures. She went on to suggest *The Taming of the Shrew* as an ideal vehicle for them as a duo.

O'Toole kissed her forehead with a promise that they'd soon meet again.

"That will happen sooner than later," she predicted. As he stood at the door, she told him, "Frankly, at the rate things are going, I think I'll never sail down the Nile on that barge of mine."

He later read that in September, the cast and crew was transferred to Rome for filming of the epic. Both Caesar and Marc Antony—that is, Rex Harrison and Burton—would be in one long, drawn-out film fiasco with Elizabeth.

From then on, whatever he learned about the collapse of Elizabeth's marriage to Eddie Fisher and her adulterous romance with Richard Burton, he read in the newspapers.

During all this time, he never heard from Elizabeth.

Within months, he had more or less recovered from his loss of the role of Marc Antony. In the meantime, he was caught up in his own international stardom, thanks to his involvement in *Lawrence of Arabia.*

In 1961, with *Cleopatra* in chaos, Taylor, with a growing reputation as an unreliable actress prone to severe and expensive illnesses, exits from London.

In London, in 1963, it was not Elizabeth, but Burton who called with an announcement: "I've just been assigned to do the film version of *Becket,* and I'm demanding that you be cast as my leading lady, Henry II, who's madly in love with me."

"Dick, my boy, that will take some bigtime acting on my part to convince movie audiences of that. But I'm game."

"Let's face it: At this moment you and I are the two hottest actors on the planet. *Becket* will be the hit of 1964, and I'll have to compete with an Irish bastard like you for the bloody fucking Oscar."

Chapter 16

Hollywood on the Tiber

A Drunken, Tabloid-Battered Trio,
Out, Feisty, and Carousing in Rome

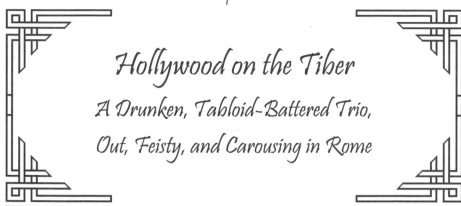

"Liz (as Cleo) and Dick (as Marc Antony) are Barging Down the Nile, and It's Sinking."

—*Peter O'Toole, on location in Rome, to Friends in London*

On location in Rome, the most famous woman of the modern world (Elizabeth Taylor) impersonates the most famous woman of the ancient world (Cleopatra), as she fine-tunes a doomed alliance with her future consort, Marc Antony (Richard Burton).

CLEOPATRA: *Without you, this is not a world I want to live in.*
ANTONY: *Everything I want to hold or love or have or be is here with me tonight.*

As details about the making of the epic film *Cleopatra* (1963) bloated the tabloids, Peter O'Toole began to regret that he had not pursued the role of Marc Antony more aggressively back when Elizabeth Taylor, from within her suite at London's Dorchester Hotel, had held out the prospect to him. He later bragged to friends, "Did you know that I was Elizabeth's first choice to play Marc Antony?"

He'd read that Spyros Skouras, head of 20th Century Fox, had predicted that *Cleopatra* would be a bigger smash after its release in the early 60s than *Gone With the Wind* had been in 1939.

On the set of *Cleopatra*, Richard Burton (left) looks down on "the cuckold," Eddie Fisher, who seems ignorant of the changing dynamics of his marriage to Elizabeth Taylor (right).

Garlanded with a million dollar contract, Elizabeth was already in Rome, having won the film's title role by beating out Joan Collins, Gina Lollobrigida, Susan Hayward, and, as absurd as it sounds, both Marilyn Monroe and Brigitte Bardot.

Elizabeth had also succeeded in getting "my fading singer," Eddie Fisher, her husband, hired for $1,500 a week as her factotum and general assistant.

Intrigued by the behind-the-scenes drama, O'Toole decided to make a secret visit to Rome without informing Siân. Only his business partner, Jules Buck, knew where he was.

Officially, although his trip to Italy involved discussing plans with Burton about their upcoming movie, *Becket,* his voyeuristic nature also wanted to see what all the scandal was about. The affair that seemed to endlessly consume

"*Taylor and Burton Dwell in Absurdity, Chaos, Infidelity, Mad Passionate Love, Betrayals, Obscene Ostentation, and Drunkenness—They're My Kind of Folks*"

—*Peter O'Toole*

"*I Should Have Taken the Role of Marc Antony, or perhaps that of Julius Caesar: A Wife to Every Husband, and a Husband to Every Wife.*"

—*Peter O'Toole*

this pair of illicit, married (to other people) lovers had captured the fascination of the world.

In Rome, local newspapers greeted him with lurid stories about how Elizabeth and Burton had taken their on-screen love affair as Cleopatra and Antony off screen, in spite of the fact Burton was still married to the long-suffering Sybil Burton, and Elizabeth was locked into "My loveless marriage to Eddie Fisher."

O'Toole checked into the Excelsior Hotel, along the via Veneto. As he remembered, "All a movie star had to do was walk along the rows of cafés [along that section of the via Veneto] and he'd get twenty invitations from aspiring starlets before he'd walked for one block."

Daydreaming about their future(s), a pensive Richard Burton and Elizabeth Taylor.

Her first opinion of him had changed. "I was determined not to become another notch on his belt," she proclaimed. Her husband, Eddie Fisher, had called Burton "an arrogant slob."

After her first night with Burton, Elizabeth confided to her secretary, Dick Hanley, "He gave me multiple orgasms."

"The Excelsior was very tolerant about lumbering." *["Lumbering" was O'Toole's British slang describing the process of bringing a hooker/ hookers into a client's bedroom.]*

Elizabeth was living with Fisher along the ancient Appian Way in the Villa Pappa, near Cinecittà. Built by Mussolini, these sprawling recording studios were the locale for the massive sets being constructed at the time for the filming of *Cleopatra.* The most elaborate of the props being built was a massive replica of a Sphinx measuring 65 feet long and 35 feet high.

O'Toole phoned Elizabeth's villa. There, Dick Hanley, Elizabeth's secretary, picked up the phone. "She's expecting you," Hanley said. "Why not drop in for drinks at five and stay for dinner?"

Villa Pappa, a sprawling ranch-style house, stood on eight acres of parkland along the Appian Way. In the household were three children, Michael, Christopher, and Liza, along with five family dogs. There was also a heated swimming pool and a tennis court.

Hanley had met O'Toole only briefly in London, but greeted him with the obligatory kiss on each cheek, and "fussed over me like I was the greatest thing since Yorkshire pudding."

The first member of the household who came out to greet him was Fisher, wearing a red satin bathrobe. O'Toole hadn't seen the singer since their meeting in London. Over a drink, Fisher told him his wife was still sleeping. "Then the poor kid poured out his broken heart to me," O'Toole later claimed.

"I feel I'm caught in a trap," Fisher told him. "I want to escape to save my sanity. I'm doing everything I can to hold onto my marriage, but it seems to be slipping away from me. Like my singing career, it seems that only weeks ago, I was the hottest entertainer in America. Now I can't seem to get a gig."

Suddenly, Elizabeth made her appearance. "She was indeed the most beautiful woman in the world, even more so than the woman I'd met in London," O'Toole said. "She'd eclipsed Jackie Kennedy as the most famous woman in the world. She exuded sex and danger. No wonder Dickie had fallen so for her. She turned those big violet eyes with those dark eyebrows on me, no doubt remembering what I looked like with an erection."

She seemed to have undergone a distinct, more imperious personality change since he'd last seen her. Surrounded with 20 servants, she was ordering them around like the empress she portrayed on the screen. At one point, she was screeching at her Italian butlers, demanding that everything be color-coordinated, from the tablecloths to the cigarette holders.

He later surmised that she seemed an emotional wreck, no doubt because she was still living with a husband she didn't love, and was, under the glare of world-wide attention, involved in a torrid affair with a married man. "All this adulation, hostile press attention, and grotesque fame were obviously taking a toll on her," O'Toole later said.

Elizabeth was visibly shaken from what she described as a near death experience the night before, when she'd gone dancing with Joseph Mankiewicz, the director of *Cleopatra.*

"My high heel came down on this match that some drunk had foolishly dropped on the floor. It ignited and set fire to the ostrich fringe on my gown. The boys in the band leaped to my rescue, or else I would have been turned into a human torch."

At this point, she brusquely ordered Fisher to "go and take care of business, since I want to talk to Peter alone."

When Fisher retreated far enough away to no longer directly annoy her, she told O'Toole that Burton wasn't in great shape either. "The first time I met him on the set, he was quivering from head to foot. There were grog blossoms (skin blemishes) all over his face. His hands were shaking so badly, I had to hold cups of coffee up to his lips."

She told O'Toole that Burton was delighted that he was in Rome and that he'd join them for dinner that night. "He's still living with that dame, Sybil."

"You mean, his wife? O'Toole asked.

"Don't be provocative," she snapped. "It's hard for me to keep up with which man I'm married to, much less other people's marital arrangements."

She excused herself to get ready for dinner and to make some emergency phone calls, turning O'Toole over to Hanley.

Hanley told him that Roddy McDowall would also be their guest for dinner that night. He and Burton had starred in *Camelot* together on Broadway, and Burton had procured for him the role of the ruthless Octavius in *Cleopatra*.

"Roddy has developed this major crush on Richard," Hanley said. "It all began when Richard let him render lip service during their run in *Camelot*."

"Lip service?" O'Toole said. "So that's what it's called this year."

Poor Roddy's been cut off now that Richard is hooked up with Elizabeth almost every night."

Burton arrived an hour later, embracing O'Toole warmly and bestowing kisses on him. "At last, I have a drinking partner worthy of me, except, of course, for Elizabeth."

He headed for the bar, where he introduced O'Toole to their newest drink of

Roddy McDowall, depicted above as Octavius in *Cleopatra*, had fallen in love with Richard Burton when they co-starred together on Broadway in *Camelot*.

McDowall told friends, "Dick is aptly named. We became so close he let me fill in his pockmarks with heavy layers of makeup. He'd suffered a severe case of acne when he turned sixteen."

choice. An "Ivan the Terrible" was a lethal blend of grappa, ouzo, and Russian vodka.

Burton had confided in O'Toole that when he'd arrived in Rome, he was prepared not to like Elizabeth. In fact, he'd told the press, "I've got to don my breastplate again to appear opposite Miss Tits."

"After being on the set for only two days, I decided I desired her. I broke her in to the Burton style of love-making in the back seat of my Cadillac."

Then he told O'Toole, "I'll let you in on her deepest, darkest secret. If she didn't shave, she'd be as hairy as an ape."

The two actors finally got around to discussing their upcoming film project, *Becket*. "Imagine me, the most immoral man who ever lived, playing the Archbishop of Canterbury," Burton said, "opposite your Henry II. Actually, I think *Becket* will be the prestige movie of the year, but not necessarily the box office champion. Both of us will probably end up being nominated for an Oscar."

In that, Burton was prophetic. Indeed, both of them would eventually compete for Best Actor of the Year for their co-starring roles in *Becket*. However, they would each lose that award to Rex Harrison for his role in *My Fair*

Lady. Ironically, Harrison was co-starring with Burton and Elizabeth, playing Julius Caesar in *Cleopatra*.

At table that night, as part of a dinner served within Elizabeth's villa, the guests included O'Toole, Burton, Elizabeth, Fisher, Hanley, and Roddy McDowall with some unknown young man.

O'Toole noticed that Elizabeth, as the household's reigning diva, treated her servants with something akin to cruelty. At one point, she called out, "We're ready for the spaghetti, asshole." For the main course, she yelled again, "Bring on the roast suckling pig, you mother fuckers."

O'Toole complimented her on the menu, beginning with the appetizer. "I don't know what it was, but it was certainly delicious."

"The tongue of flamingos," she said. "A treat for decadent Roman emperors." She

Bewitched and bothered, O'Toole, perhaps in a moment of jealousy, later told his friend, Kenneth Griffith, "*I* should be playing Marc Antony. And Elizabeth should be visiting *my* bed at night, at mid-afternoon, and an hour before dinner."

went on to inform him how the custard had been made, since she'd noticed him ordering a second helping.

"I asked my male servants to wank off into a mixing bowl in the kitchen," she said. "The cook whipped it into an egg custard mix. That's why the dessert was extra creamy."

"Male semen," Hanley sighed, dreamily. "No wonder it tasted good. From now on, I want you to commission it that way every night for dessert."

"Dream on, cocksucker," Elizabeth said.

At the end of dinner, a drunken Burton stood up on wobbly legs to deliver a long and boring Shakespearean monologue. As McDowall, Elizabeth, and O'Toole listened patiently, Fisher got up and left the table.

Watching him go, Burton interrupted his own monologue, "Eddie's mad because I raped him last night."

When he heard that, O'Toole thought at first that his friend was joking.

At the end of Burton's monologue, Elizabeth told him, "The sound of your melodious voice gives me an orgasm. It makes up for that neck of yours pitted with acne and blackheads."

"I adore your breasts," Burton shot back. "I find them ravishing, in spite of all that whale blubber."

Later, O'Toole told McDowall, "These guys might be lovers, but they obviously aren't rehearsing *Romeo and Juliet*."

Back in the living room, Elizabeth and Burton went upstairs to her bedroom. Fisher had gone out for the night. Burton whispered to O'Toole, "Stick around. After I take care of Cleo, we'll go out on the town."

In the living room, when they were alone, Hanley told O'Toole what had happened on the night Fisher was raped:

"Elizabeth and Richard got into their worst brawl," Hanley said. "Believe it or not, they call it foreplay. Sometimes they get violent with each other, certainly verbally abusive. He called her 'a fucking, sag-titted, no-talent Hollywood cunt.' Richard than began defending Fisher, telling Elizabeth that 'this man loves you, and you treat him like shit.'"

"If you feel so sorry for poor Eddie," she responded, "why don't you take him upstairs and fuck him yourself, since I've been told that originally, you wanted him instead of me, you faggot Welshman. You fucked Olivier...Why not Fisher?"

Based on her provocation, and almost on a dare, Burton grabbed Fisher and forcibly carried him up the stairs," Hanley said. "They were gone for an hour. Fisher emerged looking worse for wear, and then retreated into his bedroom."

"Richard came downstairs, and told us, 'Deed done. He must have enjoyed it. He exploded all over me.'"

"It sounds like Villa Pappa stages the best shows in town," O'Toole said. "Better than what you're likely to see at the Trevi Fountain."

"Fisher is always denying those gay rumors," Hanley told O'Toole. "But I know the truth. He may not be as gay as I am—who is?—but he likes a man every third Sunday."

In London, Burton had already confessed to O'Toole, "I am not a bona-fide, 100 percent heterosexual in spite of my reputation."

Within the hour at the Villa Pappa, Burton appeared ready to go on the town with O'Toole. "Elizabeth and I have just enjoyed our most passionate lovemaking yet. We like to get violent and denounce each other before we perform the dirty deed. She prefers it that way."

Two Drunken "Babe Magnets" on the Prowl in Rome After Dark

By midnight, in Trastevere, a neighborhood where the paparazzi would not necessarily look for them, Burton and O'Toole were wandering in and out of a long series of low, after-hours dives.

O'Toole later recalled, "I was a lightweight Irishman stacked up against a major Welshman boozer. Dickie could down double vodkas with beer chasers at an incredible rate. He belonged in the Guinness Book of Records. By four o'clock that morning, I was under the table. We got back to the Villa Pappa at 5AM, and he had to leave almost immediately for Cinecittà. I don't know how he did it."

Burton told him, "My doctor told me that Welsh liver and kidneys seem to be made of some metallic alloy quite unlike the rest of the human race. "

"I wonder what the good doctor would say about Irish kidneys and livers?" O'Toole said.

O'Toole recalled that "our kidneys were floating. Dickie came up with a magnificent idea. We made a bet to see which of us could urinate the farthest. We didn't want to mess up the [Villa Pappa's] beautiful living room, so we headed to the kitchen. We pulled out or johnnies, and each of us pissed a big stream, perhaps evocative of Niagara Falls. Burton won by a foot. The loser was supposed to suck the other's cock. All's fair in love and war. Dickie began to wank himself into an erection. I stumbled toward the door, telling him, 'I'll owe you one.'"

The next morning, after Elizabeth's cooks found the kitchen floor saturated with urine and beer, she denounced both O'Toole and Burton as "sophomores."

During O'Toole's second night on the town with Burton, Elizabeth stayed at home being comforted by Hanley. She complained of cramps in her stomach. "She's a delicate hothouse flower," Burton told O'Toole. "Between fucks, she's always involved in some health crisis."

This time, the two actors headed for the clubs on and off the via Veneto, where the paparazzi chased after them.

"Photographers weren't the only ones chasing us," O'Toole said. "Dickie and I attracted an army of women, or those who tried to pass as women." Some were prostitutes, but dozens were giving it away. Of course, Dickie was clearly the man of the hour, but I got more solicitations from good-looking young women and pretty boys than I ever had in my life. I set up two or three appointments at my suite at the Excelsior for 2AM since I planned to bug out early."

As a "babe magnet," I was in the Junior League, compared to Dickie," O'Toole said "Women just threw themselves at him. He told me that he required at least one piece of new meat a day. JFK was supposed to have made the same claim. How Dickie managed that and still satisfied all those mistresses and side detours I don't known Not only could he keep Elizabeth happy, he was also satisfying his mistresses—Jean Simmons, [Playboy centerfold] Jean Bell, Susan Strasberg, Claire Bloom, and I don't know how many others."

Burton's biographer, Tom Rubython, wrote: "Of all the men that had ever walked on the planet, it is probably true to say that Richard Burton, between the years 1948 and 1962, was the most attractive. There was virtually no woman with whom he came into contact that could resist him. The secret of his blazing magnetism was the extraordinary glint in his blue-green and 'wicked' eyes. His success in his younger years was around 95 percent. He had few morals, so it's hard to estimate the number of women he slept with, but the best guess is 2,500."

Burton told O'Toole that he'd slept with all of his leading ladies except Julie Andrews. "She almost succumbed to my manly charm," he boasted.

"I think you and I are just in the beginning of our world-class reputations, primarily that we're drunks and womanizers," O'Toole said. "Both of us have been called the natural successors to Olivier and Gielgud, without the faggot label, and both of us will no doubt be accused of selling out our genius to Hollywood and, in your case, to Dame Elizabeth."

"She's not a Dame yet," Burton cautioned.

O'Toole Goes Shopping with an "Erotic Vagrant" & Bids Adieu to the World's Most Notorious Couple

In the late morning, O'Toole arrived at Villa Pappa to take Elizabeth shopping, since she wasn't due on the set that day.

That morning, *L'Osservatore Dominicana,* the official newspaper of the Vatican, had referred to Elizabeth as "an erotic vagrant." In the aftermath of that pronouncement, she received threats on her life. Fox took these threats so seriously, they hired twenty security guards, disguising them as extras in togas and ordering them to mingle with the other actors during crowd scenes.

The paparazzi were on their trail, waiting outside the gates of Villa Pappa. Once, when Elizabeth's chauffeur-driven Cadillac left the compound and rolled into the street, they followed it into the monumental heart of Rome. There, as flashbulbs popped, O'Toole and Elizabeth got out for a stroll along via Condotti, heading for Bulgari's, the most exclusive jewelry store in all of Italy.

Never in O'Toole's experience had he encountered such aggressive photographers. At one point, one of them punched Elizabeth in the stomach as a means of capturing a candid shot of her doubling over in pain.

O'Toole struck the paparazzo in the face, bloodying his nose. Then he smashed his camera right before he and Elizabeth retreated beyond the security guard into the guarded confines of Bulgari's.

Once they were safely inside, she kissed him, calling him, "My knight in shining armor."

Later, at the top of the Spanish Steps, they shared a late lunch within the exclusive Hotel Villa Hassler. O'Toole spoke about the film he'd be shooting next with Burton, and he was shocked when ELizabeth asked him to get her one of the minor roles, perhaps a cameo, in *Becket.* "That way, I can keep an eye on Richard."

Peter said that he'd see what he could do. Two days later, when he conveyed her request to producer Hal B. Wallis, he rejected the idea, claiming, "That gal would be far too much of a distraction, and her appearance would be so startling to audiences that it would throw the picture off track."

She told him that after *Cleopatra,* she had two other projects in mind, both of them bio pictures. One of them focused on the modern dancer, Isadora Duncan, and the other on the early 20th-century actress, Sarah Bernhardt. Elizabeth held out the promise that there might be roles in both pictures for him.

[Two days later, over drinks with Burton and O'Toole, Elizabeth revealed those plans to Burton, who mocked her. "You can't dance and you can't act, so I suggest you forget both pictures."

Reacting swiftly, she picked up a valuable Chinese vase and tossed it at his head. It shattered into many pieces across the pink marble floor. As she ran sobbing from the room, he called out to her. "Ducky, I suggest you star in

The most spectacularly emotive actress in the history of late 19th-century / early 20th century theater: Sarah Bernhardt. Elizabeth wanted to portray her on screen.

Hellenic Revival...Two views of the world-famous early 20th century dancer, Isadora Duncan. Elizabeth wanted to portray her on screen.

Burton to Taylor, before she threw a vase at him: "This might be more your speed, darling...."

324

Harold Robbin's steamy bestseller, The Carpetbaggers. *That's more your speed."]*

After lunch, Elizabeth's chauffeur drove both of them back to Villa Pappa. After he let her off, the driver continued to Cinecittà, where O'Toole was escorted directly to Burton's dressing room. O'Toole found "Marc Antony" in a jockstrap having a drink. He joined him.

During their chat, he was startled at what Burton revealed about a casting drama that had occurred near the debut of O'Toole's greatest fame, during his jockeying for the lead role in *Lawrence of Arabia* (1962). Burton, it was revealed, and not O'Toole, had been David Lean's original choice to play T.E. Lawrence. Up to that point, although O'Toole was aware that such actors as Albert Finney and Marlon Brando had been considered, he'd never heard that Burton had been the director's first choice.

"After turning down that role," Burton admitted, "I realize I'd made the most catastrophic judgment of my career. I should have gone for it. After my horrible failure in another, earlier, epic, *Alexander the Great* (1956), I didn't want to devote another year of my life to some bloody film with the Arabs in the desert, getting raped by Turkish soldiers. I'm still suffering from the critical attacks on my take as that sodomite, Alexander. Some critics called it *Alexander the Bore,* and attacked my so-called pompous speeches."

After two more outrageous nights with Burton and Elizabeth, O'Toole had grown weary of being in the eye of their hurricane. He was ready to return to London. In the meantime, Fisher had disappeared without telling anyone where he was going. No one in the household seemed unduly concerned over his whereabouts.

On the afternoon of his own departure, O'Toole paid a final visit to Villa Pappa for an *adieu* to his friends.

After each of them lip-locked him, O'Toole promised he'd be waiting in "*Merrie Olde England* to welcome you back" after they finished shooting *Cleopatra,* which at the time seemed like it would drag on forever.

Earlier, he'd privately told Elizabeth that it was probably just as well that he had not accepted the role of Marc Antony. "I'd have to wear a toga and my toothpick legs

To her chagrin, Elizabeth was not the first actress with whom Burton had played swords and sandals with. Above, the demure Claire Bloom with Richard Burton in *Alexander the Great* (1956).

Burton later told O'Toole: "I was a blonde goddess in that one."

can't compete with those of Dickie."

At the airport, he was surrounded by reporters, at which time he made a statement that shocked them. At first, some of them gave the impression that they had misunderstood, as they weren't that proficient in English. O'Toole smiled and told them, "Every man needs a good husband. Dickie Burton fulfils that role for me."

The next day, the flamboyant director of *Cleopatra*, Joseph Mankiewicz outdid O'Toole. He faced the press and, in full view of reporters, groped Burton's crotch and kissed him on the mouth, with tongue, for almost a full minute. Breaking away, he smacked his moistened lips and announced, "There you are! I'm the one Richard is having an affair with, not Elizabeth Taylor."

"Elizabeth Taylor Combines the Worst of American and English Taste, and Richard Burton Is as Butch and Coarse as Only a Welshman Can Be."

—Cecil Beaton, Haute Society Photographer

The world's most famous photographer, the flamboyantly gay Cecil Beaton, became fascinated with the image of Peter O'Toole. He got in touch with him and proposed a novel idea:

With the cooperation of the best costumer in London, he proposed that O'Toole pose for him in an archive of photos devoted to leading characters from the plays of William Shakespeare.

After meeting with Beaton, O'Toole said, "I didn't like him. He spent our luncheon attacking my friends, Dickie Burton and Elizabeth."

Beaton had taken a series of pictures at a lavish black-tie ball in 1971. Elizabeth was there, posing in couture (Valentino) with a necklace from Van Cleef & Arpels entwined in her hair.

Beaton told O'Toole, "Both stars are vulgar, common, and crass. She is a monster. I loathe them. Around her neck was a velvet ribbon with the biggest diamond in the world pinned on it. On her fat, course hands, more of the biggest diamonds and emeralds; her head a ridiculous mess of diamond necklaces, sewn together, with a snood of blue and black pompons and black aisprey aigrettes. And sausage curls! I hold both of them in utter comtempt."

Cecil Beaton

After the luncheon, O'Toole politely rejected the project, claiming, "The Bard would be offended at such a tasteless idea."

Chapter 17

Becket: What Is This Thing Called Love?

The Stormy Relationship Between
A Medieval King and His Ecclesiastical Puppet

World-Class Boozers: Elizabeth Taylor Joins Burton and O'Toole

The producer, Hal Wallis, had predicted that the teaming of Oscar nominees Peter O'Toole (the left figure in both photos above) with Richard Burton in *Becket* would help create "the biggest blockbuster of the year." He was bitterly disappointed. "Perhaps if they had not been stinking drunk," Wallis complained, "*Becket* might have succeeded."

On a budget of $3 million, it took in only $5 million worldwide. However, in time, it would make millions for Paramount in home video sales.

Because of a scheduling conflict, Peter O'Toole never got to perform *Becket* on the stage in London. On Broadway, Laurence Olivier had starred as Becket, with Anthony Quinn cast as Henry II. O'Toole had long wanted to star in *Becket*, and at last the chance came through. The producer, Hal B. Wallis, called and asked to meet with him in London.

Sometimes described as "a walking, talking version of a Hollywood Studio," Wallis was one of the most successful producers in the history of movies, a mogul whose career would span half a century. He had turned out many of the biggest hit films of the Golden Age, including *Little Caesar* (1930), *Casablanca* (1942), and *Come Back, Little Sheba* (1952).

In time, his films would win more than thirty Oscars in various categories. Although he later degenerated into turning out Elvis Presley quickies, he also produced first-class dramatic movies, including costume dramas, of which *Becket* was destined to become one of the most distinguished.

"For me, the big question involves which actor will star opposite me as the Archbishop of Canterbury," O'Toole said.

"Have no fear," Wallis responded. "Tonight I'm meeting with Laurence Olivier at which time I will offer him the role. I'm sure he's aware of what's about to happen, and I bet he is salivating."

Two days later, Wallis phoned O'Toole as his contract was being negotiated. "Olivier is off the picture. In his place, I've cast Richard Burton. He says he knows you and wants to work with you."

"He's a marvelous actor," O'Toole said. "Maybe he's too good. I don't want to fall on my arse competing with the slugger."

Elizabeth Taylor was a frequent visitor to the set of *Becket*, in which Peter O'Toole (above) was cast as Henry II opposite her husband, Richard Burton, as the Archbishop of Canterbury.

As she confided to her friend, Roddy McDowall, using cockney slang, "Those two blokes are one randy pair. I can't trust them in a room with a woman. I can't even trust them in a room with each other."

"You won't," Wallis said. "Remember, you're a king, Burton merely an archbishop."

Over lunch at The Ivy *[an elegantly upscale restaurant catering to London's West End show-biz trade]*, O'Toole found him most personable, with a strong ego.

"I think *Becket* will do more for your status as an actor than *Lawrence of Arabia*," Wallis predicted. "I know talent when I see it. Just look at the stars I've made: Burt Lancaster, Kirk Douglas, Bogie, Edward G. Robinson, Montgomery Clift, James Cagney, Dean Martin, and, yes, Miss Bette Davis. I even took this untalented, low-rent actor, Ronald Reagan, and made a star out of him in *Kings Row*."

Wallis planned to budget *Becket* at $3 million, financed in part with money earned from Elvis Presley's *Blue Hawaii* (1961). Shooting was to take place in the London suburbs, at Shepperton Studios, with outdoor scenes shot in the English countryside, where the events depicted in this drama had unfolded six centuries before.

Edward Anhalt was busy at work on the screenplay that documented the stormy relationship between the English King, Henry II, and Thomas Becket, the Norman he appointed as Archbishop of Canterbury. *[In the script, Becket was inaccurately portrayed as a Saxon.]*

Becket's producer, Hal B. Wallis. "A no-no to Miss Taylor."

Anhalt, who used to grind out pulp fiction, often wrote in collaboration with his first wife, Edna Anhalt. During the war, he'd scripted a series of Army training and propaganda films. At the time, Ronald Reagan—at the time working as an Army Air Force officer in an Army film unit—was his boss.

Anhalt had won his first scriptwriting Oscar for *Panic in the Streets* (1950). Later, he was nominated again for his screen adaptation of Irwin Shaw's World War II novel, *The Young Lions* (1958), starring Marlon Brando.

Wallis told O'Toole that there had been many historical inaccuracies in Jean Anouilh's dramatic version of *Becket*, and that although these chronological discrepancies had been pointed out to him many times already, he had no plans to correct them. "We're making a movie, not a fucking history book."

"The theme will be about the friendship between you and Becket. Call it a love affair if you wish," Wallis said. "The basic plot, as you know, is about the separation of church and state. There will be great moments, but also amusing ones. Right at the beginning, Becket is your partner in wenching and drinking. We want to insert a scene where the two of you guys have spent the night fucking the same girl."

"Perhaps Burton and I should actually rehearse that beforehand," O'Toole said.

"I'm sure you could find hundreds of gals who'd like to get double fucked," Wallis said. "But I think you have talent and that is something hard to define," Wallis said. "I know it from my head to my toenails. An actor with brilliant talent registers with me immediately. It's like magic."

Their dialogue was interrupted when Wallis had to suddenly rush off to see how construction was progressing on a replica of Canterbury Cathedral, part of a movie set being built on what was then the largest sound stage in Europe.

Peter Glenville, the noteworthy English stage actor and director, was hired to helm the movie version of *Becket*. He seemed a natural choice, as he'd successfully directed a Broadway stage production of *Becket* in 1961. *[In that production, Anthony Quinn (who was later replaced by Arthur Kennedy during part of its run) played Henry and Laurence Olivier was cast as Becket.]*

Born into a theatrical family, Glenville was equally at home helming either Shakespearean or modern dramas such as *Separate Tables* by Terence

Rattigan which he went on to direct in 1964.

Before filming began, O'Toole had retreated to his beloved Ireland. He needed a quiet transition between playing the introspective desert warrior, T.E. Lawrence, and Henry II, a lusty, hellraising, and ultimately ruthless soldier/king. "I was falling apart, and I always view Ireland as the most peaceful place on the planet. When London and the world itself became too much for me, and I hovered on the verge of a nervous breakdown, I long for the green, green grass of home. Also, Siân was pregnant, and I wanted my next child to be born in Ireland, not in England."

During the first week of shooting, O'Toole had a reunion with Burton, whom he had not seen since his sojourn in Rome, where he'd spent time watching Burton's filming of *Cleopatra* in tandem with Elizabeth Taylor, with whom Burton had launched a mad affair that had attracted the attention of the world.

Since both Burton and O'Toole were drawing fire for their (oft-deserved) images as hell-raising drinkers, both of them agreed to stay off the booze for at least for the first ten days of filming. "We'll drink tea," Burton said.

"I hope I can go that long," O'Toole said. "Giving up booze is worse that abandoning sex for a week."

On the first day of the shoot, Burton learned that he had been the second choice as an actor cast as the Archbishop in the film version of *Becket.* "I heard that Glenville practically licked Olivier's ass to get him to play my role. That bastard! I'll be lovey-dovey with the fucker when we get together, but deep down, my Welsh blood is bubbling like a tea kettle."

"I think both of us can handle Glenville," O'Toole said. "My fear is that you, with your seemingly effortless acting, will show me up."

"You forgot to mention my gorgeous Welsh looks," Burton said. "The other night, Elizabeth told me I was the handsomest man who ever lived."

"Is that so? I hope makeup has enough plaster in fill in those crater-sized pockmarks in your neck. And those blackheads!"

Burton said that he'd forgiven Glenville for firing him fourteen years before as a character in a play he was directing at the time, *Adventure Story.* "The sod almost ruined my career."

O'Toole, however, noticed no lingering animosity between Burton and Glenville on the set. If anything, they had a flirtations relationship based on Burton's indulgence of (and bantering responses to) the director's homosexuality.

Over drinks with Kenneth Griffith, O'Toole told him, "Every time Dick comes onto the set, he feels up Glenville's moon-shaped buttocks and flirts outrageously with him. I suspect he's fucked Glenville in his past. You know, Burton in his early days in the theater admitted being passed around from one old sod to another in the theater, Olivier among them. "

"My fear is that Glenville will favor Burton over me in close-ups," O'Toole said.

"Have no fear," Griffith said. "I know Glenville. He's a total professional. He will drag the best performance out of both of you, although I don't envy you having to compete against Burton."

Desperately in need of an alcohol fix, Burton, late one morning, about a week into the filming, when they weren't needed on camera, said to O'Toole, "My good man, I think we deserve a little snifter." The aftermath of that exchange marked the beginning of their heavy drinking. Their days of a self-imposed sobriety had come to an end.

As filming progressed, Burton had only praise for his co-star. "Acting is a craft," he told the press. "But once or twice in a lifetime, an actor can reach a plateau that is odd, mystical, and deeply disturbing. Peter O'Toole is such an actor, possessing these strange qualities."

O'Toole also weighed in with praise for Burton. "*Becket* was a draw between Dick and me—and I had all the twiddly bits. My relationship with him is both professional and personal. We are rivals but dear friends. We compete with each other both on and off the screen, and we get along fabulously."

As a whispered aside, he went on to say, "This is not to be printed, but the reason I love Dick so much is that he lets me fuck Elizabeth—just kidding!"

In the beginning, Elizabeth visited the set every day from her temporary home in a suite at the very posh Dorchester Hotel in London. Even before her arrival on the set, Burton began his mornings with three Bloody Marys—heavy on the vodka—for breakfast.

Once, during time they shared together within the Kings Head Pub, a dining and drinking establishment on the village green of Shepperton, convenient to the movie studio, while Burton was on the phone for a long conversation with someone in Central London, Elizabeth confided to O'Toole, "I desperately want to be Mrs. Richard Burton," she said. "I'd give up my career for him. I recently gave him a $275,000 Van Gogh landscape to hang over the fireplace in our suite. I also presented him with a custom-made library of five hundred leather-bound books. Other gifts are on the way."

"He loves you, dear," O'Toole cautioned. "You don't need to buy his affection."

"Life is not exactly heaven," she said. "As you know, he's a womanizer and a heavy drinker. He also goes into these long periods of black melancholia—he calls them his 'Welsh hours.'"

Once, after Wallis, the film's producer, arrived on the set, he huddled to compare notes with Glenville, who analyzed the O'Toole/Burton/Taylor dynamic like this: "Burton is the older actor, as you know, but I think both he and

O'Toole are equal in talent. Both men can match each other drink for drink. Elizabeth is also a heavy drinker, as she shows us every day. I think her presence on the set here is a big distraction, and she only makes their drinking worse. She knows what a womanizer Burton is, and I think she shows up to check up on him. Perhaps you can speak to her."

Although he remained benign and soft spoken, Wallis heeded Glenville's request, suggesting to Elizabeth, "My dear, you should probably confine your visits to the set to every other day."

Usually, the actors could perform, masterfully, with copious quantities of alcohol pumping through their bodies. But occasionally, the consequences of their drinking were painful, indeed.

Cleopatra had its premiere in New York, and its aftermath, the reviews were devastating. Elizabeth arrived on the set of *Becket* in tears. David Susskind, the TV host, had weighed in with his judgment about how awful he thought her performance had been: "Overweight, over-bosomed, overpaid, and under-talented, Elizabeth Taylor has set the acting profession back a decade."

Newsweek proclaimed, "Miss Taylor is not the worst actress in the world with her shrill, rasping voice."

Over lunch that day at the Kings Head, both Burton and Elizabeth drank even more heavily than usual. When she excused herself to go to the women's room, Burton whispered to O'Toole: "If you know some producer who's got a role for Elizabeth, based on those terrible reviews for *Cleopatra*, he can get her for $25,000."

Burton had ordered steak-and-kidney pie, but midway through consuming it, he vomited up his lunch and part of his liquor, covering himself in his vomit. With O'Toole's help, Elizabeth got him back to his dressing room, where she proceeded to clean him up.

Ed Sullivan flew in from New York for a televised interview with Burton. Estimated at a worth equivalent to a million dollars or so in publicity for *Becket,* the interview had been scheduled for that very afternoon.

But later that day, after Burton had cleaned himself up and was brought before the TV host, Sullivan immediately perceived that he was too drunk to proceed with the interview. He went ahead anyway, asking as his first question: "This is the first time you've ever worked with Peter O'Toole, is it not?"

Burton mumbled and slurred, *"Yeah, and it will prolly fucking be the lashed."*

Sullivan tried to proceed, but knew that so far nothing recorded on tape could be aired. The interview was never televised.

Glenville had cast Siân Phillips in *Becket* as one of Burton's love interests, Gwendolen. "The only reason I got the part was because I could read music,

332

sing Welsh, and dredge up some words that the Welsh spoke in the Middle Ages."

Sometimes Siân joined O'Toole, Burton, and Elizabeth for lunch at the Kings Head Pub on the village square of Shepperton. At the first luncheon, Burton confessed that originally, he'd have preferred to have played the part of Henry II (O'Toole's role) rather than that of the commoner, Becket. Then he leaned over and kissed Elizabeth on the lips. "But her ladyship talked me out of it, claiming I'd played enough kings. She told me to hold out for the role of the Archbishop."

"Dick and I plan to make movies together in the future," Elizabeth said directly to Siân. "What about you and Peter?"

"We hate working with each other," Siân said. "We both consider it a quick way to the divorce court. Working together is bad on our nerves."

On at least one occasion, Siân joined Burton, Elizabeth, and her husband for drinks in central London at the Salisbury pub, a favorite with the theatrical crowd.

But the evening did not transpire without a rocky moment or two. Siân seemed to have negative opinions about Burton leaving his wife, Sybil, and about pursuing wealth instead of a love for the theater. Consequently, O'Toole did not press her to become involved in his frequent (and frequently alcohol-soaked) rendezvous with Elizabeth and Burton.

Siân did join them one night to see a play on St. Martins Lane in the West End. Over drinks, Elizabeth, attired in a tall turquoise hat, complained that wherever she and Burton went, they attracted mobs.

Leaving the pub they'd been in, they made their way to the theater, working their way through a dense crowd. To their distress, one woman shouted "I got so close to the whore I could spit on her!"

Inside the theater's lobby, Elizabeth renewed her complaints about the attention she invariably attracted.

In response, O'Toole quipped, "It might help a bit if you took off that fucking turquoise busby." *[His dismissal of her then-fashionable hat probably failed to soothe Elizabeth's distress. Busby (def.): A full-dress fur hat of varying shape, worn by hussars in the 19th century and by the foot guard regiments of the British army.]*

Mr. and Mrs. Peter O'Toole, hubby & wifey competitors.

For his film version of *Becket,* Glenville had assembled a stellar supporting cast, the most notable member of which was John Gielgud, cast as King Louis VII of France. On two separate occasions, O'Toole lunched with Gielgud and his relatively new lover, Martin Hensler, an interior designer from Hungary.

O'Toole found Hensler difficult, often argumentative, and rather rude to Gielgud. He later predicted to Burton that he didn't give the relationship much chance: "John has too strong an ego to put up with this guy's insults."

O'Toole was wrong. Their relationship lasted until Hensler's death in 1999, which was followed by Gielgud's death a year later.

For his brief appearance in *Becket,* Gielgud was eventually nominated for an Oscar as Best Supporting Actor. "John's appearance was brief," O'Toole said, "but it was memorable, and he performed it with great theatrical camp."

Gielgud lost the Oscar that year to Peter Ustinov for his role as the not-too-bright con man in *Topkapi.*

O'Toole was an admirer of the London actress, Pamela Brown, who played Eleanor of Aquitaine in *Becket* (1964). That was the role that Katharine Hepburn would develop four years later in O'Toole's future movie, *The Lion in Winter (1968).*

Like O'Toole, Brown had trained at RADA. He'd seen her in the London production of *The Lady's Not for Burning* (1949), with Burton, Claire Bloom, and Gielgud.

He had not seen a lot of her repertory performances, except for her role in Olivier's *Richard III* (1955). O'Toole had also gone to see her in Kirk Douglas's film about Van Gogh, *Lust for Life* (1956).

"Why don't we work together some time?" he asked her. "I hear you look standoffish, but are really quite come-hitherable."

"If you want to know what goes on behind closed doors, ask Burton," she told him. "But when I appeared in *Cleopatra,* he had no time for me in Rome."

"Perhaps Dick was busy with some other actress," O'Toole said. "That limey. Oh, what is her name? Did you know I was offered the role of Marc Antony? I deemed it not worthy of my talent."

"Please don't get me wrong," she said. "I just pretend to be promiscuous Actually, I'm a devout Roman Catholic. I divorced my first husband, Peter Copley, because of his infidelity. But I adhere to the teachings of the Church, and I can't remarry while Peter is still alive.

Gielgud as
Louis VII of France

"I was campy, but it was high camp."

So I'm shacked up with my partner, Michael Powell, the director. He gave me my first film work. We together live in sin in London, and I go to confession once a week.

"Even though I'm not a Catholic, I would go to confession," O'Toole said. "My trouble is, I have nothing to confess...And if anyone believes that, I'll sell him London Bridge really cheap."

Pamela Brown as Eleanor of Aquitaine "A sinful life."

On the set, O'Toole approached Martita Hunt, who had been cast in *Becket* as the Empress Matilda of England. "My god," he said, "it's Miss Havisham from *Great Expectations.*"

"Hello, Mr. O'Toole," she said. "That wretched role will haunt me forever. I'm also known for playing queens."

"So am I," he said. "Did you watch *Lawrence of Arabia?*"

"I'm absolutely thrilled to be working with you and Burton. But I hear you are two naughty boys engaging in all sorts of perversions. Need I have any fear for my virginity?"

"I can't speak for Dick, but I might find some use for that beak nose of yours," he said.

"You are such a naughty boy," she said. "I think everything I've heard about you is as true as the Bible."

Martita Hunt as England's Empress Matilda... "naughty queens."

O'Toole also had a brief reunion with Donald Wolfit, the distinguished actor who had appeared with him in *Lawrence of Arabia.* "We meet again," O'Toole said.

"And what a pleasure it is," Wolfit said.

O'Toole had continued to view Wolfit as one of his mentors. "I see every performance of yours I can. I literally study your every movement. Few actors can perform Shakespeare like you can. I pray I'll be half as good as you in this costume epic we're making."

"You are too kind," Wolfit said. Then he held out his hand. "Would you like to kiss my ring? I'm playing Gilbert Foliot, the Bishop of London."

An Italian actor, Paolo Stoppa, had been cast as Pope Alexander III. "Come to me, my son," he said to O'Toole, "and I will forgive you for your many sins."

Over a drink, he told O'Toole, "I get more dubbing jobs in Italian than I do acting roles. Throughout Italy, in American movies, I've been the Italian-language overvoice of Fred Astaire, Richard Widmark, Kirk Douglas, and Paul Muni."

"I'm sure you sound better than they do on the screen," O'Toole said.

Gino Cervi, another popular Italian actor, had been cast in *Becket* as Cardinal Zambelli. Although his career would encompass an involvement in a hundred films, he was best known for his role of Giuseppe Bottazzi ("Peppone"), the communist mayor in the Franco-Italian *Don Camillo* films of the 1950s and 60s.

***

Shortly after its release in 1964, *Becket* was nominated for eleven Academy Awards. They included Best Actor nominations for both O'Toole and Burton. Their joint nominations virtually canceled winning chances for both of them, thereby allowing Rex Harrison to win for his performance in *My Fair Lady.* O'Toole was furious, since he felt he both deserved (and almost won) the role of Professor Henry Higgins during its pre-production casting.

Also losing the designation of Best Actor to Harrison were Anthony Quinn for *Zorba the Greek* and Peter Sellers for *Dr. Strangelove.*

"All of us knew each other and were friends of a sort," O'Toole later told the press. "That is, we were friends until Oscar night."

Edward Anhalt was the only person associated with *Becket* to win an Oscar, in his case for Best Screenplay. *Becket's* other Oscar nominations that year were for Best Picture, Best Director, Best Supporting Actor, Best Art Direction, Best Costume Design, Best Editing, Best Score, and Best Sound.

O'Toole claimed that many of his friends in the theater had warned him not to tackle another costume drama so soon after *Lawrence of Arabia.* "They wanted me to put on a T-shirt like Brando in *A Streetcar Named Desire,* or else stub out a cigarette on the creamy thigh of my leading lady in some kitchen sink drama."

"Dick and I plan to continue our friendly rivalry, but on the stage," he said. "He'll be doing *Hamlet* in New York with John Gielgud as director, and I'll be doing *Hamlet* for the National Theatre with Laurence Olivier as director. May the best man win, and my darlings, we know who that is."

Burton as the reformed Archbishop "gone good"

Chapter 18

On a Bet, O'Toole Sets Out to Seduce
Three of the Blondest Bombshells in Showbiz—
Diana Dors,
Jayne Mansfield,
& Anita Ekberg

Conquering Britain's Dimestore Version of Marilyn Monroe,
& Replicating "La Dolce Vita" With Miss Sweden

Well-stacked and raring to mate, three blonde goddesses of international cinema (left to right) Diana Dors, Jayne Mansfield, and Anita Ekberg show off their best assets.

Surveying this "parade of pulchritude," O'Toole claimed, "Like Caesar, I came, I saw, I conquered, and I came again."

In the wake of the spectacular fame generated by *Lawrence of Arabia,* Peter O'Toole, as was the custom with big-name movie stars, was receiving sexual solicitations (and sometimes marriage proposals) from around the world.

Many of them arrived in the form of letters from Ireland, the U.S., Great Britain, Brazil and Australia. For some reason, his greatest number of marriage proposals derived from Italy, and to a lesser extent, France and Germany. Attached to their letters, many of his fans included nude pictures of themselves.

During this postal avalanche, Horizon Pictures hired Helen Lynn to digest and respond to the mail and to send out "autographed" photographs of O'Toole dressed as T.E. Lawrence. *[It was Helen who actually scribbled his "autograph" to the portraits.]*

Helen estimated that about ninety percent of the solicitations were from women who ranged in age from sixteen to seventy. The remaining ten percent were overtures from homosexuals, many of them revealing, graphically, what they'd like to do to O'Toole after they pulled off his flowing white robe.

He told Lynn, "I know all these people don't want to bed me, Peter O'Toole. They want a liaison with that guy I impersonated in the movie. They're in love with that image—dashing, romantic, and seductive enough to have inspired lust in a sodomite of a Turkish officer. I fear that under scrutiny, the real Peter O'Toole would disappoint. I'm reminded of what Rita Hayworth once said, "They fell in love with Gilda and woke up in bed with me.""

As he relayed to Lynn, "When my phone rings today, the calls will mainly be from people I've never met, although most of their names are familiar to me. They're the type of society folks attracted to movie stars. They're wealthy; they travel the world on first class airplanes or yachts; they extend invitations to the rich and famous, or they invite you into their mansions to swim in their Olympic-sized swimming pools. Some of the men will even arrange a bevy of dollybirds for your pleasure—take Hugh Hefner, for example. I hate to confess this weakness of character, but I adore people who adore me."

Toying with the Idea of Becoming Someone's "Toy Boy,"
O'Toole Is Pursued by Hundreds, Including the
Flamboyant Capitalist, Malcolm Forbes

Of his male admirers, the most formidable name—with the most financially rewarding invitation—involved an offer to visit the historic London mansion of the capitalist and magazine publisher, Malcolm Forbes. Forbes sent a chauffeur-driven Rolls-Royce to pick him up and transport him to luxurious surroundings, the stately looking, Georgian-styled Old Battersea House.

[Built immediately adjacent to the Thames on Tudor foundations in the late 17th century, it was rescued from decrepitude and demolition by Forbes in the 1970s thanks to the immediate expenditure of $750,000. After his death, his family sold it for in excess of $19 million. It was estimated that Forbes spent no more than 12 nights a year, on average, during his ownership.]

Over drinks and dinner, financier Malcolm Forbes "was the epitome of charm, grace, and wit."

O'Toole later said, "I turned down an invitation to become his plaything."

Peter decided to accept Forbes' invitation. He'd later joke to Richard Burton, "Long before our beloved Elizabeth (Taylor) was pursued by Malcolm, he went after my delectable rosebud, the tastiest on Planet Earth, or so I've been told."

He praised O'Toole's performance in *Lawrence*, claiming that the real-life character had always intrigued him. "Forbes was mesmerizing," O'Toole later told actor Kenneth Griffith, his best friend.

O'Toole had long read about the exploits of this flamboyant defender of capitalism. He was known for jet-setting, luxurious yachts competing with Aristotle Onassis, his celebrity-studded parties, his richly furnished homes, his aircraft, his fabulous art treasures, and one of the world's most comprehensive collections of Fabergé eggs, a peculiar passion of his.

Within this historically important and lavishly furnished late 17th-century home (Old Battersea House, London SW11), Forbes wined and dined Elizabeth Taylor.

He also wined and dined Peter O'Toole, but failed to seduce him.

Privately, and not known to the general public, Forbes hired some of "the handsomest men on earth to accompany him on extended holidays, preferring a cross section of beefcake from the far corners of the planet. Their points of origin ranged from Rio de Janeiro to Sydney, from Bulgaria, to the north woods of Canada, from California to Jamaica.

"He held out such adventures to me," O'Toole later claimed to Griffith. "Luxury cruises of the Mediterranean. He bought me one of the greatest deluxe motorcycles ever made to race with him through the Irish countryside.

He even suggested that I might want to accompany him on an upcoming hot-air balloon trip, beginning on the Oregon coast and traversing North America eastward to the Chesapeake Bay."

He was also invited to accompany Forbes on holiday to Lauthala, a small island he owned in Fiji. "You can run around in the nude if you wish," Forbes informed O'Toole. "There are no laws. 'Do what thou will' is the one command that applies there."

As O'Toole told Kenneth Griffith, "At no point did he make a sexual proposition to me. He has too much class for that. But it was obvious that to enjoy his generosity, I would have to sing for my supper."

"Be honest with me," Griffith said. "Weren't you tempted? I'm more heterosexual than most blokes, but I would have at least considered such an offer."

"I certainly thought about it, and had to look deep down into my soul. As a poor boy growing up in Leeds with not enough to eat every night, it was a fabulous temptation. To live the life of the Sultan's favorite in his harems around the world. To have a wardrobe of a thousand suits from Savile Row. A specially made diamond-studded Rolex costing a king's ransom. Three sports cars, custom made."

"I thought maybe I'm a whore after all," he said. "Aren't all actors whores, selling our bodies to some producer? But I'll have to turn darling Malcolm down. I finally realized that my dear old Mum didn't raise some male plaything for some obscenely rich American sodomite."

A week later, he attended a play in London's West End with Griffith. When the performance ended, the men rushed to the Salisbury pub for a few quick lagers before "last call."

There, O'Toole told him more details about the "sudden avalanche of indecent proposals I'm receiving at Horizon. It seems, darling, that everybody on the planet wants to get Lawrence of Arabia into their bed. Lately, I've been feeling like a male Marilyn Monroe, a love goddess in my own right."

"I sure hope you're feeling better than poor Marilyn," Griffith said. "The fact that she's dead is horrible. And there's a rumor going about that Robert Kennedy ordered her murder. I don't believe it was a suicide."

"Ah, my dear man, a mystery for the ages. It's odd that both Marilyn and her lover, JFK, were murdered within a year or so of each other. That reminds me. I, too, am facing death threats."

"Who, pray tell, would want to kill you?" Griffith asked. "Perhaps a jealous husband or two?"

"The threats are coming in from potential assassins in the Middle East," O'Toole said. "*Lawrence* is banned in these countries, and the idiots were told that we've made an anti-Arab film—that we've committed blasphemy against the Prophet Mohammed."

"What nonsense!" Griffith said. "Let's talk of something a bit more pleasant—those indecent proposals, for example. How many of them are you going to accept?"

"So far, none, but I'm seriously thinking about it. I've ordered the studio not to forward those letters to my home. I don't want to make Siân insanely jealous of her husband. Each night, I remind her how delicious it is to be in bed with me. That is, on those nights I'm home."

"I'd like to see some of those letters," Griffith said. "After all, I'm a secret *voyeur.* No one ever propositioned me except this Catholic priest back in Tenby. He was trying to convert me (to something, at least) since I'd been reared as a Protestant. I was a cute little devil, only nine years old, a sodomite's delight."

"I'll make a deal with you," O'Toole said. "I sometimes stay in a two-room suite at this dump of a hot-bed hotel on Earls Court. Many Londoners use it for their off-the-record trysts. If I have Horizon deliver all those letters to me there, will you spend the weekend with me in the suite, opening and evaluating them? Management there is discreet. They know I like to pop in ever so often, usually with a dollybird or two."

"You've got a deal," Griffith said. "That's the most fascinating offer I've received this year."

That weekend, O'Toole and Griffith spend hours together opening his enormous backlog of mail. It contained an array of offers and propositions, many of them obscene, and many containing nude photographs. Most of the letters were tossed aside.

"For the first time I saw just what kind of mail a big-time movie star gets." Griffith said, "Talk about Eve tempting Adam with that harmless apple. These were hard-core letters. I didn't realize how many so-called respectable women are driven sex crazed over a mere movie star. I think it changed my mind about women. I began to think about what lurked behind their ladylike facades: Perhaps a secret strumpet. As for the gay solicitations, I told O'Toole that those should be sent over to Olivier, Noël Coward, and most definitely, John Gielgud."

That Saturday night at The Nag's Head *[10 James Street in Covent Garden]*, Griffith came up with what he called "My brightest idea since I urged Wales to break away from England."

"The letters represent 'easy lays,'" he said. "A man like you needs something more dignified, more rarefied—a more daunting challenge."

"Here's what I propose," Griffith continued. "I bet you're getting more offers than Brando. *[Griffith had heard that when Marlon Brando appeared on Broadway in Tennessee Williams' A Streetcar Named Desire, he received sev-*

eral offers from big-name female movie stars.] So I'll bet you £100 that you can seduce some of the most famous sexpots on the planet. Let's see if you can seduce them with your charm and male beauty. It doesn't matter whether they're married or not."

"You're on!" O'Toole said. "I love a challenge."

"There's one condition," Griffith said.

"And what in bloody hell might that be?" he asked.

"I get to name the bombshells. And since gentlemen are said to prefer blondes, I propose that you set your sights on Anita Ekberg, Jayne Mansfield, and on Britain's own Diana Dors. I already know Dors. I have her phone number. I got my first film role after the war with her—it was her all-time first movie role. The picture was *The Shop at Sly Corner."*

[Featuring a suspenseful performance by its lead, Oscar Homolka, The Shop at Sly Corner (also known as The Code of Scotland Yard; 1947), contained a scene-stealing wiggle walk from Diana Dors, playing a blackmailer's girl-friend. Although she did not appear in the credits, crowds of her admirers came to see the film because she had a part in it.]

"The title needs work," O'Toole countered.

"When I met Diana, she was only sixteen," Griffith said. "But very fuck-able. Instead of 'Diana Fluck,' the name she was using for billing at the time, we suggested that she bill herself as Diana Dors, her mother's last name. 'What if one of the letters dropped off a marquee?' we asked."

"I accept your challenge," O'Toole said. "What fun I'll have."

"You don't think you'll be rejected, do you?" Griffith asked.

"No, dear boy, I'm not known as 'Peter the Toole' for nothing. My noble tool will penetrate all three of these overworked vaginas, giving them thrills that John F. Kennedy, Gary Cooper, Errol Flynn, or Tyrone Power couldn't. During my quest and conquest, I'll keep you posted."

A Self-Styled "Hurricane in Mink," Diana Opens "Dors" to Her London Orgies, Secretly Filming the Players With Hidden Cameras

Diana Dors, Britain's sexually charged answer to Marilyn Monroe, was among the most fascinating women O'Toole ever seduced. Actually, she seduced him. After he inaugurated a phone dialogue, she invited him to her apartment for a rendezvous.

Even during the course of her marriage to her now-estranged husband, Richard (nicknamed "Dickie') Dawson, she was notorious for her extra-marital affairs and for the orgies she staged at her residence. Geoffrey Fisher, the frequently outraged Archbishop of Canterbury, had just publicly denounced her as "a wayward hussy."

Rising to fame as a G.I. pinup girl in World War II, Dors was called "more figure than talent," during her emergence as England's reigning sex symbol of the 1950s. Like O'Toole, she'd attended RADA, but the acting styles taught there—at least in her case—didn't' seem to take. She starred in mostly second-rate films such as the tepidly percolating potboiler, *Miss Tulip Stays the Night* (1955). A favorite of the tabloids, Dors had grown up emulating such role models as Veronica Lake, Lana Turner, and Jean Harlow.

Dors was seen driving around London picking up horny young men in her expensive car. *[At the age of 20, she had set a record as the youngest-ever registered owner of a Rolls-Royce.]*

She was the first major British star to pose for semi-nude or completely nude photographs. Though not quite the equal of those within Marilyn Monroe's notorious calendar, they were widely circulated throughout Britain.

For a while, RKO had her under contract, but after they dropped her, they claimed that she had violated the morals clause she'd signed.

In Dors' living room, sipping champagne in 1964, O'Toole found her wearing a sexy semi-transparent black *négligée*.

She was rather free and candid during discussions of her marriages, including her first in 1951 *[to Dennis Hamilton]*. "He cheated on me, stole my money, beat the shit out of me, and got syphilis from some hooker he picked up in Soho. He died from it. Thank God he didn't pass it on to me."

[A biographer of Diana Dors, David Bret, wrote that Welsh-born Hamilton "was an out-and out

Diana Dors: "I'm the only sex symbol Britain has produced since Lady Godiva."

In the photo above, Diana as she appeared in *They're Happy* (1955).

Diana in her greatest role as the condemned-to-die murderess Mary Hilton in *Yield to the Night* (1956), a protest against capital punishment in the UK.

343

louse: a thug, gigolo, and serial phi-landerer, who treated even his friends and most especially his girl-friends despicably."]

Dors had just attended a show-biz party in Mayfair. "I don't know if it'll make the tabloids, but I saw Rock Hudson across the crowded room, and I pranced across the floor and slapped the fucker's face. I mean, really hard."

Diana Dors with Rock Hudson, competing for the love-making of his stand-in, the much-in-demand stud, Tommy Yeardye.

"What in hell did you have against Mr. Hudson?" he asked. "He looks rather harmless to me, a sort of pinup boy nice guy Hollywood type. You know, Tab Hunter, Troy Donahue, and that ilk from the dream factory, as it's called."

"I was madly in love with a handsome hunk, Tommy Yeardye, who was a peasant Irishman turned gigolo and highly praised in circles because of his endowment. By the time he was sixteen, he was hustling johns and rich women in London who wanted to have sex with him. His clients passed him on to their friends. He stood six foot four and was all muscles except for one stupendous organ."

She related how, in 1954, while shooting *Captain Lightfoot,* a swashbuckling adventure saga in Ireland, Yeardye had been hired as a stand-in for Hudson. "He resembled Rock in more ways than one, if you get my drift. Rock had this hunky Italian lover, 'Massimo,' but was always on the lookout for a fresh piece of meat."

Diana Dors with Tommy Yeardye. She described him as "fists like bricks, eyes like emeralds, and the cock of a horse."

"Later," she continued, "Tommy and I flew to Rome. Rock was in Italy making *A Farewell to Arms.* The bastard called me and invited me to the set. The liar told me what a fan of mine he was. As it turned out, he'd seen a photo of Tommy arriving with me at the airport. He wined and dined us. But when I was engaged on business, he came on to Tommy like gangbusters, for a repeat of everything they'd done before in Ireland. All of this was going on behind my innocent, trusting back. And I thought Tommy loved me."

"In Rome, Rock was staying in his suite at the Grand Hotel with Massimo, and Tommy was shacked up in a cheaper room with Troy Donahue, who was also in Rome at the time. He and Tommy would visit Rock's suite every night for what he called his 'tarts and Romans fuckathons.'"

"I had been signed to make this picture called *La Ragazza del Palio* or *The Love Specialist* for director Luigi Zampa," Dors said.

"While I was away in Siena making that picture, Tommy stayed behind, hoping to get work on Rock's picture. I later found out that he was the star attraction at Rock's orgies. Meanwhile, I was getting raped every day by my co-stars, Bruce

The Love Specialist (1959). Diana Dors claimed, "I endured daily rapes from my co-stars, Vittorio Gassman and Bruce Cabot."

Cabot and Vittorio Gassman, Shelley Winters' ex. So I hope that explains why I detest Rock Hudson."

"But it seems fair that while Tommy boy was plowing Rock, you were getting stuffed by Gassman and Cabot."

"We need not go into that!" she said. "People are always citing my infidelity. My point of view about that is if infidelity is so bad, then why did God invent it? He obviously wanted us to practice it, or else it would not exist."

"I think your logic is beyond challenge," he answered. "Like you, I believe in infidelity. When a man cheats on his wife, he usually returns home with flowers and chocolates and is extra nice to his old girl. So she benefits. Although I'm married myself, I tell everyone that marriage is nothing more than state-sponsored bondage."

Since at the time O'Toole was considering storming the gates of Hollywood, he was eager to hear about her adventures there and in Las Vegas. She revealed that during her time in Hollywood, she'd given birth to her second son, Gary Dawson. *[Born in 1962, he later worked as a producer on the television game show,* Family Feud.*]* "I made Liberace his godfather, knowing he'd take a personal interest in my boy, perhaps keep him in mink and diamonds as he grows older."

She spoke of her act in Las Vegas, where she hung out with the number one pinup of World War II, Betty Grable. "On the night of August 4, 1962, Betty and I got these two male dancers to escort us to the Thunderbird Hotel to see Frances Faye's show. At one point, this drunken shit called Betty's escort a faggot, and a fight broke out. The police were called. It would have made the headlines, except for one major event that editors thought was more important."

"What might that have been?" he asked.

"Marilyn Monroe was found dead in her bedroom. She knocked everything else off the front pages."

"How do you feel about her passing?"

"To be honest, I'm not exactly in mourning," she said. "I've been called a second-rate Monroe or her dime store imitation, and I'm tired of that. I'm an original, not a carbon copy of anybody else. I told the press that if Marilyn had had children to love, she would never have killed herself. Of course, that's what I said to the press. Actually, I don't think it was a suicide. I think her lover, President Kennedy, had her wiped out. But with Monroe out of the way, I'm now the only true blonde bombshell remaining."

"What about Jayne Mansfield?" he asked.

"Oh, her! I think she's a female impersonator. I hear that Mae West is also a transvestite. West might still even have her penis. Mansfield was probably born with one, but had it cut off."

Over their second bottle of champagne, O'Toole turned to Dors. "I'm a married man, and I have a terrible confession to make. I came here tonight to seduce you. My intentions are anything but honorable."

"Thank God that we got the small talk out of the way. Now we can go into the next room for some real man-on-woman stuff"

The next afternoon, Griffith wanted a rundown of the Dors seduction.

"She's good," Peter said. "Really, really good. Most experienced. She let me have it three ways. I was divinely inspired. What more could a man ask? She's got a talented serpent-like tongue that explores every inch of the male body—yes, even the rosebud."

"Dors is lascivious and vulgar, yet feisty enough to be forever intriguing. She's destined to play brassy women where every curve of her body is sinful. There is a certain cynicism about her which, in contradiction, is combined with naïveté. She is easy to manipulate. She had a large, glitzy, whorish wardrobe in her bedroom, but looks best with no clothes on at all. She thinks of herself as a female Errol Flynn. Perhaps she stole the line from someone, but her parting words to me were, 'What is life if you don't live it?'"

Two weeks later, Dors called O'Toole and invited him to one of her infamous orgies, which she occasionally staged for wannabe starlets who wanted to meet producers and directors, or else for celebrities visiting London, most often from Hollywood.

Two cameramen were hired for the occasion to "get the party going by showing hard-core porno flicks."

There were no bigtime celebrities at the orgy on the night O'Toole attended. The biggest attraction was the American movie star, Bruce Cabot, with whom Dors had filmed *The Love Specialist* in Siena.

Fay Wray with Bruce Cabot in *King Kong* (1933)

O'Toole was eager to talk to Cabot, knowing he'd been the lover and "fuck buddy" of Errol Flynn, who had died in 1959 after a spectacularly dissipated life. O'Toole fancied himself as a potential 1960s version of Errol Flynn, and as such, he wanted to learn all he could about the late swashbuckler and rogue.

He knew very little about Cabot, other than that he'd been born to a French father in New Mexico to a mother who died shortly after childbirth. He'd watched him in a revival of *King Kong* (1933), as he'd rescued Fay Wray from the clutches of the Beast. He'd heard that during the course of his career, he'd made mostly action pictures and westerns, often cast as a villain.

After Cabot had returned from the War, he'd become one of "John Wayne's Regulars," appearing in several picture with "The Duke."

Before breaking into movies, Cabot had been an oil worker, a prize fighter, a used car salesman, a real estate agent, a sailor, a door-to-door insurance salesman, and a "pig killer" in a slaughterhouse, out of which he'd emerged every afternoon at 5PM covered in blood.

Errol Flynn (depicted above) bragged to Bruce Cabot that he'd seduced between 12,000 and 14,000 young men and women.

O'Toole found Cabot fascinating. More and more, he was intrigued by Hollywood stars and the dark rumors he'd begun hearing about them. He'd been told that Cabot, near the end of World War II, had allegedly been involved, in collusion with high-ranking U.S. military commanders, in a gold-smuggling ring that shipped gold from the dying ruins of Nazi Germany to Brazil and/or the Middle East. When

Cabot's involvement in this was uncovered in Cairo, he was arrested and posted to an "end of the world" desert outpost in Mauretania, where he was assigned janitor duty in the barracks.

When his "banishment" ended at wartime's end, Cabot migrated to Hollywood.

Out of courtesy, O'Toole never asked Cabot about the second "dark rumor" swirling around him. He was said to have taken as his first wife Grace Mary Mather Smith, an African-American woman, even though interracial marriages were technically illegal at that time in the United States. She was reported to be the same actress who had starred in such all-black movies as *The Girl from Chicago* (1932).

At the time that O'Toole bonded with Cabot in London, he had made plans to travel to either Germany or Italy, seeking work in film production.

After Flynn's death, Cabot "dined out" on stories that capitalized on his late friend's exploits. "He was the ultimate Tasmanian Devil, staging orgies long before Dors started producing her own. Sometimes, he attracted really big name stars. Errol often complained that the world saw him just as a phallic symbol instead of as an actor."

"He had them all: Truman Capote, Doris Duke, Rock Hudson, Barbara Hutton, Howard Hughes, Tyrone Power, Lupe Velez, Shelley Winters, Hedy Lamarr, Carole Landis, Ann Sheridan, even Evita Péron. Sometimes, in his dressing room, he entertained four starlets at a time. He often flew to Mexico City for a little boy ass, too."

"In the 1930s, Errol and I joined this club called the Olymphiads. Our meetings were always behind locked doors. No Jews were allowed. We told truly nasty stories, got stinking drunk, and often invited naïve young girls in to get up close and personal with Flynn and/or John Barrymore, and I took their leftovers. Other members included John Decker the painter, and W.C. Fields. Also Errol's boyfriends at the time, William Lundigan and Patric Knowles. Some of our meetings were held aboard Errol's yacht, *Sirocco,* often during transits to and from Catalina Island. If only someone had filmed those orgies."

"Errol told me that he arrived in London in June of 1933 with only two shillings in his pocket, Cabot continued. "Various adventures followed. As Errol explained it, 'A pretty boy in a land of old sods doesn't have to go hungry."

"Whenever money was low in Hollywood, Errol always had a scheme to make more bucks. Once, he charged his friends and voyeurs $50 each to watch us play a mixed doubles tennis match with two busty blonde heifers. To spice up the game, all four of us got stark naked. Errol and I flopped around the courts, much to the glee of those damned voyeurs."

"One time, Errol got so mad at Bogie that he made Patric Knowles, his actor boyfriend, sign a pact. All three of us set out to fuck his slutty wife, Mayo

Methot, and we did!"

"Errol was one cocky guy, and I miss him terribly," Cabot said, "although we had our disputes. Our friendship ended badly. He hired me to make *The Story of William Tell.*"

[Starring and produced by Errol Flynn, The Story of William Tell *is an unfinished film that would have been the first instance of an independent film using the then-new technology of Cinemascope. Filming began in Italy in 1953. As a backdrop set, a £10,000 model town set was built near Mont Blanc. Ultimately, Flynn lost most of the money (approximately $430,000) he had invested into the $860,00 budgeted for production, leading to the seizure of some of his cars, personal effects, and assets.]*

"Flynn, as the film's producer, ran out of dough." Cabot continued. "He knew I was having trouble finding work in Hollywood, and he called me his 'old, old pal.' Filming was halted, and Flynn and his wife, Patrice Wymore, were stranded in Rome with absolutely no money. I sued him for back pay. I went to court and got a ruling allowing me to seize his property at his hotel. I took their two cars and his clothing. He claimed that I had betrayed him, but I needed money, too. I don't work for dirt."

"He always had this philosophy of life that stated, 'it's my life to fuck up any way I choose.'"

"Truer words were never said," O'Toole claimed. "My philosophy exactly. Now, with respect to our hostess, Miss Dors, it's time to select one of these dollybirds. Diana told me she's tight for space tonight, and that we'll have to share a double bed with our picks."

"That's fine with me," Cabot said. "Errol and I used to do that all the time, most often with only one gal—always one who was very, very young."

That night at Dors' orgy, Cabot chose an exotic beauty from Sierra Leone. O'Toole himself selected a Joan Collins lookalike, but as he later quipped to Griffith, "Except my Joan Collins was born in 1943, not 1933."

Two years later, in London, at a party that the theatrical critic Kenneth Tynan hosted for Marlene Dietrich, who was in London at the time performing cabaret, the names of Errol Flynn and Bruce Cabot surfaced. Dietrich delivered her own appraisal: "Bruce was the biggest tightwad in Hollywood, a sponger off Errol Flynn or anyone else. He was also the most stupid actor in Hollywood. He couldn't even read his lines, much less remember them. He always acted like a complete shit."

O'Toole delivered his final appraisal of Cabot like this: "After sharing a bed with him and two other young ladies, I now know why Flynn referred to him as "Jumbo.'"

In time, Dors' own son, Jason Lake, son of her third husband, Alan Lake, revealed his mother's secret hobby. She arranged for the rooms of her apartment to be equipped with hidden movie cameras. Allegedly, she told the starlets she invited to her parties to seduce the celebrities or important film industry bigwigs without obstructing the sightlines of her cameras.

Later, she would evaluate the playbacks of the pornographic clips thus generated. Friends even revealed some of her ratings: Douglas Fairbanks, Jr. got a 6½; Anthony Steele a 10; Richard Harris, 8; Oliver Reed, 9; Alan Bates, also a 9; Peter Lawford, 3; Rex Harrison a 5. Terry Thomas came in with the lowest rating of all, a 2.

"So, long before I made *Caligula,*" O'Toole told Griffith, "I was a porno star. I never learned how high Dors rated me on her scale of one to ten. Perhaps one day when I'm old and grey, her stash of porno films will surface and I'll have a reminder of how I looked and performed during what Doug Fairbanks called 'Our Salad Days.'"

A Pink Négligée & Pink Champagne at the Pink Palace—
O'Toole Visits the Pink World of the Sexbomb
Who Wanted to be His Pussycat, Jayne Mansfield

With the daunting Dors conquered, O'Toole continued his mission. The challenge of Jayne Mansfield lay in his immediate future.

Fortunately, he didn't have to travel to Hollywood to encounter her. He'd read that she had stopped off in London *en route* to East Germany (presumably because prices there were cheaper) to make her next film.

He was friends with the British actor, Anthony Quayle, whom he knew had recently co-starred with Mansfield in *The Challenge* (1959). A mediocre British film, the movie featured her as the leader of a gang of burglars. A member of her gang, Quayle falls in love with her.

O'Toole called Quayle and asked him if he could arrange a meeting for him with Mansfield. The actor said that he'd be dining with his former co-star that Saturday night at the Café Royal, former haunt of Oscar Wilde. "You're welcome to join us. I'm sure she'd like to meet Lawrence of Arabia. Maybe she'll want to make a sex comedy with you. If I see that you two are hitting it off, I'll skip out and leave you with the tab."

"Fair enough," O'Toole said.

Dubbed "The Working Man's Marilyn Monroe," Mansfield was on her way to becoming a box office has-been at the time of her meeting with O'Toole, as arranged through Quayle.

She'd recently made a sexploitation movie, *Promises, Promises!* (1963), in which she became the first major American movie star to appear nude in a film.

On that Saturday night, in a satin, ivory-colored gown with plunging *décolletage*, she made her entrance at the Café Royal wearing a sable coat. Her appearance in the main dining room caused patrons to turn and stare.

She didn't walk, but sort of sashayed.

Introduced to O'Toole, she spoke to him with "baby breath," thrusting the contents of her D-cups against his chest.

As he'd later relate to Griffith, "I couldn't wait to bite those nipples that were practically bulging out of her gown."

Jayne Mansfield "busting out all over."

He was somewhat surprised that the then-communist government of the *Deutsche Demokratische Republik* (a.k.a., East Germany) had invited her behind its closely guarded borders to make a film, *Heimweh nach St. Pauli.* She said that in the film, she'd have to sing two German-language songs: "I've been listening to old Marlene Dietrich records and rehearsing with my current lover, Nelson Sardelli."

[Of Italian descent, Sardelli had born in Brazil. She had taken up with him after the failure of her marriage to the Hungarian muscleman, Mickey Hargitay, the former Mr. Universe of 1955, a stud she stole from Mae West.]

"Nelson is the best lover I've ever had," she revealed. "Far better than Mickey. I used to think Mr. Universe was the best. But no more."

Jayne Mansfield: "I turned 1950s sex into a malignant fever."

O'Toole was rather surprised at her candid evaluation.

As he was later to learn, Mansfield never minded discussing her love affairs, asserting, "It's part of my legend, dear."

Back in her suite at The Dorchester, she called room service and ordered three bottles of pink champagne.

Two hours later, rather drunk, he found himself in her bed. As he'd later tell Griffith, "She certainly is a body beautiful. But she's no tiger in bed like Diana Dors. Even though I was making love to her, she seemed more enchanted with her own body than mine. She held up this mirror so she could get a closer look at the action below. Instead of my making love to her, I felt she was making love to herself, using me as her tool of masturbation. I know that doesn't make any sense at all. But that's what happened."

"After the deadly deed, she seemed to want me to leave. She said she had to take a bubble bath and get some beauty sleep. She didn't ask me to join her in the tub."

Long after his seduction of Mansfield, O'Toole encountered John Gielgud, who told him that he was departing for Hollywood, where he'd been cast in the film adaptation of *The Loved One,* based on the comic novel by Evelyn Waugh about the funeral system in Los Angeles.

When worlds collide: Jayne Mansfield meets the queen. She had been warned that too much *décolletage* would be looked down at, unfavorably.

"You'll never guess who else is appearing in the picture," Gielgud said. "Jayne Mansfield, Miss Dairies herself."

"That's one film I've got to see," O'Toole said.

Months later, he ran into Gielgud again in the lobby of one of London's West End theaters and asked him how filming had gone. "You lied to me," O'Toole said. "You were in it, so was Robert Morse, even Milton Berle and Rod Steiger. There was also a bevy of faggots—Tab Hunter, Roddy McDowall, even Liberace, but no Jayne Mansfield."

"The poor, busty thing is all heartbroken," Gielgud answered. "All her footage landed on the cutting room floor."

Presumably, O'Toole would never have sex with her again. However, when he was in Los Angeles, she called him to set up a rendezvous. *Variety* had run a story with the information that O'Toole was about to appear with Peter Sellers in a movie called *What's New Pussycat?* (1965). It would be Woody Allen's first feature film wherein he functioned as both an actor and its screenwriter. The script, an updated version, with music, of a French bedroom farce, contained four roles for sexy actresses.

Mansfield reached O'Toole within his suite at the Beverly Hills Hotel. An invitation was extended to The Pink Palace, her home, a 40-room Mediterranean-style mansion at 101000 Sunset Boulevard. She had acquired it in 1957 from its previous owner, the crooner, Rudy Vallee.

The subsequent night, she arrived to retrieve him at the hotel's entrance in a pink Cadillac Eldorado Biarritz convertible, the only pink Cadillac in Hollywood at the time. *[Elvis Presley had bought one in 1955, but his was in Memphis.]*

Back in England, O'Toole would gossip with Griffith about the details associated with his arrival at her home.

Mansfield had painted everything there pink. Pink champagne flowed from a fountain. At one point, she led him on a tour, showing off her heart-shaped (pink) bathtub and her upholstered-with-fur (and dyed pink) toilet seats.

Together, they went for a swim in her heart-shaped pool. Whereas she stripped down completely, he opted to retain his bathing trunks. As twilight fell, pink fluorescent lights illuminated statues of cupids in various poses.

At dinner, her cook had dyed, with food coloring, the mashed potatoes pink. And naturally, the drink of choice was (*what else?*) pink champagne.

With money inherited from her grandfather, she'd purchased the mansion for $78,000. A former construction worker, Hargitay directed, with her guidance, the building's massive renovation. It included the installation of a waterfall.

Jayne: A money shot in her money dress.

"I detest the color of pink," she confessed to O'Toole as the evening wore on. "But I need it for my image. My favorite colors are actually black and white, but that's not sexy. Who wants to see me wearing the colors nuns wear? Pink is sexy. I've gotten more press mileage out of pink than that Kim Novak ever has with her lavender."

She sadly spoke of John F. Kennedy's assassination in Dallas. "Jack and I were lovers," she confessed. "He wasn't very good at it. Once he blasted off, a woman didn't exist for him."

She claimed that JFK's brother-in-law, Peter Lawford, had introduced them in 1957 in Hollywood when he was still a senator from Massachusetts. He came to visit her on the set of *Will Success Spoil Rock Hunter?*

She revealed that the last time she'd had a rendezvous with JFK was at a villa in Palm Springs. "I was pregnant at the time with Maria."

[Mariska Magdolna Hargitay, born in 1964 from the union of Jayne Mansfield and her husband, Hungary-born bodybuilder Mickey Hargitay, is a well-respected, award-winning actress best known to modern readers for her role as a New York City sex crimes detective on the NBC television series Law & Order, Special Victims Unit.*]*

"The President seemed fascinated by my belly...even more than he was with Suzi."

["Suzi" was Mansfield's pet name for her vagina, something he'd learned from her back in London.]

He rubbed my belly and kissed it," she said. "When I told him I thought I was going to give birth to a girl, that really excited him. He bent me over and entered me from behind while he felt my belly."

"My darling," O'Toole said. "I think you've told me more than I need to know, real insider information. But that's not why I think you've invited me here tonight. You've got something else on your mind. I just know."

"How right you are," she said. "I want you to use whatever influence you have to get me any one of those four girl roles in *What's New Pussycat?* I just know I can play any of those parts better than any other actress in Hollywood. Let's face it: "Marilyn Monroe is no longer available to steal roles from me like *Bus Stop."*

The evening drifted off with his weak promise that he'd see what he could do. She told him that she'd arranged for a taxi to take him back to his hotel, as she had to go to see the late show at a club where her lover, Nelson Sardelli, was singing. "I don't want Nelson to catch me with you. He might get suspicious."

During the course of the next three or so days, when she didn't hear from him, she called O'Toole at his hotel, where the reception staff informed her, "Mr. O'Toole is no longer in residence. He left no forwarding address."

He never saw Mansfield again, and was horrified to learn of her tragic death, at the age of 34, from head trauma in the aftermath of a car accident in June of 1959. From the relative safety in the back seat of the vehicle she was riding in, her three children survived with minor injuries.

The Pink Palace was later sold to Ringo Starr and then to Mama Cass Elliot. Its last owner was singer Engelbert Humperdinck, who, in 2002, sold it to a developer who demolished it.

In Rome, O'Toole Chases Anita ("Miss Sweden") Ekberg, The Orgasmic Fantasy from Fellini's La Dolce Vita

Ever since he'd seen Anita Ekberg in Federica Fellini's *La Dolce Vita* (1961), O'Toole had been fascinated by the buxom star. She'd parlayed a "Miss Sweden" title into a career as an internationally famous actress. Her performance as Sylvia, the unattainable dream woman dancing without inhibition in Rome's Trevi Fountain, had electrified audiences around the world.

After his seductions of Mansfield and Dors, Ekberg remained O'Toole's final challenge. He hoped that his cachet as *Lawrence of Arabia* would allow him to slip into the bedroom of this blonde goddess like some panting version of Casanova.

354

He'd seen her performance in the 1955 ABC TV version of *Casablanca,* in which she'd played Isla, a role immortalized in its original (1942) version by Ingrid Bergman, another Swedish actress. *[In his comparisons of the two versions, O'Toole preferred the original, Ingrid Bergman version.]*

Gossip columnists had kept the world up to date on the many dramas associated with Ekberg's staged press antics and her frequent romantic escapades with celebrated men who had included Gary Cooper, Errol Flynn, Yul Brynner, Tyrone Power, and Rod Taylor.

O'Toole had flown to Rome to spend some time with Richard Burton and Elizabeth Taylor, who were falling in love during their filming of *Cleopatra.* O'Toole had also sought out his friend, Anthony Steel, who was living in Rome at the time. Conveniently, Ekberg also lived in Rome. O'Toole knew that Steel and she had been married from 1956 to 1959, but had jointly endured a bitter divorce. He'd read that she'd married another actor, Rik Van Nutter (aka Clyde Roberts), and that she was rumored to have been unfaithful to him.

In Rome, O'Toole first had dinner with Steel. Although O'Toole had maintained a breezy, light friendship with him, the two actors also had a certain rivalry that became more visible when O'Toole became romantically involved with Patricia Roc, one of the most beautiful screen actresses in Britain, and the former lover of Ronald Reagan.

Steel never married Roc, but he eventually fathered a son with her.

The once popular, well-muscled actor, who was twelve years older than O'Toole, said he feared that he was on the downside of his movie

Federico Fellini's 1960 *La Dolce Vita* electrified the world and made stars of Italy's Marcello Mastroianni and Sweden's busty Anita Ekberg.

When she jumped into Rome's Trevi Fountain, it instantly became one of the major sightseeing attractions of Rome

Anthony Steel, Britain's Mr. Beefcake, invited O'Toole to enjoy the charms of his ex-wife, Anita Ekberg.

355

career, "I'm taking whatever roles come along." He said he felt comfortable living in Rome, and that didn't know when, if ever, he might return to England.

"I'm very bitter about Anita. She bad-mouthed me in the press. She claims I used to beat her, which is a total lie. She did say that when I'm not falling down drunk, I can be charming and cultured. But she claims that after one drink, I start arguments that usually go violent."

"We've already shared a bottle of wine, and you haven't beaten the shit out of me, yet," O'Toole said.

When he explained that Ekberg might be ideal for a role in *What's New Pussycat?* Steel said, "We're not speaking, but I know who handles her career. I'll call him and let him get in touch with the bitch about this."

After dinner, Steel and O'Toole embraced on a romantic cobblestone square in the heart of Rome. "Until I return to Rome, or else you dare to face the cold winds of Britain again," O'Toole kissed him on both cheeks, "goodbye, darling, and good luck to you."

Two nights later, O'Toole received a phone call at the Hotel Excelsior on the via Veneto. "This is Anita Ekberg," she said in a sexy, husky voice. "I hear you want to see me."

"Indeed, I do. Thanks for getting back to me so soon."

"The prospect of appearing in a movie role with Sellers and you would be any girl's fantasy. Speaking of fantasies, I'm dreaming about you right now. Years from now, historians of cinema will cite two pivotal scenes—*Me* in that damn fountain and *you* in your flowing robes racing across the desert to kill some Turks."

She gave him her address in Rome, and told him to come over that evening since she was free. "My new husband is out of town. I live right outside the city. Take a taxi. He'll know the way."

After giving him her address, she rang off.

In her villa, over drinks, he sat across from her. She was so voluptuous, so elusive...

"Everyone always wants to talk about that *Dolce, Dolce* picture," she said. "So let's get that out of the way. It was a frigid March day in Rome. The city does get cold. I was wearing a strapless dress, as you remember, and I was freezing."

"To prepare himself for the cold, Marcello (Mastroianni) had downed a fifth of vodka. He also wore a wet suit under his clothes. He fell down several times during filming, he was so drunk. This caused endless delays, turning me into a block of ice. By the time Fellini was satisfied, my legs were frozen. I had to have three grips lift me out of the Trevi Fountain. I could no longer feel anything in my legs. So much for that god damn romantic scene that thrilled the world."

"My career never went the way I wanted it to," she continued. "My greatest heartbreak was when I lost the role of Honey Rider in the first James Bond film, *Dr. No* (1962). I lost it to that dreadful Ursula Andress."

"That's amazing," he said. "I also lost a role in *Dr. No.* My god, we almost became lovers on screen."

The day before O'Toole met her, she'd told the Roman press, "I don't know if paradise or hell exist, but I'm sure hell is more groovy."

She also told the reporter, "I was the one who made Fellini famous. Not the other way around."

"My greatest fear is that this blonde bombshell craze has ended. The 1960s seem to call for waif-like creatures. Take Audrey Hepburn. Is she really a boy?"

"I don't truly know," O'Toole quipped. "But I look forward to finding out for myself at some future date."

"My outlandish publicity may actually run me out of the business," she said. "I feel like I'm portrayed as a freak."

"That's why I'm here," he said. "I'm doing this film, as you know, with Peter Sellers. It's *What's New Pussycat?* There are four good roles in it for a woman. They call for the women to be sexy, but any of the roles would show off your comedic talents. Are you interested in my recommending you to the director, Clive Donner?"

"I'd give my left breast to be in something like that—well, not really... Yes, I'd love for you to recommend me. After your spectacular appearance in *Lawrence of Arabia,* you're much sought out. I understand the girls really go for you."

O'Toole found her to be a rather serious actress with strong points of view about her image.

"I'm more than some curvaceous thing on the screen, but I never get a chance to prove myself. I'm told my range is limited. I end up linked with those blonde stereotypes like the murdered Marilyn Monroe or that horrible cow, Jayne Mansfield. I've even been called the Swedish Diana Dors—how disgusting, how depraved. Diana Dog Dors."

"Some producers are trying to find financing for a film about

Gorgeous, seductive Anita Ekberg, the Ice Goddess of the North, complained to O'Toole: "My outlandish publicity may actually run me out of the business. I feel like I'm portrayed as a freak."

Marlene Dietrich—now that's a role I could play. One creepy little guy wrote that Jane Russell and I are the personification, like Marilyn, of exaggerated female sexuality. As a blonde bombshell, I'm called 'pneumatic.'"

As O'Toole later recalled to Griffith, "What can I say about Anita Ekberg, the lover? She's all woman. She's not an athlete in bed like Diana Dors. But she delivers. She's very sensual, like she was in *La Dolce Vita.* She doesn't go in for kinky sex, but likes it the old-fashioned way. Well, maybe she *is* a bit kinky. When she felt that I was about to explode, she demanded that I do so between her breasts. 'After all, I'm a married woman,' she told me."

"Later, she said that if she ever got pregnant, she wanted her kid to look like Van Nutter, not some little pint-sized Peter O'Toole."

"The hundred pounds is yours," Griffith said. "You won it fair and square. You don't mind if I delay paying you for a month or so, do you?"

"I don't mind at all."

"By the way, are you really going to recommend her for one of the female roles in *What's New Pussycat?*"

"Hell, no! That was merely a tool of my seductive technique. I heard two nights ago that Clive Donner has already cast the women's roles. Are you ready for this? He's contracted Capucine, Paula Prentiss, Ursula Andress, and Romy Schneider. I'm going to try to bed all of them, but no more bets."

"Keep me posted."

"Who knows?" O'Toole said. "I might be chasing after Ursula Andress, beating that handsome devil, John Derek, my major competition. Either I'll get lucky or I won't. If bad luck sets in, after my winning streak with blondes, I might have to rape Woody Allen for relief."

"That would be a fate worse than death," Griffith said. "Could you imagine? Any man, woman, or child going to bed with a nerd who looks like Allen? Of course, he has talent."

Chapter 19

O'Toole Launches Britain's National Theatre With Hamlet—"The Worst Play Ever Written"

Its Director, Lord Laurence Olivier, Wanted Three Things from His Star:"Kisses, Sodomy, & the Best Hamlet Ever"

O'Toole's MacFlop (or "MacDeath") is Reviewed as "The Worst Performance in the History of the British Theatre"

At London's Old Vic in 1980, Peter O'Toole was disastrously cast as Macbeth. Before opening night, he said, "I will be either brilliant or plain, but I won't be mediocre. I'm prepared to walk out on that stage to face the lions eager to devour human flesh."

When Laurence Olivier cast Peter O'Toole as Hamlet in 1963 at the National Theatre, he told his wife, Joan Plowright: "I'm taking a considerable risk, and I hope I don't turn out to be a jerk. He's a known boozer and world-class hellraiser."

One night, two world class boozers, Richard Burton and Peter O'Toole, sat in a London pub, the Salisbury, "until neither of us was entirely sober," as O'Toole recalled. "After Dick's long sonnet to Elizabeth Taylor's tits, we got around to talking *Hamlet.* Both of us despised the play. In fact, I called it the worst play written since the dawn of time. But he and I were always masochists. Some nights we whipped each other's bare asses with belts, and you think I'm making that up. As masochists—catch my scene in *Lawrence of Arabia*—we agreed to do *Hamlet* again and get it out of our systems."

O'Toole as Hamlet with "poor Yorick" at the National Theatre's opening in 1963

"Before we sobered up the next day, we tossed a coin. On Broadway, John Gielgud would direct Burton in *Hamlet* when not trying to suck his dick, and Olivier would direct me in *Hamlet* in London when not trying to suck my dick."

After his pact with Burton, O'Toole the next day walked into Olivier's headquarters at the National Theatre. *[Positioned on the South Bank of the Thames, midway between the London Eye and the Tate Modern, the National Theatre opened in 1963 through the efforts and funding of the Arts Council of England. Today, one of its three auditoriums is named after (Lord) Laurence Olivier. At the time, since the massive theater was still being built, Olivier's headquarters were temporarily housed within a prefabricated hut.]*

O'Toole announced to Olivier that he was going to play Hamlet in the West End. Would Olivier direct?

Recognizing that he needed a big-name star, and that after the recent release of *Lawrence of Arabia* (1963), O'Toole was the biggest star in the world, Olivier agreed, but only if O'Toole would launch the play as the premiere performance within the National Theatre that upcoming autumn. O'Toole re-

"Theatre Critics are Slimy Bitches in Heat. . . They Don't Recognize Genius."
—Peter O'Toole

"The Press Turned on Me. They Brought Machine Guns to the Theatre."
—Peter O'Toole

sponded that he'd be delighted.

As the newly appointed Director of the National Theatre, Olivier had beat out Sir John Gielgud and Sir Ralph Richardson.

By ignoring the actors at Stratford-upon-Avon, who desperately wanted part of the spotlight, Olivier "serious pissed us off," one actor said.

Olivier countered that he needed "fresh blood and star power, both of which O'Toole represented, based on the success of *Lawrence of Arabia* and *Becket*. To me, Peter O'Toole represents the new generation of actors in the British Theatre."

At the Bristol Old Vic, O'Toole had appeared only in the shorter version, but for this grand opening of what was envisioned as the very essence of Britain's theatrical tradition, Olivier was demanding *Hamlet's* full, unabridged, five-hour version. The "five hour monster" would run nonstop every night except Sunday, with two afternoon matinees.

Even though O'Toole did not like to perform in the same play as his wife, Siân Phillips, Olivier nonetheless offered her the role of the teenaged Ophelia, even though she was thirty at the time. Apparently, O'Toole talked him out of casting Siân, and subsequently, Olivier hired Rosemary Harris instead.

As later related by Max Adrian, who played Pelonius, "O'Toole joined us in the cast with the stage still littered with rubble and mortar. There was a bloody enormous hole in one wall, which allowed the winds to blow in with hurricane force from Waterloo Road. It was frightfully uncomfortable and chaotic."

O'Toole was reported as "blissfully immune to the gravity of the enterprise, blithely indulging in practical jokes such as filling the dressing room showers with ice."

He was prone to idol worship of Olivier at the time, asserting that he had knelt at the veteran actor's shrine for years. "He sat on the top of Mount Everest and waved down at the Sherpas. He speaks from Olympian authority. I

Laurence Olivier as Macbeth

Laurence Olivier as Hamlet in 1947, at the very moment when a postwar Britain, battered and bruised, was re-affirming its cultural identity through what was going on in "The British Theatre."

know lesser farts in bigger organizations who brandish their puny accomplishment like a club."

In the final analysis, after he grew impatient with Olivier's commands, O'Toole said. "Larry tried to stretch me much farther than human skin will stretch. I did not fulfill his expectations. He asked too much from me. I've been bullied in life by bigger louts than Larry Olivier. He was faint in his praise, yet one afternoon in front of the cast, he told them, 'For the first time in living memory, we have seen the real Hamlet.'"

O'Toole as Hamlet with Rosemary Harris as Ophelia at the National Theatre in 1963.

O'Toole told Kenneth Griffith, "It's useless to argue with Olivier. He is the most persuasive bastard to ever draw breath. He almost convinced me that I was duty bound to plug him nightly. Such an old sod."

Later, O'Toole infuriated Olivier when he told the press that the veteran actor did not have much to contribute as a director. "He should stick to acting. He belongs in the stable as head stallion."

Unlike the rest of the cast, whose actors were bearded, O'Toole appeared clean-shaven with his hair dyed white.

He had not wanted to appear that way until he had to face "that gray-eyed myopic stare that can turn you into stone," a reference, of course, to Olivier's steely gaze.

One actor, 23-year-old Michael Gambon, cast as a spear-carrier, liked O'Toole's appearance, calling him "a god with bright blonde hair."

Throughout the production, Olivier constantly called O'Toole "Dear Boy" and kissed him frequently. It was obvious to the cast that the veteran actor desired O'Toole sexually. The only problem was, O'Toole did not view his director as a desired object for sex.

To O'Toole's surprise, Olivier's favorite word was "fucking."

"The fucking lights, the fucking curtain, everything was fucking," O'Toole claimed. "It not that, then bloody."

At one tense moment, O'Toole told Olivier, "I've been bullied by bigger shits than you." Then he walked off the stage. No doubt, he was referring to David Lean during the filming of *Lawrence of Arabia*. But the next day, he showed up on time and tried to do what Olivier wanted.

Olivier spared his praise, almost never giving it. He often expressed disappointment with O'Toole in rehearsal. Under such a stern taskmaster, O'Toole seemed to grow less and less confident before opening night.

Gielgud had recently slipped in to watch a rehearsal, and after his departure, O'Toole heard a rumor that backstage, Gielgud had confronted Olivier, telling him, "This dear Irish laddie is just not Hamlet. He won't do. Cut your losses and fire him."

Olivier refused to heed Gielgud's advice.

When O'Toole's friend, James Villiers, came backstage, he shared his doubts about Olivier. "I think on the one hand he wants me to succeed. Yet on the other hand, he hopes I'll go down in flames so that he can remain the definitive Hamlet...even though Gielgud claims that distinction for himself."

Poisoning the trough of anyone who dared to play Hamlet in his wake?

Gielgud as Hamlet, speaking in a voice defined as "a silver trumpet muffled in silk."

After nearly a century of struggle, the National Theatre had begun its life at London's Old Vic, where it had claimed squatter's rights.

October 22, 1963, represented a historic night for British Theatre. The curtain opened to reveal O'Toole performing the lead role in *Hamlet.* He'd been directed by the actor whose Hamlet had once been praised as the finest ever.

It was one of the most challenging moments of O'Toole's theatrical career. "I got through performing *Hamlet* by drinking four pints of beer before going onstage."

Actor Derek Jacobi, cast as Laertes, said, "O'Toole was wallowing in booze, terrifying me. I had to fight him in the last scene. If he gave me a wink, and he usually did, this wild Irishman meant a very hard fight. It was even dangerous to be sitting in the front row when he flashed out his sword like Douglas Fairbanks."

This bravado swashbuckling was dismissed by Edmund Gardner, the critic from the *Stratford-upon-Avon Herald.* He sniffed: "O'Toole holds his rapier like a billiard cue." The *Sunday Telegraph's* reviewer predicted, "Young men will now act *Hamlet* in their bathroom. Such narcissism is understandable in private. On stage, the actor who allows himself to fall in love with the role cannot avoid wallowing in self-indulgence."

Siân, who was in the audience on opening night, later claimed "Hamlet was a pale shadow of the performance O'Toole had given at the Bristol Old Vic. Larry seemed intent on making O'Toole look like a clean cut, well-dressed, young master. O'Toole went along with everything—pudding basin haircut, Lord Fauntleroy collar. I thought O'Toole was badly served by Larry."

During rehearsals, O'Toole had carefully followed all of Olivier's intricately plotted moves onstage. But on opening night, O'Toole betrayed the director and performed the role as he would have directed, instead.

Watching in horror, Olivier later poured out his woes to the critic Kenneth Tynan, whom he had seemingly forgiven "for all the bloody crap" he had written about Vivien," a reference, of course, to Olivier's former wife, Vivien Leigh.

"We'd mapped out the rhythms so carefully," Olivier said. "The scene that follows the graveyard has to go like lightning to bring it off. And O'Toole would be so sleepy in it that members of the audience, who had not fallen asleep, did so soon enough. They were now all asleep. He just didn't understand that he was fucking up my *Hamlet.* He was absolutely fucking up his chances for the last scene in the play, which was so all-important."

After the curtain went down, O'Toole told reporters, "I was sick with nerves. If you want to know what it's like to be lonely, really lonely, try playing Hamlet."

As he had stated in the program, Olivier viewed *Hamlet* as a "precursor" to *Look Back in Anger's* anti-hero, Jimmy Porter, a role played by O'Toole at the Bristol Old Vic in 1957.

The Times found Olivier's claim "curiously belittling," stating that O'Toole "had been miscast as Hamlet. *The Times* went on to say, "Mr. O'Toole is an electrifying outgoing actor, and it is a surprise to see him make his first appearance with his features twisted onto melancholy."

A visiting critic from the leading newspaper in Birmingham wrote, "The Prince's blondness and his curiously comic trousers are disconcerting."

When O'Toole read that, he said, "Bloody hell! Attacking my blondness. The fucking Prince of Denmark is a Dane. Blonde hair is not unknown in Denmark."

As Ophelia, Rosemary Harris got mixed reviews, one critic calling her "the most real and touching Ophelia." But writing for *The Evening News,* critic Felix Barker found her "an embarrassing deb who has had too much gin."

The Observer accused Olivier of "giving a heavyweight role to a lightweight actor."

Reporter Samantha Ellis wrote: "Olivier's weighty production warranted a weighty set: a monolithic staircase that left the *Daily Sketch's* critic "trying hard not to be grossly hysterical, such was his joy regarding this 'blinding piece of revolving poetic engineering.' In fact the Revolve problem proved so troublesome that it was nicknamed The Revolt. On opening night, the trap door jammed, and stagehands had to rush on to squirt it with oil."

R.B. Marriott, for *The Stage,* described O'Toole as a "magnificent prince," but other critics were not convinced. One reviewer said that O'Toole's "virile and pulsating performance left the audience bewildered about the true purpose of all the sound and fury."

Another wrote, "It is hard to think of a young actor less able to imply impotence than O'Toole."

Reporter Sylvia Morris commented on O'Toole's performance in previous Shakespearean plays, including that of Shylock in *The Merchant of Venice,* and Petruchio in *The Taming of the Shrew.* She said, "Nobody would wish Peter O'Toole the fate of Henry Irving, who died in the lobby of the Midland Hotel in Bradford just after coming off stage, or of Edmund Kean, who collapsed on stage into the arms of his son, Charles, while they were appearing in *Othello.*"

Harold Hobson of *The Sunday Times* claimed that "the manly, richly spoken *Hamlet* of Mr. O'Toole matched Sir Laurence's conception of the role." He also claimed that the Bard's words were given "their just weight and colour and measure."

The London *Times* called O'Toole's performance "ordinary, his features twisted."

Another reviewer was cruel. "Peter O'Toole has blown the launch of the National Theatre with a disgraceful performance of *Hamlet.*"

For the most part, the performance of Michael Redgrave as Claudius garnered raves.

To his friends and to his wife, O'Toole blamed the failure on Olivier. "I was too much under his influence, and he gave me bad advice. He beguiled me with his bloody tricks—wigs, short skirts, the uncut version."

Many critics claimed that as Hamlet, O'Toole "was too much of an angry young man, too rebellious."

The iconic play that had been conceived and configured as the premiere of England's National Theatre devolved into a personal humiliation for O'Toole. It ran for nine weeks.

With matinees scheduled and with long, almost unendurable hours on stage, delivering difficult lines in front of demanding audiences, O'Toole soon neared a state of complete exhaustion.

One night, a member of the cast gave him a tablet from a silver Victorian pillbox she always carried around. When it took effect, he recalled, "I was walking on the ceiling for two days and two nights. I was cuckooing and crowing from the rooftops, hurtling about and gamboling and jumping rope. I never shut my trap. I wept at the weather forecasts, even when they predicted sunny skies over England."

By play's end, O'Toole, in his words, "had been worn down to a pulp. I had dangerously lost weight and was on the verge of a nervous breakdown."

According to the *Daily Express,* stage celebrities loved the new-born theater. Lionel Bart told a journalist that he was hoping to make *Hamlet* into a musical.

Michael Redgrave to Olivier: "I was the only good thing in *Hamlet.*"

In a spoof, one reporter responded, "*Hamlet* as a musical?" I suggest Doris Day for Ophelia and Robert Goulet for Hamlet."

In 2013, the year O'Toole died, he made headlines when he opted not to show up for the National Theatre's 50th anniversary gala. Many other actors—including Rosemary Harris, Judi Dench, Maggie Smith, and Michael Gambon—agreed to reprise scenes from some of their best-loved roles.

Although O'Toole turned down the invitation for the 50th anniversary gala, Queen Elizabeth accepted. Reportedly, she was heard to say, "O'Toole should have come here tonight. I should have commanded him."

Macbeth, the Blood-Soaked Thane of Glamis
"O'Toole Makes Macbeth Sound like Bette Davis in 'What Ever Happened to Baby Jane?'"

"From its first performance on August 7, 1606, Shakespeare's bloody master-piece, Macbeth, *has been considered accursed by actors. On that first opening night, the young boy scheduled to play Lady Macbeth fell ill and died—and the Bard himself had to step into the role. At a more recent performance in London in 1934, the noted Shakespearean actor, Malcom Keen, suddenly lost his voice—and his replacement was hospitalized after one performance, with severe chills. Three years later at the Old Vic, Laurence Olivier broke a sword onstage during his performance. It flew into the audience, striking a patron, who suffered a heart attack."*

—*Fred Hauptführer*

"At his best, which is very good indeed, Peter O'Toole is an actor of great presence and power, constantly swimming against the tide. A romantic in nature, he finds much to criticize in the contemporary theatrical scene and can unleash laser beams of invective against the citadels of mediocrity. There's passion and violence behind the handsome mask.

"Flamboyant, a jeune premier in the classical mould, a tough matinée idol, a compelling and elegant actorish actor who needs firm handling. His destiny lies not in the mundane, but in the heroic. He is in the old-fashioned slang sense a major 'lardy,' a barnstorming character possessed of unlimited charm, which disarms the unwary."

—*Bryan Forbes, Director of* Macbeth

Aware of the risks in a role that was perhaps jinxed, Peter O'Toole, 48, set out to appear as Macbeth at London's Old Vic. He told reporters, "I was born to play this role. I've been obsessed with it. I felt the jinx when I was 17 and failed it at an audition. *Macbeth* is a brute. It is the famous brute."

***

It was Friday the 13th in late September, 1980, in Ireland. In his Toyota, O'Toole had left his home in Connemara in Ireland to drive to a rehearsal hall to meet the cast of *Macbeth*, due to open in London at the Old Vic.

Speeding at eighty miles an hour, as was his custom, he was racing along a cliffside road bordering the Atlantic.

At one point, he lost control of his car and crashed into a stone wall. Fortunately, it was thick and blocked his vehicle from plunging off the cliff down into the ocean.

After that harrowing experience, in which he had miraculously escaped with only minor injuries, he decided never to call the play *Macbeth* again. From then on, would order the cast to refer to the jinxed play as "Harry Lauder."

[Henry "Harry" Lauder (1870 – 1950) was a Scottish vaudevillian and comedian. Relentlessly cheerful, he was perhaps best known for his long-standing hit "I Love a Lassie" and for his international success. Described as "Scotland's greatest ever ambassador" by Winston Churchill, he eventually became the highest-paid performer in the world, and the first Scottish actor/performer to sell a million records.]

The next day, after O'Toole recovered and joined the other cast members, he was told that on the opening night of *Macbeth* in 1937 in London, Lilian Baylis, the founding *doyenne* of the Old Vic, suffered a fatal heart attack and died instantly.

Days later, Frances Tomelty, Sting's wife *[she was married to Sting from 1976-84]*, who had been cast as Lady Macbeth, was nearly killed when she was speeding on her motorcycle and hit a bump in the road and was thrown twelve feet. She was bruised and bloodied, but emerged with no broken bones.

"I almost ended up like your friend, T.E. Lawrence," she told O'Toole after she'd recovered from the accident.

At the time, Sting was dating an actress, Trudie Tyler *[whom he eventually married in 1992]*. He'd used his influence to get her cast as the First Witch in *Macbeth*. On the fourth day of rehearsals, he had to rush her to the nearest hospital. Her appendix had burst.

"We're getting off to a good start." O'Toole told the cast. "Which one of will be the first to die?"

As he flew to London, O'Toole had finally persuaded Fox to release his latest film, *The Stunt Man,* which had been shot in 1978 and held up for two years before its release. The executives at Fox didn't know what to make of the quirky movie in which O'Toole had been cast as a (presumably insane) film director.

When *The Stunt Man* was released in 1980, it had only a limited run, never finding a major audience. Yet sufficient numbers of members of the Academy saw fit to nominate O'Toole for the sixth time as Best Actor.

The prize that year went to Robert De Niro for his performance in *Raging Bull.*

O'Toole as Macbeth, with Trudie Tomelty as His Lady. "She wasn't really Milady. I just borrowed her for a while from Sting."

***

In London during rehearsals for *Macbeth*, O'Toole immediately tangled with Timothy West, an actor himself who for two years had signed a contract as artistic director of the Old Vic. But O'Toole was given unprecedented power as an associate producer there.

"I knew at the beginning that I was the wrong partner for O'Toole," West later wrote in a memoir. "We clashed over everything. What he wanted was a compliant business associate who would laugh with him, and make rude jokes about subsidized theatre. I just was not his man."

A member of the cast likened O'Toole and West as "a fighting man and a wife heading for the divorce court. It didn't help that O'Toole mockingly referred to West as Eddie Waring."

[Widely satirized for his folksy but controversial deliveries during his long career as a rugby commentator with the BBC, Eddie Waring was sometimes cited as a negative stereotype of what Londoners sometimes ridicule as the provincialism of northern England.]

At one point, O'Toole outrageously barred West from the Old Vic, even though he was its artistic director.

Bryan Forbes was brought in to direct, although he was known primarily for his film work. He wrote both novels and non-fiction, and had been head of film production for EMI at the Elstree Studios outside London.

He was a great admirer of O'Toole, who soon let Forbes know who was in charge of production. "It's my way or the highway," O'Toole told Forbes when he greeted him.

O'Toole said, "I want to present the bloodiest Macbeth in the history of the theatre. At one point I plan to come out dripping with blood and gore. Did you know if you stab a man, his blood can spurt as much as fifteen feet

Two views of Timothy West (left) in 2010, and (right photo), playing Falstaff.

into the air? Isn't that something, old darling? For the sword fight, I'm having the finest sword made in Toledo, Spain, delivered here. I'll be ready to behead Macduff."

Forbes found his star in a weakened condition, still recovering from the life-threatening operation on his intestines, during which, it was rumored, various tumors had been removed. Macbeth was widely acknowledged as one of the most physically challenging roles in the British theater.

Bryan Forbes with Katherine Ross in an episode of *The Stepford Wives*.

The new director was immediately drawn into the long-simmering feud between West and O'Toole. Forbes recalled, "I felt I'd stumbled into a nest of vipers."

O'Toole had first spotted actress Frances Tomelty at the Belfast Theatre. He thought the wife of Sting would make the ideal Lady Macbeth. "I was knocked out by her manner and the fierceness of her eyes. She fitted exactly what I had been carrying around in my head for months—a bloody eagle, tall and dark."

During the course of the play, O'Toole and Sting became good friends.

[At the time, the English musician, activist, and philanthropist— also known as Gordon Matthew Thomas Sumner—was the leader of the rock band The Police.*]*

Months later, Sting would write his hit song, "Demolition Man" during a sojourn with

Bryan Forbes with Margaret Thatcher

369

O'Toole in Connemara.

Throughout most of the run of *Macbeth*, O'Toole dated Trudie Styler, cast as the rather glamorous First Witch. But somewhere along the way, Trudie caught the eye of Sting, although he was married to Tomelty at the time. But following his divorce from her, Styler became Sting's second wife.

Reporters found out about O'Toole's link to Styler during the run of the play and asked about it. "I'm divorced from Siân Phillips, and I have no plans to get married again—for ever and ever."

"What about your romantic life?" asked a journalist from *The Daily Mail*.

"The odd little thing here and there, no more, no less," O'Toole responded. "I'm good at picking fast women and slow horses."

Cast as Banquo, the very robust, very large Brian Blessed became O'Toole's close friend during rehearsals.

Trudie Styler with her husband, Sting, at a benefit for the Rainforest Foundation.

"I dated her before Sting got around to her," O'Toole claimed.

"He's a massive man with massive humor," O'Toole said. "A skilled fighter, amazing, exciting, and hugely intelligent. He's very sexy, with a deep voice. When he calls out to you, the whole house shakes. He's built like a bear and absolutely terrifies me, darling."

Princess Margaret Suggests "More Bloody Blood"

Princess Margaret, whose favorite Shakespearean play was *Macbeth*, could not attend O'Toole's opening night because of a conflicting engagement. So through O'Toole, she arranged to attend one of the final rehearsals.

[Glamis Castle in Scotland has long enjoyed a legendary link to British royalty. It's made clear at the beginning of the tragedy, that Macbeth is the Thane (Lord) of Glamis. Queen Elizabeth, the Queen Mother, was reared here. Her daughter, Elizabeth II, spent a lot of her childhood here. And Princess Margaret, the Queen's younger sister, was born here, becoming the first Royal Princess born in Scotland in three centuries. The existing castle was built in stages from the 14th to the 17th centuries, with many of its luxurious interiors dating from the 18th and 19th centuries, based on massive expenditures from

the Earls of Strathmore, heirs by marriage to a coal-mining fortune.]

By 1980, O'Toole had long ago ended his affair with the princess, but their friendship had remained intact.

After watching the rehearsal, she came backstage to congratulate him. But she had a suggestion. In spite of the fact that O'Toole had emerged in one scene dripping with stage blood, Margaret Rose called "for more Kensington gore, more bloody blood."

[Kensington gore was the British name for stage blood, the type used in all those old British Hammer horror films.]

"We use lots of it in all those demonstrations for the St. John's Ambulance Brigade," she said. "It's so realistic."

Margaret Rose in 1969

"I was born in Glamis Castle," Margaret had jokingly told O'Toole, "and I've come to remove Macbeth's curse."

Twenty minutes before the curtain went up, Forbes dropped into O'Toole's dressing room, finding him sitting there naked except for the *Gauloise* he was smoking.

"Peter, dear boy," Forbes said. "Aren't you leaving it a bit late not getting into your bloody outfit? They've called the quarter."

"Can't wear it, darling," O'Toole said. "My outfit is hopeless."

"A little late to tell me," Forbes said. Not knowing what to do, Forbes sought out Brian Blessed, a close friend of O'Toole's.

When O'Toole emerged on stage with glasses, he wore a slime-green jogging suit and gym shoes. An uncomfortable murmur emerged from the audience, everyone seeming to suspect that he was drunk.

During the performance, laughter rang through the audience. There were whispers of "*Macbeth* the Comedy."

One reporter later noted, "Passing in front of the theater, a pedestrian would have thought that the Old Vic was having a Jerry Lewis Festival."

"Prepare for the worst," O'Toole had warned the cast.

Timothy West said it might have been worse. Originally, O'Toole wanted inflatable scenery, blow-up backdrops from an Irish company that could "fit into the boot of the car."

The designer had arrived from Ireland and carefully set up his inflatables. "The curtain rose to reveal a dimly lit collection of black phalluses swaying in the wind," West wrote in his autobiography.

When, mercifully, the curtain went down on opening night, critics rushed to file the most disastrous reviews O'Toole had seen during the course of his career. Some of them retitled the production "*MacDeath*" or "*MacFlop*."

"Campy, rowdy, overblown," O'Toole's *Macbeth* was described as "the most ridiculous thing I have ever seen on the London stage," wrote the Dublin-based critic Sean O'Hara about his fellow Irishman. His review was broadcast.

The first review to reach O'Toole from Fleet Street attacked the play as "ludicrous, about as subtle as a battering ram."

Jack Tinker of the *Daily Mail* wrote "O'Toole's voice was a combination of Bette Davis in *What Ever Happened to Baby Jane?* and of Vincent Price "hamming up a Hammer horror film. The three witches are transformed into glamorous extras felled from some abandoned *Brides of Dracula.*"

The prestigious *Sunday Times* trumpeted, "Mr. O'Toole's performance is deranged."

One by one, the attacks increased their venom. Critic Michael Billington claimed "O'Toole delivers every line with a monotonous tenor bark as if addressing an audience of deaf Eskimos."

Nor did blood-drenching O'Toole impress Robert Cushman. "Chances are he likes the play, but his performance suggests that he is taking some kind of personal revenge on it."

Another review claimed that "Eradicating the unnecessary tragic aspects that have always weighed down the play, the cast sent the first night audiences home rocking with laughter."

When the last attack from Fleet Street was read, O'Toole announced, "I came unstuck publicly and bloodily. Public crucifixion is not fun. My nose is bleeding as I think of it. Yet audiences packed the stalls for the spectacle. It took many months, but we finally got it right."

Under heavy fire, O'Toole defended himself, saying that was the way that the play should have been performed—"rather broadly, my darling, back in Shakespeare's day." Then, with a deliberate barb aimed at the Royal Shakespeare Company, he railed against the "bloodless, boring character of subsidized theatre in England."

News about the disastrous opening night of O'Toole's *Macbeth* reached Katharine Hepburn in New York. She phoned O'Toole at his home in Hampstead. "Peter, dear, if you're going to have a disaster, make it a big one!"

While touring the United States with *Camelot,* Richard Burton phoned the next day.

> BURTON: I hear you've had a bit of stick from the critics. How are the houses?
> O'TOOLE: Packed.
> BURTON: Then remember, my boy, you are the most original actor to come out of Britain since the war and fuck the critics. Think of every

four-letter obscenity, six-, eight-, ten-, and twelve-letter expletives and ram them right up their envious arses, in which I'm sure there is ample room. I love you.

O'TOOLE: I love you too, Dickie boy.

Conditions got even worse on the third night of *Macbeth*. The Old Vic received a bomb threat and the theater was emptied. After a search, the scare was dismissed as a hoax. About an hour later, the curtain went up, but shortly thereafter, another bomb threat was called in. This time, the theater was emptied, and the price of every ticket was refunded at the box office.

Five months later, O'Toole issued his own final verdict. "I was a total fuck-up. It was a disaster. To think about it makes my nose bleed. Banging into the scenery, forgetting my lines, and coming out one night in tennis shoes, wearing my glasses were not what The Bard had envisioned."

William Shakespeare

O'Toole as Hamlet in 1963, for the launch of Britain's National Theatre

Britain's National Theatre, on the River Thames' South Bank

Chapter 20

O'Trouble South of the (U.S.) Border

Chasing Iguanas With Burton and Taylor in Mexico

O'Toole's Torrid, Tequila-Soaked Nights With Ava Gardner & a Mexican Spitfire; His Portrayals of Eccentrics in Distress: A Romanian Aristocrat Fleeing World War 2,, & Robinson Crusoe Fleeing from Savages

Peter O'Toole flew to Mexico to visit his friends on the set of *The Night of the Iguana.* He fell in love with a local Mexican girl, and witnessed first hand the off-screen dramas that unfolded "South of the Border."

"Everybody was doing everybody else and drinkng an agave brandy stronger than tequila. Ava Gardner called it 'cactus piss.'"

Richard Burton and Elizabeth Taylor were snapped by a *papparazzo* as they were leaving a bar in Puerto Vallarta.

Elizabeth told O'Toole, "I was dead when I encountered Richard on the set of *Cleopatra* in Rome. It was a case of Prince Charming kissing the Sleeping Princess, who'd slept through four years of marriage to that fucking *schmuck*, Eddie Fisher."

Before flying to Puerto Vallarta in Mexico to join his friends, Elizabeth Taylor and Richard Burton, Peter O'Toole dined with Tennessee Williams at Barney's Beanery in L.A. on Santa Monica Boulevard.

"I always come here because of the sign," the playwright said, pointing to the wall where a sign read "FAGOTS *(sic)* STAY OUT."

Iguana

"From the outside, I thought this *cantina* was ready for the bulldozer," O'Toole said. "Now that I'm inside, I'm convinced of it."

The waiter had seated Williams in his favorite corner, the exact spot where Jean Harlow, Gary Cooper, and Clara Bow used to dine. Williams told O'Toole that since he was headed for Mexico, he should consider ordering tacos and enchiladas.

O'Toole had accepted an invitation to join Burton, who had been cast in the leading role in the screen adaptation of Williams' play, *The Night of the Iguana.* It was clearly understood that he would not be performing opposite Elizabeth (who would basically be relegated to the role of a spectator on the set), but with Ava Gardner and Deborah Kerr. The production would be directed from a locale near Puerto Vallarta by John Huston.

During its run on Broadway, *The Night of the Iguana* had starred Bette Davis (wearing an orange fright wig) and Margaret Leighton. In the stage version, Patrick O'Neal had played the male lead, that of a defrocked priest working as a tour guide to a group of (obnoxious) American tourists on a bus tour of Mexico.

That afternoon, whether it was true or not, Williams claimed at Barney's that he'd recommended O'Toole for the role that eventually went to Burton. "Of course, the producer went for the marquee name, and Burton was selected in your place."

"The stage version of *Iguana* did not win the Tony," Williams said. "Those idiots gave it to your friend, Robert Bolt, for that middle-brow British historical play, *A Man for All Seasons.*" [*Williams knew that Bolt had also written the script for* Lawrence of Arabia.*"*

"I fear I'm becoming *passé* in the American theater," Williams confessed to O'Toole. "My pseudo-literary style of writing seems to be fading."

In his self-assessment, Williams was right. *Iguana* would be his last and final hit on Broadway.

"To me, you will always be Broadway royalty," O'Toole said. "I can't imagine you ever being deposed."

"I wouldn't be the first queen who lost her throne," Williams said.

Scripted and On Camera, O'Toole Kills Cannibals
Off-Screen and Unscripted, He Devours Flesh of Another Kind

After drinks on the Sunset Strip, Williams gave O'Toole a kiss and promised to meet with him again in Puerto Vallarta, "when we both call on our world-famous Elizabeth."

***

Unannounced, O'Toole slipped into Puerto Vallarta, the then-undiscovered fishing port on Mexico's Pacific coast, where he became a guest of the Burtons at their villa. Over drinks, Elizabeth told him that their recent arrival at the local airport had devolved into pandemonium. "The press treated us like we were the Beatles," she said.

"The press here is against us," Burton said. "Some people in the government are demanding that we be deported."

[Previously, Burton had told the Mexican press, "This is my first visit to Mexico. I hope it will be my last."]

"And, ducky, what brilliant thing did you say to the press?" Burton asked Elizabeth.

She answered, "I told them, 'I have always wanted to come back to fucking Mexico. I like fucking Mexico.'"

O'Toole laughed uproariously.

"I was not the first choice to play the defrocked priest," Burton said. "Huston wanted Marlon Brando, and the producer, Ray Stark, wanted your friend, Richard Harris, or even William Holden."

After a night of heavy drinking, O'Toole was shown to his bedroom after being told their neighborhood near the port was called Gringo Gulch, because a number of expatriate Americans had purchased homes here.

"I call this place *La Casa de Zoplotes,* or *the House of Buzzards,* because we're near a garbage dump," Elizabeth said.

The next morning, before O'Toole got up, Burton had left for the set. He shared breakfast with Elizabeth before they headed by boat to the isolated peninsula of Mismaloya, where the actual shooting was happening. It was inaccessible by road to other parts of the Mexican mainland.

Casa Kimberly, in Puerto Vallarta, was the residence purchased by Richard Burton and Elizabeth Taylor. Linked by a bridge, her home was on the north side of a narrow street, and his was on the south.

Elizabeth sold the house in 1990, leaving most of her personal possessions behind. Today, it's operated as a B&B, the rooms named after some of her leading films.

With her, O'Toole waded through chickens, naked children, and mange-encrusted mongrel dogs. He carried a picnic basket for lunch with Burton.

377

Once they were on the set, he renewed his acquaintance with Huston, who was in Puerto Vallarta with his mistress, Zoe Sallis.

Huston startled him by telling O'Toole, "I'm considering casting you and Ava in one of my upcoming films, but I'm not ready to spill the beans just yet."

To O'Toole at the time, that sounded like an idle non-commitment.

"I'm glad to be working with Ava again," Huston said, "since our last film, *The Killers*. She's still as untamed as ever, earning her hedonistic reputation. She drinks, smokes, and dances, smokes, and then fucks into the wee hours. Right now, she's auditioning some Mexican beach boys."

Depicted above is Deborah Kerr, one of *Iguana's* co-stars, with her husband, screenwriter Peter Viertel, the former lover of Ava Gardner, another of the film's co-stars.

Commenting on the potential for explosive, off-the-record confrontations, Kerr said, about her husband, "I try to keep him away from temptation."

Over coffee, O'Toole was introduced to Deborah Kerr. She whispered to him, "I'm the only one on the set who isn't having a clandestine affair. My husband, Peter Viertel, is here. But before me, he had an affair with Ava."

"Who hasn't?" O'Toole asked.

"You too?" I should have known," Kerr said.

O'Toole was drawn to Kerr, finding her the most grounded and sympathetic of all the people working on the film. She referred to the dozens of lurid press reports being filed at the time as "moronic muck."

"I feel like Hannah Jelkes, the character I'm playing in the movie. Nothing human disgusts me unless it is unkind or violent."

She had nothing but praise for her fellow actors, calling Gardner "funny and rich and warm and human as well as beautiful. She brings just the right kind of self-mockery to her role. Elizabeth is generous and sweet, friendly, also warm and impulsive. Richard is sensitive and great fun, with the sense of humor and humility of a really great artist."

After his first talk with Kerr, O'Toole grabbed her and kissed her, which startled her. "The next time we meet, and I'm sure we will, and providing you're not married to Peter, and I'm not married to Siân, let's you and I get married. You're the kind of woman I've searched a lifetime for and never found, the very epitome of good English breeding and refinement."

"Stewart Granger told me the same thing, so why did he run off with Jean Simmons?"

"A question for the ages, my darling," he said.

Huston also introduced O'Toole to Sue Lyon, who played the much chaperoned nymphet in *Night of the Iguana.* To O'Toole, the night before, Burton had confessed, "I've already made it with her, and I think Elizabeth suspects something."

Lyon had arrived in Puerto Vallarta with her boyfriend, Hampton Fancher III. He was once described as "a tall, pale youth ravaged by love." In reference to anyone's attempt to win her affections, he had warned Burton, "I tend to be murderously inclined."

O'Toole told Lyon, "I will forever detest Stanley Kubrick for not giving me the James Mason role opposite you in *Lolita* (1962). I'm sure we would have had great sexual chemistry on the screen. No one could have acted more repulsed by love-starved Shelley Winters than me. And as for jailbait you, I would have been most convincing as a pedophile."

At three o'clock, Gardner appeared on the set since she hadn't been needed earlier that day. Seeing O'Toole, she ran up and gave him a passionate kiss. "Remember me, shugah?"

"You are unforgettable," he told her, embracing her warmly.

"I do repeats, darlin'," she said.

"I was counting on that."

In the distance, they witnessed Elizabeth and Burton having an argument. She turned to O'Toole. "Elizabeth and Richard are the Frank Sinatra and Ava Gardner of the 1960s."

She told him, "John hasn't come on to me like he usually does. Perhaps I'm losing my appeal. I hope he's cured. He seduced this Neo-Nazi woman in London who gave him syphilis. He calls it 'the Hitler clap.'"

That evening, O'Toole dressed in a white suit for dinner and descended the stairs of the Burton/Taylor villa. As he passed the entrance to their bedroom, he heard the sounds of their argument, eerily evoking a battle in one of their future movies, *Who's Afraid of Virginia Wolff?* (1966).

It was clearly audible that the fight was

John Huston (left) with Tennessee Williams on the set of *Iguana*.

Iguana's playwright told its director, "I'm here shacked up with the last hustler-lover of Marilyn Monroe. José Bolaños. He wants me to make him a movie star."

379

over his "fucking Ava Gardner, that Tarheel Bitch," in Elizabeth's screeching accusation.

Downstairs, O'Toole joined the popular columnist James Bacon, a fellow guest who was in Puerto Vallarta to cover the shooting of the film. He was telling Huston that the other night, he had witnessed Burton downing twenty-five straight shots of tequila, using Casa Blanca beer as a chaser.

Bacon informed O'Toole that Tennessee Williams had arrived in town that afternoon.

When asked by a member of the press about the ongoing rosters of Burton/Taylor scandals, the playwright answered, "They are artists on a special pedestal and therefore bourgeois morality does not apply to them."

"That's my credo exactly," O'Toole told Bacon.

"Elizabeth today told me there are more press guys in Puerto Vallarta than iguanas," Bacon said. "I'm going to be kinder in my stories than the Mexican press boys will be in theirs."

He showed O'Toole an article that had appeared about the filming of *Night of the Iguana* in the Mexican newspaper, *Siempre,* translating it for him as follows: "We deplore the wanton sex in its many variations, the heavy drinking, the use of drugs, the illicit vice, and carnal bestiality of that gringo garbage that has descended on our country—a motley crew of gangsters, nymphomaniacs, and heroin addicts."

Out on the terrace, Huston told O'Toole, "I've dealt with Bogie, so I know how to handle difficult, temperamental personalities. Williams is an odd bird, always in flight. He can also 'fly' off the handle at just a perceived insult. Not only that, but he's an eccentric, a sex addict, a pill pusher, an alcoholic, and, perhaps, a genius. I'm sure he'll soon be buying every good-looking hustler hanging around the bars."

At around midnight, a tequila-soggy O'Toole went to bed. He decided that Elizabeth and Burton had made up, judging by the sounds of love-making emanating through their walls.

The next day, he journeyed, once again by boat, to the peninsula for another day of filming. There were no picnic baskets to carry, as Elizabeth had arranged for the food to arrive later.

Long ago and far away from their present filming gig in Puerto Vallarta, Elizabeth and Michael Wilding had actually been married AND produced a Michael, Jr.

Right before the noon break, he was startled to see Michael Wilding arriving with the foodstuff. Elizabeth's divorced husband had been hired as an assistant to Burton's agent, Hugh French. This former luminary of the English box office had been reduced to a role as "gopher" on the set of *Night of the Iguana*. He'd just arrived from Los Angeles, accompanied with containers of chili from Chasen's in Los Angeles, purveyors of some of Elizabeth's favorite foods.

Frank Merlo (left) and Tennessee Williams were photographed at their home in Key West, where he had written *The Night of the Iguana*.

"Three packages of cigarettes a day have done Frankie in," Williams told O'Toole.

"Imagine having chile and beans flown from California to Mexico," O'Toole marveled in front of Huston. "Isn't that like shipping coal to Newcastle?"

Accompanying Wilding was a beautiful Swedish actress, Karen von Unge, whom O'Toole assumed was Elizabeth's replacement.

That night at their villa, Burton and Taylor invited O'Toole to yet another of their dinner parties, this one in honor of the arrival of Tennessee Williams. He'd flown in on the arm of a very young Frederick Nicklaus, who Williams was billing as "the world's greatest living poet." *[Williams had stashed José Bolaños in a separate villa.]*

Before the Burtons made their usual very late arrival at (their own) dinner party, O'Toole got to drink and talk once again with Williams.

Perhaps as a means of flattering him, the playwright proclaimed, "In so many ways, you are the very *persona* who could interpret some of my more difficult roles, especially those I plan to write in the future. Don't tell Elizabeth this, but I always believed that you'd have been far better than her friend, Monty Clift, as the doctor in *Suddenly, Last Summer*. I heard that you were considered as a standby in case poor drugged-out Monty couldn't make it through the film. I found his performance very wooden. With those shaking hands of his, he couldn't have performed a lobotomy on anyone. You would have brought to the role the sensitivity and dimension it needed."

Williams went on to say that in the future, he'd like to see him star in a play he was working on, *The Milk Train Doesn't Stop Here Anymore*.

"Its main character is Flora Goforth, a once-celebrated actress who is now an indefatigable dying monster, dictating her memoirs to her secretary."

"I want you to play Christopher Flanders, a sweet-talking 'angel of death,' the author of a slim volume of poetry and the maker of mobiles. He's an interloper at Flora's villa. He trespasses on her privacy. He hopes to bring her some kind of salvation that will assuage her desire, and ease her out of life. You would be both a seer and a seducer, a saintly angel and a predatory hustler, combining the elements of con man and mystic."

"I envision you as a reed thin, willowy, almost ethereal character," Williams continued.

"It sounds like my name is written all over the character," O'Toole said.

O'Toole was pre-empted by Tab Hunter for the role of a young gigolo to...

"You dear man," Williams said. "On this tequila-soaked night, let's seal our understanding with a lover's kiss, even though we're not lovers. I can dream, can I not?" Then he kissed O'Toole on the lips before wandering off to the living room to join the other guests.

[A few months later, in 1964, O'Toole read that The Milk Train Doesn't Stop Here Any More *was being produced on Broadway. He tried to get through on the phone to Williams, but his calls were never returned.*

Under casting news, he read that Tallulah Bankhead would play the dying monster—no doubt based on her own life—with Tab Hunter, the golden Blonde Adonis of all those 1950 movies, as the hustler/poet.

...The spectacularly temperamental Tallulah Bankhead. Might O'Toole have handled the diva better than Hunter as the itinerant Angel of Death?

"Tab Hunter!" O'Toole exclaimed. "I can't believe it."

"My humiliation wasn't over. Later, I heard that Burton and Taylor were making the movie version of that play, the title by then changed to Boom! *It was the miscasting of the decade."*

"So much for the promises of a drunken playwright."]

The following afternoon, in Puerto Vallarta, O'Toole and Elizabeth went to the beach. She wore a white bathing suit evocative of the one she'd worn during her famous beach scene in

The Milk Train Doesn't Stop Here Anymore flopped. Perhaps O'Toole might have made it work.

Suddenly, Last Summer.

After less than an hour, they were attacked by *chigoes,* tropical fleas that burrow into the skin. By nightfall, both of them were so irritated and itchy that they could not sleep. She could not arrange an appointment with a doctor until 9AM the following morning.

In the doctor's office, he had to surgically remove the invading parasites from deep within their skin. He warned them that if they had not completed this procedure, that the fleas might have multiplied and invaded their bloodstreams.

In spite of this and other difficulties, O'Toole fell in love with Puerto Vallarta, sharing Burton's enthusiasm for the place. He had also enjoyed sampling three prostitutes who had come up from Acapulco to service *Iguana's* film crew.

A three-way? In Puerto Vallarta? Fueled by agave tequila? If only it had been filmed.

Burton told him that he and Elizabeth had paid only $40,000 for a sprawling villa in Gringo Gulch, and that he knew of one that O'Toole might buy for even less.

"And servants can be had here for virtually nothing," Burton claimed.

Before his return to Los Angeles, O'Toole had agreed to become a property owner in Mexico.

For his final night, Gardner invited O'Toole and the Burtons to the Casablanca Bar. Elizabeth had known Gardner since their days as MGM contract players. They'd often seduced the same man, notably Frank Sinatra. Perhaps Elizabeth had forgiven Ava for seducing Burton during the filming of *Iguana.* Perhaps not. But at the last minute, she backed out, blaming her nonappearance on a bout of *"turista."*

O'Toole, however, joined Gardner and Burton at the bar. Up until then, Gardner had been flirting with O'Toole, and he'd flirted back. But Ava had failed to extend an invitation to him to spend the night with her at her rented villa.

At the Casablanca Bar, she looked ravishing. She introduced O'Toole to the local version of moonshine, a throat-scalding liquor distilled from the agave plant. Known locally as *raicilla,* Gardner called it "cactus piss—and it's stronger than tequila."

As a trio, these famous stars then proceeded to get intoxicated.

Behind the bar was a string of cabins that were usually rented out as hot beds.

By midnight, Gardner suggested that the three of them retire together to a cabin. "There's a fire raging inside me," she told them, "and I think that it will take two stout-hearted men, a Welshman and an Irishman, to extinguish the flame."

As O'Toole later informed Jules Buck, his business partner, "Ava was right. It took the both of us to satisfy her that night. At least I got a chance to see up close and personal Burton's love-making techniques. I even learned a lesson or two."

Buck said, "Oh, my God, with all those reporters swarming all over Puerto Vallarta, the jerks missed the hottest story of all, a three-way with you, Richard, and Ava. If only it had been filmed."

Robinson Crusoe Vs. His Man Friday, O'Toole Interacts With Hollywood's Then-Hottest Action Hero

Jack Gold, the London-born film and TV director, successfully negotiated with Jules Buck for O'Toole to star in a 1975 remake of the Daniel Defoe novel, *Robinson Crusoe,* scheduled for shooting in Mexico.

Entitled *Man Friday,* it would represent a substantial reworking of the Defoe novel, a sort of role reversal wherein O'Toole's Crusoe would be a blunt, stiff, and somewhat inflexible Englishman. In marked contrast, Crusoe's "Man Friday" would show more intelligence, more diplomacy, and greater amounts of empathy.

Defoe had published *Robinson Crusoe* in 1719. In time, it became a worldwide bestseller, spawning future se-

In *Man Friday,* Peter O'Toole (standing) captures Richard Roundtree, who was awaiting death and consumption by cannibals.

Before the end of the film, which some critics viewed as an ironic commentary on cultural imperialism, O'Toole, as Robinson Crusoe, morphs him into a servant, teaches him to speak English, and converts him to Christianity.

quels for the stage and ultimately, for film and TV.

Many readers thought the book was based on a true story, but in reality, it was a work of fiction formatted as an autobiography. A castaway, Crusoe spends years on a tropical Caribbean island (probably Tobago, the sister island of modern-day Trinidad). Here, he encounters cannibals, captives, and mutineers.

The film's screenplay had been adapted by Adrian Mitchell from the script of his successful 1973 play. O'Toole knew this English poet, novelist, and playwright, as they had lived concurrently in the north of London and on occasion, took walks together.

[A dedicated pacifist, Mitchell was known as a peacemaker whose work demolished royalty and satirized cultural fashions. He was a noted figure on the British Left and the foremost poet of the "Ban the Atomic Bomb" movement. He was also the first to publish an interview with the Beatles. In London, The Guardian had cited Mitchell for successfully combining the "legacies of William Blake and Bertolt Brecht, which coalesce with the zip of Little Richard and the swing of Chuck Berry."

It was Mitchell who famously translated, from German into English, for staging by the Royal Shakespeare Company, The Persecution and Assassination of Jean-Paul Marat as Performed by the Inmates of the Asylum of Charenton Under the Direction of the Marquis de Sade, *a title usually shortened to* Marat/Sade, *by Peter Weiss. Critics defined it as an overview of class struggle and human suffering.]*

Mitchell convinced O'Toole that his role in *Man Friday* would be a career-defining moment and an attack on the "lunacy of western civilization. I see an Oscar in your future, not just a nomination."

O'Toole with Roundtree in *Man Friday.*

Its screenwriter, Adrian Mitchell, had convinced O'Toole that the film would become a career-defining event for him and an attack on the "lunacy of Western civilization. I see an Oscar in your future, not just a nomination."

***

At O'Toole's household, in preparation for his filming of *Man Friday,* Siân and daughters, Kate and Pat, helped him pack for his trip. He was eager for a return to Mexico, having fallen in love with it based on his previous visit to the set of the film version of *The Night of the Iguana.*

In a memoir, Siân expressed her feelings of how she felt about sending O'Toole off to Mexico. "When the day came to say goodbye to him, I felt I was saying goodbye to him forever. I had been incapable of making him understand what I felt, how urgently I needed to be with him now. He had a hard task ahead of him, and I could read the determination in his face and in the set of his shoulders. He would not yield to weakness. He would survive whatever the cost. I admired him for that, but I was admiring him as I would a stranger and that left me desolate."

In Hollywood, before continuing on to Mexico, Gold, in his capacity as director, introduced O'Toole to his co-star, Richard Roundtree, cast as his Man Friday. After meeting him, O'Toole said, "That buck is nobody's man except his own. What a guy, a formidable powerhouse to act opposite."

Even dressed like this, O'Toole —whose diction always remained perfect—managed to convey the ironies and eccentricities of a British Imperialist.

Roundtree was known as "the first black action hero," for his portrayal of the private detective, John Shaft, in the 1971 movie, *Shaft.* Its success had led to two sequels whose style eventually came to be identified as *"blaxploitation"* movies.

After appearing with O'Toole, Roundtree would go on to star as the slave, Sam Bennett, in the 1977 TV series, *Roots.* He would also play opposite Laurence Olivier in *Inchon* in 1981.

Having rehearsed for a week in Hollywood, filming in Mexico took only five weeks.

It included some health problems for each of its two stars. Once afternoon, an exhausted O'Toole fell asleep on the ground, only to wake up, screaming, shortly thereafter. He had fallen asleep on an active ant colony, whose members were in a stinging mood. "I was practically devoured," he later said.

Roundtree became dangerously sick for three days with a fever, but recovered.

Throughout the shoot, O'Toole complained of stomach cramps, Gold dismissing his concern and blaming it on the Mexican diet. "Down here, the Mexicans call it 'Montezuma's revenge,'" Gold said. But soon, O'Toole would realize that his pain had nothing to do with the local cuisine.

He enjoyed working with the crew, often joking with them or perhaps delivering impressions of famous English stage performers.

Watching the final cut, Gold had higher hopes for the film than O'Toole did. It was the British entry in the Cannes Film Festival of 1975.

Six minutes of the film were cut, including a controversial scene where

O'Toole commits suicide at the end by pressing his toe onto the trigger of his musket.

There had been talk of Academy Award nominations until the reviews came in. Most of them were harsh, relieved only occasionally by praise.

Rotten Tomatoes described *Man Friday* as "a subversively satirical variation on the Robinson Cruse tale, a cheeky critique of colonization, race relations, and class struggle."

Roger Ebert called the film "an unfortunate attempt to turn it into a fable for our times. Instead of a story of survival, we get a metaphor in which everything in the movie has to serve the ultimate, and murky, meaning."

During the second week of *Man Friday's* filming in Mexico, O'Toole had fallen in love for the second time in his life.

O'Toole Confronts Quentin Crisp—England's Most Stately Homo—One Who Opposes Gay Liberation

In Hollywood during rehearsals and pre-production of *Man Friday*, Jules Buck, O'Toole's business partner, and the star himself confronted a star of a different stripe. He was the flamboyant homosexual, Quentin Crisp, who had widely defined himself as "England's Most Stately Homo."

In 1975, Jack Gold directed two films, not only *Man Friday*, but *The Naked Civil Servant*, a TV movie based on the 1968 autobiography of Quentin Crisp, starring John Hurt.

In his brief talk with Crisp, O'Toole found him "absolutely enchanting, a creature from another time." He invited the flamboyant writer and raconteur to dinner with Buck and himself, planning to "turn heads at Chasens" as they marched in, led by the *maître d'*.

Over dinner, which Crisp called a Roman feast, the aging Englishman told them stories about his life, which he had begun as an effeminate young man walking the streets in full makeup, with lipstick, which he later called "Betty Grable fuck-me." He wore open-toed sandals as a means of showing his painted toenails, which sometimes matched his fingernail polish.

He claimed he earned his living as a "rent boy for sodomites" and also by posing nude for art classes. "One woman artist told me that I was very thin, with skin so white it almost had a greenish tinge," Crisp claimed.

Crisp's opinions shocked O'Toole, who did not shock easily.

Despite being a victim of homophobic street attacks for years, Crisp was still opposed to gay liberation. "What do they want liberation from? What is there to be proud of? I don't believe in rights for homosexuals. Homosexuality is a terrible disease."

O'Toole would adhere to that outrageous opinion, plus others, for years.

[Another of Crisp's controversial critiques focused on Princess Diana, wife of Britain's Prince Charles. Crisp said, "She was Lady Diana before she was Princess Diana, so she knew the racket. She knew that royal marriages have nothing to do with love. You marry a man and you stand beside him on public occasions, and for that you never have a financial worry until the day you die."

When the Princess died in a car crash in Paris in 1997, Crisp asserted, "Her fast and shallow lifestyle led to her demise. She could have been the Queen of England—and she was swanning about Paris with Arabs. What disgraceful behavior. Going about saying she wants to be the Queen of Hearts. The vulgarity of it is so overpowering."]

Of Quentin Crisp, O'Toole said, "I thought I was dining with Oscar Wilde reincarnate. Even when Joan Collins paraded in with her party, she did not upstage Crisp. All eyes were on our table."

At the end of the dinner, when Buck went to talk to the manager about an upcoming private party, Crisp told O'Toole, "During World War II, I provided lip service to at least a thousand Yanks during the black-outs in London. My seductions inspired my love of all things American. Their kindness and open-mindedness to me made me adore them. If you'd like to experience what all those G.I.s enjoyed during the war, perhaps you'll invite me back to your hotel tonight?"

"As enticing as that sounds, I must respectfully decline," O'Toole said.

In 1976, O'Toole went to see Crisp make his debut as a film actor in the Royal College of Art's low-budget production of *Hamlet.* He played Polonius in the same production of Shakespeare's play in which Helen Mirren appeared as Ophelia.

In 1992, O'Toole also went to see him play Elizabeth I, outfitted in full Tudor drag, in *Orlando* (1992).

Once, during an interview, O'Toole was asked what book he was reading at the time. He answered, "*How to Become a Virgin,* by Quentin Crisp."

O'Toole Falls in Love with His Mexican "Cactus Flower—
"The Spitfire Who Stole My Heart"

One morning in Puerto Vallarta, during the filming of *Man Friday,* after a night of heavy drinking, O'Toole wandered into the Buena Vista Café. Richard Burton had told him that the best cure for a Mexican hangover was two raw eggs whipped into a large beer. The Welsh actor had frequently promoted it as his most effective cure during his filming of *The Night of the Iguana.*

Taking his order was one of the most beautiful young women he'd spotted anywhere in Mexico. She'd never seen any of his films, but she'd heard that he was a big-time movie star. She filled his order for beer, and then suggested that he needed something more substantial "to put some meat on your bones."

He later told Buck, "My new friend doesn't speak English like Dame Sybil Thorndike, but we can at least communicate. I've just met her, and I've already expanded her vocabulary. She's also taught me some words in Spanish they don't teach you in Spanish classes."

He described Malinche Verdugo as "a pint-sized bundle of dynamo energy with the spirit of Lupe Velez. She has the hyper mannerisms of Bette Davis, the fractured English of Carmen Miranda, and her sights are set on becoming a Hollywood star. As for beauty, Dolores Del Rio comes to mind. Both Malinche and Del Rio have faces that look as if they'd been dipped in porcelain. She's the kind of girl who should have run off with a Mexican *bandito* named Durango, but she's ending up with an Irishman named Peter, who is no spring chicken."

"How old is she?" Buck asked. "I hope you're not pulling another Errol Flynn, shacking up with a jail-bait fifteen-year-old."

"She's legal," O'Toole said. "Perhaps twenty years my junior. I've promised her that if she'll be my true love, I'll use all my star power to make her a big star. I also told her I'm a movie producer and a partner with you in Keep Films. That impressed the hell out of her."

"When do I meet this Mayan goddess?" Buck asked.

"Tomorrow," O'Toole said. "I want you to wear a black French beret and smoke your cigarette through the longest cigarette holder you can come up with. The cliché of a director/producer would come in handy to help me lure her into my web."

O'Toole had not exaggerated. Verdugo almost lived up to her star billing. Buck later described it, "Most of the stars were the ones dancing in the eyes of my love-sick friend. After only a weekend with Malinche, Peter seems to have fallen madly, passionately in love. Too bad he nabbed her before I put my mark on her."

O'Toole became a regular client at her *cantina* for breakfast, lunch, and dinner. His nights were spent in her arms. When passion ebbed one evening, he invited her to a local hot spot that called itself by its English name, *Tijuana*

Nights. The pink neon letters spelling out its name had both the "U" and the "N" burnt out.

They entered the place through mock western-style swinging doors, the type John Wayne or Gary Cooper used to pass through before encountering a saloon filled with hard-drinking, gun-slinging desperados.

The lighting was dim and the room was packed with scruffy-looking men, each of whom seemed to evoke extras from a South-of-the-Border movie. A coven of a dozen scantily clad prostitutes worked the bar. A few expatriate gringos of various sexual persuasions hung out downing tequila, some of them being targeted by Mexican hustlers in tight pants.

Loud music was playing, as a big-bosomed Mexican woman—dressed only in a red G-string with sequins—danced to its beat, playing with the meaty lobes of her breasts.

O'Toole ignored her, concentrating only on Verdugo.

At the end of her act, the men around the bar tossed pesos at her, which she eagerly scooped up. O'Toole left a dollar bill.

Later, he and Verdugo danced to the rock music that pounded out from the jukebox. The place smelled of sweaty men, stale beer, and urine.

O'Toole searched the eyes of the other men, who were only too aware that he had the prize catch of the evening. As he'd later tell Buck, "Malinche was the only lady there. The other women looked like tramps, some Hollywood costume designer's idea of how a Tijuana whore dresses."

That night, O'Toole had more than his share of tequila and complained of stomach pains. Verdugo said she could take him to this Mexican doctor she knew, but he turned down her offer, claiming he'd feel better in the morning after he drank another beer with raw eggs.

After his first week with Verdugo, O'Toole confessed, "I don't think I've ever desired a woman this much in my life. I have this need to devour her, one nibble after another. I can't imagine having to tell her goodbye. Already, I've promised to take her to England, as soon as I can make adjustments."

When he scheduled a long weekend off duty from filmmaking, O'Toole rented a car so he and Verdugo could explore the countryside. He would later tell Buck, "I've found my second home country."

"Mexico has gotten under my skin. The sunsets with my Cactus Flower are spectacular, a series of streaks in the sky of purple, crimson, magenta, and indigo."

"Nothing beats waking up in the arms of my love goddess. It would take the rosy glow of dawn and a Michelangelo to capture the radiance of my Mexican Mona Lisa."

"You sound inspired by a Nat King Cole song," Buck said.

With her as his guide, O'Toole discovered offbeat Mexico, as she led him to places where American tourists never trod. They dined in *cantinas*, with locals who smoked non-filtered cigarettes. "Wherever we went, we encountered Mexicans in overly worn clothing and weathered faces. For lunch, she found freshly baked bread for me, luscious fruit, and bottles of wine."

"Except for this nagging pain in my abdomen, it would have been a perfect honeymoon."

"You didn't marry her, did you?" Buck asked. "That's bigamy."

"I don't plan to marry ever again if Siân leaves me," O'Toole said. "I'm a free spirit. I don't want to be in contractual bondage to a woman."

When the filming of *Man Friday* was wrapped, Buck gave him some good news. He'd also arranged for O'Toole's next film, *Foxtrot,* to be shot in Mexico

"After a brief trip to England and a reunion with Siân, you'll soon be back in the arms of your Mexicali Rose."

Grateful to Be Alive, A Sober, Post-Operative O'Toole "Foxtrots" on a Tropical Island with Charlotte Rampling

It would be months before O'Toole returned to Mexico and the arms of Verdugo. In London, in 1975, he faced a series of operations wherein parts of his intestines were removed, followed by weeks of recovery. His drinking days were over, as alcohol, according to his doctors, would be poisonous and life-threatening to his overtaxed system.

Flying back to Mexico, he was met by Verdugo, who welcomed him into her arms again. He told her what had happened to him. She found him in a weakened condition, promising that the good food, fresh air, and sunshine of Mexico would bring him renewed vigor.

He held out a promise to her. "I've made arrangements to take you to England with me. I'm arranging for you to take acting lessons at the Bristol Old Vic You're going to fulfill your dream of becoming an actress, perhaps bigger than Dolores Del Rio herself."

He had returned to Mexico because Roger Corman of New World Pictures had offered O'Toole the lead in *Foxtrot (aka The Other side of Paradise.)*

O'Toole liked the script, although

Foxtrot
Charlotte Rampling with her "Romanian" partner, Peter O'Toole

391

he knew that by accepting the role, he would suffer a loss of prestige. Corman—an American independent producer, director, and actor from Detroit—was known mainly for his trashy exploitation films.

Yet this maverick of the cinema world also had a distinguished film career as well. He had been instrumental in launching the careers of such young filmmakers as Ron Howard, Martin Scorsese, James Cameron, and Francis Ford Coppola. He'd also helped launch the careers of a number of actors, including Dennis Hopper, Sandra Bullock, Bruce Dern, and Robert De Niro. He'd told them, "If you do a good job for me in this film, you'll never have to work with me again."

Corman had been a pioneer in counter-culture films such as *Women in Cages* (1971). In 1966, he'd made the first biker movie, *The Wild Angels,* co-starring Peter Fonda and Nancy Sinatra. Corman's *The Trip* (1967), written by Jack Nicolson and also starring Fonda, became a "defining moment" in the psychedelic film craze that swept through the 1960s.

O'Toole also came to admire Corman's role in bringing to the United States the works of such foreign directors as Ingmar Bergman, François Truffaut, and Federico Fellini. In a decade, New World Pictures won more Oscars for Best Foreign Film that all other studios combined.

In *Foxtrot,* O'Toole would star with two distinguished actors, Charlotte Rampling and Max von Sydow.

Due to his health crises and subsequent surgeries, he'd been out of work for months, and was eager to return to the screen. He'd wanted more time to prepare for the role, but had been too weak.

In Cabo San Lucas, he said, "I had to lock myself away for days at a time just to concentrate on my lines."

He also claimed, "It seemed that everybody in Mexico had heard what a heavy drinker I was. I couldn't go anywhere without people offering me glasses of tequila. I had to turn them down, much to my disappointment. I told them that alcohol would poison my already dangerously weakened system. I was limited to five cigarettes a day, and I had been a chain smoker. Not only that, I could not even drink coffee, take aspirin, or even an Alka-Seltzer when Mexican beans gave me too much gas."

The director, Arturo Ripstein, understood O'Toole's physical limits and did

Charlotte Rampling with Peter O'Toole in *Foxtrot.*

"She was startlingly beautiful," he said. "One of my favorite actresses. But there was nothing romantic between us. She was married to actor Bryan Southcombe, and I had my Mexican taco."

not ride him hard. Whenever he wasn't needed, he let O'Toole and Verdugo search the surrounding region for Precolombian artifacts, which he wanted for shipment back to England.

Cast in *Foxtrot* as a wealthy Romanian aristocrat, Liviu, O'Toole flees from Europe on a yacht as nations are plunged into World War II. With his wife, Julia (portrayed by Rampling), he's accompanied by his servants, Van Sydow and "Eusebio" (played by Jorge Luke), plus a retinue of staff.

They retreat to a tropical island, where the couple lives in luxury in a tent-like "manse" set directly on the beach. They have ample provisions.

Their idyllic life is uprooted when "friends" arrive on another yacht to take over their compound and decimate their supplies. In a frenzied shooting party, these guests kill every animal on the island.

The yachting party departs with all of their servants, except for Von Sydow and Luke.

In the aftermath of their guests' "rampage," Liviu and his wife send their yacht away for supplies, but it never returns. There is no way that O'Toole can communicate with the outside world. With provisions diminishing, three men and one woman are left on the island. The chemistry of this quartet seems to foment mistrust, greed, and jealousy.

During the course of filming, O'Toole had many conversations with Von Sydow, an actor he respected. In time, he would win two Academy Award nominations. His mentor had been the Swedish director, Ingmar Bergman, with whom Von Sydow would make nearly a dozen films, his first being *The Seventh Seal* (1957). American audiences would remember Von Sydow mainly for his interpretation of Jesus Christ in the all-star epic, *The Greatest Story Ever Told* (1965).

At the time O'Toole had first met him, Von Sydow was living in Rome, where he was appearing in a number of Italian films and hanging out with Marcello Mastroianni, at the time the hottest male heartthrob in Italy.

O'Toole had seen Rampling in her breakthrough film, *Georgy Girl* (1966), in which she played a saucy, gadabout flatmate to poor, plain and ordinary Georgy.

Max von Sydow: "In *Foxtrot*, I play a villain but I can also do the best Jesus Christ of any other actor."

He complimented her on her cynical scene in a hospital bed with her newborn gurgling beside her in a crib. "I remember you saying, 'I hate it. It's hideous.' That took balls on your part. Aren't mothers supposed to adore their infant darlings?"

Rampling and O'Toole talked about their screen images and their marriages. Both of them agreed how dangerous, even narcissistic, it was to fall in love with their images.

"As you know, I'm married to an actress, Siân Phillips," O'Toole said.

"And I'm married to an actor," she responded.

"Not a good idea to be married to someone in the same profession, wouldn't you agree?" he asked.

"I agree."

[In 1976, Rampling would divorce Southcombe.]

O'Toole told Rampling that he was well aware that he was spending too much time away from Siân, and Rampling must have known of his affair with the Mexican woman because he constantly brought her to the set.

Charlotte Rampling
One of the most consistently hip and brilliant actresses of her generation.

"When I'm back in London with Siân, we put up a good front," he claimed. "I mean, we go to dinner parties, work in our vegetable garden in Hampstead, stuff like that."

He did admit that he was "not a bra-burning feminist. At home, I'm an Irishman, meaning I'm free to roam, expecting the wife to tend to home and hearth and bring up my daughters."

"Both Pat and Kate have independent streaks like I do," he said. "I think both of them consider me a good father, but they always object to my opening and reading their mail. I can't imagine why."

After its completion, in 1976, *Foxtrot* went into limited release in the United States and was not shown at all in England. In *The Hollywood Reporter,* Arthur Knight defined it as a masterwork, lauding it as a "visual and aural experience. No picture could look better or feel better. O'Toole is simply incredible as the jaded aristocrat. Lacking, however, are the well springs of emotion that might make it all happen."

That paper's rival, *Variety,* attacked the film, describing it as "chic, stylish, and ultimately hollow. It often lapses from wild irony into cornball melodrama."

O'Toole later delivered his own review: "*Foxtrot* wasn't very good, was it? There's a dearth of good scripts these days. However, I'm grateful to be back before the cameras again. After all those life-threatening surgeries, it's good to be alive."

Chapter 21

Lord Jim

O'Toole Suffers Three Months in Hell

Hostile Critics & a Psychotic Politician

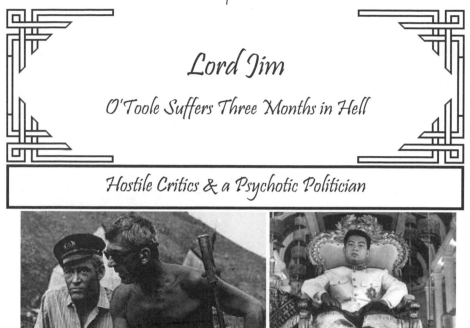

Peter O'Toole with director Richard Brooks, fighting reptiles, insurrection, bats, spiders, and...

...the spectacularly corrupt and probably insane Sihanouk of Cambodia.

For years, director Richard Brooks had labored over a screen treatment of *Lord Jim,* the novel published in 1900 by Joseph Conrad. Modern Library ranks it as 85th on the 100 best English-language novels of the 20th Century.

Married at the time to the English actress Jean Simmons, Brooks was a multi-talented artist. A son of Philadelphia, he was a film director, novelist, scriptwriter, and occasional movie producer.

His hits had included *Blackboard Jungle* (1955) with Glenn Ford; *Cat on a Hot Tin Roof* (1958), with Elizabeth Taylor and Paul Newman; and *Elmer Gantry* (1960), which brought its star, Burt Lancaster, an Oscar. It also won Brooks an Oscar for Best Adapted Screenplay.

Brooks flew to London to meet with O'Toole and his partner at Keep Films, Jules Buck, to see if O'Toole would accept the starring role of Jim in a film he envisioned as a 1965 release.

Brooks informed them that director Victor Fleming had first made a silent version of *Lord Jim* in 1925. It had starred Percy Marmont in the title role, supported by Shirley Mason as Jewel, the love interest, and Noah Berry as Gentleman Brown.

Neither O'Toole nor Buck had read Joseph Conrad's turn-of-the-century novel, so Brooks—with the understanding that it would be shot as a "big Technicolor extravaganza"—quickly outlined the scenario to them.

Based on a true event, *Lord Jim* (the protagonist's surname is never given) is a young, hardworking, deferential, and ambitious English seaman in Britain's Merchant Marine. He becomes first mate aboard the *Patna*, a ship brimming with Muslim pilgrims *en route* to their *hajj* (holy pilgrimage to Mecca).

At first, Peter O'Toole had reservaions about accepting the role of Lord Jim, feeling the character too closely evoked that of T. E. Lawrence.

"If I take the part, I'm in danger of becoming known as a tall, blonde, dramatic actor playing men filled with self-doubt. The type who stands by the sea and looks mournfully at the distant horizon. It seems that Lord Jim, like Lawrence of Arabia, is another tortured soul."

At one point during the voyage, during a violent storm, the ship begins to sink. The captain, along with Jim and the crew, decide to flee aboard one of the limited and inadequate roster of lifeboats, abandoning their ship, leaving it to sink and the Muslims to drown.

Jim, as part of a wrenching moral dilemma that will dominate the rest of his life, either jumps or is pushed into one of the lifeboats (the scenario is deliberately unclear), hitting his head and becoming unconscious as the lifeboat leaves behind the hapless passengers.

The lifeboat carrying a remorseful Jim along with the (less morally traumatized) crew eventually reaches safety. Later, they learn that the ship's passengers, many on the verge of death, were rescued by a passing French ship.

During a trial by a British military tribunal, although the captain and his

His Feud with Cambodia's Genocidal Despot, Prince Sihanouk

"Snakes in My Soup, Cobras in My Path,

& Bloodsucking Mosquitoes as Big as Bats"

crew manage to evade punishment, Jim makes a full confession and remains—alone, abandoned, and despised—to face charges. In abject disgrace, he is stripped of his rights, his post, and presumably, his pension, and thrown out of the British Navy.

Infused with guilt, he spends the rest of his life avoiding contact with Western (i.e., corrupted) society and trying to redeem his blemished honor.

At this point, the novel evolves into an action/adventure story set within the fictional island-nation of Patusan, presumably part of the Indonesian archipelago.

When he frees the local residents from the control of a cruel, bloodthirsty warlord, Jim becomes a hero and savior to the natives, who revere him and elevate him to "Lord Jim." And a native girl (Jewel) falls in love with him, helping to integrate him into the "savage but noble and unpolluted" non-European society he's adopted as his refuge from his personal history.

Ultimately, Jim's past catches up with him, and, in actions that some fans of Joseph Conrad attribute to the self-sacrifices of Christ, he offers

A fall from (British Imperial) Grace. "If not the Oscar itself, I should at least have been nominated for one."

his life (submitting willfully to a fatal bullet in his heart) as retribution for his cowardice during his ill-fated stint as an officer aboard the *Patna*.

Shooting was scheduled in locations that included Hong Kong, Singapore, and exotic Cambodia, with studio filming conducted at Shepperton Studios outside London.

"At the age of thirty-three, I don't want to become a perpetual juvenile, an aging Tab Hunter or Troy Donahue. You've seen the face of these blondes so often on the screen. As they move deeper into their thirties, makeup no longer conceals Father Time, but they're still hanging on to yesterday. Not me. I need to face greater challenges."

Brooks finally persuaded him to accept the role, even though he didn't immediately supply him with a finished script. Nevertheless, O'Toole came to trust his director, although he refused to become involved in a scene containing a homosexual rape, since that would have adhered too closely to the plotline of *Lawrence*.

He admired how Brooks—during his directorship of *Cat on a Hot Tin Roof*

(1958)—had chafed at the Production Code, fighting with censors and ultimately being forced to camouflage the latent homosexuality that Tennessee Williams had written more graphically into the pages of his play.

In time, O'Toole claimed that Brooks "was a hard-driving taskmaster, difficult to work with and forever angry, but the man had talent. A powerful ego is mandatory for a great director. Richard and I had our clashes, but they never went beyond threatening to kill each other."

In London, the director assembled a supremely talented cast, some members of whom O'Toole knew, others whom he met for the first time. Stars included James Mason, Curt Jürgens, Eli Wallach, Jack Hawkins, Paul Lukas, Akim Tamiroff, and the beautiful Israeli actress, Daliah Lavi as "The Girl" (i.e., Jewel).

Greeting his cast, Brooks said, somewhat undiplomatically, "I'm sure all of you have your own ideas about what kind of contribution you can make to this film. What you can do to improve it and make it better. But keep your ideas to yourself. It's my fucking movie, and I'm going to make it my way."

Daliah Lavi with O'Toole at the film's premiere.

At the time O'Toole had agreed to play Lord Jim, he was appearing in London's West End as *Hamlet* (it opened in October of 1963), directed by Laurence Olivier as the first-ever performance within the then-newly constructed National Theatre, on the South Bank of the Thames.

After the curtain came down on the production's final performance, O'Toole celebrated its demise with an all-night binge with his friends. They included James Villiers and Kenneth Griffith.

The next day, in the early dawn, he headed for Heathrow for the flight to the British colony of Hong Kong.

"As I boarded the plane, I had so many holes in me that I felt I would start oozing booze," O'Toole said.

In his enigmatic way, he was referring to both his heavy drinking that night and to the fact he'd suffered through nearly twenty inoculations against foreign tropical diseases he might be exposed to in Cambo-

Emulating the Agonies of Christ

O'Toole mourning the death of a child, and comforted by "The Girl" as played by Daliah Lavi.

dia and the Far East.

In Hong Kong, O'Toole checked into the deluxe Peninsula Hotel. "After flying into Hong Kong, the next bloody day, Brooks had me in a blazing small boat with a coolie paddling like some crazed idiot. What is Hong Kong? It's Manchester with slanted eyes."

When his remark was translated and published in a local newspaper, some local commentators referred to it as "racist."

Some clients of the Peninsula Hotel opted to arrive there in chauffeur-driven Rolls-Royces. In contrast, O'Toole outraged the hotel's management by arriving, rather theatrically, in a rickshaw. Then, he invited the coolie who had pulled the rickshaw into the hotel's lobby, where they raucously drank together until two that morning. After the coolie departed, O'Toole stumbled and fell down, and had to be carried to his suite.

Prince Sihanouk Evicts O'Toole from Cambodia— "As if I Would Ever Want to Return to This Hellhole"

After the completion of filming in Hong Kong, Brooks' cast and crew headed off to Cambodia, where O'Toole would experience "the worst three months of my life."

At their remote and rural location, Brooks had to spend $600,000 to build a 50-room extension onto the shabby small hotel where they would lodge.

From the very beginning, O'Toole detested everything. "The bloody place was more expensive than Claridges [*the most expensive hotel in London*], ten flaming quid a night and a poxy room at that. As for what they ridiculously called a cuisine, it was grotesque, not fit for human consumption."

"On my first day, I was walking down this jungle path and came upon this gigantic black cobra, eyeball to eyeball. I heard the snake can outrun a man. Not that day. With feet of Mercury, I fled the scene."

"Snakes were always a problem," he continued. "The natives have a name for one of the deadliest of the local snakes. In English, it translates as a 'Two-Step' In other words, the venomous fiend bites you. You take two steps, and you're dead!"

[*O'Toole was probably referring to the Krait snake, a brightly banded, extremely venomous nocturnal elapid snake native to Southeast Asia.*]

O'Toole also claimed that he had been attacked by mosquitoes "the size of bats. When they attack you, they somehow managed to suck out an entire pint of your blood."

Their location was near Cambodia's world-famous ruins of Angkor Wat.

[Intricately carved, the lavishly ornate Angkor Wat complex, which dates from the 11th century, was first a Hindu, later a Buddhist, temple. The largest religious monument in the world it was famously visited by Jacqueline Kennedy in November of 1967. She was accompanied by Lord Harlech, and there were false rumors that the couple planned to marry in Cambodia.]

In advance of filming, the set decorators had to create a small village with straw huts on stilts, shops, a public hall, and a schoolhouse.

"The Cambodians charged triple for everything," O'Toole claimed. "The locals also stole everything that wasn't guarded or nailed down. Prince Sihanouk skimmed all the profits, anyway. His Majesty, if I may call the sleazeball that, and I were destined to become bitter enemies."

***

After hard-working, sweaty, and confusing days filming, O'Toole socialized with his fellow actors after dark.

Eli Wallach had been his friend since the making of *Lawrence of Arabia.* In Hollywood, he had played Mexican *banditos,* an Okinawan, a Greek jewel thief, a Latin American dictator, and even the redneck Southern owner of a cotton gin trying to seduce a teenaged virgin in Tennessee Williams' *Baby Doll* (1956).

According to Wallach, "In the movies, I used to watch villains heat a sword, then press it into the flesh of Errol Flynn to get him to confess. Now, here I was, in the jungles of Cambodia, doing the same thing to Peter O'Toole!"

[A year later, in 1966, Wallach and O'Toole would make yet another picture together, How to Steal a Million, *co-starring Audrey Hepburn.]*

O'Toole's main drinking buddy was Jack Hawkins, cast as Marlowe, the naval officer who narrates *Lord Jim* in that distinctively

Two views of a Despot

Sihanouk (top photo) against a frieze left behind by the French, and (lower photo) during the militarization of Cambodian villagers armed only with wooden weapons.

400

throaty voice of his. Critics would later denounce him as "a sizable bore, static, and long-winded."

O'Toole spent an occasional evening with James Mason, shocking the distinguished actor by telling him that he would have much preferred Mason's role as Gentleman Brown, the 19th Century buccaneer. "I still haven't forgiven you for stealing the lead in *Lolita* from me. I'm sure I would have been more convincing as a pedophile. I tell everybody that."

Warlord Eli Wallach with Daliah Lavi, the film's leading lady. The on-site makeup department shaved two inches off his hairline to make him look more "ethnic."

"My dear man, I, too, have missed out on roles I wanted," Mason said. "I was committed to playing Svengali opposite Jane Wyman as Trilby, but the film never made. I was also earmarked as the male lead in *La Duchess de Langeais.* It was conceived as a comeback picture for Greta Garbo. Alas, she backed out at the last minute."

[Ironically, it would be O'Toole who would eventually star in Svengali, *a TV movie shot in 1983 that co-starred Jodie Foster.]*

As Gentleman Brown, Mason was later ridiculed as "almost comic as a bowler-hatted, bearded type."

At the time he worked with O'Toole in *Lord Jim*, Mason was in the process of ending his famous marriage to Pamela Mason. Although he would

Seeing the ruins of Angkor Wat, O'Toole proclaimed, "The glories of Cambodia were of another day. Today, it's a hellhole."

marry again *[in 1971 he wed Clarissa Kaye, the Australian film and stage actress]* Mason was bisexual. In the bar, while waiting for Mason to arrive, a young hustler from Vietnam admitted he was "servicing" Mason. He told O'Toole that as a nine-year-old, he had rented himself out to French sailors during their occupation of Saigon.

"I didn't get to know Curt Jürgens, although he seemed to have led a fascinating life," O'Toole said. "I did learn that in 1944, he was sent to an internment camp in Hungary. The Nazis called him 'a political unreliable.'" He was taller than me, standing 6'4". I meant to ask him what Brigitte Bardot meant when she nicknamed him *[based on his imposing height and bulk] l'armoire normand* ('The Norman Wardrobe.') He had appeared with her in *Et dieu créa la femme (And God Created Woman;* 1956). I also wanted to ask Jürgens if he ever fucked Bardot. I meant to do that myself, but never seemed to find the time."

Critics later pounced on Jürgens' performance in *Lord Jim,* interpreting his role as Cornelius as "a ponderous Germanic go-between whose melodramatic involvement is greater but less clear than what was laid out in the book."

As Jewel, Daliah Lavi was O'Toole's romantic interest. *[Born in what was then known as Palestine, to Jewish parents from Germany and Russia. Fluent in six languages, Lavi's career took off in 1960, when she started appearing in large number of European and American productions, including gigs as a pop singer in Germany.]*

She was lambasted with "All you can do is look at her and wonder," wrote one reviewer. "It's hard to understand a word she says."

Paul Lukas, cast as "Stein," a seafaring trader, though damned by faint praise, actually fared the best with the critics. One of them merely referred to him as "gentle."

O'Toole met Lukas during his waning years, near the end of a career which had included roles in many box office hits in the 1930s and 40s. He'd won an Oscar as Best Actor for his role in *Watch on the Rhine* (1943), with Bette Davis, beating Humphrey Bogart that year for his role in *Casablanca.*

Paul Lukas...In the twilight of a distinguished career

O'Toole had sympathy for Lukas, as he was suffering a memory loss and had difficulty with his scenes. At one point, in frustration, he lashed out at both Brooks and the crew.

That night, he told O'Toole, "I just had *Fun in Acapulco* (1963) with Elvis Presley. Now I have the unenviable job of being the owner of a boatload of gunpowder, and I want you to undertake the dangerous job of transporting it up the river. Let's face it: I've had better parts. My role in *Lord Jim* is the part the studio gives you as they're escorting you out the door."

[In 1971, O'Toole was saddened to learn that in August of that year, Lukas had died in Tangier, Morocco, while searching for a place for his retirement.]

In *Lord Jim,* Akim Tamiroff played a clown named Schomberg. "Orson Welles liked Akim, so we hired him,"

Curt Jürgens...Did he really seduce Brigitte Bardot?

O'Toole said. "Welles had cast him in *A Touch of Evil* (1958) as a slovenly Mexican crime boss, a movie I went to see merely as a means of watching a cameo performance by Marlene Dietrich."

"We also hired Akim for *Great Katharine* (1968). He didn't have to imitate a Russian accent. He already had a thick one."

From his sweat-drenched, bug and snake-infested film locale, O'Toole not only continued to attack Cambodia, but also loudly criticized Prince Sihanouk.

[Norodom Sihanouk (1922 – 2012) functioned as the despotic King of Cambodia from 1941, when he seized control from the Vichy-controlled colonial French, off and on, until 2005. During that period, depending on many factors associated with the genocidal Pol Pot regime and the complicity and/or collaboration of both the French and the Americans, he held power for two separate terms as king, two as sovereign prince, one as president, two as prime minister, as well as numerous positions as leader of various governments-in-exile. During O'Toole's filming of Lord Jim, Sihanouk was moving into position as puppet head of state for the genocidal Khmer Rouge government, making and breaking alliances with, among others, North Vietnam, North Korea, and the People's Republic of China.]

Not seeming to appreciate (or fear) that he was in the country under the autocratic regime of a brutal dictator, O'Toole spoke freely to the press. "There is a pulse of political violence simmering just below the surface, here," he said.

A reporter for *Life* magazine visited the set of *Lord Jim*. Deploring the local conditions, O'Toole told him that during dinner the previous night, "I found a snake in my soup."

On national radio, Sihanouk denounced O'Toole for making such a claim, charging him with an attempt to destroy the Cambodian tourist industry.

Critics Blast O'Toole's Lord Jim
After Hours Aboard Flights from Cambodia to New York, O'Toole Collapses on Johnny Carson's The Tonight Show

On the Cambodian film set, during the final months of 1963, there had been animated, anxiety-filled predictions that a violent revolution was brewing. Early in 1964, Sihanouk ordered Brooks to remove his crew from Cambodia before March 12, leaving them less than six weeks to complete the film. To adhere to that ultimatum, the director worked the cast and crew overtime to finish their location shooting before the deadline.

When the political situation devolved into gunfire, Siân Phillips and

O'Toole fled from the remnants of their film set to a local airport, where a large photograph of Sihanouk dominated one of the walls, to catch a flight bound for Hong Kong. At the sound of gunfire, they retreated into a small toilet, where they hid until their small plane was ready to take off.

O'Toole later made a flippant remark: "Huddling in fear of our lives in that public lavatory was less stressful than playing Stratford."

The day after O'Toole fled from Cambodia, he was ordered never to return. He told the press, "Have no fear, Sihanouk, you bloody bastard, I'll never come back. Incidentally, the whores Sihanouk flies in from Paris call him 'Prince Tiny Meat."

The press did not print those remarks.

Throughout the 1970s, O'Toole continued his personal attack on the controversial prince (or king). He charged Sihanouk with crimes against humanity, citing that he was the titular head of the Khmer Rouge when he operated as a puppet of Pol Pot, the military dictator who supervised the extermination of nearly two million Cambodians. O'Toole called it a holocaust. He went on to accuse Sihanouk of sending assassins to London to murder him. That charge was never proven.

From Hong Kong, Siân and O'Toole transferred to Tokyo, with the intention of arriving in New York for the premiere of *Becket,* and in response to invitations from both Johnny Carson and Ed Sullivan to appear as a guest on their respective shows.

In spite of O'Toole's aversion to air travel, he and his wife flew across the North Pole, stopping in Anchorage, Alaska, for refueling. "In the airport, I got a bowl of chili," he claimed. "For the rest of the flight to New York, I had the runs."

Checking into a suite at the St. Regis in Manhattan, he had time only to shower and dress for what turned out to be a notorious appearance on *The Tonight Show* with Johnny Carson.

When he arrived on Carson's set, he had been deprived of sleep for sixty hours.

To Carson and his millions of viewers, O'Toole appeared drunk. He mumbled incoherently for about three minutes, appearing unable to utter a coherent sentence.

Finally, as the cameras rolled, he collapsed, falling onto the floor and breaking his glasses. He picked himself up and walked off the set, the first time any guest had ever done that to Carson.

Cancelling his scheduled appearance on *The*

Heeeeeeere's Johnny!
But where's Peter O'Toole?

Ed Sullivan Show, he took the first flight back to London. "I arrived in a box," he said.

***

Lord Jim had its premiere on February 15, 1965 at the Odeon Leicester Square, a Royal Command performance in the presence of Queen Elizabeth, the Queen Mother, and Princess Margaret.

The royal guest that attracted O'Toole's eye was Margaret, who was most gracious to him, perhaps overly so. As he later told Kenneth Griffith, "I think I read too much into her greeting. As she moved down the reception line, she probably forgot all about me."

In a phone call to Griffith late the following afternoon, O'Toole said, "How wrong I was. I've just gotten off the phone, where I spoke to the Princess herself. She wants to see me, privately, for tea."

For his interpretation of Lord Jim, O'Toole was attacked by critics, one of them defining his performance as "imperfect, inexcusable, and overly indulgent." The *London Observer* claimed, "Peter O'Toole ingratiates himself with his audience in the most shameless matinee idol manner."

One reporter asked him, "What did you think of the final cut of *Lord Jim?*"

"I really can't give an opinion. I never saw the picture."

Many critics cited *Lord Jim* as an overlong and uneven adaptation of Conrad's murky novel about honor, human frailty, and redemption.

The acerbic Bosley Crowther of *The New York Times* delivered one of the devastating reviews: "The performance of Mr. O'Toole is so sullen, soggy, and uncertain, especially toward the end, that it is difficult to find an area of recognizable sensitivity in which one can make contact with him. One hardly knows whether to pity or feel contempt for him. He seems to know, however. He appears constantly on the verge of bursting into tears."

Despite years of Brooks' devoted attention to its execution, despite the film's creditable acting by O'Toole, *Lord Jim* misfired at the box office.

In O'Toole's words: "At the end of the film, I took a bullet in the heart. And when the critics finished with me, I felt another bullet in my not always reliable heart."

Representing the True Grit of His Majesty's Navy:
Peter O'Toole as Lord Jim.

Chapter 22

Peter O'Toole's Secret Affair with Margaret Rose, "The Black Sheep" of the House of Windsor

"Margaret Brought Sex Appeal to the Royal Family, and Shoved them Kicking & Screaming into the Modern World."
—Peter O'Toole

"From the souks of Marrakech to the sands of the Grenadines, the Princess fell in love with Lawrence of Arabia—and got me." —Peter O'Toole	"Beautiful, vivacious, & violet-eyed, Margaret Rose was the Diana of her day & not above a little canoodling from time to time." —Her ex-Lover, Peter Sellers

Peter O'Toole's friendship with Princess Margaret had begun the night he was introduced to her at the Royal Command performance of his latest film, *Lord Jim* (1963). That was also the night that he'd been greeted by Queen Elizabeth and the Queen Mother.

Those two stately royal personages had already moved on down the reception line, but Margaret Rose of York had sent him a signal with a flicker of her eye that she'd like to get to know him better, which she did the following afternoon, when he showed up for tea at her residence within Kensington Palace.

As her many biographers have noted, some of Margaret's affairs became scandalous. Others never appeared on the radar screen.

Although there were a few tabloid links tying O'Toole to Margaret, they were never considered a romantic item—"just good friends."

However, when Peter Sellers, O'Toole's friend, became romantically involved with Margaret, it had catalyzed scandalous headlines in the tabloids.

When Sellers learned that, like himself, O'Toole was also enjoying Margaret's favors, the two actors discussed her. Whereas O'Toole was discreet, Sellers was more outspoken.

Young Margaret and her older sister, Elizabeth, are shown here with their protocol-obsessed grandmother, Queen Mary, who seems determined not to screw it up with them the way she had with her son, Edward VIII and his "unacceptable" wife, the American divorcée, Wallis Simpson.

He said that Margaret was more of a sex goddess than the beautiful but notorious Britt Ekland, to whom he'd become engaged in 1964.

Sellers told O'Toole, "I know why Margaret is attracted to you. She has always been drawn to men of dubious sexuality. After seeing *Lawrence of Arabia*, she knew you had a gay streak in you. It was so obvious right there on the screen."

Since O'Toole was a married man (Siân Phillips), both he and Margaret thought it discreet to become involved surreptitiously.

"*From Danny Kaye, ex-lover of Laurence Olivier, to the disgraced politician John Profumo, Her Royal Highness was imbued with a zest for life inherited from her great-grandfather, Edward VII, and his 7,000 sexual "conquests."*

—Margaret's ex-friend Gore Vidal, who entertained her in Ravello

She confided that after Charles and Princess Anne were born, she knew she would never become Queen of England. "Therefore, I saw no reason to be a slave to a throne I would never occupy."

O'Toole's romantic liaison with Margaret might never have been revealed if he had not confided all the details to his friend, Kenneth Griffith, whom he had called in to write his biography before beginning a series of surgical procedures to remove tumors from his intestines in the mid-1970s.

At that time, Griffith was fully aware of O'Toole's relationship with the Royal Princess, since he had kept him abreast of the affair. Griffith later speculated that it was not a very serious romance, "but a diversion, a mere diversion."

Margaret Rose, lovely and vulnerable, with early signs of ironic humor and probably smarter than the rest of her clan.

O'Toole was very candid with Griffith, telling him, "Frankly, I think members of the Royal Family are a bore, with the exception of Margaret Rose. She is a true *femme du monde.* She can be imperious at times, demanding all the royal privileges to which she is entitled. At other times, she can be the most amusing person in a room."

He claimed that she had a wicked wit and was brilliant at mimicry.

"She does a better impression of Elizabeth than Elizabeth does of herself."

He praised her impersonation of Vivien Leigh as Scarlett O'Hara in *Gone With the Wind.* "She could even do Marilyn Monroe and Ethel Merman."

When he met her, he was aware of the tragedies she'd suffered during her life, much of it previewed in the British tabloids.

In her twenties, her fun-loving ways had been dimmed when she'd fallen into an unlucky romance with Group Captain Peter Townsend of the Royal Air Force, a Battle of Britain hero. She had fallen in love with him when he served as an equerry to her father, King George VI.

It was believed that he was the love of her life, but there was a hurdle, which at the time seemed grave, indeed.

He was a divorced man.

Elizabeth, as the Supreme Governor of the Church of England, forbade divorce. Bowing to the demands of the moral code of that day, Margaret agreed to give up her dashing and handsome war hero. However, she continued to see him on and off in secret for a number of years.

In 1960, five years before she met O'Toole, she'd married a photographer, Anthony Armstrong-Jones, who was himself a child of divorced parents. Their tempestuous marriage had produced two children. A commoner, he was given the title of Earl of Snowdon, and henceforth referred to as Lord Snowdon.

From what O'Toole gathered, it was not a happy union. Writing in *The New York Times Magazine,* at around the time O'Toole met her, British journalist Charles Hussey noted that Margaret could move rapidly and alarmingly from "a gaiety that was sometimes febrile to Hanoverian gloom."

"The Black Sheep of the Royal Family," Margaret had become part of "Swinging London" that had emerged in the 1960s. She was devoted to the music of Louis Armstrong, who referred to her as "one hip chick." She also adored the music of the Beatles, John Lennon nicknaming her "Priceless Margarine."

She once confessed to the French author and filmmaker, Jean Cocteau, "Disobedience is my joy."

Love thwarted by royal command: The dashing Peter Townsend.

In post-war Britain, which was rather dismal, Margaret tried to recapture some of the glamorous spirit of the pre-war era. She took frequent trips to Paris and was seen dancing the night away in the most fashionable clubs of London, many of them in Mayfair.

Margaret confessed to author Andrew Duncan, "When my sister and I were growing up, she was made out to be the goody-goody one. That was so boring to write about, the press had to create me as being as wicked as hell."

During her time with O'Toole, Margaret always complained about being watched by British Intelligence and the security brigades assigned to protect her. "I like to pull a bit of Scottish wool over their eyes," she confessed. "Slip around and do things I shouldn't."

She revealed tidbits of her life,

Margaret with Princess Elizabeth in 1948, having made the choice to wear "post-war respectable clothing."

sharing royal secrets. She said that in the mid-1950s, British Intelligence discovered that Prince Philip maintained a "love nest" in Mayfair, using it as a locale for cheating on Her Majesty. "He was the main villain who ended my relationship with Townsend, yet he is the one who carries on with all these illicit affairs. When he went to Mexico, he

Waving from the balcony of Buckingham Palace after Margaret's royal wedding to Anthony Armstrong-Jones

had this torrid affair with Merle Oberon, who always chased after him."

Margaret loved the theater and its performers. She told O'Toole that in 1948, she'd gone to see one of Danny Kaye's shows in London. She raved about him so much that she persuaded both her mother and father to come to see him perform.

In her romantic association with actor/comedian Danny Kaye (left), Princess Margaret had to face the formidable competition of Sir Laurence Olivier (right).

The King and Queen were so impressed that they invited Kaye to dinner at Buckingham Palace. "He asked if he could bring Laurence Olivier, and we said we'd be delighted. I soon discovered they were lovers."

She also claimed that, "Danny was an obvious bisexual, because he and I also got together for mutual enjoyment. That seriously pissed off Sir Laurence, who exploded in all his queenly anger. He even threatened, years later, to seduce Lord Snowdon to get even with me. And would you believe it, after Kaye went back to Hollywood, I began a relationship with John Profumo."

[Brigadier John Dennis Profumo, later married to the well-liked British actress, Valerie Hobson, was a British politician of Italian origin. He held a number of important government posts in the 1950s, becoming Minister of State of War (outside the Cabinet) and a member of the Privy Council.

In 1963, he was a centerpiece of the British decade's biggest sex scandal, a controversy known as "The Profumo Affair." It led to his resignation and helped to topple the Conservative government of Harold Macmillan.

Profumo had become sexually involved with a 19-year-old-model, Christine Keeler, who was at the same time intimately linked to Yevgeni Ivanov, a senior naval attaché of the Soviet Embassy. As events unfolded, the indiscretions, which included multiple orgies at some of the most prestigious country homes in the U.K., mushroomed into a situation with implications for Britain's national security.

Profoundly disgraced, Profumo resigned and spent the rest of his life as a volunteer cleaning toilets at Toynbee Hall, a charity based in the East End of London.]

During the moments she spent with O'Toole, Margaret complained frequently about her marriage to Lord Snowdon. "Prince Philip didn't want me to marry him, finding him too effete."

In the months before their wedding in 1960, there was a suspicion that Snowdon might be a homosexual, and Buckingham Palace had him investigated. They discovered that he had a number of gay friends—in fact, the best man he'd selected for his wedding turned out to be gay. Armstrong-Jones was immediately ordered to find another best man—this time one with straight credentials.

Margaret defied royal protocol and smoked in public and sniffed cocaine in private. She also drank too much Scotch, and associated herself with "artistic bohemian friends," who danced in her large drawing room within Kensington Palace. O'Toole attended at least three of these parties, noting the open hostil-

PROFUMO QUITS OVER CHRISTINE

But who gets to wear the better costume? Christine Keeler, above, as a performer at Murray's Nightclub, and...

...John Profumo in Privy Council drag.

NEWS OF THE **WORL**

Confessions of Christine

BY THE GIRL WHO IS ROCKING THE GOVERNMENT

TODAY the News of the World starts publishing the full confessions of 21-year-old Christine Keeler, the girl who has rocked the Government, the model whose life is high and not-so-high society has set the world talking.

On Pages Four and Five will be found the first real and authentic account of the startling events which culminated in the resignation of Mr. John Profumo, the War Minister. SHE TELLS . . .

ity festering between Lord Snowdon and the Princess.

One night, in front of all the guests, Lord Snowdon shouted at Margaret, "I hate you!" and stormed out of the palace for points unknown.

Despite the many roles which followed O'Toole's success as Lawrence of Arabia, he was always identified with that role.

Perhaps Rudolf Nureyev had O'Toole's Lawrence in mind when he propositioned him sexually at one of Princess Margaret's bohemian parties in Kensington Palace. Depicted above is Nureyev playing Rudolf Valentino as the Sheik in Ken Russell's 1977 film.

"I wouldn't say that Her Majesty ran the best disco in town, but her parties were always lively," O'Toole claimed. "One night, Rudolf Nureyev asked me to dance. Not wanting to look square, I accepted. He'd seen *Lawrence of Arabia* and thought I was gay. At one point in the middle of the dance, he took my hand and placed it over his ample crotch. He whispered in my ear, 'All that can be yours tonight.'"

"It could, Rudi," O'Toole said, "but I fear I wouldn't know what to do with it."

On another occasion at a dinner party hosted by Margaret for eighteen guests at Kensington Palace, Lord Snowdon rose to his feet and deliberately spilled the contents of his wine glass onto the linen-covered dining table. He glared at Margaret. "You look like a Jewish manicurist."

She shouted back at him, "You're speaking to her Royal Highness, Princess Margaret. And don't you damned well ever forget that!"

Then he stormed out of the dining room.

Sometimes, she'd call O'Toole at two or three o'clock in the morning just to have someone to talk to. She'd told him that she always carried around a silver pillbox that had belonged to Queen Victoria. It was filled with Mogadon *[a heavy sedative]* tablets. "If it gets too much for me, I'll swallow all of these little devils."

"A lot of people thought Margaret was suicidal," O'Toole told Griffith. "I think it was not that, but a *cri de coeur.*"

O'Toole and Margaret Rose Bathed in the Aura of the Arabian Knights

In the late 1960s and early 70s, whenever Princess Margaret could no longer tolerate the pressures of London, she'd sometimes slip away to the most deluxe private home in Marrakech, Villa Taylor, originally constructed in all its grandeur during the 1920s and 30s by an American heiress to a railway fortune. It lay in the Ville Nouvelle (also known as Gueliz), within sprawling gardens, on the outskirts of the old city walls.

On one occasion in the 1970s, she invited O'Toole to join her in this retreat from the world. He flew to Gibraltar, then to Marrakech to join her. This was his second trip to Morocco, following in the wake of his first visit to shoot the battle scenes in the Sahara for *Lawrence of Arabia.*

·   Both Margaret and the elegant Countess de Breteuil *[known to her friends as "Boul"],* the owner of the retreat, were there to greet O'Toole when he arrived.

In 1986, the aging countess shared details of that long ago visit with the authors of this book, along with their traveling companion at the time, society doyenne Virginia Peirce. The three of them were staying in the Villa Taylor as her house guests, during research they were conducting for an up-coming edition of the well-known travel guide, *Frommer's Morocco.*

[The countess was used to entertaining famous guests in her extraordinary villa. No guests were more famous than the wartime leaders, Franklin D. Roosevelt and Sir Winston Churchill, who had se-cretly arrived here in 1943 during their famous

Sybaritic R&R at the most ex-clusive retreat in Morocco, The Villa Taylor

Casablanca Conference. Under heavy security, they had been driven from Casablanca to Marrakech for a short stay at the Villa Taylor.

The countess assigned Princess Margaret the Churchill Suite, with its bath-tub practically the size of a small swimming pool. O'Toole occupied the ad-joining suite with connecting doors.

"You cannot come to Morocco without seeing Marrakech," Churchill had told Roosevelt. "Let us spend two days of sheer delight within its confines. You must see the sun set over the snows of the Atlas Mountains."

From Casablanca, with soldiers stationed at strategic spots along the way, the two leaders were driven 150 miles across the desert.

Once there, Churchill stoked himself with brandy before climbing six floors to the villa's tower, where he painted the scene before him, the only painting he had time to create during the war.

Roosevelt, restricted as he was to his wheelchair, had to be carried up the stairs to the tower in the arms of the strongest member of his security detail. He later told Churchill, "It was worth it."]

Throughout the day, when not making love in the Churchill Suite, O'Toole and the Princess found charming nooks into which they would retreat, many with elaborate Moorish carvings and decorations, and paneling in shades of sunflower yellow, navy blue, and mint green.

In the garden, they discovered banks of violets mixed with petunias and other flowers. They wandered at leisure through the bougainvillea, geraniums, and orange trees, past bubbling fountains crafted from black marble. Behind the villa's "pinky-red" masonry walls, they felt safe from the prying eyes of the media.

O'Toole later told his actor friend, James Villiers, in London, "Living at the Villa Taylor was the closest I will ever come to knowing the life of a sultan torn from the pages of *Arabian Nights."*

After lunch and a siesta, enjoyed in Churchill's former bed, they went for a swim in the sparkling pool as the unforgiving sun beat down on the ancient minarets of the desert city.

For their first night at the villa, Margaret had requested that she and O'Toole be served the same dinner shared by Roosevelt and Churchill. Boul's chef willingly obliged, presenting them with an exquisite meal that included both lobster and fork-tender filet mignon served with a pâté salad.

It was the dessert that was an object of splendor: a *pièce montée,* as Louis XIV had dubbed it. Standing three feet high, it was a reproduction, crafted from nougat of the Koutoubia Tower whose soaring bulk, completed in 1199, dominated the skyline of Marrakech. A candle was placed inside the dessert confection, and a substructure of spun sugar represented the Atlas Mountains in the distance.

Before dinner, O'Toole had found his drink of choice, which he ordered every night, enjoying a few too many. It was the same drink served to the two wartime leaders, the bartender's special concoction which to him tasted like a "mixed breed": i.e., something halfway between a Sidecar and the kind of gin martini the Queen Mother liked, sometimes to excess, every evening.

When it was time to go, O'Toole had already told Margaret farewell within the confines of her Churchill Suite. He warmly embraced and kissed *la comtesse,* who told him, "My door will always be open to you."

"I think I've been living in a daydream," he said. "As a little boy in the ghetto of Leeds, I dreamed of living with a Princess in a fairytale castle. Here, my dream came true."

Forbidden Pleasures Way Down South in the Grenadines

In 1975, O'Toole had made a film called *Foxtrot* with Charlotte Rampling. It opened under the radar screen, without a lot of publicity, and wasn't released in Britain. It was the tale of a Romanian aristocrat who escapes to a Caribbean island to avoid the horrors of World War II.

In real life, about two and a half years before the release of that film, O'Toole escaped to the Caribbean island of Mustique for a secret rendezvous with Princess Margaret.

Part of the island nation of St. Vincent, Mustique, one of the Windward Islands, is the pearl of the Grenadines, a tiny archipelago of secluded lagoons, coral reefs, and long stretches of nearly deserted beaches.

At the time, Mustique was a privately owned island controlled by a consortium of business people. Its "King" was the spectacularly eccentric Colin Tennant (aka, Lord Glenconnor), a close friend of Princess Margaret. He made Mustique a celebrity favorite, attracting movie stars, rock stars, and the very wealthy.

Mustique had as its social center the exclusive retreat of the 18th Century Cotton House, a very upscale, very chic, colonial British West Indian-style hotel decorated by Oliver Messel.

Real estate developer, lifestyle guru, courtier to the House of Windsor, eccentric, and "King of Mustique," Lord Glenconnor, aka Colin Tennant

Tennant gave the Princess a ten-acre plot of land overlooking the sea. He agreed to construct an exclusive villa for her called *Les Jolies Eaux* (Pretty Waters), as it opened onto the blue waters of a bay. It was here that Margaret could pursue what the press later referred to as a "louche way of life."

Her neighbor was Mick Jagger, whom she'd met in 1967 when he was dating Marianne Faithful. Although the Princess always denied it, locals assumed that Margaret and Jagger were having an affair. They were often seen together late at night holding hands at Basil's Beach Bar.

Many of her friends on the island were not welcome within her orbit back in London. Jagger, of course, was the exception. Margaret was reported to have snorted cocaine with him in his dressing room before he went on to present a concert at Earls Court Stadium.

O'Toole had heard of the uninhibited and sometimes exhibitionistic parties on Mustique, and he eagerly accepted an invitation to visit "this pirate's den of sexual perversion where I heard libidos ran amuck, and where Margaret let her hair down to partake of all the fun."

To be discreet, she didn't invite him to stay at her villa, but Tennant arranged a separate villa for him about half a mile away. "I loved the long walks along the beach," O'Toole later told Kenneth Griffith. "Especially in the moonlight, especially with Margaret, who always wore these skirted bathing suits, invariably in pink."

At the Beach Bar, O'Toole pronounced the seafood "the best in the Caribbean," even though he had no basis of comparison. With Margaret, he showed up on Monday night for the live music. Reportedly, he was stunned to see David Bowie and Margaret sing a duet, although that could have been exaggeration in the press. If Margaret didn't actually sing with him, she was known to play the piano while such major stars as Jagger provided the vocals.

Back in London, O'Toole told Griffith, "I saw a side of Margaret I'd never seen before. I wouldn't say she was as much of a hellraiser as myself, but she knew how to have hellish fun. She felt safe in Mustique, away from the prying eyes of the tabloids, although eventually, those sods caught up with her antics."

Anyway, it was a hell of a lot of fun. Margaret, before her features hardened with the pain of life, was quite a beautiful woman, far prettier than the queen and miles more striking than her niece, horse-faced Princess Anne.

"I'll always treasure our walks along the rustling palm trees, seeking out that secluded cove for lovemaking. Think Burt Lancaster and Deborah Kerr on the beach in *From Here to Eternity.*"

The private parties O'Toole attended on Mustique were far more notorious than the antics at the Beach Bar, which staged a weekly "jump-up" as it was called, followed by a Caribbean barbe-

Mick Jagger--although by Royal standards, Jagger was more socially acceptable in Mustique than in London, Margaret, rather indiscreetly, entertained the rock musician in London, anyway, at rendezvous that were sometimes augmented with "blow."

417

cue.

The "biggest" attraction was John Bindon, an actor/bad boy from the East End of London, who had a criminal past. He had a party trick of balancing four half-pint glasses on his erect penis. When she first saw the act, it was said that Margaret "squealed with delight."

[Later, when he returned to London, Bindon agreed to be interviewed by Noel Botham, the author of Margaret, The Last Real Princess. Bindon claimed that he shared many a sultry night with Margaret. "I'd give the Princess a nine for technique and a bloody great fifteen for enthusiasm. She wasn't at all shy about coming out with what she wanted."

Bindon also claimed that the Princess invited him for several return engagements within Kensington Palace. As related to Botham, "I thought I was a goer, but if I'd have let her, she'd have me at it all bloody night. And the same the night after. What a player!"]

Back on Mustique, the days passed too quickly for O'Toole and he told Margaret goodbye, promising to meet again in London.

He took the boat to St. Vincent where he was able to board a plane that landed

John Bindon playing a gangster in a bit part in *Quadrophenia* (a non-musical film from 1979 inspired by a rock opera from The Who. Although Sting made an appearance in the film near its end, Bindon had only a very minor walk-on part.

Wearing a t-shirt that glorified cocaine, and presumably showing off his party tricks and evaluating the enthusiast quotients of Margaret Rose, Bindon is shown here with the Royal Princess on Mustique.

him eventually in Miami. Although he had promised to return to the island again, there is no record that he ever did, although he retained fond memories of his interlude there.

Eventually, Margaret's privacy was invaded, as the "seawall" around Mustique was penetrated by the press and increasing numbers of mass-market tourists.

In 1973, Margaret, 43, met and fell in love with toy boy Roddy Llewellyn, 25. He, too, was invited to Mustique.

Her liaison with him became a scandal when someone stole a candid photo that she'd taken of the young man on the beach. It was a full frontal nude, which ended up in the pages of London's *News of the World*.

Years later, after losing many bruising battles for control of the island, Lord Glenconnor summed up the glory days of Mustique. "It was a place where inhibitions could be cast off. Princess Margaret, O'Toole, Bowie, Prince Andrew, Jagger, Raquel Welch, Richard Avedon, Tommy Hilfiger, everybody mixed freely with the locals and assorted flotsam and jetsam that washed up on our shores. Whenever nosy reporters arrived, I put them on the next plane out. I was the arbiter of style and the judge of who should be allowed to share in our fun, which, I must admit, got a bit rowdy at times."

Princess Margaret and the Notorious Gangster, "Big John," The Most Dangerous Man in Britain

Whereas it seemed acceptable for Princess Margaret to carry on an affair with the notorious John Bindon on the private enclave of Mustique, O'Toole was unpleasantly surprised to learn that she chose to continue this dangerous liaison in socially conscious London.

Various of Bindon's girlfriends reported that late at night, he often received a summons for a Royal Command performance in Margaret's sumptuous bedchamber at Kensington Palace, where he was slipped in and out discreetly.

In addition to Margaret, many of "Big John's" other girlfriends were familiar to readers of British tabloids. They included Playboy "Bunny Girl," Serena Williams. He was also sleeping with Angela Barnett, the future wife of pop star David Bowie. None of his girlfriends, however, was more notorious than the hooker, Christine Keeler, the female star of the Profumo Affair.

Bindon had launched himself into London society during his twelve-year relationship with model/actress Vicki Hodge, a beautiful, blue-blooded blonde who was a baronet's daughter. It was through Hodge that Bindon was originally introduced to Margaret Rose.

Hodge's previous romances had included dalliances with Rod Stewart and Yul Brynner, among others. But Bindon became her favorite. She said he was "tall, broad, with an air of menace, coupled with boyish charisma that rendered him irresistible."

Born in London in 1946, Hodge became known as a "tabloid femme fatale," in the wake of her "kiss-and-tell" confession about her affair with Prince Andrew. During his stationing aboard the HMS *Invincible,* Andrew had spent ten days of shore leave in Barbados in the arms of this beauty. She later revealed all the steamy details to the *News of the World* in London, which paid her £40,000. Others of her lovers included Ringo Starr and actor Elliott Gould, who had married Barbra Streisand.

Hodge's most infamous affair was with Bindon himself, whom she'd met in 1968 when he had a small role in *Performance* with Mick Jagger, a film not released until 1970.

Kiss and Tell: Vicki Hodge, the baronet's daughter.

Hodge introduced Bindon into *tout* London, where he met Margaret Rose, who soon became enchanted with him—and not just for his stupendous endowment. Reportedly, she liked his cockney accent, his slang, and his dirty jokes. She once told O'Toole, "His bawdy humor would have appealed to Henry VIII."

The son of a cabbie in Fulham, Bindon led a gang of street urchins at the age of ten and soon landed in prison for stealing live ammunition. Throughout his life, he would go in and out of jail. At one point, he was linked to John Hobbs, the glamorous international antiques dealer.

One of Bindon's former gang members told the press, "Big John has a temper that can explode into violence at any second. Watch out!"

As he grew older, Bindon ran a protection racket, shaking down West London pubs, and he maintained connections to two of the most feared gangs in London.

In addition to all his criminal activity, he wanted to be an actor, playing villains, of course.

John Huston found him a delight—"He could make a horse laugh"—-and cast him in his film *The Mackintosh Man* (1972), with Paul Newman. Stanley Kubrick found Bindon "a hell of a character" and hired him to appear in *Barry Lyndon* (1975). Bindon eventually became the bodyguard of the film's star, Ryan O'Neal.

At one point, Princess Margaret called O'Toole, asking him, as a favor to her, to find acting jobs for Bindon. He promised to speak to his partner, Jules Buck, who co-owned Keep Films with him. Buck came up with some small jobs, even stunt work, but no speaking parts.

Buck's commissions allowed Bindon to at least claim that he was still making films

In 1977, when money was tight, he signed as a bodyguard to tour with Led Zeppelin on the band's U.S. tour. But he soon got involved in violent disputes and was dismissed.

The following year, Bindon was paid £10,000 to stab gangster Johnny

Drake nine times outside a pub in Putney. Amazingly, he was tried but found not guilty.

Bindon later told the press, "The jury found me an all-around good geezer and gave me a pass."

Despite his nonchalance, Bindon's reputation had been seriously damaged, and both O'Toole and Margaret eventually dropped him.

He ended his days renting "me mammoth organ to rotting old sods." In 1993, he succumbed to AIDS.

O'Toole briefly considered attending his funeral, mainly to see who would show up. Some two hundred people did. He told Kenneth Griffith, "Big John was no dumb bloke. He put his time in and out of jail to good use. He knew Shakespeare better than I did, and he certainly knew English history better than I did. You name him—the Duke of Wellington or Oliver Cromwell—John could tell you all about them."

Griffith shared drinks and at least three pub dinners with O'Toole and Bindon and remembered him differently. "He was a very vulgar man, a braggart. He once told us that he planned to seduce the Queen herself. He said that he heard that what one sister went for, the other might, too."

"He was a bigger hellraiser than O'Toole, who seemed fascinated by this character. But then, O'Toole always sought out the *demimonde.*"

"When Big John met someone," Griffith continued, "the conversation soon drifted to his claim to fame, a 14-inch penis with a circumference of 6 ½ inches. He was mighty proud of that thing of his."

"One night, Big John told us that the first time he entered a prison shower, he was shown into a communal room where some twenty prisoners were showering. 'I looked around and surveyed the scene as all eyes turned to look at what I was swinging. That was the first time I realized that God did not create all men equally.'"

Carlton Television produced a documentary for ITV, *The Secret Life of Princess Margaret,* which was broadcast in 2005 and which corroborated the links between Margaret and the notorious gangster. The most recent broadcast of the Margaret/Bindon link was *The Princess and the Gangster* which aired in February of 2009.

Around the same time, Margaret was the unwitting and unwilling focus of a central plot device in the crime movie, *The Bank Job (2008),* based on the robbery, in 1971, of the Baker Street branch of Lloyd's Bank in London. In the caper, numerous safe deposit boxes were ransacked. As part of its plot line, the film developed the unsubstantiated claim that among the items stolen were compromising photographs of Bindon cavorting with Margaret on the beach at Mustique, and that the robbery was motivated by someone's wish to secure the pictures.

***

"In 1975, as I lay dying, talking to my old friend, Kenneth Griffith, I told him that after Mustique, Margaret and I went our separate ways and into the arms of others," O'Toole once related at a dinner party Elizabeth Taylor hosted for him at her chalet in Gstaad.

"We remained friends," O'Toole said. "Other than James Villiers and Dickie (Burton), she was about the only one who rallied to my side after my disastrous attempt to bring *Macbeth* to the Old Vic."

"I know this sounds as corny as hell, but, as I told Griffith, 'I borrowed a line from Bogie in the closing reel of *Casablanca,* and told Margaret that, regardless of what the future holds for us, we would always have Marrakech and we would always have Mustique.'"

Chapter 23

Arrevederci Roma!

Problem Paparazzi & Barbara Steele

O'Toole Plunges into a Torrid Romance with
"Miss Dracula," The Queen of British Horror Movies.

In a Roman Street Brawl, O'Toole Assaults a Famous Photographer and Ends Up in Jail

In Rome, Peter O'Toole became enchanted with Barbara Steele (center photo) who enjoyed a cult following among the Italians for her horror flicks.

She confided in him that, "I'm called the working-for-rent kind of actress. Actually, I never wanted to be a movie star. My dream was to become the female Picasso."

O'Toole was stationed in Rome during his filming of John Huston's "sword and sandal" epic, *The Bible* (1966), in which he had interpreted the role of "the Three Angels." Among others, the picture had starred Ava Gardner.

Every time they entered or exited from the grounds of Cinecittà, he and the other stars were aggressively pursued by paparazzi, the most aggressive photographers in the world. Gardner especially had her privacy invaded.

In Rome, he was staying at the exclusive Hotel Excelsior along the via Veneto. "After all, this is where the movie stars stayed."

On his second night in town, he'd retired early—and alone—stripping down and getting under the sheets to read a script that had been sent to him.

"Long ago, I'd been warned that the paparazzi in Rome would stop at nothing to get incriminating pictures," O'Toole said. "At that time, I viewed them as only a minor annoyance. I didn't know to what ends they would go to get a picture."

Suddenly, there was a knock on the door. "Housekeeping," a woman's voice called out in English with a slight German accent. He had ordered more towels from room service and had been expecting the maid.

Then, without receiving an invitation to enter, she used a passkey to unlock and open his door. Barging into his bedroom, she raced toward his bed, a big, buxom blonde who was "jaybird naked," as he'd later recall.

She was closely trailed by two paparazzi, who snapped photographs of him, as he shouted for them to get out.

He pressed a button summoning security, and within minutes, two of the hotel's security guards arrived to remove the invaders.

In the aftermath of the incident, the night manager arrived with champagne, roses and apologies. "You know I'll be splashed across the tabloids in the morning!" O'Toole raged. "Now get out! I need some sleep!"

The next day, he emerged from his depression when he was introduced to a Cheshire-born actress, a green-eyed, raven-haired beauty who was working in films in Rome at the time.

She was Barbara Steele, the world's reigning "Queen of Horror Movies," sometimes known as "Miss Dracula" or "The Queen of Terror." She had a large cult following throughout Italy.

O'Toole was captivated by her charm and beauty. He began to date her. *[Perhaps a stronger word is needed.]*

With Support from Other Movie Stars, O'Toole Organizes a Film Boycott of Italy

He quickly discovered that she had a sharp wit and a sense of self-mockery, at one point informing him, "I swear I'm never going to climb out of another coffin."

Her breakout role had arrived when the Italian director Mario Bava had cast her in Black Sunday (1960), now hailed as a film classic.

Steele had starred in a string of horror films, including the 1962 *The Horrible Dr. Hichcock* and—released around the same time, *The Ghost,* an adaptation of Edgar Allan Poe's short story, *The Pit and the Pendulum.* During a period she spent in the U.S., director Don Siegel had cast her opposite Elvis Presley in a low-budget western, *Flaming Star* (1960), but after a dispute, she'd walked off the set and was replaced by Barbara Eden.

Among the first words uttered between Steele and O'Toole was his saying to her, "I hear you have a cult following"

"You can't eat off cults," she responded.

O'Toole had read about her in the press, one reporter claiming, "Barbara Steele is the premiere actress in the world to have starred, survived, and excelled in the male chauvinist domain known as the horror film."

In *Black Sunday* (1960), Barbara Steele's breakout role, a vampire/witch, destroyed by her brother, returns several centuries later to wreak vengeance on her descendants.

A film reviewer had written, "Above all else, her eyes most definitely have it. Wide open, terrified as she screams lustily inside some torture chamber, hypnotic as she lures men to their deaths, incandescent as she devours whatever is in her path."

She had experimented with London and Hollywood before turning to Italy for her popularity. "The film blokes in Britain are embarrassed by women. They feel anybody with any kind of femininity, womanliness, should have a Parisian accent. I could never be the red-cheeked English lassie they wanted."

"I also tried Hollywood, but they wanted me to be one of their plastic dolls on the factory conveyor belt, dyed blonde, of course. I was told that they would have to pin my ears back and that I didn't have any *décolletage.* Talking about my failures is such a frigging drag."

She admitted that at one point, Cary Grant wanted to put her under personal contract.

"But I thought he was gay," O'Toole said.

"Perhaps he had an off night," she answered.

"Back in Britain, Grant wanted to put me under something, too," O'Toole said.

O'Toole developed his own take on Steele's movies: "She makes those thud' n' blunder type of films. You know, where things go *eek!*—or *ecce!*—in the night. She is devilishly beautiful, with a profane figure to match."

[Years later, after O'Toole made the XXX-rated Caligula *for Tinto Brass in Rome, he encountered Steele at a party in London.*

She told him that Brass had once wanted her to make a totally pornographic movie, but it never came about.

"I don't know what your experience has been, but many actresses have told me that they allow their leading men to penetrate them under the sheets during their love scenes," she said.

"I think that should be mandatory in such scenes and written into the bloody contracts," O'Toole said. "No more faking it."]

On some of their evenings together, trailed by aggressive paparazzi, O'Toole and Steele made the rounds of Roman bars together.

They were often joined by his friend, Albert Finney, even though they'd been rivals for lead roles in certain movies. *[Finney had turned down the lead role in* Lawrence of Arabia *before it was awarded to O'Toole.]*

In time, both actors would share their amusement at one director who had attributed their joint "failures" to their inability to display "a certain feminine vulnerability."

Karel Reisz had written "What we prize in Garbo is her masculinity, and what we prize in Olivier and Chaplin is their femininity. If it's there in Finney, he has suppressed it, even if he has played 'camp' quite amusingly from time to time. So, in the rarified atmosphere of great, great stars, he's not on that level. But I think that O'Toole hasn't utilized that side of his personality either, so Finney is in good company."

"Bloody Hell!" O'Toole said after reading that. "Did Reisz see *Lawrence of Arabia?* Femininity! Hell, gays saw me as a flaming faggot!"

Sometimes joining them during their bar hopping was Dave Cowley, a man who doubled on some occasions as a security guard and personal bodyguard. Half-Italian, he had grown up in Clerkenwell, a London neighborhood known as "Little Italy."

He had contended as a Featherweight/Lightweight in the boxing rings of Britain in the 1930s. In 1938, as war clouds loomed over Britain, he became that country's lightweight champ. In all, he'd won 128 fights, losing 40. "He was our bodyguard," O'Toole said, "except he wasn't there on the night I truly needed him."

In spite of being hounded by hordes of paparazzi along the via Veneto, O'Toole took Steele almost nightly to his favorite watering hole, Harry's Bar.

Another of his favorite watering holes along the fabled, celebrity-haunted strip of the via Veneto was Café de Paris. Whenever possible, he tried to end his evenings there.

At around 3AM one morning, O'Toole and Steele were leaving the café after a final nightcap. As they emerged onto the street, a cluster of paparazzi moved in on them.

O'Toole always remembered the most aggressive of the lot, a young man who looked like a late teenager. Right in O'Toole's face, he exploded a flash-bulb which temporarily blinded him.

He tried to shake free of this photographer, but he was intent on trailing Steele and him, along with a horde of other photographers, back to their hotel. At one point, the aggressive teenager shot a picture almost directly in Steele's face, blinding her.

Infuriated, O'Toole, who was not a violent man on most occasions, punched the man really hard, bloodying his nose. He fell back onto the pavement, severely injuring his head when he fell. Blood began gushing from his wound, soaking his face.

Along with other paparazzi, a crowd soon gathered, and O'Toole was recognized. The angry passers-by screamed threats at him. Within minutes, the security police patrolling the via Veneto arrived, slapping O'Toole into handcuffs and hauling Steele off to jail, even though she was a victim and had not participated in the violent encounter.

At police headquarters, both O'Toole and Steele were subjected to intense questioning before being locked up.

In two, maybe three hours, both of them were set free. Lawyers from Cinecittà had been summoned to police headquarters and secured their release.

At the hospital, the wounded paparazzo, Rino Barillari, received five stitches to his head as a means of sealing the wound he'd sustained during his fall to the pavement.

[Beginning with this disastrous encounter with O'Toole, Barillari would go on to become the unofficial "King of the Paparazzi" during Rome's reign as "Hollywood on the Tiber." During his long and stress-inducing future, Barillari would claim many more "victims": Ingrid Bergman, Jacqueline Kennedy, Brigitte Bardot, Anna Magnani, Al Pacino—even the Pope.

During the course of a career spanning more than fifty years, Barillari would make 162 visits to the emergency wings of hospitals for treatments of work-related assaults and injuries. During that period, he suffered eleven broken ribs and a serious knife wound, and 76 of his cameras would be smashed.]

Back at the Excelsior, O'Toole and Steele slept until noon, when they were awakened by a loud pounding on their door. Throwing a robe around his nude body, O'Toole answered the door and encountered two police officers. A precinct captain informed him that he had been formally charged with assault and battery.

He was ordered not to leave Rome and informed that within the hour, other officers would arrive with a court order from a local judge to confiscate his luggage and his passport.

"Not even a change of underwear left for me?" O'Toole asked.

After they left, O'Toole went into action. He immediately called his stunt double, Peter Perkins, who bore an amazing resemblance to him. When he wasn't working with O'Toole, Perkins bred dogs in Ireland.

He wanted Perkins to disguise himself with one of his suits, his glasses, and cap, and then appear in the lobby of the Excelsior, paying his bill. In the meantime, with Steele accompanying him, he would slip out the hotel's rear entrance and make a run for the airport.

Before leaving the hotel, as a fine-tuning of his disguise, he put on the fake beard he'd previously disguised himself with during his filming on the set of *The Bible*.

Steele agreed to accompany him by taxi to the airport. When they got there, before he kissed her goodbye, she told him, "It's easier to find someone to make love to than somebody you'll want to wake up with in the morning."

"How true, my darling girl," he said, before giving her a passionate farewell kiss.

Unlike most of his unwilling subjects, Anita Ekberg, "The Queen of the Trevi Fountain" in *La Dolce Vita*, was said to adore Rino Barillari, the "King of the Paparazzi."

Here, he is photographed with Ekberg in 1982 upon her return to the Trevi Fountain.

Airborne and en route to Paris, O'Toole imagined that 'the Bogeys,' as he called them, were right at that moment arriving at The Excelsior to confiscate his passport and his luggage.

Before he landed in France, he concocted a plan to boycott future films that called for location shooting in Rome. "We'll cost the fuckers millions of dollars for treating me like this."

He'd begin with the most obvious of his potential allies, each a victim of the paparazzi, and systematically contact everyone on the list. Topping his list of victims were Elizabeth Taylor, Ava Gardner, Richard Burton, and Frank Sinatra. He also called others of his show-biz friends—actors, directors, and producers to enlist their collaboration.

Conveniently, Burton and Elizabeth were already in Paris, staying at the Lancaster Hotel. They'd been the most abused victims of "those paparazzi vultures."

Problem Paparazzi Incite O'Toole's Enraged Demands For The Film Industry's Boycott of Rome

During the filming of *Cleopatra,* hordes of paparazzi had camped out at Cinecittà, creating chaos for the production. They were hoping to get a candid shot of "the illicit lovers," Burton and Elizabeth, together. The Vatican had already denounced Elizabeth as an "erotic vagrant."

When Burton and Taylor had dined at the Tre Scalini, on the Piazza Navona, they were surrounded by screeching photographers, some of whom even followed Elizabeth to her chalet in Gstaad. Eager to sell newspapers, the photographers had practically engulfed them every time they ventured outside.

It was their rabid pursuit of the two stars that caused Federico Fellini, while filming *La Dolce Vita*, to rename his intrusive reporter, "Paparazzo," a name that translates from the Italian as "buzzing insect." It soon became a term understood in dozens of languages.

Sinatra's battles with the press and the paparazzi were legendary. Based on his bad experiences there, he made it a point to no longer visit the via Veneto. Whenever he did, the paparazzi rushed him, and there was a lot of pushing, shoving, and cursing.

"These creeps have ruined my visits to Rome," he claimed. "I can't even take a leak without some jerk following me to the men's room, hoping to get a picture of my dick."

An eavesdropper in the Vatican was paid to report on his meeting with His Holiness. Sinatra bowed to kiss the pope's ring.

POPE: Are you a tenor?
SINATRA: I'm a baritone.
POPE: And what operas do you sing?
SINATRA: I don't sing opera, your holiness.
POPE: Where did you study?
SINATRA: I never studied.

Before the paparazzi began focusing on Burton and Taylor, they'd been relentless in documenting the nuances of Sinatra's romance with Ava Gardner.

"The vicious animals gave me no peace, especially after Ava flew to Rome to shoot *The Barefoot Contessa* (1954) with Humphrey Bogart."

"I feel I can't step out the door," Sinatra said. "In Rome, I can no longer eat at my favorite trattoria because they'll disrupt any place I go to get a plate of spaghetti."

At one point, the paparazzi pursued him so violently he suffered bouts of insomnia and depression. These freaks are nothing but henchmen and goons."

Sinatra told O'Toole, "I refused to come into Rome when I was making *Von Ryan's Express* (1965)." Outside Rome, the studio had leased an eighteen-room villa for him, complete with helipad. On one occasion, he fled to a retreat high in the Dolomite Alps as a means of escaping from them.

Later, during discussions with the producers of his upcoming movie, *What's New Pussycat?,* O'Toole got them to switch the venue of their location shooting from Rome to Paris.

"I had the star power back then and could get away with that," he said. "With me leading the charge, we were hoping to cost Rome millions of dollars in lost revenues."

Chapter 24

What's New Pussycat?

Chasing Dollybirds, O'Toole Takes Over from Warren Beatty

As a "Babe Magnet," O'Toole Confronts Four of the Most Alluring Babes in Entertainment: Romy Schneider, Paula Prentiss, Ursula Andress, & Capucine

Cast as a womanizing and sex-obsessed fashion editor, Peter O'Toole played a "babe magnet" in *What's New Pussycat?*. Later, caustic critics bitchily proclaimed that the original choice for the role, Warren Beatty, would have been more convincing, as he was both sexier and better looking than O'Toole.

In response to these barbs, O'Toole said, "What a cruel blow. It's driving me to drink!"

When Peter O'Toole and Peter Sellers—each a hot box office star—were first introduced by Kenneth Griffith, neither of them knew that they would one day be starring in the biggest box office comedy of that time, *What's New Pussycat?* (1965).

Griffith had arranged a meeting with the understanding that Sellers, who was attending a play at the Duchess Theatre in London, would meet Griffith with his friend, O'Toole, on the pavement outside the theater after the conclusion of a play. O'Toole and Griffith were to wait for him in the lobby.

As the theatre emptied, O'Toole and Griffith waited and waited, but Sellers did not come out. The theater emptied, but still no Sellers. Finally, they went inside and, according to Griffith, found him hiding in the theater, reluctant to meet O'Toole. Griffith suggested that he seemed too shy or timid.

This seems hard to believe.

He also claimed that he and O'Toole went "crawling on our hands and knees" between the seats of the theater searching for Sellers. If this claim is true, then Sellers much have been in a poor mental condition at the time, perhaps heavily medicated because of his ongoing ill health. Surely, he wasn't intimated meeting someone of O'Toole's stature, as he had been introduced to some of the most famous figures in the world, including British royalty. His affair with Princess Margaret was gossiped about.

Whatever happened that night, and however their initial logistics unfolded, Sellers agreed to have dinner with Griffith and O'Toole.

"I planned to add Capucine to my list of seductions," Peter Sellers told O'Toole. "Princess Margaret, Mia Farrow, Sophia Loren, Liza Minnelli....I got around. But I struck out with Capucine. She told me I was really in love with my mother."

A bedroom farce: Woody Allen, Romy Schneider, Peter O'Toole

The three men journeyed by taxi from London's theater district to a Turkish restaurant in Chelsea, arriving at the doorstep just as it was shutting down. When he spotted Sellers and O'Toole, the owner relented, and as a "special after-hours dispensation," agreed to let them into his restaurant. The kitchen had shut down, but he provided them with skewers of beef and a charcoal brazier set directly on their table.

> *"I'm Trapped between Dr. Strangelove (Peter Sellers) &*
> *Lawrence of Arabia (Peter O'Toole)"*
>
> *— Woody Allen*

The debut of their collaboration on *Pussycat* was based on a link to Siân Phillips, O'Toole's wife, who was ultimately deeply disappointed in her lack of any involvement in the final product.

Originally the agent, Harvey Orkin, had given Siân a copy of the script, which she read almost immediately at her home in Hampstead. Apparently, she evaluated it as exciting comedy with a possible lead for her husband.

O'Toole liked the script, also interpreting it as potential vehicle for himself as the male lead. The original *Pussycat* script had been written by Woody Allen. In it, in addition to his role as scriptwriter, Allen also made a screen appearance—the first of his then-youthful career.

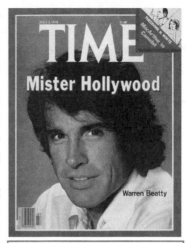

Warren Beatty, "sitting securely on the throne of Hollywood" as shown by this cover of TIME magazine, July 3, 1978.

A few days after reading the script, O'Toole read that *Pussycat's* producer, Charles Feldman, had already cast Warren Beatty in the role O'Toole had wanted.

[Feldman, as producer, a former lover of Marilyn Monroe, had already turned out such acclaimed films as The Glass Menagerie *(1950), and* A Streetcar Named Desire *(1951), both of them based on plays by Tennessee Williams.]*

Ten days later, however, Beatty dropped out.

The film's title had been inspired by the way Beatty typically answered many of his phone calls. *[What's New Pussycat?]* It was speculated in the press that Beatty dropped out because the role he'd been commissioned to play—that of a notorious womanizer—paralleled his own life too closely.

However, Donner later claimed that Beatty rejected any involvement in the film because Feldman insisted on casting Feldman's former girlfriend (Capucine) into a key role.

Shortly thereafter, O'Toole contacted Feldman, who suggested that he should discuss the creative aspects of the upcoming film with Allen. It was then agreed that Allen would come for a dialogue with O'Toole in his home in Hampstead.

Siân later recalled Allen's arrival: "He was small, droll, and settled cautiously in a corner of our Green Room."

She also remembered how, when her husband came downstairs to meet Allen, he rather rudely dismissed her and immediately went into a huddle with Allen.

Siân lamented, "There went my role. My part was later given to Capucine.

I was mortified at first, but didn't appreciate that O'Toole loathed nepotism. It was a measure of his slightly cockeyed respect for me that he strenuously avoided doing me any professional favors."

O'Toole recalled his first meeting with Allen in his Hampstead living room. Allen informed him, "I'm a militant Freudian atheist."

"The best I could come up with was that I was a 'retired Christian,' as I had so often repeated. Not as good as Allen's line."

Groucho Marx. "He wudda been funny, but he dropped out."

***

In *Pussycat,* the role of the crazy, manic psychiatrist, Dr. Fassbender, was originally to have been played by Groucho Marx. But like Beatty before him, Marx then dropped out, too.

Feldman, as the film's producer, left himself open to a major financial risk when he cast Sellers into one of the film's key roles, but he really wanted him. "The insurance companies would not insure Sellers, treating him like the Black Plague, because he'd recently suffered a heart attack—the eighth in a series of seven previous heart attacks. In discussing it, Sellers frankly admitted to Feldman, "Eight times, I've risen from the dead just as they were hammering the nails into my coffin."

This was not the first time Peter Sellers had been cast as a zany eccentric. Here he is as the potentially genocidal *Dr. Strangelove.*

"If he had died during the shoot, I would have had to cover the losses myself and reshoot his scenes with some other actor," Feldman said. "I prayed that would not happen. I ordered Sellers to work only five hours a day, and I clustered all of his scenes together so they could be shot in slightly more than two weeks.

Sellers, in collaboration with the wardrobe department, decided he would appear in all his scenes wearing a Beatles wig, but what he thought would add to the film's comedy backfired. When the film was released, one critic wrote, "Seller's wig looks like some discard that Laurence Olivier left behind in his dressing room after appearing as Richard III."

Other critics defined it as a "Prince Valiant" wig, something similar to what Robert Wagner wore in the Technicolor and Cinemascope action/adventure extravaganza, *Prince Valiant* (1954).

Sellers and O'Toole tossed a coin for which of them would get star billing. Sellers won.

In order of their billing, the rest of the cast included a then relatively unknown Woody Allen, and four of the most sought after actresses of that era: Romy Schneider, Capucine, Paula Prentiss, and Ursula Andress. It was announced that the movie would be shot mostly in Paris.

Londoner Clive Donner, a defining figure in New Wave British cinema, was hired to direct *Pussycat,* his first American film. He'd made his breakthrough in 1963 with his direction of the film version of *The Guest [In the U.K., it had been entitled* The Caregiver*]*, based on a play by Harold Pinter. It had starred O'Toole's friend, Alan Bates, and was financed in part by Elizabeth Taylor, Richard Burton, Noël Coward, and Sellers himself.

Critics laughed at Peter Sellers' wig. In photo above. Robert Wagner plays Prince Valiant (1954) opposite Janet Leigh.

In the zany context of *Pussycat*, O'Toole, cast as Michael James, wants to remain true to his *fiancée* Carole Werner (Schneider), but he's distracted by the fact that every woman he meets falls madly in love with him. They include a parachutist, Rita (as played by Andress), who literally falls from the sky into his vintage automobile. Prentiss, who also falls in love with him, plays a neurotic American stripper.

Disaster looms when all of these manic and extroverted characters, each unaware of the others' presence, check into the same small hotel for a weekend in the French countryside.

***

During the shoot, O'Toole said "I was comfortable, not cozy, working with Sellers. We had a few sharp words, but that happens on any shoot. For the most part, we were *simpatico.* Sellers was in ill health. Yet his dynamic personality shone through. Dynamic, hell. It came out his pores, almost frighteningly."

That's my judgment of him. Sellers didn't agree. Off screen, he told me he had no personality at all, which, of course, was not true."

Over dinner, O'Toole told Sellers

Looking for pussy, but seemingly rather frightened when confronted with it, Peter Sellers (left) and Peter O'Toole survived this zany comedy.

that to prepare for his role, he had screened all the movies of W.C. Fields that he could, since he admired the way that vaudevillian pratfaller had performed.

O'Toole went on to say that his previous appearances in comedy had been rare. His favorite being his interpretation at the Bristol Old Vic of Alfred Doolittle, Eliza's father, in George Bernard Shaw's *Pygmalion,* first performed in 1913.

O'Toole also complimented Sellers for his bizarre role in the film *Lolita,* expressing once again that he had wanted the James Mason role.

As Dr. Fassbinder, psychiatrist to the character played by O'Toole, Sellers offers little aid, as he's too busy stalking another of his patients, the character played by Capucine.

O'Toole had long wanted a key role in a comedy. "But in my first time out, did I have to face off against Sellers, the funniest man alive? Not to mention Woody Allen?"

"The movie was full of hot and cold running dollybirds," O'Toole said. "What an array of beauties. More than a flaccid prick could handle. At least I was cast in a movie where I wasn't in love with a camel or with Richard Burton." He was referring, of course, to his previous films, *Lawrence of Arabia* and *Becket.*

Romy Schneider, the Vienna-born actress, was O'Toole's main love interest in *Pussycat.* The year she met O'Toole, she was just emerging from the ruins of a love affair with the French matinée idol, Alain Delon. Later, she'd marry Harry Meyen, the German director and actor.

According to O'Toole, "Romy was out of my league and involved with others, but I was saddened by her early death in 1982. At first, suicide was suspected, but it turned out to be cardiac arrest. She was forty-four."

Raised in San Antonio, and of Sicilian descent, Paula Prentiss was married

Pussycats, from upper left: Prentiss, Schneider, Andress, Capucine, Allen, O'Toole, and Sellers.

to actor Richard Benjamin when she starred in *Pussycat.* During its filming in Paris, she suffered a nervous breakdown, which would keep her out of films for five years. She returned to work with her husband in the short-lived TV series, *He & She.*

Those writers who compile lists of "Who's Had Who" in Hollywood often cite Ursula Andress as one of O'Toole seductions. Of course, that is possible, but there isn't any strong evidence to indicate they were lovers. It is irrefutable is that Andress was nearing the end of her 1957 marriage to former matinee idol John Derek. She'd married the handsome actor in the wake of her ill-fated affair with the doomed James Dean.

Andress had become famous as a shell diver, "Honey Rider," an object of desire in *Dr. No* (1962), one of the early

Manic energy and humor that was sometimes strained. Here, O'Toole escapes from a *gendarme* and a crowd whose members were made up to resemble historic figures from France's cultural past.

The character in the foreground was made up to resemble the 19th century novelist Émile Zola, for anyone quick enough to recognize him.

James Bond films based on a character created by Ian Fleming. From the warm waters of the Caribbean rose this vision of loveliness wearing a white bikini and armed with an oversized diving knife strapped to her hip.

After the release of *Dr. No*, she'd spend the rest of her life identified as "the quintessential Bond girl."

But it was not Andress upon whom O'Toole would focus his romantic fantasies, but Capucine. He told Sellers, "I think Ursula is a little too much woman for me."

Capucine had become well known after her comedic role in *The Pink Panther* (1963), co-starring Sellers and David Niven. In Paris, around the time she'd met Audrey Hepburn, she'd modeled for the House of Dior and Givenchy. The two women bonded and became friends until Capucine's tragic ending (see chapter 25).

Capucine reminded O'Toole of Audrey Hepburn, with whom, a year later,

437

he'd appear in *How to Steal a Million* (1966).

"An obvious nonconformist, she *[Capucine]* was always elegantly attired as if she'd stepped off a high-fashion runway. Her features were classic. She was very independent. I was stricken."

He later confessed his infatuation to Kenneth Griffith and a few other trusted friends, who he knew would be discreet around Siân.

"On screen, she projected a calm demeanor, a real ice queen, but I set out to melt the ice," O'Toole told Griffith.

Lovely Paula Prentiss as a neurotic American stripper

As a hip, attractive, and intuitive woman, Capucine was immediately aware of O'Toole's sexual interest in her, claiming, "From the first hour we met, he kept looking at me like I were a suspicious-looking trunk, and he was a monstrous customs agent."

In Paris, O'Toole and Siân booked a suite at the swanky Hotel George V, a second home to many visiting movie stars. Jules Buck, O'Toole's co-producer in Keep Films, flew in to join them.

The two men often went on the prowl together after dark. One evening, O'Toole stumbled in drunk and told some bizarre story about how he'd beaten up a *gendarme [French police officer]*. He claimed it was all part of a comedy act in a night club.

The story didn't make sense to his wife. She told him, "Just so long as you didn't get arrested. I thought you abhorred violence."

When not needed on the film set, O'Toole went shopping for art, or whatever. Meanwhile, Siân with her rail-thing fashion model body sought deeply discounted clothes from the House of Dior. Worn by its models during fashion shows, some of the garments were sold inexpensively as used samples of the previous season's styles.

Over Allen's objections, O'Toole and Sellers inserted their egos into the script, aggressively rewriting scenes, stage business, and dialogue. At one point, O'Toole made the astonishing statement, "Peter and I jotted down our rewrites on the back of a pack of contraceptives."

Regardless of who wrote them, some lines emerged as hilarious. At one point, Capucine says, "I'm a physical woman. I feel I come from a family of nymphomaniacs, including my father and my two brothers."

In another scene, Sellers as Dr. Fassbinder suggests to participants in a group therapy session he's leading, *"Vy don't ve all take off our clothes? It's so modern."*

Prentiss, as the neurotic American stripper, informs O'Toole that "I am a semi-virgin. In Paris, I'm a virgin, but in America, I am not." Then she announces, "I feel faint. Excuse me for a minute. I'm going into the bathroom to take an overdose of sleeping pills."

Audiences were delighted with the unexpected appearance in the film of Richard Burton—then at the height of his fame. Spotting Burton, O'Toole asks, "Are you Richard Burton?

"No," Burton answers. "I'm Peter O'Toole."

"God bless you," O'Toole replies. "You must be the greatest man who ever lived."

Sellers had recently married the Swedish actress Britt Ekland. When O'Toole met her, he noticed that she was deep into her pregnancy and said, "Married such a little time, and already he's gotten you into trouble!"

In January of 1965, Sellers and Ekland announced the birth of a daughter, Victoria.

What's New Pussycat? was shot between October of 1964 and January of 1965. Ticket sales exploded nationwide after its premiere in Manhattan on June 22, 1965. In France, it was released as *Quoi de neuf, Pussycat?*

After *Pussycat's* release, Allen went public with his displeasure over the final cut, calling it "a move of the quintessential Hollywood machine. They executed this project with everything that everyone hates about Hollywood films. People who have no sense of humor decided what's funny and what's not. People putting their girlfriends in roles. *[It was] t*he worst nightmare one could think of."

"But I survived," Allen went on to say, "despite having to work on a comedy with *Dr. Strangelove* and *Lawrence of Arabia."* He then announced that *Pussycat* would be the last film in which he would appear that he did not direct.

The film's theme song, "What's New Pussycat?," by Burt Bacharach (music) and Hal David (lyrics), was belted out with sex appeal and verve by Tom Jones. It became a hit record whose wording went a long way in promoting the film. It was later nominated for an Academy Award.

In addition to the theme song recorded by Tom Jones, the film included Dionne Warwick singing "Here I Am," and Manfred Mann warbling "My Little Red Book."

When filming was wrapped, Feldman thanked O'Toole for working overtime and beyond the terms laid out in his contract. In gratitude, he presented him with a new red Rolls-Royce Silver Cloud III. Siân wondered how long it would take before her husband smashed it up.

O'Toole thanked Feldman for his lavish gift, but suggested that he would have preferred a new Ferrari Superfast, which was not available in any dealership at the time. *[Featuring twelve cylinders and speeds of up to 171 mph, only 36 of them were ever made, one of them famously associated with Prince Bernhard of The Netherlands.]*

***

O'Toole would make only a brief, uncredited, appearance in another Sellers movie, *Casino Royale* (1967), a James Bond spoof that also starred Orson Welles, Ursula Andress, Woody Allen, Deborah Kerr, Charles Boyer, William Holden, George Raft, and Jean-Paul Belmondo. David Niven played an aging secret agent who'd been pulled out of retirement to confront a menace from the international crime ring, SMERSH.

In one scene, one hundred bagpipers paraded across the screen. As a joke, O'Toole, who played the bagpipes, appeared, uncredited, in the scene as Bagpiper #101. The director of that scene, John Huston, didn't notice O'Toole in the lineup until he watched the rushes.

Shortly after that, O'Toole learned from Sellers that he was walking off the picture, refusing to appear ever again on the same set with his co-star, Orson Welles.

"Sellers was going through a really paranoid period of his life," O'Toole said. "Not trusting anyone, even reliable me."

O'Toole and William Holden, meeting that day on the set during the filming of Casino's 1967 version, bonded like two friends who had much to talk about, namely their joint affairs with Audrey Hepburn and Capucine.

[Featuring additional (and astonishing) action scenes, Casino Royale, *starring Daniel Craig, was later remade in 2006.]*

Chapter 25

O'Toole's Combustible Liaison With
Capucine
"The World's Most Beautiful Transsexual?"
Or Was It Just a Rumor?

During the Filming of "What's New Pussycat?"
He Discovers That She's Deeply In Love with Audrey Hepburn

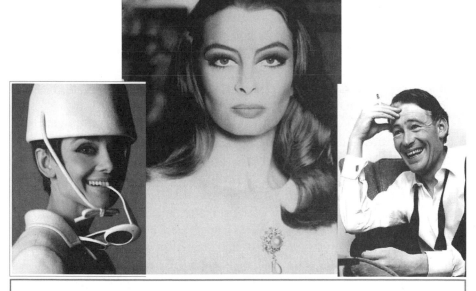

Love Triangle: Audrey Hepburn (left), Capucine, and Peter O'Toole. When he met Capucine, she said she hated her real name (Germaine). In France, it's as common as Gladys.

He asked her what Capucine meant. "It's French for nasturtium," she said. She also told him, "I used to think I needed a man to define myself. No more."

During his filming of *What's New Pussycat* (1965), Peter O'Toole fell under the spell cast by the enchantress, the French actress, Capucine.

He agreed with the Italian director, Federico Fellini, who in the 1960s and 70s blazed across the screen like a shooting star before flickering out. "She had a face to launch a thousand ships, but she was born too late." Fellini said.

Capucine was the best friend of Audrey Hepburn. Collectively, they were known as "the two most beautiful faces of the 20th Century."

Born in 1928, in Toulon, along the Mediterranean coast of France, she would grow up to become a high-fashion model and later an actress. Her greatest fame derived from her role in *The Pink Panther* (1963), and *What's New Pussycat?* (1965). Both films had starred Peter Sellers. On the set of *Pussycat,* she was introduced to O'Toole.

Capucine modeling Givenchy's *haute couture* in Paris

He immediately commented that she reminded him of the bust of the Egyptian Queen, Nefertiti, which he had seen in a museum in Berlin. "My first photographer compared my high cheekbones to that of an early Picasso painting," she said.

Right away, he realized that she was not modest, and that she had the necessary ego to become a big star.

Discreetly, within a week of meeting her, he launched an affair with her. A few nights later, Sellers delivered a startling revelation, asserting that Capucine was a transsexual. He'd heard that on the set of *The Pink Panther.* This rumor may have made its first published appearance in 1991, in James Parish's *The Hollywood Book of Death,* an overview of the circumstances associated with the demises of about a hundred entertainment industry icons.

Capucine never admitted to being a transsexual, although near the end of

---

"If you were more of a woman, I would be more of a man. Kissing you is like kissing the side of a beer bottle."

—Laurence Harvey to Capucine during their filming of Walk on the Wild Side (1962)

her life, she confessed to "some surgical read-justment," whatever that meant. She did admit that she was a lesbian. In spite of her affairs with men who included producer Charles Feldman and actor William Holden, she claimed she had always been in love with Audrey Hepburn.

O'Toole was not daunted by the transsexual rumors, because he'd been intimate friends with April Ashley, Britain's most famous transgendered person, during his filming of *Lawrence of Arabia* in Spain a few years before. *[For more on this, refer to Chapter 14.]*

Transsexuals, in fact, had often intrigued him. He told Sellers, "I like it when they've got it cut off."

Capucine, older, still modeling, and still looking fabulous

Capucine shared with O'Toole her secrets of stardom. "Every time I get in front of a camera, I think of it as an attractive man I am meeting for the first time. I find him demanding and aloof, so I must do all in my power to interest him."

At the age of nineteen, Capucine made her 1949 film debut in the French picture, *Rendez-vous de juillet*. On the set she met actor Pierre Trabaud. They would marry the following year, although the union was a disaster, lasting for only six months.

Trabaud was brilliant at voices, and was the eternal French-language voice of the cartoon sailor, Popeye. He was also the French-language voice of Daffy Duck and even Marlon Brando in the French release of *On the Waterfront* (1954).

The major source of the transgendered rumor about Capucine came from her one and only husband himself. He never discussed it with members of the press, but he asserted to his male friends in Paris that when he'd married Capucine, she was a transvestite who later underwent male-to-female surgery in a hospital in Geneva. Although in some ways it appears as a bizarre act of slander, the accusation that she'd been born a male with an undeveloped penis has to be given some credence.

Throughout his life, Trabaud preferred sex with transvestites or transsexuals and was rather frank about his preference. His belief was that drag queens and transsexuals "give a man a better time in bed than a regular woman. They do more, give more of themselves, know more ways to pleasure a man."

He compared his pursuit of transvestites or transsexuals to study men in ancient Egypt who preferred to sodomize a man who had had both his penis and his testicles removed. "Those Egyptian men knew that a completely cas-

443

trated male who could get no enjoyment with the front part concentrated all their sexual energy into their rear door," Trabaud said.

The comparison doesn't quite hold up, but that was his expressed belief.

Death came to Trabaud in 2005, when he was living in France's Hauts-de-Seine region. He went to his grave maintaining what was either the truth or else an enduring and consistent campaign of slander about his former wife.

As his relationship deepened, O'Toole quickly discovered that Capucine's first and most preferred topic of conversation was Audrey Hepburn.

Pierre Trabaud. A preference for *Travesti*?

Director Billy Wilder defined the bonding of Hepburn with Capucine as "the greatest female friendship of the 20th Century." In one reckless moment, Audrey told the director, "To know the other half of me, you must know Capucine. She supplies me with my daily oxygen."

In 1967. Susan Hayward appeared with Capucine in the 1967 crime comedy, *The Honey Pot.* Hayward claimed that Capucine told her, "Audrey and I on many a night have rescued each other from the brink of suicide."

When both Audrey and Capucine strutted their stuff on runways as models in Paris, they met and soon swore to each other to become "best friends for life."

Audrey Hepburn as the prostitute, Holly Golightly, in Truman Capote's *Breakfast at Tiffany's*

Born in Belgium on May 4, 1929, Audrey was the daughter of a banker and a Dutch baroness, both of whom were Nazi sympathizers.

During their struggling days, Capucine and Audrey shared an apartment while they both pursued careers as models. That presumably was the beginning of their lesbian link, promoted more by Capucine's desires than by those of Audrey.

In 1952, Capucine got a two-week job modeling the latest clothes aboard a French cruise ship. She shared a cabin with a stunning 17-year-old dancer, who was working in the chorus of the ship's nightclub. Her name was Brigitte Bardot.

When Audrey or Capucine wandered into "deep, deep darkness, a stairway to a dark gulf," as Audrey characterized it, "Cap *[i.e., Capucine]* and I were there for each other."

Capucine told O'Toole, "I rescued Audrey when actor Ben Gazzara walked out on her."

Obviously I wasn't in love," Gazzara later asserted. "I was flattered that someone like that would be in love with me. But I didn't know how deeply in love she was with me until I left her. She told others, not me, that I had broken her heart." After Gazzara's departure, she wanted to kill herself.

According to what he confessed to O'Toole, when Holden began *The Country Girl* with Grace Kelly, he switched his affection to the blonde goddess.

When Holden bonded with O'Toole on the set of *Casino Royale,* they became instant friends. "Let's go on drinking, and get really plastered like I used to do with Ronald Reagan before he married Nancy and reformed."

O'Toole told Kenneth Griffith, "When I talk to Capucine, she tells me how much she loves Audrey Hepburn. And when I talk to William Holden, he tells me that he's still in love with her."

Holden had fallen for Audrey when Billy Wilder had cast both of them in *Sabrina* (1954).

"What happened?" O'Toole asked. "With your marriage to Brenda (aka Ardis)?"

"I was ready to leave my wife for Audrey," Holden said. "She told me, "I bet we can make beautiful babies together."

He admitted when he told her that he'd had a vasectomy, it signaled the end of their affair. "She wanted children."

In 1954, shortly after ending it with Holden, Audrey met and married actor Mel Ferrer.

"After Audrey dropped me, I fucked my way around the world," Holden admitted to O'Toole. "My goal was to screw a girl in every country I visited" Holden said. "I'd had practice at being a whore. When I was a young actor starting out in Hollywood, I used to service actresses who were older than me. I'm a whore. All actors are whores. We sell our bodies to the highest bidders."

In 1982, Capucine made a softcore movie, *Aphrodite,* appearing in a nude scene. I was by now clear that *The Pink Panther* sequels had not rescued her floundering career.

Throughout her life, she'd suffered from manic-depression and a bipolar disorder. In 1990, having operated from a base in Lausanne, Switzerland, for a number of years, she committed suicide at the age of 59, jumping to her death from the window of her eighth floor apartment.

The New York Times reported that her only survivors were the three cats she left behind. Before her fatal jump, she left plenty of food out for her felines.

O'Toole had heard plenty from both Capucine and Holden about their largely unrequited love for Audrey.

Ironically, in O'Toole's next movie, *How to Steal a Million* (1966), he would fall for the charms and allure of this Belgian waif too.

Chapter 26

How to Steal a Million

"Our Rail-Thin Bodies Would Make a Perfect Fit in the Boudoir"

—O'Toole to Audrey Hepburn,

On and Off the Screen, O'Toole Pursues His Little Gamine ("That Boyish Figure, Those Doe Eyes") "And to Hell with Her Roving Husband!"

Fun, light, witty, and elegant, *How to Steal a Million* provided a marvelous change of pace for its stars, Peter O'Toole and Audrey Hepburn. When work shut down for the day, O'Toole found nights with Audrey, "delectable."

1965 had been a busy year for Peter O'Toole, as he'd made both *Lord Jim* and the wildly successful *What's New Pussycat?* His voice had even been used as background narration in Vincente Minnelli's *The Sandpiper,* starring his friends, Elizabeth Taylor and Richard Burton.

While filming *Pussycat* in Paris, O'Toole learned that scenes from *The Sandpiper* were being shot on an adjacent set. He decided to pay a surprise visit to Burton.

He met with Minnelli and asked him if he could be inserted into a scene—"a small walk-on, pretty please?"

As a prank, the director agreed. An upcoming scene called for two drunks to interrupt the amorous maneuvers of Burton and Elizabeth.

O'Toole agreed to appear as one of the drunks. Suddenly, in the midst of a love scene, Burton heard the drunken but distinctive voice of O'Toole shouting at him in flawed, grammatically incorrect Welsh.

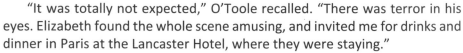

Elizabeth Taylor co-starred with Richard Burton in *The Sandpiper* (1965), with O'Toole sneaking in for a brief cameo.

Originally, the role was conceived as a vehicle for Kim Novak, with Sammy Davis, Jr., playing one of her lovers, but the producers decided that the world was not ready for that type of casting...at least not back then.

"It was totally not expected," O'Toole recalled. "There was terror in his eyes. Elizabeth found the whole scene amusing, and invited me for drinks and dinner in Paris at the Lancaster Hotel, where they were staying."

Over far too many drinks, she explained that for the past many months, she had been off the screen, devoting herself instead to Richard, the children, and his career.

"Because of my near-death experiences, insurance companies treat me like the bubonic plague. Finally, we got these roles in *The Sandpiper,* the company deciding to take a risk on me."

"We know we're not making an artistic masterpiece," Burton said. "But we dance when we see greenbacks, a million for Elizabeth here, only half a mil for me."

She had surprised O'Toole by telling him that originally, she had requested Sammy Davis, Jr., as her other suitor, a bohemian sculptor, in *Sandpiper*. "Marty *[i.e., Martin Ransohoff, the film's producer]* nearly had a stroke. He said my casting idea was way ahead of its time, and told me to check with him

Gregory Peck, William Holden, Cary Grant, & Gary Cooper
Scored First. Now It's O'Toole's Chance.

in fifty years. I was fully prepared to give Sammy a sloppy wet one on screen."

"Surely, that would have caused riots in Mississippi and Alabama," O'Toole said.

"Instead of Sammy, they cast Charles Bronson," she said. "What woman in her right mind would want to kiss that thing?"

"I'm not sure, but I think that Ransohoff had the hots for Kim Novak," Burton said. "But before the beginning of filming, they broke up. So instead of getting to fuck the lavender blonde, I have to make love to this old girl here, instead."

"Poor baby," O'Toole said.

"Many stars are showing their tits on screen, but not Elizabeth," Burton said. "If she ever did that, there would be pandemonium at the cinema. So instead of showing the real thing, Minnelli got this sculptor, Edward Kara, to get Elizabeth to pose nude for him. He chis-

The image above shows sculptor Edward Kara "releasing the image of Elizabeth Taylor" locked inside this block of redwood, with the intention of using it as a prop in *The Sandpiper*. Elizabeth posed nude for it.

eled out a tantalizing nude replica of her from a 2,200-pound redwood log. When I first saw it, I masturbated on it."

"Why in bloody hell would you want to do that?" Elizabeth asked, "when you could have the real thing?" Men...I'll never understand them."

Both Burton and Elizabeth were eager to learn of O'Toole's next projects, and he discussed them in detail, soliciting their advice.

"For the moment, I'm switching to comedy," O'Toole said. "I'm meeting Audrey Hepburn tomorrow night to discuss our upcoming movie."

"You're a lucky man—that is, if you don't like tits," Burton said. "As Elizabeth can testify, I am a tit man."

"My friend, Peter Finch, had a part in *The Nun's Story* (1959)," O'Toole said. "He told me that Audrey—like Grace Kelly, is terribly prim and proper. But once you lure her into taking off her panties, she becomes a hot tamale."

"You men are disgusting pigs," Elizabeth said. "You have one-track minds. Sex, sex, sex. Not me, baby. *I* should have starred in *The Nun's Story.* When Richard married me, I was a virgin."

He discussed with them his upcoming role in *How to Steal a Million,* slated for direction by William Wyler, and co-starring Audrey.

"Cary Grant would have been ideal in the part—better than me—thirty years ago," O'Toole said. "When he made *Charade* with Audrey in 1963, he could easily have been her grandfather. I think Wyler wanted someone new, something different this time around. I really want to have a chance to work with Audrey."

"Do you mean work with Audrey or a chance at Audrey?" Burton asked.

O'Toole Begins Losing Desirable Roles
(Sherlock Holmes and the Duke of Wellington) to Other Actors

During O'Toole's talk with Burton and Elizabeth, he revealed a number of film projects under consideration, while expressing a desire to return to the stage in *King Lear.*

His plan involved "zipping through some lightweight fluff and then to make a really serious film with Dickie, or Ritchie, as I sometimes call him."

He was referring to a film in pre-production called *Waterloo,* where he would play the Duke of Wellington, and Burton would be cast at Napoléon.

Both actors wanted to take on these challenging roles within a film that Dino de Laurentiis planned to launch as an Italian-Russian co-production. John Huston had expressed an interest in directing the picture.

Then, like so many film projects conjured up by actors, producers, and directors, their version of *Waterloo* met its Waterloo.

[A film entitled Waterloo *was eventually released in 1971 as an Italian-Russian project, with direction by Sergei Bondarchuk. As the Duke of Wellington, a role originally intended for O'Toole, he cast Christopher Plummer. Rod Steiger played Napoléon.]*

Fully aware that O'Toole was still under contract to him, Sam Spiegel, sent him the script for a movie called *The Chase,* a depiction of sin and sex in a small Texas town. Although the leading character had not yet been cast, supporting actors who had already signed for roles in the film included Jane Fonda, Robert Redford, E.G. Marshall, and Angie Dickinson.

O'Toole rejected the role. "Imagine me, an Irishman playing some cowboy with a Texas drawl. Sam must be out of his mind."

When he later heard that the role had gone to Marlon Brando, O'Toole said, "That is a switch. Usually it's the other way around. I take Brando's sloppy seconds. He did, as you know, turn down *Lawrence of Arabia.*"

He had angered Spiegel by his rejection, which later cost him a role he really wanted to play. A surprise call came in from director Billy Wilder, who had scored such successes as *Sunset Blvd.* (1950) with Gloria Swanson and *Some Like it Hot* (1959) with Marilyn Monroe.

Wilder had long been obsessed with the character of Sherlock Holmes, a detective who was both a violinist and a cocaine addict.

Wilder had conceived of a Technicolor musical, with a score by Lerner and Loewe, that he predicted would become a bigger success at the box office than 1965 film version of *The Sound of Music,* starring Julie Andrews.

Wilder wanted O'Toole to play Holmes. And even though he'd had difficulties with Peter Sellers in past projects, he thought Sellers would be ideal as Dr. Watson.

But difficulties arose right from the beginning. When Sellers' agent informed him of Wilder's offer, the actor said, "I wouldn't be in the same room as Wilder." *[Sellers still resented his horrible treatment by Wilder on the set of Kiss Me, Stupid.]* Then another problem arose.

Furious at O'Toole for turning down *The Chase,* Spiegel, who still had an unfulfilled open contract vindictively refused to allow him to appear in the Wilder film.

Wilder, however, did not abandon his vision about Sherlock Holmes. Eventually, in 1970, he released his *The Private Life of Sherlock Holmes.* Instead of O'Toole, the role had gone to Robert Stephens, a leading actor at Britain's Royal National Theatre, who was married to actress Maggie Smith at the time. Colin Blakely was cast as Dr. Watson, in the role intended for Sellers.

In 1983, O'Toole lent his voice to the character of Sherlock Holmes in three animated films: *Sherlock Holmes in the Valley of Fear, Sherlock Holmes in a Study in Scarlet,* and *Sherlock Holmes in the Sign of Four.*

***

In 1966, John Huston had cast O'Toole as "Three Angels" in his epic film, *The Bible: In the Beginning.* His co-stars, among others, included Ava Gardner.

In 1967, Huston came back again with yet another offer for O'Toole. He was toying with the idea of making a movie based on the life of the Elizabethan explorer, William Adams (1564-1620), a navigator and sailor who was the first Englishman ever to reach the shores of Japan, and the first Western Samurai. Adams had been the inspiration for the character of John Blackthorne in James Clavell's best-selling novel, *Shogun.* O'Toole admired the achievements of Adams, claiming that he was the only Elizabethan who traveled to foreign shores without planning to pillage and plunder.

Huston hired the blacklisted, Left-leaning screenwriter, Dalton Trumbo, to write the script. Huston later told O'Toole, "So Dalton was a communist. Who really gives a fuck? He's written the perfect script, probably the finest one that has ever breathed."

As O'Toole's co-star, Huston began negotiating with Toshiro Mifune, at the time the most famous actor in Japan and the one best known to western audiences. Mifune's fame was partly based on his long association (1948-

1965) with filmmaker Akira Kurosawa, who turned out such hits as *Rashoman*. *[Released in 1950, it's known for a plot device which involves various characters providing alternative, self-serving and contradictory versions of the same incident.]*

Mifune also played Toranaga in the TV mini-series, *Shogun*. By then, Huston had long ago abandoned his idea of producing and/or directing a full-length film based on the life of Adams.

Huston would make one final attempt to cast O'Toole and Burton in a film together, *The Man Who Would Be King*. Based on a short story by Rudyard Kipling, it had originally been intended as a vehicle for Clark Gable and Humphrey Bogart. Later, Frank Sinatra expressed an interest in playing one of the leads.

[In an ironic exploration of fame, celebrity, imperialism, and religion, it follows two rogue adventurers, outcasts and runaways from His Majesty's British army in India who, in the late 19th-century set off in search of adventure and end up as kings of Kafiristan (in modern Afghanistan), thanks to having convinced the locals that they are gods.]

But once again, no deal could be reached with either Burton or O'Toole. Eventually, a memorable interpretation of *The Man Who Would Be King* was released in 1975, starring Sean Connery and Michael Caine.

In Paris, O'Toole Has a Rendezvous with a Goddess, Audrey Hepburn, Thin, Chic, and Alluring

Months before filming began on *How to Steal a Million*, a meeting between Audrey Hepburn and O'Toole was arranged in Paris at the bar of the Ritz Hotel, a former retreat of Ernest Hemingway and F. Scott Fitzgerald.

Just in advance of that meeting, when O'Toole disembarked from a plane in Paris, he stumbled and almost fell down the ramp.

He was battered and in bad condition. In London, his doctor had warned him that if he did not stop drinking, he'd face an early death. But on holiday with Siân, he had continued to drink. "My life is my own. I can't allow some doctor, or anyone for that matter, to dictate how I should live it."

For years, he'd read what other men had to say after their interchanges with Audrey, and he welcomed the opportunity to form his own opinion.

When Billy Wilder had directed her in *Love in the Afternoon* (1937), with Gary Cooper, he said, "Tit-ism has taken over the country. But Audrey Hepburn single-handedly may make bosoms a thing of the past."

Theater critic Walter Kerr proclaimed, "She is every man's dream of the nymph he once planned to meet." Orson Welles had dubbed her "the patron saint of anorexics."

O'Toole would always remember their inaugural meeting in the bar of the Ritz. "There she sat like a vision. There was something unreal about her, perhaps like a dream. She had carefully groomed for our meeting like the character of Nicole Bonnet she was set to play in the movie—dress by Hubert de Givenchy, bejeweled by Cartier, and coiffed by Grazia de Rossi into a helmet-like beehive."

How to Steal a Million celebrated the aesthetics of Paris. The photo above highlights the grand mansard gables of Paris' *belle époque* as much as it did the physicality of Hepburn and the character playing her charlatan father, Hugh Griffin.

She had nothing but praise for Givenchy: "His designs are the only clothes in which I am myself. He is far more than a couturier. He is the creator of a personality."

"You're in good company, sweetheart," he said. "Grace Kelly, Elizabeth Taylor, Jacqueline Kennedy. If I ever decide to become a cross-dresser, perhaps he'll whip up a frock or two for me."

She'd appear in Givenchy throughout most of the filming, with the understanding that she'd abandon her chic wardrobe only once during the shoot. In that scene, she'd disguise herself in an unflattering smock of a museum's cleaning woman. When he sees her wearing it, O'Toole's character wryly comments, "Well, it gives Givenchy a night off."

When O'Toole complimented her on her glamorous look, she disagreed. "I don't think I'm glamorous at all. Ava Gardner and Elizabeth Taylor are glamorous, but I'm not, not at all."

He provocatively told her, "I have just appeared in a play at the Piccadilly Theatre in London. It was called *Rock a Cock Horse* 1965)."

Hepburn wearing Somalian leopardskin before it was defined as an endangered species and—consequently—illegal.

"Is that an invitation?" she asked, subtly flirting with him, and raising an eyebrow.

As Audrey's biographers and profilers have suggested, this delicate hot-house flower was a bit deceiving. Behind the façade beat the heart of a woman with a healthy sexual appetite, not opposed to a brief romance here and there, despite her marriage to actor Mel Ferrer at the time.

After Siân Phillips came to Paris and was introduced to Audrey, she wrote, "I didn't much like her husband at the time. He installed her in Paris, sent her out to work, and decamped, all over Europe, having, as far as I could see, a fine old time."

Siân was right. At the time O'Toole met Audrey, Ferrer had flown to the French Riviera, where he was enjoying a brief fling with actress Jean Seberg in a villa outside Cannes.

Audrey and O'Toole discussed their upcoming film, and he seemed delighted that William Wyler had cast him opposite her. "Wyler has certainly done well by you."

Wyler had previously directed her in *Roman Holiday* (1953), opposite Gregory Peck. Yet in spite of the success of the picture, she seemed disturbed by its critical reception.

GIVENCHY

Top photo: Audrey with the designer forever associated with her image and career: Hubert de Givenchy, and— lower photo—as the focal point of one of his ads.

"Some no-nothing critics claimed that we were not sex symbols, that we made a very unerotic pair."

"We'll change that perception in this flick," he said.

"Is that a promise?" she asked in her most flirtatious voice. "Perhaps we should begin rehearsals tonight."

"He couldn't believe how candid she was. There was no doubt: She was propositioning him. "Audrey Hepburn, star of *The Nun's Story* (1959), was actually inviting me between her sheets," he later said. "I'd been a little shaky earlier in the day, but this was one challenge I could not refuse."

After her wildly successful role in *Roman Holiday,* Wyler went on to direct her in the 1962 release of *The Children's Hour,* a study of the destructive after-effects of gossip and malice in a small town, in which Audrey had co-starred with Shirley MacLaine.

During their meeting, O'Toole with Hepburn went on to discuss his upcoming role in *How to Steal a Million* as Simon Dermott, a so-called society cat burglar. [*Spoiler alert: As is eventually revealed, O'Toole's character is really that of a private detective investigating her father (played by Hugh Griffith), who he knows is a notorious art forger.]*

"You know, of course, we're appearing in marshmallow-weight hokum," he said.

"I do indeed," she answered. "After all, I starred in *Charade* (1963) with Cary Grant."

"I welcome a silly little romantic caper," he said. "I was in danger of becoming known only as a dramatic actor, particularly after *Lawrence of Arabia* and *Lord Jim.* I don't want to get locked into playing only characters filled with self-doubt and suffering from a tortured mind."

"At last, I've met an actor who is as thin as I am," she said.

"That means our bodies were made for each other," he said in his most seductive voice. "We're a perfect fit."

"That remains to be seen," she said. "Frankly, I worry about our age difference. Will it show on the screen?" I don't want to appear as some older woman chasing a younger man."

"Come on now," he said. "I've learned that you are only three years older than me. But with my dissipated face—which comes from sharing a pint with a friend every now and then—I look at least old enough to be your father, although I doubt if my seed would ever spawn a lovely thing like you. Let's face it: You're hailed as the most beautiful woman in the world."

"Don't flatter me," she said, "or I might follow you anywhere. I've been feeling inadequate as a woman, and your appreciation thrills me."

After a dinner in the dining room of the Ritz, she invited him to her suite for a nightcap. He was amazed at how homelike and personalized it looked, as if she'd decorated it herself.

She told him that as she moved from city to city, she always shipped around twenty large trunks and crates filled with her possessions, including vases, paintings, and her favorite photographs, "Being surrounded with my things makes me feel at home. When I'm ready to leave a city, I repack everything and ship it on to my next destination."

"An expensive way to travel," I'd say," he said. "Sometimes I grab a flight without even a change of underwear."

"I believe that an actress has to be at least a little bit in love with her leading man and *vice versa*. If you're going to portray love on the screen, it's hard to fake it. There have been too many examples of a leading man and a leading lady who

Audrey Hepburn married her philandering husband, Mel Ferrer, in 1954. Here, she's shown with him as her co-star in King Vidor's *War and Peace* (1956), based on the famous novel by Tolstoy.

It would be filmed again, far more successfully, in 1968.

loathed each other and had to play a kissing scene, looking like they wanted to puke. Loving your leading man during filming is one thing. Carrying it beyond the set after shooting is over is yet another story."

Each of these two upcoming co-stars seemed to interconnect. "We were like-minded souls," O"Toole recalled, "sharing some of the same problems, especially in our marriages."

She was surprisingly frank with him, perhaps having already learned that her husband was sexually and emotionally involved in a liaison with the young and emotionally troubled Seberg. "My marriage with Mel has become more of a professional relationship than a romantic love affair. He's always devising projects for himself where I would be his co-star. He's hardly a box office magnet, and he views me, in his words, as 'very bankable.'"

"If my marriage continues, our love-making might be limited just to the screen. He does visit my bed twice a month, invariably on a Saturday night."

"Saturday night seems to be a worldwide ritual," O'Toole said. "I read that more sex occurs on Saturday night than any other evening of the week. That's understandable. Sunday is the Sabbath and Monday, when you have to face the real world, is just too depressing."

By the way, are you aware that tonight is Saturday night?" she asked.

"I am indeed," he answered. "It is foremost in my mind. I believe in respecting the traditions of a Saturday night."

Back in London, O'Toole's voyeuristic friend, actor Kenneth Griffith, wanted to hear the intimate details of his friend's fling with Audrey. Griffith had long harbored a crush on "that delicate flower of a woman."

O'Toole admitted that after their inaugural meeting, he visited her suite at the Ritz three nights in a row. "She's a woman of passion, and she carries on a seduction with style and grace, the same qualities she brings to the screen. She is a lady on camera or off."

He also added, "She's the kind of woman I've dreamed about all my life and never expected to meet. Of course, she's out of my reach and not available. Even so, she embodies everything I desire in a woman, and on some bad hair days, I don't like women at all."

"There is not the slightest suggestion that we will divorce our spouses, although we both seem to realize our marriages are ultimately doomed. In many ways, Audrey and I are perfect for each other. We are both sensitive to each other's desires and wishes. In a sustained relationship, now long could that politeness and deference survive?"

"She would not be able to put up with my drunken binges, my womanizing, and my errant ways, and I would probably find that in the end, marriage to this dream princess might suffocate me."

"She seems too good to be true. Therefore, I feel there is something unreal about her charm offensive. Perhaps she's covering up a darker side of herself. From toast and coffee at breakfast to a midnight glass of champagne, she seems like a goddess. But no woman is a goddess."

"Of course, when making love to her, I fancied myself as George Peppard seducing Holly Golightly in Truman Capote's *Breakfast at Tiffany's*. I read his little novel. Capote's Holly is not the one pictured on the screen. On camera, Audrey projected romance, vivacity, and sweetness. But Capote's Holly was a tough little hooker with a certain bitchery and with a streak of cold brutality. Perhaps that is the real Audrey hiding behind all those lovely masks that she puts up to conceal herself from the world."

"Alas, I will never get to know Audrey Hepburn? I will never be able to answer an intriguing mystery: Who is that real woman lurking behind that incredible façade?"

Iconic Audrey, Iconic Givenchy.

Depicted above is the dress she wore in *Breakfast at Tiffany's*. It was auctioned in 2006, an unknown bidder buying it for about 600,000 Euros, making it the most expensive dress in the world.

***

On the Set of a Film Devoted to Art Forgeries
O'Toole Confronts His Co-Stars:
A Nude Art Forger (Hugh Griffith)
and a Fading Matinee Idol (Charles Boyer)
After George C. Scott is Fired,
Eli Wallach Is Hired as His Replacement

Even before he received the final shooting script, O'Toole read the short story, *Venus Rising,* on which *How to Steal a Million* was based. It had been written by George Bradshaw, who had scored a big hit with the script for one of O'Toole's favorite movies, *The Bad and the Beautiful* (1952), starring Lana

Turner and Kirk Douglas.

After receiving a copy of the script, O'Toole met with director William Wyler. He was a bit apprehensive. Interpreting Wyler as "Old Hollywood," O'Toole wondered how his more modern style of acting might clash with the veteran director, who had begun his involvement in films during the age of silent movies. Wyler had received the bulk of his acclaim during the studio-dominated "Golden Age of Talkies" for having directed everyone from John Barrymore to Bette Davis.

William Wyler, the critically demanding scion of Hollywood's fast-fading "golden age"

Wyler had already directed two of O'Toole's all-time favorite movies, *Mrs. Miniver* (1942) and *The Best Years of Our Lives* (1946). He'd also directed Laurence Olivier in *Wuthering Heights* (1939).

"Larry told me you taught him screen acting on that film," O'Toole said to Wyler. "Perhaps you'll teach me screen acting for this little caper we're trying to pull off."

"Perhaps," Wyler said, noncommittally.

During filming, O'Toole, for the most part, worked smoothly with Wyler, except for an occasional flare-up. During one scene, Wyler shouted at O'Toole, "Stop your fucking wide-eyed emoting. Who in hell do you think you are? Joan Crawford?"

The screenplay had been written by Harry Kurnitz, a playwright, novelist, and prolific screenwriter, who had previously written scripts for some of Errol Flynn's swashbucklers and for some of Danny Kaye's comedies. His most famous and best-acclaimed movie script was *Witness for the Prosecution,* the 1957 Billy Wilder film that starred Tyrone Power and Marlene Dietrich.

Kurnitz would die of a heart attack two years after the release of *How to Steal a Million.*

During the first week of shooting, producer Fred Kohlmar came onto the set and invited O'Toole for lunch. The producer wanted to hear from O'Toole himself what he thought of the script.

"It's very derivative," O'Toole said candidly, "but I hope we can make it our own, without evoking too many memories in movie fans of pictures gone by."

"Never fear," Kohlmar said. "I'll see that we come up with some original twists."

This veteran of film production had previously assisted both Samuel Goldwyn and Darryl F. Zanuck. He'd also produced pictures by such celebrated directors as diverse as John Ford (a closeted homosexual) and George Cukor (a more obvious one).

For a film associated with art, art forgeries, and art appreciation, Wyler had hired Alexandre Trauner, a talented, avant-garde Hungarian eccentric who lived in Paris at the time as the film's art director. Trauner went everywhere with his dachshund. Previously, he had designed the richly evocative sets for the rue Casanova in *Irma la Douce* (1964), starring Shirley MacLaine.

Key elements of *How to Steal a Million* transpired within a museum, so for efficiency's sake, a fake art gallery was replicated within the studio. For decorating its walls, Trauner hired young Parisian artists to create a series of *faux* paintings from Old Masters who included da Vinci, Rembrandt, Picasso, El Greco, and Tintoretto. The most stunning film prop was the so-called replica of a 30-inch sculpture, supposedly by Cellini, *Venus Rising.*

Most of the movie's plot revolves around the choreographed theft of the phony *Cellini Venus* from a maximum security Paris museum. It is a fake, created by Audrey's screen father, a congenial art forger (Hugh Griffith). To many reviewers, the plot evoked that of *Topkapi* (1964). *[Starring Melina Mercouri, Peter Ustinov, and Maximilian Schell it depicted a stylishly larcenous gang of world-class jewelry thieves plotting to rob the Topkapi Museum in Istanbul.]*

Many of *To Steal a Million's* exterior shots were filmed on the streets of Paris during August, when thousands of Parisians had abandoned the city for their vacations, a period in the French capital when permission to film in outdoor locales was easier to obtain.

Although the film dealt with a robbery, its production crew suffered an actual robbery from five masked Parisian bandits. One night, they broke in to the studio and cracked open the safe where Wyler kept the payroll, making off with $20,000, which represented a week's salary to the crew. The thieves also stole several valuable *objets d'art* used within the movie, including two *col de cygne* vases. The heist was never solved.

Originally, George C. Scott was assigned the role of David Leland, a rich American art collector who had wanted to marry Audrey, although as the plot unfolds, he seems more interested in acquiring the Venus sculpture than he does in walking down the aisle with her.

Two views of the divine Melina Mercouri (daughter of the 30-year veteran mayor of Athens) and (in lower photo) Peter Ustinov in *Topkapi* (1964), a roughly equivalent romantic comedy-cum-heist film set in a more exotic (Istanbul) locale.

459

On the first day of shooting, Scott was due on the set at 11AM, but he didn't turn up until five that afternoon.

"We've missed you," Wyler said sarcastically to the errant actor. Scott was then asked to go to his dressing room, where makeup and wardrobe assistants awaited him.

However, when time came for him to appear on the set, an assistant told Wyler, "Scott has disappeared. He just stormed out of this dressing room, and no one has seen him since."

"I've had it with the monster, Wyler said. "What ego! He's fired as of NOW."

Then Wyler called Eli Wallach, who at the time

Tough, egocentric, and difficult to direct, George C. Scott walked off the picture early,

was appearing in a play, *Luv,* in London. He wanted the role, but had to go through a lot of maneuvers to free himself from his commitments so he could fly to Paris.

In 1965, Wallach had co-starred with O'Toole in *Lord Jim,* and both actors admired each other's work.

Over dinner with him, O'Toole recalled his first meeting with Wallach. It had been associated with Wallach's appearance in the London production in 1954 of *The Teahouse of the August Moon,* a performance attended by Elizabeth, Prince Philip, and Winston Churchill.

"You were short of stagehands," O'Toole reminded him. "So your producer asked RADA *[The*

Eli Wallach, holding the (fake) version of a (nonexistent but purported) Cellini's Venus.

Royal Academy of Dramatic Arts, the school attended by O'Toole at the time] to send over volunteer stagehands. So during your performance, Alan Bates, Albert Finney, and I were handing your actors props and helping you on with your jockstraps, or whatever."

"I didn't remember that, but I will if I ever write my memoirs," Wallach said. "I'd call you guys a trio of the most distinguished stagehands in the history of the London theater."

Wallach did remember O'Toole, Finney, and Bates in his memoirs, and he also recalled working with Audrey. "She was as beautiful as Venus coming out of her half-shell. In one scene, I had to kiss her. She was a mile taller than me. But she volunteered to take off her shoes."

During the filming of *How to Steal a Million,* O'Toole met and had several talks with the fading matinée idol of yesterday, Charles Boyer. The French actor had been cast as De Solnay, O'Toole's boss.

Boyer's style, enhanced as it was with heavy-lidded eyes and a seductive Gallic accent, seemed to belong to a Hollywood of long ago. He had co-starred with some of the reigning queens of the silver screen: Bette Davis, Greta Garbo, Paulette Goddard, Claudette Colbert, Irene Dunne, Marlene Dietrich, and Hedy Lamarr. It was based on his performance with Lamarr in *Algiers* (1938) that Boyer became genuinely famous for a line he never actually delivered on screen—"*Come wiz me to ze Cashbah.*"

The art of illusion: French-accented Charles Boyer, sultrily inviting the object of his desire to the casbah?

"You're never a star until you're parodied," O'Toole told him.

"My role in this caper movie we're making is as drab as it is small," Boyer complained. "I seem to be only assigned to cameos these days."

"That day will come for me too," O'Toole predicted.

Boyer seemed aware that O'Toole and Audrey were having an affair. He did not specifically mention that, but said, "Sex on a movie set is almost taken for granted in this business. I've appeared with the most seductive women on the planet, but I never seduced them, except in one case."

"Please tell the voyeur in me who that was," O'Toole asked.

"I'm not a kiss-and-tell type of man, BUT since you asked, it was my co-star, Katharine Hepburn, when we made *Break of Hearts* in 1935."

"My God, you've stormed the most heavily guarded, the almost impregnable citadel in all of Hollywood," O'Toole said. "I'm impressed."

"They call me the last of the cinema's great lovers. Actually, I wasn't—at least not off screen. I'm past the age of falling in love," Boyer said. "Love is something that happens to younger, more foolish men. When I was young, I could not afford to fall in love. I know it was selfish of me, but I avoided it. Besides, I think a man's greatest and most enduring affair is with himself."

One night in Paris, Boyer invited O'Toole to his favorite Left Bank bistro, with the understanding that they'd rendezvous before dinner in Boyer's dressing room. O'Toole noticed that all day, Boyer had lit one cigarette after another, revealing to O'Toole that on a regular basis, he smoked six packages a day.

As O'Toole later recalled, "Boyer was still interested in his appearance. I could not believe it. As he was undressing, his wig came off first, then the lifts in his shoes, and finally, his most secret undercover garment, a corset."

At the time these interchanges with O'Toole, Boyer recorded an album, *Where Does Love Go?*, a medley of mostly famous love songs delivered in a half-singing, half-spoken style. "I'm told that it's Elvis Presley's favorite album. He listens to it all the time."

Boyer was the husband of British actress Pat Paterson, whom he'd wed in 1934, a union that lasted forty-four years. Their only child, Michael Boyer, committed suicide in 1965 at the age of 21 playing Russian Roulette after separating from his girlfriend.

Boyer himself would commit suicide on August 26, 1978, two days after his wife's death from cancer.

An eccentric actor, Hugh Griffith, depicted above as Hugh Bonet, cast as an eccentric art fraud:

Audrey Hepburn, horrified, to the character playing her father: "The Cellini Venus is a fake!"

Griffith, as Bonet, to Hepburn: "We don't use that word in this house!"

***

One night in the bar of the George V, O'Toole had drinks with Hugh Griffith, who had been cast as Charles Bonnet, Audrey's eccentric, art-forging father. He had long admired him.

O'Toole congratulated Griffith for winning an Oscar for Best Supporting Actor in *Ben-Hur* (1959), and told him that he should have won another one for *Tom Jones* (1963), for which he was nominated.

O'Toole had also seen Griffith in *King Lear.* He discussed the possibility that he'd consider playing the role of *King Lear* himself.

Griffith said that he had first appeared in a production of *King Lear* at the Bristol Old Vic in 1956. "I was too young, callow, and inexperienced to know what Shakespeare was saying then. I was also drunk most of the time."

"Welcome to the club," O'Toole responded. "I'm drunk all the time. It's the only way to get through life."

As O'Toole recalled, "Hugh was a real pisser, perhaps England's most notorious boozer. A brilliant actor, but an unreliable bad boy. When he'd consumed enough brandy, he was capable of performing any outrageous stunt. But his favorite drink was Black Velvet—you know, champagne with Stout."

As he'd told O'Toole, "Whenever I have to play a drunk scene, I always down a number of Black Velvets. Does some moron of a director think I can fake a drunkard scene with bloody tea?"

After three hours of heavy drinking, an intoxicated O'Toole helped guide Griffith back to his room at the very posh George V. where he left him. But as he was leaving the lobby, the night manager at the hotel approached him.

"Sir, one of our bellboys has caught your friend, Mr. Griffith. He's wandering nude up and down the hall. He's taken one of our DO NOT DISTURB signs and crossed out the NOT. He uses the sign to cover up his genitals. Please come upstairs and help us subdue him."

Although he wasn't in great shape himself, O'Toole agreed and finally got Griffith back into his bed, where the actor immediately passed out.

The final scenes of *To Steal a Million* were shot during the closing weeks of 1965.

It was during this period that a drama between O'Toole and Audrey took place offscreen.

Did O'Toole Impregnate Audrey Hepburn? Their Fans (and their Spouses) Will Never Know

During their final weeks of filming, Audrey admitted to O'Toole, "I'm pregnant, and I haven't told Mel yet." She had been working overtime, and it was obvious she wanted to finish the picture before signs of her pregnancy showed.

She told him that whereas he might be the father, she could not be sure. At the inception of her pregnancy, she'd had sex with both O'Toole and her husband. "Perhaps we won't know until the child I born," she said. "Then we'll see which one of you he most resembles."

"I'd be honored to bear you your child," she continued. "If it's a son, I imagine he'd grow up to be as talented as you."

"He'd also inherit your genes, combining talent with beauty."

Throughout her final days on the set, O'Toole pleaded with Wyler to ease up on the many demands he was making on her, without telling him the reason why. The director did not listen to him.

On the final day of filming, O'Toole retired with her to her dressing room, where he held her in his arms and kissed her goodbye. Her husband, Mel Ferrer, had arrived on the set and was conferring with Wyler. The moment her work was completed, he planned to drive her back to their home in Switzerland.

"I'll always be there for you, great lady," O'Toole told her. "If you ever need me, call me. I'll come running, even if it's across continents."

"Mel and I will spend Christmas together, and I hope it will save our marriage. The idea of a divorce horrifies me. Maybe the baby will bring us closer together."

He agreed to keep in touch by phone. He wanted to know how the final weeks of her pregnancy were going, as she'd miscarried several attempted childbirths in her past.

He called her every week. It was with great sadness that he learned that in January of 1966, she'd been rushed to a clinic in Switzerland, where once again, she had miscarried.

Shortly after that, she announced her intention of taking a four-month retreat from contact with most of the world, for rest and recuperation.

In a phone dialogue, he said to her, "Wherever you go, you'll always have my love. I have the memory."

"The saddest words in life are what might have been," she said. "Perhaps one day our paths will cross again."

He held out the prospect of their making another picture together and continuing their affair in the future.

That didn't happen.

Critics Evaluate "How to Steal a Million"
Is It "a Strawberry Shortcake?"
Or a Gay and Gamine Rip-Off of Topkapi?

After working with Wyler, O'Toole agreed with Charlton Heston's assessment of the director. *[Wyler had helmed Heston in the technically complicated* Ben-Hur *(1959).]*

"Doing a film for Wyler is like getting the works in a Turkish bath." Heston said. "You damn near drown, but come out smelling like a rose."

Released in 1966 by 20th Century Fox, *How to Steal a Million,* despite mixed reviews, generated a respectable box office, mainly because of the star power of Audrey.

The monthly magazine, *Film Bulletin,* suggested that the picture would have benefitted from a director other than Wyler. It went on to dismiss O'Toole as "more winsome than winning."

The powerful critic Pauline Kael defined the film as "just blah."

Kael's chief rival, film critic Judith Crist, described it as "an absolute strawberry shortcake of a film." She interpreted Audrey and O'Toole as "an utterly delightful pair of respectable thieves."

Audrey received her usual praise from critics, one of them writing about her "fawnlike charm," and described her walking style as that of "a tiny tiptoe teeter."

Sight and Sound claimed, "Wyler hasn't got the touch any more. *How to Steal a Million* is terribly wordy and slow."

Bosley Crowther of *The New York Times* dismissed the plot as unbelievable, including O'Toole's role as a "society burglar." He called the scheme that O'Toole's character devised to steal the Cellini statuette as "clearly preposterous."

Newsweek accused Audrey of "trading too heavily on her usual selection of charm, and *Time* magazine dismissed the movie's glossy tone. Their critic wrote, "Everything that is going to happen happens according to long-established rules of the game, from the first skittish encounter to the last eager kiss."

Eventually, word reached O'Toole that Audrey had returned to work for director Stanley Donen, who had cast her in the stylishly romantic 20th Century Fox film, *Two for the Road* (1967) *[From their headquarters in the south of France, a jet-setting couple, in random order, reflect on their respective infidelities during their troubled ten-year marriage.]* Rumors had spread to London that she was involved in a torrid affair with her handsome co-star, O'Toole's friend, Albert Finney.

Audrey Hepburn, resuscitating a marriage with Albert Finney in *Two for the Road (1967)*

Chapter 27

The Lion in Winter

An Anti-Camelot Drama Evoking
"Who's Afraid of Virginia Wolff"
O'Toole At War with Katharine Hepburn

"She's a Cross Between Medusa and Tugboat Annie"

When *The Lion in Winter* first opened as a play on Broadway, it had flopped. Katharine Hepburn had gone to see Rosemary Harris "purr and scratch" her way through the role of Eleanor of Aquitaine. According to Hepburn, "She played it too broad for the screen."

When O'Toole read the script, he told Hepburn: "These Plantagenet barbarians might well be an upper-class family of today. Their sexual hang-ups, their endless bickering, their greed, betrayals, and deceit."

"Then let's give it hell." Hepburn said.

The flamboyant producer, Joseph E. Levine, had long wanted to cast Peter O'Toole in a movie, but had never found the right vehicle for him. In 1966, he'd gone to see *The Lion in Winter* at the Ambassador Theater on Broadway.

Written by James Goldman, it had starred Robert Preston as Henry II and Rosemary Harris as Eleanor of Aquitaine. The next day, Levine acquired the film rights.

Levine had already seen O'Toole and Richard Burton in the film, *Becket.* He liked O'Toole's portrayal of Henry II and thought he'd be ideal cast once again as an older version of the same medieval king.

He called O'Toole and pitched this new casting idea to him. This time, the actor didn't need to see a script. All he

"It's terrifying working with Katharine Hepburn," O'Toole told the film's director, Anthony Harvey. "Sheer masochism. She's been sent by some dark fate to nag and torment me."

wanted to know was that playwright James Goldman was adapting his own Broadway hit to the screen.

"My terms are steep," O'Toole warned Levine.

"Don't worry, baby, we'll butter your buns. Lots of money."

"Who in hell are you going to get to play Queen Eleanor? She's about sixty in the role."

"Only one actress in the world can pull off this part," Levine said. "No, not Bette Davis. Not Joan Crawford, not Greer Garson. Only that butchy dyke, Katharine Hepburn, can yank this rat out of the bag."

"Hepburn would be divine," O'Toole said. "She and I will eat up the screen."

"Not only that, but it'll be another Oscar for her," Levine said. *[He was referring to her 1967 performance with a dying Spencer Tracy in* Guess Who's Coming to Dinner?.*]*

The die was cast for a historic pairing, an event noteworthy in the history

"If this *#@&** Costume Drama Isn't a Hit, I'll Hang Up My Jockstrap."

—Peter O'Toole

of cinema. It brought together Hepburn—a fiercely independent, patrician, original, and forever memorable actress—with O'Toole. "Spencer is an Irish drunk," Hepburn told Levine. "I'm sure I can handle working with another Irish drunk like O'Toole."

O'Toole's (i.e. Henry's) Christmas Message to Hepburn (Eleanor): "Shall We Hang Holly or Each Other?"

Goldman was working all day, every day, and throughout most of his nights preparing a rough draft of the shooting script for Hepburn and O'Toole. He was known for basing his plays, novels, and screenplays on historic or literary figures, depicting such characters as Anna Karenina, Tolstoy, and Czar Nicholas II. His dialogue had been described as "witty, intelligent, pithy, and often mercurial."

This was evident when Hepburn and O'Toole read Goldman's first draft. When Hepburn, as Eleanor, learns that her dysfunctional family has been engaged in sodomy, patricide, treason, and incest, she says, "Well, what family doesn't have its ups and downs?"

On another occasion, she says of her husband, Henry II, "His bed is his province. He can people it with sheep for all I care. Which, on occasion, he has done."

The autocratic Henry at one point quips, "What shall we hang? The holly or each other?"

Levine had awarded Hepburn and O'Toole with the unique contractual privilege of selecting not only their director but their supporting players as well.

O'Toole had met Hepburn before: She had recommended him as a possible replacement and safeguard against the very real possibility that Montgomery Clift—for reasons associated with his physical and emotional health (or lack thereof)—might have to abandon his involvement in the filming of *Suddenly, Last Summer* (1959).

A murky family amid murky medieval politics: O'Toole, as Henry, kissing his mistress, Alais Capet (Jane Merrow) In full view of his (about to be re-imprisoned) queen, Eleanor of Aquitaine.

469

Some reports claim that at first, Hepburn, still in mourning over the loss of her long-time companion, Spencer Tracy, rejected the role. But her closest friends denied that, asserting that the star immediately recognized the dramatic power of Eleanor of Aquitaine. Hepburn told her friend, Lauren Bacall, "A role like this comes along once in a generation."

Director Anthony Harvey, with Kate, frantically replicating the marital strife of....

Before the debut of rehearsals, O'Toole flew to New York to meet with Hepburn and discuss the script. Their working together was viewed as ranking up there with Stanley meeting Livingstone in the vast expanses of Africa.

O'Toole reminded her that Levine had given both of them the choice of their own director, and then went on to declare that he preferred Anthony Harvey.

"And who in hell might this Harvey creature be?" she asked him.

A Londoner, Harvey was mostly known as a film editor, but he'd directed *Dutchman* in 1966, a movie whose direction had deeply impressed O'Toole.

[Dutchman was an independent British film based on Amiri Baraka's taut drama about a rebuffed flirtation that ultimately resulted in a murder on a New York subway car. Shirley Knight and Al Freeman,

...Eleanor of Aquitaine and her husband, the English King, Henry II.

Jr. were cast as a psychotic white woman and a "minding his own business and uninterested" black man. When he doesn't rise to her sexual challenge, she teases and taunts him until he slaps her. Reacting violently, she stabs him with a knife, killing him. In the confusion that follows, she moves on and out, presumably to find another victim.]

The only available screening of *Dutchman* was within an all-night theater on Manhattan's Lower East Side at midnight. O'Toole and Hepburn had to stumble over winos and empty liquor bottles, passing dopeheads, to enter a tawdry cinema that smelled of urine. Some members of the audience used the theater as an all-night crash pad.

Hepburn later recalled, "Peter and I were the only ones in the audience who came to see the actual movie. The rest of the audience was engaged in sexual couplings of all known persuasions."

After seeing the movie, Hepburn told O'Toole, "It's absolutely riveting. It grabs you by the throat. Harvey showed exactly the approach that your material needs. Not that old glossy MGM stuff, cold people living in cold castles. *Lion* is the very antithesis of sentimentality. This is no *Ivanhoe* or crap like that. This is a play about an estranged wife still trying to hold onto her dignity, a ferocious mother hen still guarding her chicks."

In announcing her acceptance of the role, she told reporters, "Eleanor of Aquitaine, in case you didn't read a history book, was the most famous woman of the Middle Ages. She must have been tough as nails to live through eighty-two years of turmoil. She was full of beans. She and her husband, Henry II, were big-time operators who held the fate of England and France in their paws. She was a schemer, plotting against her husband, who imprisoned her for life. She gave birth to children who were from hell. My kind of lady."

O'Toole also talked to the press, informing them that he was thrilled once again to be cast as Henry II. "This Henry will be quite different, older, more worldly wise, more astute, having suffered pain. Survival will be etched on my face."

When O'Toole met with the film's producer, Levine, he told him, "Kate is getting long in the tooth, but since Eleanor in the movie is pushing sixty, that should be just fine. Before you meet her, I must warn you: She comes on like a battle ax, but she's got a heart of gold."

"As a married pair," O'Toole continued, "we'll be the odd couple of the year. When I told her I was still in my early thirties, she told me that all my heavy drinking made me look dissipated and far older. She said that whereas she was still trim and fit, at the rate I am going, I'll be dead by the time I'm forty."

"I've decided that Katharine Hepburn," he continued, "is a cross between Medusa and Tugboat Annie."

When Hepburn met with Levine, she told him, "I saw O'Toole flounce around in the desert in those white robes. He didn't have a woman in that picture to challenge him. He's got one now. Spencer could always hold his own against me, but I don't know about O'Toole. I chew up minor actors and spit them out for breakfast."

Henry and Eleanor: Lions in Any Season

Henry II (1133-1189): Chroniclers have recorded that his eyes "were bright and in anger, fierce and flecked." An energetic and sometimes ruthless ruler,

Henry—who ruled England from 1154-1189—was also designated as the Duke of Normandy and Lord of Ireland. At various times, depending on the outcome of the many battles surging around Western Europe during the High Middle Ages, he also ruled over Wales, Scotland, and Brittany.

Henry II of England, founder of a dynasty

Shortly after he inherited the French province of Anjou in 1151, he married Eleanor of Aquitaine, heiress to vast tracts of land in what is today the Atlantic seaboard of France. Her previous marriage to Louis VII of France had been annulled based on her failure to bear him a son after fifteen years of marriage.

Henry, now firmly linked with Eleanor, then engaged in military conflicts with Louis VII that dragged on for decades. Henry's vast territories were collectively known as the Angevin Empire, which stretched from the Pyrenées to Ireland, encompassing roughly half of medieval France, all of England, and some of Ireland.

He and Eleanor, as founders of the Plantagenet Dynasty, had eight children together. Usually scruffily dressed, Henry was described by chroniclers of that day as "good looking, red-haired, freckled, and with a large head and short, stocky body, bow-legged from riding." An impulsive ruler, he was known for his outbursts of temper.

Eleanor of Aquitaine (1122-1204): A monumental figure in history, throughout the High Middle Ages, Eleanor was the richest and most powerful woman in Western Europe. Contemporary sources cited her beauty, calling her "the embodiment of charm."

She was queen for nearly 46 years. Based on her marriage to King Louis VII, she became the Queen Consort of France (1137-1152). Later, based on her marriage to King Henry II, she became Queen Consort of England (1154-1189).

Three of her sons by Henry became kings.

She was imprisoned in 1173 for having supported her young son Henry's revolt against his father (her husband). She was not released until the senior Henry died.

Their son, Richard I (see below) eventually ascended the throne of England. When he headed

A pious view of Eleanor of Aquitaine, holding her own in a world ruled by men.

off to the Holy Land as part of the Third Crusade, Eleanor, as Regent, ruled England in his place. When her son was captured, she personally traveled to Germany to negotiate his ransom.

Richard I ("the Lionheart; 1157-1199); was King of England from 1189 until his death. The third son of Henry II and Eleanor, he was also the Duke of Normandy, an enormously powerful rank in an era when memories of the Norman invasion of England, in 1066, were still vivid.

Coeur de Lion (Richard the Lionhearted) loved Philip II of France.

Richard was said to have been the lover of King Philip II of France. His homosexuality has long been a topic of debate among historians, although his reputation as the toughest of Henry's sons remains intact.

He eventually married Berengaria of Navarre, but that appears to have been an attempt to gain territory. The couple remained childless.

Geoffrey II, Duke of Brittany (1158-1186): The fourth son of Henry II and Eleanor, Geoffrey Plantagenet has been characterized "as the brains of a ghastly family, a cold, amoral schemer with calculating machinations." The Norman/Welsh chronicler Gerald of Wales (1146-1223) labeled him "a hypocrite in everything, a deceiver, and a dissembler."

Geoffrey II, Duke of Brittany: A rebellious son slated for an early grave.

A fascinating figure of much complexity, he deserved his own movie instead of a minor role in *The Lion in Winter.*

When he was fifteen, Geoffrey joined his brothers in rebellion against their father. Henry II later forgave his ambitious, greedy, and errant son, but demanded, in 1181, that he marry Constance, the heiress of Brittany, as a means of ensuring England's control over that lush and fertile domain in nearby France.

Geoffrey became extremely intimate with Prince Philip of France, and he spent much time with him at his court in Paris. Philip eventually elevated Geoffrey as his *seneschal [a feudal steward in charge of an estate(s).]*

When Geoffrey died at the age of twenty-seven, Philip was so grief-stricken that, according to contemporary accounts, he attempted to jump into the coffin during the burial of his beloved intimate.

Philip II of France (1165-1223): The first ruler to be designated as "King of France," Philip, a member of the Capetian Dynasty, was the son of Louis VII and his third wife, Adela of Champagne. His greatest achievements included a role in the breakup of the Plantagenet's Angevin Empire, the construction of a fortified wall around Paris; and the solidification of financial security to the political entity known forever after as "France."

Phillip II of France... Loving Henry II's sons until he turned against them.

Philip befriended all of Henry II's sons and used them to foment rebellion against their father. He later turned against both Richard and John after their accessions to the throne of England.

John, King of England (1166-1216); The youngest son of Henry II and Eleanor, John ruled England from 1199 until his death, but he lost the Duchy of Normandy to Philip II of France. A baronial revolt at the end of his reign led to his being forced to sign the Magna Carta.

Scholastics do not give John rave reviews as a ruler. The historian Ralph Turner defined him as a man with "distasteful, even dangerous personality traits, including pettiness, spitefulness, and cruelty." John often appears as the villain in films and novels depicting his hatred and ill treatment of Robin Hood. He didn't fare much better in the script for *The Lion in Winter*, despite his having been described as Henry's favorite son.

John, King of England... "A spoiled brat, sulky, sullen, with a sniveling slack jaw."

In succession, he married two women each of whom were named Isabelle. They included the Countess of Gloucester (married 1189, annulled in 1199); and the Countess of Angoulême (married 1200), when she was nine years old. That marriage endured until his death. Although he was said to have been abusive to his wife, they had five children, including Henry III, who became King of England in 1207.

He was known to have had many mistresses, many of them married noblewomen. In his conflicts with ecclesiastics of his era, the church hierarchy denounced him as "sinfully lustful."

Princess Alais (also spelled Alys) **Capet: (1160-1220),** was the daughter of Louis VII through his marriage to Constance of Castile, and half-sister of Philip II of France. As a child, she had been sent to be reared in the English court, later becoming the mistress of Henry II, the father of the man (Richard, at the time, Count of Poitou, and later elevated to the rank of Richard I) she had been officially "contracted," from the age of nine, to marry.

She was passed around like a pawn from prince to prince. Henry had plans to annul his marriage to Eleanor and marry Alais himself. She particularly objected to John, telling his father (her lover, Henry II) that "he smelled of compost."

Ultimately, she didn't marry any of Henry's sons. At the age of thirty-three, she wed Guillaume de Ponthieu, bearing him three children before dying at the age of forty.

Lions in Winter: Reel Characters (i.e., Supporting Players)

O'Toole played a key role in the casting of the film's supporting players. Hepburn didn't want well-established actors, referring to them as "either eccentrics or skeletons." O'Toole "trawled" English repertory companies including his *alma mater*, the Old Vic in Bristol, looking for fresh new talent. Most of the actors he solicited were available (and jumped at the chance for an involvement in the film), although in the case of Anthony Hopkins, Laurence Olivier had to be persuaded to release him from his commitments to the National Theatre.

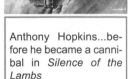

Anthony Hopkins as Richard the Lionheart: Making his film debut, this Welsh actor went on to become one of the greatest and highest paid of British stars. In time, he'd win an Oscar for his stunning portrayal of Hannibal Lecter in *The Silence of the Lambs* (1991).

Anthony Hopkins...before he became a cannibal in *Silence of the Lambs*

Beginning as an understudy for Oliver, he later starred in such movies as *The Elephant Man* (1980) and *Mutiny on the Bounty* (1984), where he played the detested commander, William Bligh, opposite Mel Gibson cast as Fletcher Christian, leader of the mutineers.

John Castle as Prince Geoffrey: Trained at RADA, this English actor also made his screen debut In *The Lion*

John Castle...any role, any time.

in Winter, garnering critical acclaim. *Hamlet* remained his favorite stage role, and he would later work with O'Toole again in *Man of La Mancha.* A versatile actor, he could play any number of characters, even the villain in *RoboCop* (1993).

Nigel Terry as Prince John: This English actor is best known for his portrayal of King Arthur in *Excalibur* (1980). In *The Lion in Winter,* he was cast as a carica-

Nigel Terry... teenaged upstart

tured, contemptible, and spastic adolescent. He broke into show biz in repertory companies, most notably The Old Vic in Bristol, later appearing in many plays for the Royal Shakespeare Company. In Derek Jarman's *Caravaggio* (1986), he played the title role. On a trivia note, he was the first baby born in Bristol after World War II, emerging from his mother's womb a few minutes after Britain's involvement in the war officially ended.

Timothy Dalton as King Philip II: Dalton is another Welsh actor who made his screen debut in *The Lion in Winter,* playing a sensitive, regal, and embittered French King. He is known today mainly for his starring

Timothy Dalton, before the world focused on him as 007.

roles in such films as *License to Kill* (1989). He also played Rhett Butler in the TV miniseries, *Scarlett* (1984), the original sequel to Margaret Mitchell's *Gone With the Wind.*

Dalton has also appeared in many BBC productions, starring as Heathcliff in a remake of *Wuthering Heights* (1970), a role originally created by Laurence Olivier. His most bizarre screen appearance involved the role of one of the husbands of the 85-year-old Mae West in *Sextette.*

Dalton never married, but had a long relationship with the English actress, Vanessa Redgrave, with whom he appeared in the 1971 *Mary, Queen of Scots.*

Jane Merrow as Princess Alais: This English actress was born to a German refugee father in Herefordshire. A graduate of RADA, she played the French-born mistress of Henry II in *The Lion in Winter.* For it, she was nominated for a Golden Globe as a supporting actress, but

Jane Merrow as Alais Capet discusses love and marital dischord with Eleanor of Aquitaine (Hepburn)

476

lost to Ruth Gordon for *Rosemary's Baby* (1968). Later, Merrow settled in the United States, where she frequently appeared in such TV dramas as *Mission Impossible* and *Hart to Hart.*

Her best line in *The Lion in Winter* was delivered as a petulant objection to her proposed marriage to Henry's (i.e., her lover's) son John. "I don't like your Johnny. He's got pimples and he smells of compost."

Drunken Orgies Under the Starry Nights of Provence

During pre-production, film locales were selected in appropriately mildewing medieval monuments and castles in Ireland, France, and Wales. Rehearsals began at the Haymarket Theatre in London.

O'Toole provocatively informed his fellow actors, "The gloves are off. It's every man for himself. I plan to steal every scene I'm in. Catch me if you can. Show me what you can do."

Over lunch with Hepburn, he said, "I realize, working with handsome young guys like Dalton, that time is marching on for me. A whole new generation of actors is emerging, many quite talented. I'm no longer the pretty young blonde running around in the desert."

"Oh, dear heart," Hepburn answered. "You're preaching to the choir. The whole world has changed a thousand times since I starred with John Barrymore in *Morning Glory* (1933), for which I won my first Oscar."

"Why don't you exercise more?" she asked him. "Go bike riding with me in the early morning in Regents Park."

"Actually, I do exercise," he said, "by high jumping to conclusions."

Early in the rehearsal process, the film's director, Anthony Harvey, joined them for lunch. He told them he got his start in show-biz playing Cleopatra's younger brother in *Caesar and Cleopatra* (1945), a British film adapted from a play written in 1901 by George Bernard Shaw. It had co-starred Vivien Leigh and Claude Rains. He recalled, "The London Blitz was on and one night in an air raid, the studio caught fire. Vivien had a miscarriage, but (for me as an actor) it was a wonderful start. The director told me I was cast because I had Vivien's eyes."

Hepburn was friendlier to Harvey than she'd been during a previous encounter with him. A few days before, in his capacity as the film's director, he'd arrived at rehearsals and presented her with a lush bouquet of red English roses. She rejected them because she claimed they had wires in them. She'd also told him, "Don't even try to be friends with me."

During rehearsals, Hepburn glided into her role of Eleanor, crafting a deadly monolith of mother love and colliding, inevitably, with her wicked, scheming sons. She seemed to genuinely morph into the chillingly ruthless matriarch of "a clan in which love works like cancer."

Packed with filial betrayals, *The Lion in Winter* is about family warfare, as every one of the king's sons sets out to betray him. Each of the sons is eventually disowned in this royal jockeying for power. Each son wants to grab the crown from Henry. Parent is pitted against parent, with Eleanor preferring Richard, and with Henry favoring John.

Lion in Winter is not an accurate historical document that reflects what actually happened at Chinon in France's Loire Valley during Christmas of 1183. The family gathering that supposedly took place there never happened, except in the original playwright's (Goldman's) fantasy.

The king's first heir, young Prince Henry, has died months before, and his wife, Eleanor, has been sent to prison in the Salisbury Tower in England.

For reasons of his own, Henry has granted her a special dispensation for release at Christmas, assuring her, "It's only for the holidays."

Goldman's dialogue between Eleanor and Henry is razor-sharp and frequently vindictive.

Eleanor tells him, "I could peel you like a pear and God himself would call it justice."

As depicted in the film, years before their reunion, Henry had abandoned Eleanor's bed. He is living with Princess Alais, his much younger mistress.

Filming began at the Brau Studios in Dublin, where the Irish government—based on its eagerness to attract capital and creative artists from abroad—eagerly welcomed the movie's cast and crew.

Interiors were shot here before moving on to locations in the South of France, a region peppered with photogenic fortresses and medieval châteaux.

In one drafty castle, O'Toole noticed Hepburn wearing a tattered wool sweater between takes.

"If you've fallen on bad days, I can afford to buy you a new Scottish woolen sweater. The one you're wearing looks as if it were half eaten by rats."

"I wear it as a good luck charm," she said. "It belonged to Bogie."

Almost from the beginning, Hepburn loudly objected to O'Toole's lifestyle, which consisted mainly of boozing down bottles of Irish whiskey. She lectured him, "You don't eat enough. You need some blood-red meat to put some weight on that skeletal frame of yours. All you do is drink. From now until the end of this picture, I'm going to call you an appropriate name: Pig!"

"And from now on, I'm going to call you Old Nags," he answered.

He discussed Hepburn with Harvey. "At first, I thought the bitch was going to steal every scene. I was wrong. She's like a bloody poultice, literally pulling a performance out of you."

From the beginning, he noted that Hepburn tried to direct the picture and rewrite the script. "You have me sitting by a fire," she told Harvey. "That isn't Eleanor. You should depict her out chopping wood."

When Harvey told her about O'Toole's appraisal, Hepburn said, "Balderdash! We'll make a fine pair, because I'm on to him, and he's on to me."

One afternoon, Hepburn carefully watched O'Toole perform one of his more emotional scenes. At its end, she approached him, saying "I think I've seen enough of your acting style to define it. You're a female impersonator."

"Oh, Katharine, dear heart, that appellation surely belongs to you."

She spat on the ground, turned her back to him, and walked away.

Deep into their filming, O'Toole began to feel that playing Henry had aged him. At one point, he asked Siân Phillips, "Just how old am I?"

She answered that he was pushing forty.

Then he denounced her. "You god damn lying whore! Get out of my sight!"

Sometimes, the relationship between Hepburn and O'Toole grew violent. In one scene, she needed her makeup man and was told he was in O'Toole's dressing room. She barged in without knocking, and socked O'Toole in the jaw before hauling off the makeup man by his ear.

As retribution for her criticism of his drinking, O'Toole waited until she was called before the camera and otherwise occupied. Then, he gathered up all the empty beer and liquor bottles he could find and dumped them onto the front seat of her car. "My aim," he told Harvey, "was to convince cast and crew that Hepburn was a raging alcoholic."

When shooting resumed in the south of France, O'Toole opted for temporary housing in Arles, a sleepy city on the Rhône sometimes called "the soul of Provence." Vincent van Gogh had painted some of most memorable art here, including *Starry Night.*

O'Toole stayed in a suite within the Hotel d'Arlatan, the former residence of the comtes d'Arlatan de Beaumont.

His hellraising came to the attention of the hotel's management after many complaints were lodged about it. It seemed that he was importing prostitutes from Marseille for drunken orgies.

Because of all these difficulties, Levine, at one point, decided to hold back $200,000 of his $750,000 salary. Later, O'Toole had to have him hauled into a U.S. courtroom, where a Supreme Court justice in Albany, Gerald Culkin, ruled in O'Toole's favor.

After that, he retreated to Les Baux de Provence, 12 miles northeast of Arles, a town that Cardinal Richelieu (1585-1642) had defined as "a nesting place for eagles." Surrounded by mysterious, shadowy rock formations overlooking the southern Alpilles, within one of the most arid regions of Europe, O'Toole found a (temporary) refuge.

At one of Les Baux's hotels, O'Toole found a management team which had long catered to off-the-record Parisians who come here for illicit holidays. Consequently, no one challenged O'Toole's "morality," even after he became sexually involved with three local girls who, it was revealed, were virgins.

One evening during his stay in Les Baux, O'Toole drank heavily. In a scene filmed earlier that day two barges, each of them a prop in the filming, had collided, bashing and seriously injuring one of his fingers. He was very upset.

Even later, over dinner, he was still very nervous, smoking one Gauloise after another and continuing his heavy drinking.

He retreated to bed with a lit cigarette and fell asleep. The bed caught on fire, and the fire department was summoned. Three firemen stormed into his bedroom to extinguish the blaze.

Stark naked, O'Toole jumped to his feet and rushed up to the chief fireman, startling him by giving him a sloppy wet one directly on the mouth.

During his final day of shooting, O'Toole told Harvey, "I haven't seen all of Hepburn's films. My god, she was making them when I was in the womb. But I think her take as Eleanor will be one of her finest performances, if not her finest. She was damn good opposite Bogie in *The African Queen,* but in this one, she's better. She was strong yet vulnerable as the queen, a difficult act to pull off. Imperious, cold-blooded, and scheming, but also needing, she never struck a false note."

Despite Critics' Praise for "That Lion," O'Toole Nonetheless Suffers His Third Oscar Loss

The Lion in Winter premiered on October 30, 1968 to critical acclaim.

With a few brickbats tossed its way, it received rave reviews, *The Daily Mirror* praising it as "an altogether triumphant achievement in picture-making.

It became the 12th highest-grossing film of 1968. Critic Roger Ebert commented on the authenticity of the sets, "with their dogs and dire floors, rough furskins and pots of stew, pigs, mud, dungeons, and human beings."

John Allen in *The Christian Science Monitor* found that *"The Lion in Winter* emphasizes Mr. O'Toole's talents." Bruce Bahrenburg in *The Newark (NJ) Evening News* found that "O'Toole gives the character a boisterous regal depth." Judith Crist of *New York* magazine pronounced his performance as "superb."

In 2015, a latter-day review of the film appeared in *The Guardian* in London. "Anthony Harvey's 1968 Plantagenet family soap opera has savage catfights, drippy suitors, a fruity Peter O'Toole, even a proto-*Brokeback Mountain* moment. What more could one ask for?"

The film received seven nominations for Oscars, winning not only for Hepburn (Best Actress) but for James Goldman (Best Adapted Screenplay) and John Barry (Best Musical Score.).

For the first time in the history of the Academy, two actresses won with a tie vote. As it happened, Hepburn shared her award with Barbra Streisand for her role in *Funny Girl.*

For Hepburn, it would be her third Oscar win, presented the year after her Oscar win a year before for her role in *Guess Who's Coming to Dinner?* She had co-starred in that film with Spencer Tracy, who lost his Oscar bid to Rod Steiger for *In the Heat of the Night.*

For Hepburn, at least, the win did not represent the "winter" of her retirement from films. It was, instead, a kind of Indian Summer for an actress whose future roles, both cinematic and for TV, would carry her into her ninth decade.

O'Toole was nominated for an Oscar but lost to Cliff Robertson for his role in *Charly*, in which he played a man with impaired intellectual skills. Other actors up for the award included Alan Arkin for *The Heart is a Lonely Hunter;* Alan Bates for *The Fixer;* and Ron Moody for *Oliver!.*

The Lion in Winter was nominated for Best Picture but lost to *Oliver!,* a film based on the classic novel by Charles Dickens.

Harvey was nominated for Best Director, but lost, although he did win a Best Director award from the Directors Guild.

Eventually, Harvey would helm both O'Toole and Hepburn again; O'Toole in *Svengali* and Hepburn in a dark comedy about euthanasia, *The Ultimate Solution of Grace Quigley (1985).*

Margaret Fruse was nominated for costume design, her wardrobes described as "a kind of Mordor-Romanesque."

The Lion in Winter won a Golden Globe award as Best Picture of the Year, with O'Toole winning as Best Actor.

He told a reporter, "Meeting Kate Hepburn was one of the great experiences of my life. If it had been twenty-five years before, I would have broken Spencer Tracy's fingers to get at her.

One of the rare moments where Hepburn's Eleanor, presumably just before he carts her back to prison, appears submissive to her Henry

Consistently betrayed by her children, Hepburn, as Eleanor, evokes a female version of the tragic King Lear

The saga of Eleanor and Henry continued to fascinate other actors in other productions of Lion in Winter. Here, Glenn Close and Patrick Stewart team up in Showtime's 2014 remake of *A Lion in Winter*

Chapter 28

Goodbye, Mr. Chips

Laurence Olivier, Rex Harrison, & Richard Burton Reject any Involvement in Remaking It, but O'Toole Commits Himself to a "Trendy and Experimental" Musical Version

Playing a Stodgy Latin Teacher, He Marries a Music Hall Soubrette (Petula Clark), Whose Questionable Past Shocks the University's "Bluenoses"

As a schoolmaster cheered by his hat-waving students, Peter O'Toole rode to his fourth "Best Actor" Oscar nomination, but lost once again.

Terence Rattigan's screenplay was a radical departure from the famous James Hilton novella of 1934. In the latest version, the time frame moved forward decades, beginning in the 1920s and ending in the 1960s.

Near the end of the turbulent 1960s, the choreographer and Broadway director-turned-moviemaker, Herbert Ross, decided that he wanted to create a filmed musical remake of *Goodbye, Mr. Chips,* scheduling it for release in 1969.

The previous year, he had worked as choreographer and director of the musical numbers for the cinematic version of *Funny Girl,* starring Barbra Streisand.

Of course, he knew that Robert Donat in the original, 1939 version of *Goodbye, Mr. Chips,* would be an almost impossibly tough act to follow. Donat had won the "Best Actor" Oscar in one of the most highly competitive Academy Awards competitions in Hollywood history, beating Clark Gable in his greatest role, that of Rhett Butler in *Gone With the Wind.* He also trounced Laurence Olivier in his greatest role, that of Heathcliff in Emily Brontë's *Wuthering Heights.* Other formidable competition came from James Stewart, nominated that same year for his engaging performance in the title role of *Mr. Smith Goes to Washington.*

Ross's first choice for the casting of Mr. Chips was Laurence Olivier, who at first thought he might be able to handle the musical numbers. Ultimately, however, Olivier decided it was not a project he wanted to tackle.

Ross then conceived the idea of casting Rex Harrison as the male lead opposite Julie Andrews. Previously, that duo had been lavishly praised for their co-starring roles in the Broadway version (1956-1962) of *My Fair Lady.* [Ironically, Andrews lost the role of Eliza Doolittle to Audrey Hepburn when the play was adapted into a movie for release in 1964.]

"In the decades to come, my version of Mr. Chips will be more appreciated." In that assessment, O'Toole was right on target.

The original 1939 version of *Goodbye, Mr. Chips,* was already a word-renowned film classic—the kind that bolstered British resolve in the battles of World War II. It was a hard act to follow.

Depicted above: Greer Garson and Robert Donat.

O'Toole and Burton Compete for the Oscar with a "Midnight Cowboy," but John Wayne Guns Them All Down with True Grit.

For a number of reasons, Harrison dropped out of the running for an involvement in *Mr. Chips,* followed shortly thereafter by Andrews, who had previously scored huge hits in *Mary Poppins* (1964) and later, for *The Sound of Music* (1965).

After that, Ross interested Richard Burton in the role, and wanted to sign Samantha Eggar for the female lead. But when Eggar dropped out, he offered the role to Lee Remick, who turned it down for another assignment.

Transitioning from a nightclub singer to the wife of a schoolmaster, Petula Clark in *Goodbye, Mr. Chips*

Ross then came up with the idea of signing singer Petula Clark to the role. When Burton heard about this twist in the casting, he, too, bolted, claiming, "I will not appear opposite a pop singer as my leading lady." *[In the original, 1939, version of the film, the female lead had been played by the endlessly dignified Greer Garson.]*

As a final choice, Ross called Peter O'Toole, who accepted.

The new script involved an aged, stiffly dignified teacher and (former) headmaster of an elite English prep school, who recalls his career, the changing fortunes of his students, and his personal life as they unfolded over the decades.

For supporting players, Ross signed the distinguished English actor, (Sir) Michael Redgrave, to

Carnaby Street, Swinging London, "Downtown," and the 60s—all of it accessorized with the charm and vigor of Petula Clark.

play the headmaster at the school. O'Toole's long-suffering wife, Siân Phillips, was contracted to appear as the best friend of Katherine Bridges (Petula Clark), a one-time music hall *soubrette* who plays Mr. Chip's fiancée and (later) wife. In the exaggerated mannerisms she exhibited in the enactment of her role, Siân obviously based her interpretation of Katharine's *confidante,* Ursula Mossbank, on the stage and screen star, Tallulah Bankhead.

Ross was married at the time to the ballerina Nora Kaye, who had been hired to choreograph Clark's musical numbers. About a year after Kaye's death in 1987, Ross would famously marry Lee Radziwill, sister of Jacqueline Kennedy Onassis.

O'Toole was insecure about tackling a famous role that had brought such international acclaim to Donat. When O'Toole signed for it, although Donat had already been dead for a decade, his memory (and memories of how he had played the role) lingered on.

As one reviewer wrote, "It is just as well that Donat is dead, since he wouldn't have to live to see O'Toole take over a role he made famous."

O'Toole's insecurities became even more acute when he picked up the morning papers in London to read that Lord Fisher, the former Archbishop of Canterbury, a former headmaster at Repton, had denounced him as the director's choice to play Mr. Chips.

City sophisticate Siân Phillips playing opposite her real-life husband in *Goodbye, Mr. Chips.*

[Repton, a prestigious, now-coeducational prep school in the English Midlands, had been founded in 1559 on the site of an Augustinian priory originally built in the 12th century.]

Fisher told *The Times* of London, "No, no, no, to Peter O'Toole. I have a very firm idea of the sort of man Mr. Chips was, and O'Toole cannot possibly play him."

The press immediately called O'Toole for his response: "I don't want to engage in combat with the esteemed Archbishop. After all, he communes every day with God himself. I feel that if I were heavenly enough to appear as not one, but three angels in John Huston's *The Bible,* then surely I would be a candidate worthy enough to portray a school teacher."

It was not the acting, or even the inevitable comparisons to Robert Donat, that terrified O'Toole, but the musical numbers. Ross, however, assured him that they would be seamlessly woven into the plot, and not be configured as show-stopping extravaganzas evocative of something from an MGM film from the 1930s and 40s.

O'Toole mocked himself: "Before members of the audience hear me sing, someone should shout FIRE! so they'd have a chance to rush to the exit doors. I decided to sing—if you'd call it that—in a slightly cracked voice, like an aging school teacher. Surely no one would suggest

Lord Geoffrey Francis Fisher, Baron Fisher of Lambeth, Archbishop of Canterbury from 1945 to 1961, presided over both the wedding (in 1947) and the coronation (in 1953) of QE2.

But were his mean and hurtful opinions about Peter O'Toole's casting in *Mr. Chips* really necessary?

me as a replacement for our beloved but doomed Judy Garland, whom we lost in 1969."

The film's musical director, Leslie Bricusse, asserted, "Peter thought he could sing. But he couldn't really hear how his voice sounded to other people. Unfortunately, I could."

Knowing that he would be compared unfavorably to Donat, O'Toole decided to create a distinctively rumpled look. He donned a pair of spectacles that looked as if they'd been salvaged from a five-and dime store. And he grew a brushy mustache that was later compared to that of an SS colonel.

O'Toole met with Rattigan for story conferences. He'd known the gay playwright ever since he'd written *Ross* (1960), a stage play based on the life of T. E. Lawrence. In 1962, Rattigan had been diagnosed as having leukemia. Although he had temporarily recovered, O'Toole noted that although he bravely tried to carry on with his work on the script, he was actually very ill.

O'Toole eventually met and bonded with Clark, finding her most compatible as his co-star, love interest, and *[in the movie, at least]* wife.

Born near London in Surrey, England, Clark, the same age as O'Toole, was the centerpiece of a career that spanned seven decades. She'd launched herself as a singer on the BBC Radio during World War II, when she became known as "England's Shirley Temple." British soldiers adopted her as their mascot, emblazoning replicas of her smiling face on their tanks as they rolled eastward across Europe for battles with the Nazis.

When O'Toole met her, during the aftermath of the overwhelming early success of The Beatles, the press identified her as "The First Lady of the British Invasion," based on the resounding success of singing hits which had included "Downtown" (1965) and "I Couldn't Live Without Your Love" (1966).

Among the first things on the director's agenda was location shooting in Italy. Cast and crew flew to Naples and its surrounding region of Campania. There, O'Toole was pursued by the *paparazzi,* many of them driving down from Rome specifically to follow his off-screen embarrassments and adventures. His reputation as a hellraiser had preceded him, and the tabloids were obsessed with associated scandals and photos.

Petula Clark, in scenes with O'Toole, often got better reviews than he did. The usually acerbic Rex Reed called her a new Jean Arthur, "with her soft, sweet smelling, dimpled doughnut with powdery cheeks and witty anxiety."

He found O'Toole, "prim and angular."

For the most part, O'Toole was protected by his friend, the ex-boxing champion, David Crowley, who owned Peter's favorite bar, Dave's Dive, in Rome on the fashionable via Veneto. "Dave did a fab job of protecting me from the flesh-eating jackals of the press," O'Toole said.

The biggest scandal erupted after a drunken O'Toole picked up two prostitutes in a sleazy bar and brought them back to his suite at the very upscale Excelsior Hotel. The two women were spotted exiting from the hotel just before dawn. A tabloid falsely asserted that one of them was only fourteen years old, and demanded, in print, that the police charge O'Toole for the seduction of a minor.

As it turned out, although she looked much younger, the prostitute was actually twenty years old.

Hoping to avoid any more scandal, Ross asked O'Toole to give up drinking. "I will go on the wagon," he promised, "except for Dom Perignon. As everybody knows, especially Elizabeth Taylor, champagne is not alcohol."

That night, O'Toole, accompanied by Crowley, headed for the bars again. At one, he reportedly downed a fifth of Irish whiskey.

During location shooting in Naples, an already ailing Rattigan suffered an attack of appendicitis that nearly killed him. He was rushed to the hospital, where doctors determined that his appendix had burst. It later became gangrenous.

Visiting him at the hospital, O'Toole found the conditions there—especially the hygiene—horrendous. He shared his sense of alarm with Ross, and the director used his influence to transfer the ailing playwright to an exclusive private clinic.

After his medical emergency, Rattigan recovered, but would remain in a weakened condition and ill health until his death in 1977.

"There go I if I don't mend my wicked, wicked ways," O'Toole told Crowley. "Perhaps I shouldn't make Errol Flynn my role model. I mean, that Tasmanian Devil was dead of a heart attack at the age of fifty."

When their filming in southern Italy was finished, cast and crew returned to England and their new location: The ancient town of Sherborne in the shire of Dorset. It was here that Sir Walter Raleigh had lived before his fall from fortune.

Siân accompanied O'Toole to Sherborne, where they rented a house and treated the shoot as something akin to a vacation.

At the time, builders were constructing a vacation home for them in Connemara, in Ireland. O'Toole said, "I wanted a retreat not only from the horrors of the world, but from the horrors of my own mind, and Connemara is the most peaceful place on earth."

When he wasn't scheduled for appearances on the set, O'Toole and Siân explored Dorset, visiting Cerne Abbas, a village to the south where Thomas and Maria Washington, uncle and aunt of George Washington, had lived. They also visited Sherborne Abbey, one of the great churches of England, dating from 705 A.D., and Sherborne Castle, which Sir Walter Raleigh had built in 1594. They dined at the Eastbury Hotel, a Georgian Building with a walled garden dating from 1740.

In real life, whoremongering O'Toole was not as restrained and scholastic as his professorial role of Mr. Chips demanded.

O'Toole preferred "salmon caught in the wild," and he liked his roast duckling cooked with honey. For the most part, he kept his drinking under control, although he became known to publicans in the area. Sometimes, he drove over to Dorchester, a town made famous by Thomas Hardy, for a few pints of lager in the Kings Arms Hotel, an establishment in business for three centuries.

Local schoolboys were hired on the set of *Goodbye, Mr. Chips* as extras. O'Toole bonded with some of the older boys. Over lager, he told them that if they really had wanted to prepare for life, they should have enrolled with him at that "roughhouse penitentiary I went to in Hunslet, Leeds. We turned out hardened criminals—ax murderers, rapists of nine-year-old girls, serial killers, and just plain quirky blokes who were panty sniffers, Peeping Toms, prostitutes, robbers, pimps selling black poontang, and blonde coozes operating fuck pads in Soho."

Michael Redgrave: A Great Actor in Turmoil
"Degrading Myself with Hustlers"

Michael Redgrave (1908-1985), one of the widely acknowledged great actors of Britain, had been designated to interpret the role that Paul Henreid, as headmaster, had made famous in the original version of *Goodbye, Mr. Chips.*

O'Toole had long been an admirer of the veteran actor's talent and continued to tell people, "Michael is my mentor. It was because of his performance in *King Lear* that I became an actor."

[He often cited how he and a male friend had hitchhiked from Leeds to Stratford-upon-Avon to see Redgrave perform as King Lear in 1953.]

"We had no money, so we slipped in after the curtain went up," O'Toole claimed. "We spent the night in this pasture, where we found a haystack. My friend went to sleep, but the odor bothered me. It was a dung heap covered with straw. The next morning at breakfast, we ordered blood pudding at a little caff. The owner said if we'd leave, he'd give us the breakfast for free. In other words, we didn't smell like Chanel No. 5."

"Some actors don a wig to make themselves old," O'Toole told Redgrave. "But you moved us ever so gently into a clinical study of senility. You portrayed a King long broken and knowing it. At limes, you seemed to be seeking a refuge from intolerable reality. In the final scene, you were more moving that any actor I've seen on the stage. You made Lear live for me."

"Oh, my dear boy, if only you wrote reviews of all my plays," Redgrave said. "Now kiss my lips and be done with you, as I've got to get ready to face the cameras."

In 1963, O'Toole had appeared as *Hamlet* and Redgrave as Claudius at the Old Vic in London. By the time they came together for the filming of *Goodbye, Mr. Chips,* O'Toole and Redgrave had become *confidants.*

The older actor talked freely to O'Toole about his emotional problems, both alcohol-related and sexual.

"I always felt a kindred spirit in Peter," Redgrave told his actress daughter, Lynn. "When we first met, I tossed off the usual proposition, and he ever so politely turned me down. At least we got the sex thing out of the way right from the beginning of our friendship."

Redgrave often spoke of "my dark side." He admitted he'd spent too many nights "debauching himself in Turkish baths, especially those in Liverpool. He claimed that in London, he often cruised Knightsbridge, picking up hustlers "to degrade myself. The next morning, I would wake up with a sense of self-disgust," he confessed.

In spite of his constant homosexual infidelities, Redgrave remained married to actress Rachel Kempson from 1935 until she died, the marriage spanning some fifty years. One of the most glamorous and admired actresses in England, Kempson had an amazing tolerance for her husband's tawdry adventures in the subterranean gay world. She was always ready to welcome him back home after his absences.

Talented, bohemian, avant-garde, socially prominent, and homosexually repressed:

Michael Redgrave with his wife, actress Rachel Kempson, in 1953.

Sometimes, he arrived on the doorstep of their home badly beaten up.

She also had to cope with Redgrave's drinking. Some directors claimed that he extended a play's length by at least fifteen minutes whenever he showed up drunk, forgetting his lines and speaking very slowly.

The Redgraves, who included both Lynn and Vanessa, were one of England's most talented theatrical families. In 2006, O'Toole would star with Vanessa in *Venus*.

"Michael always lived in fear of exposure in the British press," O'Toole said, "dreading the fate that had descended on his colleague, John Gielgud, who had been arrested in a public toilet. Yet, in spite of that, Redgrave kept returning to forbidden pleasures and always loved to be paddled, I mean, REALLY paddled, before performing some sex act on a poor wretch selling his body for a pound or two."

"O'Toole Becomes a Stooped, Celluloid-Collared, Floppy-Hatted, Baggy-Kneed, Crumpled & Creased Semi-Myopic"

—Critic Max Caulfield reviewing Goodbye, Mr. Chips

Evoking the half singing/half speaking style that Rex Harrison had delivered in the musical interludes of *My Fair Lady*, O'Toole pulled off the musical numbers of *Goodbye, Mr. Chips*. The songs included the not-particularly-memorable "Where Did My Childhood Go?" and "What a Lot of Flowers."

For the fourth time, he was nominated for an Academy Award, this time for his contribution to *Goodbye, Mr. Chips*. He was competing against his friend, Richard Burton, for his performance as King Henry VIII, a role O'Toole had coveted, in *Anne of a Thousand Days,*

Also in competition with him were Dustin Hoffman and Jon Voigt for their roles in *Midnight Cowboy,* the story of a male prostitute selling his wares on the grimy streets of Manhattan. All of them lost to John Wayne for *True Grit*. O'Toole, however, later won a Golden Globe as the year's Best Actor.

During the time he spent working on *Goodbye, Mr. Chips*, O'Toole was prepping himself for his involvement in his next film project, which he thought would be the role of Shylock in Shakespeare's *The Merchant of Venice*. He had scored a hit and rave reviews when he'd performed the role at Stratford-upon-Avon.

During pre-production, the administrative lineup within MGM went through a major re-adjustment. The newest roster of "suits" who were running things there concluded that MGM would be denounced as "anti-Semitic" if they continued bringing into production a character like Shylock to the screen. Although the project was dropped, O'Toole wasn't notified until weeks later.

He lived in dread of the reviews he'd receive for his role of Arthur Chipping when *Goodbye, Mr. Chips* was released by MGM in November of 1969.

Most of the film's original musical numbers had been deleted before the public ever saw the film. Even Petula Clark, by far the cast's best singer, emerged in the final cut with only two songs. Critic Rex Reed attacked Leslie Bricusse's score, opining, "To insinuate that Bricusse's plodding score is merely dreadful would be an act of charity."

Reviews were generally lackluster, although the pairing of O'Toole with Petula Clark was generally praised. Vincent Canby in *The New York Times* wrote: "O'Toole has never been better. Having been forced to abandon his usual mechanical flamboyance, he delivers Chips with an air of genuine, if seedy, grandeur that shines through dozens of make-up changes. He talks with such charm that I almost suspected he was lip-synching Rex Harrison's voice."

London's *Daily Mirror* wrote: "Peter O'Toole gives a most impressive performance—quiet, subtle—but he isn't Mr. Chips."

Writing in the *Chicago Sun Times,* Roger Ebert found the mating of O'Toole and Clark "exactly right. He succeeds in creating a character that is aloof, chillingly correct, terribly reserved, and charming all the same."

Archer Winsten of the *New York Post* pronounced O'Toole's performance "a gem," and Richard Schickel found that together, O'Toole and Clark "make the old thing work—and make it worthwhile."

Goodbye, Mr. Chips.

Chapter 29

Under Milk Wood, On the Cheap

An Unholy Trio of the Busiest (and Booziest) Superstars —Richard Burton, Elizabeth Taylor, & O'Toole— Conspire to Film a Play by Dylan Thomas

"La Liz" Plays a Tart—"Type Casting" Her Enemies Called It— In This Hodgepodge of Boom Box Histrionics and Lewd Giggles

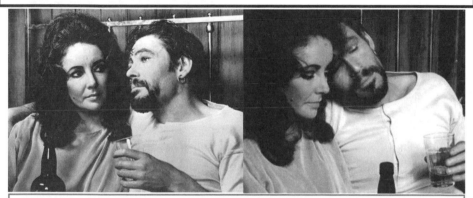

In the film version of the Dylan Thomas play, *Under Milk Wood,* Peter O'Toole, throwing caution to the wind, decided to join the most documented, the most fascinating, the most passionate, the most flamboyant, and the most exhibitionistic couple in the world.

"Why not?" he asked. "They invited ridicule, of course, but their turbulent marriage attracts jaded imaginations of lesser mortals around the globe. We will not see their likes again. I wanted to be part of that circus."

"To begin at the beginning. It is spring, moonless night in the small town, starless and bible-black, the cobblestones silent and the hunched courters'-and-rabbits' wood limping invisible down to the sloeblack, slow, black, crowblack, fishingboatbobbing sea."

—Excerpted from *Under Milk Wood,* by Dylan Thomas

For his 45th birthday, Richard Burton, accompanied by Elizabeth Taylor, had been invited to Buckingham Palace, where he was awarded with an honorific—Commander of the British Empire—by Queen Elizabeth II. He had hoped for a knighthood, but that would have been against British tradition. Having carefully defined points outside the U.K. as his permanent home, he was a "tax exile" at the time, making him ineligible for knighthood.

The Swansea-born Dylan Thomas was "imprisoned" for a night by *Under Milk Wood's* producer, Douglas Cleverdon, who reportedly locked him inside a recording studio until he completed the final readings of his play.

Andrew Sinclair, who had been in charge of only one previous film, had purchased the screen rights to what had originally been written as a radio drama in 1954, Dylan Thomas' *Under Milk Wood,* the most famous work of that Welsh playwright and poet. Sinclair had written a screenplay and planned to direct. He knew that the work had long been a favorite of Burton, who in 1954 had been one of the actors in the work's original manifestation for the radio.

Sinclair was also a novelist, critic, historian, and biographer whose previous works had included biographies of Che Guevara, Dylan Thomas, Jack London, John Ford, Francis Bacon, and J. Pierpont Morgan.

Revered in Wales as a modern-day cultural hero, Dylan Thomas, with a style emulated, perhaps, by his Welsh compatriot, Richard Burton, showed self-destructive patterns that contributed to his early death.

"The Greatest Actor in the World" (Burton)
Vies With "The Greatest Actor in the World" (O'Toole)

O'Toole Seduces "The Most Glamorous Whore
in the History of Welsh Prostitution."

Elizabeth Taylor had informed a reporter that she had frequently played recordings of *Under Milk Wood's* original radio format, confiding that "hearing the rich music of Richard's voice can make me experience an orgasm."

She once told Ava Gardner, in Puerto Vallarta, Mexico, "The sound of that voice can give me a better orgasm than his unreliable, flaccid Welsh dick when he's come to bed after consuming three quarts of vodka in a day."

With the very clear understanding that it would be filmed in Wales as a celebration of the region's heritage, Sinclair had raised £300,000 to finance this low-budget film.

No Welsh play ever had such colorful characters. O'Toole had already been assigned the role of the blind and aging Captain Cat, who dreams of his deceased shipmates and lost lover, Rosie Probert (Elizabeth Taylor), who was a harlot. Long dead, she is remembered only in his dreams. He comments on the goings-on and repressed passions (and anguish) that preoccupy the residents of a Welsh fishing village, which he loves. Despite the fact that he is blind, he gives every impression, during moments of stillness, that he's staring out the window, reflecting on the memories of time passed.

Captain Cat is aware of other town residents who include Mr. Waldo, a rabbit catcher, barber, herbalist, cat doctor, and quack, who reflects on his mother and on his several failed and unhappy marriages. Waldo is a notorious alcoholic and general troublemaker who's involved in an affair with Polly Garter, an innocent young mother, who dreams of her many babies. During the day, she scrubs floors and sings of her lost love.

One of these was Burcher Beynon, who dreams of riding pigs and shooting wild giblets. During the day, he enjoys taunting his wife about the questionable meat he scavenges and sells—owl's flesh, and the eyes of a dog are among his more exotic offerings.

Mae Rose Cottage, seventeen and never been kissed, dreams of meeting Mr. Right. Her day is spent in the field daydreaming, and drawing lipstick circles around her nipples.

Since O'Toole had already been assigned the drama's male lead, the only role suitable for Burton was that of "First Voice," (i.e., the narrator). The obvious role for Elizabeth was that of the harlot. *[This kind of role was not necessarily new for her. She'd previously won an Oscar for her interpretation of a prostitute in* BUtterfield 8 *(1960).]*

When Sinclair heard that Burton and Elizabeth could spend only ninety days in the U.K., and that their status as foreign residents (and tax exiles) would become null and void if they remained longer than that, he arranged a meeting with Burton at his rented home.

There, he found the walls covered with modern paintings, including works by such internationally famous artists as Rouault and Modigliani.

"Richard tried to lord it over me," Sinclair said. "How do you like my Monet and things? We have a better one on our yacht, anchored in the Thames."

He was referring to the *Kalizma,* which housed Elizabeth's four beloved dogs. They were not allowed to come ashore.

"Oh, I see," Sinclair said. "These are only your traveling pictures."

At one point, Burton turned his most intense gaze upon Sinclair. "You do know I am the greatest actor in the world, don't you?" he asked.

"I've just visited O'Toole," Sinclair said. "He told me *he* is the greatest actor in the world."

Andrew Sinclair directing Burton in Wales. The director defined Burton as "a true Welshman, who all his life wore a bit of red to commemorate the Welsh flag. He once told me his greatest pleasure at night was to wander the hills of Wales and listen to the calling of the owls."

Burton told Sinclair, "I know the film won't make any money. But in a sense, I'm paying my debt to Dylan by doing it."

"I adore Peter," Burton said. "Every time we meet, we tongue kiss. But we are also rivals. I often end up getting the parts he wants. But he always forgives me when we unite, extending that serpentine tongue of his instead of a handshake."

After dining aboard their yacht that night with Sinclair, the couple agreed to work with O'Toole on filming.

Sinclair had raised a budget of £300,000, and each of the three superstars had agreed to work for 10,000 pounds each.

Based on her role, Elizabeth was cited as "the most glamorous hooker in the history of Welsh prostitution."

However, in his first meeting with Burton and Taylor, Sinclair sensed potential trouble. Shortly after his arrival on their yacht, the "Battling Burtons" broke into a fight, at one point approaching the edge of violence. Reportedly, Burton at the time was overly medicated and with frayed nerves, and both were suffering from alcoholism, perhaps experiencing withdrawal symptoms.

At least one other visitor to their yacht, Rex Harrison—who had appeared with them as Julius Caesar in *Cleopatra* (1963)—reported that Burton and Taylor "lived off each other's nerves."

Harrison claimed that Burton had just returned from Wales, and during the course of their dinner, "Elizabeth accused him of seducing a little Welsh girl

496

who worked on the film. 'I have my fucking spies,' she shouted at her husband. They were almost ready to break into a fight, and I feared Elizabeth would not be camera ready because of a potential for bruises and black eyes that makeup wouldn't conceal."

In Wales, on the film set, O'Toole and Burton entertained the Welsh playwright and actor, Emlyn Williams. Burton spent much of the evening complaining "about what a bitch Elizabeth was."

"I told you not to marry her," Williams said. "She was—and is—nothing but a third-rate chorus girl."

Before the evening ended, Williams invited Burton to go back to the house where he was living for a three-way. "I've picked up this Welsh drifter who has a body that is lithe, smooth, sweet, and very, very tasty."

The gay playwright and actor, Welsh-born Emlyn Williams, always claimed: "I discovered Richard Burton. He had horribly pock-marked skin, yet sculptural cheekbones. His accent was as thick as the mist over Snowdon. Yet he had a startling beauty and keen intellect. He was not only very handsome, but very very sexy. Rather cold-bloodedly, I set out to seduce him."

Burton turned down the invitation. "Emlyn, I don't do that any more."

O'Toole's Welsh-speaking wife, Siân Phillips, was cast as the fastidious Mrs. Ogmore-Pritchard, the owner of a guest house, who seems driven by memories, and nostalgia for, the hours she spent nagging each of her two long-dead husbands.

Members of the cast included Vivien Merchant, who was married at the time to playwright Harold Pinter. Other actors in the cast included Ruth Madoc, Angharad Rees, Ann Beach, Glynis Johns, Victor Spinetti, and David Jason, making his film debut.

It was like arranging a weekend with Howard Hughes, Queen Elizabeth II, and Puck," Sinclair said. "Everyone in the cast was under the spell of Dylan Thomas' words. His voice seems to sing through all the other voices in an incantation."

As Captain Cat, O'Toole altered his appearance by growing a beard and a mustache which he dyed red. Some time before, his nose had been nipped by plastic surgeons, but for his role in *Under Milk Wood,* he used a fake nose to make him look like he did before his cosmetic surgery.

Back in London, O'Toole was joined by his co-producer, Jules Buck. Buck later told friends, "With Burton fucking country lasses, Peter resumed his long dormant affair with Elizabeth."

At this point in her very grand career, she had become a diva, refusing to travel to Wales from London because of back pains.

One night, early in the filming, she invited O'Toole for a sleepover. "Just because I have back trouble doesn't

Siân Phillips, who had always been famously associated with Wales, played the landlady who nags the spirits of her two dead husbands.

mean that other parts of my body are out of commission," she reportedly said to him.

O'Toole told Buck, "I wonder what it would have been like if I had accepted the role of Marc Antony in *Cleopatra*. I might have ended up as Elizabeth's husband, with all those millions and the Krupp diamond, too."

Burton later praised his wife for her Welsh accent in the film. In the meanwhile, Sinclair was less than pleased because he'd been forced to spend £600—half of his total costume budget—on three designer nightgowns for his temperamental star.

In the movie, the Welsh town depicted on screen bore the name "Llareggub, whose name, when its letters were spelled backwards, became "Bugger all."

The gorgeous and elegant Siân Phillips overlooked her husband's infidelities with his other co-star.

During the shoot, Elizabeth and Burton continued to feud, but not in front of the press. She told *The Ladies' Home Journal*, "Richard is the ocean. He is the sunset. He is such a vast person. He has such a huge personality. He is capable of being so many people, of doing so much. How can I describe him with a single word? He is truly magnificent."

"Despite his drinking, Burton was the ultimate professional," Sinclair said. "My only problem was at which distance I was to shoot him to cover up his bloodshot eyes."

Burton told the press, "The play is about religion, sex, and death—a comic masterpiece."

As a footnote, O'Toole spent the latter part of the film with his eyes closed because he could no longer tolerate the contact lenses he'd beem forced to wear in earlier segments of the shoot.

Between scenes one afternoon, Burton, in the presence of O'Toole, informed Sinclair, "It's a good thing for you that I'm sober."

"Define sober," the director said.

"Only one bottle of vodka a day."

More rowdy, as cameras rolled, than a Welsh rugby play-off.

Elizabeth Taylor, Peter O'Toole, and Richard Burton, in their tribute to the power and poetic sensitivities of Wales, formed "The Unholy Trio."

After his scenes and times with Elizabeth, O'Toole bragged to Jules Buck, "Elizabeth told me that I was the only man she preferred in bed to Burton."

His co-producer found that hard to believe. He knew that O'Toole was given to bragging, boasting to one of his short-term partners, "If there's not a dame on this set I can't screw, my name's not Peter O'Toole. Emphasis on 'Tool.'"

[He had repeated that boast many times.]

After a weekend in Wales with Burton, O'Toole told him, "My greatest sexual thrill involves going to bed with you and some girl at the same time."

Burton was suffering guilt throughout the film. He told O'Toole that the play's author, Dylan Thomas, had asked him for a loan of £200 pounds. Burton turned down the impoverished poet and playwright's request, even though he had lent him money before.

Burton later surmised, "Dylan Thomas went to America to earn money on the lecture circuit. He drank himself to death one night in 1953 in Greenwich Village at the White Horse Tavern. I blame myself for his death."

"There is only one Welshman more talented than me," Burton said. "And that was Dylan."

After the release of their rendering of *Under Milk Wood*, Critic Leslie Halliwell wrote, "Everything is much too literal—a real place instead of a fantasy."

Elizabeth and O'Toole, according to Jules Buck, were jealous when Burton, as narrator, received the best reviews. Judith Crist, the prestigious movie critic for *New York Magazine,* wrote, "The film is a triumph of visualization of the verbal visions and vignettes the poet created. No question that Burton was born to recite Thomas' luxuriant and flowing poetic realities and lusciously lifting prose. His voice was over the screen, penetrating to the very heart of the matter."

Elizabeth was devastated by her reviews, especially one that claimed, "her film career is waning, as is her acting talent."

Expressing the general negativity of her experience with the production, she later said, "The best thing I can say about my appearance is that I was viciously attacked and knocked off the charts."

As anticipated, the film was an utter failure at the box office when it premiered. It played to mostly empty houses at a few art theaters. Despite its casting of three major stars, its gross was only one million dollars. Sinclair failed to sell it to television.

The entire film was shot in just forty days, mostly on location in the Gwuan Valley in Wales. The townspeople appeared as extras.

With only hours to spare before they'd lose their status as tax exiles, Elizabeth and Burton kissed and embraced O'Toole goodbye before they left Wales aboard a private jet to Paris.

In parting, Burton told O'Toole, "*Under Milk Wood* never leaves me. Awake or asleep, the voices in the play sound throughout my head a thousand times."

After their departure, Sinclair told O'Toole, "Richard's voice seems to contain all the passion and powers, all the weariness and weaknesses, of our kind. To hear him speak is to listen to the human condition."

After hearing this, O'Toole asked, "What about *my* voice? Do I sound like a pansy?"

He received the most positive reinforcements from Caitlin Thomas, the poet's widow. She approached him and gently touched his arm. "Your film is just what Dylan would have liked."

"That was my greatest compliment," he said.

***

O'Toole survived Burton, who at the age of fifty-eight died of a brain hemorrhage in 1984. Elizabeth lived to be nearly eighty years old, dying at seventy-nine in 2011 from congestive heart failure.

O'Toole's passing in 2013 was greeted with the headline: DEATH OF A HELLRAISER.

Some of their fans believed that Dylan Thomas, had he been alive, should have written their eulogies.

Chapter 30

The Ruling Class

England's Church Leaders Accuse O'Toole
of Cinematic Blasphemy

O'Toole Portrays Jesus Christ as a Paranoid Schizophrenic

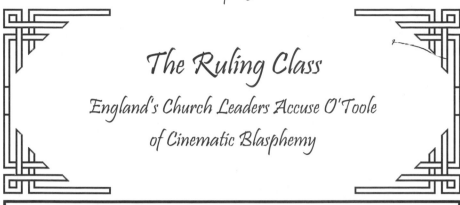

"One critic wrote that when it came to playing an elegant aristocratic lunatic, no actor does it better than *moi,*" said Peter O'Toole.

"It seemed natural to offer me *The Ruling Class,* this black comedy about a deranged earl. Derek Godfrey, poor thing, starred in the stage version, but was not much challenge for me. The play is a comedy with tragic relief. My partner, Jules Buck, and I acquired the rights for just £55,000."

After his return from Brazil and the filming of *Murphy's War* (1971), O'Toole checked into a hospital close to his residence in Hampstead.

He was visited by Peter Medak, an avant-garde Budapest-born director who wanted to discuss acquiring the rights to a new play by Peter Barnes entitled *The Ruling Class.*

"Peter was supposed to have given up liquor," Medak said, "but when I came into his room, he was devouring Beluga caviar and Russian vodka."

Eventually, after his exit from the hospital, O'Toole accompanied Medak to see the stage version of *The Ruling Class* being performed at the time in London's West End. Medak urged O'Toole, through Keep Films, to acquire the film rights.

After the performance, Medak and O'Toole went on a pub crawl through the sprawling neighborhoods between Soho and Hampstead. Since British pubs were legally required to respect the U.K.'s licensing hours, O'Toole had to pound on doors to persuade some publicans to open their premises for them. According to Medak, all that O'Toole needed to do involved knocking heavily and announcing "'Peter's here!' Amazingly, a publican would open the door to serve us after hours."

Eventually, O'Toole purchased the movie rights to *The Ruling Class* from its author, Peter Barnes, for £55,000. Then he commissioned him to personally adapt his work to the screen for a release in 1972. O'Toole later said, "Barnes's best line comes when I am asked why I'm so certain that I'm God. 'Simple,' I say. 'When I pray to him, I find myself talking to myself.'"

O'Toole later referred to Barnes as "an eccentric misanthropist who devours every film book at the British Museum. If you want to know who fitted and designed Charlie Chaplin's jockstrap—he called his Thing the eighth wonder of the world—Barnes will come up with the culprit."

The Ruling Class was produced by Jules Buck, who was in partnership with O'Toole in their shared venture, Keep Films, Ltd. Committed to not exceeding their budget of $1.4 million, O'Toole, as an actor, worked for free, hoping to get rich from his share of the box office receipts.

To the outrage of the church, and Christians in general, O'Toole starred in a blonde wig as an eccentric who fancies that he is "The Holy Trinity All in One." He demands to be called by any of the nine billion names signifying God.

"Like Jesus Christ himself, I was nailed to the cross and crucified. Not really, darlings. Don't be a silly ass."

The ailing actor, Jack Hawkins, O'Toole's longtime friend and co-star in *Lawrence of Arabia,* was listed as co-producer.

In *The Ruling Class,* defining it as a "black comedy," O'Toole spearheaded a cast of veteran English actors who remained optimistic by the success of its

Marlon Brando, for His Role in The Godfather, Steals the Oscar from Peter O'Toole, but Then Rejects It

theatrical version in London's West End.

But whereas its stage presentation generated a rollicking box office, its status as a scathing cinematic indictment of both organized religion and the depravity of the English aristocracy generated major protests, not only from the British Establishment, but from organized religion too.

Its plot was preposterous, and not to be taken seriously, despite its inclusion of an occasional murder. It opens with the death of the 13th Earl of Gurney, who dies from accidental asphyxiation during some kinky sex. The earl's title is passed to Jack Gurney (O'Toole), a psychotic who imagines he is Jesus Christ, and who makes it a point every night to sleep upright on a cross. As a raving but very articulate lunatic, O'Toole made a striking appearance with his flowing blonde hair, a beard, a monk's robe, and tennis shoes.

As the plot thickens, Jack's unscrupulous uncle, Sir Charles (William Mervyn), arranges for Jack to marry his mistress, Grace (Carolyn Seymour). His hope is that the newlyweds will produce a son, so that Sir Charles can then bestow the title (Earl of Gurney) on his nephew and commit Jack to a mental institution. But the plan, as could be predicted, backfires.

Sir Charles' wife, Lady Claire (Coral Browne), hates her husband. Plotting against him, she commissions a psychiatrist (Michael Bryant), with the hope that he can cure the 13th Earl's (i.e., O'Toole's) mental illness.

Dr. Herder introduces Jack (O'Toole) to a psychiatric patient (Nigel Green), who also fancies himself as Christ. Herder, who envisions himself as "The Electric Messiah," subjects Jack to electroshock therapy.

When the aging and embittered Lady Claire tries to seduce him, Jack murders her. Then, with the sly skill of a major psychopath and with no remorse whatever, he frames the estate's communist butler (Arthur Lowe).

Grace, Jack's wife, eventually gives birth to a baby boy, but it doesn't, as had been hoped, cure Jack's madness. Instead of Christ, he now declares himself as Jack the Ripper.

In Parliament's House of Lords, in his capacity as the Earl of Gurney, O'Toole delivers a fiery speech calling for capital punishment for even minor infractions. Not recognizing

Depicted above, the 13th Earl of Gurney, auto-asphyxiated and accessorized with his British Army uniform and a tutu.

him as insane, his colleagues in Parliament applaud wildly.

Back at his estate, his Lordship, the Earl (O'Toole) murders Grace for expressing her love for him. Her terrified scream is played out against the sound of a baby cooing. "I'm Jack, I'm Jack," the boy cries out, seemingly having inherited the insanity of his father.

Exterior shots were filmed at the sprawling estate of Harlaxton Hall in Lincolnshire. *[Built in 1837, it's a monumental mixture of Jacobean, Elizabethan, and baroque architecture that's been featured as the setting, in addition to* The Ruling Class, *of several other feature films and TV series.]* Interior scenes were filmed within baronial sets replicated on sound stages at Twickenham Studios outside London.

Women We Love:

Coral Browne as the very rich, very sophisticated, and very jaded, Lady Claire

During filming, O'Toole ordered the crew to install a fully stocked bar in his dressing room, with plenty of bottles of Irish whiskey. Coral Browne said. "All the crew drank like fish. By the time they returned from lunch, they

O'Toole as the new, also crazed, Lord Gurney

were all besotten. I don't know how any of them managed to stand up, much less make a film."

During the course of the filming, the Hungarian director, Medak met and fell in love with Seymour, the actress playing Grace, marrying her a year after *The Ruling Class's* 1972 release. During the course of his career, he would direct many distinguished stars, including George C. Scott and some of O'Toole's friends, Richard Burton, Richard Harris, and Oliver Reed. He tended to respect actors, referring to them as "musical instruments."

"I survived all of them," he once said, "even Peter O'Toole. We had laughter, we had drama."

Appearing in *The Ruling Class* as the acquiescing Bishop, the Scottish actor, Alastair Sim, was one of the most distinguished in British cinema. *The* (London) *Times* had described Sim's "treacherously sweet smile, triple takes, and unheralded spasms of apoplectic fury."

Sim's talent was almost matched by Arthur Lowe, who played the butler. He was best known for his performance as Captain George Mainwaring in the hit sitcom about Britain's Home Army during World War II, *Dad's Army,* whose eighty episodes, regularly attracting as many as eighteen million viewers, were broadcast on the BBC between 1968 and 1977.

During the course of the shoot, Lowe and O'Toole became drinking buddies. "He didn't know when to stop," O'Toole said. "He seemed to drink all the time. On occasion, he was known to pass out on the stage during a performance."

Other actors in the cast included Harry Andrews, who despite his status as a talented Shakespearean actor, usually played tough military officers in films,

Born in Nairobi, but educated in Britain, William Mervyn was better known for his TV appearances, where he often was cast as rich members of the aristocracy.

Also cast in *The Ruling Class* in a small role was South African-born Nigel Green. His commanding demeanor often landed him in military roles that had included *Zulu* (1964) and *Tobruk* (1967). He and O'Toole immediately recognized each other as hellraisers, and they became drinking buddies.

Green, who had served in The Royal Navy during World War II, had studied at RADA before going on stage in the Old Vic.

"When he starred with me as 'the Electric Messiah,' I had no idea Nigel was performing his last role," O'Toole said. "He died shortly thereafter at the age of forty-seven. The coroner said it was from an overdose of sleeping pills, but I knew better. He committed suicide."

"He was separated from his wife, Pamela Gordon, and he told me he felt 'so very, very much alone.' I spoke to him right before he killed himself, and volunteered to come over and sit with him. But he told me he wanted to be alone 'to wallow in my self-pity and get lost down some lonely street.' That's the last I ever heard from him."

Coral Browne was one of O'Toole's favorite actresses. When the English production of *The Man Who Came to Dinner,* then touring the provinces after a successful run on Broadway, ran out of money, she borrowed some from her dentist and purchased the rights. After successfully producing it later at the Savoy Theatre in London, she virtually lived off the royalties from that and from subsequent productions ever after. When she appeared as the campy Vera Charles in *Auntie Mame* (1958) opposite Rosalind Russell, Brown developed a gay cult following.

"This Aussie dame was a tornado and utterly fascinating," O'Toole said. "I think I fucked her, but was too drunk to remember. The only thing I never understood about her was her marriage (1974-1991) to Vincent Price, who was gay as a goose."

[Upon Browne's death in May of 1991, the Australian performer, Barry Humphries, was asked to deliver her eulogy, some lines from which are repli-

cated below. Humphries was famous for appearing on stage in drag as his alter ego, Dame Edna Everage, the gaudily dressed, acid-tongued, egomaniacal, and internationally fêted "Housewife Gigastar."]

"She Left Behind an Emptiness
A Gap, a Void, a Trough.
The World is Quite a Good Deal Less
Since Coral Browne Fucked Off."

On location near Harlaxton Hall, O'Toole shared a house with actor James Villiers, who played a small role. They staged nightly parties that were so outrageous that they aroused the ire of the townspeople. "James and I invited a coven of tramps, hobos, trollops, pederasts, and Satanists," O'Toole claimed.

At one point, they decided to whip up a batch of cocktails, filling a large punch bowl with alcohol poured liberally from every bottle in the house. O'Toole and the other guests tried, but no one could down a complete glass of "punch" without risk of vomiting.

"In the class system of England, I was at the bottom rung of the ladder, and James was at the top," O'Toole said. Villiers was from an upperclass background and a descendant of the Earls of Clarendon. In theatrical circles, he was known for what one critic called his "plummy voice and ripe articulation."

"He (Villiers) was the British answer to Vincent Price," O'Toole claimed. "No one could display supercilious arrogance like he could. He was made for plays written by Oscar Wilde."

"I adored James, though others were put off by his manner. He became my friend and confidant. I told him secrets about myself that I never shared with anyone, certainly not my wife, not even Kenneth Griffith. Regrettably, I later learned that as James got older, he no longer believed in the motto, 'Loose lips sink ships.' He told too many, and dined out on too many Peter O'Toole stories."

"We became friends at RADA when we were very young and always remained close," O'Toole said. "He was most often cast as cold, somewhat effete villains."

A favorite role he played was that of King Charles II in the BBC series, *The First Churchills* (1969).

Villiers, jokingly or otherwise, once said, "Peter and I sometimes slept naked in bed together. But we were not a pair of poofs, although many of our friends thought we were banging each other. We may have had sex, however. If so, we were so drunk, we probably thought that body in bed with us was that of a woman."

In Rupert Everett's autobiographical memoir, *Red Carpets and Other Ba-*

nana Skins, published in 2007, he described an encounter with Villiers in an Indian restaurant in 1985. "He was leglessly drunk, booming orders and insults to the poor, long-suffering waiter in a strange breathy vibrato that was pitched for the upper circle."

"James probably had a few and imagined that we were back on the set of *The Ruling Class,*" O'Toole said.

The film was released at a time when sex and violence characterized hundreds of films of the 1970s. O'Toole later said, "I'm no prude. God knows I've fucked my way through the boudoirs of the world, and I never met a drink I didn't down. In London, the only bedchamber I've never invaded is that of Her Majesty. I'm proud that our film contains no violence, except for a harmless murder or two, and the sex is light. I did not have to show my erection. We were frolicsome and oh so gay. What *The Ruling Class* does is attack the closed heart, the closed mind. These are the dangers we face today."

Many critics asserted that the performances of Sim and Lowe were substantially better than that of O'Toole, which infuriated him. "I surround myself with some of the best talent in England. But what did they do? Sim and Lowe upstaged me. Both of them took delight in pissing on my grave."

He had quite a different reaction when he saw Michael Bryant perform his best scene. After he finished, Bryant found O'Toole weeping on the sidelines. When he asked why, O'Toole said, "I adore you in that scene, darling. Nothing moves me like great acting."

In 1972, when *The Ruling Class* went into general release, the leading church leaders of England accused O'Toole of "blasphemy." The church objected to his imagining himself as the Holy Trinity, all in one, and the satirical aspects of getting himself crucified.

Catherine Bramwell Booth, a descendant of the founder of The Salvation Army, denounced O'Toole in *The Times.* "Is there no power in all the land able to prevent the intrusion into any program of such beastly travesty of Him Whom I Hold Most Holy?"

The critic for *The Los Angeles Times* defined *The Ruling Class* as "snail-slow, shrill, and gesticulating." *The New York Times* pronounced it "fantastic fun," and *Variety* called it "brilliantly caustic."

Because of O'Toole's blonde hair, Vincent Canby compared his look to that of the murderess, Barbara Stanwyck, in *Double Indemnity* (1944). For *Time* magazine, Jay Cocks wrote: "The film will be remembered for Peter O'Toole's Jack Gurney, a performance of such intensity that it may trouble sleep as surely as it will haunt memory—funny, disturbing, and finally, devastating. O'Toole finds his ways into the workings of madness, revealing the anger and consuming anguish at the source."

Cecil Wilson of the London *Mail* wrote: "Madness was never my idea of a joke. But there are disarming shafts of logic in the lunacy of Peter O'Toole, wild-eyed and nobly spoken. He sweeps titanically through a delirium of slapstick, melodrama, song and dance."

Critic John Simon of *The New York Times* wrote, "There is Peter O'Toole, as mercurial as he is incisive, a Jack who does the most outrageous things with a bemusedly introspective air, who gives absurd romantic-heroic stature and makes crude farce so dainty and elegant that the film acquires another dimension by his mere presence."

United Artists acquired the film's distribution rights. Meeting with Jules Buck at Mr. Chow's Restaurant in London, an executive from the studio informed him that before UA touched it, the film would have to be heavily edited. Enraged, Buck jumped up and punched the executive in the nose, bloodying it.

The next day, Buck bought the rights back from United Artists and turned the film over to Avco Embassy for distribution. Even this supposedly more lenient and indulgent distributor planned to cut six of *The Ruling Class's* most controversial minutes from its running time.

The commercial failure and the controversies associated with *The Ruling Class* virtually ended the partnership of Buck with O'Toole. In a reckless decision, O'Toole decided to buy up the distribution rights, because he objected to the way executives were distributing the movie and failing to promote it. It cost him about all of his fortune, some one million British pounds. "I almost ended up in debtors' prison," he said.

During that year's Oscar race for Best Actor, O'Toole was pitted against both Michael Caine and Laurence Olivier for their roles in in *Sleuth;* and against Paul Winfield for *Sounder.*

All three of them lost to Marlon Brando for his role in *The Godfather.* That night at the Oscars, in front of 85 million viewers, Brando, through a spokeswoman—a full-blooded member of the Cherokee tribe wearing full native dress—declined the award.

[Brando justified his rejection of the Oscar as follows: "The motion picture community has been as responsible as any for degrading the Indian and making a mockery of his character, describing him as savage, hostile and evil. It's hard enough for children to grow up in this world. When Indian children see their race depicted as they are in films, their minds become injured in ways we can never know."]

Responding to Brando's rejection of an Oscar, O'Toole was furious. "I wanted that prize, I really wanted that prize. Brando, the asshole, turns it down. What an insult to the Academy, which keeps humiliating me. I've now lost the bloody thing five times. When will they ever learn?"

Chapter 31

Man of La Mancha

The Impossible Dream, for Peter O'Toole and Sophia Loren, Becomes an Unendurable Nightmare

"My Co-Star, Luscious Loren—I Called Her Scicolone—Was a Lovely Bitch. I Loved the Cow. In the Rape Scene, She Kneed Me in my 'Orchestras.'"

Peter O'Toole signed to play the dual role of Cervantes/Don Quixote in *The Man of La Mancha*.

As Don Quixote, O'Toole encounters the plunging *décolletage* of Sophia Loren in the film that critic Leonard Matlin called "A BOMB" based on "beautiful source material that was raped, murdered, and buried."

Released in 1972, the film version of *Man of La Mancha* was a spectacular flop.

At the time he signed to play its dual role of Cervantes/Don Quixote, it seemed that everybody in London and New York seemed to be singing "The Impossible Dream."

One could turn on any radio and hear renditions as diverse as versions sung by Frank Sinatra, Elvis Presley, Jacques Brel, and Plácido Domingo, all of them dreaming The Impossible Dream.

At an Off-Broadway theater in Manhattan, one that opened onto Greenwich Village's Washington Square, the play starred Richard Kiley in the role whose cinematic version eventually went to O'Toole, and Joan Diener as Aldonza/Dulcinea.

The play was such a hit that at times, it generated a bigger box office gross than equivalent musicals in bigger, splashier theaters uptown.

Dale Wasserman had scripted the play based on a plot suggested by the 17th century Spanish classic, *The Ingenious Gentleman Don Quixote of La Mancha* (aka *El Ingenioso Hidalgo Don Quijote de la Mancha*) by Miguel de Cervantes. The music for its 20th century adaptation into a stage musical was written by Mitch Leigh with lyrics by Joe Darion.

"I cooked spaghetti for Marshal Tito. I dined with the Queen of England. I starred with Marcello Mastroianni, Charles Chaplin, Marlon Brando, and William Holden. And, yes, I made a film with Peter O'Toole."

— Sophia Loren

The gay actor, James Coco, was hired to play a dual role as Cervantes' manservant and Don Quixote's squire, Sancho Panza. Since at the time, O'Toole was not a box office guarantee, United Artists signed Sophia Loren to portray the scullery maid and part-time prostitute, Aldonza, and also Dulcinea, the noblewoman whom Quixote idolizes.

As author Donald Zec noted, Sophia Loren "was totally unprepared for the barnstorming bhoyo from Connemara, who spoke like a character created jointly by Sean O'Casey and S. J. Perelman."

"The O'Toole technique with superstars, to prevent his ego from being left out in the cold, is to feed them a mixture of honey and prussic acid. If his needling strikes a nerve, the lean face with the almost lidless eyes under streaky yellow hair, smiles penitently in search of a forgiving bosom."

A New Yorker, son of a shoemaker, Coco was overweight and prematurely bald, a physicality that was ideal for that of the practical but dim-witted character he was portraying.

Coco had already won a Tony nomination for his performance in the Neil Simon hit, *The Last of the Red Hot Lovers* (1969).

O'Toole flew to Rome for the shooting, checking into the swanky Excelsior Hotel, a favorite haunt of visiting movie stars, on the via Veneto. During the first week, his friend, Peter Sellers, arrived and asked to be allowed to sleep on the sofa in the living room of O'Toole's suite. *[Sellers and O'Toole had become friends when they'd co-starred together in What's New Pussycat? (1965).]*

Sellers was very depressed at the time, and in trouble with Britain's Inland Revenue for his failure to pay back taxes. Perhaps to get rid of him, O'Toole suggested that he return to London and hide out with his wife, Siân Phillips, at their home in Hampstead. "Those Revenue blokes won't find you there." Sellers accepted the invitation, and flew to London, arriving on Siân's doorstep.

Even as a stage presentation, *Man of La Mancha* had already had a troubled production history. Albert Marre had directed the stage version, and the upcoming film's trio of producers—Arthur Hiller, Saul Chaplin, and Alberto Grimaldi—eventually asked him to helm the film, too.

Although he was skilled at directing plays, Marre had never helmed a motion picture before. He angered the producers by using up part of the film's budget through the organization of elaborate screen tests for the possible leads, as he didn't seem satisfied with the producer's choices of O'Toole and Loren. He tested both Kiley and Diener *[Diener was married to Marre at the time]* holding out the possibility that they might repeat their stage performances in the movie version.

Before too long, executives from United Artists became angry with Marre and booted him out the door.

O'Toole was delighted when the producers hired the gay British director, Peter Glenville, who had helmed Richard Burton and himself so successfully in *Becket* (1964), a project that won Academy Award nominations for both of them.

Although *La Mancha's* film producers had paid "a large amount" *[the actual figure was not announced]* for the film rights to the stage musical, Glenville ignored that and began writing a script inspired directly from the Cervantes novel, which was in the public domain. Envisioning the film as a nonmusical, he wanted to eliminate the songs associated with the project's success as a play. O'Toole was delighted, as he had always harbored deep insecurities about his ability to sing.

He was disappointed when Glenville was fired. In his place, the Canada-born Arthur Hiller was hired to transform Glenville's (non-musical) script back into a musical. O'Toole was contemptuous of Hiller, calling him "Little Arthur."

Working with Hiller, the play's original author, Dale Wasserman, restored nearly all of the songs from the stage play, including, of course, the by-now widely satirized "The Impossible Dream."

Despite the putdowns from O'Toole, Hiller boasted a fine and profitable record in filmmaking, having produced the box office bonanza, *Love Story* (1970), starring Ryan O'Neal and Ali McGraw. As it turned out, however, his style of directing was not suited to musicals.

O'Toole complained, loudly and frequently, that Hiller seemed more interested in "keeping things rolling along" and not spending a great deal of time reshooting scenes which his actors perceived as inadequate. Hiller's priority involved bringing the project in on time and under budget, perhaps as a means of ensuring that the studio would hire him again.

In Hiller's defense, the film script called for flashbacks and fantasy scenes, and it was hard to keep the audience oriented on the many nuances that were unfolding. At one point, perhaps out of earshot of Hiller, O'Toole asked, "Where is Vincente Minnelli or Stanley Donen now that we need him?"

In contrast, Hiller's evaluation of

Peter O'Toole (left) and James Coco as Don Quixote and his faithful squire, Sancho Panza, bravely chase windmills across the plains of La Mancha.

With his pointed beard and piercing eyes, O'Toole captured the essence of the crazy Knight Errant. But his armor was made of plastic.

Miguel de Cervantes, forever associated with the cultural legacy of Spain.

O'Toole was, "He can't sing and he knows he can't sing."

Ultimately, except for some mostly spoken lines, O'Toole's voice was dubbed by Simon Gilbert, a *bona fide* musical comedy singer.

Every morning, O'Toole reported to work at the film studios at Dinocittà. *[Associated with the films of director Dino de Laurentiis, Dinocittà was an independent subdivision of the financially troubled Cinecittà Studio. Built by Mussolini before World War II, Cinecittà was the site for the filming of, among others, Ben-Hur (1959). O'Toole was already familiar with the layout, virtues, and drawbacks of Dinocittà, as he'd already appeared as "Three Angels" in an epic,* The Bible, *filmed there by John Huston and released in 1966.]*

O'Toole Fails in His Attempt to "Conquer" Sophia Loren, Who Directs Her Love toward Richard Burton Instead

From the moment he met her, O'Toole was dazzled by the natural beauty of Sophia Loren. "Even in peasant dress, playing a whore, her loveliness was luminous." He nicknamed her "Scicolone." *[Loren's father was named Riccardo Scicolone.]*

When Loren joined Coco and O'Toole between scenes for games of poker, he saw a different side to her personality. "A sharp cardplayer, she'd lose her cool, becoming a gesticulating, cursing, scratching Neapolitan, particularly as the stakes rose. I think she concealed aces in her tits."

"However, she was one lovely bitch. I loved the cow, perhaps more than Cary Grant did when they made *The Pride and the Passion* (1957) together; or my friend, Peter Sellers, when they shot *The Millionairess* (1961)".

"The one question I was never to answer is if my other friend, Omar Sharif, got lucky when they co-starred together in *More Than a Miracle* (1969). I heard that Alan Ladd, who made *Boy on a Dolphin* (1957), found her too much woman for him. He later claimed that acting with her was 'like being bombed by watermelons.'"

Loren told O'Toole, "Everything you see, I owe to spaghetti."

In the film's famous rape scene, Loren faced ten groping pairs of hands. "She punched and

Sophia Loren with Cary Grant in *The Pride & the Passion* (1957). All the passion was not confined to the screen.

513

kicked everybody at least once, and I can tell you she kneed me in my orchestras," O'Toole claimed. "It was two days before I could clank balls again."

One night in Rome, O'Toole left his hotel attired in a tunic and wearing alligator skin boots, each of them dyed emerald green in honor of Ireland. His plan that night involved making love to Loren.

Sophia Loren's long and eventful run of filmmaking with Richard Burton, *Brief Encounter* (left) and *The Voyage* (right)

Admitted into her quarters by her maid. He found Loren "in a Madonna scene. She was with her son, Cipi (i.e., Carlo Ponti, Jr.)."

She remembered O'Toole's entrance. "He stood at the door, his arms outstretched like some Christ figure on the cross. He was totally mad in that creative, affectionate kind of madness that changes your way of seeing the world."

Loren interpreted O'Toole as "an extraordinary actor. He had an uncontainable, nonconformist intelligence. He was as funny as a great comedian, and as intense as a character in a tragedy. It was wonderful working beside him. I hung on every word, filled with admiration. When he acted, it sounded like he was singing. And yet, when he really did have to sing, he had trouble. Neither of us was a professional singer, and we were aware of this. To be honest, we were scared out of our wits."

"For me," Loren continued, "*La Mancha* was a rough ride. Not just the singing, but the conflicts with Hiller, and my own feeling, halfway through the movie, that I was failing in my scenes. I fear my impossible dream was becoming an unendurable nightmare for me."

During the course of filming, Loren came to O'Toole and revealed that she was pregnant, and that she'd be racing to complete the film before her condition became visible.

Although she found him charming, O'Toole's visit to Loren's villa never led to a seduction.

[Edoardo Ponti, Loren's son, was born on January 6, 1973, and O'Toole visited her shortly after she was able to receive him. "My Don Quixote came to see me with an extraordinary ostrich egg, signed, 'With all my love, Peter.' I kept it on my nightstand for a long time, the surreal memory of a dear, eccentric

514

friend."]

United Artists released *Man of La Mancha* in English. For the Italian market, it was dubbed and renamed *L'Uomo della Mancha.*

Unlike the play, which seemed to have almost universally loved, the film version came under heavy artillery fire.

Time magazine led the attack, defining the movie as "especially vulgar," even attacking "The Impossible Dream," citing it as "surely the most mercilessly lachrymose hymn to empty-headed optimism ever since *Carousel's 'You'll Never Walk Alone.'"*

Its rival, *Newsweek,* also denounced the film, claiming that "the whole production is based on the cheapest sentiment."

Vincent Canby of *The New York Times* was much kinder, claiming that O'Toole and Coco "beautifully acted" their roles.

Roger Ebert raised a point: "I always thought there was a flaw in the logic of *Man of La Mancha.* What good does it do to dream The Impossible Dream when all you're doing is killing time until the Inquisition chops your block off?"

As for O'Toole, Ebert wrote "He is a film actor of considerable talent, granted. But what possesses directors to cast him in musicals?"

***

In 1972, when O'Toole heard that Loren was making two movies with Burton, he wrote to her from his home in Ireland, "The news I'm getting in Ireland is that you have abandoned me for a bandy-legged, pock-marked little Welshman."

In 1973, Burton made *The Voyage* with Loren, although it was not released until 1977. It was to be Vittorio de Sica's last film.

In 1974, the pair also co-starred in a made-for-TV movie, *Brief Encounter,* a remake of the famous 1945 David Lean movie starring Trevor Howard.

When Burton flew into England, he invited O'Toole to have drinks with him in the bar of The Dorchester. The Welsh actor told his friend that he'd had "a lovely, lovely visit" with Loren and her family at the Vila Sara.

Loren confirmed that in a memoir: "He (Burton) could talk of no one but his love of the beautiful, violet-eyed Cleopatra. Their first marriage to each other had reached a crisis that would lead to a divorce in 1974. They remarried in 1975, only to divorce once more, for good this time, in 1976."

After making films together, Loren and Burton became close friends. Weeks after his second divorce from Elizabeth, he wrote to Loren: "I've completely recovered from my recent madness and have rarely felt so content. Elizabeth will never be out of my bones, but she is, at least, out of my head. Such love I had has turned to pity. She is an awful mess and there's nothing I can do about it without destroying myself. I love you."

According to Loren, Burton was never more than a beloved family friend, called "Uncle Richard" by her son, Carlo Ponti, Jr.

O'Toole never bought that, although he had no proof. He told his friends, James Villiers and Kenneth Griffith, "At times, I love the bloke (Burton) dearly. But at other times, I would whack off that overused dick of his. He not only gets roles I want, but he also takes desirable women, namely Elizabeth Taylor, Ava Gardner, and Sophia Loren."

"At her Villa Sara Burton told me that Sophia nursed him back to health after his break from Elizabeth. I wish she'd place me between those lovely melons of hers and nurse me back to something."

Imprisoned, James Coco (left), Peter O'Toole, and Sophia Loren confront their destinies. Loren played the prostitute Aldonza to O'Toole's Don Quixote, aided by his squire, Panza.

At the end of the shoot, O'Toole approached Loren and kissed her on both cheeks. "I want to give you the greatest gift a man can give a woman."

"What might that be?" Loren asked. "You're offering yourself?"

"No," He opened a plastic bag. "A pile of shark's teeth."

Chapter 32

O'Toole's "Wand of Lust"

Gets Recharged While Hungering for the "Peyton Place Hotties"

"I Want to Be Joan of Arc's Ski Bum,"

—Peter O'Toole, Before Launching an Affair with Jean Seberg—

"The Blonde Queen of the Black Panthers" (FBI)

O'Toole's Flirtations With Mia Farrow, and the Tragic Sharon Tate

(Who's About to Be Stabbed 16 Times)

Peyton Place Bad Girl Barbara Parkins	Mia Farrow "Not just Sinatra"	Harassed by the CIA, Jean Seberg	The actor whose first and last names BOTH had phallic implications	Witty and unstable: Rachel Roberts

In London for a quick visit, producer Joseph E. Levine called Peter O'Toole in 1974 when he'd been off screen for more than two years. O'Toole's lack of work was at least partially attributed to the disastrous 1972 release of *Man of La Mancha* with Sophia Loren.

It was true that same year (1972), he'd made *Under Milk Wood* with Elizabeth Taylor and Richard Burton, but that movie, based on Dylan Thomas' play, had flopped. Also in the same year, he had been nominated for an Oscar for *The Ruling Class*, but that quirky film had hardly been a box office bonanza either.

In spite of some previous differences, Levine had continued to admire O'Toole as an actor, and he was "always searching for the right showcase for you, baby," as he continued to promise. He was still glowing in the success of the film he'd produced, *The Lion in Winter* (1968), with the formidable Katharine Hepburn, but so far, he had not come up with an equivalent vehicle.

Joseph E. Levine, producer and showbiz hustler

Over dinner and drinks, Levine pitched story ideas to O'Toole, but no script appeared that was camera ready. "I get an idea for a film every time I take a shower, which is three times daily," Levine said. "You see, I have to take that many showers because I don't like the smell of the woman I've just had on my body. It makes my flesh crawl. When I'm through with a pussy, I want her out the door, hopefully never to return. Like *Tyrannosaurus rex*, I prefer fresh flesh on the hoof."

Over dinner, Levine recalled their first projected film together, a project that preceded his acquisition of the film rights to *The Lion in Winter* (1968). The picture was *The Ski Bum,* a film released in 1971. Together, Levine and O'Toole strolled down memory lane, recalling what went wrong with *The Ski Bum:*

Hoping to Dance All Night with

Audrey Hepburn,

O'Toole Competes for Roles with Rex Harrison

In a Film About Terrorist Kidnappings, Otto Preminger Sacks

Robert Mitchum

— "That Drunkard" —and Replaces Him With Peter O'Toole

Rachel Roberts

O'Toole's Long-Time Affair with "The Fourth Mrs. Rex Harrison"

[One afternoon in 1967, O'Toole sat in his living room reading a bad script and recovering from an all-night binge. To cure his hangover, he'd consumed three Bloody Marys before 10AM.

His Welsh actor friend, Kenneth Griffith, had been his house guest for the week, and he was reading another script that had been sent over by producer Arthur P. Jacobs, who in 1969 would cast O'Toole in Goodbye, Mr. Chips.

Levine, son of an immigrant Russian tailor, wasted no time with small talk. "Have I got a great role for you, baby. It's Romain Gary's The Ski Bum. *You'll be terrific in it. I see an Oscar in your future. I want you so much that I'm willing to let you choose the director, and even the leading lady. Of course, if I know you, you'll pick a broad you can fuck both on and off the screen."*

"Mr. Levine, what a privilege to talk to such a fine showman like you," O'Toole said. "Before I commit myself, is there a thing called a script—or should I read the novel? If I like it, I'm sure our people will work out some equitable financial terms."

"Great," Levine said. "I'll announce to the press in the morning that I've signed you for this multi-million-dollar production to be shot in Switzerland."

"Mr. Levine, please," he said. "It's best to put the horse in front of the cart. The script."

"Okay, but don't think I'm jumping the gun, because I just know that once you've seen the script, you'll be salivating for the role. Of course, the script needs work. Sidney Carroll is laboring over it, even as we speak. Writers are usually bums or drunkards, so it's hard to get the fuckers to do what you want. Do I know scripts? After all, I'm the smart-assed son of a bitch who discovered this nothing Jap film, Gojira *(1956). I changed the god damn title to* Godzilla, King of the Monsters, *and the public ate it*

Nihilism, American style. No one would ever think of snow bunnies in the same way ever again.

O'Toole Co-Stars With the Sexy Blonde Mermaid, Daryl Hannah, Who's Shacked Up with JFK Jr. ~ O'Toole Predicts Their Futures as "President and First Lady of the United States."

up."

"I heard you brought the world Hercules (1959)," O'Toole said, not concealing the cynical tone in his voice.

"That, too," Levine said. "Okay, the fucking flick was sleazy. I call it my 'WOP Loincloth-and-Beefcake' movie. Throw in musclemen, broads, a shipwreck and a dragon for the kids, and you've got yourself a hit."

"Congratulations," O'Toole said. "You sound like the huckster supreme."

"But I've got class, too," Levine said. "Look what I did with that Neapolitan broad, Sophia Loren, the one with the big tits. She walked away with a fucking Oscar for Two Women (1961). I told the director, Vittorio de Sica, to throw in a scene where Loren and her daughter are raped by Moroccan soldiers. Presto! AN OSCAR! I'll do the same for you in The Ski Bum, even without tits."

"Look, I'm making a star out of Dustin Hoffman in The Graduate," Levine said. It's playing everywhere, making millions. I wanted Doris Day for the female role of Mrs. Robinson, but the bitch turned me down. I got Anne Bancroft instead."

"Send me the script," O'Toole repeated, "and I'll get back to you."

Within an hour, an emerald green Rolls-Royce pulled up at O'Toole's doorstep. From it emerged a chauffeur who looked like Arthur Treacher, in an olive-green uniform, who delivered a copy of The Ski Bum's rough script.

O'Toole spent the rest of the night studying it. Although it was a bit raw in spots, he recognized its potential. He told Siân Phillips, his wife, "I think it's good drama, a strong characterization."

He called Levine the next day and accepted the role.

"Welcome to my happy family, baby," Levine said. "You can trust me, sweetheart."

***

[During pre-production of The Ski Bum, Levine encountered endless delays, including snow conditions—"the god damn snow won't cooperate. Thank you, God." There were problems with the script, casting difficulties, and Levine's growing disenchantment with the director, Anatole Litvak, who had once been married to Miriam Hopkins.

Finally, with The Lion in Winter ready to be shot, Levine abandoned The Ski Bum altogether, signing a new contract with O'Toole for Lion.

After additional delays and complications, The Ski Bum finally went before the cameras and was released in 1971. It starred Zalman King. Charlotte Rampling, and Joseph Mell. The film turned out to be a murky and convoluted interpretation of the Romain Gary novel. In some markets, its title was changed *to* Point Zero.*]*

O'Toole needed a vacation, and he eagerly accepted an invitation to visit Cannes, where Levine had booked a suite for him at the Carlton. There, he was to meet Jean Seberg and her husband, the Lithuanian-French author, Romain Gary, whom she'd married in 1963 following her short (1958-60) union with François Moreuil, a French lawyer. Shortly after her divorce, she told the press, "Marriage to Moreuil was a violent affair."

Griffith, who had an acting career of his own, served between gigs as O'Toole's "Man Friday," though he detested that label.

Jean Seberg with the brilliant, multi-faceted, multi-national Romain Gary

[Ironically, Man Friday *became the name of a film that O'Toole, as Robinson Crusoe, would make in 1975.]*

Winging his way to the south of France, in anticipation of meeting the author and also the film adaptation's potential co-star, O'Toole read the final chapter of *The Ski Bum.*

The novel was the story of Lenny, an American who escapes his homeland to pursue some vague dream in the Swiss Alps. He is seeking oblivion and trying to avoid being sent to Vietnam. In essence, he is running away from himself. He doesn't want to speak to anyone, which is fine because he is not fluent in either French or in *Schweitzerdeutsch.*

He spends time skiing and coming to grips with his demons. When summer comes and the snow melts, he migrates to Geneva, where he meets Jess Donahue, daughter of the American Consul.

She, too, is trying to run away from herself, perhaps to join a *kibbutz* in Israel.

Gary wrote his novel in 1964, and although years passed before Levine got around to reading it, he promoted it aggressively as "the perfect vehicle" for Seburg co-starring with O'Toole.

After O'Toole, with his friend and "assistant," Griffith, arrived in Geneva, they discovered that the original novel, *The Ski Bum,* had been re-released, in French, as a new edition with a different name. *Adieu, Gary Cooper* was a trendy concession to the publisher's belief that its character of Lenny would evoke, for French readers, at least, the Golden Age American movie star.

On their first night in Geneva, O'Toole and Griffith dined with Seberg and her husband, Gary. O'Toole was mildly surprised to discover him so much older than his wife. (Sporting a 24-year difference in their ages, he was born in 1914,

Seberg in 1938.) Although he later characterized them as "The Odd Couple," O'Toole found both of them fascinating.

Gary was more than a novelist, having worked as a respected film director and as a French diplomat in Bulgaria, Switzerland, and Los Angeles. He had also won the prestigious Prix Goncourt twice, once in 1956 under a pseudonym (of which he had many), and again in 1975 under his own (adopted) French name. Born in what is now Vilnius, Lithuania, he claimed to have been the son of Mina Owcznska, a Litvak actress, and his father (perhaps) was the noted film star Ivan Mazzhukhin.

After the Nazi occupation of France, Gary fled to England, where he served under Charles de Gaulle with the Free French Forces in North Africa. He flew missions with a bombardier crew, and later received many medals for his bravery in combat.

When O'Toole met him, he'd already written *Les racines du ciel*.

[Winner of the Prix Goncourt in 1956, it was translated and distributed as The Roots of Heaven *in 1957. In 1958, it was adapted, also by Gary, into the John Huston film that starred Errol Flynn and the French chanteuse, Juliette Greco, mistress of Darryl F. Zanuck. Zanuck went on to hire Gary to write the script for the all-time greatest World War II epic,* The Longest Day *(1962), with an all-star cast spearheaded by John Wayne.*

As The Duke later and uncharitably said, "I won the war, fighting alongside some stout-hearted men like Robert Mitchum, but mostly it was a pack of homos.

Wayne was no doubt referring, con-temptuously, to such co-players as Peter Lawford, Sal Mineo, and Roddy McDowall, among others.]

During their time together in Geneva, O'Toole found Seberg a compelling presence, a blonde beauty whom many Americans assumed was French. *[She'd been born in a small town in Iowa, the daughter of a substitute teacher and a pharmacist.]*

Gary was very forceful in outlining how he wanted his wife and O'Toole to play the key roles in *The Ski Bum*. For the most part, O'Toole agreed with him.

That dinner marked the beginning of O'Toole's on-again, off-again friendship with Seberg that would last until her death in 1979.

Darling of the French "New Wave," the Iowa-born expatriate, Jean Seberg, captured the spirit of sexual liberation vital to the then-prevalent French vision of cinematography.

O'Toole recalled, "Jean was an utterly fascinating creature of her time, a young woman who set out to live her life on her own terms—and to hell with the worst of the world. She was even more mixed up that I was."

Very early in their burgeoning friendship, he learned that she'd had a brief fling with actor Mel Ferrer, who had been married to Audrey Hepburn at the time.

O'Toole recalled that when he'd filmed *What's New Pussycat?* in Paris with the waif-like beauty, Hepburn had told Ferrer goodbye because he had to go to Cannes to meet with some producers, seeking backers for a script he had been developing to star both himself and Hepburn. His absence had given O'Toole the chance he needed to move in on Hepburn, who became pregnant during the shoot.

As he got to know Seberg, O'Toole was surprised to learn that both of her husbands had directed her in films. Moreuil, although primarily an attorney,had helmed her in *La récréation (Playtime)* in 1961 *[Seberg, estranged from Moreuil during the making of that film, recalled its production as "pure hell."]* Seven years, later, her second husband, Gary directed her *Les oiseaux vont mourir au Pérou (Birds in Peru; 1968).*

As O'Toole became more and more involved with Seberg over the passage of time, he found her very candid in speaking of her own life. "My loss of virginity was so very, very American," she said. "I was seventeen at the time, and he was the captain of the football team. The dirty deed took place at a local drive-in movie when we were watching a film about invaders from outer space."

"Mel Ferrer, with his cheating heart, was just one of the men Jean went through," O'Toole told Griffith. "She believed in loving them and leaving them. Sometimes, she bedded marquee names like Warren Beatty and Clint Eastwood, perhaps Dennis Hopper. Her range was versatile, and she didn't mind crossing the color line—take Sammy Davis, Jr., for example, or Masai Hewitt, the leader of the Black Panthers. One of her lovers, the actor, John Maddox, disappeared into the so-called Bermuda Triangle. One winter, I encountered her in Davos with that French skier, Jean-Claude Killy."

Once, in Nice, while dining with O'Toole, Yves Boisset, the French director, was rather frank about Seberg when she excused herself to go to the ladies' room. "It is very important to Jean that she appears, excuse the expression, fuckable. In her depression, she turns to men for reassurance. She could have sex in an elevator between the third and fourth floors."

Near the end of her life, she told O'Toole, "When I first arrived in France, I used to be treated like a little princess. A director, or whomever, would send a black limousine for me. They don't do that anymore."

O'Toole was never drawn into the murky political world of Seberg, with whom he indulged in an occasional affair, usually lasting no more than a weekend. A favorite point of rendezvous was La Colombe d'Or (The Golden Dove) in St-Paul-de-Vence, a restaurant forever associated with the painters of the early to mid-20th-century *avant garde.* Both Seburg and O'Toole loved modern paintings by such artists as Picasso and Dufy.

O'Toole interpreted Seberg as disillusioned with Hollywood, telling him that "most of the scripts I'm offered border on porno."

Actually, she wasn't offered that many scripts, because in essence she had been blacklisted in Hollywood, in ways equivalent to that endured for a time by Jane Fonda. Seberg also became one of the best-known targets of the FBI's COINTELPRO project. Fueled by the contexts and paranoias of the Cold War, it harassed, intimidated, defamed, and discredited her, with stated intention of "cheapening her image with the public," according to information later released as part of the Freedom of Information Act.

Not a rich woman, Seberg nonetheless provided money for the Black Panthers, the NAACP, and Native American groups such as the Meskwaki Bucks.

In the summer of 1979, Seberg was living with Ahmed Hasni, an Algerian part-time actor and soccer player. He'd persuaded her to sell her apartment on the rue du Bac in Paris for 11 million francs, in cash, which he pocketed himself.

On the night of August 30, 1979, she disappeared. Hasni told the police that only the month before, she'd tried to kill herself by jumping in front of a Paris Metro (subway) train rushing toward her.

On September 9, her decomposing body was found wrapped in a blanket in the back seat of her Renault in Paris' 16th Arrondissement. By her side was a bottle of barbiturates and an empty bottle of mineral water. Her note in French read: "Forgive me. I can no longer live with my nerves."

The following year, Gary committed suicide. In a note to his publisher, he claimed he did not kill himself over the loss of Seberg, but did so because, "I feel I can no longer produce literary works." In it, he also associated himself with what might have been the favorite of his many pseudonyms, Émile Ajar.

In London, O'Toole told the press, "It is a sad day with the passing of Ms. Seberg, a remarkably young lady who always fought against injustice, of which she suffered greatly at the FBI's tarnishing of her reputation. It was said that a Black Panther fathered her child, although the poor infant, who died in childbirth, was born white as snow."

"Ferrer was a real creep," O'Toole told Griffith. "He

Evasive genius
Romain Gary (aka Émile Ajar): Death by Suicide

524

tried to capitalize off Audrey's fame to promote himself in films. He got Audrey Hepburn before I did, and he also managed to seduce Jean before I did."

***

Both Jean Seberg and Joseph E. Levine played important roles in Otto Preminger's last-minute decision to cast O'Toole in the 1975 thriller, *Rosebud*.

Sometime in the late 1960s, Seberg had introduced O'Toole to Preminger at the Cannes Film Festival. As the trio enjoyed a drink together, O'Toole complimented Preminger on his past achievements, the best-known of which was *Laura* (1944), starring Gene Tierney.

[O'Toole later told Seberg, "John F. Kennedy was so wrong to have dumped a woman like Tierney.]

O'Toole had also seen Frank Sinatra's brilliant performance playing an addict in the Preminger-directed *The Man With the Golden Arm* (1955).

"You got Frank for that," O'Toole said, "but oh, if god had only given it to me."

"I was god, and I'd never heard of you at the time," Preminger told him.

Preminger and O'Toole went on to discuss their mutual acquaintance, Sam Spiegel, who had produced *Lawrence of Arabia* (1962).

"I knew him back in 1935 when he traveled with me from Vienna to Paris, where I made my way to Le Havre and America aboard the *Normandie*. I also knew him when he called himself S.P. Eagle, because he'd signed too many bad checks using his real name, Sam Spiegel.

Preminger shared memories of 1957, when Seberg made her film debut in the George Bernard Shaw's *Saint Joan,* which Preminger had directed. "I spent $150,000 on a talent search," he told O'Toole and came up with this lovely blonde thing from the cornfields of Iowa. I must have tested 18,000 hopefuls. The press called it a *Pygmalion* experience, a Henry Higgins/Eliza Doolittle situation known only too well to you."

"I have two memories of that film," Seberg said. "I was burned at the stake on camera, and later burned

Black Panther pinup Jean Seberg, depicted here as Saint Joan.

525

at the stake by critics."

"I believe everyone should have a second chance," Preminger continued, "so I cast Jean in *Bonjour Tristesse* (1958). Audrey Hepburn wanted the role but I preferred to take a risk with Jean because I believed in her." [*Bonjour Tristesse (Hello, Sadness) was a 1958 British-American, English-language film, directed and produced by Preminger from a screenplay by Arthur Laurents based on novel written in 1954 by the noted French feminist, Françoise Sagan.*]

"This time, the reviews were so atrocious, it almost ended my career," Seberg said.

"The next thing I knew, this little girl had fled to France and such New Wave directors as François Truffaut and Jean-Luc Godard were hailing her as the best actress in Europe," Preminger said.

"I played roles about women I didn't understand and had no interest in," Seberg said. "But the critics liked my characters, even when I was cast in *Lilith* (1964) with Warren Beatty."

"Please, for once, give me the inside information," Preminger said. "Is Beatty hung like a horse or like a rooster? Girls I've known are on opposite sides."

"I prefer not to discuss a man's penile size," Seberg answered. "I think it's vulgar, like talking about a woman's bra size."

"But those are the two favorite topics of conversation in Hollywood, my dear, as you already know," Preminger said.

When it was time to leave, Preminger shook O'Toole's hand. "Perhaps when the timing is right, I'll call you one night. I'll say, 'Mr. O'Toole, I've just read this script, and it has Peter O'Toole written all over it.'"

"I will be breathing anxiously until that night arrives, kind sir," O'Toole said.

Preminger was taken aback by what happened next. Unfamiliar with O'Toole's habits, he gasped when he received the actor's familiar tongue kiss as a goodbye.

It wasn't Seberg but Joseph E. Levine who alerted O'Toole that the role of Larry Martin in the 1975 thriller, *Rosebud*, had become available.

But Seberg did introduce him to John Cohan, the celebrity seer to the stars, who one day would have an impact on O'Toole's life and decisions.

Barbara Parkins...a sexual obsession

"Good Girl/Bad Girl" Barbara Parkins
Becomes the Object of O'Toole's Affection

When the Canadian-American actress Barbara Parkins decided to move to England in 1968, O'Toole seemed to have developed a sexual obsession for her.

The native of Vancouver, British Columbia, was twelve years his junior. A beautiful brunette, she had once studied ballet. Having emigrated to Hollywood, when she was sixteen, with her mother, she'd broken into show business as a backup singer and dancer in the nightclub acts of such stars as comedian George Burns.

When gigs were not available, she worked as a uniformed usher in a movie theater, earning money to pay for her drama lessons.

In the 1960s, she became a household name because of two projects—the ABC primetime television series, sexy, seductive *Peyton Place,* based on the Grace Metalious novel; and the 1967 film adaptation of Jacqueline Susann's best-selling 1966 novel, *Valley of the Dolls.* Although at the time it was contemptuously dismissed as "trash," the public devoured it. In terms of sales, scandal, and notoriety, it became the 1960s' equivalent of *Fifty Shades of Grey.*

It was because of this exposure that O'Toole became intrigued by Parkins' image on the screen.

In *Peyton Place,* Parkins played the small town's "bad girl with a fast reputation," Betty Anderson. Originally, the script called for a short-lived character who would die ("as bad girls should") in a car crash. But audience response was so supportive of her character that the producers decided to keep her on as an ongoing player in the series. Parkins described her role as "the salt and pepper of the stew."

She became the only actress in the long-running series (1964-69) to remain as a vital part of the ongoing storyline. She was eventually nominated for an Emmy as Best Actress in a Lead Role in a Dramatic Series, losing to Barbara Stanwyck for her "anchoring role" in *The Big Valley.*

In *Peyton Place*, Dorothy Malone, along with Farrow and Ed Nelson, led a cast of some 200 actors. Some of them were highly visible stars of that day who appeared as part of short-lived cameos. Examples included Dan Duryea, Leslie Nielsen, Lee Grant, and Gena Rowlands. It also helped launch the careers of such upcoming stars as Mia Farrow and Ryan O'Neal.

***

527

The 1967 film, *Valley of the Dolls,* was based on the 1966 novel of the same name. *[At the time, the word "dolls" was a slang term associated with "downers," especially such barbiturates as Nembutal.]*

The novel had been famously written by Susann, whom author Truman Capote had denounced on the Johnny Carson show as "looking like a truck driver in drag."

The movie starred not only Barbara Parkins but Patty Duke, the doomed Sharon Tate, Lee Grant, and the best actress of all of them, the talented and fiery redhead from Brooklyn, Susan Hayward. She played a character that some critics suggested was a composite of both Judy Garland and Ethel Merman. Ironically, Garland had been originally cast in the Hayward role, but was later fired.

Parkins starred as Anne Welles, a naïve small town character called "the good girl with a million dollar face and all the bad breaks." After her creation of the character, Susann said that she had based the character on herself, and that she had been drawn to Parkins because "she looked like me, or at least the way I used to look—dark and intense with that distinctive voice."

O'Toole knew little of Parkins' private life, reading in the papers that she was romantically linked to his longtime friend, Omar Sharif. She was also said to have dated Adam West (star of the Batman series) and Marcel Marceau (French master of the art of mime).

In London in 1968, Parkins was a bridesmaid at the wedding of Sharon Tate to director Roman Polanski. It was then that she decided to move to London, claiming that she preferred the atmosphere of that city, with its ancient traditions, as well as its "Swinging London" scene.

In addition to seeing her on TV and in the movies, Parkins caught O'Toole's lusty eye when she posed, topless, for the May, 1967 issue of Hugh Hefner's *Playboy*.

***

As mentioned, O'Toole had been introduced to celebrity seer John Cohan by the psychic's friend and *confidante*, Jean Seberg. A friendship developed, and the actor O'Toole occasionally consulted Cohan for one of his "readings."

Immodestly yours,
Barbara Parkins

"Peter always had a serious drinking problem, and I told him I could help him, but only when he was sober," Cohan said.

At one point in their relationship, Cohan met O'Toole in New York at Donahue's Restaurant and Bar.

It was here that O'Toole revealed his "passion" for Parkins, and he asked Cohan if he should pursue her.

The seer strongly advised against it. "She is someone whose behavior is that of a person who likes to let it all hang out, so to speak. She is definitely with the 'now' scene, that's for sure."

"But I like that about her," O'Toole claimed.

Cohan seemed aware of O'Toole's self-destructive lifestyle, and he advised that a possible romantic attachment to Parkins would only accelerate his own downward spiral. "Stay away from Parkins," Cohan strongly advised. "It could be your downfall. That woman, though beautiful, is heavy duty main-

Celebrity psychic to the stars, John Cohan

tenance. Your nerves could never endure a relationship with her."

O'Toole listened attentively and finally agreed, although admitting, "It's hard to turn down temptation. I was never good at that. If Eve had tempted me as Adam, I would not only have taken a bite from the apple, but eaten the whole damn luscious thing."

He remembered Cohan's final words. "Ms. Parkins is a definite no-no."

Two other women associated with Parkins, however, intrigued O'Toole even more—Sharon Tate and Mia Farrow, both of them friends and co-stars of Parkins.

O'Toole's "Fires of September" Are Still Burning, but Sharon Tate & Mia Farrow Show No Interest in the Flames

Toole had seen Parkins at parties attended by Sharon Tate and "Mama Cass" Elliot.

The first time he'd met portly Mama Cass, she'd bluntly asked him, "Wanna fuck, big boy?" He'd turned her down after politely requesting a rain check.

Although he admired the energy and singing style of Mama Cass, he was much more attracted to two of Parkins' other friends, Mia Farrow, with her delicate beauty, and especially Sharon Tate, whom he labeled as "the most beautiful woman in the world."

During the run of Peyton Place, Parkins may have used Farrow, an emerging star, as a role model. Parkins certainly followed Farrow through all her turbulent affairs and marriages, first to Frank Sinatra and later to pianist-composer André Previn. In time, she developed a notorious long-time relationship with Woody Allen.

At one time, Farrow arrived on the set of *Peyton Place*, telling the cast that she'd accompanied Salvador Dalí to watch an orgy taking place in a loft in Greenwich Village.

Parkins had also heard about her affairs with Eddie Fisher, Peter Sellers (the actor kept O'Toole abreast of that romance), and Roman Polanski, who had directed her in *Rosemary's Baby* (1968), even though she was married to Sinatra at the time.

Sellers had given Farrow a stern lecture when he discovered that she had experimented with mescaline with John Phillips (of the Mamas and the Papas) during her affair with him. Another of her lovers had been Sven Nykist, the noted, Stockholm-based cinematographer.

At one point, O'Toole had expressed an interest in Farrow himself and had urged Sellers to introduce him to the star. But he never did. However, O'Toole, in London, encountered Ava Gardner, with whom he'd had a fling, and she gave him her candid opinion of Sinatra's marriage to Farrow: "I always knew Frank would end up in bed with a little boy. Dean Martin told me that he has Scotch older than Farrow."

When Farrow heard Gardner's derogatory appraisal of her physicality, she said in her own defense, "I may not have Ava's famous tits, but I can match bottoms with any other woman in Hollywood—just ask Frank."

After Polanski had seduced Farrow, he said, "There are 127 varieties of nuts. Mia is 116 of them."

***

O'Toole had seen Tate at three different parties, and on their third meeting in London, he'd propositioned her. He was drunk and she turned him down. He later told Sellers, "Steve McQueen got lucky, even her hairdresser, Jay Sebring, the only hairdresser in Hollywood who isn't gay. But my old bag of bones didn't turn her on at all."

Like most of the rest of the world, O'Toole over breakfast read of the shocking events of August 9, 1969, at the home Tate shared with Polanski, her husband.

The so-called "Charles Manson family" had broken into their home during one of their parties, stabling Tate sixteen times in the stomach. She was 8 ½ months pregnant at the time.

Mia Farrow, during the peak of her fame and chic.

Four others, including her hairdresser, Sebring, were also brutally murdered, sending panic across Hollywood. Security guards were in such demand that many men had to be imported from Florida.

Deeply shocked by the murders, O'Toole on his next visit to Hollywood, brought white carnations to the grave site of Sharon Tate at the Holy Cross Cemetery in Culver City.

He agreed with Joan Didion's assessment that the Swinging Sixties abruptly ended on the night of August 9, 1969, based on the events that transpired at that home on Cielo Drive.

Tate's last completed film, *Twelve Plus One,* released in 1969 after her death, co-starred Orson Welles, with Tate, because of the notoriety of her murder, receiving top billing.

In London, O'Toole met Welles at the National Theatre, in the lobby after attending a production at the same venue where, in October of 1963, he had disastrously played *Hamlet.* He discussed the Tate murder with Welles, who claimed that he was at work on a script about Charles Manson and the murders.

"My biggest dilemma right now involves who to cast as Charles Manson," Welles said. "I can't decide if I should offer you the role or give it to Tony Perkins."

[Like so many of Welles' projects, including the unfinished The Other Side of the Wind, *his script about Charles Manson, tentatively entitled* Pig!, *was never finished. The police had discovered the word "Pig" scrawled on the front door of the murder house in Tate's own blood.]*

***

O'Toole liked the music of Mama Cass and went to see her in 1974 when she performed in two weeks of sold-out concerts at London's Palladium. The event represented the height of her solo career.

He went backstage, where she greeted him warmly, liplocking with him. "You sure don't look like Lawrence of Arabia anymore, but you can still put your shoes under my bed anytime," she said to him.

"An offer I just might take you up on," he jokingly responded.

On July 29, that same year, he picked up the papers to read that she was dead. Mama Cass had died at the tender age of thirty-two. She'd had a heart attack. An urban legend was spread that she choked

Sharon Tate..."Kill me, but save my baby!"

531

to death on a ham sandwich. A partially eaten sandwich was found beside her bed, but an autopsy showed that there was no food blocking her windpipe at the time of her death.

Thirty years later, when O'Toole was in his beloved city of Dublin, he attended a 2004 stage production, *The Songs of Mama Cass,* listening to Kristin Kapelli performing most of the vocals. Afterwards, he told a reporter, "When I'm down and out, I mean really down and out, in the pits, so to speak, I listen to Mama Cass. Somehow 'Dream a Little Dream of Me' pulls me back from the brink. We differed in one respect, however. Mama Cass sometimes came on shot up with heroin. *[In contrast],* when I was per-

Mama Cass Elliot in her solo act

forming *Hamlet* or *Macbeth,* I preferred to drink four large lagers before the curtain went up."

O'Toole Learns Elizabeth Taylor's Darkest Secret

Celebrity Psychic John Cohan not only offered O'Toole advice, but over a period of time, he became privy to many of the secrets of other stars, including those of O'Toole's friend, Elizabeth Taylor, with whom he'd co-starred in Dylan Thomas's *Under Milk Wood* in 1972.

One of the violet-eyed beauty's darkest secrets, as described below, was known to Cohan:

While Elizabeth was undergoing exploratory surgery and told she could have no more children, rumors surfaced about one of the unsolved mysteries of her life. Stories spread that she'd had a "love child" in the early 1950s. But details of the rumored birth would not be revealed in print until after her death when stories about it were published in such newspapers as London's *Daily Mail.*

In addition to being her psychic, Cohan was a friend and confidant to Elizabeth for many years. During one of their sessions, she told him that she'd once given birth, out of wedlock, to a baby girl named Norah.

According to rumors, since such a birth would have destroyed any actress's career during the more uptight 1950s, she was forced, based partly on the urging of both MGM executive Benny Thau and her mother, Sara, to give the baby away.

"Money changed hands," Elizabeth told Cohan. "Norah was adopted by a family in Ireland."

The child, now a mature woman, of course, knows that Elizabeth was her mother, but is said to resent her for abandoning her. She was once quoted as saying, "I want nothing to do with Elizabeth Taylor."

Cohan's revelations were published by Cindy Adams, a columnist for *The New York Post*. Adams admitted that she could not confirm either the accuracy of the story or the existence of the daughter, "but I'm reporting it because one can't ignore the story in case there's some truth."

Elizabeth admitted to Cohan that at the time of the birth, she was involved with three different men and therefore could not be certain who the father was.

"I am still guilt ridden about having to abandon my child, even to this day," she said to Cohan. She also extracted from him the promise that he was to "say nothing about Norah until I'm gone."

The celebrity seer also had other insightful revelations. He said that he and Elizabeth were mutually involved in a short affair "between her marriages to Richard Burton. She told me I was a much sweeter and darling lover than Richard ever was. 'He was too rough at times,' she claimed."

She also admitted that Mike Todd had been "the love of my life, my soul-mate—and not Richard."

As a final bombshell, she claimed, according to Cohan, that she believed that Burton had died from some AIDS-related disease.

Cohan has been a celebrity psychic to the stars for more than three decades. During much of that time, he has supplied Adams with his yearly predictions, which have turned out to be surprisingly accurate.

More revelations about the stars can be found in his memoir, *Catch a Falling Star: The Untold Story of Celebrity Secrets*, published in 2008.

In his book, he has much to reveal about Natalie Wood, Merv Griffin, River Phoenix, John F. Kennedy, Jr., and Elvis Presley. He even writes about what Mick Jagger and Rudolf Nureyev were caught doing at the Flesh Palace Disco in Manhattan. He also writes about his dear friend,

Young Elizabeth Taylor from around the time of her alleged abandonment of Norah

murder victim Nicole Brown Simpson, as well as "the love of my life," Sandra Dee.

Otto Preminger Fires Robert Mitchum.
In His Place, He Hires O'Toole to Chase Palestinian Terrorists

In March of 1974, the temperamental director, Otto Preminger, launched pre-production of his upcoming film, *Rosebud.* (It was eventually released in 1975.) The script was by his own son, Erik Lee Preminger, a child he'd fathered with Gypsy Rose Lee, the most famous stripper in America at the time. For decades, he had not acknowledged his son.

Erik based the script on a best-selling novel by Paul Bonnecarrère, with Joan Hemingway, Ernest's granddaughter, sharing writing credits. United Artists had already agreed to distribute *Rosebud,* which Preminger viewed as "a love gift to my beloved son Erik."

In spite of the lovefest being cele-brated between Erik and Otto, father and son would have many conflicts during pro-duction.

Film locations would include Corsica, the southern coast of France (specifically Juan-les-Pins), Berlin, Paris, Hamburg, Haifa, Tel Aviv, and various points within the Israeli desert.

Preminger needed a big name star to carry the film, and consequently, he went after Robert Mitchum, who eventually signed for the key role.

Robert Mitchum with his wife, Dorothy, as they looked in 1944

According to the plot, Martin, a re-porter for *Newsweek,* secretly works for the CIA as he travels across the globe. He's summoned by Israeli intelligence to help locate five girls, each the daughter of a wealthy family, who have been kidnapped by terrorists from the Palestinian Libera-tion Army during their cruise aboard a lux-urious yacht named *Rosebud,* from which derives the name of the movie. *[It was probably an ill-chosen name. Many view-*

Robert Mitchum, as he looked in 1975—tougher, meaner, and more beat-up—with Charlotte Rampling

ers thought Rosebud pertained to the closing scene of the Orson Welles' classic film, Citizen Kane (1941)]

Mitchum and Preminger had known each other for years, the actor admitting, "Otto and I used to go whoring together when we went out on press junkets."

Flown to France, Mitchum greeted reporters in Juan-les-Pins. He appeared drunk. "I'm only making this crap because I need the dough."

A reporter asked him about the females co-starring with him in the picture. In response, Mitchum answered, unchivalrously, "I don't give a flying fuck, just so long as they have tits."

During the same interview, an obviously homosexual reporter from Nice asked, "Are you happy to be working in France?"

"Not particularly," Mitchum said. "But you could make it ever so gay if you'd meet me after the conference to suck on my big dick."

Finally, in a rage, Mitchum stormed out of the room. "Fuck all of you," he yelled at reporters. "I'm not here to sell your fucking newspapers."

The first day he showed up to begin shooting, Mitchum was tanked up on *pastis*. A reporter visited the set. "I've got a story for you," the actor said. "Did you know that I taught isometric farting to Gina Lollobrigida? And I once visited Eleanor Roosevelt at this big barbecue at Hyde Park. I slipped upstairs, stripped down, and put on one of her see-through nighties. Noël Coward was on my tail, his tongue hanging out, panting for me. Just as he was giving me the blow-job of my life, in walked Eleanor."

Preminger was disappointed to find Mitchum drunk, and horrified by the negative publicity he was generating. Since time was running out, and his budget limited, he tried to shoot the scene that day anyway. It took place in a map room where Israeli agents were trying to pinpoint the location of the kidnapped heiresses.

Growing impatient, Mitchum whipped out his penis and urinated on the arm of the map pointer. He turned to Preminger. "I'm just trying to guide the fucker in the exact location on the map, Otto."

The director dismissed him for the day. "Sober up, Bob."

But the following morning, Mitchum showed up staggering, having spent the night drinking with some Corsican fishermen.

He'd been summoned to the set for a shoot in the early morning. It was 6AM. He mocked Preminger. *"Vath aff you gotten me out out here at this fucking hour of ze nacht?"* he asked.

The famous director could take no more. He came up to Mitchum and shook his hand. "We can't go on like this, Bob."

Mitchum glared at him. "Bon voyage, baby. I'm out of this stinking hellhole. Tell France and the French to kiss my crusty ass."

When Mitchum reached Hollywood, he heard the news that O'Toole had replaced him. "That's like subbing Ray Charles with Helen Keller," he said.

Looking Like the Grim Reaper Is About To Haul Him to the Grave, O'Toole Shows Up in Corsica to Film Rosebud

By sheer coincidence, on the same morning Preminger fired Mitchum, a call came in for Preminger from Joseph E. Levine concerning another possible script. Preminger told Levine that he'd fired Mitchum, and that "I've got just forty-eight hours to come up with a star."

"I've got the ideal candidate," Levine said. "Peter O'Toole."

"Another god damn drunk," Preminger said.

"No, I've recently talked to him. His doctors have ordered him to give up drinking, and he's sober."

"I'll take your word for that, Joe, baby," Preminger said.

Within the hour, he'd reached O'Toole at his home in London's Hampstead section. He was out of work and eager to appear before the cameras again.

Preminger made his pitch.

In response, O'Toole said, "I'll be on the next plane to Marseille. And then on a boat to take me into your loving arms, darling."

When he arrived, both Erik and his father were disappointed at how dissipated O'Toole looked. But unlike Mitchum, he had at least arrived on the set sober.

"He looks at death's door," Preminger told Erik after O'Toole went into makeup. "The Grim Reaper is on his way."

A journalist was on the set, planning to write a book about the making of *Rosebud,* believing at the time that it was going to become "the hottie film of the year."

Day after day, the unnamed journalist watched O'Toole emote in front of the camera, recording his

Two Premingers: Otto and his son, Erik

impressions. "O'Toole played Lenny Martin as a sort of dandy, very neurotic, almost precious, just borderline gay, and perhaps secretly ill. He certainly looks ill. Unlike his usual direction, Preminger seems to be giving him free rein. In some scenes, O'Toole even improvised his own dialogue. He seems nervous, his hands shaking. I fear he's lost confidence in himself as an actor. Perhaps because of all those operations he's endured."

In spite of his having miscast the film's leading male twice in a row, Preminger showed greater skill in his hiring of supporting players.

These included the English actor/director, Richard Attenborough, the villain of the movie. As O'Toole would later say of him, after he directed the Best Picture of 1983 (*Gandhi*), "Lord Attenborough's

Two views of Peter O'Toole as a diffident "action hero" in *Rosebud*

achievements are so splendid that it's vulgar to even mention them."

In *Rosebud,* Attenborough played Edward Slaot, the treacherous head of Black September, the terrorist group.

Cliff Gorman was cast as Yafet Hemlekh. He'd "stolen" the gay movie *The Boys in the Band* (1970), and had won a Tony Award in 1972 for his portrayal on Broadway of the controversial comedian, Lenny Bruce.

In *Rosebud,* Gorman was cast as a high-powered Israeli agent. Some other cast members included Peter Lawford as Lord Carter, and Raf Vallone as George Nikolaos.

The oddball casting was John Lindsay, cast as Senator Donnovan.

[Lindsay was the handsome and debonair 6'4" politician, who had represented Manhattan's East Side "Silk Stocking District" for seven years in Congress, eventually becoming the two-term mayor (1966-1973) of New York. He presided over a city in upheaval—a landscape defined at the time by racial unrest, anti-war protests, and citywide strikes.]

Preminger told O'Toole, "His Lordship, the Mayor, got carried away when we negotiated his fee. He thought he was Elizabeth Taylor, demanding a million for *Cleopatra.* I brought him back to earth again."

***

When the cast and crew of *Rosebud* moved to Paris for location shooting there, O'Toole suddenly became ill with abdominal pains and was rushed to the American Hospital. There, undergoing extensive examinations and treatment, he was confined for two weeks.

O'Toole with "Hizzoner," the former Mayor of New York City, John Lindsay, in *Rosebud*.

"Our figures are identical," O'Toole said to him.

Preminger had no other choice but to allow the *Rosebud* crew "to live it up in Paris at my god damn expense."

When O'Toole did return to work, he was in a weakened condition and asked for shorter working hours.

For one location's shooting, Preminger made an agreement with Tom Curtiss, whose apartment was positioned directly beneath the well-known restaurant, La Tour D'Argent *[quai de la Tournelle, Paris 5e]* with its view of the flying buttresses of Notre Dame Cathedral, dramatically illuminated at night. The specialty in the restaurant was *caneton* (pressed duck).

Shortly before filming began, a bomb scare erupted into hysteria on the film set. A messenger, who turned out to be a street vagrant, walked up to O'Toole, handed him a letter marked URGENT, and disappeared. O'Toole read it quickly. Its writer asserted that a bomb and been planted within Curtiss's apartment, and that it was about to explode. O'Toole showed the letter to Preminger, who immediately called the police. Arriving on the scene within a few minutes, five *gendarmes* ordered that the entire building be evacuated. Preminger, fearing that the letter had been sent by Palestinian militants asserting that *Rosebud* was a propaganda film designed as an assault on their ideologies and their cause. Preminger clearly expressed his belief to the police that "This is clearly a threat from Arab terrorists."

In the letter, O'Toole was denounced as a "renegade Irishman and a traitor to the IRA." The letter went on to berate him for appearing in a film that attacked the Palestinian quest for freedom, claiming, "The Palestinians are in the same boat as the Irish."

In the midst of all this upheaval, Curtiss arrived on the scene. He was a reporter for the Paris-based *International Herald Tribune,* and also a close friend of Kenneth Tynan, one of London's leading theater critics, who was visiting Curtiss in Paris at the time, but staying elsewhere, in another apartment.

It was Curtiss who admitted that the letter to O'Toole had been a hoax. He said that it had been written by Tynan "just to spook out O'Toole." He also claimed, "It's such a parody that we never realized any fool would take it seriously."

Preminger denounced both Curtiss and Tynan, defining the prank as "vicious, stupid, and cruel."

When O'Toole learned that the bomb scare was a hoax, he became violent, rounding up "two slabs of beef" from among the grips. He learned the address of the apartment where Tynan was staying in Paris' 5th Arrondissement. With the two men, he set out to get Tynan.

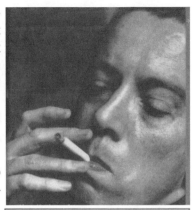

"Kicking the critics in the balls"

The ultimate Queen-bitch of the U.K.'s drama critics, Kenneth Tynan.

At his address, Tynan let O'Toole and the two grips inside his apartment. He was unsuspecting.

Once inside, O'Toole ordered the two men to hold Tynan down while he beat him viciously, repeatedly kicking him in the testicles after Tynan fell onto the floor.

One of the grips later claimed, "I thought O'Toole was going to kill this faggot Englishman. We had to stop him and force him out the door before the police were summoned."

Tynan was rushed to the American Hospital, occupying the same room that O'Toole had recently vacated. He was held for observation for two days and nights, during which time he planned to file assault-and-battery charges against O'Toole. He was talked out of it, because he, too, could have been arrested as the source of the fake bomb scare.

Tynan later said, "O'Toole was a god damn coward, thinking he was demonstrating his machismo. What machismo? I was held down by two bruisers while he beat me up. Sheriff O'Toole with his steel-blue eyes kicked the cowering Apache (that's me). He concentrated on my balls."

***

At the end of *Rosebud*'s filming, O'Toole said, "Working with Preminger was a trip. In Berlin, he went around mumbling some shit, claiming 'The real Nazis were the Austrians, and I should know because I'm Austrian.'" At one point, while directing me in a scene, he refused to get out of his car. He just lowered the window and barked orders at me."

539

After its release, *Rosebud* was ridiculed by the critics. Dilys Powell was the kindest, welcoming O'Toole upon his return to the screen. "As a CIA man, he plays his role with a lackadaisical composure dead right for the infallible agents of spy fiction. One hopes to see him again in a role of the same sort."

Temperamental and brilliant: Otto Preminger

Preminger came in for harsh criticism, reviewers suggesting that his glory days were behind him.

One critic mocked O'Toole's voice, claiming "consonants aspirated somewhere between the mannerisms of Charles Laughton and Bette Davis."

Writing in *The Village Voice*, Andrew Sarris claimed that "the treatment of Arab terrorist plot material is by turns disconcertingly casual and coldly ambiguous."

Arthur Thirkell in London's *Daily Mail* claimed that *Rosebud* was "confused, rambling, and is totally lacking in suspense." The *Daily Mail* chimed in: "The drama is curiously flat, unmotivated. O'Toole could have acted a little more as if he meant it."

In *The New Yorker,* Penelope Gilliatt wrote: "It would have taken Hitchcock perhaps to divert our attention from the film's missing moral comprehension of the story. The ethical questions raised are tempestuously ignored in the tantrums of narrative minutiae."

In *Variety,* A.D. Murphy proclaimed, "Absolutely nothing in the film itself evokes even remotely the fire, the passion, fanaticism, and commitment of the political forces which at this very moment in early 1975 could precipitate another global war."

***

Long before Barbara Parkins appeared on O'Toole's radar of sexual obsession, he became intimately involved with the self-destructive Welsh actress, Rachel Roberts. While both were working at the Bristol Old Vic, they began a romance that would endure countless other love affairs and their own marriages, his to Siân Phillips (married 1959-1979) and hers to two actors, Alan Dobie (1955-1961) and, more famously, Rex Harrison (1962-1971).

By the late 1950s, O'Toole regarded Harrison as "my rival in the boudoir, on the stage, and on the screen. I detest the bastard, though we are polite when we encounter each other."

Five years before she married Harrison, Roberts had appeared at the Bristol Old Vic with O'Toole, starring in a strange musical whose title was alternately promoted as either *Oh, My Papa,* or *Oh, Mein Papa.*

When previewed in Bristol, it got rave reviews. Not so when it opened in London's Garrick Theatre on Charing Cross Road.

Roberts had a solo, and she performed a singing duet with O'Toole. Both of them faced boos and catcalls from the stalls, but bravely carried on until the final curtain.

As O'Toole later told his actor friend, James Villiers, "That night, after such a panning, Rachel and I fell into each other's arms back at her place. We enjoyed the comforts of the damned before going back on the stage the following night. Okay, so we weren't Nelson Eddy and Jeanette MacDonald."

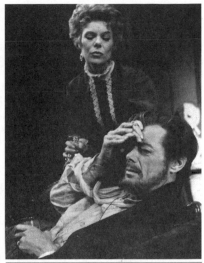

Rex Harrison ("Mr. Bad News for Women") with Rachel Roberts in Chekhov's *Platonov* at London's Royal Court Theatre in 1960.

Born in Llanelli in Wales in 1927, Roberts had been reared in a strict Baptist background. Like O'Toole, she later deserted the church for a rather promiscuous life in London, where she enrolled in RADA.

It wasn't until she appeared with Albert Finney in *Saturday Night and Sunday Morning* (1960) that she became prominent, winning a British Academy Award.

"I got to bed her before that 'Angry Young Man' in the film, my dear friend Finney," O'Toole boasted to Villiers.

Roberts followed her success by co-starring in *The Sporting Life* with Richard Harris in 1963.

"Once again, Rachel was mine before Harris plugged her with his overripe dick, which has been down more holes than a gopher," O'Toole said.

Roberts had become involved with Harrison when both of them had appeared in Chekhov's *Platonov* at London's Royal Court Theatre on Sloane Square. That was back in 1960.

At the time, Harrison said, "As a Welsh lassie, Rachel expected all Englishmen to be a lot of nits and, of course, she found them so."

At the end of the run of the play, Harrison invited her to Portofino, his vacation retreat on the Italian Riviera.

Roberts' marriage to Harrison was a turbulent union characterized by violence, daily arguments, and occasional moments of passion in the boudoir.

"Why did he want to marry you?" O'Toole once provocatively asked her.

"It was because of my fried bread, his favorite food," she answered. "He claimed I made fried bread just like his dear old Mum did, and he couldn't face the morning without his black coffee and that damned fried bread."

As she moved deeper into her marriage with Harrison, Roberts kept O'Toole abreast of the ups and downs of her relationship with him. "I am a woman of my own achievements," she said. "It is difficult for me to attend a party with Rex and be introduced as the *fourth* Mrs. Rex Harrison. I hate that."

"At times, he frightens me," she claimed. "His eyes narrow to slits. They are like embrasures in a fortress of the Middle Ages, behind which archers fire poison arrows and pour boiling oil."

One night in London, when O'Toole dined with Elizabeth Taylor in her suite at the Dorchester, Taylor's characterization of the Harrison/Roberts marriage in some ways paralleled the impression of biographer Patrick Garland, who wrote: "Their marriage has its own strangely tormented erotic sexuality, heightened by argument and alcohol, generated by competition and jealousy, compounded by fears of failure and loneliness."

Years later, Elizabeth also told O'Toole that she feared Roberts' marriage to Harrison was deteriorating rapidly. On a visit Elizabeth had made to Portofino with Richard Burton, aboard their yacht, Harrison had descended from his home (the Villa San Genesio) to greet them. He'd seemed disillusioned with everything, including his once beloved villa, which he had named for the patron saint of actors.

He told her that his former butler had attempted to assassinate him with a shotgun after he'd been fired. "He also sabotaged my Jeep. Rachel told me that villagers hate me. But she pronounced it *haaaate*. All my servants have gone on strike. The road to my villa is blocked off. Repairs are never made. I have to walk to the port for champagne on ice. By the time I get it up the hill, the ice has melted and the champagne is hot."

Elizabeth told O'Toole that Roberts got so drunk one night at a dinner party aboard her yacht "that the bitch tried to masturbate my dog."

Near the end of his marriage to Roberts, Harrison encountered O'Toole at a theater party given in a flat in Mayfair. He told O'Toole that "Rachel is a sad, pathetic figure, a poor thing who never quite found herself. She never attained that elusive thing called stardom, as I did. She hates me for that. It's the bitch in her that gets onto me." With those words, he turned and walked away.

If he knew of O'Toole's ongoing affair with his wife, Harrison was always too polite to mention it.

***

In the late 1970s, O'Toole had seen Roberts less and less, although they occasionally got together. She explained that divorce from Harrison was in-

542

evitable. "For a while, our marriage worked. We lived like a Lord and His Milady. Portofino, Paris, Rome, yachts, hanging out with Elizabeth Taylor and Richard Burton. But my life was passing me by. I was wasting my talent. Life can't be just a pleasure trip. I felt like a turnip. He was always putting me down."

After Roberts' divorce from Harrison in 1971, they had continued to see each other periodically. O'Toole noticed that in spite of the fact that she'd left him, she, at least on occasion, wanted him back.

In her paranoia, she confided to O'Toole that, "Rex is slowly poisoning me. He's making me very sick."

"Bloody hell!" he told her. "Don't go around him. Don't eat in his presence. Don't accept a box of chocolates. We both saw what he did to poor Doris Day in *Midnight Lace* (1960). He's a born killer."

Roberts would commit suicide on November 26, 1980. Police in Los Angeles reported that she was suffering from depression and alcoholism, and that she had swallowed lye, alkali, and some unidentified substance. Combined with her intake of liquor and barbiturates, she'd died after her body collapsed onto the kitchen floor, where it was found surrounded by shards of broken glass. She'd fallen through a decorative glass partition that separated the kitchen from her dining room. She was fifty-three at the time. Her death was defined as a suicide.

For Harrison, Roberts' death obviously brought back memories of the suicide of his former mistress, blonde-haired Carole Landis, who had swallowed an overdose of sleeping pills and had died at her home on Capri Drive in Hollywood on July 5, 1948.

O'Toole called his celebrity seer, John Cohan, to report that on the night of her death, Roberts had phoned him and begged him to come over to her house.

"I was in bed with these two dollybirds, and I didn't want to break away," O'Toole confessed. "She'd called me before, late at night, filled with anguish. I just gave her my love and put down the phone, thinking she'd had too much to drink and would be all right in the morning. Over breakfast, I heard the news on TV."

"I have such guilt over not coming to her aid," O'Toole said to Cohan. "It's a guilt I'll no doubt live with for the rest of my life."

In 1992, in commemoration of her death, O'Toole joined a crowds of mourners when her ashes, along with those of her best friend, Jill Bennett, were scattered across the Thames. Director Lindsay Anderson scattered the ashes during a boat trip on the river. Her professional colleagues joined in the service, and the musician Alan Price sang "Is That All There Is?"

"O'Toole and I Get Along Like a House on Fire"
"Sexy Rexy is No Longer Sexy—He's Far Too Old!"
—George Cukor on his casting vision for My Fair Lady (1964)

Originally, Elizabeth Taylor, while she was still married to Eddie Fisher, had discussed with O'Toole his playing Marc Antony opposite her in *Cleopatra*. *[For more on this, refer to Chapter 15.]* Of course, that didn't work out, and O'Toole always regretted that the role went to Burton. Even so, he retained his friendship with Burton, seemingly forgiving him, repeatedly, for taking other roles that "should have been mine," he said.

But Harrison was the one actor he could never forgive for "stealing the role of Henry Higgins from me" in the film version of *My Fair Lady (1964)*. O'Toole had to wait twenty years, until 1984, to play Higgins on stage at the Shaftesbury Theatre in London.

Jack Warner didn't want Harrison for the 1964 film version, fearing that "Grandpa would not sell one ticket at the box office." Warner had worried about the age difference between Harrison and his co-star, Audrey Hepburn. In misstating the case, Warner had claimed, "My God, Harrison was born back in 1908, before the invention of the light bulb, the automobile, or the telephone."

Subsequently, Warner called Cary Grant and pitched the role to him. Grant turned him down. "Not only will I not play Higgins, but I refuse to go see it if you don't let Harrison repeat his stage role. You should also cast Julie Andrews in the film, too."

[Andrews and Harrison had co-starred together on Broadway in My Fair Lady's *1956 production.]*

Eventually, as his second choice, Warner decided that O'Toole would be perfect for the part. He contacted O'Toole, who told him, "For me, Henry Higgins is a dream role. I'd love to do it."

After that, Warner called the film's director, George Cukor, in Switzerland, where he was staying at the home of Noël Coward in Les Avants, in the Vaud region of French-speaking Switzerland, near Montreux. Cukor told him he thought that the casting of O'Toole would be a splendid idea.

He even volunteered to direct O'Toole in a screen test if the actor were willing, either in London or in Hollywood.

In London, O'Toole announced to the press that the role of Henry Higgins "was more or less assigned to him. It's ideal for me, very Shavian," a reference to an admirer of or devotee of the works of George Bernard Shaw. "Basically, Henry Higgins is a bully. I can play that."

After reading that, Harrison went into a panic. He called the composer, Alan Jay Lerner, who assured him, "I will turn down every actor, including O'Toole, until Warner casts you."

As it turned out, O'Toole foolishly demanded far too much money. Warner was known as a cheapskate, so in the end, he agreed to cast Harrison, telling Cukor, "We can get him cheap. Let Audrey Hepburn be responsible for box office."

Throughout the rest of his life, O'Toole regretted losing the role. "It was my own bloody damn fault. I was too greedy. From now on, I think I'll tell the next producer who comes along that I'll work for food."

That same year (1969), Elizabeth Taylor alerted O'Toole that Richard Burton had signed to appear as a homosexual hairdresser in a two-character play called *Staircase,* which was being made into a film.

Written by Charles Dyer, it was the story of an aging gay couple who own a barber shop in the (unfashionable) East End of London. The action takes place during the course of a single night as they discuss their loving but often volatile relationship.

When O'Toole called Burton about the role, he said that he'd already spoken to Harrison, who had agreed to play his homosexual lover. "He told me that if I were game, so was he."

For the role, 20th Century Fox paid Burton $1.25 million, with Harrison getting $1 million.

When O'Toole went to see *Staircase,* he found it a "dismal failure." He also noted that it did almost no box office, critic Roger Ebert referring to it as "an unpleasant exercise in bad taste."

***

When summing up his longtime competition with Rex Harrison for that and for other roles, O'Toole said, "Every actor has a Rex Harrison in his life, someone to compete against. It's true in most fields, sports, ballet, the stage, and especially in politics. Dare I include the boudoir? We both got Vivien Leigh. He got Lana Turner and Merle Oberon, but I bedded Ava Gardner and Elizabeth Taylor. So who's the man?"

Staircase, with Rex Harrison (left) and Richard Burton. Could O'Toole have saved the picture?

O'Toole's Co-Star in High Spirits "Carries on a Torrid Romance With the Sexiest Man Alive—But Not With Me"

—Peter O'Toole

Following his role in the 1987 *The Last Emperor,* O'Toole appeared in only one movie the following year. In *High Spirits,* a fantasy comedy, he was cast as Peter Plunkett, the financially strapped owner of a decaying Irish castle that he was forced to convert into a bed and breakfast.

To attract business, he advertised it as "the most haunted castle in Europe," instructing his staff to appear as ghosts at night, with special effect to frighten his American visitors. As it turns out, the castle is really haunted.

Ever since he was a boy, O'Toole had believed in ghosts, as had his drunkard father. On many a night around the fireplace, his father had told him stories of things that go bump in the night. "We Irish believe in ghosts and the Wee People," O'Toole said. "It's in our blood. On a cold and windy night, only a ghost story will do. My dad told some pretty damn good yarns, and, if I must say so, very convincingly. I was afraid to go to my bedroom alone."

Before filming began, O'Toole went to consult with his celebrity seer, John Cohan. He wondered if Cohan could show him how to get in touch with spirits or ghosts. Would these spirits feel that his upcoming movie was making fun of them? If so, he feared that they might retaliate by sabotaging his movie, perhaps having some of the cast, maybe himself, meet up with an unfortunate accident.

Cohan more or less "greenlighted" the project, assuring O'Toole that he and the cast would be safe from accidents during the shoot. "I gave him my blessing to go ahead, as I did not foresee any tragedy looming."

"More than that, I gave him my lucky rosary which Mother Teresa had presented to me. I told him that if he wore it, it would protect him from the evil spirts wanting to do him harm. From that day forth, he carried the rosary as a good luck charm."

Neil Jordan had been assigned to direct the picture for distribution by TriStar Pictures, with a running time of 99 minutes. Jordan was also a screenwriter. In 1992, he would win an Oscar for Best Original Screenplay for his *The Crying Game,* a film about an IRA terrorist and a transgendered woman.

Jordan lined up a strong supporting cast, including Steve Guttenberg, Beverly D'Angelo, Jennifer Tilly, Liam Neeson, and Peter Gallagher. But the cast member who attracted O'Toole's attention was the blonde goddess, Daryl Hannah. She played Mary Plunkett, one of the castle's real ghosts, opposite

Neeson as Martin Brogan, another ghost and her lover.

Hannah's real lover was no ghost. She was embroiled at the time in at torrid affair with John F. Kennedy, Jr. He'd originally met her at La Samanna, a deluxe hotel on the French side of St. Martin in the Caribbean. Apparently, he'd regarded the teenager as "no more than a toothpick."

But when he saw her again,

High Spirits: O'Toole with Daryl Hannah and Steve Guttenberg

years later, she was twenty-seven years old and had blossomed into a young woman of charm and beauty and had definitely filled out. In fact, *McCall's* had named her one of the "Ten Best Bodies in America." She stood almost six feet tall, with a bone structure defined as "Teutonic."

"The one time I met John Jr., he told me that he wanted to be an actor like myself," O'Toole said. "He claimed that both Peter Lawford and Rudolf Nureyev were encouraging him in that ambition."

"My mother is against it," he said. "She wants me to run for the office of President of the United States on Day. I don't think she approves of my taking an actress for my wife."

"Well, Ronald Reagan seemed to do all right by bringing a reformed actress to the White House," O'Toole said.

Gossip columnist Michael Gross wrote, "Like Jackie, Hannah was patrician. She was also a film queen like Marilyn Monroe, so there were facets to her that would have appealed to JFK Junior's father."

At the time, JFK Jr. started dating Hannah, she was involved with musician Jackson Browne, and JFK Jr. was still intimately linked

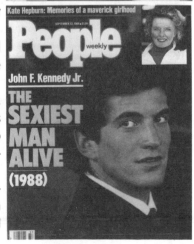

to Christina Haag.

Called a "tomboy's tomboy," Hannah shared JFK's interest in outdoor sports such as sailing off the coast of Martha's Vineyard, or skiing at Telluride, Colorado.

She nicknamed JFK Jr. "Helmet Head" because of his perfect head of hair.

"I found JFK Jr. a mesmerizing figure," O'Toole recalled to his friends. "He was some sort of tabloid Casanova, and I'd heard about his wild sex life. No doubt he was following in the footsteps of John F. Kennedy. Daddy had his blonde, Marilyn Monroe, and Junior had his blonde, Ms. Hannah. I also heard all the gossip that on a dark, rainy night, the gender of his partner didn't matter that much to the handsome lad."

During filming, JFK Jr. stayed in constant touch with Hannah, whom O'Toole called "his maiden fair." The young beau sent her dozens and dozens of long-stemmed red roses. One afternoon, when he telephoned her, "Daryl seemed really pissed off," O'Toole claimed. "I heard her accusing him of hiring a call girl in her absence. Of course, I could have been mistaken. Could this have been the beginning of Trouble in Paradise?"

Years later, in discussing *High Spirits,* he said, "I, along with my fellow cast members, got it wrong about that President of the United States and his First Lady thing. Alas, most of our dreams are not fulfilled, only to be dreamed when we then have to wake up and face the nightmare of this thing called life."

O'Toole as master of ceremonies, summoning ghosts in a haunted castle in Ireland

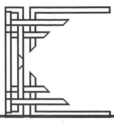

Chapter 33

Caligula

From the Emperor of Porn, O'Toole Is Offered, and then Portrays the Depraved and Syphilitic Emperor Tiberius

In one of the most artful of screen makeup jobs, Peter O'Toole (right) played Caligula's great-uncle, the half-mad, syphilitic *débauché*, Emperor Tiberius, who killed nubile youths for his own amusement after he'd had sex with them.

Originally the film was to be called *Gore Vidal's Caligula.* The author wanted to turn it into something of a homosexual romp, depicting the decadence of Ancient Rome. "I want to show that freedom and liberalism are aberrations in the history of the world, and without due vigilance, America and Britain are likely to get their own modern version of Roman royalty," Vidal said

In London, Peter O'Toole was startled to hear that Bob Guccione was on the other end of the phone, calling from his suite at the Savoy Hotel.

The publisher of *Penthouse* was one of the most controversial media persons in the United States and Britain. Picking up the receiver, O'Toole said to Guccione, "If you're calling me to pose for a nude centerfold, the answer is an emphatic no."

"I've got a better offer," Guccione said. "How would you like to play the Emperor Tiberius in an epic to be shot in Rome?"

"That sounds mighty intriguing," O'Toole said.

"If you'll meet me at eight tonight in the Savoy Grill, I'll discuss all the details with you."

Although a more ardent reader of Hugh Hefner's *Playboy* than Guccione's *Penthouse,* O'Toole had long admired Guccione as a champion of freedom of the press.

Before having drinks and dinner with him, he read some recent articles about him that traced his amazing, trail-blazing career. A breaker of taboos, an outrage to bluenoses trying to maintain some semblance of Victorian taste in a rapidly changing, permissive society, Guccione had created a pornographic empire.

As a struggling artist, he had taken out a loan for $1,170 for the establishment, in 1965, of a magazine that featured female nudes in positions far more explicit than those within *Playboy.* "I wanted to be the first publisher to depict the clitoris," he announced to the press.

Forbes listed him as one of the world's richest men, with a fortune spiraling toward $400 million. Each edition of his magazine, at its peak, reached nearly five million readers. His art collection, filled with works by Dalí, Picasso, Matisse, and Renoir, among others, was worth some $150 million.

Over drinks, O'Toole encountered a flamboyant publisher that to him evoked a "libidinous pornographer," as he later described his encounter to his ever-loyal confidant, Kenneth Griffith.

Penthouse founder and publisher Bob Guccione, "The Caesar of sex magazine gurus," believed in breaking taboos and outraging the so-called "guardians of taste." He made millions before drowning in a slough of bad investments, one of which involved financing the controversial pornographic epic, *Caligula.*

Most movie houses refused to show it.

Dark, haunted eyes stared at O'Toole from under thick, grizzled brows. "He was tanned, really, really tanned," O'Toole told Griffith. "Either from the Palm Beach sun, or else from a sun lamp in a massage parlor attended by barebreasted Amazons."

Guccione was dressed in an Italian silk suit with a black silk shirt open to

550

the waist, exposing a hairy chest. Around his neck was a series of gold chains, many of them containing charms. He showed one charm which was a depiction of the first-ever cover of *Penthouse;* yet another was a miniature replica of a man's genitals.

"This was a reproduction of my cock and balls," Guccione said. "My dick is big enough, but, like all men, I wish it extended at least another two inches."

Two years older than O'Toole, Guccione revealed that he had been born in Brooklyn to parents of Sicilian roots. As an altar boy, he had considered the priesthood. "But as a teenager, my testosterone won out, and I began to deflower what virgins remained in Brooklyn. By eighteen, I was married."

In one of the most artful examples of screen makeup, Peter O'Toole played Tiberius in *Caligula*. He was a syphilitic *débauché* who killed people for his own amusement. In later life, O'Toole, in his own judgment, came to resemble how he had appeared on the screen as Tiberius.

He seemed very familiar with the geography of London, and O'Toole soon learned why. In 1960, he'd settled here, running a dry-cleaning business. "I sold plnup pictures of mostly naked women as a sideline." For a while, he became a cartoonist for *The London American,* where he feuded with his editor, Derek Jameson. "He constantly complained to me, 'Bob you can't put tits and arse on the front page, or we'll all end up in the nick.'"

He launched *Penthouse,* a magazine he described as devoted to "sex, politics, and protests."

"My kind of man," O'Toole said.

"I'm the enemy of all feminists and conservatives," he said. Although I'm a publisher, my real interest in life is as a painter. I'm damn good. Better than Picasso."

"I've revolutionized men's magazines," he said, "Hefner wasn't showing pubic hair. From the beginning, I showed female genitalia, beginning with fuzzy pictures of the pudenda, without the inner labia parted. Now, I'm showing sharper views of the vulva."

"It took a while to get around to male genitalia, including erections."

"As you may know, in media, I'm known for breaking down barriers to censorship. I want to show actual oral, vaginal, and anal penetration. I also pioneered girl-on-girl shots. I know guys like to watch how much lesbians like each other's pussies. In the trade, we call it 'going pink.' I plan to break the final taboo."

"My god, man, what else is left for you to do?"

"I want to depict female models urinating," Guccione said. "That would cross the last frontier in men's magazines. What I'd really like to show is a man urinating into the face of a bitch, but that may be too much. Lezzie feminists wouldn't like it."

"I can't imagine why," O'Toole said, sarcastically.

"Working together, we'll get to know each other better," Guccione said. "I'd like to invite you to my parties. You'll learn that I believe in open marriages, and so do my guests."

"So do I, dear man," O'Toole said. "What man likes to walk around with a ball and chain?"

Guccione revealed that he was prepared to spend as much as $20 million on a film epic that graphically portrayed the decadence of Imperial Rome. "If it's successful, I'll do other biopics. I have two in mind, *Catherine the Great,* and a biopic based on Defoe's *Moll Flanders.* Perhaps there would be roles in both movies for you if you get through our first venture. I saw your film, *Great Catherine* (1968), so you already know your way around a Russian court."

"What are you calling your Roman epic?" O'Toole asked. "Perhaps just *Tiberius* would be enough, since even the name of that madman suggests all sorts of wicked things."

Then very much in vogue, Lina Wertmüller

"You don't understand," Guccione said. "I'm hiring you to perform a cameo. The movie is to be called *Caligula* in honor of the main character."

"You mean, my successor, my great nephew?"

"Exactly. You know your ancient Roman history, I see."

"Who do you have in mind to play Caligula?" O'Toole asked. "Of course, it would have to be an actor younger than me."

"I'd prefer an English actor. He's got to agree to appear in a full frontal nude scene. You know most of the major actors. Who would you recommend?"

STANLEY KUBRICK'S Clockwork Orange

"Over here, we call it the Full Monty," O'Toole said. "The obvious choices would be either Alan Bates or Oliver Reed. After all, they showed their family jewels in *Women in Love* (1969). Alan is only two years younger than me, but Reed was born in 1938."

"Actually, I was thinking about pitching the role to Malcolm McDowell," Guccione said. "Do you know how

Clockwork Orange

Malcolm McDowell in his (previously) most famous role as a psychotically violent sociopath.

he's hung?"

"I never gave him a blow-job, but he might go for it. After all, he made *A Clockwork Orange,* so he might be up for doing anything. He and I both grew up in Leeds."

"Right as we speak, Lina Wertmüller is at work on the script," Guccione said. "I'm thinking of asking her to direct the picture as well."

"I admire her work," O'Toole said.

[At that time in the mid-1970s, the director was enjoying an international vogue. She was called "a modern Aristophanes and a Chaplinesque defender of humble individuals."

An article by Ellen Willis had appeared about her in Rolling Stone, making her a very dubious candidate for Caligula: "She is a woman hater who pretends to be a feminist. Her basic appeal is a clever double-dealing that allows high-minded people to indulge their lowest-minded prejudice."]

In the days that followed, Guccione stayed in frequent contact with O'Toole. One afternoon, he called from New York. "I detested Wertmüller's script. She and I had a big row. I'm asking John Huston to direct. I'll get back to you when I've found out his reaction. In the meantime, I've hired Gore Vidal to come up with a script. He and his lover live in Rome, and he's said to be an expert and scholar on ancient Greek and Roman history."

"A wise choice, I'm sure."

In the meantime, O'Toole was researching whatever he could on Tiberius, who ruled the Roman Em-

"It was not my Caligula. It should be called Bob Guccione's Caligula."
— Gore Vidal

Tiberius of ancient Rome... All known perversions

pire from 14-37 A.D. Tiberius was the stepson of Augustus, the paternal uncle of Claudius, and great-grand uncle of Nero. He also was one of Rome's greatest generals.

In his later years, TIberius became reclusive on the island of Capri, where he was said to have indulged in "the most wicked of all known perversions." Pliny the Elder labeled him "the gloomiest of men." Caligula, his adopted grandson, became his successor after his death in 37 AD.

O'Toole had agreed in advance that he would have to wear grotesque make-up for his depiction of the depraved Emperor during the final stages of his venereal disease. He amused himself swimming with his "minnows and little fishes," nubile youths ages 9 to 13, who swam below the waters to tantalize his rotting sex organs. For amusement, Tiberius liked to watch degrading sexual scenes, including both children and deformed people.

Before leaving for Rome, O'Toole speculated to his friends, "How in hell will Guccione and Vidal depict such debauchery of the court? They'll certainly have to sanitize the stories of Tiberius and Caligula to bring that pair to the screen. Otherwise, *Caligula* will degenerate into hard-corn porn."

As it turned out, he was correct.

Tango Dancing with an Ethiopian Beauty
Rivalry with a Deposed King

Before leaving for Rome, O'Toole had to subject himself to five days of hospital tests in order for Guccione to get adequate insurance for *Caligula*. Press reports had revealed that his health had deteriorated greatly, and that he might be in no condition to stand up to the rigors of making a motion picture. "These gentlemen wanted to make sure that I wouldn't croak until I'd shot my final scene. Before subjecting myself to makeup, I saw a sketch of how I'd look as Tiberius. I was literally to play a walking cadaver."

On a Saturday morning, he received the news that the doctors in London had deemed him in sufficiently good health to complete the film. One doctor had scribbled at the bottom of his report, "Even though we're passing on him at the moment, don't sign any long-term contracts with him."

Once in Rome, O'Toole had arranged, through a real estate agent, to rent a villa on the ancient Appian Way. He installed himself there two weeks before the actual shooting began. Since he had been long separated from his wife, O'Toole took up with a stunning model, born in Ethiopia.

Emeliya Jamal was tall

King Constantine II of Greece, born 1940, on the occasion of his marriage (1964) to his triple third cousin, Princess Anne Marie Dagmar Ingrid of Denmark, with whom he eventually produced 5 children

and statuesque, and had emerald green "cat eyes," with the suggestion that she might have had some Italian blood in her. She preferred to travel around Rome in native Ethiopian dress, wearing tribal jewelry.

Her former lover was the bisexual ex-King Constantine of Greece.

Since he was in "exile" from his wife, "O'Toole openly dated Jemal, wandering around at night hand-in-hand among the historic squares and fountains of Rome, always ending with a *gelato* at Tre Scalini along the Piazza Navona overlooking Bernini's "Fountain of the Four Rivers."

He later referred to his liaison with the Ethiopian beauty as "my ten-night romance." It all ended when O'Toole arrived at his villa late one afternoon after meeting with the *Caligula* crew at the studio.

In his living room sat an unexpected visitor. O'Toole didn't recognize him, but knew that name when Jemal introduced him as King Constantine II of Greece. Of course, he was no longer king, as he'd fled into exile in Rome after his government's collapse, the abolition of the monarchy, and the takeover of Greece by a military junta in 1973.

O'Toole quickly figured out what was going on. His Majesty had arrived on the scene to reclaim Jemal.

Constantine seemed most gracious, immediately recognizing O'Toole as a man of the world familiar with such scenes when it came to romance and illicit relationships. O'Toole responded with ease and sophistication, and even went and poured the king a drink.

Sipping his drink, Constantine congratulated O'Toole on *Lawrence of Arabia*. "What a magnificent piece of work! Fabulous!"

He then informed O'Toole that he was moving Jemal to a secret address three miles north of Rome. "You, kind sir, will always be welcome to come and visit, perhaps for a dinner."

"It would be an honor, Your Majesty," O'Toole said, knowing that there would be no invitation forthcoming.

A boy servant O'Toole had hired moved Jemal's luggage into the trunk of the king's car, which he was driving himself.

O'Toole was aware that the king had a good reason to maintain a hideaway. Jemal had told him that he had a desire for young Greek, or, in this case, Roman boys, a secret passion he shared with his friend, Aristotle Onassis.

Before departing, Constantine warmly shook O'Toole's hand. "Regardless of what you read about me in the future, I will always be King of the Hellenes, and I will always be a Prince of Denmark."

"I once played a Prince of Denmark," O'Toole said. *"Hamlet."*

"I'm sure you were magnificent in the role," the king said. "Perhaps far better than myself."

A week later, reporters and paparazzi caught up with Jemal on a shopping trip along via Condotti. She was asked why she was no longer being seen with O'Toole.

"Mr. O'Toole and I broke up because after love-making, he would get up and force me to dance the tango with him for an hour."

When O'Toole wasn't occupied with love-making or dancing the tango, he studied Spanish, not Italian. He'd purchased a tract of land in Mexico and planned to erect a vacation retreat there. By doing so, he would be following in the footsteps of Elizabeth Taylor and Richard Burton.

Late in 1963, Elizabeth and Burton had arrived in Puerto Vallarta to film Tennessee Williams' *The Night of the Iguana* in which he co-starred with Ava Gardner and Deborah Kerr. Elizabeth had arrived on the set to "supervise" Burton and to try to keep him out of the beds of both Gardner and that Lolita nymphet, Sue Lyon.

On his first visit to Mexico, O'Toole had admired the lifestyle of its people, although his characterization of its people subjected him to criticism, some critics calling him a racist: "I like the lazy lifestyle, the philosophy of life that suggests there is nothing you should do today that can't be put off until *mañana*. Mexico seems my kind of place. That wicked man, Errol Flynn, used to come here to leave deposits in beautiful young boys. As for me, I have a soft spot in my heart for olive-skinned, compliant maidens who can be lured into deflowering by an Irish rogue like me before getting married, looking virginal in white at the altar."

His life as a "married bachelor" was about to end. Another international beauty soon descended into his life.

He spoke of his current dilemma one night at Gilli's, a café near the Piazza della Repubblica dating from 1789. Marcello Mastroianni had invited him here for drinks under Venetian chandeliers. Both actors admired each other's work. O'Toole said, "I seem to end up with Marlon Brando's leftovers—first, *Lawrence of Arabia* after he turned it down, and now his former girlfriend washed up from the debris of *Last Tango in Paris.*"

Malcolm McDowell, Catacombs, Caligula, and Chicken Gizzards

Long before he co-starred with him in *Caligula,* Malcolm McDowell, who played the insane emperor, first met Peter O'Toole in 1965 at a "bring-a-bottle party" in Hampstead. He recalled McDowell as "an extraordinary-looking man with flaxen hair, jeans tucked into his boots, looking every inch a Greek god."

When O'Toole died, McDowell shared his memories of the actor with *The*

Guardian: When both of them met John Gielgud, also cast in *Caligula,* O'Toole said to him, "Hello, Johnny! What is a knight of the realm doing in a porno movie?"

McDowell recalled being summoned to the set with O'Toole at midnight, when the extras were "engaging in every sexual perversion in the book."

"Peter asked me if they were doing the Irish jig. I looked over to discover two dwarves and an amputee dancing around some girls splayed out on a giant dildo."

The most revolting scene occurred with Mc-Dowell and O'Toole when they encountered an inattentive Roman sentry. "Caligula," O'Toole (as Tiberius) asked. "Do you think this man is drunk?" When assured that he was, O'Toole, as Tiberius, orders two sentries to restrain him and to tie up his foreskin. Wine was then forced down his throat, enough so that his belly looked like that of a pregnant woman near term.

At that moment, O'Toole was supposed to take his sword and ram it into the sentry's bloated stomach, which was fronted with a goat's bladder filled with blood, wine, and chicken gizzards. When they spilled onto the floor, they evoked the sentry's decimated innards.

O'Toole inserted the sword under the sentry's breastplate, and then snapped it with such force that it hit the extra in the face, knocking him out.

Instead of piercing the goat's bladder, he cut only the cord that positioned it into place around the sentry's waist. Instead of spilling out the sentry's simulated intestines, it plopped onto the floor and rolled along like a bouncing beach ball.

Observing what had happened, O'Toole said, "I think she's dropped her fucking handbag!"

Malcolm McDowell, defiant and about to become Emperor of Rome.

The English actor, Malcolm Mc-Dowell, played the title role as the depraved Emperor Caligula. His slightly startled look was defined by critics as "emotionally greedy."

He was not ashamed to appear fully nude in the movie. Thanks to his striptease in *Caligula,* the star of Stanley Kubrick's *Clockwork Orange* developed a whole new fan base.

After seven takes, he finally got it right, puncturing the goat-skin bladder, causing the grisly blend of wine, blood, and gizzards to (supposedly) flow from the sentry's dying bowels.

Between takes, O'Toole told McDowell how he collected Etruscan jewelry and ancient artifacts: "I break into the tombs at night as a grave-robber. I then enter a tomb and sift very gingerly through the drains with my fingers. I know that when these ancient bodies decomposed, all the artifacts are eventually washed into these drainpipes."

"Gore Vidal Imagines Everyone as a Homosexual," Charges Caligula's Director, Tinto Brass

On a Monday morning, a chauffeur-driven limousine arrived at O'Toole's rented villa to transport him to the studio at Cinecittà, where *Caligula* was to be filmed. There, he was introduced to Tinto Brass, the film's newly appointed director. Guccione had designated him to helm the picture after John Huston rejected his offer.

As O'Toole recalled, "I didn't exactly hate the director on sight, but after working with him for a few days, I did. I mocked him behind his back, nick-naming him 'Tinto Zinc.' As a director, his usual instruction was to 'turn over,' and that was about it."

Guccione had hired Brass on the basis of his 1976 film, *Salon Kitty,* in which he fused explicit sex scenes with dramatic re-enactments of specific historic events.

[Salon Kitty was an erotic drama, among the prototypes of the "Nazi-sploitation genre," set in an expensive brothel in Berlin. According to the plot, the bedrooms were wiretapped, and the whores were trained as spies, gathering various incriminating data on "rebellious" or disloyal members of the Nazi hierarchy during World War II.]

Within the hour, Brass had delivered a blistering attack on Vidal's original script. "Everybody in the goddamn

Bob Guccione hired Giovanni ("Tinto") Brass, depicted above, to helm his controversial *Caligula.* He';d been impressed with how daring Brass had been with his 1976 release of *Kitty Salon,* which fused explicit sex scenes with so-called "historical drama."

Before the filming of *Caligula* was over, Brass and Guccione were locked into a major battle.

The director also ridiculed Gore Vidal's original script.

movie, according to Vidal, is supposed to be engaged in homosexual acts. Clearly, that is his fantasy of ancient Rome. I personally have nothing against gays, but *Penthouse* fans of Guccione want to see straight sex on the screen."

"Vidal did write a scene focusing on conventional hetero sex, but even that was tinged with depravity, since it depicted the co-dependent, incestuous passion between Caligula and his half-sister Drusilla," Brass said. Guccione paid Vidal $200,000 for the script, and it's a piece of shit. I'm rewriting it. Instead of *Gore Vidal's Caligula,* I want him to retitle it *Tinto Brass's Caligula.* If challenged, I'll denounce Vidal in the press as an aging arterisclerotic."

In his attack on Vidal, Brass claimed that Vidal had depicted Caligula as a good man driven to madness by absolute power. "In my rewrite, I'm depicting him as a born monster."

"That is pure delight to hear, darling, but I really want to know how Tiberius is being written," O'Toole said.

"We're still working on that. There's one sequence being debated. On the island of Capri, Tiberius was known for sodomizing nine-year-old boys. After he'd gotten their asses all bloody, he ordered his guards to toss the youths over a cliff to certain death."

"How utterly enchanting," O'Toole said, mockingly. "Such a scene would surely guarantee me that long, elusive Oscar, which is certainly overdue me."

"In a perfect world," Vidal told the press, "Tinto Brass would be washing windows."

After hearing that, Brass countercharged, claiming, "If I really get mad at Vidal, I will publish the original script he submitted to us. It was laughable, it was

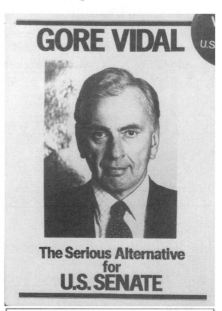

GORE VIDAL U.S

The Serious Alternative for U.S. SENATE

During the filming of *Caligula*, having seen *Lawrence of Arabia*, Gore Vidal assumed that Peter O'Toole was gay.

He invited him to his apartment in Rome and, as a sexual favor, agreed to provide him with one of the golden boys of Rome, a hustler, "for your enjoyment, following in the footsteps of the Emperor Tiberius."

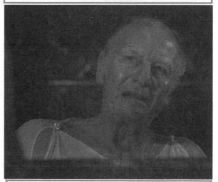

Nerva, dying, after slitting his wrists in a hot bath, as portrayed by John Gielgud, one of the great Shakespearean actors of the English Stage, in "my first porn film."

so horrible."

O'Toole was amazed at the impressive lineup of stars who had contracted with Guccione to star in the movie. Malcolm McDowell had agreed to play the star role of Caligula.

John Gielgud, cast as Nerva, a trusted friend of Tiberius, commits suicide at the prospect of having Caligula proclaimed as the new emperor. Gielgud would maintain his artistic dignity throughout the curse of this bacchanialian, orgiastic film. His farewell to Tiberius (and to life itself) begins when he slits his wrists and submerges himself into a bath of hot water.

Unaware of the sex scenes that Guccione would later insert into the context of the film, Gielgud, after seeing the final cut, announced, "*Caligula* is my first porno movie."

Back in London, he told his friend Noël Coward, "I didn't regret making the movie. After all, Guccione had rounded up at least one hundred of the best-looking and the best hung young Romans, a feast for any old Queen. Nearly all of them were available."

Helen Mirren would play Caesonia, "the most promiscuous woman in Rome," who marries Caligula. Mirren was to appear in most scenes dressed like a flamboyant drag queen of the ancient world. Maria Schneider was cast—temporarily, as it turned out— as Drusilla, Caligula's half-sister.

Appearing in a porno flick did not prevent Mirren in 2003 from receiving a Damehood in the Order of the British Empire for services to the performing arts.

She would later define the film as 'an irresistible mix of art and genitals."

McDowell, cast as the depraved emperor, had a slightly startled look in many scenes, which some critics would label as "emotionally greedy." He was not ashamed to appear fully nude.

Helen Mirren was cast as the nymphomaniacal Caesonia, "the most promiscuous woman in Rome" and later, the wife of Caligula.

In later years, Mirren was destined to play (brilliantly) more demure roles, including a 2006 portrayal of Queen Elizabeth *Segundo* in *The Queen.*

Thanks to his striptease, he developed a whole new fan base, which included author Truman Capote. He told the press, "I can't abide anything written by Gore Vidal. But I went to see

Caligula just to get a glimpse of Malcolm's cock."

"For me, seeing his penis was the highlight of the movie, rivaled only by his beautiful ass on ample display. He gazed at the camera with all the loaded essence of charm, insolence, and trickery."

After Brass's harangue, he informed O'Toole that he was having lunch with Maria Schneider at the Taverna Flavia, which had enjoyed its heyday during those heady days in the 1950s when Rome was sometimes defined as "Hollywood on the Tiber." Flavia attracted such dignitaries as Frank Sinatra, Mario Lanza, and Elizabeth Taylor.

"I saw Maria—in fact, I saw a lot of her in *Last Tango in Paris* with Brando, who made an ass of himself, literally—and I was impressed with her," O'Toole said.

"Perhaps you'd like to join us," Brass said. "Meet our Drusilla in person."

"How delightful for McDowell," O'Toole said. "That means the lucky bloke will at least get to screw her on screen. Perhaps off-screen as well. Maybe I, too, will get lucky."

Peter O'Toole had become enchanted with Maria Schneider, seen in the upper photo with Marlon Brando, after her appearance in the controversial film, *Last Tango in Paris*.

O'Toole later said, "She was like a little Lolita, only more perverse." She had been cast as a twenty-year-old *petite bourgeoise* named Jeanne. Meeting Brando during her search for an apartment in Paris, she becomes involved with him in the throes of what director Bernardo Bertolucci labeled "a vertical position."

"In Rome," Peter said, "Maria and I carried out what Brando had only started in Paris."

"Perhaps, like you said," Brass noted, "But you can't be sure. She's part lezzie, maybe a whole lot lezzie. You don't look like you have any tits."

"Perhaps my charm will win her over," O'Toole said.

He would later recall how Maria Christine Schneider entered his world, looking very much like she did when at the age of nineteen she had starred in Bernardo Bertolucci's *Last Tango in Paris* (1972).

When she made her entrance into Flavia, she'd just finished portraying "The Girl" in Michelangelo Antonioni's *The Passenger* (1975), opposite Jack Nicholson.

Introduced to O'Toole, she politely shook his hand. As she sat down to order a Campari, she confessed, "After seeing *Lawrence of Arabia,* I had a dream that very night. I dreamed you were a desert Shiek and I, a virgin in a white dress. In my dream, you kidnap me and ride away with me on this beautiful white stallion. We arrive at this large white tent in the desert, where you take me inside and proceed to perform depraved acts on my ravaged body."

"Perhaps we can make your dream come true," he told her.

All the Actors (including O'Toole's Bodyguards) Get Naked Only Tiberius and Nerva Are Allowed Togas

At Cinecittà, on the first day of one of his scenes as Tiberius, O'Toole met the film's co-producer, Franco Rossellini, a handsome intense young man. Of all the people working in production, he found the young man the most agreeable, an initial impression that was more or less verified when he accepted his invitation to dinner at his favorite trattoria, Ristorante Rugatino, where the paparazzi often photographed him with his friends, Anthony Franciosa and Shelley Winters, during their marriage.

The son of the famous composer, Renzo Rossellini, he was also the nephew of film director Roberto Rossellini, who had married screen legend Ingrid Bergman after a scandalously adulterous affair that had virtually destroyed (at least temporarily) her Hollywood career.

Franco was often photographed with Bergman's daughter, Jenny Ann Lindström, and there were rumors published in the press about an impending marriage.

Franco revealed that he and Roberto had launched a TV series based on the notorious life of Caligula. However, their finances were low, and it appeared that the series would be the most lavish production since Richard Burton, with Elizabeth Taylor, left town after the filming of the ill-fated *Cleopatra* in 1963.

Franco flew to New York to meet with Bob Guccione at his elegant private home, because he'd expressed interest in being co-producer of the film and putting up the millions needed for production.

"So that's how the *Penthouse* playmates got involved," Franco said. "I don't want anyone to know this, but Roberto, against my wishes, is planning to sue Guccione and Vidal for plagiarizing his material from our doomed TV series.

[Although threatened, based on the advice of his lawyers, Roberto's lawsuit was eventually dropped.]

The next day, O'Toole dined with Mc-Dowell, whom he had known in London. Mc-Dowell told O'Toole that he had insisted that a provision for script approval be written into his contract, and that consequently, he was personally rewriting each of his lines and scenes from the Vidal script. "I want to get rid of all of Caligula's cruelty

Invasive Sex as an Abuse of Power

Despite his dream of portraying "a kinder, gentler, Caligula," isn't that Malcolm McDowell on the right, brutally asserting his authority, as the depraved Emperor, over a bridegroom, just a few minutes after his wedding?

and homosexuality," he said. "My Caligula, at least as I am conceiving him, will have the character of an anarchistic *provocateur.*"

"Whatever that might be, my good man," O'Toole said, as he was becoming increasingly bewildered by the film he'd contracted to make.

McDowell told O'Toole, "Originally, Tinto Brass was asked by Paramount to direct me in *A Clockwork Orange* (1971).

"He had a scheduling conflict, and that's when Stanley Kubrick stepped in. Critics protested that my *Clockwork Orange* was too strong to stomach. What in hell will they say about *Caligula?*"

Months later, O'Toole commented on McDowell. "He may have shown his fine British dick in *Caligula.* I don't really know, since I never saw the complete film. Nor do I intend to. All I know is that the time I saw Malcolm, he was attired in this fetching gold *lamé* number, and looked marvelously fuckable. I was sure his appearance in *Caligula* would guarantee him an international gay following, like it did for me in *Lawrence of Arabia.* But the camp boys are out of luck. Malcolm is straight. Even so, based on that gold *lamé* number, I dubbed him 'Tinkerbell' for the rest of the shoot."

"On the subject of wardrobe, John Gielgud and I were the only actors allowed to wear our togas. But what sane person would want to see either of our bodies in the nude? John and I sat around between takes looking at all those lilywhite bottoms with their appendectomy scars."

Gielgud surprised O'Toole by telling him that he had originally been offered the role of Tiberius, but had turned it down. "Too depraved for my taste."

"Three of the young women really turned me on," O'Toole confessed to his friend Kenneth Griffith back in London. "I asked all three of them to visit me at my villa for an orgy. I even offered to pay each of them the equivalent of $200 U.S. dollars. All of them rejected me in horror. I finally figured out why. I was in my Tiberius cadaver makeup, looking like I was going to cause each of them to become as syphilitic-looking as I was."

Every day, O'Toole had to rise in the middle of the night to be driven to Cinecittà, where he had to endure three long and tedious hours submitting to the labors of makeup artists.

"Three queens fussed over me trying to turn me into an aging, cadaverous syphilitic."

[O'Toole made one movie after another at the dawn of the 21st Century. His harsher critics claimed. "Had he played Tiberius today, he would not need any makeup."

Since O'Toole, as Tiberius, was supposed to be partially paralyzed, Brass assigned him a naked girl (defined in the script as "Sumerian,") to lean on from start to finish.

Throughout the course of the filming, *paparazzi* were disguising themselves and sneaking in to snap forbidden pictures.

O'Toole was assigned ten bodyguards, each of whom also functioned as extras in the film. "To my utter amazement, I looked around one day and saw all ten of them stark naked except for their 'Robin Hood hats.' Sometimes, when they watched some of the scenes being shot, they got impressive erections. I told them they would have to ask Gielgud to service them, as I preferred a hole to a protrusion."

Brass also assigned him another beautiful woman as his personal assistant. "She followed me around wherever I went, even invading the privacy of my toilet. It seemed that Tiberius always had a beautiful servant girl to wipe him after he'd done his business. I nicknamed her 'Betsy, the Collapsible Crutch.'"

On the third day of the shoot, Brass told him that Maria Schneider had bolted from the picture. "For some reason, she demands to talk to you. I gave her the address of your villa. Perhaps you can bash some sense into her dizzy brain."

Last Tango in Rome: Sodomizing Maria Schneider O'Toole Succeeds Where Brando Failed

Two nights after her disappearance from the set, a distraught Maria Schneider slowed up unannounced at O'Toole's villa, where he was spending a lonely night. She was sobbing, and he invited her in to offer her whatever comfort he could.

She told him what he already knew: That she'd bolted from the cast of *Caligula* based on her refusal to be filmed in the nude. Her point of view was equivalent to problems she'd caused as a temperamental nineteen-year-old, playing opposite Marlon Brando in Bernardo Bertolucci's *Last Tango in Paris* (1972).

"After *Last Tango,* I vowed never to appear nude on camera ever again," Schneider said. "But I realized that Brass was about to violate our agreement about no nudity when he ordered the makeup department to ensure that any pimples on my ass were covered up."

He was startled by her naïveté, wondering why, with such elevated standards of modesty, she'd accepted the role of Drusilla in the first place. He felt that she must have known that nudity would be required in an epic that included multiple re-enactments of ancient Roman orgies.

To some degree, he was already aware of Schneider's reputation, having followed her exploits in the tabloid press. In 1974, she had defined herself publicly as a bisexual. He knew that she'd gone through a turbulent life which had included some episodes of drug addiction. She'd been through some near-death experiences with overdoses, and there had been at least one suicide attempt.

"Bertolucci robbed me of my youth," she told O'Toole. "He violated me and exploited my relative innocence on the screen."

O'Toole had been fascinated by the career of Marlon Brando, ever since he'd taken the role of T.E. Lawrence from him, and he was eager for any inside information that Schneider might have about the fabled Method actor. He decided to ask her a question the press had been fretting about for years: "Did you and Brando ever make it together?"

"No," she said. "He was more like a daddy to me. I never felt any sexual attraction to him. He was almost fifty, and he was only beautiful to his waist—certainly not below the belt. Not for me, at least!"

"I found much of the dialogue amusing, especially when Brando tells you that you're going to take 'a flying fuck on a rolling doughnut.'"

"I sometimes mocked his flabby body, but, if you remember, he issued a dire warning: 'In twenty years, you'll be playing football with your tits.'"

Maria claimed that she and Brando never figured out what *Last Tango* was about. "Bertolucci told us it was a reincarnation of his own prick," she said. "He also said Marlon and I were prolongations of said prick."

"Marlon and I got along during the filming because we are both bisexuals and understand each other. We had a certain incestuous link."

"What on earth was that?" he asked.

"I'm the illegitimate daughter of Daniel Gélin, the French actor. Ironically, my father and Brando had been on-and-off lovers for years. At least Marlon got to make love to my father, a pleasure denied to me."

She claimed that originally, Bertolucci had intended to photograph both Brando and herself frontally nude. In Brando's memoir, *Songs My Mother Taught Me,* he backed up Schneider's claim.

Why Maria Showed It All, & Why Brando Didn't, During Their Tango Together in Paris

In his autobiography, *Songs My Mother Taught Me,* Marlon related what had been a painful incident for him:

"I had one of the more embarrassing experiences of my professional career when we were making this film [Last Tango in Paris] *in 1972. I was supposed to play a scene in the Paris apartment where Paul meets Jeanne and be photographed in the nude frontally, but it was such a cold day that my penis shrank to the size of a peanut. It simply withered. Because of the cold, my body went into full retreat, and the tension, embarrassment and stress made it recede even more. I realized I couldn't play the scene this way, so I paced back and forth around the apartment stark naked, hoping for magic. I've always had a strong belief in the power of mind over matter, so I concentrated on my private parts, trying to will my penis and testicles to grow; I even spoke to them. But my mind failed me. I was humiliated, but not ready to surrender yet. I asked Bernardo to be patient and told the crew that I wasn't giving up. But after an hour I could tell from their faces that they had given up on me. I simply couldn't play the scene that way, so it was cut."*

At one point, Bertolucci insisted that Brando and Schneider engage in penile-vaginal intercourse on film. Brando objected to the command, claiming that, "We don't want our sexual organs to become characters in the film." He recalled one scene within the movie of simulated buggering, in which, "I used butter, but it was all *ersatz* sex."

Although Brando refused to "fuck Maria on camera," author Norman Mailer felt that the director should have prevailed. Upon seeing the film, Mailer expressed his disappointment. "Brando's cock up Schneider's real vagina would have brought the history of cinema one huge march closer to the ultimate experience it has promised since its inception—that is, to embody life."

After talking and drinking at O'Toole's villa until around 2AM, Schneider asked if she could spend the night.

"My guest room is filled with all sorts of junk," he said. "But you're welcome to sleep either on the sofa here, or in my bed. If you opt for the latter, I promise to let you stay on your side of the bed with me on mine. I promise not to touch you all night."

"Cut the shit," she admonished him. "Why do you think I want to stay over? I need to be held, to be touched, to be comforted, to be loved. I've been through hell."

No one knows exactly what happened during those pre-dawn hours before the sun rose over the Vatican. He did mention it to Kenneth Griffith when he returned to London. But all he had to say was, "I succeeded where Brando failed in *Last Tango.* I entered Maria from the rear, her portal of choice, it seemed."

Back at his villa, when O'Toole woke up beside Schneider, he found her trembling. "She had an awful case of the shakes, and we decided she needed to enter a clinic. After a call to Vidal, he recommended one, and I took her there. I held her close and kissed her goodbye, never to see her again."

She stayed one week in the mental hospital. He called to learn that her lover, photographer Joan Townsend, was with her, looking after her.

He later said, "Poor Maria Schneider. Some people are not meant to be celebrities. At times I wonder if I am such a person."

Gore Vidal, as Pimp, Wants to Treat O'Toole to Some of the Roman Pleasures Enjoyed by Caligula

Receiving an unexpected call from Gore Vidal, O'Toole accepted an invitation to visit his apartment in Rome. He showed up at exactly 8PM on the evening of the following day. Vidal introduced him to Howard Austen, Vidal's lover and longtime companion.

"Welcome to Rome," Vidal said. "What better place to await the end of the world than The Eternal City?"

As the evening wore on, O'Toole began to realize why he'd been invited here. Vidal not only wanted to give him his take on what *Caligula* should have been, he also wanted to pick up tidbits of information about what was going on at Cinecittà, a studio from which he had been barred.

The author explained that in his script, he had set out to capture Rome in the First Century. "I wanted to make the viewer experience the smells, the depravity, the brutal imperial regime, the struggle for survival. To experience life on the screen as it was lived in those heady days."

He said he'd been heavily influenced by Albert Camus's play, published in 1944, *Caligula*. "My aim was to show how this rather ordinary boy was placed in extreme situations with his own family wanting to kill him. Even as a youth, he was terrified, fearing assassination. In the end, his greatest fear came true."

At the time of his dinner with Vidal, the writer was engaged in a public battle between Tinto Brass and himself, with Guccione thrown in as a side attraction.

Vidal relayed that he had called Brass a "sex maniac," charging him with filming a hardcore porno flick that would not be able to find a major distributor. "I hear that many of the acts he's shooting are illegal, especially because of their use of underaged children. I have suggested that Roman authorities shut down production and send all those responsible to prison."

O'Toole had read those same charges in the tabloid press. He wondered if the original source had been Vidal himself.

Vidal pointedly asked O'Toole, "Do you know what in hell is going on?"

"Only this: Brass is going around threatening to sue you for defamation of character."

"I may sue him as a plagiarist," Vidal claimed. "He's told the press that he and McDowell have rewritten my script. When did McDowell become a screenwriter all of a sudden? I have a spy on the set. He tells me that many of my original lines and a lot of my story and stage directions have been kept."

"I really don't know," O'Toole said. "All I know is this god damn bloody *Caligula* is getting real nasty, very nasty."

In time, all the Brass vs. Vidal lawsuits, threatened or filed, would fall into some murky legal limbo. Nothing ever came of them.

To conclude the evening, the talk turned to sex, specifically sex in Rome. Vidal shared his views on the subject. "There is a difference between Roman boys and American boys. American boys have dirty assholes but clean feet. Roman boys have clean assholes but dirty feet."

As the talk progressed, O'Toole realized that Vidal was relating to him as a homosexual or possibly as a bisexual. As he later claimed, "I didn't want to be a troublesome guest, and tell him that I was neither gay nor bi. At first, I thought he might be setting me up for a three-way with Howard Austen and himself. But then I realized I was far too old for either of them. As a generous host, what he planned to do involved fixing me up with some desirable conquests."

"Perhaps he was just talking. If he actually went through with something, I figured I could gracefully bow out without alerting Vidal that my sexual proclivities lay elsewhere."

Two nights later, Vidal kept his promise. Arriving at O'Toole's villa was what he would later describe as "one of the most enchanting boys to walk the streets of Rome. He was a golden boy, incredibly beautiful. Nero would have freaked out."

"I offered the young man a drink and explained my situation. I asked him to keep my secret from Vidal—let him think the best of me—and in return, I gave him the equivalent of a hundred dollars in *lire*."

The boy seemed pleased, telling O'Toole that he was glad he didn't have to perform because he had a midnight rendezvous with one of the leading politicians of Italy.

Departing from the city a week later, with a touch of nostalgia and bitterness, O'Toole summed up his experiences. "I truly believe the glory that was Rome was of another day."

Penthouse Commandeers Caligula

Guccione Banishes Soft Core Porn, Demanding Raw Sex & Big Erections

Back on the set at Cinecittà, O'Toole was introduced to a British-born actress, Teresa Ann Savoy, whom Brass had hired as Schneider's replacement in the role of Drusilla.

O'Toole had never heard of her, but was quickly told about her background. As a teenager living in Italy, she'd appeared in the October, 1973 edition of the Italian adult magazine, *Playmen*. Before that, she had fled her home at the age of sixteen, living for a while in a hippie commune in Sicily.

She had been cast in a recent role in *Private Vices, Public Virtues* (1975), the story of Crown Prince Rudolf, son of the Austro-Hungarian emperor, Franz Joseph. Savoy had starred as the Baroness Mary Vetsera, Rudolph's lover, who —according to some historians and the scriptwriter— was a hermaphrodite.

"I hope Rudolf was bisexual," O'Toole

From Nazi prostitute to a depraved ancient Roman sensualist: Two views of Teresa Anne Savoy, the left-hand figure in the lower photo.

told Brass. "That way, he could enjoy a man and a woman all in one body."

Brass had cast Savoy in his 1976 *Salon Kitty,* in which she played a member of the League of German Maidens, a pro-Nazi youth organization. She had starred as a spy who poses as a prostitute to gain incriminating evidence against other Germans for the SS.

Unlike Schneider, Savoy had no problems about appearing nude on camera.

During his final days at Cinecittà, O'Toole witnessed the backstage frenzies of an epic film in chaos. "Everybody seemed to have adopted the slogan, 'When in Danger, When in Doubt, Run in Circles, Scream and Shout.'"

Guccione flew from New York to Rome to confront Tinto Brass. He'd seen the first rushes and was horrified, claiming that this was not the film that he had instructed his director to shoot.

"I wanted to see the actors actually engaged in intercourse—not all this fake shit," he shouted, with O'Toole listening in. "Don't you think modern audiences are sophisticated enough to know the difference between a real fuck and merely the mock?"

The die was cast. A battle as epic as the film ensued. O'Toole later said, "Thank God I was leaving and flying back to the mere craziness of London, which lacked the insanity of Rome."

On the way out, he said, "I'm not ashamed of having made a shilling or two in a blue movie. Of course, from what I later saw, and that was only a few clips, *Caligula* was boring rubbish, entirely unerotic. Talk about scripts. What bloody script? Gielgud and I were told to improvise our lines as Nerva and Tiberius. I don't know. McDowell may have written his lines or not. All I know is that Guccione didn't get his ultimate wish. Perhaps he didn't even present his request to his star. But he confided to me that his secret desire involved having Malcolm show off his erection in a close-up."

Astonishingly Tasteless?

A scene from *Salon Kitty* (1976), a quasi-historical thriller directed by Tinto Brass, featuring Teresa Ann Savoy, in an erotically saturated spin on what officers of the Nazi SS were doing between genocidal exterminations.

Guccione told O'Toole, "I've hired *Penthouse* Playmates and Pets as extras. Brass seems intent on hiring women with withered bodies. I also want plenty of male nudity, including erections, so we can attract horny women and gay guys. I know what women want. Most of them tell me that they can't really assess the power of a man just by showing them nude. Many men are growers, not showers."

"I hired two queens as my casting directors for the male extras. I instructed them to hire young men with at least nine, preferably ten, inches. Some 200 men showed up at Cinecittà for my casting call. They were told they had to produce erections. Some of them jerked off for the queens, others preferred the queen to volunteer their mouths, which they were only too glad to oblige."

"You should have made an entire movie featuring clips of the casting auditions," O'Toole advised. "I'm sure such a film would have made millions."

Guccione ultimately dismissed Brass, taking over the filming of *Caligula* himself. His intention involved transforming it from a serious political parable into a hard-core porn movie.

As outrageous as *Caligula* was, it was a prayer meeting compared to how the sensationalist Roman press was describing it. The orgies were said to be real, not simulated, and nine-year-old boys and girls who were even younger were rumored to be participating. Some of the female extras were said to be filmed servicing horses.

In one scene, McDowell was falsely rumored to have revived a custom that once was common during the heyday of the Roman Empire. Six comely boys were strung up by their feet and brutally sodomized by Caligula and his guards. All of this was just some reporter's fantasy.

There were calls for the Roman police to raid Cinecittà and to shut down production.

"I'm being defamed," Vidal protested to the press. "I have nothing to do with what's going on there. Blame Tinto Brass. If not him, Bob Guccione. He's the real culprit."

Right before he left, O'Toole was introduced to the Oscar-winning artist, Danilo Donati (famous for the art direction in Fellini's *Satyricon* and *Casanova*). He had been brought in as costume and set designer. In preparation for the filming of *Caligula,* he set about creating a Felliniesque fantasy, designing skimpy costumes for all the actors, including in some cases four-foot-long phalluses, held in place with rubber straps and belts, as inspired by the erotic frescoes discovered in the volcanic ruins of Pompeii.

"I was glad to see the project end," O'Toole said. "Everyone except Malcolm, Helen, John, and me were suing each other. Vidal was among the first to file a suit to have his name taken off the picture. Brass followed."

After he was dismissed, Brass sued both Guccione and Franco Rossellini for "improper dismissal and breach of contract."

He actually won, but never collected any damages, seemingly entrapped in a tangled legal web of complications and counter challenges from *Penthouse* lawyers in the Italian and U.S. courts. The case dragged on seemingly without end. Brass, as reported in the press, finally said, "Tired of the whole thing, I threw up my hands and surrendered. I don't want to speak of *Caligula* ever again."

The most serious lawsuit Guccione faced was from actress Anneka Di Lorenzo, cast as Messalina. She sued him for sexual harassment, winning $60,000 in compensatory damages and $4 million in punitive damages.

On an appeal, the punitive damages were determined by a judge as not recoverable, and as a result, the bulk of the penalties were invalidated.

Based on delays, confusion, ineptitude, and litigation, *Caligula* did not appear in theaters until late in 1979. Franco Rossellini,

Sapphic Trysts in the Emperor's Court

Depicted above: Lori Wagner as Agrippina and Anneka di Lorenzo as Messalina.

Di Lorenzo sued Guccione for sexual harassment, but after years of litigation, collected very few of the damages she won.

in the meantime, took advantage of Cinecittà's elaborate sets replicating ancient Rome and made use of them as backdrops for an independent film he was producing based on the scandal and blood-soaked life of Messalina. To Guccione's rage, his movie made it into theaters before Guccione could release *Caligula,* thereby pre-empting some of the fire and passion of *Caligula* with equivalent visuals from competing film.

Like Gielgud, O'Toole claimed that his scenes as Tiberius were shot before the film mutated into an XXX-rated movie. Even though he had not yet seen the complete finished version, he publicly denounced *Caligula.*

When he heard about O'Toole's denunciations, Guccione told the press, "O'Toole was far too drunk during the shoot to know what he was doing."

Reacting to that, O'Toole threatened a lawsuit, claiming that he had never been drunk on the set, and that he had "gone on the wagon" prior to the debut of filming because of a major health crisis.

Still angry with Guccione for the drunk charge, O'Toole announced that he was going to finance a rival magazine to *Penthouse,* entitling it *Basement.* He boasted, "It will be ten times more lurid than *Penthouse,* even more explicit than Larry Flynt's *Hustler.* Features will include 'Rodent of the Month,' and also 'Toe Rag of the Year.'" *[Of course, O'Toole was speaking sardonically and elliptically, having no intention of actually launching such a magazine.]*

Reviews of *Caligula* were harsh, Roger Ebert asserting that *"Caligula* is sickening, utterly worthless, shameful trash. People with talent allowed themselves to participate in this vulgar travesty. Disgusted and unspeakably depressed, I walked out of the film after two hours of its 170-minute length."

Acerbic Rex Reed denounced the film as "a trough of rotten swill." Writing for *The Daily Mail*, Jay Scott compared *Caligula* unfavorably to *The Realm of the Senses*, describing that movie as a better treatment of extreme sexuality. *"Caligula* doesn't really work on any level. It is a boondoggle of landmark proportions."

[Realm of the Senses (1976), by Japanese filmmaker Nagisa Ôshima is a graphic portrayal of sexual desire as expressed amid the costumes, protocols, and tensions of Imperial Japan on the verge of war. Set in 1936, it depicts a man and a woman (Tatsuya Fuji and Eiko Matsuda) consumed by a transcendent, destructive love in an era of escalating government control.]

David Denby, a New York critic, defined *Caligula* as "an infinitely degraded version of Fellini's *Satyricon.* Another critic, Leslie Halliwell, denounced *Caligula* as "a vile curiosity, of interest chiefly to sado-masochists." *Time Out London* labeled it "a dreary shambles."

Guccione had hoped to make $100 million off *Caligula,* but it grossed only $24 million, a million dollars less than its production costs.

If a movie-goer wanted to see the full version of the film, he or she would have to have attended its original screening in New York in 1979. Today, new generations of movie-goers will have to be satisfied with countless "butchered" versions of the film, including the 2007 three-disc special edition released by Image Entertainment. This edition, for example, left out some of Guccione's more explicit sex scenes, including a lesbian tryst and various sexual couplings during the Imperial bordello sequence. One scene that was omitted involved Caligula ordering a newly married couple into his lavish bedchamber and raping each of them as part of their honeymoon tryst.

In 1982, Guccione's personal fortune of $400 million had positioned him as one of the richest Americans, according to *Forbes* magazine. But at the time of his death in 2010, he was hovering close to bankruptcy because of a series of bad investments.

As the 21st Century moves on, *Caligula* remains one of the most infamous cult movies ever released, although dozens of countries around the world still forbid it to be shown. However, so eagerly is *Caligula* sought out that many private viewings of the smuggled video are screened, usually in secretive defiance of local obscenity laws.

"Oh, my God!" O'Toole said, shortly before his death. "In some circles— in rather low-rent parts of town—*Caligula* is my most famous film, even more famous than *Lawrence of Arabia.*"

Chapter 34

The Stuntman

With Chilling Restraint, O'Toole Plays a "Probably Insane" Film Director

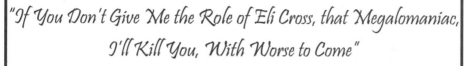

> "If You Don't Give Me the Role of Eli Cross, that Megalomaniac, I'll Kill You, With Worse to Come"
> — Peter O'Toole to the Richard Rush, Director of The Stunt Man

In *The Stunt Man* (1980), Peter O'Toole plays a crazed director, Eli Cross. He seems to be fondly holding his stunt man, Cameron (actor Steve Railsback) in his arms. But Cameron wonders if he's really plotting dangerous stunts that will ultimately lead to his death.

Blowing smoke rings before giving them the finger, O'Toole played the role of a maniac director based on David Lean.

"I was at home in the role," he said, "eccentric and autocratic. How so like me. But audiences were confused. One minute they were in the real world; another minute in Cross' movie being filmed."

The Stunt Man (1980) began as a "labor of love" for Richard Rush, the man who would eventually direct it. He'd read the novel by Paul Brodeur and became intrigued with its plot of an egotistical movie director who will sacrifice almost anyone and everything during his pursuit of high-risk actions on camera. Rush was very eclectic in his taste for literature, having grown up reading everything from *Batman* comics to Marcel Proust's *Remembrance of Things Past*.

"Like the director, Eli Cross, I played in *The Stunt Man*, I will do anything for the sake of art."

The Stunt Man was a big departure for the author who wrote it. Brodeur, until then, had been known as a science and technical writer exposing the hazards associated with asbestos, household detergents, depletion of the ozone layer, and microwave radiation.

Based on Brodeur's novel, Rush wrote a film scenario and then sent it to every major studio in Hollywood, along with some minor ones. One by one, each of them rejected it, not really knowing what it was—comedy, satire, drama?

Right from the beginning, Rush wanted O'Toole to star in the movie. "He was always my favorite actor," Rush said.

Fellow directors warned Rush against casting O'Toole, claiming that 'he's box office poison." His previous two pictures had been financial disasters.

Defying them, Rush sent his scenario to O'Toole, who read it three times in one night. He fell in love with the role of the director, Eli Cross. He later told Rush, "The part is practically autobiographical. I'm mad, impulsive, profane, reckless, a genius, and a megalomaniac. My favorite line in the script is when Cross says, 'If God could do the tricks that we can do, he'd be a happy man."

O'Toole told Rush, "I'm a literate and an articulate man. If you don't let me play the part, I will kill you, with worse to come. "

Rush told him that for a role model of the character he'd be playing, he might use either Orson Welles or John Huston, perhaps a combination of both of them. O'Toole preferred to use David Lean, with whom he'd sweated during all those months under the blazing sun of Jordan, Southern Spain, and Morocco during the filming of *Lawrence of Arabia* (1962).

Finally, Rush found a financial backer in Melvin Simon Productions, a cor-

Using The Gipper's Sexual Legend as a Role Model,
O'Toole Rents Ronald Reagan's Former Hollywood Love Nest

poration heavily invested in real estate, especially shopping malls.

Rush wasn't the only one interested in bringing *The Stunt Man* to the screen: both Arthur Penn and François Truffaut had expressed interest. Rush also had to defend the title from Burt Reynolds, who wanted to make a movie with the same title (but not the same plot). In the end, Reynolds decided to call his film *Hooper* (1978), in which he cast himself as a stuntman.

Steve Railsback was a 5'10" actor noted for his "dangerous, chameleon-like portrayals. He has the scariest-looking pair of eyes in the business."

As a novel, *The Stunt Man* had been written in 1970, but it would not be filmed until 1978. Up to that point, Rush's best known movie was *Trebbie and the Bean (1974),* a minor hit as a police buddy comedy/drama starring James Caan and Alan Arkin.

Lawrence B. Marcus was hired to write the final screenplay, a project that would bring him an Academy Award nomination for screenwriting. Up to that time, some of his better known films included *Justine* (1956); and *Going Home* (1971) starring Robert Mitchum.

He told O'Toole that he had worked as a scriptwriter on the 1968 film, *Petulia,* starring Julie Christie and George C. Scott, directed by Richard Lester.

Barbara Hershey, the female lead, was known for performing outrageous and image-altering stunts. One of them involved breast feeding her child during a widely televised appearance on *The Dick Cavett Show.*

"I wrote thirty-five pages, then sent Lester a script telling him how silly I thought the plot was. 'I quit,' I wrote, as part of the letter I attached."

Lester fired back, "Love the pages; hated the letter; keep working."

"I had less luck when I wrote a film script for Jim Morrison of *The Doors*," Marcus said. "He read it and then burned my only copy."

In anticipation of filming, O'Toole migrated from Ireland and the U.K. to Hollywood for the filming of *The Stunt Man.* He told his close friend and fellow actor, James Villiers, "I rented a rather rundown apartment that the landlord claimed had once been inhabited by Ronald Reagan during his bachelor days."

"The old guy still remembers young Reagan," O'Toole said, "telling me that hot blondes were seen coming and going, everybody from Marilyn Monroe to Doris Day. He said that after his divorce from Jane Wyman, Reagan entered his second horndog period, his first being when he first arrived in

Hollywood, fucking everyone from Lana Turner to Betty Grable.

"Every night as I slept in Reagan's bed, I imagined myself screwing the honey blondes of my era. Marilyn wasn't around anymore, but I found a lot of hot-to-trot tamales. I didn't go after them. They chased me."

"I heard that in this apartment, William Holden and his best friend, Reagan, often shared the same woman," O'Toole told Villiers. "A cozy arrangement I might say, evocative of my many love trysts with Dickie Burton."

Ronald Reagan with his "Juke Girl," Ann Sheridan. O'Toole used him as a role model.

Other than that played by O'Toole, the film's most important role was that of Cameron (Steve Railsback), a Vietnam War veteran desperately trying to avoid recognition by the police, who may have caused the death of one of the film's stuntmen.

Appearing on the set where a movie is being filmed, Cameron (Railsback) meets Cross (O'Toole), who realizes that he is escaping from the police and, based on a motivation which that may derive from the fact that Cross is insane, offers him a job performing extremely dangerous stunts. They are so hazardous that Cameron suspects that Cross is planning to kill him.

The most alarming of the risky stunts is scheduled near the film's climax when Cameron is ordered to drive a vintage Duesenberg off a bridge into a river. From his position, trapped in the car under twelve feet of water, Cameron is supposed to escape, although to an increasing degree, he fears it has been rigged so that he will die inside the submerged car.

Along the way, Cameron falls in love with the film's female lead, Nina Franklin (Barbara Hershey), Cross's discarded mistress.

The Stunt Man—a film whose plot involves the making of a film—unfolds on the set of a movie about flying daredevil pilots of World War I. Everything that moves, breathes, or wiggles is subjected to the cinematic scrutiny of Cross, with O'Toole delivering a heavily mannered performance, very arch, articulate, acidic, and fey.

Many scenes were filmed at the historic Coronado Hotel, just outside San Diego. That same hotel had provided the background for many of the scenes in the 1959 hit comedy starring Marilyn Monroe, *Some Like it Hot*.

Hailing from Dallas, Railsback was awarded one of the major roles of his career. Previously, he had studied at the Actors Studio in New York. With direction from Elia Kazan, he had starred in plays by Tennessee Williams.

"Bring on those weird, warped character parts," he once said. Such was the case when he played Charles Manson in the 1976 hit TV mini-series, *Hel-*

ter-Skelter.

Barbara Hershey, in the female lead, was hailed by the *Chicago Tribune* as "one of America's most versatile actresses," equally at home in westerns, dramas, and comedies. In time, Martine Scorsese would cast her as Mary Magdalene in *The Last Temptation of Christ* (1988).

Prior to her appearance in *The Stunt Man,* during one of the low points of her career, the press had depicted her as "a kook who's always high on something." In 1972, she had married actor David Carradine.

Sharon Farrell, playing Denise, the film's other female lead, was also controversial. Later in her life, she wrote her autobiography, *Hollywood Princess from Sioux City, Iowa,* detailing her love affairs with Bruce Lee, Che Guevara, and Steve McQueen, and her "working relationship" with O'Toole. She asserted that, "Che was the great love of my life. But if I'd stayed with him, I'd probably be dead by now."

Married four times, Farrell had only one child, a son named Chance Boyer. After his birth, she suffered an embolism which caused her heart to stop beating for four minutes. That caused brain damage, physical impairment, and loss of memory. Steve McQueen befriended her when she was cast with him in *The Reivers* (1969), and he advised her to keep her impairments a secret.

At the end of her run as a Hollywood princess, in her final interview, she told a reporter, "I had a good run. I did it all. Now, I'm just looking for another way to get off the planet."

Alex Rocco, cast in *The Stunt Man* as Cameron's props and stunt coordinator, had previously appeared as a gangster in *The Godfather* (1974), playing Moe Greene, the top Jewish mobster in Las Vegas.

***

One of the best real-life stuntsmen in the film industry at the time, Chuck Ball was assigned a role in *The Stunt Man* too. He'd been a veteran of many films and TV sagas, including *Wagon Train* with Ward Bond. In *The Stunt Man,* as stated, he played himself in a small role, all 6'6" of him. During his stint in the U.S. Navy, he'd been a champion boxer and expert swimmer.

"My job is to make sissy actors look like real he-men by performing their dangerous stunts for them. My motto is 'Ride tall, stand tall, and give it your all.'"

The Stunt Man's theme song, "Bits & Pieces," was sung by Dusty Springfield, the English pop star, a blue-eyed songstress known for her distinctly soulful and sensual sound. During the "Swinging Sixties," accessorized with a peroxide blonde bouffant, heavy makeup, and lavish gowns, she became the best-selling female singer in the world.

"*The Stunt Man* was not released, it escaped." Or so remarked O'Toole during his appraisal of that movie's performance at the box office. He was referring to its limited release, in 1980, in the United States, where it attracted small audiences. Nevertheless, it brought him his sixth Academy Award nomination as Best Actor of the Year.

It opened in Seattle, where it attracted favorable critical acclaim, and it was also shown at film festivals in Montréal and Dallas. With such a good press, 20th Century Fox agreed to distribute it, but printed only 300 copies. It had premieres in Chicago, New York, and Los Angeles, as well.

Kenneth Turan of *The Los Angeles Times* wrote that the director's career "seems to be followed by the kind of miserable luck that never seems to afflict the untalented."

[In 2001, Rush would make a documentary that detailed some of the confusion and ironies associated with the making of his 1980 film. It was entitled The Sinister Saga of The Stunt Man.*]*

One of the deans of New York film critics, Pauline Kael, hailed *The Stunt Man* as "a virtuoso piece of kinetic moviemaking," rating it as one of the year's best films and praising O'Toole's performance as "peerless."

Roger Ebert, however, didn't like it, saying, "There was a great deal to admire, but there were times I felt cheated."

Janet Maslin, writing in *The New York Times,* cited "the film's cleverness, which is aggressive and cool. The gamesmanship is fast and furious, but gamesmanship is almost all it manages to be."

When asked what he felt his chances were of winning an Oscar that year, O'Toole said, "I always ring the bookies in Las Vegas. I'm the son of a racetrack bookie, and I'm never known as an odd-on favorite. In all my years of not winning, bloody hell to that talk that it's an honor just to be nominated. It's not, it's a bore, and I'm fed up. Second prize is no prize."

At the 1980 Academy Award presentations, O'Toole once again faced tough competition, especially from John Hurt, who had delivered a brilliant performance as *The Elephant Man.* O'Toole viewed Jack Lemmon's *Tribute* as lesser competition, but feared that Robert Duvall might get the prize for his performance in *The Great Santini.* Finally, through a Las Vegas bookie, he bet $1,000 that Robert De Niro would win that year's Best Actor award for *Raging Bull.* "I won the bet. Of all the bets I've made in my life, that was one thousand dollars I wanted to lose."

Rush received an Oscar nod for Best Director, and both he and Marcus were nominated for Best Adapted Screenplay.

Having been budgeted at six million to produce, the film ended up grossing seven million, a dismal failure at the box office.

Chapter 35

My Favorite Year

O'Toole's Oscar Nomination as a Boozy, Woman-Chasing, Washed-up Matinee Idol with Parallels to Errol Flynn

O'Toole Wants to Star in a Film About an Aging Matinee Idol Falling for a 15-Year-Old Nymphet

As Alan Swann, fading matinee idol, Peter O'Toole appears in *My Favorite Year* as dryly *soigné,* a pie-eyed, woman-chasing, forgetful, drunken matinee star of yesteryear.

In his portrayal of the sloshed actor, O'Toole drew upon his own life experiences mingled into a stew with elements from the last days of the ravished Errol Flynn. Like the charismatic trouper he is, Swann can rise from his stupor "on cue," transforming himself, as cameras roll, into a charismatic celebrity pouring out streams of humor, wit and dapper charm.

That is best reflected in a scene when he enters Manhattan's swanky Stork Club, setting feminine hearts aflutter.

In London, Peter O'Toole was licking his wounds from the massive critical assault he'd endured for his performance in the 1980 production of *Macbeth* on the stage at the Old Vic Theatre.

To his attention, a script arrived from Hollywood producer Michael Gruskoff, wanting him to star in a comedy/drama entitled *My Favorite Year,* a film eventually released in 1982. He sat down and read the screenplay by Dennis Palumbo.

It traced the misadventures of a fading matinee idol, the alcoholic Alan Swann, who, though washed-up, was about to make an appearance on a live TV variety show.

At first, O'Toole decided to reject the role. Arriving as it did in following the worst failure of his life in Shakespeare's *Macbeth*, he feared that the character of Alan Swann would be too close to his own.

Set in 1954, the movie was based on the twilight years of Errol Flynn.

When Gruskoff did not get an immediate response from O'Toole, he called him in London, urging him to take the role. Three other producers were involved, including Art Levinson, Mel Brooks, and Joel Chernoff. "All of us want you to play the role. We don't have an American actor who could look convincing using a sword. A sword fight is the highlight of one of the scenes of the movie."

"I did practice fencing when I was a student at RADA," O'Toole told him.

[The events in My Favorite Year *would be almost entirely fictional, but*

When this picture was taken, doctors told Errol Flynn that he had less than a year to live. In the press, he was treated cruelly, with unflattering descriptions of his gray complexion and sagging, overweight body. Despite the obvious decline of his health and his looks, he retained his impish, romantic spirit.

"Errol Flynn wrote a book, *My Wicked, Wicked Ways,*" O'Toole said. "Like my hero, I lived hard, squandered money, and pretty much behaved as I damn well chose."

"After a lifetime of hellraising, you'd think I'd be in a home or at least in a wheelchair. But I'm still trucking, still outrageous, and still causing trouble wherever I go."

A Mob of Crazed, "Mad Dog" Extras Attacks O'Toole in an Out-of-Control Crowd Scene Evoking "Day of the Locust"

O'Toole was told that the movie and its suppositions had been based on the experience of some TV writers, including Brooks, who had once worked for the Sid Caesar va-riety program, Your Show of Shows. *Flynn had appeared in an episode of that series, and his stint was, for the most part, uneventful.]*

After some strong persuasion, O'Toole agreed to sign for the role. At around the same time, the Oscar nominations were an-nounced for films released during 1980. O'Toole was nominated for an Oscar based on his performance in *The Stunt Man.*

Later, Brooks chastised Gruskoff claiming, "We could have gotten O'Toole a hell of a lot cheaper if you'd signed him before the Oscar nominees were an-nounced."

With his luggage packed, O'Toole flew west to Hollywood to make another film.

Along for the trip, he had accu-mulated a huge amount of reading material, mostly books about Flynn. Gruskoff had suggested that

That's Show-Biz: Two other spectacularly dissi-pated, frequently inebriated actors in the tradition of Errol Flynn:

John Gilbert (left) and John Barrymore, showing the profile for which he became famous.

Errol Flynn: King of the Costume-Drama Swash-bucklers, O'Toole's role model.

he could also draw on the lives of two other famously alcoholic actors, John Gilbert and John Barrymore.

En route to California, O'Toole fell more and more under the spell of the fictional character of Alan Swann. He felt the role would give him a chance to live out on the screen his fantasies about the former swashbuckler, Errol Flynn, born in Tasmania. His favorite quote from Flynn was based on something he had told the press, "I like my whiskey old and my women young."

A defendant in three statutory rape cases, Errol Flynn had married three times, but never found satisfaction in just one woman. Shortly before his death, he estimated that he had seduced anywhere from 12,000 to 14,000 people. Adding to his notoriety, a judge in London had declared, "As a sexual athlete, Flynn may have attained Olympic standards."

Although thousands of these sexual interludes had transpired with unknowns, Flynn had also welcomed plenty of "marquee names" into his bed—Joan Bennett, Jane Wyman, Truman Capote, Howard Hughes, Barbara Hutton, Rock Hudson, Hedy Lamarr, Tyrone Power, Gloria Vanderbilt, Laurence Olivier, Ann Sheridan, Shelley Winters, Carole Landis, Lupe Velez, even Evita Péron. "I'm just a god damn phallic symbol to the world!" Flynn had claimed.

He was quoted as saying, "I only know if I touch the arm of a girl or a woman who fires me, I have to go as far as I can, or as far as she will let me."

O'Toole felt that Flynn had set the standard for modern action heroes in such films as *Captain Blood* (1935); *The Adventures of Robin Hood* (1938); *Dodge City* (1939); and *The Sea Hawk* (1940).

"Would you believe it? I spent years chasing after Ronald Reagan (above, left), who used to be good looking," Errol Flynn (right) told his former roommate, actor Bruce Cabot.

"I thought I almost had him one drunken night back in '42 when we made *Desperate Journey.* But I could never get a rise out of him."

To O'Toole, Flynn was a high-living hellraiser who packed at least a dozen lifetimes into one short but highly eventful life. "He was incredibly beautiful in the 1930s, with an astounding physique. He was the quintessential hedonist. He had a special thing for under-age girls and beautiful boys. I could skip the boys, but the girls sure sounded seductive. He possessed all those fine qualities I admire in a man—sexual pervert, lovable rebel, obscene lecher, ace seducer, boastful cocksman, charming rogue, world-class drunkard—all in all, one of a Hell's Angels of the front ranks."

When he arrived in Hollywood, O'Toole was asked if he could convincingly play a drunkard on film now that he'd given up booze. "Only ninnies make booze the excuse for their wild escapades. I can still make whoopee, darling, but now I do it with sobriety. It is not necessary to pickle myself into unconsciousness. After all, my name is not Oliver Reed."

While reading about the exploits of Flynn, O'Toole became intrigued by the final months of his life. He actually wanted to appear in a movie based on the last two years of Flynn's life, when he was more or less washed up as a Hollywood star. And whereas O'Toole knew that he was too old to appear in a role about Flynn during his heyday, he was utterly convinced that he had the right physicality and the emotional depth to portray the actor in his final months.

During his research of the role he'd be playing, O'Toole read *The Big Love* by Florence Aadland, an autobiographic tale that relayed the history of Flynn's November-to-May affair with Aadland's beautiful and alluring 15-year-old daughter, Beverly. More than that, it relayed a chronicle of an obsessive and tragic passion imprisoned within the glitter and garish glamor of Hollywood during the Marilyn Monroe 1950s.

O'Toole was still bitter that he hadn't been cast as the pedophile in *Lolita,* the 1962 film about the impossible love of a middle aged college professor for a way-underaged nymphet. The cherished role of Humbert Humbert, as originally defined by Vladimir Nabokov, eventually went to James Mason. O'Toole staunchly believed that with the right script, he could be far more convincing as a man with an obsessive romantic and sexual lust for a young girl than Mason was.

In his worst movie, made in Cuba during his dying days, Errol Flynn appeared with his teenage nymphet, Beverly Aadland, in *Cuban Rebel Girls.*

Casting himself as Flynn, O'Toole wanted to star in their saga, a chronicle of an obsessive and tragic passion, a portrait of the garish, glittering California of the 1950s, when the American dream was created, or at least reinforced, on a studio back lot.

"I would like to personally audition an array of depraved young girls from Hollywood High—all actress wannabes—for the role of the nymphet I seduce."

After the filming of *My Favorite Year* was wrapped, O'Toole made several attempts to acquire an existing script (or catalyze the creation of a new one) that incorporated the doomed love affair between Errol Flynn and Beverly Aadland. As it happened, every script he read was either inadequate, unfinished, or hopelessly riddled with problems. Many writers, confronted with the taboos raised by the subject, interpreted it as "too delicate," and backed away.

[In 2013, as O'Toole faced his final curtain, a movie documenting the love between Flynn and Aadland was finally released. It starred Kevin Kline as Flynn, Dakota Fanning as his teenage lover, and Susan Sarandon as Beverly's rapacious stage mother, Florence.

Near the time of his death, O'Toole remarked, "Errol left us in 1959, and I'm soon to depart this sordid sinkhole called Earth. The question is, who in bloody hell is going to replace us?"

585

"I'm Not Afraid to Make an Ass of Myself," O'Toole's Supporting Cast Includes a Playboy Centerfold, Lauren Bacall's Screen Lover, a Transvestite Husband, & Bea Arthur's Abused Spouse.

In Hollywood once again, O'Toole had a reunion at a social event with Anthony Harvey, who had stressfully directed him in *The Lion in Winter*.

[Back then, before the release of that film way back in 1962, O'Toole had driven across London to pound on the door of Harvey's home in Chelsea. Once there, he threatened the director with violence if he did not restore certain cuts he'd made within the context of that film.]

After a twenty-year interlude, Harvey encountered a more mellow, post-operative O'Toole. "There was anger there," Harvey recalled. "But there was also a new gentleness, some inner strength that shone through. He could actually sit down and talk things over with me without making any threats."

"In *My Favorite Year*," Harvey continued, "he took many chances and wasn't afraid to make an ass of himself on camera. Perhaps some of the anger had been cut out of his gut during surgery. That hellraiser of yesterday seemed to have disappeared."

The New York actor, Richard Benjamin, was making his debut as a director with *My Favorite Year*.

Joe Bologna as an egomanical, high-testosterone TV talk show host

Married to the actress, Paula Prentiss, Benjamin was primarily known for his acting roles in such films as *Goodbye, Columbus* (1969), based on the novel by Philip Roth; *Catch-22* (1970), from the Joseph Heller bestseller; and *The Sunshine Boys* (1975), written by Neil Simon.

O'Toole had seen only one of his director's films, *Portnoy's Complaint* (1972), in which Benjamin played the title

O'Toole with his young and inexperienced "handler." Mark Linn-Baker

role. "I read that only because I heard it was about a masturbator, a subject with which I was intimately acquainted," O'Toole said.

The New York Times would eventually interpret Benjamin's directing style as "steady and affable, occasionally inspired, always snappy and never less than amusing."

During filming, Benjamin had only praise for O'Toole's acting, lauding his comedic talents. "When he enters a room, you know a star has arrived. When you look at the rushes, his star quality shines through. He's a thoroughbred among actors. Often, he gets it right on the first take. I had always associated him with drama, but I came to

Richard Benjamin directed Peter O'Toole in *My Favorite Year*.

realize his potential for comedy. He even improved on our script, improvising some of the situations himself."

The film's narrator and co-star, Mark Linn-Baker, was cast as Benjy Stone, a junior comedy writer during the early days of live television in the 1950s. In the film, Benjy tells the story of his favorite year, an interlude whose focal point involved meeting his screen idol, Alan Swann (O'Toole).

Fully aware of Swann's reputation, the host of the TV show on which O'Toole has been hired to appear is King Kaiser (Joseph Bologna). Kaiser orders Benjy to keep Swann sober and out of trouble until his performance is complete. That task evolves into a "job from hell itself" for the poor, bewildered writer.

As a depiction of Swann in his younger days, film clips were inserted from two O'Toole films—*Lord Jim* (1965) and *Great Catherine* (1968).

O'Toole later met the film's executive director, Mel Brooks, the comedian, producer, and screenwriter. As O'Toole later said, "I found him a vulgar, pushy man. I knew he was married to Anne Bancroft, and that in Hollywood they were known as 'The Beauty and The Beast.' Brooks was very Brooklyn, very Jewish. He was brash and superficial, a real *schmuck* as they say. I was told he liked fart jokes."

O'Toole worked smoothly with his co-star, Linn-Baker, who effectively played straight man as a foil for O'Toole's outrageous flamboyance. His character seemed based to some degree on Woody Allen, with whom the actor had worked in films that had included *Manhattan* (1979).

"An unusual event occurred with Benjy and me," O'Toole said. "It seemed torn from the pages of the Nathanael West novel, *Day of the Locust,* about Hollywood's nether world. Extras were hired for a mob scene. I was supposed to be surrounded by fans. The scene took place in an apartment house corridor."

"Maybe the extras were drugged, or out of their bloody minds. Maybe they were striking for higher pay, better lunches, bigger roles. All I know is that we were assaulted by this pack of mad dogs. One cheeky prick grabbed me by my right ear and wouldn't let go until I belted the jerk in his fat gut. The crowd was rabid, out of control. We escaped with our lives, but very battered."

On film, Benjy goes on a rollercoaster ride with Swann, one episode of which involves an early-morning ride through Central Park on a stolen police horse.

Sexy and Fabulous at any Age: Lainie Kazan...a former *Playboy* centerfold

Born to a Russian Ashkenazi father and a Turkish Sephardic mother in Brooklyn, scene-stealer Lainie Kazan plays Benjy's Jewish mother. The character she plays is married to a Filipino former bantamweight boxer, Rockie Carroca (Ramon Sison). Partly as a means of keeping him out of trouble, Benjy escorts Swann to one of his family's dinners, an invitation with many comic overtones.

Kazan—a gutsy and talented singer who had posed for a *Playboy* spread in 1970—had been the understudy for Barbra Streisand in *Funny Girl* on Broadway. Critics would later credit her with "one of the great Jewish mother roles in screen history."

How to Handle a Movie Star: O'Toole being wheeled into a meeting at studio headquarters.

A Californian, Cameron Mitchell, played Karl Rojeck, a corrupt union boss who threatens Kaiser for parodying him in a series of comic skits. When Kaiser refuses to stop televising the skits, "accidents" begin to break out across the set.

One of the funniest actors to ever graduate from the Actors Studio in New York, Mitchell had been a young member of the Alfred Lunt and Lynn Fontanne National Theatre Company.

Over the years, Mitchell had starred with some of the biggest names in Hollywood, including John Wayne, Wallace Beery, Doris Day, James Cagney, Lana

Cameron Mitchell Bacall's lover, only on the stage, or maybe not.

Turner, Spencer Tracy, and Clark Gable. One of his most successful films, *How to Marry a Millionaire* (1953), co-starred Marilyn Monroe, Betty Grable, and Lauren Bacall. In that film, he played Bacall's lover.

Cast as Benjy's love interest, interpreting the role of K.C. Downing, was a Chicago-born actress, Jessica Harper. Woody Allen had liked this actress so much that he'd cast her in both *Love and Death (1975)* and *Stardust Memories* (1980).

Love in Bloom on Madison Avenue: Jessica Harper with Mark Linn-Baker

A Toronto actor, Lou Jacobi, had also worked with Allen, interpreting the role of a transvestite husband in *Everything You Always Wanted to Know About Sex (But Were Afraid to Ask),* released in 1972. In *My Favorite Year,* Jacobi had the role of Benjy's uncouth Uncle Morty.

Sy Benson (Bill Macy) played a fussy straight man, providing contrast to the shenanigans of the other writers on the TV Variety show. This New Englander was best known for playing Wal-

Bill Macy, shown here with a mocking Bea Arthur in the 70s-era sitcom, *Maude.*

ter Findlay, the long-suffering husband of the title character in the 1970s hit TV series, *Maude,* starring Beatrice Arthur.

Selma Diamond spoke in the high ranges of her raspy Brooklyn voice. She had been one of the original writers for Sid Caesar in his ground-breaking TV series, *Your Show of Shows*. She told O'Toole, "I don't act. I just appear as myself." In *My Favorite Year,* she had a small but memorable role as a wardrobe mistress.

My Favorite Year opened in 1982 in more than 700 theaters across the United States and Canada, eventually grossing $20 million. Many critics interpreted it as a comic Valentine to the unpredictable early days of live TV variety shows.

After reading some of the many flattering reviews, O'Toole said, "My old ticker of a heart started beating again after the mauling I'd been getting from the critics."

A leading New York film commentator, Pauline Kael, found the film's lighting "gummy," the shot of Broadway "a blur," and the staging "creaky and klonky." Yet she lauded "the bubbling spirit" of the film, and defined O'Toole's performance as "astounding."

Kael also wrote, "I can't think of another major star, with the possible exception of Ralph Richardson, who would have the effrontery to bring this performance off."

When the 1982 nominations for the Motion Picture Academy's Best Actor were announced, O'Toole's name was among them for his work in *My Favorite Year*. It would be his seventh nomination in that category.

He faced stiff competition from, among others, Paul Newman in *The Verdict;* Jack Lemmon for *Missing;* and Dustin Hoffman for his interpretation of *Tootsie,* a role he played in drag. The Oscar for Best Actor ultimately went to Ben Kingsley for his portrayal of *Ghandi,* which also won the Academy Award as Best Picture that year as well.

Chapter 36

Robbing Jodie Foster from the Cradle

O'Toole Pursues Her Off-Screen During
Their Filming of "Svengali"

O'Toole Fulfills Foster's Need for Comfort, After John Hinckley, in an Effort to Impress Her, Shoots Ronald Reagan

In the made-for-TV movie, *Svengali* (1983), Jodie Foster and Peter O'Toole played May-to-December lovers. Some critics praised the chemistry between them, others found the mating "disgusting, almost perverted," labeling O'Toole "a dirty old man lusting after a teenager."

Shot in New York in 1982, the film was the third remake of the famous George du Maurier movie, *Trilby,* in which a singer falls under the hypnotic spell of her manager and voice coach.

Did Jodie and O'Toole become off-screen lovers? The jury is still out on that one.

     "**Peter O'Toole** didn't exactly save my life, but he was wonderfully loving and supporting of me when we co-starred in *Svengali,*" said Jodie Foster. She was referring to a CBS-TV movie telecast in 1983.

     During her first three years at Yale University, Foster had made no films. When the *Svengali* script arrived, she liked it and wanted to star in it, looking forward to working with an Oscar-nominated star as O'Toole. During the winter of 1982, she would commute from her lodgings near Yale (in New Haven, Connecticut) to Manhattan by train, studying her lessons on the passenger train.

At the time, she was in a sort of post-traumatic shock, recovering from the aftermath of John Hinckley, Jr.'s attempted assassination, on March 30, 1981 at 2:25pm, of the newly elected U.S. President, Ronald Reagan. Hinckley had fired six times at Reagan with a .22 caliber Röhm RG-14 revolver, as Reagan left the Hilton Hotel in Washington, D.C., following his speech at an AFL-CIO conference. He wounded police officer Thomas Delahanty and Secret Service agent Timothy McCarthy. He had also critically wounded Reagan's Press Secretary James Brady, leaving him paralyzed and in a wheelchair for the remainder of his life.

When millions of Americans saw this picture of John Hinckley, Jr., pointing a revolver at his temple, they urged him, "Pull the trigger, John boy. You deserve to die!"

Right before his assassination attempt, Hinckley had sent Foster a note, claiming that he would "abandon this idea of getting Reagan in a second if I could only win your heart and love and live out the rest of my life with you."

After the assassination attempt, Hinckley was arrested and committed to St. Elizabeth's, a psychiatric hospital in Washington, D.C., under heavy guard. Once there, he proclaimed that the attempt on Reagan's life had been an attempt to win the hand of Foster. "My killing of Reagan, if I'd succeeded, would have been the greatest love offering in the history of the world."

He claimed that at the time of the shooting, he was very upset with Foster for not returning his phone calls.

He also told the Secret Service that his role model in his presidential assassination attempt had been Lee Harvey Oswald, who had shot John F. Kennedy in Dallas in November of 1963.

Charged with thirteen offenses in 1982, Hinckley was found not guilty by reason of insanity. He had been diagnosed with narcissistic and schizoid personality disorders and dysthymia.

When the Press Asked O'Toole Whether Jodie "Bats for the Other Team," He Answered: "She's Far Too Good for a Mere Man"

***

When Foster arrived on location in Manhattan for the filming of *Svengali,* she found that it was being shot in one of the most dangerous parts of the city. Transvestite prostitutes plied their trade nearby, and pyromaniacs set cars on fire in the parking lot adjacent to one of film sets.

In contrast to her usual nature, Foster became confidential with O'Toole shortly after meeting him, as she interpreted him as a trusting soul filled with compassion for the ordeal she'd been forced to endure.

"When I heard that Hinckley tried to kill Reagan to impress me, I cried and cried and then cried some more. I was overwrought, hysterical, laughing, then crying, then laughing uncontrollably at this pathetically love-struck boy who'd been harassing me."

[In the wake of the Hinckley assassination attempt, another young man, Edward Richardson, stalked Foster at Yale, planning to assassinate her. But he finally decided against it, telling police, "She was just too pretty."]

When she'd heard about Hinckley's assassination attempt, "My body jerked in painful convulsions," Foster wrote in an article for *Esquire.* "I hurt. I was no longer thinking of the president, of the assailant, of the crime, of the press. I was crying for myself. Me, the unwilling victim. The one who would pay in the end."

She told O'Toole, "I had to draw upon all my resources, 'playing cowboy," a tough kid act I'd put on for everybody else's benefit."

He held her in his arms and comforted her, more big brother or loving father than lover.

The script for *Svengali* had arrived in her life just when she needed a distraction. "I was getting restless. Just school was not enough. I did want something to take my mind off Hinckley. Thank

Jodie Foster appears as a pedophile's dream in *Taxi Driver* (1976), starring Robert De Niro, in a *Götterdämmerung* world, a gory New York story about a sick man's lurid descent into violence.

John Hinckley was inspired by the vision of Jodie Foster, a teenaged hooker in tight hot pants and a halter top. "Fifteen dollars for fifteen minutes."

God he didn't kill the president."

"For the first time, I was in love with a project, that *Svengali* movie," she said. "It made me fall in love with acting again. It cured me of my insecurities: It healed my wounds."

Day by day, O'Toole helped her through her trauma. On his part, he may have fallen in love with her—"at least for a few days of my life"—as he later claimed to Kenneth Griffith and James Villiers, his actor friends back in London.

Hinckley had originally become obsessed with Foster when he saw her performance in *Taxi Driver* (1976). She had played a child prostitute opposite Robert De Niro. In the movie, the disturbed protagonist, De Niro, sets out to assassinate a presidential candidate.

At first, Hinckley had planned to assassinate Jimmy Carter, but he ultimately decided he'd get more publicity by assassinating the newly elected Reagan instead.

He began to write messages, even poems, to Foster, slipping them under the door of her dormitory room at Yale. He got to speak to her on a few occasions, recording her voice for eerie, perhaps erotic, playbacks later.

Robert Halmi was *Svengali's* producer, and Anthony Harvey was its director. Both of them came up with the unique casting of "odd couple" lovers, O'Toole and Foster, with the very talented Elizabeth Ashley thrown in "for extra spice."

The movie was a variation on the romantic novel, *Trilby, published by George du Maurier in 1894. [One of the most popular novels of its time, and first available as a serialization in Harper's Magazine, it was set in a romanticized version of Paris in the 1850s. It's the story of three British artists and their interconnection with Svengali, a rogue musician and hypnotist. Its female protagonist, Trilby, is tone-deaf. "Svengali would test her ear, as he called it, and strike the C in the middle and then the F just above, and ask which was higher; and she would declare they were both exactly the same." Svengali hypnotizes her, and as part of the process, transforms her into a co-dependent (on him) musical star of the operatic stage.]*

In the modern-day film incarnation of that book, the *Svengali* script has O'Toole cast as Anton Bosnyak, a mercurial, temperamental voice coach whose speaking voice goes in and out of a Hungarian accent. His agent, Eve Swiss (Ashley) takes him to a seedy rock club, where he hears a singer, Zoe Alexander (i.e., Foster, who used her own voice for the replication of

Zoe's songs.)

Reluctantly, but driven by his perception that she nurtures a formidable talent, Anton takes her on as his latest pupil, demanding her nonstop pursuit of perfection and warning her that "Art is a form of bondage."

As a singer, critics suggested that Foster was "Janis Joplin-ish, with a pleasant Bette Midler quality."

As the film progresses, Foster falls for her older vocal coach. As "baggage" from her earlier life, she also has a young boyfriend, who, when he hears of her affair, tells her, "I didn't know you were into wrinkles."

Elizabeth Ashley: "In *Svengali*, Peter O'Toole should have gone for me, not Jodie. He looked far older than her father."

The Florida-born actress, Elizabeth Ashley, impressed O'Toole. Before meeting her, Tennessee Williams had told him that "Elizabeth Ashley is my favorite actress." Of course, the playwright's view of his favorite actor or actress changed from season to season. But Ashley did receive a Tony nomination for the Broadway revival, in 1974, of *Cat on a Hot Tin Roof*, in which she played a voluptuously sexy version of Maggie the Cat.

When O'Toole met her, Ashley was just emerging from James McCarthy— her third unsuccessful marriage. Before that, she'd wed, in succession, two other handsome actors, James Farentino and heart-throb George Peppard, who had appeared with her in Harold Robbins' steamy *The Carpetbaggers* (1964).

O'Toole resonated with Ashley's very frank and usually iconoclastic opinions, delivered offhandedly in a husky voice that was sometimes riddled with expletives.

"If you're an old woman, we live in a culture that assumes you're a whipped dog," she told him. "But an old woman who is not a whipped dog can be right dangerous."

She told him that when she was older, she'd like to tackle two of Tennessee William's most famous stage characters: "Instead of Maggie the Cat, I'd like to be Big Mama in *Cat on a Hot Tin Roof*. I'd also like to play the scary mother, Amanda Wingfield, in *The Glass Menagerie*."

[In 2001 and 2005, respectively, Ashley indeed would play both of these characters on stage.]

"In spite of my three marriages," she told O'Toole, "I'm a wanderer and a loner."

"So am I," he said. "One day, I plan to return home...if only I knew where it was."

The cast and crew assumed that O'Toole and Foster were having a May-

December romance. Some newspaper accounts accused him of robbing the cradle. They were seen walking around Manhattan holding hands and looking like an odd but loving couple. Candid snapshots by *paparazzi* suggested some intimacy. The film's publicity department churned out the suggestion that they had become "fast friends." One writer suggested that was a "code for the nudge-nudge, wink-wink suggestion."

Foster did not comment on any intimate relationship with O'Toole. Not then, not today.

O'Toole was asked by one reporter for an insight. In his usual enigmatic fashion, he said, "I keep an open mind and an open pair of arms. There is nothing on earth as good as a man and a woman."

Although not commenting on an affair (or lack thereof), O'Toole referred to Foster as "a gutsy little bird—a gorgeous snot-nose. As an acting team, we are absolutely spot-on. The set is covered with fuzz, and there are always doggy people after her. It's tremendously unfair that this nice, talented girl should have become the target of every nutter in the land."

"When I hooked up with Jodie, my straw-colored hair had turned to gray, and I had a cadaverous figure and evoked the Grim Reaper, but Jodie didn't seem to mind."

Reviews of *Svengali* were not favorable, one critic defining it as "a dull, pointlessly updated rendition. O'Toole and Foster fail to light any sparks whatsoever. You don't believe them together for an instant."

In their review of *Svengali, The New York Times* found O'Toole "looking more emaciated and acting more eccentric than ever. He delivers his lines with a quirkiness that suggests a wicked parody of some English ham actor." John O'Connor, who wrote that review, went on to assert, "He retains vestiges of the dashing lead man of *Lawrence of Arabia* or *Becket.* He is still certainly an imposing presence. But he has become disconcertingly bizarre, almost impossibly theatrical. His performance is embarrassingly similar to John Barrymore in his last films. *Svengali* is fascinating, but, finally, silly."

Years later, O'Toole was asked about Foster's gender preferences, the implication being that those lesbian rumors about her were true. "Jodie is too good a plum pudding for a mere male," was all that Peter had to say.

[Foster broke up with her long-time partner, a movie producer, Cydney Bernard, in 2003, after a relationship that had lasted since 1993. In April of 2014, she married Alexandra Hedison, an actress and photographer, who had previously been in a relationship with Ellen DeGeneres from 2001 to 2004.]

Chapter 37

Peter O'Toole's Final Curtain

Lawrence of Arabia Rides Into the Sunset, Shouting
"I've Done Everything & Everybody"

A Hellraiser Joins Fellow Hellions "Down Under"

In 2003, the Academy honored Peter O'Toole with a lifetime achievement award, but he was reluctant to accept it. "I'm still in the game," he expressed to the Academy. "Let me win one outright for Best Actor!"

Two weeks later, he received notice that an Oscar would be presented to him whether he liked it or not. His children admonished him, "Don't be like Marlon Brando and turn it down. Show up, for God's sake. It's the highest honor you can win."

He turned up that night. As watched by millions, his Oscar was presented by the elegant Meryl Streep, who whispered in his ear, "I've been nominated for, and lost, far more Oscar nominations than you have."

Back home in London, his long time friend, Kenneth Griffith, belittled him for accepting "this ridiculous award. Bloody hell! By now, you should have had at least ten Best Actor Oscars."

In 1981, O'Toole was appearing in *Masada,* the hit TV series where he played an Imperial Roman general, Cornelius Flavius Silva. As commander of Rome's 10th Legion in 73 AD, he confronts Jewish zealots, who have retreated to the isolated but impregnable fortress of Masada. His orders are to crush them.

Rallying his demoralized troops through the sheer force of his personality, he continues the siege, spearheading the hammer-like resolve of the Roman Empire, at great expense. At the very moment when Roman victory is inevitable, his face betrays his anguish as the Jews on the hill commit mass suicide. O'Toole was nominated for an Emmy and a Golden Globe for his brilliant performance.

***

"I didn't get to play the Roman general, Marc Antony, opposite Elizabeth Taylor in *Cleopatra,* but my day finally came. At least I was a Roman general in *Masada."*

That same year, O'Toole met a beautiful and well-known model, Karen Brown. Early the following year, they had set up housekeeping together. His relationship with Karen is still shrouded in mystery, and attempts to reach her have failed.

One source claimed that she was with O'Toole for ten months before they split. Another states their turbulent relationship lasted until 1987, at which time they were definitely living apart.

Once O'Toole said, "I was married one time to the actress Siân Phillips. I will never marry again."

Yet there are reports of a secret marriage, and Karen was sometimes in-

O'Toole Meets a Beautiful Model

THEIR SON

& Their Endless Custody Battles

troduced as Karen O'Toole.

Maybe one day, a marriage license will surface—perhaps not. O'Toole's relationship with Karen is mainly significant in that their union produced O'Toole's only son, Lorcan [Gaelic for Lawrence] Patrick O'Toole, born March 17, 1983. He came into the world in Dublin because his father wanted him to be born an Irishman.

Today, he's an actor with a small resumé and is the half-brother of Kate and Patricia O'Toole, whose mother is Siân. O'Toole also has a grandchild, Jessica, born to Patricia.

Originally, Karen had custody of Lorcan, with O'Toole given visitation rights. By 1985, the little boy was being shuttled across the Atlantic, living mainly with Karen but allowed to visit his father in London.

Later in life, O'Toole began a tumultuous affair with a beautiful model, Karen Brown. Together, they had a son, which led to a bitter custody battle that made the tabloids (see above).

Once, during a visit to England, O'Toole refused to return Lorcan to America. After hiring a tough lawyer, Karen appealed to a judge to have O'Toole declared in contempt of court. Her lawyer warned that he might be fined $1,000 for every day he failed to return the kid.

O'Toole capitulated, putting Lorcan on the next plane to New York. Before they departed for the airport, O'Toole held him in his arms in his garden in Hampstead and wept. "I don't know when we'll meet again, son, perhaps on some far and distant shore. But I love you, love you, my dear boy."

One time in Manhattan, O'Toole "kidnapped" Lorcan and flew him east to Bermuda. When Karen found out where he was, she arranged with a lawyer in Bermuda to block O'Toole's attempt to fly Lorcan on to England. As the boy and O'Toole were boarding a plane for London, authorities intervened and Lorcan was flown back to New York and delivered to New Jersey and his

Like his father, Lorcan O'Toole grew into an elegant man, also an actor, like his father. Ultimately, O'Toole got his son back, saying, "After many a court battle, I now have the right to bring up my son before he becomes an old man like me. It was a struggle, but justice has prevailed."

mother's arms once again.

Karen's lawyer, Raoul Felder, told the judge, "One parent is an international movie star, the other a homebody. His mother wants her son to be brought up as a typical American boy. You don't have to be Freud to see the boy might be better off with roots."

But their fight over custody of the child had only begun.

In 1987, during O'Toole's Broadway run of *Pygmalion,* when four-year-old Lorcan was living with Karen in New Jersey, he was allowed to come to New York and stay with his father in his hotel suite.

Amanda Plummer, O'Toole's co-star in *Pygmalion,* told the press, "Peter dotes on his son. Oh, God, to see those two together! Peter's eyes shine when he is with his boy."

O'Toole could hire lawyers, too. He appealed to a higher court in America and by 1988, he'd won Lorcan back. He could attend school in London, seeing his mother on holidays.

When Lorcan grew up, he became an actor, following in his father's footsteps. His older half-sister, Kate O'Toole, had already set the example for him, becoming an award-winning actress herself.

Lorcan has appeared in such films as *The Boxer* (1997), *Mrs. Palfrey at the Claremont* (2005), and *Knife Edge* (2009).

At last report, Lorcan's mother is now Karen Dempsey and living in Aiken, South Carolina. She presented Lorcan with a half-sister, Morgan Dempsey, who inherited her mother's beauty. Morgan is an interior designer operating a business in California.

"So I Lost the Tony for Pygmalion. What Is a Bloody Tony?"

In 1987, O'Toole made his Broadway debut at the Plymouth Theatre in *Pygmalion.* At the time, he was being plagued with a highly publicized lawsuit with Karen over the custody of his son.

Peter O'Toole as Henry Higgins in George Bernard Shaw's *Pygmalion*—an ode to British diction and the late Victorian era.

In 1984, he had appeared in the same role, that of Professor Henry Higgins, at the Shaftesbury Theatre in London's West End. Even before that, in 1957, he'd had a key role as Eliza Doolittle's father in a 1957 production of *Pygmalion* at the Bristol Old Vic.

Had things gone his way, he would also have starred as Henry Higgins in *Pygmalion's* movie adaptation, *My Fair Lady* (1964). The film that eventually starred Rex Harrison and Audrey Hepburn, O'Toole's former flame.

Although some reviewers compared his Professor Higgins unfavorably to that of the more famous portrayal by Harrison, O'Toole's reviews for the most part were good.

On opening night, he'd received a standing ovation when he strutted out onto the stage in his Edwardian finery to do justice to George Bernard Shaw's memorable role. *The New York Times* claimed that he'd made "goo-goo eyes at the audience." He told a reporter, "Shaw called Higgins an imperious baby, and I think that's a good note."

A reporter from *People* magazine went to interview him, describing what O'Toole looked like:

"A gaunt, towering Irishman pushes open the living room door. The face is wan and ravaged, the web of broken blood vessels testimony to his past as Richard Burton's rival in roistering. The spirit, however, is evidenced by his bright red shirt; green, red, and cream blazer; and green-and-pink tie. He remains undaunted."

When later he was asked about his snub by the judges at the Tony Awards for the year's Best Actor Award, he retorted, "I've been snubbed seven times by the Academy for an Oscar. What's another snub? By the way, what is this bloody thing called a Tony? Never heard of it. But then, I'm new to Broadway. Perhaps Richard Burton knows what a Tony is. He knows everything else, to hear him tell it."

He also confessed, "I'm no longer a playboy. It had become a bore. The pleasure wasn't worth the pain."

O'Toole Finally Wins an (Honorary) Oscar. "Always a Bridesmaid"

After seven near-misses, it finally happened in 2003, when the Academy of Motion Picture Arts and Sciences invited him to Hollywood to accept an honorary Oscar for Lifetime Best Actor Achievement.

O'Toole notified the Academy that he would show up to accept the honor. But he also wired, "I'm still in the game. I'd rather win the bugger outright."

He would be nominated one more time for a (conventional) Academy Award based on his performance in *Venus* (2006). Once again, for the eighth time, he lost, this time to Forest Whitaker for his performance in *The Last King of Scotland.*

In Hollywood, O'Toole faced a bevy of reporters, telling them, "I'm really being awarded for being an Oscar bridesmaid and the poster boy of a hell-raiser. Although old and tattered tonight, like some roses in a Victorian *pot-pourri*, I remain a reformed but unrepentant Bad Boy."

"I am happy to be an inspiration for a new generation of actors. I was delighted to hear that Tom Cruise viewed me as a role model."

"The kid is sort of cute, dancing around in his jockey shorts in *Risky Business* (1983). Had I been of a different sexual orientation, I might have gone for him."

VENUS: O'Toole's Ultimate Expression of Unrequited Love

"Imagine an Old Sod Like Michael Redgrave Producing a Daughter Like Vanessa!"

—Peter O'Toole

In the Dotage of His Twilight Years, O'Toole Lusts After a Nude Aphrodite in an Art Class

O'Toole's role in *Venus,* a 2006 British comedy/drama, culminated in his eighth Oscar nomination and—as events would demonstrate—his last serious opportunity for designation as Best Actor.

In February of 2007, at the Kodak Theatre in Hollywood during the 79th annual Academy Award presentations, O'Toole would lose that award, as he had lost equivalent awards at seven earlier Oscar ceremonies during the course of his long career.

[At O'Toole's first Academy Award ceremony, during February of 1963, the

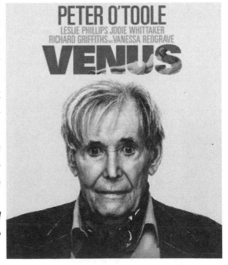

602

audience's emotional attachment to Lawrence of Arabia virtually dominated an event held at the Santa Monica Civic Auditorium Despite its designation as 1962's Best Picture, O'Toole as an actor faced stiff competition from that year's winner, Gregory Peck for his role in To Kill a Mockingbird. The other nominees had included Burt Lancaster (Birdman of Alcatraz), Marcello Mastroianni (Divorce, Italian Style), and Jack Lemmon (Days of Wine and Roses).

Forty-four years later, at the Award ceremony honoring the best film venues of 2006, when O'Toole was nominated for his role in Venus, his competitors included Leonardo DiCaprio (Blood Diamond); Ryan Gosling (Half Nelson); and Will Smith (The Pursuit of Happiness). Ultimately, it was Forest Whittaker who walked off with the Best Actor Oscar for his interpretation of The Last King of Scotland. The event marked O'Toole's eighth and final Best Actor nomination over a span of forty-five years as an actor.

In the interim, other actors who beat O'Toole for the coveted Best Actor award had included Gregory Peck (To Kill a Mockingbird; 1962); Rex Harrison (My Fair Lady, 1964); Cliff Robertson (Marty, 1968); John Wayne (True Grit, 1969); Marlon Brando (The Godfather, 1972); Robert De Niro (Raging Bull, 1980); and Ben Kingsley (Ghandi, 1982).]

Venus, a tender exploration of the dignified wisdom that sometimes accompanies old age and the noisy recklessness that sometimes accompanies youth, was an oddity within O'Toole's repertoire. Although many observers assumed it would represent O'Toole's last filmmaking attempt, he'd continue acting virtually until his death in 2013.

Helming the production was Roger Michell, born in Pretoria, South Africa. He had approached O'Toole with an offer to cast him as the male lead, an elderly actor, Maurice, on the verge of his own death.

As a director, Michell had already generated a host of prestigious credentials, having worked with playwrights

In *Venus*, Jodi Whittaker plays Maurice's (O'Toole's) unrequited love. She humiliates him when she brings a lover into his flat and asks him to take a walk so they can have sex. He returns and kicks them out. A scuffle follows, and she knocks the aging Maurice down on the floor, injuring him. With remorse, she returns to look after him.

In the final reel, both of them are at seaside at Whitstable in Kent. He sits down to look out at the water. "Now we can really talk," he tells her. Leaning on her, he dies.

John Osborne and Samuel Beckett. In 1985, he'd held the coveted directorship of the Royal Shakespeare Company. His greatest commercial success had been the romantic comedy, Notting Hill (1999), co-starring Julia Roberts and Hugh Grant, which became the highest-grossing British movie of all time.]

In *Venus,* Maurice, despite his recurring battles with prostate cancer, still lusts after his friend Ian's great-niece Jessie (Jodie Whittaker). Ian (Leslie Phillips), an aging actor, warns him that Jessie is a troublemaker and a nuisance.

Motivated by his unexpressed and unrequited love, Maurice maneuvers Jessie into modeling nude for an art class in a pose inspired by his favorite painting, *The Rokeby Venus* by Velázquez. As their relationship unfolds, Maurice and Jessie become more deeply engaged in a co-dependent bond punctuated with various degrees of passivity and aggression.

Maurice (O'Toole) escorts the object of his affection to the National Gallery to expose her to *The Rokeby Venus* (depicted above), painted between 1647 and 1651 by the great Spanish court artist, Diego Velásquez.

Inspired by the painting, he wants Jessie (Jodi Whittaker) to pose nude for his art class.

Although she keeps him relentlessly at bay, Jessie represents the last love of Maurice's life.

And whereas she lives with him, she only lets him hold her hand or perhaps smell her neck. Eventually, she cons him into letting her commandeer his flat as a love and mating nest for herself and her young boyfriend.

O'Toole's character (Maurice) remains sexually and emotionally unfulfilled, a study in romantic altruism. He dies at the end of the film.

Venus' script had been written by the brilliant Pakistani writer Hanif Kureishi, whose exploration of intimacy and infidelity were attractive to Michell, who had had a long professional relationship with him. Born in London, and widely applauded as one of the leading writers of the contemporary U.K., Kureishi began his career in the 1970s, writing porno under a pseudonym. *The (London) Times* in-

Hanif Kureishi, author of the Venus filmscript, was a brilliant Anglo-Pakistani writer.

Sharp of wit, he had views on almost everything, referring to England as "a wilderness of monkeys" and suggesting that "anything good in art has to be a little pornographic."

604

cluded Kureishi on its list of the greatest British writers since 1945. *The New York Times* called him "a post-colonial Philip Roth." Kureishi's biggest hit came in 1985 with his screenplay for *My Beautiful Laundrette,* about a gay Pakistani-British boy growing up on the rough-and-tumble streets of downscale London in the 1980s.

When O'Toole was introduced to Kureishi, he found him an intriguing figure, "a Pakistani kid who liked Jimi Hendrix, took drugs, and was devoted to hot sex. He had stories to tell of being 'a Paki,' a kid of color from a mixed marriage experiencing racial discrimination on the tough streets of London."

After reading Kureishi's script for *Venus,* O'Toole called it "off the wall—that's why I like it so much."

In his casting of the *Venus*, Michell hired a strong back-up cast of supporting players. Whittaker, cast as Jessie, was a Yorkshire-born actress who had risen to prominence. At the time O'Toole met her, she was getting ready to marry the American actor Christian Contreras.

A Londoner with a strong Cockney accent, Leslie Phillips, cast as O'Toole's friend, Ian, had been born into poverty. He ended up playing plummy English charmers with an exaggerated and eccentric upper-class accent in the style of Terry Thomas. Eventually awarded a voiceover role ("The Sorting Hat") in the *Harry Potter* series, he achieved great success in one of Britain's most successful series of low-budget movies, the *Carry On* films. *[Inspired by the bawdy traditions of vaudeville, 31 of these were released between 1958 and 1992, bearing names like* Carry On, Nurse! *and* Carry On Up the Khyber.*]*

Phillips described some of his early days in show business, where he performed in the "murkiest, rat-infested old playhouses and music halls of the North of England." Eventually, he moved into films portraying "lecherous twits with suave chat-up lines."

For his role as Ian in *Venus* , he was nominated for a BAFTA award for Best Supporting actor.

Another veteran actor, Yorkshire-born Richard Griffiths, is better known for another film release *The History Boys* 2006). He played the role of Hector, a professor in a boy's prep school, whose most obvious flaw involved a fondness for groping his male students while riding behind them on their motorbikes. Griffiths later became even more

Venus: Jodi Whittaker. For her role in *Venus*, she was nominated as "Most Promising Newcomer." From there, she went on to make many other films, including seven in 2011 alone.

famous playing Harry Potter's priggish, judgmental, and dim-witted uncle, Vernon Dursley.

[After Venus, Griffiths appeared in the stage revival of Peter Shaffer's Equus *in London at the Gielgud Theatre, and on Broadway at the Haymarket. In these revivals, he co-starred with Harry Potter himself, actor Daniel Radcliffe. According to Griffiths, "Everybody in the audience was flocking to see what Harry Potter's penis looked like in his nude scene. And what a noble tool it was to gaze upon! It truly would make an old queen's mouth water."]*

Enduring but Low-Key Love
Vanessa Redgrave with O'Toole

Veteran professional Vanessa Redgrave was cast in *Venus* as O'Toole's long-suffering wife, Valerie. O'Toole had long been a friend of her distinguished father, actor Michael Redgrave.

A celebrated stage actress, Vanessa had already starred in some eighty films. She was a six-time Academy Award nominee, winning an Oscar for Best Supporting Actress for her title role in the historically evocative *Julia* (1977) about a woman murdered by the Nazis for her anti-Fascist activism prior to the outbreak of World War II. In that film, she had co-starred with Jane Fonda, who played the Left-leaning and endlessly trenchant playwright and social critic, Lilian Hellman.

The year *Julia* was released, Redgrave had funded and narrated a documentary film, *The Palestinian,* about the goals and platforms of the Palestine Liberation Organization. When she was nominated—and later won—an Oscar for her role in *Julia,* members of the Jewish Defense League burned effigies of her and picketed the Academy Awards, protesting both Redgrave herself and her support of the Palestinian cause.

Redgrave remains the only British actress to win an Oscar, Emmy, Tony, Olivier, Cannes, Golden Globe, and Screen Actors Guild awards. Playwrights Arthur Miller and Tennessee Williams proclaimed her as "the greatest living actress of our times." In a poll of industry experts, Redgrave was ranked as "the ninth greatest stage actor/actress of all time."

In *Venus,* playing O'Toole's discarded wife, Valier, Redgrave's role was small but memorable. She wears black and an old sweater and glasses with square-shaped lenses. Greeting her estranged husband at the door of their flat, she needs a cane and holds a cat, her sole companion, in her arms.

O'Toole heads for the kitchen to cook supper, while she watches one of his old movies on the telly. She calls into the kitchen that he used to be handsome. When an actress appears on the screen, she yells at him, "There is the woman who took you away from me."

When he yells at her that the food is burning, she shouts back, "You will burn, Maurice."

As her biographer, Dan Callahan, so accurately put it, "This is barely a performance, just a few stray pieces of dialogue an opening for movement that Redgrave takes up and fuses together into a totally convincing, troubling portrait of a limited first wife filled with unreasoning anger."

O'Toole said that Jane Fonda in her 2005 autobiography best captured the essence of Vanessa Redgrave, the actress.

"There is a quality about Vanessa that makes me feel as if she resided in a netherworld of mystery that eludes the rest of us mortals. Her voice seems to come from some deep place that knows all suffering and all secrets. Watching her work is like seeing through layers of glass, each layer painted in mythic watercolor images, layer after layer, until it becomes dark. But even then, you know you haven't come to the bottom of it."

"O'Toole told his fellow actor, Griffiths, "To think an old sod like Michael Redgrave could have produced a daughter like Vanessa."

Redgrave's marriage to director Tony Richardson had ended in 1967, when he'd left her for French actress Jeanne Moreau. Redgrave then became romantically involved with the strikingly handsome Franco Nero when they met on the set of the film version of *Camelot* in 1967. On Broadway, it had starred Richard Burton and Julie Andrews. As one writer said, "Nero's love-struck blue eyes matched up ideally with Vanessa's own startled blue peepers."

After emotionally bonding and then separating for many years, during which they both had love affairs with other people, they reunited and married on the last day of 2006, around the same time that Redgrave was filming *Venus* with O'Toole.

Venus opened with a limited release in the United States right before Christmas of 2006. For the most part, it received positive reviews, eventually being nominated for five British Independent Film Awards.

Decline of an Empire (a.k.a. Katherine of Alexandria)
Peter O'Toole Emerges from Retirement to Star in a Roman Epic But Dies Before He Screens Its Final Cut

Footage of His Final Performance is Completed
A Few Hours after His Death.

In August of 2012, a month before his 80th birthday, Peter O'Toole announced his retirement from both the stage and the film world.

"It is my belief that one should decide for oneself when it is time to end one's stay. It is time for me to chuck the sponge. The heart for it has gone out of me: It won't come back. So I bid the profession a dry-eyed and profoundly grateful farewell."

True to his word, he disappeared—for a few months, at least.

In May of 2013, less than a year later, he surprised his friends and fans with an announcement. "I'm tossing off my tattered bedroom slippers for sandals, swords, and sands to appear in an upcoming drama, *Katherine of Alexandria.*

[Before the film's release in 2014, a year after O'Toole's death, its title was changed to Decline of an Empire.]

At the time, he was struggling to complete the third volume of his memoirs, a book that would have included an overview of the most tantalizing parts of his life. Regrettably, he never finished it.

O'Toole had accepted the role of Cornelius Gallus (70 BCE-26 BCE), an ancient Roman poet, orator, and politician. Gallus' verses about the death of Julius Caesar were considered a benchmark of satire. Almost nothing from his poetry survives, but his contemporaries viewed him as the first of the elegiac poets of ancient Rome. He wrote four books of elegies chiefly about his mistress, whom he called

A film release of a product burdened with two distinctly different names.

"Lycoris." *[In reality, Lycoris was a poetic pseudonym for Cytheris, a notorious actress of her day, a woman known for having "deflowered" legions of young men.]*

In *Katherine of Alexandra,* at least, Gallus was a minor character. The movie revolves around the "Virgin Martyr," Katherine (sometimes spelled Catherine) of Alexandria (282-305 AD), who was martyred in the early 4th Century on the orders of the pagan Emperor Maxentius.

[A Christian at the age of fourteen, she converted hundreds of people to the then-relatively new religion. Eleven hundred years later, Joan of Arc cited Katherine as her most important role model.

Sometimes the saint is known as "Catherine of the Wheel," because Maxentius condemned her to death on a spiked "breaking wheel," a circular device to which the victim was fastened before an executioner systematically broke enough of his/her bones to eventually kill him or her. Rumor had it that the wheel shattered at Katherine's touch. In desperation, Maxentius then condemned her to be beheaded by a Roman soldier. Known for the hundreds of witnesses she converted to Christianity throughout her imprisonment—including, by some accounts, Maxentius' wife—Katherine remains one of the most important saints of the Christian heritage.]

Michael Redwood made his directorial debut with this film, and also wrote its script. He was flattered that O'Toole heartily endorsed his script, claiming, "If anyone alters Michael's screenplay other than to add a full stop, shoot the bastards with my permission."

"That was such a compliment for me as a first-time screen writer," Redwood said.

"I was quaking in my Liverpudlian boots before I met O'Toole," the director recalled. "But after his high praise for my script, I adored him."

"I set out to create an intelligent screenplay and to seek out Britain's finest actors, including *Lawrence of Arabia* himself," Redwood said.

Hailing from the north of England, Redwood had entered show business via the music industry, working with such artists as Eric Clapton. In the early 80s, he ventured into the

Illustration of a Christian-era execution, on a wheel,

609

world of film, on such productions as *Romancing the Stone* and *The Whistle Blower,* before writing and directing *Katherine of Alexandria.*

The movie hinged not on O'Toole but on the actress cast into the lead role of Katherine. Redwood chose an unknown from Romania, Nicole Kenilheart, for the lead. "No one had ever heard of it," O'Toole said. "Where did Redwood come up with her?"

She later said, "I was terrified of working with an Oscar-nominated star like O'Toole. But he made everything easy, and he put me at ease. I felt like I'd known him for a very long time. He taught me not to panic and to be myself. I feel very privileged to be starring in such a film with him. Millions of actors would die to have been put in my position."

"When I first met O'Toole, he asked me a lot of questions. I recall, his first one was, 'Is it true that vampires still come out at night in Transylvania?' We searched for something we might have in common. Oddly enough, it was that at the age of six, we both came down with

Two views of Nicole Kenilheart as Katherine of Alexandria. The film's director said, "When Katherine is tied to that infamous wheel, with a bloody crown of thorns on her brow, I want her to evoke a female Jesus Christ."

some dreadful illness. We had to be locked away from our families for a month."

"I was playing a virgin in the film."

Reportedly, O'Toole told her, "If I were at least ten years younger, I could cure you of that awful affliction."

He also asked her, "What training did you have to undergo to become a virgin?"

At one point during a scene, Redwood instructed O'Toole to make Kenil-heart smile. He whispered something into her ear. She smiled.

Redwood later asked him what he'd whispered to her. "It is unprintable," O'Toole responded.

To round out the cast, Redwood assembled an array of talented British actors, none more famous than Edward Fox, who played the Emperor. He and O'Toole had become friends when they'd starred in the TV movie, *Gulliver's Travels* in 1996.

"Peter and I were old friends," Fox said. "Some of the best performances I've ever seen on stage have been given by him. I hope this isn't his final film before he retires again."

"In spite of his ill health, Peter came across like a firecracker. He delivered a performance of great intensity, and was frightfully good. By the time the film was completed, however, he was not well. He rather locked himself up and kept away from things."

Both Fox and O'Toole discussed acting, the older actor agreeing with the younger one's assessment. "I think acting is somewhere in the genetics of people. It exists in most people, if not all. Formal education has rather tended to knock that on the head, and replace it with more academic requirements. The strain of passion and feeling within people needs to be developed much more than it is at the moment."

Jack Goddard played one of the key roles as Constantine the Great. He was not just a Welsh stage actor, following in the footsteps of Richard Burton, but a music industry writer as well.

Before accepting the role, he "boned up" on the historical figure of Constantine, who ruled the Roman Empire from 305 AD to 337 AD, and was the first Roman ruler to convert to the previously illegal religion of Christianity. The Byzantine Empire hailed him as its founder. A half-millennium later, the Holy Roman Empire (800-1806 AD) viewed him as one of its most venerable figures.

The multi-talented actor, playwright, and theater director, London-based Steve Berkoff, was cast as Liberius. Best known for his villainous roles, he had played General Orlov in the James Bond film, *Octopussy,* and later starred as Adolf Hitler in the TV mini-series, *War and Remembrance.* The irony of that was that he came from a Jewish family with roots in Romania and Russia.

Drama critic Aleks Sierz once characterized Berkoff's "in-yer-face" style as:

"The language is usually filthy, characters talk about unmentionable subjects, take their clothes off, have sex, humiliate each other, experience unpleasant emotions, and become suddenly violent. At its best, this kind of

theater is so powerful, so visceral, that it forces audiences to react. Either they feel like fleeing the building or they are suddenly convinced that it's the best thing they've ever seen."

Cast as Marcellus, Dudley Sutton was an English actor trained at RADA. He told O'Toole, "I was kicked out because of my interest in rock 'n' roll." He came to the attention of audiences after he starred as a gay biker in *The Leather Boys* (1964). He also became famous for marrying the American actress, Marjorie Steele, in 1961. She had previously been married to the A&P heir, Huntington Hartford.

Joss Ackland, in the role of Rufus, was a London actor, who has enjoyed a long career in film and TV, appearing in some 130 productions. Other than O'Toole, over the course of his career, he appeared with Alec Guinness, Demi Moore, Nigel Hawthorne, and Anthony Hopkins, along with Maggie Smith, Judi Dench, and Tom Courtenay at the Old Vic.

Samantha Beckinsale, a Londoner, played Vita. By 1990, she'd become a household word in England, when she was cast as Firefighter Kate Stevens in the popular television drama, *London's Burning,* which ran from 1986 to 2002.

O'Toole did not want to make the commute from Pinewood Studios into London every night, so he set up camp in a big tent on the studio grounds. He had a female assistant, known only as "Lucy," tending to his every need.

"In spite of his age and health, he took a great interest in how the film was shot," Redwood said. "He insisted on having his input on camera angles and shooting. After every take, he'd ask, 'Can we see a replay?' It slowed us down, but it was a pleasure really, He was a true professional."

"One characteristic which appears to have stood out on the set was his irresistibly naughty sense of humor. He would make the whole crew laugh. If he were filming a scene, he would say things afterward like: 'You've fucked that up and I'm going to tell everybody.'"

"He narrowly escaped death many times in his life, and during filming, he had a few setbacks," Redwood said. "But as in his life, he's made more comebacks than a phoenix with repetitive strain injury. If he were unwell, he never showed it. He brought a crackling energy on set with him."

"He played a death scene which ended up on the cutting room floor," Redwood said. "You could literally see the life drain out of one eye and the other, which is a long-one-and-a-half minute shot of him lying on the ground. It's a great shot because he is smiling just as he dies. I don't think I've seen him do a better performance than he has in this film."

O'Toole is featured in nearly half an hour of the overall 106-minute film.

Redwood said, "Peter never lived to see the movie. We arranged for a copy to be shown to him in his hospital bed, but it didn't arrive in time. We missed him by forty-eight hours."

The Once Penniless Boy from Leeds
Draws Up a Will to Dispose of 4 Million Pounds

After his death on December 14, 2014, when O'Toole's will was read, it shocked many of his fans. The bulk of his estate was left to his elder daughter, actress Kate O'Toole, 53. Most of the remainder went to his son, Lorcan, 31. Left out was his younger daughter, Patricia, 50. The two girls had been born during his marriage to Siân Phillips. Lorcan, his son, was born to his girlfriend, Karen Brown.

Kate got the lion's share of £1.1 million, and all of O'Toole's property in Ireland. Lorcan received £760,000. And it was stipulated that Patricia's 14-year-old daughter, Jessica, was to receive £360,000 when she turned 18.

It was reported that O'Toole had been estranged from Patricia for many years—no reason given. Even though she'd been left out of the will, she was said to have profited from partial ownership of Keep Films, the movie company he'd formed with his partner, Jules Buck.

At the age of 81, Peter O'Toole, hellraiser, sexual outlaw, and Irish rebel, had died in London's Wellington Hospital after a long illness.

His funeral was held at the Golden Green Crematorium, the services attended by his longtime friend, Sting. After the service, a wake was held in his London home.

In his will, he asked that his ashes be interred in the Actors Church of St. Pauls in Covent Garden. The rest of his ashes, according to his will, were to be interred on his land in Eyrephort near Clifden in County Galway in Ireland.

Tributes poured in from around the world. Prime Minister David Cameron cited his brilliant performance in *Lawrence of Arabia,* praising that film as his alltime favorite.

At the time of his acrimonious split from his wife, Siân Phillips, she had claimed he was "a dangerous, disruptive human being."

At the time of O'Toole's death, she was appearing as Lady Bracknell in Oscar Wilde's *The Importance of Being Earnest* for the Shakespeare Theatre Company.

"It was a big shock to me, when Peter died," she told reporters. "I do miss him. I somehow thought he would be there forever. He hadn't been well for a long time, but he seemed to be going on. We weren't in touch, but, even so, I was very upset because I wasn't expecting his death."

She had long ago deserted him for a much younger man, actor Robin Sachs.

O'Toole's last public utterance concerned what he wanted written on his tombstone. "Here lies Peter O'Toole. He made the best French toast."

"Otherwise," he said. "I have no memories I wish to share except one. Back in my days as a hellraiser, it was such fun to go pub crawling in London and wake up in Mexico."

Ω

Peter Seamus O'Toole
1932-2013
Rest in Peace

THE AUTHORS

DARWIN PORTER

As an intense and precocious nine-year-old, **Darwin Porter** began meeting movie stars, TV personalities, politicians, and singers through his vivacious and attractive mother, Hazel, a somewhat eccentric Southern girl who had lost her husband in World War II. Migrating from the depression-ravaged valleys of western North Carolina to Miami Beach during its most ebullient heyday, Hazel became a stylist, wardrobe mistress, and personal assistant to the vaudeville comedienne Sophie Tucker, the bawdy and irrepressible "Last of the Red Hot Mamas."

Virtually every show-biz celebrity who visited Miami Beach paid a call on "Miss Sophie," and Darwin as a pre-teen loosely and indulgently supervised by his mother, was regularly dazzled by the likes of Judy Garland, Dinah Shore, Veronica Lake, Linda Darnell, Martha Raye, and Ronald Reagan, who arrived to pay his respects to Miss Sophie with a young blonde starlet on the rise— Marilyn Monroe.

Hazel's work for Sophie Tucker did not preclude an active dating life: Her *beaux* included Richard Widmark, Victor Mature, Frank Sinatra (who "tipped" teenaged Darwin the then-astronomical sum of ten dollars for getting out of the way), and that alltime "second lead," Wendell Corey, when he wasn't emoting with Barbara Stanwyck and Joan Crawford.

As a late teenager, Darwin edited *The Miami Hurricane* at the University of Miami, where he interviewed Eleanor Roosevelt, Tab Hunter, Lucille Ball, and Adlai Stevenson. He also worked for Florida's then-Senator George Smathers, one of John F. Kennedy's best friends, establishing an ongoing pattern of picking up "Jack and Jackie" lore while still a student.

After graduation, as a journalist, he was commissioned with the opening of a bureau of *The Miami Herald* in Key West (Florida), where he took frequent morning walks with retired U.S. president Harry S Truman during his vacations in what had functioned as his "Winter White House." He also got to know, sometimes very well, various celebrities "slumming" their way through off-the-record holidays in the orbit of then-resident Tennessee Williams. Celebrities hanging out in the permissive arts environment of Key West during those days included Tallulah Bankhead, Cary Grant, Tony Curtis, the stepfather of Richard Burton, a gaggle of show-biz and publishing moguls, and the once-notorious stripper, Bettie Page.

For about a decade in New York, Darwin worked in television journalism and advertising with his long-time partner, the journalist, art director, and distinguished arts-industry socialite Stanley Mills Haggart. Jointly, they produced TV commercials starring such high-powered stars as Joan Crawford (then feverishly promoting Pepsi-Cola), Ronald Reagan (General Electric), and Debbie Reynolds (selling Singer Sewing Machines), along with such other entertainers as Louis Armstrong, Lena Horne, Arlene Dahl, and countless other show-biz personalities hawking commercial products.

During his youth, Stanley had flourished as an insider in early Hollywood as a "leg man" and source of information for Hedda Hopper, the fabled gossip columnist. On his nightly rounds, Stanley was most often accompanied by Hedda's son, William Hopper, a close friend of Ronald Reagan's.

When Stanley wasn't dishing newsy revelations with Hedda, he had worked as a Powers model; a romantic lead opposite Silent-era film star Mae Murray; the intimate companion of superstar Randolph Scott before Scott became emotionally involved with Cary Grant; and a man-about-town who archived gossip from everybody who mattered back when the movie colony was small, accessible, and confident that details about their tribal rites would absolutely never be reported in the press. Over the years, Stanley's vast cornucopia of inside Hollywood information was passed on to Darwin, who amplified it with copious interviews and research of his own.

After Stanley's death in 1980, Darwin inherited a treasure trove of memoirs, notes, and interviews detailing Stanley's early adventures in Hollywood, including in-depth recitations of scandals that even Hopper during her heyday was afraid to publish. Most legal and journalistic standards back then interpreted those oral histories as "unprintable." Times, of course, changed.

Beginning in the early 1960s, Darwin joined forces with the then-fledgling Arthur Frommer organization, playing a key role in researching and writing more than 50 titles and defining the style and values that later emerged as the world's leading travel accessories, *The Frommer Guides,* with particular emphasis on Europe, California, New England, and the Caribbean. Between the creation and updating of hundreds of editions of detailed travel guides to

England, France, Italy, Spain, Portugal, Austria, Germany, California, and Switzerland, he continued to interview and discuss the triumphs, feuds, and frustrations of celebrities, many by then reclusive, whom he either sought out or encountered randomly as part of his extensive travels. Ava Gardner and Lana Turner were particularly insightful.

One day when Darwin lived in Tangier, he walked into an opium den to discover Marlene Dietrich sitting alone in a corner.

Darwin has also ghost written books for celebrities (who shall go nameless!) as well as a series of novels. His first, *Butterflies in Heat,* became a cult classic and was adapted into a film, *Tropic of Desire,* starring Eartha Kitt, among others. Other books included *Razzle-Dazzle,* about an errant female movie star of questionable morals; and an erotic thriller, *Blood Moon,* hailed as "pure novelistic Viagra, an American interpretation of Arthur Schnitzler's *La Ronde.*"

Darwin's novel, *Marika,* published by Arbor House, evoked Marlene Dietrich for many readers.

His controversial novel, *Venus,* was suggested by the life of the fabled eroticist and diarist, Anaïs Nin. His novel, *Midnight in Savannah,* was a brutal saga of corruption, greed, and sexual tension exploring the eccentricities of Georgia's most notorious city.

His novel, *Rhinestone Country,* catalyzed a guessing game. Which male star was the inspiration for its lovable rogue, Pete Riddle? Mississippi Pearl praised it as "like a scalding gulp of rotgut whiskey on a snowy night in a bowjacks honky-tonk."

Darwin also transformed into literary format the details which he and Stanley Haggart had compiled about the relatively underpublicized scandals of the Silent Screen, releasing them in 2001 as *Hollywood's Silent Closet,* "an uncensored, underground history of Pre-Code Hollywood, loaded with facts and rumors from generations past."

Since then, Darwin has penned more than eighteen uncensored Hollywood biographies, many of them award-winners, on subjects who have included Marlon Brando; Merv Griffin; Katharine Hepburn; Howard Hughes; Humphrey Bogart; Michael Jackson; Paul Newman; Steve McQueen; Marilyn Monroe; Elizabeth Taylor; Frank Sinatra; John F. Kennedy; Vivien Leigh; Laurence Olivier; the well known porn star, Linda Lovelace; all three of the fabulous Gabor sisters, plus Tennessee Williams, Gore Vidal, Truman Capote, Jacqueline Kennedy Onassis, Jane Wyman, and Ronald and Nancy Reagan.

As a departure from his usual repertoire, Darwin also wrote the controversial *J. Edgar Hoover & Clyde Tolson: Investigating the Sexual Secrets of America's Most Famous Men and Women,* a book about celebrity, voyeurism, political and sexual repression, and blackmail within the highest circles of the U.S. government.

He has also co-authored, in league with Danforth Prince, four *Hollywood Babylon* anthologies, plus four separate volumes of film critiques, reviews, and commentary.

His biographies, over the years, have won more than 30 First Prize or runner-up awards at literary festivals in cities which include Boston, New York, Los Angeles, Hollywood, San Francisco, and Paris.

Darwin can be heard at regular intervals as a radio commentator (and occasionally on television), "dishing" celebrities, pop culture, politics, and scandal.

A resident of New York City, Darwin is currently at work on two biographies slated for release in 2015 and early 2016. These include *Bill & Hillary—So This Is That Thing Called Love;* and *James Dean—Tomorrow Never Comes.*

DANFORTH PRINCE

The publisher and co-author of this book, **Danforth Prince** is one of the "Young Turks" of the post-millennium publishing industry. He's president and founder of Blood Moon Productions, a firm devoted to researching, salvaging, compiling, and marketing the oral histories of America's entertainment industry.

One of Prince's famous predecessors, the late Lyle Stuart (self-described as "the last publisher in America with guts") once defined Prince as "one of my natural successors." In 1956, that then-novice maverick launched himself with

$8,000 he'd won in a libel judgment against gossip columnist Walter Winchell. It was Stuart who published Linda Lovelace's two authentic memoirs—*Ordeal* and *Out of Bondage.*

"I like to see someone following in my footsteps in the 21st Century," Stuart told Prince. "You publish scandalous biographies. I did, too. My books on J. Edgar Hoover, Jacqueline Kennedy Onassis, and Barbara Hutton stirred up the natives. You do, too."

Prince launched his career in journalism in the 1970s at the Paris Bureau of *The New York Times.* In the early '80s, he resigned to join Darwin Porter in researching, developing and publishing various titles within *The Frommer Guides*, jointly reviewing the travel scenes of more than 50 nations for Simon & Schuster. Authoritative and comprehensive, they were perceived as best-selling "travel bibles" for millions of readers, with recommendations and travel advice about the major nations of Western Europe, the Caribbean, Bermuda, The Bahamas, Georgia and the Carolinas, and California.

Prince, along with Porter, is also the co-author of several award-winning celebrity biographies, each configured as a title within Blood Moon's Babylon series. These have included *Hollywood Babylon—It's Back!; Hollywood Babylon Strikes Again; The Kennedys: All the Gossip Unfit to Print;* and *Frank Sinatra, The Boudoir Singer.*

Prince, with Porter, has co-authored such provocative biographies as *Elizabeth Taylor: There is Nothing Like a Dame.*

With respect and a sense of irony about "When Divas Clash," Prince and Porter also co-authored *Pink Triangle: The Feuds and Private Lives of Tennessee Williams, Gore Vidal, Truman Capote, and Members of their Entourages*, as well as *Jacqueline Kennedy Onassis: A Life Beyond Her Wildest Dreams.*

Prince is also the co-author, with Darwin Porter, of four books on film criticism, three of which won honors at regional bookfests across America, including Los Angeles and San Francisco. Special features within these guides included the cinematic legacy of Tennessee Wiliams; the implications associated with strolling down *Sunset Blvd.,* that "Boulevard of Broken Dreams"; behind-the-scenes revelations about the making of *Ben-Hur,* starring Charlton Heston. From *Flesh* to *Trash*, he previewed many of Andy Warhol's films and "unzipped" Marlon Brando. He also took a cinematic look at the legacy of Greta Garbo in the re-release of her movies of long ago, revisiting *Mata Hari,*

Anna Christie, Queen Christina, Anna Karenina, Camille, and *Ninotchka,* among many others.

Prince, a graduate of Hamilton College and a native of Easton and Bethlehem, Pennsylvania, is the president and founder (in 1996) of the Georgia Literary Association, and of the Porter and Prince Corporation, founded in 1983, which has produced dozens of titles for both Prentice Hall and John Wiley & Sons. In 2011, he was named "Publisher of the Year" by a consortium of literary critics and marketers spearheaded by the J.M. Northern Media Group.

According to Prince, "Blood Moon provides the luxurious illusion that a reader is a perpetual guest at some gossippy dinner party populated with brilliant but occasionally self-delusional figures from bygone eras of The American Experience. Blood Moon's success at salvaging, documenting, and articulating the (till now) orally transmitted histories of the Entertainment Industry, in ways that have never been seen before, is one of the most distinctive aspects of our backlist."

Publishing in collaboration with the National Book Network (www.NBN-Books.com), he has electronically documented some of the controversies associated with his stewardship of Blood Moon in more than 50 videotaped documentaries, book trailers, public speeches, and TV or radio interviews. Any of these can be watched, without charge, by performing a search for "Danforth Prince" on **YouTube.com**, checking him out on **Facebook** (either "Danforth Prince" or "Blood Moon Productions"), on **Twitter** (#BloodyandLunar) or by clicking on **BloodMoonProductions.com**.

During the rare moments when he isn't writing, editing, neurosing about, or promoting Blood Moon, he works out at a New York City gym, rescues stray animals, talks to strangers, and regularly attends Episcopal Mass early every Sunday.

BLOOD MOON PRODUCTIONS

Entertainment About How America Interprets Its Celebrities

As described by *The Huffington Post*, "Blood Moon, in case you don't know, is a small publishing house on Staten Island that cranks out Hollywood gossip books, about two or three a year, usually of five-, six-, or 700-page length, chocked with stories and pictures about people who used to consume the imaginations of the American public, back when we actually had a public imagination. That is, when people were really interested in each other, rather than in Apple 'devices.' In other words, back when we had vices, not devices."

Reorganized with its present name in 2004, Blood Moon originated in 1997 as the Georgia Literary Association, a vehicle for the promotion of obscure writers from America's Deep South. For several decades, Blood Moon and its key players (Darwin Porter and Danforth Prince) spearheaded the research, writing, and editorial functions of dozens of titles, and hundreds of editions, of THE FROMMER GUIDES, the most respected name in travel publishing.

Blood Moon maintains a back list of more than 30 critically acclaimed biographies, film guides, and novels. Its titles are distributed by the National Book Network (www.NBNBooks.com), and through secondary wholesalers and online retailers everywhere.

Since 2004, Blood Moon has been awarded dozens of nationally recognized literary prizes. They've included both silver and bronze medals from the IPPY (Independent Publishers Association) Awards; four nominations and two Honorable Mentions for BOOK OF THE YEAR from Foreword Reviews; nominations from The Ben Franklin Awards; and Awards and Honorable Mentions from the New England, the Los Angeles, the Paris, the Hollywood, the New York, and the San Francisco Book Festivals. Two of its titles have been Grand Prize Winners for Best Summer Reading, as defined by The Beach Book Awards, and in 2013, its triple-play overview of the Gabor sisters was designated as Biography of the Year by the Hollywood Book Festival.

For more about us, including access to a growing number of videotaped book trailers, TV and radio interviews, and public addresses, each accessible via **YouTube.com,** search for key words "Danforth Prince" or "Blood Moon Productions." Or click on **www.BloodMoonProductions.com;** visit our page on Facebook; subscribe to us on Twitter (#BloodyandLunar); or refer to the pages which immediately follow.

Thanks for your interest, best wishes, and happy reading. Literacy matters! Read a book!

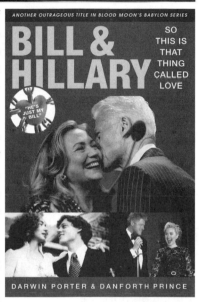

James Dean

Tomorrow Never Comes

Live Fast, Die Young

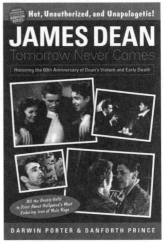

Stunning, provocative, candid, page-turning, *Tomorrow Never Comes* presents James Dean as never before.

America's most enduring and legendary symbol of young rebellion, Dean continues into the 21st Century to capture the imagination of the world. Bars from southeast Nigeria to Patagonia are named in his honor.

From his climb from the dusty backroads of Indiana to the most formidable boudoirs of Hollywood, his saga is electrifying.

Dean, a strikingly handsome heart-throb, is a study in contrasts: Tough but tender, brutal at times but remarkably sensitive; a reckless hell-raiser badass who could revert to a little boy in bed.

He claimed that sexually, he didn't want to go through life with one hand tied behind his back. The rampant bisexual proved that with Marilyn Monroe, Rock Hudson, Elizabeth Taylor, Paul Newman, Natalie Wood, Shelley Winters, Marlon Brando, Steve McQueen, Ursula Andress, Montgomery Clift, Pier Angeli, Tennessee Williams, Susan Strasberg, and (are you sitting down?) Tallulah Bankhead and J. Edgar Hoover. Woolworth heiress Barbara Hutton wanted to make him her toy boy.

Tomorrow Never Comes is the most penetrating look at James Dean to have emerged from the wreckage of his Porsche Spyder in 1955. He flirted with Death until it caught up with him. Ironically, he said, "If a man can live after he dies, then maybe he's a great man."

Before setting out on his last ride, he also said, "I feel life too intensely to bear living it."

Tomorrow Never Comes presents a damaged but beautiful soul.

LOVE TRIANGLE

Ronald Reagan, Jane Wyman, & Nancy Davis

Most of the world remembers Ronald Reagan and Nancy (Davis) Reagan as geriatric figures in the White House in the 1980s. And it remembers Jane Wyman as the fierce empress, Angela Channing, in the decade's hit TV series, *Falcon Crest*.

But long before that, two young wannabe stars, Ronald Reagan and Jane Wyman, arrived in Hollywood as untested hopefuls. Separately, they stormed Warner Brothers, looking for movie stardom and love—and finding both beyond their wildest dreams. They were followed, in time, by Nancy Davis, who began her career posing for cheesecake in a failed attempt by the studio to turn her into a sex symbol.

In their memoirs, Ronald and Nancy (Jane didn't write one) paid scant attention to their "wild and wonderful years" in Hollywood. To provide that missing link in their lives, Blood Moon's *Love Triangle* explores in depth the trio's passions, furies, betrayals, loves won and lost, and the conflicts and rivalries they generated.

A liberal New Deal Democrat, Reagan quickly became a handsome leading man in "B" pictures and a "babe magnet." Reagan himself admitted he developed *"Leading Lady-itis"* even for stars he didn't appear with. He launched a bevy of affairs with such glamorous icons as Lana Turner, Betty Grable and Susan Hayward, even a "too young" Elizabeth Taylor.

He eventually married Jane, but he was not faithful to her, enjoying back alley affairs with the likes of "The Oomph Girl," Ann Sheridan. Jane, too, had her affairs on the side, notably with Lew Ayres (Ginger Rogers' ex) while filming her Oscar-winning *Johnny Belinda*.

After dumping Reagan, Jane launched a series of affairs herself, battling Joan Crawford (for Hollywood's most studly and newsworthy attorney, Greg Bautzer); and Marilyn Monroe (for bandleader Fred Karger, marrying him, divorcing him, marrying him again, and finally divorcing him for good.)

Reagan's oldest son, Michael (adopted), later said, "If Nancy knew that one day she would be First Lady, she would have cleaned up her act." He was referring to her notorious days as a starlet in the late 1940s and early 50s, when the grapevine had it: "her phone number was passed around a lot." The list of her intimate involvements is long, including Clark Gable, whom she wanted to marry; Spencer Tracy; Yul Brynner; Frank Sinatra; Marlon Brando; Milton Berle; Peter Lawford; Robert Walker; and others.

Love Triangle, a proud and presidential addition to **Blood Moon's Babylon Series**, digs deep into what these three young movie stars were up to decades before two of them took over the Free World.

LOVE TRIANGLE: Ronald Reagan, Jane Wyman, & Nancy Davis

Darwin Porter & Danforth Prince

Hot, scandalous, and loaded with information the Reagans never wanted you to know.

6" x 9" with hundreds of photos.   ISBN 978-1-936003-41-9

JACQUELINE KENNEDY ONASSIS

A Life Beyond Her Wildest Dreams

After floods of analysis and commentary in tabloid and mainstream newspapers worldwide, this has emerged as the world's most comprehensive testimonial to the flimsier side of Camelot, the most comprehensive compendium of gossip ever published about America's unofficial, uncrowned queen, **Jacqueline Kennedy Onassis**. Its publication coincided with the 20-year anniversary of the death of one of the most famous, revered, and talked-about women who ever lived.

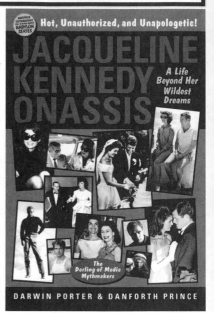

During her tumultuous life, Mrs. Onassis zealously guarded her privacy and her secrets. But in the wake of her death, more and more revelations have emerged about her frustrations, her rage, her passions, her towering strengths, and her delicate fragility, which she hid from the glare of the world behind oversized sunglasses. Within this posthumous biography, a three-dimensional woman emerges through the compilation of some 1,000 eyewitness testimonials from men and women who knew her over a period of decades.

An overview of the life of Mrs. Onassis is a natural fit for Blood Moon, a publishing enterprise that's increasingly known, worldwide, as one of the most provocative and scandalous in the history of publishing.

"References to this American icon appear with almost rhythmic regularity to anyone researching the cultural landscape of America during the last half of The American Century," said Danforth Prince. "Based on what we'd uncovered about Jackie during the research of many of our earlier titles, we're positioning ourselves as a more or less solitary outpost of irreverence within a landscape that's otherwise flooded with fawning, over-reverential testimonials. Therein lies this book's appeal—albeit with a constant respect and affection for a woman we admired and adored."

Based on decades of research by writers who define themselves as "voraciously attentive Kennedyphiles," it supplements the half-dozen other titles within Blood Moon's Babylon series.

JACQUELINE KENNEDY ONASSIS—A LIFE BEYOND HER WILDEST DREAMS
Darwin Porter and Danforth Prince
Biography/Entertainment   6" x 9"   700 pages with hundreds of photos
ISBN 978-1-936003-39-6   Also available for E-readers.

Marilyn at Rainbow's End
Sex, Lies, Murder, & the Great Cover-Up

This book illustrates why *Gentlemen Prefer Blondes*, and why Marilyn Monroe was too dangerous to be allowed to go on living

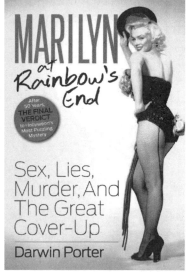

Less than an hour after the discovery of Marilyn Monroe's corpse in Brentwood, a flood of theories, tainted evidence, and conflicting testimonies began pouring out into the public landscape.

Filled with rage, hysteria, and depression, "and fed up with Jack's lies, Bobby's lies," Marilyn sought revenge and mass vindication. Her revelations at an imminent press conference could have toppled political dynasties and destroyed criminal empires. Marilyn had to be stopped...

Into this steamy cauldron of deceit, Marilyn herself emerges as a most unreliable witness during the weeks leading up to her murder. Her own deceptions, vanities, and self-delusion poured toxic accelerants on an already raging fire.

Winner of literary awards from the New York, Hollywood, and San Francisco Book Festivals

"This is the best book about Marilyn Monroe ever published."

—**David Hartnell**

"Marilyn was a highly complex personality, both the dewy-eyed innocent, only semi-aware of her own seductiveness that we saw on the screen in *The Princess and the Showgirl,* and the half-crazed, over-medicated slut portrayed in the pages of this book were quite real aspects of that unique woman. Porter's book explores it all in detail and concludes with an account of her death that would certainly have gotten him a pair of cement overshoes or a bullet in the head had he published it 30 years ago."

—**Toby Grace**

MARILYN AT RAINBOW'S END, SEX, LIES, MURDER, AND THE GREAT COVER-UP, BY DARWIN PORTER
ISBN 978-1-936003-29-7 Temporarily sold out of hard copies, but still available for E-Readers

PINK TRIANGLE

The Feuds and Private Lives of Tennessee Williams, Gore Vidal,
Truman Capote, and Famous Members of their Entourages
Darwin Porter & Danforth Prince
Softcover, 700 pages, with photos ISBN 978-1-936003-37-2 Also Available for E-Readers

The *enfants terribles* of America at mid-20th century challenged the sexual censors of their day while indulging in "bitchfests" for love & glory.

This book exposes their literary slugfests and offers an intimate look at their relationships with the *glitterati*— MM, Brando, the Oliviers, the Paleys, U.S. Presidents, a gaggle of other movie stars, millionaires, and dozens of others.

This is for anyone who's interested in the formerly concealed scandals of Hollywood and Broadway, and the values and pretentions of both the literary world and the entertainment industry.

"A banquet... If *PINK TRIANGLE* had not been written for us, we would have had to research and type it all up for ourselves...Pink Triangle is nearly seven hundred pages of the most entertaining histrionics ever sliced, spiced, heated, and serviced up to the reading public. Everything that Blood Moon has done before pales in comparison.

"Given the fact that the subjects of the book themselves were nearly delusional on the subject of themselves (to say nothing of each other) it is hard to find fault. Add to this the intertwined jungle that was the relationship among Williams, Capote, and Vidal, of the times they vied for things they loved most—especially attention— and the times they enthralled each other and the world, [*Pink Triangle* is] the perfect antidote to the Polar Vortex."
—Vinton McCabe in the NY JOURNAL OF BOOKS

"Full disclosure: I have been a friend and follower of Blood Moon Productions' tomes for years, and always marveled at the amount of information in their books— it's staggering. The index alone to *Pink Triangle* runs to 21 pages—and the scale of names in it runs like a *Who's Who* of American social, cultural and political life through much of the 20th century."
—Perry Brass in THE HUFFINGTON POST

"We Brits are not spared the Porter/Prince silken lash either. PINK TRIANGLE's research is, quite frankly, breathtaking. PINK TRIANGLE will fascinate you for many weeks to come. Once you have made the initial titillating dip, the day will seem dull without it."
—Jeffery Tayor in THE SUNDAY EXPRESS (UK)

THOSE GLAMOROUS GABORS
Bombshells from Budapest, by Darwin Porter

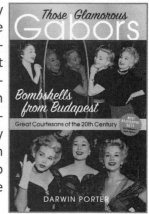

Zsa Zsa, Eva, and Magda Gabor transferred their glittery dreams and gold-digging ambitions from the twilight of the Austro-Hungarian Empire to Hollywood. There, more effectively than any army, these Bombshells from Budapest broke hearts, amassed fortunes, lovers, and A-list husbands, and amused millions of *voyeurs* through the medium of television, movies, and the social registers. In this astonishing "triple-play" biography, designated "Best Biography of the Year" by the Hollywood Book Festival, Blood Moon lifts the "mink-and-diamond" curtain on this amazing trio of blood-related sisters, whose complicated intrigues have never been fully explored before.

"**You will never be Ga-bored...this book gives new meaning to the term compelling.** Be warned, *Those Glamorous Gabors* is both an epic and a pip. Not since *Gone With the Wind* have so many characters on the printed page been forced to run for their lives for one reason or another. And Scarlett making a dress out of the curtains is nothing compared to what a Gabor will do when she needs to scrap together an outfit for a movie premiere or late-night outing.

"For those not up to speed, Jolie Tilleman came from a family of jewelers and therefore came by her love for the shiny stones honestly, perhaps genetically. She married Vilmos Gabor somewhere around World War 1 (exact dates, especially birth dates, are always somewhat vague in order to establish plausible deniability later on) and they were soon blessed with three daughters: **Magda**, the oldest, whose hair, sadly, was naturally brown, although it would turn quite red in America; **Zsa Zsa** (born 'Sari') a natural blond who at a very young age exhibited the desire for fame with none of the talents usually associated with achievement, excepting beauty and a natural wit; and **Eva**, the youngest and blondest of the girls, who after seeing Grace Moore perform at the National Theater, decided that she wanted to be an actress and that she would one day move to Hollywood to become a star.

"Given that the Gabor family at that time lived in Budapest, Hungary, at the period of time between the World Wars, that Hollywood dream seemed a distant one indeed. The story—the riches to rags to riches to rags to riches again myth of survival against all odds as the four women, because of their Jewish heritage, flee Europe with only the minks on their backs and what jewels they could smuggle along with them in their *decolletage*, only to have to battle afresh for their places in the vicious Hollywood pecking order—gives new meaning to the term 'compelling.' The reader, as if he were witnessing a particularly gore-drenched traffic accident, is incapable of looking away."

—New York Review of Books

Softcover, 730 pages, with hundreds of photos   ISBN 978-1-936003-35-8

INSIDE LINDA LOVELACE'S DEEP THROAT

DEGRADATION, PORNO CHIC, AND THE RISE OF FEMINISM

DARWIN PORTER

An insider's view of the unlikely heroine who changed the world's perceptions about pornography, censorship, and sexual behavior patterns

The Most Comprehensive Biography Ever Written of an
Adult Entertainment Star and Her Relationship with the Underbelly of Hollywood

Darwin Porter, author of some twenty critically acclaimed celebrity exposés of behind-the-scenes intrigue in the entertainment industry, was deeply involved in the Linda Lovelace saga as it unfolded in the 70s, interviewing many of the players, and raising money for the legal defense of the film's co-star, Harry Reems. In this book, emphasizing her role as a celebrity interacting with other celebrities, he brings inside information and a never-before-published revelation to almost every page.

The Beach Book Festival's Grand Prize Winner: "Best Summer Reading of 2013"

Runner-Up to "Best Biography of 2013" *The Los Angeles Book Festival*

Winner of a Sybarite Award from HedoOnline.com

"This book drew me in..How could it not?" Coco Papy, *Bookslut.*

INSIDE LINDA LOVELACE'S DEEP THROAT
Softcover, 640 pages, 6"x9", with hundreds of photos.
ISBN 978-1-936003-33-4

DAMN YOU, SCARLETT O'HARA

The Private Lifes of Laurence Olivier and Vivien Leigh

Darwin Porter and Roy Moseley

Scarlett O'Hara, Desperately in Love with Heathcliff, Together on the Road to Hell

Here, for the first time, is a biography that raises the curtain on the secret lives of **Lord Laurence Olivier**, often cited as the finest actor in the history of England, and **Vivien Leigh,** who immortalized herself with her Oscar-winning portrayals of Scarlett O'Hara in *Gone With the Wind,* and as Blanche DuBois in Tennessee Williams' *A Streetcar Named Desire.*

Dashing and "impossibly handsome," Laurence Olivier was pursued by the most dazzling luminaries, male and female, of the movie and theater worlds.

Lord Olivier's beautiful and brilliant but emotionally disturbed wife (Viv to her lovers) led a tumultuous off-the-record life whose paramours ranged from the A-list celebrities to men she selected randomly off the street. But none of the brilliant roles depicted by Lord and Lady Olivier, on stage or on screen, ever matched the power and drama of personal dramas which wavered between Wagnerian opera and Greek tragedy. *Damn You, Scarlett O'Hara* is the definitive and most revelatory portrait ever published of the most talented and tormented actor/actress coupling of the 20th century.

*"**Damn You, Scarlett O'Hara** can be a dazzling read, the prose unmannered and instantly digestible. The authors' ability to pile scandal atop scandal, seduction after seduction, can be impossible to resist."*
—THE WASHINGTON TIMES

ISBN 978-1-936003-15-0 Hardcover, 708 pages, with about a hundred photos and hundreds of insights into the London Theatre, the role of the Oliviers in the politics of World War II, and the passion, fury, and frustration of their lives together as actors in Hollywood.

PAUL NEWMAN

The Man Behind the Baby Blues, His Secret Life Exposed

Darwin Porter

Drawn from firsthand interviews with insiders who knew Paul Newman intimately, and compiled over a period of nearly a half-century, this is the world's most honest and most revelatory biography about Hollywood's pre-eminent male sex symbol.

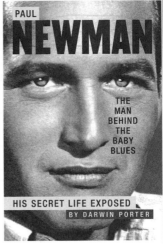

This is a respectful but candid cornucopia of once-concealed information about the sexual and emotional adventures of an affable, impossibly good-looking workaday actor, a former sailor from Shaker Heights, Ohio, who parlayed his ambisexual charm and extraordinary good looks into one of the most successful careers in Hollywood.

Whereas the situations it exposes were widely known within Hollywood's inner circles, they've never before been revealed to the general public.

But now, the full story has been published—the giddy heights and agonizing crashes of a great American star, with revelations and insights never before published in any other biography.

"Paul Newman had just as many on-location affairs as the rest of us, and he was just as bisexual as I was. But whereas I was always getting caught with my pants down, he managed to do it in the dark with not a paparazzo in sight. He might have bedded Marilyn Monroe or Elizabeth Taylor the night before, but he always managed to show up for breakfast with Joanne Woodward, with those baby blues, looking as innocent as a Botticelli angel. He never fooled me. It takes an alleycat to know another one. Did I ever tell you what really happened between Newman and me? If that doesn't grab you, what about what went on between James Dean and Newman? Let me tell you about this co-called model husband if you want to look behind those famous peepers."

—**Marlon Brando**

Paul Newman, The Man Behind the Baby Blues, His Secret Life Exposed
Hardcover, 520 pages, with dozens of photos. **ISBN 978-0-9786465-1-6**

J. Edgar Hoover and Clyde Tolson

Investigating the Sexual Secrets of America's Most Famous Men & Women

Darwin Porter
How the FBI Investigated Hollywood

This epic saga of power and corruption has a revelation on every page—cross dressing, gay parties, sexual indiscretions, hustlers for sale, alliances with the Mafia, and criminal activity by the nation's chief law enforcer.

It's all here, with chilling details about the abuse of power on the dark side of the American saga. But mostly it's the decades-long love story of America's two most powerful men who could tell presidents "how to skip rope." (Hoover's words.)

"Everyone's dredging up J. Edgar Hoover. Leonardo DiCaprio just immortalized him, and now comes Darwin Porter's paperback, *J. Edgar Hoover & Clyde Tolson: Investigating the Sexual Secrets of America's Most Famous Men and Women.* It shovels Hoover's darkest secrets dragged kicking and screaming from the closet. It's filth on every VIP who's safely dead and some who are still above ground."

—Cindy Adams, The New York Post

"This book is important, because it destroys what's left of Hoover's reputation. Did you know he had intel on the bombing of Pearl Harbor, but he sat on it, making him more or less responsible for thousands of deaths? Or that he had almost nothing to do with the arrests or killings of any of the 1930s gangsters that he took credit for catching?

"A lot of people are angry with its author, Darwin Porter. They say that his outing of celebrities is just cheap gossip about dead people who can't defend themselves. I suppose it's because Porter is destroying carefully constructed myths that are comforting to most people. As gay men, we benefit the most from Porter's work, because we know that except for AIDS, the closet was the most terrible thing about the 20th century. If the closet never existed, neither would Hoover. The fact that he got away with such duplicity under eight presidents makes you think that every one of them was a complete fool for tolerating it."

—Paul Bellini, FAB Magazine (Toronto)

Winner of Literary Awards from the Los Angeles & the Hollywood Book Festivals
Temporarily sold out of hard copies, but available for E-Readers. ISBN 978-1-936003-25-9

MERV GRIFFIN

A LIFE IN THE CLOSET

DARWIN PORTER

Merv Griffin began his career as a Big Band singer, moved on to a failed career as a romantic hero in the movies, and eventually rewrote the rules of everything associated with the broadcasting industry. Along the way, he met and befriended virtually everyone who mattered, including Nancy Reagan, and made billions operating casinos and developing jingles, contests, and word games. All of this while maintaining a male harem and a secret life as America's most famously closeted homosexual.

In this comprehensive and richly ironic biography, Darwin Porter reveals the amazing details behind the richest, most successful, and in some ways, the most notorious mogul in the history of America's entertainment industry.

"Darwin Porter told me why he tore the door off Merv's closet.......*Heeeere's Merv!* is 560 pages, 100 photos, a truckload of gossip, and a bedful of unauthorized dish."

Cindy Adams, The NY Post

"Darwin Porter tears the door off Merv Griffin's closet with gusto in this sizzling, superlatively researched biography...It brims with insider gossip that's about Hollywood legends, writ large, smart, and with great style."

Richard LaBonté, BOOKMARKS

Merv Griffin, a Life in the Closet, by Darwin Porter. Hardcover, with photos.
ISBN 978-0-9786465-0-9. Also available for E-Readers.

THE KENNEDYS

ALL THE GOSSIP UNFIT TO PRINT

A Staggering Compendium of Indiscretions Associated With Seven Key Players in the Kennedy Clan

Darwin Porter & Danforth Prince

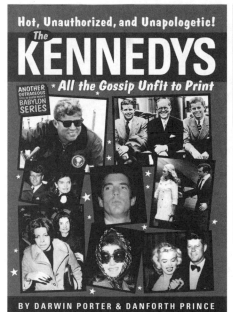

The great enemy of truth is very often not the lie—deliberate, contrived, and dishonest, but the myth—persistent, persuasive, and unrealistic."
—John F. Kennedy

A Cornucopia of Relatively Unknown but Carefully Documented Scandals from the Golden Age of Camelot

"Pick this book up, and you'll be hard-pressed to put it down"
—Richard Labonté, *Q-Syndicate*

The Kennedys were the first true movie stars to occupy the White House. They were also Washington's horniest political tribe, and although America loved their humor, their style, and their panache, we took delight in this tabloid-style documentation of their hundreds of staggering indiscretions.

Keepers of the dying embers of Camelot won't like it, but Kennedy historians and aficionados will interpret it as required reading.

BLOOD MOON Productions, Ltd.

BLOOD
MOON
Productions, Ltd.